CW00870715

CASSELL DICTIONARY OF
Modern Britain

CASSELL DICTIONARY OF Modern Britain

CIRCA
Research & Reference Information

CASSELL

Cassell Publishers Limited
Wellington House
125 Strand
London WC2R 0BB
England

First published 1995

Distributed in Australia
by Capricorn Link (Australia) Pty Ltd
2/13 Carrington Road, Castle Hill, NSW 2154

British Library Cataloguing-in-Publication Data
A catalogue record for this book is available from the British Library

ISBN 0-304-34588-1

Compiled and typeset by CIRCA Research and Reference Information Ltd, Cambridge

Printed and bound in Great Britain by Mackays of Chatham PLC, Chatham, Kent

CONTENTS

INTRODUCTION

This is a dictionary of modern Britain in the broadest sense, covering a diversity of topics including politics and government, economics and business, Northern Ireland, foreign affairs and Europe, education, housing, health, the criminal justice system, religious affairs, the environment, scandals, media and the arts as well as the people whose names have become part of the language of postwar society. In addition the index of personal names provides another route into the web of entries associated with particular individuals. The dictionary's coverage is for the period 1945 to mid-1995.

Within the limits of a single volume, we have tried to include as many current terms as possible, concentrating on those which users are most likely to encounter. Inevitably there will be omissions, for which we apologise.

Cross-references are indicated by the use of **bold** typeface. Entries for organizations are usually to be found under their acronyms. Where the headword or its initial element is a numeral, as in **300 Group** or **1992**, the entry can be found in the alphabetical sequence (under 'three hundred' or 'nineteen' in these examples).

The dictionary incorporates a number of appendices covering a range of topics from election results to exchange rates, from the prison population to average incomes. Where an appendix has a direct relevance to a particular entry, this is indicated by *See also* . . . at the end of the entry.

We owe an enormous debt to all our colleagues at CIRCA and are especially grateful to Robert Fraser and to Philippa Youngman, who was responsible for the book's final production.

Finally, a word of thanks to John and Joanna.

Tanya Joseph
D. J. Sagar
Cambridge, July 1995

EDITORS

Tanya Joseph is a regional editor for CIRCA. She co-edited the *Cassell Dictionary of Modern Politics* and was a major contributor to *Political Parties of Africa and the Middle East*. She has has contributed to several other books, including *The World's News Media* and *Political Parties of Asia and the Pacific*.

D. J. Sagar is a founder member of CIRCA and has edited, co-edited and contributed to many books, including the *Cassell Dictionary of Modern Politics*, the *ITN Fact Book* and the *Economist Dictionary of Political Biography*. He is a contributor to the *Annual Register*.

CONTRIBUTORS

Rupert Dickens is a journalist and a regular contributor to *Keesing's UK Record*.

Roger East is a founder member of CIRCA. He is the editor of *Keesing's Record of World Events*, author of *Revolutions in Eastern Europe* and co-author of *From the Six to the Twelve: The Enlargement of the European Communities*. He co-edited the *Cassell Dictionary of Modern Politics* and numerous other reference works, including the *ITN Fact Book* and the *Economist Dictionary of Political Biography*.

D. S. Lewis is a regional editor for CIRCA and has contributed to numerous books, including the *Cassell Dictionary of Modern Politics*, the *ITN Fact Book* and the *Economist Dictionary of Political Biography*. He is the author of *Illusions of Grandeur*, editor of *Korea: Enduring Division*, and joint editor of *Political Parties of Asia and the Pacific* and *Political Parties of the Americas and Caribbean*.

Frances Nicholson is a regional editor for CIRCA. She is co-author of *From the Six to the Twelve: the Enlargement of the European Communities*, and has edited the *Political and Economic Encyclopaedia of Western Europe*. She contributed to the *ITN Fact Book* and is a contributor to the *Annual Register*.

Charles Phillips is a freelance writer and a regular contributor to *Keesing's UK Record*.

Jolyon Pontin is a regional editor for CIRCA, specializing in the politics of Central and Eastern Europe and the CIS. He was a contributor to the *Cassell Dictionary of Modern Politics*.

Farzana Shaikh is a regional editor for CIRCA. She has written on Islam, is author of *Community and Consensus in Islam: Muslim Representation in Colonial India, 1860–1947* and edited *Islam and Islamic Groups*. She was a contributor to the *Cassell Dictionary of Modern Politics*.

William Stallard is a college lecturer in management and business studies, and a freelance writer. He has contributed to *Keesing's Record of World Events* and is a regular contributor to *Keesing's UK Record*. He was also a contributor to *Political Scandals and Causes Celebres since 1945: an International Reference Compendium*.

Martin Upham is editor of *Trade Unions and Employers' Organizations of the World*, co-author of *Western European Economic Organization* and a contributor to *Keesing's UK Record*. He is currently writing an official history of the Iron and Steel Trades Conference.

CIRCA Research and Reference Information Ltd specializes in reference works on international politics, economics and current affairs, producing a variety of books, periodicals, ad hoc reports and electronic data. Books produced by CIRCA include the *Cassell Dictionary of Modern Politics*. CIRCA is responsible for researching, writing and editing the long-established monthly *Keesing's Record of World Events*, and is also the publisher of the bi-monthly *Keesing's UK Record* and *People in Power*.

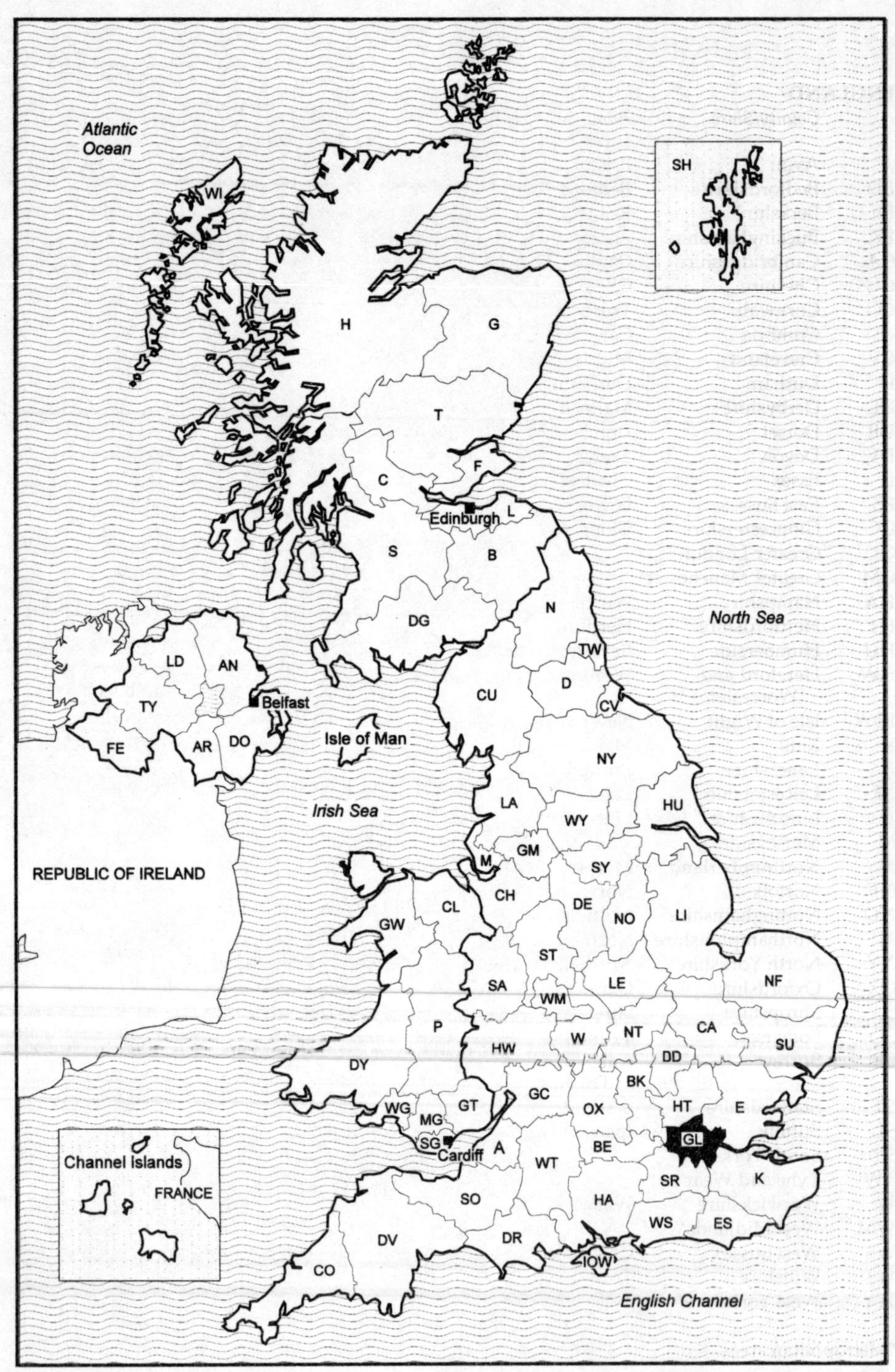

Atlantic Ocean
WI
SH
H
G
T
F
C
Edinburgh
L
S
B
DG
N
North Sea
TW
LD
AN
TY
Belfast
D
CU
CV
FE
AR
DO
Isle of Man
NY
LA
Irish Sea
WY
HU
GM
M
REPUBLIC OF IRELAND
SY
CH
CL
DE
GW
NO
LI
ST
SA
LE
NF
WM
P
NT
CA
W
SU
HW
DD
DY
BK
GC
WG
GT
HT
E
OX
MG
GL
SG
Cardiff
A
BE
Channel Islands
WT
SR
K
FRANCE
SO
HA
WS
ES
DV
DR
IOW
CO
English Channel

KEY TO MAP

ENGLAND

	County/Shire	*Administrative centre*
A	Avon	Bristol
BD	Bedfordshire	Bedford
BE	Berkshire	Reading
BK	Buckinghamshire	Aylesbury
CA	Cambridgeshire	Cambridge
CH	Cheshire	Chester
CO	Cornwall	Truro
CU	Cumbria	Carlisle
CV	Cleveland	Middlesbrough
D	Durham	Durham
DE	Derbyshire	Matlock
DR	Dorset	Dorchester
DV	Devon	Exeter
E	Essex	Chelmsford
ES	East Sussex	Lewes
GC	Gloucestershire	Gloucester
GL	Greater London	
GM	Greater Manchester*	
HA	Hampshire	Winchester
HT	Hertfordshire	Hertford
HU	Humberside	Beverley
HW	Hereford and Worcester	Worcester
IOW	Isle of Wight	Newport
K	Kent	Maidstone
LA	Lancashire	Preston
LE	Leicestershire	Leicester
LI	Lincolnshire	Lincoln
M	Merseyside*	
N	Northumberland	Morpeth
NF	Norfolk	Norwich
NO	Nottinghamshire	Nottingham
NT	Northamptonshire	Northampton
NY	North Yorkshire	Northallerton
OX	Oxfordshire	Oxford
SA	Shropshire	Shrewsbury
SO	Somerset	Taunton
SR	Surrey	Kingston upon Thames
ST	Staffordshire	Stafford
SU	Suffolk	Ipswich
SY	South Yorkshire*	
TW	Tyne and Wear*	
W	Warwickshire	Warwick
WM	West Midlands*	
WS	West Sussex	Chichester
WT	Wiltshire	Trowbridge
WY	West Yorkshire*	

*Metropolitan areas.

WALES

	County	*Administrative centre*
CL	Clwyd	Mold
DY	Dyfed	Carmarthen
GT	Gwent	Cwmbran
GW	Gwynedd	Caernarfon
MG	Mid Glamorgan	Cardiff
P	Powys	Llandrindod Wells
SG	South Glamorgan	Cardiff
WG	West Glamorgan	Swansea

SCOTLAND

	Region/Islands	*Administrative centre*
B	Borders	Newtown St Boswells
C	Central	Stirling
DG	Dumfries & Galloway	Dumfries
F	Fife	Glenrothes
G	Grampian	Aberdeen
H	Highland	Inverness
L	Lothian	Edinburgh
O	Orkney	Kirkwall
S	Strathclyde	Glasgow
SH	Shetland	Lerwick
T	Tayside	Dundee
WI	Western Isles	Stornoway (Lewis)

NORTHERN IRELAND

	County	*Administrative centre*
AN	County Antrim	Belfast
AR	County Armagh	Armagh
DO	County Down	Downpatrick
FE	County Fermanagh	Enniskillen
LD	Londonderry	Londonderry
TY	County Tyrone	Omagh

THE DICTIONARY

A-LEVELS

The Advanced Level examination introduced in 1951 to replace the Higher School Certificate. A-levels, originally the second level of the General Certificate of Education (**GCE**), are taken in individual subjects, usually at about the age of 18, and are a partial qualification for entrance to university and to many of the professions. The nearest Scottish equivalent is the Certificate of Sixth Year Studies. A-levels have remained more or less unchanged since their inception, and have been criticized for encouraging specialisation in too narrow a range of subjects at too early an age.

Advanced Supplementary (A-S) level examinations were introduced in 1987 as an alternative to, and to complement, A-level examinations.

AAM

Anti-Apartheid Movement, an organization founded in 1959 to increase awareness of apartheid. Sympathetic to the African National Congress (ANC), it brought together South African exiles and British activists. It played a key role in campaigns to implement and maintain the sports, cultural and economic boycott of South Africa, including the particularly successful campaign against buying South African fruit. It also organized demonstrations and street protests, lobbied parliament and sought to attract media attention to events in South Africa. One of its most successful campaigns was that in 1988 to mark the 70th birthday of the then imprisoned Nelson Mandela, which culminated in a mass rally in London's Hyde Park attended by an estimated 200,000 people. Following the ending of apartheid, AAM decided to transform itself into a solidarity organization for the 11 countries of southern Africa (Angola, Botswana, Lesotho, Malawi, Mozambique, Namibia, Swaziland, Tanzania, Zambia, Zimbabwe and South Africa). The new organization, Action for Southern Africa (ACTSA), was launched in October 1994.

ABATEMENT *see* BUDGET REBATE

ABC TRIAL

The failed prosecution under the **Official Secrets Act** of Crispin Aubrey, John Berry and Duncan Campbell in 1977–8 – the initials of the trio's surnames provided the trial's name. Berry was accused of giving sensitive information to journalists Campbell and Aubrey when a corporal in army Signals Intelligence, but all significant charges were dropped and the only outcome was a suspended prison sentence for Berry.

This was the last prosecution authorized by the **Labour** government under the Official Secrets Act. The Act itself was reformed and partially relaxed in 1989 in the wake of a number of controversial episodes, in particular the **Spycatcher affair**.

ABERFAN

A village in South Wales, scene of a coalmining landslip disaster in October 1966. Around 150 children and some of their teachers died when an avalanche of waste, rocks and sludge slid down from a spoil tip and engulfed their primary school. An inquiry report published the following August placed blame for the disaster on the National Coal Board (later **British Coal**), which was criticized for its total lack of a tipping policy.

ABORTION ACT

The 1967 basis for the legalization of abortion. Sponsored by the **Liberal** (now

Liberal Democrat) MP David Steel, this act, which came into force in April 1968, effectively permitted the termination of pregnancy within 28 weeks, under given conditions and subject to certain safeguards. A major attempt was made through the unsuccessful **Alton Bill** in 1988 to reduce the limit to 18 weeks, while the Human Fertilization and Embryology Act 1990 set a general 24-week limit but provided for a number of exceptions.

See also Appendix VI.

ACAS

The Advisory, Conciliation and Arbitration Service, set up by the UK government in 1974 when the improvement of industrial relations and of collective bargaining was seen as a key political issue. ACAS provides a free service, offering advice (on invitation) and dealing with some 50,000 conciliation cases a year; it issues codes of practice on industrial relations; and it has referred to it, for arbitration, issues such as dismissal and discipline, pay and conditions of employment, grading, and annual pay rounds.

ACCESSION

The term usually used formally whenever a state becomes a member of an international organization, but generally understood in the UK to refer to joining the European Communities (now the **EU**). This accession took place on 1 January 1973, almost a year after signature of the accession treaty. With the simultaneous accession of Ireland and Denmark, the **Six** became the **Nine**.

ACID HOUSE PARTIES

Unauthorized parties, often held in city warehouses, where thousands of young people gathered to dance. Such parties became common in the late 1980s (in the aftermath of the so-called 'summer of love') and, largely because of the heavy consumption of illegal drugs (especially acid – LSD – and ecstasy), created a furore among **tabloid** journalists and right-wing **MPs** and were a particular target of police activity.

ACID RAIN

A damaging consequence of air pollution, the excessive acidity of rain or snow which can destroy forests, damage crops, upset the chemical balance of lakes and rivers and corrode buildings. Acid rain contains sulphuric and nitric acids, formed from airborne pollutants which are mainly the emissions of sulphur dioxide and nitrogen oxides from power stations burning fossil fuel. Although acid rain is a localized phenomenon, it can be caused by pollutants emitted hundreds of miles away; acid rain falling in Scandinavia is widely attributed to coal-fired power stations in the UK. The damaging effects of acid rain has been used by champions of nuclear power as an **energy source**, to support their case that nuclear energy is more 'environmentally friendly' than coal.

ACQUIS COMMUNAUTAIRE

(French, 'the community's attainments') The corpus of existing laws and regulations applied collectively by member states of the European Union (**EU**) at any given time, either generally or in a specific field of activity. New members are required to accept the *acquis communautaire* upon accession, and to arrange its incorporation within their own national laws and regulations, except where they are granted specific **derogations** or transitional arrangements. In preparation for the creation of the European Economic Area (**EEA**) embracing the 12 EU countries and five of the **EFTA** countries from January 1994, the EFTA participants had to pass some 1,500 laws through their national legislatures in order to adopt the *acquis communautaire* in the relevant fields.

ACTION FOR SOUTHERN AFRICA *see* AAM

ACTSA *see* AAM

ADAM SMITH INSTITUTE

A right-wing **think tank** founded in 1976 by its president, Madsen Pirie, widely known as 'Dr Mad' because of the fervour of his views. The Institute regards the cross-party acceptance in the UK and widespread adoption internationally of **privatization** as its greatest success, and is no longer as keen to advance its (disputed) claim to have originated the **poll tax**. It remains extremely influential over the **Major** government, with a direct feed into **Downing Street**. In early 1995 it claimed to have sent the **Prime Minister** a list of 50 policies for possible inclusion in the next **Conservative** manifesto. The main feature of the list was, apparently, welfare reform.

ADAMS, GERRY

(b. 1948) President since 1978 of **Sinn Féin**, the political wing of the **IRA**, and one of the leading participants in the ongoing **Northern Ireland** peace process. His career as party leader has encompassed more than one attempt on his life, periods of internment and imprisonment, his long-term exclusion from mainland **Britain** (until October 1994), and the banning of his voice – as a member of a proscribed organization – from radio and television over a six-year period to 1994. Adams was elected to the **House of Commons** as a *Sinn Féin* member in 1983, but refused to take his seat, stating that he did not recognize the legitimacy of the institutions of British rule; he was defeated in 1987 by the **SDLP**. A high-profile visit to the USA in early 1994 marked his emergence as a key interlocutor if the republican movement was to gain a full political role within the democratic process. This expectation, given dramatic effect by the announcement in August 1994 of a permanent IRA **ceasefire**, was further borne out by the talks between *Sinn Féin* and the UK government in December 1994 and the issuing of the **joint framework document** of February 1995.

ADEN

The Yemeni city and port situated on the Gulf of Aden. Aden was occupied by Great Britain in 1839 to provide a chandling station on the vital route to India. In 1937 the city became a Crown Colony and the Yemeni interior a Protectorate, where tribal leaders retained nominal authority. Aden was amalgamated with the Protectorate in 1963 to form the Federation of South Arabia. The last British troops withdrew in late 1967 and the independent People's Democratic Republic of Yemen (South Yemen) was proclaimed with Aden as its capital. With the unification of South and North Yemen in May 1990, Sana'a became the national capital, although Aden remained the country's commercial centre.

ADJOURNMENT OF THE HOUSE

A procedural technicality permitting half-an-hour's debate each day in the **House of Commons** on matters concerning **MPs'** constituents or of general immediate interest.

ADVERTISING STANDARDS AUTHORITY

The organization established in 1962 which regulates advertising throughout the whole range of non-broadcast media, including newspapers, magazines, advertising posters, the cinema and direct mail. An independent body funded through a levy on display advertising, the Authority promotes a high standard of advertising by enforcing the British Code of Advertising Practice. The Code's basic principles include ensuring that all advertisements are 'legal, decent, honest and truthful', that they are written and designed with a degree of responsibility and duty towards consumers, and that they measure up to principles of fair competition. The Authority can recommend that advertisements which breach the Code are amended or withdrawn, and publishes regular reports on its investigations of complaints.

ADVISORY, CONCILIATION AND ARBITRATION SERVICE *see* ACAS

AEEU

The Amalgamated Engineering and Electrical Union, a major manual-craft-based **TUC**-affiliated union with substantial membership in the **motor industry** and engineering. It originated in 1851 as the Amalgamated Society of Engineers, and in the twentieth century has always been one of the UK's largest unions. Structurally the union is characterized by a high degree of elective democracy with much power being exercised by (local) district committees; at national level there is a tension between the union's president and its general secretary. By the 1970s it had grown into the Amalgamated Engineering Federation with four sections – construction, engineering, staff and draughtsmanship. With more than one million members it was said to exercise considerable influence during the 1974–79 **Labour** administration. Rationalization into a single union proved litigious, and the process resulted in secession by the draughtsmen's section as the Technical, Administrative and Supervisory Staffs (TASS). In 1992 the union (now unified under an earlier name – the Amalgamated Engineering Union) achieved a difficult merger with the electricians' union (the Electrical, Electronic, Telecommunication and Plumbing Trades Union – **EETPU**), thereafter adopting its present name. Politically the AEEU tends to occupy a position on the right of the labour movement and successive leaders, whether presidents such as Bill Carron, Hugh Scanlon and Bill Jordan or general secretaries such as John Boyd, Terry Duffy and Gavin Laird, have normally been reliable allies of Labour Party leaders.

THE AFFLUENT SOCIETY

A term made popular by the US economist, John Kenneth Galbraith, in his 1958 book of the same name. 'The affluent society' was a description of one in which the majority of the population could satisfy their basic needs, with enough 'disposable income' left over to enable them to become consumers. Galbraith posited the notion that, in the acquisitive society of the 1950s, there was a stark contrast between 'private affluence and public squalor'. He provided an authoritative and coherent economic and social philosophy for those who believed that such a contrast was the consequence of a rich society neglecting to provide for those social utilities which the market-place could not of itself supply. Galbraith concluded that an affluent society ought to be able to turn its attention in other directions, to show concern for collective needs and social well-being.

AFRO-WEST INDIAN UNITED COUNCIL OF CHURCHES

A predominantly black Pentecostal grouping, it was founded in 1976 as a federation of black-led churches which aimed to promote a sense of 'Unity without Conformity', and to 'work together on tackling social and educational issues'. The overwhelming majority of its members are from Jamaica or of Jamaican origin and are drawn mainly from black-led Pentecostal churches. Since the mid-1980s the Council has claimed the support of increasing numbers of young blacks who regard it as an instrument of anti-**racism** and political self-expression.

AGE OF CONSENT

The legal minimum age at which an individual may consent to have sexual intercourse. In the UK the age of consent for heterosexual sex in 16; for homosexual sex it is 18, having been reduced from 21 under the 1994 Criminal Justice and Public Order Act. Gay rights campaigners continue to demand legal parity with heterosexuals.

AGENDA 21

A 'blueprint for action' adopted at the 1992 Earth Summit in Rio, setting out the measures which governments, **UN** organizations, development agencies and other bodies need to take in order to ensure sustainable development and the reversal of environmental degradation. Agenda 21 aims to provide a framework within which these objectives may be accomplished, although its recommendations are not binding.

AGR

The Advanced Gas-cooled Reactor, a British-designed type of nuclear reactor which uses for fuel enriched uranium containing 2 per cent of fissile uranium-235. AGRs constituted the second generation of reactors in the UK nuclear energy programme and, being able to operate at higher temperatures, they doubled the capacity of the first generation Magnox reactors. The plan to build AGRs was announced in 1964, but owing to delays from parliamentary and government enquiries and numerous design and costing problems the first AGRs came into operation only in 1976. In subsequent years AGRs were touted as less susceptible to cooling failure than the competing **PWR** design.

AGRICULTURAL SECTOR

That sector of the economy based on farming. The proportion of the workforce employed in agriculture has fallen dramatically during the twentieth century to stand at just below 2 per cent in the early 1990s. However, massively increased productivity has meant that the UK, more than three-quarters of whose land area is farmed, now produces more food than in the nineteenth century and roughly half of the country's requirements. The contribution of agriculture to total national output is 1.5 per cent. The UK's membership of the European Communities since 1973, has entailed the adoption of the **EC's** common agricultural policy (**CAP**) with its controversial system of price supports.

AID

Assistance in the form of money, goods or training and other services, intended to support development programmes and projects in the Third World, or for disaster relief. The UK government's foreign aid programme is administered through the Overseas Development Administration (**ODA**), a somewhat confusing acronym since it is also the standard abbreviation for the term 'official development assistance'.

The UK (like most aid donor countries) is well below the **UN**'s target of providing 0.7 per cent of **GNP** as official development assistance; ODA in 1993 was 0.31 per cent of GNP. Aid may be in the form of loans, on favourable terms, but the trend is increasingly towards grants; by 1993, nearly 94 per cent of UK ODA was in grant form. Just over half of UK ODA is bilateral (government to government) and the rest multilateral (the UK's contributions for aid via the **EU**, **UN** organizations, the World Bank, and regional development banks). Non-governmental organizations (**NGOs**) such as **Oxfam** are also active in lobbying for aid, fundraising, and running projects worldwide.

AIDS

Acquired Immune Deficiency Syndrome, a disease attacking the human immune system as a result of infection by the human immunodeficiency virus (**HIV**), which usually leads to death from opportunistic infections. First identified in the early 1980s, HIV is transmitted in body fluids, primarily by sexual activity but also among intravenous drug users and when infected blood is given in transfusions, notably to haemophiliacs. According to official figures the number of people in the UK to have contracted AIDS rose by 442 to 10,304 in the last quarter of 1994. Of these 890 (8.6 per cent) were women and 7,019 (68 per cent) had died. A total of 1,789 new cases were notified during 1994, an 11 per cent increase on 1993: although the majority of cases continued to occur in the Thames health regions, covering London, the rate of increase was faster in the rest of England and Wales than in the London area and in Scotland.

AIIC *see* ANGLO-IRISH INTERGOVERNMENTAL CONFERENCE

AIMS OF INDUSTRY

An organization whose purpose is to defend, and promote public belief in, free enterprise, and to oppose excessive state and governmental intervention in the economy. It was founded in 1942. Throughout its existence it has been opposed to **nationalization**, and during the 1980s and early 1990s it has seen its cause of **privatization** largely implemented. It has been in the forefront of campaigns to combat what it has seen as subversive influences in the field of industrial relations, and drew up a controversial 'blacklist' of alleged political agitators. It does not have direct party political affiliations, although some **Conservative MPs** are among its most ardent supporters.

AIRBUS INDUSTRIE

The European aircraft consortium, which brings together manufacturers in France, Germany, Spain and the UK. The Airbus project began in the 1960s as a Franco-German initiative. By the mid-1990s the company produced seven different models (300, 310, 319, 320, 321, 330 and 340) with the French generally manufacturing the front sections of the fuselage, the Germans the bulk of the fuselage, the Spanish the tail and **British Aerospace** (the UK partner with a 20 per cent stake in the company) the wings; engines are supplied by a variety of producers.

AK-47

An automatic or semi-automatic assault rifle most closely associated with guerrillas and terrorist organizations, including the **IRA**. The weapon, also known by the name of its designer, Mikhail Timofeyevich Kalashnikov, went into production in the Soviet Union in 1947. The design specification was passed on to

China and to Soviet allies in the Warsaw Pact and the weapon itself supplied to pro-Soviet guerrilla groups. Consequently the rifle, capable of firing 600 rounds per minute, is notoriously cheap and widely available – an estimated 50 million have been made.

ALDERMASTON

The site of the Atomic Weapons Research Establishment. Between 1958 and 1963 the anti-nuclear campaign group **CND** organized annual four-day marches between London and Aldermaston The first demonstration began in London, while in subsequent years the march ended in a mass rally in Trafalgar Square.

ALLIANCE

The campaigning coalition of the **SDP** and the **Liberal Party** from 1983 until 1987. The Alliance parties agreed not to run competing candidates in the **general election** of 1987 and the party's two leaders, David Steel and David **Owen** – the **two Davids** – consistently appeared together and contrived to maintain an appearance of unity on policy. The Alliance ultimately ended with unification of the two parties to form the **Social and Liberal Democrats** in 1988, to the chagrin of David Owen, who refused to join the new party.

ALLIANCE PARTY

A small, non-sectarian and non-doctrinaire party of the centre in **Northern Ireland**. The Party was founded in 1970 with the express purpose of attracting support from both Catholic and Protestant sections of the community. Under the leadership of John Alderdice it has seen limited electoral success and is not currently represented in the UK Parliament. Alderdice welcomed the **Downing Street Declaration** of December 1993 as a basis for political progress in the province.

ALLIED RAPID REACTION CORPS

One of the products of **NATO's** re-examination of its role in the 1990s after the end of the **Cold War**. The new mixed-nationality 'corps-sized' formation, made up of units from different European NATO members, based in Germany and under UK command, was agreed in May 1991 and inaugurated in October 1922, and was expected to be operational by the end of 1994. There would also be a small Immediate Reaction Force, based on NATO's existing Mobile Force. The primary purpose was to ensure that troops were held ready to respond if a member state's security were threatened, but the possibility existed that NATO members would agree to the corps being used for specific 'out-of-area' actions, under the auspices of the **WEU** or, prospectively, the **EU**.

ALLIED RAPID REACTION FORCE *see* MOBILE THEATRE RESERVE

ALLIES

A general term, used in the pre- and immediate post-1945 period for the countries which emerged victorious in the Second World War, defeating the Axis Powers (Italy, Germany and Japan). However, the **Cold War** soon divided the Soviet Union from the Western Allies, while the differently configured Atlantic Alliance also took shape, with Italy as a founder member of **NATO** and West Germany joining in 1955.

ALTON BILL

An attempt to restrict the availability of abortion in the UK. David Alton, a **Liberal** (and subsequently **Liberal Democrat) MP**, introduced a bill in the **House of Commons** to limit to 18 weeks the then current 28-week period within which abortions might legally be performed in **Great Britain** under the 1967 **Abortion Act**. Although the Abortion (Amendment) Bill received a relatively narrow majority on its second reading on 22 January 1988, it failed to complete its remaining stages in parliament. Disagreeing with his party's more tolerant attitude to abortion, Alton withdrew from his frontbench responsibilities.

See also Appendix VI.

AMALGAMATED ENGINEERING AND ELECTRICAL UNION *see* AEEU

AMNESTY INTERNATIONAL

The human rights organization founded in 1961 by two London-based lawyers, Peter Benenson and Sean MacBride. Amnesty International, which claims over 1,000,000 members worldwide, was awarded the Nobel Peace Prize in 1978. It campaigns for (i) the release of prisoners of conscience, defined as those imprisoned because of their beliefs, or because of their ethnic origin, colour or gender, and who have neither used nor advocated violence; (ii) the prompt and fair trial of political prisoners; (iii) the abolition of 'cruel' punishments, including torture and the death penalty; and (iv) an end to 'disappearances' and extrajudicial executions. Amnesty's main campaign technique is to encourage its members to write directly to officials to protest at particular cases of human rights abuse.

ANGLICAN EVANGELICAL ASSEMBLY

The representative body of the fundamentalist tradition within the **Church of England**. Founded in the early 1980s, its origins lie in the Church of England Evangelical Council (CEEC) (itself created in 1960), which sought to unite Anglican evangelical leaders from various strands within the movement. In 1987–8 its members played a key role, in alliance with sections of the **High Church**, in opposing a motion in the **General Synod** allowing the admission of homosexual clergy.

ANGLICANISM

The body of beliefs, with emphasis on personal faith and the authority of the scriptures common to the Protestant Reformation, of the **Church of England**. Its development as a creed is generally attributed to Henry VIII's proclamation of 1534 which established royal supremacy over the Church and rejected the authority of the Pope and the Church of Rome. The Thirty-Nine Articles, adopted in their final form in 1571, together with the Book of Common Prayer of 1662 define the Anglican position. There were estimated to be about 1,200,000 practising Anglicans in Britain in 1992 and some 70,000,000 worldwide, living in 450 dioceses in 164 countries.

ANGLO-CATHOLICISM

A movement within the **Church of England**. Its adherents trace their origins to the Oxford Movement of 1833, which sought to dilute the Protestant character of the Anglican Church by the adoption of principles and practices intended to unite all Christian churches. These included the espousal of the doctrine of apostolic succession and an accompanying emphasis on an exalted priesthood and ceremonial pomp more commonly associated with the **Roman Catholic** church. Anglo-Catholics emerged as a powerful force during the **Thatcher** era when many sided with other prominent **High Church** adherents to denounce the apparently liberal drift of the Church of England, particularly its approval of the **ordination of women**. One of its most prominent representatives at the time was Gareth **Bennett**.

ANGLO-IRISH AGREEMENT

An agreement between the UK and Irish governments in November 1985 on the issue of **Northern Ireland**. Under its terms the two governments affirmed that any change in the status of Northern Ireland would come about only with the consent of the majority of the people of Northern Ireland. The agreement, the most important political initiative since the collapse of the **Sunningdale Agreement**, established an **Anglo-Irish Intergovernmental Conference** (AIIC) which has met at frequent intervals in the following years to deal with political matters, with security and related matters, with legal matters and with the promotion of co-operation across the border between Ireland and Northern Ireland.

ANGLO-IRISH INTERGOVERNMENTAL CONFERENCE

A body established under the terms of the 1985 **Anglo-Irish Agreement** which aimed to facilitate and promote dialogue between the **UK** and Irish governments. To the dismay of hardline **unionists**, the conference has met regularly either in London, Dublin or Belfast, with representatives of both the UK and Irish governments (most notably the UK **Northern Ireland** Secretary and the Irish Foreign Minister) discussing issues of mutual concern, including proposals for devolution arrangements within the province, cross-border security, problems in respect of **extradition** legislation, current terrorist controversies and the administration of justice.

ANGRY BRIGADE

A small radical group in existence in 1968–71, which carried out several bombings in January–June 1971, directing its protests mainly against new industrial relations legislation, consumerism, and militarism. The Angry Brigade's name, and its association with anarchism, student protest and youth culture, encouraged an exaggerated view of its threat to the **Establishment**, compounded by the simultaneous emergence of the Baader-Meinhof terrorist group in West Germany. Six members of the group were arrested in Stoke Newington, London, in August 1971, and four of them received 10-year sentences in December 1972 for conspiracy to cause explosions, after a protracted and high-profile **Old Bailey** trial.

ANGRY YOUNG MAN

A term used to denote writers and artists in the 1950s whose radical views, style and choice of subject matter was sharply at odds with the cultural orthodoxy of post-war Britain. The expression was particularly associated with John Osborne, whose mould-breaking play *Look Back in Anger* singled him out as the archetypal angry young man. Although it is still used, the term was made somewhat anachronistic by the more general challenge to prevailing conventions posed by youth culture in the 1960s and 1970s.

ANIMAL LIBERATION FRONT

A militant animal rights and **anti-vivisection** organization. As distinct from the **RSPCA** it promotes direct action, and since the late 1970s it has been associated with sabotage attacks on centres experimenting on animals, releasing laboratory animals into the wild, attacking research scientists and fire-bombing shops selling furs. Front members were among those demonstrating in Shoreham, Brightlingsea and other southern ports against **live exports** in early 1995.

ANNAN COMMITTEE

The Committee on the Future of Broadcasting, chaired by Lord Annan, whose report was issued in 1977. The Annan Committee was the most substantial government inquiry to date into British broadcasting, and the Annan Report contained a good deal of evidence and factual information on the major issues. The Report made clear its apprehension about the 'glorification of violence' shown generally on television. On impartiality, Annan judged that broadcasters should allow the fullest range of opinions and views, that account should be taken of the weight of opinion of the 'established view', and that there should be a recognition of constant changes to the range and weight of opinion.

ANNUS HORRIBILIS

(Latin, 'horrible year') At a lunch given in her honour by the Lord Mayor of London on 24 November 1992, Queen **Elizabeth II** described 1992 as her 'annus horribilis' – a play on the phrase 'annus mirabilis' meaning a remarkable or wonderful year. This was a reference to the failure of the marriages of three of her children, which had culminated in December in the announcement of the separation of her oldest son Prince **Charles** and Princess **Diana**, and to the extensive fire a few days previously at **Windsor Castle**. 1992 was also a year when the issue of royal taxation and the **Civil List** came under widespread scrutiny.

ANTARCTIC TREATY

An agreement signed in December 1959 to promote peaceful international scientific co-operation in Antarctica. In addition to the **UK** the signatories to the treaty were Argentina, Australia, Belgium, Chile, France, Japan, New Zealand, Norway, South Africa, the former Soviet Union and the USA. There have been 26 subsequent accessions, including 10 consultative memberships. Current territorial claimants to Antarctica include Argentina, Australia, Chile, France, New Zealand, Norway and the UK. Since the mid-1980s concern over the degradation of Antarctica's natural environment and over the deterioration of the **ozone layer** above the continent has led to calls for Antarctica to be declared a 'world park', a step which would restrict commercial mining and drilling. However, a protocol to ban mining in Antarctica for 50 years, signed in October 1991, still remains to be enforced.

ANTI-MARKETEERS

Conservative MPs and peers, generally right-wingers, who opposed the **accession** of the UK to the **EEC** in 1973 (although only 15 MPs defied the Conservative **whip** and voted against accession); and those who presently go further than **Eurosceptics**, by demanding radically revised conditions for continued membership of the **EU** or even withdrawal. The **Labour** MPs – such as Peter Shore – who campaigned for a 'no' vote in the 1975 **referendum** on renegotiated terms for the UK's membership of the Community, were also described as anti-marketeers.

ANTI-NAZI LEAGUE

A **left-wing** organization in the UK formed in the 1970s to oppose the activities of militant right-wing and racist parties and organizations. The League lost its prominence in the 1980s, but was revived in January 1992 to counteract the growth of the **BNP**. It was involved, together with other organizations such as Youth Against Racism in Europe, in demonstrations in September–October 1993 in east London and outside the BNP headquarters.

ANTI-SEMITISM

Hostility towards Jews. Endemic to most parts of Europe throughout the medieval and modern periods, anti-Semitism frequently manifested itself in institutionalized discrimination against Jews and popular outbursts of violent hostility (pogroms). In the late nineteenth century racial – as opposed to religious-cultural – anti-Semitism was developed by racial theorists and social Darwinists. This found its most complete expression in the Nazi Holocaust. Since 1945, although widely discredited, both cultural and racial anti-Semitism have continued to exist, the latter being a common characteristic of fascist and neo-Nazi parties currently in existence in the UK and throughout the rest of Europe. The charge of anti-Semitism has also been used as a slur against critics of Zionism and Israeli policies in the Middle East.

ANTI-VIVISECTIONISTS

Animal rights campaigners committed to ending the dissection of living animals in medical or industrial experiments. Some of those fighting against animal experiments, such as the **Animal Liberation Front**, have used threatening and violent behaviour against scientists and have attacked laboratories.

ANTON PILLAR ORDER

A form of civil search warrant enabling a solicitor to search the premises of a defendant and to seize disputed property. The first orders enabling a plaintiff to take such action were granted in 1974 and were designed to enable film and record companies to seize pirated copies of video and audio cassettes which were in breach of copyright law. Anton Pillar orders can be used in conjunction with a **Mareva injunction**, and have also been used in cases of serious financial fraud.

The name derives from an action brought by the then West German firm Anton Pillar AG – the first case in which the **Court of Appeal** approved the use of such orders and laid down guidelines for their use. In 1985 the **High Court** awarded £10,000 damages in trespass against solicitors who were over-zealous in their execution of the order.

AONBs

Areas of outstanding natural beauty – areas of England, Wales and Northern Ireland so designated in order to preserve their character and natural features, including landscape and wildlife. Development within them is restricted. AONBs have been created since 1956 under the National Parks and Access to the Countryside Act 1949, which also provided for the creation of the **National Parks** and **SSSIs** (sites of special scientific interest).

APOSTLES

An exclusive group at Cambridge University founded in the early nineteenth century. In the early 1930s some members of the Apostles were recruited to work clandestinely for the Soviet intelligence services, most notably Guy **Burgess** and Anthony **Blunt**.

APPRENTICE BOYS

A **Northern Ireland** Protestant organization which takes its name from the so-called 'no surrender' gesture of the 13 apprentice boys who closed the city gates of Londonderry (**Derry**) on the army of James II in 1688. The Apprentice Boys hold their anniversary march in the city on 12 August, involving thousands of members from all parts of the province together with some from mainland **Great Britain** and from overseas. The march has been banned many times because of the violence and riots which it has often generated.

ARCHBISHOP OF CANTERBURY

The Primate of All England, and as such the most high-profile of national religious leaders. The primacy of what is now the supreme archbishopric of the **Church of England** over the archbishopric of York (the only other archdiocese of the Church of England) was recognized in 1072. In the fourteenth century the Pope endorsed this position by designating York Primate of England, and Canterbury Primate of All England. Since the mid-sixteenth century the Archbishop of Canterbury has assumed the prerogative of crowning the monarch and consecrating the sovereign to the office of 'supreme Governor on Earth' of the Church of England. The current Archbishop of Canterbury, the Most Rev. George Carey, is the 103rd incumbent of the post.

AREAS OF OUTSTANDING NATURAL BEAUTY *see* AONBs

ARMALITE

An automatic rifle favoured by paramilitary republican forces in **Northern Ireland**. It was widely used in the **republicans'** struggle with their Protestant **loyalist** opponents and against the UK armed forces, but was later largely replaced by the Kalashnikov **AK-47**. The phrase 'the ballot box and the Armalite', coined in 1981, continued to be used to indicate the strategy of aiming to secure eventual victory by violent as well as constitutional means.

ARMS CONTROL

A term often paired with disarmament, as in the title of the US Arms Control and Disarmament Agency which was created to handle such issues from 1961 onwards, and applicable to conventional weapons as well as to nuclear, chemical and biological warfare. Throughout the **Cold War** the emphasis was on arms control rather than actual disarmament until the **START** and **CFE** agreements of the early 1990s. Arms control efforts related variously to limiting the geographical spread of weapons deployment (the 1959 Antarctic Treaty, the 1967 Latin American Treaty of Tlatelolco, the 1987 Pacific Rarotonga Treaty, and the Outer Space Treaty and Seabed Treaty of 1967 and 1970); preventing the deployment of new weapons and systems (the 1972 Biological Weapons Convention, the ABM Treaty, the INF Treaty and the Geneva negotiations on chemical weapons); and controlling the development and proliferation of technology (the 1963 Partial Test Ban Treaty, and the 1968 Nuclear Non-Proliferation Treaty (NPT)).

ARMS RACE

The rapid and competitive build-up of weapons by states which regard themselves as adversaries. An arms race may occur in a regional context (as in the Middle East or the Asian subcontinent), while at the global level the nuclear arms race between the superpowers was a feature of the **Cold War**, marked by periods of particular intensity in weapons development and production. The arms trade, a major export earner for certain countries, is the principal beneficiary of an arms race. Some analysts have also sought to explain the superpower arms race in terms of the power of the military-industrial complex in the domestic economy and politics of both superpowers.

ARMS TO IRAQ *see* SCOTT INQUIRY

ARTS COUNCIL OF GREAT BRITAIN

An independent body established in 1946 to be the principal channel for the government's support of the arts, operating under a Royal Charter. It was independent of government and was registered as a charity, although it was funded by an annual government grant. The Council's objectives were to improve the knowledge, understanding and practice of the arts, to increase the accessibility of the arts to the public and to advise government departments, local authorities and other bodies on the arts. In April 1994 the Scottish and Welsh Arts Councils became autonomous, and the Arts Council of Great Britain became the Arts Council of England. The Arts Council is responsible for distributing funds raised by the **national lottery** to the arts, crafts and film.

ASHDOWN, PADDY

(b. 1941) Leader of the **Liberal Democrats** since 1988. Ashdown guided his party, formed in March 1988 by the merger of the **Liberal Party** with the **Social Democratic Party**, into a period of relative calm. Ashdown had enjoyed a successful career in the Royal Marines, emerging in 1971 as a captain; he then completed short spells in the diplomatic service and industry. He entered the **House of Commons** in 1983 after taking the hitherto safe **Conservative Party** seat of Yeovil for the Liberals. In 1983–8 he served as his party's spokesperson on trade and industry, education and science, and **Northern Ireland**. Despite electoral setbacks, Ashdown has revitalised Liberal Democrat policies, which now include an acceptance of the free market and greater competition and, most recently, the abandonment of 'equidistance'.

ASIAN 'FLU

An influenza epidemic stemming from a particularly virulent strain of the virus, originating in Asia, which occurred in the autumn of 1957. At its height, in September, several hundred people were dying each week from the 'flu and from pneumonia and bronchitis. A vaccine was distributed at the beginning of October, and by early November the epidemic had receded.

ASLEF

The Associated Society of Locomotive Engineers and Firemen – the rail drivers' union, founded in 1880, which organizes most drivers employed by the railway companies and by London Underground. It is fiercely independent and has periodically mounted industrial action in defence of working practices.

ASSOCIATION OF CHIEF POLICE OFFICERS

The staff associations for Chief Constables, Deputy Chief Constables and Assistant Chief Constables of **police** authorities and for officers of the rank of Commander and above in the Metropolitan Police and the **City** of London Police. ACPO representatives played a full part in the often critical response of the police profession to government plans for its reform, which had been recommended in the **Sheehy Report** on the structure and management of the police force and which were contained in the Police and Magistrates' Courts Act 1994. There are two separate bodies, the Association of Chief Police Officers of England, Wales and Northern Ireland and the Association of Chief Police Officers in Scotland. *See also* Appendix VI.

ASYLUM

Refuge sought by someone fleeing political, religious, racial or other persecution or harassment in another country. Traditionally the UK was seen as a haven for the politically persecuted, whether they were Jews fleeing Russia at the beginning of the twentieth century, or individuals fleeing the communist states or conflicts in the other parts of the world. However, the end of the Cold War and the generally increased mobility of individuals has led to perceptions that asylum seekers are often **economic migrants** in disguise. The number of asylum seekers in the UK has risen gradually, from about 5,000 in 1988 to 22,000 in 1990. By 1991 the number was 44,800, although since then the number of applications has fallen to 24,600 in 1992 and 22,370 in 1994.

In 1987 the government imposed a £1,000 fine on carriers for each passenger brought to the UK without proper papers; this amount was doubled in 1991. In November 1991 the government also introduced the Asylum and **Immigration** Appeals Act, which came into force in July 1993. This Act seeks to streamline the applications process, but at the same time gives all those refused entry the right of appeal before deportation. The Act also lists factors that the **Home Office**, which had hitherto enjoyed a high degree of discretion, must take into account when considering asylum applications. The new system has done little to speed up the process, although since the Act came into force the number of refusals has risen dramatically and correspondingly '**exceptional leave to remain**' has fallen, with only a very small number of applicants being granted formal **refugee** status. Those awaiting a decision on their application may be held in detention centres such as that at **Campsfield**.

AT THE EDGE OF THE UNION *see* REAL LIVES

ATTLEE, CLEMENT

(1883–1967) **Prime Minister** from 1945 to 1951, a **Labour** politician noted for terse comment and businesslike style. Attlee, a former Mayor of Stepney (in London) and **Cabinet** Minister, was Labour Party chairman (leader) from 1935 to 1955. After shifting Labour towards support for rearmament before 1939, he led Labour into coalition in 1940 under Winston **Churchill** and later served as **Deputy Prime Minister**, chairing the Cabinet in Churchill's absence. Labour withdrew from the coalition in June 1945 and in July went on to win its greatest **general election** victory, winning 393 seats. The new government included Ernest **Bevin**, Stafford **Cripps**, Herbert **Morrison** and Aneurin **Bevan**, beside whom Attlee cut a modest figure; however, he remained Prime Minister for six years, enacted an ambitious legislative programme, and kept popular support. His reforming government oversaw the **nationalization** of the **coal industry**, the gas industry, electricity generation and supply, and the railways; the establishment of the National Health Service (**NHS**); and Indian independence. As leading ministers aged or fell ill and later legislation (such as nationalization of the **steel industry**) proved controversial, Attlee remained in command, winning a second victory (albeit with a much reduced majority) in 1950. Internal differences now opened up between those favouring rearmament and those declining to fund it from public expenditure cuts. The resignations of Bevan, Harold **Wilson**, and John Freeman in objection to the proposal of Hugh **Gaitskell**, the **Chancellor of the Exchequer**, to introduce health charges sharpened disunity: Labour was narrowly defeated in a general election of October 1951. Attlee remained party leader, but after Labour, weakened by the fierce internal battle between left and right, lost the 1955 general election he retired, accepting an earldom.

ATTORNEY GENERAL

The government's chief law officer and adviser on legal matters. The holder of the post appears in court in civil cases affecting the public interest, and directs the prosecution of significant criminal cases. An **MP**, he or she (although as of 1995 no women had served in this office) is appointed by the **Prime Minister** and becomes a member of the **Privy Council**. The Attorney General must give consent before proceedings are begun in certain criminal cases – for example, those brought under the **Official Secrets Acts** of 1911 and 1939. He or she has the right to refer to appeal cases in which the sentence passed appears to be too lenient. In **Scotland** the **Lord Advocate** performs similar, although broader, functions. The Attorney General is assisted by the **Solicitor General**.

Sir Nicholas Lyell has served as Attorney General since April 1992.

AUSTERITY BUDGET

The emergency measures taken in 1947 by the **Labour** government to counteract the deteriorating external financial situation. During 1947 post-war credits extended by the USA to support the British economy were diminishing fast. They had been extended under an agreement requiring sterling to become convertible in July; when this took place, it exposed sterling's weakness further. Convinced by the **Chancellor of the Exchequer**, Hugh **Dalton**, of the need to cut imports the **Prime Minister**, Clement **Attlee**, presented an austerity programme on 6 August. It included an extension of the miners' working day by half an hour, cuts in food imports from hard-currency areas and reduction in the basic petrol **ration**, as well as a 75 per cent tax on US films. When the position of sterling continued to deteriorate, arrangements for the convertibility of sterling into dollars was suspended (on 19 August), and on 23 August further restrictions were announced, including a reduction in the meat ration and the abolition of the basic petrol ration.

See also Appendix V.

AUTUMN STATEMENT

The annual statement of public expenditure plans as presented by **Chancellor of the Exchequer** each autumn. The statement includes expenditure by both central and local government, and shows the way in which public spending is allocated between the different departments of state, together with changes to such allocations over a rolling three-year programme. The aim of the **Conservative** government has been to maintain rigid control of public spending so that total spending as a percentage of **GDP** declines. Where public spending is greater than revenue, a shortfall – or public-sector borrowing requirement (**PSBR**) – is created. The autumn statement was for the first time in November 1993 combined with government's revenue plans – hitherto presented at Easter – thus producing a unified **budget**.

AWACS

Airborne Warning and Control Systems aircraft. These aircraft are airborne jamming-resistant radar stations and command and communications centres, and their radar can 'peer' about 300 km over the horizon. The US E-3 Sentry, based on the Boeing 707, is distinctive by the radome dish mounted on top. A similar aircraft based on the **Nimrod** was originally planned for the RAF, but insuperable problems caused its cancellation in 1987.

B SPECIALS

The colloquial name given to the controversial Ulster Special Constabulary, a now-disbanded auxiliary police force in **Northern Ireland**. The B Specials (numbering some 8,000 personnel, effectively all Protestant) were established in the early 1920s and were widely seen by the Catholic community as representing an oppressively military and sectarian element of the Royal Ulster Constabulary (**RUC**). They were disbanded in 1970, when their military role was assumed by the Ulster Defence Regiment (UDR) and their police duties by a new RUC reserve force.

BABIES ON BENEFIT

A controversial television documentary broadcast in September 1993 as part of **BBC**'s *Panorama* series. The programme focused on the issue of young women who have children and who claim **welfare benefits**. It contained interviews with teenagers who deliberately had babies in order to be able to claim benefit, women who had a second child to obtain a council flat, and women who preferred to remain as independent single mothers. Following the broadcast the National Council for One Parent Families made a complaint to the **Broadcasting Complaints Commission** that the programme was unfair on six separate counts. In September 1994 the Commission ruled that the programme had been 'unfair and unjust'. The BBC responded by broad- casting live a denunciation of the adjudication and announcing that it would seek a judicial review of the ruling, on the grounds that the National Council for One Parent Families was not directly involved in the programme and that therefore its complaint should not have been considered.

BABY BOOM

An expression used to describe any sudden increase in population, but particularly the population rise in the UK (and the USA) between the late 1940s and the early 1960s attributed to the combination of the ending of the Second World War and the rapid expansion of the economy. Consequently 'Baby Boomer' is used to describe the generation that came of age and joined the workforce in the 1970s. The term itself only gained currency in the 1970s.

BACK TO BASICS

A strategy adopted by the **Conservative Party** in late 1993. Back to Basics was a bid by **Prime Minister** John **Major** to reaffirm the party's fundamental values, thereby re-establishing the public's trust in politics, appealing to basic values neglected by politicians, and – crucially – re-establishing a consensus within a party preoccupied by its divisions over European policy.

Emphasis was placed not only on a free-enterprise economy but also on the basic social values of self-discipline, respect for the law, concern for others, individual responsibility and traditional education, while **family values** were also seen as fundamental. The strategy quickly began to unravel as personal, business and sexual scandals rocked the party and exposed it to accusations of hypocrisy. The many scandals included the cases of **MP** Stephen Milligan, who died accidentally in 1994 of auto-erotic asphyxiation, MP Tim Yeo, who was found to have fathered a child through an adulterous liaison, and two Conservative MPs involved in the **cash for questions** scandal. Party managers had dropped the Back to Basics slogan by late 1994.

BACKBENCHER

A member of the **House of Commons** or **House of Lords** who is not a member of the government or of the principal opposition team of parliamentary spokespersons. By extension, the term is also used to mean rank-and-file parliamentarians in other countries. The representative body of Conservative backbenchers is the **1922 Committee**.

BAKER, KENNETH

(b. 1934) **Conservative** Home Secretary under John **Major** from November 1990 to April 1992. Prior to his appointment as Home Secretary he had served briefly as Conservative Party chairman during the period of turmoil that preceded Margaret **Thatcher**'s defeat as party leader. He had been a loyal servant to Thatcher, serving under her at local government, environment, and, most controversially, education, where he laid the groundwork for the series of educational reforms that included a **national curriculum** and the right of schools to **opt out** of local authority control.

BAKER DAYS

Five days in the school year set aside for teachers in state schools for in-school training and associated activities. They were introduced in 1986 by the then Education Secretary, Kenneth **Baker**, as part of his new set of conditions of service for teachers. Of the five days only one – the first of the academic year – is now a set day, compared with three when Baker days were first introduced.

BALANCE OF PAYMENTS

An account reflecting inflows of money into the UK when goods or services are sold abroad, and outflows of money from the UK when goods or services are bought from another country. The balance of payments has a number of component parts. Within the current account, the balance of (visible) trade shows the difference between exports and imports of goods, while the balance of invisible trade relates to international transactions in services such as banking, insurance and tourism. The capital account involves movements of capital (or money) between countries, and includes government loans, borrowing and lending overseas by UK banks, and investment between the UK and other countries. The UK has traditionally run a deficit on its visible trade which has usually been offset by a surplus on the invisible account.

BALCOMBE STREET SIEGE

An incident in central London in December 1975, when four **IRA** members held two hostages for a week until finally surrendering. The gunmen, who had been pursued by police, entered a flat and took the two occupants hostage; the building was then surrounded by unprecedented numbers of armed police. All four men were sentenced to life imprisonment in February 1977, for murder and other offences, and also received concurrent 21- and 20-year sentences for their part in other serious offences in 1974–5.

BALTIC EXCHANGE

The Baltic Mercantile and Shipping Exchange, a worldwide market located in the **City** of London for buying and selling cargo space on ships and aircraft. Its origins lie in a sixteenth century company of English merchants trading with ports on the Baltic Sea. The Exchange, a listed building, was the target of an **IRA** bomb in April 1992, when it was sufficiently badly damaged for the decision to be taken in July 1995 to demolish it.

BAN THE BOMB!

A slogan used by **CND** and other organizations opposed to nuclear weapons. First coined by members of the World Peace Council in the 1950s, it came into wider usage after being chanted by CND supporters on the first **Aldermaston** march.

BAND AID

The charity formed by musicians Bob Geldof and Midge Ure in December 1984 in response to the famine in Ethiopia. The pair wrote the song 'Do They Know It's Christmas?' and arranged for prominent musicians and technicians to donate their services to record the song; it reached Number One in the UK hit record chart on 14 December. All proceeds for the sale of the record went to the charity, which focused on self-help schemes as well as emergency relief. Band Aid also organized **Live Aid** in 1985.

BANDING *see* STREAMING

BANK OF ENGLAND

The semi-independent central bank and financial regulator. The Bank of England was established in 1694 as a private body and was nationalized by the **Labour** government under the Bank of England Act 1946. This and subsequent Acts of 1979 and 1987 gradually extended its power to regulate the banks. By legislation of 1844 it has sole power to issue legal tender in England and Wales. The Bank assists the government in raising capital by issuing gilt-edged stock, thus helping to fund the public deficit. It also acts in two important ways to assist the management of the economy: it influences interest rates by setting its own rate (formerly known as the bank rate and later as minimum lending rate), thus counteracting **inflationary** or deflationary pressures; and it uses gold and foreign currency reserves to intervene in the foreign exchange markets and act on the value of sterling. In order to reduce political influence on the timing of interest rate adjustments, an independent Bank has been proposed; although bank rate changes continue to be agreed by **Chancellor of the Exchequer** and the Governor of the Bank, timing is now left in the hands of the Bank. The transparency of economic policy management was increased in 1994, when it was decided that the minutes of monthly meetings between the Chancellor and the Governor should be published.

BAOR

The British Army of the Rhine, until 1994 the principal component of UK armed forces in continental Europe, based in the former West Germany. Its strength included one corps headquarters, one armoured divisional headquarters, three brigade headquarters, infantry battalions and artillery regiments. Following the advent of German unification in October 1990, nearly 50 years of British presence in Germany ended in September 1994 with the withdrawal of the remaining British service personnel.

BAR COUNCIL

The General Council of the Bar, the governing body for all practising and retired barristers in **England** and **Wales**. Its role is to maintain standards and to safeguard the independence of the Bar and to represent it in all public consideration of the administration of justice. It played an active role in debates about the reform of the legal system in the early 1990s. The governing body in **Northern Ireland** is the Honourable Society of the Inn of Court of Northern Ireland and that in **Scotland** is the Faculty of Advocates.

BARBER, ANTHONY

(b. 1920) Barber replaced Iain **Macleod** in July 1970 as **Chancellor of the Exchequer** of the **Conservative** government. Barber's chancellorship encompassed **decimalization** (1971), entry into the **EEC** (1973) and the adoption of **VAT** (1973) as well as the introduction of a **three-day week** for industry in early 1974 to cope with the miners' strike. After the Conservative defeat in the 1974 **general election** Barber entered the **House of Lords** as a **life peer**.

BARINGS BANK

The merchant bank whose spectacular collapse in February 1995 highlighted the risks of over-exposure in the volatile **derivatives** markets. Baring Brothers & Co Ltd, founded in 1762, was closely identified with the British **Establishment** and numbered Queen **Elizabeth** among its customers, but failed to keep proper control over the activities of Nick Leeson, a young financial market operator at Baring Futures Singapore. Leeson's apparent golden touch encouraged the bank to transfer £760 million to fund his speculation in financial derivatives, but his deals came badly unstuck over a downturn on the Japanese stock market. He absconded (and was later arrested in Germany), leaving the bank liable to meet contracts whose eventual cost might exceed £10 billion. With the **Bank of England** and the **City** unable to make an open-ended commitment to bail it out, Barings was placed in administration on 26 February 1995 and was sold off the following month to the Dutch bank ING.

BARLOW CLOWES

The fund management group whose collapse in 1988 resulted in nearly 20,000 investors losing up to £191 million. The company was formed in 1973 and specialized in bond-washing, a tax avoidance loophole which was finally closed by the government in March 1985. The company nevertheless continued to operate under a number of different guises, and complex methods were used to divert clients' cash. Peter Clowes gained a controlling interest in James Ferguson Holdings, a public company listed on the **London Stock Exchange**, which then went on to acquire the Barlow Clowes businesses. The collapse of the house of cards was precipitated by **Black Monday**, the stock market crash in October 1987; Ferguson shares, which had peaked at 192p, fell continuously to 46p by May 1988, when they were suspended. The suspension coincided with the decision of the newly formed **Securities and Investment Board** to place Barlow Clowes into liquidation. Clowes was sentenced to 10 years' imprisonment for fraud in 1992 and his computer expert Peter Naylor got 18 months. In December 1989 the government accepted an **Ombudsman's** report pointing to **DTI** maladministration and deficiencies over supervision, regulation and licensing. It agreed to establish a £150 million compensation fund for Barlow Clowes depositors, who had believed that their money had been safely invested in government bonds. In July 1995 the official DTI report into the affair declared that the fundamental cause of the collapse of the company was the fraudulent activity of those involved, Clowes in particular. However, it listed missed opportunities by the DTI, regulators and professional advisers to detect the fraud.

BASIC LAW

The 'mini-constitution' for **Hong Kong** after sovereignty reverts from the UK to China in 1997. The Basic Law was drawn up following the Sino-British Joint Declaration of 1984, and the final draft was approved by the Chinese National People's Congress in 1990. Its status was thrown into some uncertainty, however, when the new British Governor, Chris Patten, announced proposals in October 1992 for more rapid democratization. Patten's proposals were openly opposed by the Chinese authorities. Despite this opposition, partial direct elections to the colony's Legislative Council (Legco) are in the process of being phased in.

BASTARDS

Prime Minister John **Major**'s unofficial term for **Eurosceptic** opponents both in **Cabinet** and on the **backbenches**. Major's off-the-record comments following an interview in July 1993 with **ITN**'s chief political correspondent Michael Brunson were recorded and leaked to the press. Major blamed the government's difficulties on the 'poison' from 'the dispossessed and the never-possessed' on the Conservative backbenches and implied that he would not sack 'three right-wing members of the Cabinet' (widely thought to refer to Peter Lilley, Michael **Portillo** and John Redwood) because he would not like 'three more of the bastards out there [on the backbenches]'.

BATTLEBUS

The **Liberal Party**'s campaign bus during the **general election** of 1979, which was made the focus of its campaign. The battlebus travelled the country bristling with Liberal politicians, journalists and media celebrities. Despite considerable publicity the campaign culminated in a reduced share of the vote for the Liberals.

BAZOFT, FARZAD

A British journalist who was hanged in Iraq as a spy in 1990. Bazoft was working for the *Observer* Sunday newspaper when he was arrested in September 1989 after travelling to a weapons base outside Baghdad to investigate reports of a large explosion. The Iraqi authorities claimed that he was found carrying soil samples from the base. Bazoft was sentenced to death on charges of spying for the UK and Israel and, despite international appeals for clemency, was hanged on 15 March 1990. The UK recalled its ambassador and applied limited sanctions as a protest. The episode added further strain to UK-Iraqi relations.

BBC

The British Broadcasting Corporation, responsible for the operation of **public service broadcasting** in the UK, governed by a **Board of Governors** appointed by the government. It was incorporated in December 1926 under Royal Charter, which governs its constitution and finances. The latter comes from a combination of a **licence fee** levied on those owning television sets, and funding from Parliament for the **BBC world service**. The BBC broadcasts via two national television services, BBC1 and BBC2, and five national radio networks as well as 38 local radio stations, within a constantly changing broadcasting environment. In the November 1992 **Green Paper** on the BBC's future, the **Conservative** government indicated that a rethink about the nature and priorities of public service broadcasting was required; although the licence fee was an 'oddity', no one had come up with a better idea. In a **select committee** report on the BBC published in December 1993, the **House of Commons** recommended that the BBC should be granted a new 10-year charter on the expiry of the current one in 1996. The committee wanted to see the licence fee retained for the moment, and rejected advertising on the BBC on the grounds that it would harm the profitability and survival of independent television and Channel 4.

BBC BOARD OF GOVERNORS

A group of 12 people responsible under the terms of the **BBC** Charter for establishing and outlining Corporation policy guidelines on broadcasting and related matters, appointing the **Director-General of the BBC** and other senior staff and maintaining high standards of broadcasting throughout the range of scheduled programmes. Appointed by the **Prime Minister** for a five-year period, the governors are currently seeing the BBC through radical changes, partly due to **broadcasting legislation** and partly through criticism from a variety of sources about the BBC's accountability and doubts about its ability to protect the public interest.

BBC WORLD SERVICE

The overseas radio broadcasting service provided by the **BBC**. Widely recognized as the largest international radio station in the world, with some 130 million listeners a week, the World Service broadcasts 880 hours of programmes a week in English and 38 other languages. Programmes include news, current affairs and political comment, together with sport, music and drama. The service's running costs are not included in the licence fee and are paid for by a parliamentary grant-in-aid, but control over editorial content rests with the BBC. Since 1994 the World Service has also broadcast television programmes to viewers worldwide.

BBFC (British Board of Film Classification) *See* CENSORSHIP

BCCI

The Bank of Credit and Commerce International, which collapsed spectacularly in July 1991. Founded originally in 1972 by Agha Hassan Abedi, in 1990 BCCI came under the majority control of the family of the ruler of Abu Dhabi. By that time it had some 800,000 depositors with deposits worldwide of some US$20,000 million. In 1991 it became apparent that the bank was insolvent as a result of suspected massive fraud which also involved the financing of drug trafficking and money-laundering. A number of senior officers were charged with various offences connected with the collapse, but some of these were outside the jurisdiction of the relevant courts. The Abu Dhabi authorities offered a US$1,700 million compensation settlement, whereby creditors would have received a return of about one-third of their deposits over a period of time. A handful of depositors held out in the Luxembourg courts for more favourable treatment, and in early 1994 the Abu Dhabi authorities proposed a revised settlement.

In the UK an inquiry into the collapse of BCCI, chaired by Lord Justice Bingham, published its report in October 1992. It gave a comprehensive account of BCCI's history and the events leading to its collapse. The supervisory role of the **Bank of England** came under particular scrutiny, the report recommending that the Bank should improve its internal communications, establish a special investigations unit and improve its legal unit. Among other recommendations were those covering European Union (**EU**) law, international banking supervision and the duty of auditors to provide information to the Bank of England.

BEAN FIELD *see* THE CONVOY

BEAST OF BOLSOVER

A nickname for Dennis **Skinner, Labour MP** for Bolsover.

BEATLEMANIA

The popular hysteria surrounding British pop group the Beatles in 1963–4, particularly on their first tour of the USA. The band, known as the 'Fab Four', were followed by an adoring army of largely female teenage fans and received almost continual coverage in the press. The Beatles – George Harrison, John Lennon, Paul McCartney and Ringo Starr – were often disrespectful and outspoken in interviews and inspired concerned comment from members of the political and social **Establishment** as well as adulation from their fans. The group split up in December 1970 and hopes for a reunion were dashed following the 1980 murder of Lennon. However, in 1995 the remaining three released two new songs.

BEECHING AXE

The radical pruning of railway lines deemed uneconomic. The term refers to the policies adopted as the result of a report by Richard Beeching (later Lord Beeching), who was appointed by the Conservative government in 1961 as chair of the new British Railways Board with the task of modernizing the railway service. In his report published in March of the following year he recommended the closure of about one-third of the existing railway route mileage and some 2,000 passenger stations, the rationalization of the remaining routes and a greater concentration on effective freight traffic.

BEECHING ROYAL COMMISSION

The Royal Commission on Assizes and Quarter Sessions. The commission, under the chairmanship of Lord Beeching, was set up in 1966 to inquire into the administration of judicial assizes and quarter-sessions. It reported in 1969, recommending radical changes in the structure of the courts and the administration of justice in England and Wales.

BELGRANO

An Argentinean battle cruiser, the *General Belgrano*, which was sunk in controversial circumstances on 2 May 1982, ending any hope of a negotiated settlement in the **Falklands conflict**. Of the 1,093 people aboard, 321 sailors and two civilians were killed and others perished at sea. The attack, by the British nuclear submarine HMS *Conqueror*, took place when the *Belgrano* was on a heading 55.18S,61.47W, taking it away from the British-imposed 200-mile total **exclusion zone** around the Falklands. The British government claimed that the ship was not steaming to port but to an intermediate point to await further developments, and justified the attack as in keeping with an earlier warning that ships within or outside the zone might be attacked if considered to pose a threat.

BENN, TONY

(b. 1925) A senior **left-wing Labour Party** politician. Anthony Wedgewood Benn was elected to Parliament as member for Bristol Southeast in 1950, but his career in the **House of Commons** was disrupted when he inherited the Viscountcy of Stansgate on the death of his father in 1960. Legislation introduced by Benn himself allowed peers to renounce their titles and Benn returned to the **House** as a Bristol **MP** from 1964 until 1983, and as MP for Chesterfield since 1984. Benn served as a member of the **NEC** from 1962 until 1993. He unsuccessfully contested the leadership of the party in 1976, when he was defeated by acting leader and **Prime Minister** Jim **Callaghan**, and in 1988, when Neil **Kinnock** was re-elected; he unsuccessfully contested the deputy leadership in 1970 and 1981. In government, Benn served as Postmaster General and Minister of Technology in the **Wilson Cabinets** in 1964–70, and held the

Trade and Industry and Energy portfolios in 1974–9.

Benn has fought a rearguard action against the revisionists and **modernizers** of the Labour Party and been a formidable advocate of **nationalization**, strong trade unions, the **welfare state, unilateralism** and democratization. He was the driving force behind Labour's move to the left in the early 1980s, and has been president of the **Campaign Group** since 1987. In the House of Commons he has championed the rights of parliament. Benn's detailed diaries have been published in stages since 1987.

BENNETT, GARETH

Author of a controversial, unsigned preface to the 1987–8 **Crockford's Clerical Directory**. A fellow and chaplain of New College, Oxford and a renowned **Anglo-Catholic**, he committed suicide in December 1987 after it emerged that he had been responsible for writing the traditionally anonymous preface. In it Bennett castigated the then **Archbishop of Canterbury**, Robert Runcie, for lacking moral purpose and capitulating to an unrepresentative liberal elite within the **Church of England**. The allegations emerged in the midst of mounting episcopal criticism of the severity of **Conservative** government policy on questions of personal morality and social welfare.

BENSON ROYAL COMMISSION

The Royal Commission on Legal Services in England and Wales, chaired by Sir Henry Benson, whose report, published in October 1979, said that the existing distinction between solicitors and barristers should be maintained. It also recommended that solicitors should retain their near-monopoly in the provision of conveyancing services, and defended lawyers against public criticism that they charged extortionate fees.

Ten years later measures in the Courts and Legal Services Act 1990 were significantly at odds with the Benson Report's recommendations. The Act transformed the relationship between barristers and solicitors by widening solicitors' rights of audience, and permitted banks and building societies to offer conveyancing services.

BENTLEY AND CRAIG

Two youths, one of whom was hanged for murder in 1953 even though it was his friend who fired the fatal shot. The case concerned Derek William Bentley and Christopher Craig who broke into a confectionary warehouse in November 1952. The two were spotted and apprehended by police, but not before Craig had wounded one policeman and shot dead another. Bentley, who was 19 but was said to have a mental age of 10 or 11, was sentenced to death for being 'concerned' in the murder, the prosecution case hinging on the claim that Bentley had shouted 'Let him have it!', apparently encouraging Craig to shoot. Craig, who at 16 was too young to receive the death penalty, was detained indefinitely. Despite appeals which won widespread popular support, Bentley was hanged on 28 January 1953, while Craig was released in 1963. Since his execution, Bentley's sister Iris has campaigned tirelessly for his case to be re-opened. In July 1993 the Home Secretary Michael **Howard** granted a limited pardon, accepting that the decision to hang Bentley was 'clearly wrong', but denied that a full pardon would be appropriate. Iris, however, continued to press for a royal pardon and in May 1995 announced that she had received leaked **Home Office** papers which strengthened her belief that her brother had been the victim of a miscarriage of justice.

Capital punishment was abolished in the UK in 1965.

BERKELEY RULES

The rules devised by Humphry Berkeley, the then **MP** for Lancaster, on which the first election for the leadership of the **Conservative Party** were held in 1965, when Edward **Heath** defeated Reginald **Maudling** by 150 votes to 133 to succeed Sir Alec **Douglas-Home**. Hitherto, the leader had 'emerged' following machinations within the **magic circle** of the party hierarchy. While they were an important step towards party democracy, the Berkeley rules were felt to be flawed, and another system, devised by Sir Alec Douglas-Home, was used for the first time in 1974, when Margaret **Thatcher** defeated Heath.

BERLIN AIRLIFT

The 1948–9 operation by the **Western Allies** to supply Berlin when overland links were cut by the occupying Soviet forces. Berlin, the capital of pre-war Germany, lay in the eastern part of Germany which had been liberated by the Red Army in 1945. Berlin itself had been divided into four sectors, administered respectively by the Soviet Union, the USA, the UK and France under the **Four-Power Agreement**, and linked to western Germany by road and rail. Reacting to the introduction of the Deutschmark into Allied-occupied zones, which they feared would bring the collapse of the eastern German currency, the Soviets announced on 24 June 1948 that the Allies no longer had jurisdiction in Berlin. The overland links to western Germany were cut. The Western Allies began the airlift on June 26 to sustain the blockaded city, and kept it going until 11 May 1949, when the Soviets agreed to reopen the overland link.

BERMUDA CONVENTION

The 1946 agreement between the UK and the USA governing each other's access to civil air transport routes across the North Atlantic and the Pacific Ocean and in the Caribbean. This Air Transport Agreement, which also covered fares, was greatly revised in 1966, at a time of considerable expansion of civil air traffic. Both sides accorded each other increased landing and associated rights at this time. A second revision in 1977 (Bermuda Two) extended the agreement to further routes, allowed 'dual designation' of carriers by the two sides on certain routes, provided for the phasing out of the USA's 'fifth freedom' to pick up passengers in London and Hong Kong, and incorporated an existing bilateral agreement on charter services.

BEVAN, ANEURIN 'NYE'

(1897–1960) The radical, charismatic **Labour** politician who rose from humble origins to become the architect of the **NHS** and the left's abiding hero. 'Nye' Bevan was born in Tredegar in south Wales, and by his late teens was already a noted union activist, having begun work in the coal mines at 13. In 1926 he led the Welsh miners during the General Strike, earning a reputation as a brilliant orator. As the **MP** for Ebbw Vale, Bevan remained in opposition to the wartime coalition government but in 1945 he was appointed as Minister of Health in the government of Clement **Attlee**, supervising the establishment of the NHS in 1948. He resigned in 1951 over NHS charges proposed in the **budget** and became the champion of a radical Bevanite alternative to the revisionist leadership of the **Labour Party**. Bevan was heavily defeated by the reformist Hugh **Gaitskell** in the party leadership contest of 1955, but returned to the Labour front bench as Shadow Foreign Secretary in 1956, and – to the frustration of many on the left – declared his opposition to **unilateral disarmament** in 1957.

BEVANITES

Labour Party supporters of Aneurin **Bevan**, often also associated with the **Tribune Group**.

BEVERIDGE REPORT

The key document laying down the framework for the development of the **welfare state** in the UK. The report, drawn up by the eminent economist Sir William (Lord) Beveridge and published in 1942, recommended principally a universal and compulsory scheme of sickness and unemployment benefits and retirement pensions and the payment of family allowances, as well as a national health service. The coalition government in 1944 accepted the main recommendations, which were then implemented by the post-war Labour government and came into force generally in 1948.

BEVIN, ERNEST

(1881–1951) The pioneer of modern trade unionism and one of the architects of the modern **Labour Party**. Orphaned as a young child, Bevin left school at 13 and educated himself. He became an official of a dockers' union in 1911 and was the principal founders of the **TGWU**, of which he was general secretary in 1921–40. He joined the wartime coalition as Minister of Labour and National Service and became a senior figure in the War **Cabinet**. Bevin served as Foreign Secretary in the government of Clement **Attlee** in 1945–51, and as such was a key figure in postwar international politics, showing himself to be eager to strengthen defence and economic links with the USA and Europe, but at the same anxious not to undermine the **Commonwealth**.

BIG BANG

The transformation of the London Stock Exchange in October 1986. This reflected the advent of global stock and bond trading networks and of international round-the-clock trading. In particular it abolished barriers between the different categories of stockbrokers and jobbers, opened up ownership of stockbroking firms to foreign participants, and rapidly led to the closure of the Stock Exchange's trading floor in favour of computerized share transactions. These major changes came only 12 months before **Black Monday**, the global equity market crisis.

BIG BROTHER

The fictional leader of the totalitarian state depicted in George Orwell's political novel **1984**. Big Brother's role shared features common to leadership cults of both right and left. The state's propaganda machine built a cult of personality, ascribing to Big Brother semi-divine status as a morally pure, all-knowing, all-powerful being. The term has become synonymous with dictatorship and the police state.

BIG ISSUE

A weekly magazine launched in 1992 which campaigns on behalf of the **homeless**. It gives an opportunity to homeless people to air their views and opinions, and carries articles on homelessness itself, missing persons and current political controversies, together with music, club, theatre, film, art and book reviews. It is sold nationwide by homeless and formerly homeless people who buy the magazine for 25 pence and sell it to the public for 70 pence. Vendors receive training, and sign a code of practice. It is funded by business sponsorship, advertising and sales, and has provided housing, training and employment initiatives to help homeless people. In the 1995 Birthday **honours** list, John Bird, the editor of *Big Issue*, was awarded the MBE in recognition of his work to help the homeless.

BIG THREE

The three principal Second World War allies from 1941 to 1945 – the USA, the Soviet Union and the UK – whose leaders met to co-ordinate military strategy and to agree upon a structure for the post-war world, notably in Tehran in late 1943, in Yalta in February 1945, and in Potsdam in July–August 1945.

BIG FOUR

A common term used to describe the four largest high street banks, namely NatWest, Barclays, Midland and Lloyds. At the end of 1994 the Big Four between them had more than 8,000 branches, a market capitalization of over £44,000 million and employed more than 200,000 staff. However, their monopoly over high street banking is being gradually broken as an increasing number of building societies take on banking functions.

BIG FOUR

Originally a term referring to the Second World War alliance of the USA, the Soviet Union, the UK and China as represented by Chiang Kai Shek's nationalist Kuomintang government. The term Big Four was also applied to the USA, the Soviet Union, the UK and France, the countries which jointly administered Germany and Austria following the conclusion of the war in 1945.

BIG FIVE

The original **Big Four** wartime Allies, plus France, which, despite having refused an invitation to be one of five sponsors of the **San Francisco Conference** in April–June 1945, nevertheless participated on an equal footing in the meetings of the sponsoring powers. The Big Five then became the five permanent members of the **UN Security Council**, with veto powers.

BILL OF RIGHTS

A bill proposed by civil rights campaigners which would enumerate an individual's rights in the absence of a written **constitution** spelling out fundamental freedoms. Pressure groups such as **Liberty** and **Charter 88** argue in favour of a bill of rights on the grounds that until a citizen's civil and political rights are clearly set out in this way, the Courts are the only place where oppressive government action against individuals may be checked. However, politicians from both sides of the **House of Commons** have at different times argued that a bill of rights would challenge the sovereignty of Parliament.

In the meantime, although the UK has ratified the **European Convention on Human Rights**, this Convention has not been incorporated into UK law and cannot therefore be applied by UK courts. Consequently individuals seeking redress must exhaust national remedies before they can appeal to the **European Court of Human Rights** – a time-consuming, expensive and cumbersome process.

BINGHAM AFFAIR

David Bingham, a junior officer in the Royal Navy, was in 1972 convicted of selling official secrets. At his trial Bingham confessed that after encountering financial difficulties he had leaked Fleet Operations Tactical Instructions to the Soviet Union for a £2,800 payment. He received a 21-year sentence, of which he served seven years.

BINGHAM REPORT

The September 1978 report of the British inquiry into alleged sanctions-busting operations to supply the **UDI** regime in **Rhodesia**. In his report Thomas Bingham QC concluded that there had been some breaches in particular of the oil embargo. It also implied that **Prime Minister** Harold **Wilson** had been aware of the continued supply of oil to the Smith regime by Shell, BP and Total. This was denied at the time.

BINGHAM REPORT *see* BCCI

BIODIVERSITY

A contraction of 'biological diversity' – the immense variety of the world's plants, animals and habitats. There are estimated to be 30 million distinct species, some 1.4 million of which have been recorded to date. Present trends indicate, however, that 10 per cent of the world's species may be lost by the year 2000 because of damage to natural habitats from phenomena such as **acid rain** and **deforestation**. Concerns about species loss underlie the 1992 Biological Diversity Convention agreed upon at the Earth Summit.

BIO-ETHICS

The moral issues arising from both recent and potential medical and scientific developments. These issues relate to such practices as scientifically assisted human reproduction, including surrogacy, **IVF** and artificial insemination; research on human embryos; tissue transfer and organ donation; and genetic engineering. The 1984 **Warnock Report** established the ethical ground rules for such assisted reproduction.

BIRMINGHAM SIX

A group of six men – Patrick Hill, Richard McIlkenny, Johnny Walker, William Power, Gerard Hunter and Hugh Callaghan – wrongly imprisoned in the UK for **IRA** activities. Following the IRA bombing of two public houses in Birmingham in November 1974, the six were in August 1975 sentenced to life imprisonment for the murder of the 21 victims. Persistent campaigns for a review of their case eventually bore fruit in March 1991 when all six were freed on appeal and their convictions were overturned as unsafe and unsatisfactory in the light of new evidence. This cast doubt on the reliability of forensic evidence as well as the veracity of police officers involved in the initial interviews. Their release followed that of the **Guildford Four** in October 1989. Within hours of their release Home Secretary Kenneth **Baker** announced the establishment of a **Royal Commission** on **Criminal Justice** on the grounds that the Birmingham Six Case raised a number of serious issues relating to the criminal justice system. Among the proposals made in the Commission's report, published on 6 July 1993, was the creation of a tribunal to examine alleged miscarriages of justice.

BIRT, JOHN

The **Director-General of the BBC** since December 1992. Under his stewardship the **BBC** has entered a phase of radical change with an apparent emphasis on the production of more commercially successful ventures (including radio and television programmes as well as magazine publication and the sale of audio and video tapes) rather than quality broadcasting, a move which has brought him into conflict with several respected broadcasters. One of the innovations introduced by Birt has been the controversial **producer choice**. Birt's personal conduct has also been the subject of controversy: in February 1993 the *Independent on Sunday* revealed that, in an arrangement which had prevailed since his appointment as deputy director-general, Birt was not a member of BBC staff but was being paid through a private company (John Birt Productions Ltd.) in order to gain tax advantage. Within days of the revelation Birt confirmed that he was to join the Corporation as a staff member.

BIS

The Bank for International Settlements, the 'central bankers' bank'. Founded in 1930, it promotes co-operation between central banks and provides additional facilities for international financial operations, as well as a forum for often informal discussions on monetary co-operation in general. There are 33 countries represented in the bank (18 west European – including the UK – 10 central and east European and five others).

BISHOPSGATE BOMB

A bomb explosion on 24 April 1993 near Bishopsgate in the City of London, the financial heart of the capital, in which one person was killed and more than 40 injured. The bomb, placed in a truck, was estimate to contain 10 pounds of **semtex** and a tonne of chemical explosive. It caused damage estimated at between £300 million and £400 million, with the Hong Kong and Shanghai Bank, the NatWest Tower and the fifteenth-century St Elthelburga church taking the main impact. The **IRA** later claimed responsibility for the bomb.

BITOV AFFAIR

Oleg Bitov, a Soviet citizen, sought asylum in Italy and then in the UK in 1986. He later returned to his homeland, claiming that he had been kidnapped and drugged by the US Central Intelligence Agency (CIA).

BLACK AND ASIAN SOCIALIST SOCIETY

see BLACK SECTIONS

BLACK ECONOMY

That part of the economy based on illegal or undeclared transactions. In a broader sense it is applied to all transactions not reflected in official statistics, including avoidance of tax by exploiting legal loopholes.

BLACK MONDAY

The first day of the 1987 global equity crisis. Following a week of unsettled conditions on the US stock markets, the Dow Jones industrial average index fell on 19 October 1989 by over 500 points, while in London the **FTSE-100** index dropped by about 250 points (over 10 per cent). There was a marked knock-on effect in most other major financial centres. The crash in share prices appeared to have been triggered by lack of investor confidence in the US government's determination to tackle its budget deficit, and by increasing international fears over the underlying strength of the US economy.

BLACK ROD

An official of the **House of Lords**, formally known as the Gentleman Usher of the Black Rod, responsible for security, accommodation and services in the upper chamber. His most prominent role is to call members of the **House of Commons** to attend the **Queen's Speech** in the House of Lords.

BLACK SECTIONS

The groups set up at constituency level in the **Labour Party** in the mid-1980s by those who wanted special representation for Black members. Essentially a feature of the Labour Party in London and other urban areas, the establishment of Black Sections caused a major rift in the party. Their supporters argued that Black Sections were the best way to involve Afro-Caribbeans and Asians in mainstream politics. However, opponents regarded them as a form of apartheid and the **NEC** and the Party Conference repeatedly refused to endorse them. Eventually it was agreed that Black Sections would be dissolved and in 1993 the Black and Asian Socialist Society, a group affiliated to the

Labour Party and open to all ethnic minorities, was founded.

BLACK WEDNESDAY

The day in September 1992 when sterling, and the Italian lira, withdrew from the exchange rate mechanism (**ERM**) of the European Monetary System (**EMS**). During the first part of September money markets in Western Europe had been very unsettled, and on 16 September sterling came under particularly violent speculative pressure. The UK authorities tried unsuccessfully to defend the pound, introducing large temporary increases in interest rates and spending huge amounts of the official reserves. On the night of 16–17 September, however, it was announced that sterling would no longer be kept within the permitted margins of fluctuation within the ERM, to which the UK had first adhered as recently as October 1990, and that the Italian lira would also float within the ERM.

BLACKBIRD LEYS ESTATE

A local authority housing estate in Oxford, central England, which in September 1991 was the scene of rioting in response to police attempts to stop the activities of **joy riders**. Other riots and looting occurred at about the same time in Birmingham, Cardiff and Tyneside, and were closely followed by the publication of official figures showing record crime levels. This led to calls for tougher sentencing and laws and also to public criticism of the police's apparent inability to control **young offenders**. Six metropolitan police authorities complained that government **capping** of local authorities' spending had led to cuts in their budgets and resulted in staffing shortages.

BLAIR, TONY

(b. 1953) Leader of the **Labour Party** since July 1994. Blair was privately educated and studied at the universities of Edinburgh and Oxford. Having been called to the Bar in 1976, he was elected as **MP** for Sedgefield in 1983. He achieved success as **Shadow** Home Affairs spokesman in 1992–4 by seizing the agenda on law and order issues, traditionally regarded as a **Conservative** area of interest, with the slogan 'tough on crime, tough on the causes of crime'. Blair became, with his friend and ally Gordon **Brown**, a leading Labour **modernizer**. Following the premature death of Labour leader John **Smith**, Blair was elected leader with 57 per cent of the vote. The party clearly hoped that the telegenic Blair would win support from **middle England** and in the south. In a striking first speech to a Labour conference as party leader, Blair called for a radical revision of **Clause IV** of the party's constitution, and, in a significant victory over the party's left wing, achieved his goal at a special party conference in April 1995. His apparent unwillingness to give details of his policies has led detractors to give him the nickname 'Tony Blur'.

BLAKE, GEORGE

(b. 1922) A Soviet agent who escaped to the Soviet Union. Blake, a former Royal Navy lieutenant, was recruited in 1948 as a Soviet spy by Guy **Burgess**, worked in the Far Eastern Department of the Foreign Office (later the **FCO**) and was later employed in a consular capacity in Korea, where he was in Communist captivity during the Korean War. He was recalled to the UK in April 1961 and in May was convicted on five charges under the Official Secrets Act and sentenced to 42 years' imprisonment, the longest sentence imposed on a spy. In 1966 he broke out of Wormwood Scrubbs and made his way to East Germany with the help of Patrick Pottle and Michael Randle; at their trial in June 1991 on charges relating to his escape these two did not contest the facts, but asserted that they had helped Blake escape for humanitarian reasons, and the jury unanimously found them not guilty. Blake later emerged in Moscow, where he has since lived.

BLANKET PROTEST *see* DIRTY PROTEST

BLASPHEMY

Irreverence towards a deity or the use of profanity. In the UK it is both a statutory and common law offence, but only with regard to Christianity. It was most recently invoked in 1977 during a successful private prosecution brought by Mary Whitehouse against the magazine *Gay News*, which had published a poem by James Kirkup, 'The Love that Dare Not

Speak its Name', which apparently portrayed Christ as the object of homosexual love. In 1989 the application of the blasphemy law to other religions practised in the UK became a subject of intense controversy when the publication of the novel **The Satanic Verses** by Salman Rushdie, deemed by large numbers of Muslims to be blasphemous in its treatment of the Prophet Muhammad, fuelled a campaign in favour of extending the law. They were opposed by human rights groups, most notably Article 19, which have consistently denounced the law against blasphemy as archaic and urged its complete abolition.

BLOCK VOTE

The exercise by British trade unions of a determining vote at **Labour Party** conferences. Traditionally voting strengths within the Labour Party conference have been based on affiliations. In the case of affiliated trade unions this has ensured that votes based on their total membership have together far outweighed those of constituency delegates; moreover, the preponderance of certain large unions has meant that individual general secretaries have often single-handedly determined the outcome of votes on crucial policy matters and the election of the party leader and deputy leader. Reforms agreed in 1992 modified this situation so that the unions' overall voting strength at the annual conference was reduced from about 87 to 70 per cent, and in 1995 Labour leader Tony **Blair** signalled his desire to reduce the strength of the block vote to 50 per cent. In 1993 **omov** (one-member-one-vote) was introduced for the selection of parliamentary candidates, where again trade unions had hitherto in many instances played a decisive role.

BLOOD DONORS *see* NATIONAL BLOOD AUTHORITY

BLOODY SUNDAY

A day of appalling conflict in the **Bogside** area of Londonderry (**Derry**), **Northern Ireland**, on 30 January 1972. A massive confrontation occurred when a technically illegal **civil rights** march disintegrated into fierce skirmishes with the security forces who had been ordered to make arrests; 13 civilians were killed, but the Widgery tribunal later effectively exonerated the security forces. The incident caused a storm of protest, including an attack on the British embassy in Dublin. It also increased support for the **IRA**, with many locals joining its ranks, while the fundraising activities of **NORAID** and other groups were boosted.

BLUE CHIP GROUP

A Conservative dining club formed by Tory liberals of the 1979 generation, including Chris Patten and William Waldegrave. An informal grouping, it brings together several blue-blooded **MPs** belonging to the **One Nation** school of **Tories** including Nicholas Soames and Lord Cranborne, who headed John **Major**'s campaign for the party leadership in June 1995, reflecting the **Prime Minister's** links with the group.

BLUE STREAK

A British rocket which in the 1950s was expected to provide a capability independent of US technological expertise to launch British nuclear warheads against targets in the Soviet Union. The rocket's basic shape and performance was derived from the US Atlas intercontinental ballistic missile (ICBM). Its military role was eventually scrapped when, at the 1962 **Nassau conference**, the **Macmillan** government opted for US-made Polaris submarine delivery systems in tandem with Vulcan bombers rather than the more vulnerable strategic option of ground-based rockets. With an eye to the civilian satellite market, Blue Streak was nevertheless launched 11 times (1964–71), either individually or as the first stage of the Europa rocket, the collaborative effort of the European Launcher Development Organization (ELDO) set up by Belgium, France, West Germany, Italy and the UK in 1964. Due to technical and management problems, the ELDO was finally wound up in 1973 and the Europa project abandoned. Leadership in European rocketry then passed to France with the formation of the **ESA** and the development of the Ariane launcher.

BLUNKETT, DAVID

(b. 1947) A **soft-left** Labour politician. Blind since birth, Blunkett graduated from Sheffield University and later became a tutor in industrial relations at the Barnsley College of Technology. He was elected leader of Sheffield City Council in 1980, achieving national prominence in the **Labour Party** campaign against Conservative reforms of **local government**. Blunkett was elected to Parliament as member for Sheffield Brightside in 1987 and proved effective as Labour spokesman in 1988–92 on the **poll tax**, since when he has served as Shadow spokesman on health and education. The popular Blunkett backed Tony **Blair** for the leadership of the party in 1994, and occupies a key role in the party as a limited **modernizer** with **left-wing** roots.

BLUNT, ANTHONY

(1907–83) A Soviet spy unmasked only in old age. Blunt was a member of the exclusive Cambridge University **Apostles** debating society, several of whom were recruited in the 1930s by Soviet intelligence as spies. After Guy **Burgess**, Donald **Maclean**, and Kim **Philby**, he was the long sought-for 'Fourth Man' of the spy ring, whose identity was long unknown and then suppressed. Blunt, an art historian, was Director of the Courtauld Institute of Art from 1947 to 1974, knighted in 1956 and appointed Surveyor of the Queen's Pictures in 1952. The security services had interrogated Blunt on several occasions after the 1951 escape of Burgess and Maclean, but without result. In 1964, however, they confronted him with new evidence and he confessed to assisting in Soviet spy recruitment up to 1945, to a part in the escape of Burgess and Maclean and to further spying in 1951–56. In return for his co-operation in providing information about Soviet intelligence activities, Blunt was promised (and given) absolute immunity from prosecution and publicity. He continued to be employed in the Royal Household. Only in November 1979, on the eve of publication of a book, *The Climate of Treason* by Andrew Boyle, which implicated him, was Blunt named in **Parliament** by the **Prime Minister**, Margaret **Thatcher**. He was then stripped of his knighthood.

BMA

The British Medical Association, an organization representing members of the medical profession which aims to further their interests and to promote the health of the public. The BMA has sometimes opposed government policy, as during the establishment of the **NHS** in 1946–8, when the Association at first advised its members not to join the service. The BMA later opposed some of the **Conservative** government's market-led reforms to the NHS in the late 1980s and early 1990s.

BNFL

British Nuclear Fuels plc, a state-owned company owning two nuclear power stations and providing services for the rest of the nuclear industry such as waste management, **decommissioning** and fuel manufacturing and reprocessing. It was established as a public company in 1971 to take over all the nuclear fuel business of the production group of the then Atomic Energy Authority (AEA). BNFL operates the major nuclear site at **Sellafield**, west Cumbria, which includes the Calder Hall **Magnox** nuclear power station as well as the controversial **Thorp** reprocessing plant and two other fuel reprocessing plants.

BNP

The British National Party, an extreme right-wing party which campaigns on an overtly **racist** platform demanding, for example, the repatriation of **immigrants** and blaming black people, whether British or not, for **unemployment** and high levels of **inner city** social deprivation. It also calls for the reintroduction of **capital punishment**.

The BNP was formed by John Tyndall as a breakaway group from the **National Front**, first as the New National Front and from April 1982 as the BNP. It has since contested **elections**, putting up candidates at general and local elections. It has had negligible success, although in September 1993 it won a local council seat in a **by-election** in Tower Hamlets, a deprived area of London with high rates of unemployment, a huge housing shortage and large black, predominantly Asian population. While condemned by both the **Liberal Democrats**, who controlled the local authority, and the **Labour Party**, the Liberal Democrats were accused by Labour of having effectively assisted the BNP victory by also distributing racist leaflets during the campaign. The party lost the seat in the May 1994 local elections.

BOARD OF DEPUTIES OF BRITISH JEWS

An officially recognized representative body of British Jewry, made up of representatives from synagogues and from some secular organizations. It originated in 1760, gaining statutory recognition half a century later, and deals principally with the government and other public bodies and with the Jewish community, the public and the media. Based in central London, its official title is the London Committee of Deputies of the British Jews.

BOARD OF TRADE

A permanent committee of the **Privy Council** established in 1696 by King William III, which was reformed in 1786 to become a conventional government department, and which in 1970 merged with the Department of Technology to become the Department of Trade and Industry (**DTI**). Although the Secretary of State for Trade and Industry also holds the title President of the Board of Trade, the title was not much used in recent years until April 1992, when it was revived by Michael **Heseltine**. The membership of the Board consists of its President (i.e. the Secretary of State); the First Lord of the Treasury (i.e. the **Prime Minister**); the First Lord Commissioner of the Admiralty – the Paymaster General of Her Majesty's Forces and Treasurer of the Royal Navy; the **Chancellor of the Exchequer**; Secretaries of the State or their representatives; the **Speaker** of the **House of Commons**; the **Archbishop of Canterbury**; the Bishop of London; the **Master of the Rolls** and the Secretary of the Board (i.e. the **Permanent Secretary** at the DTI). It last met as an entity on 21 March 1986 to mark its bicentenary; this was the first time it had met as such since 1850. However, since 1901 the Board's quorum has been one, so that it can therefore be regarded as being in constant session.

BOAT PEOPLE

The term applied in the UK to Vietnamese refugees who fled their homeland by sea following the end of the Vietnam War in 1975 and landed in Hong Kong and various countries in south-east Asia, with the eventual aim of gaining residency in the UK and other Western countries. The majority of boat people who left during the immediate post-war period were middle-class southerners, but by 1978 they were joined by an increasing number of peasants and urban workers and thousands of Hoa (ethnic Chinese). Most were denied political refugee status (being deemed **economic migrants**) and were forced either to live in camps established at their place of arrival or to return to Vietnam. Under an agreement reached at a Geneva conference on Vietnamese refugees held in March 1995, the 18,000 boat people remaining in camps in south-east Asia would be repatriated by the end of 1995, while the 22,000 in Hong Kong would depart by early 1996. The Vietnamese government agreed to simplify its cumbersome repatriation procedures and accept some 3,600 returnees a month.

BODY SHOP

A **UK**-based manufacturer and retailer of cosmetics and skin care products made from natural materials founded by Anita Roddick in 1976. In 1995 the company had over 1,200 stores in 45 countries. The Body Shop has a public commitment to socially and environmentally responsible policies such as energy efficiency and an ethical approach to trade with the developing world, but during 1994 this was the subject of press investigation and criticism by some investors who claimed that the company did not put these ideals into practice.

BOGSIDE

An area of Londonderry (**Derry**) in **Northern Ireland** with an almost exclusively **Roman Catholic** and **republican** population. On 13 August 1969 its siege by **loyalists**, supported by the **B-specials**, marked the start of the **Troubles**. On 30 January 1972 (**Bloody Sunday**) a massive confrontation with the security forces left 13 civilians dead; the Widgery tribunal, however, effectively exonerated the security forces of any general breakdown in discipline in their actions.

BOOKER PRIZE

The UK's major literary prize, sponsored by Booker McConnell, the multinational conglomerate. Awarded annually since 1968, the Booker jury awards £20,000 to the best full-length novel in English, written by a citizen of the **UK**, the **Commonwealth**, the Republic of Ireland or South Africa. In recent years the Booker has become a major media event and in sales terms a place on the short-list has a major impact on the marketability of a book. However, in recent years the prize has often been clouded in controversy. In 1994 it was won by the Scottish writer James Kelman for *How Late It Was, How Late*, but the jury almost disintegrated during the selection process and the choice was roundly condemned by self-appointed guardians of pure English who objected generally to Kelman's usage of Glaswegian vernacular and, in particular, to his repeated use of the words 'fuck' and 'cunt'.

BOOT CAMPS *see* YOUNG OFFENDERS

BORRIE COMMISSION *see* SOCIAL JUSTICE COMMISSION

BOUNDARY COMMISSIONS

Four bodies, constituted under the Parliamentary Constituencies Act 1986, which are responsible for keeping the parliamentary constituencies in their parts of the UK under review. In March 1995 the Commissions published a report of the review carried out after the 1992 **general election** to take account of population changes over the past 20 years. It proposed 180 major and 170 minor boundary changes and an expansion of the **House of Commons**, increasing the number of **MPs** from 651 to 659 with additional seats allocated to Wales (with two extra MPs), Northern Ireland (one extra) and England (five extra). The recommendations of the report were subsequently approved by the House of Commons.

BOW GROUP

A policy research organization associated with the **Conservative Party**. Formed in 1951 as an intellectual counterbalance to the **left-wing Fabian Society**, it has provided a wealth of progressive policy initiatives for the Conservatives, and a number of prominent members of Conservative governments have been Bow Group members. Around one-third of Conservative **MPs** are members.

BRADFORD COUNCIL OF MOSQUES

A Bradford-based federation of mosques. It was established in 1980 with the aim of acting as a link between Bradford City Council and the city's sizable Muslim community and of liaising between mosques under the control of different Islamic factions. In 1989 its then leader, Sher Azam, catapulted the organization to prominence after he decided to spearhead the campaign to ban Salman Rushdie's novel *The* **Satanic Verses**. Since then the Council has played an active part in seeking the extension of the law of **blasphemy**, currently applicable only to Christianity, to cover Islam and other non-Christian religions.

BRADFORD FOOTBALL FIRE

Fire which swept through the main stand of Bradford City football club on 11 May 1985, killing 59 spectators and injuring a further 150. The fire was caused by a match or cigarette being dropped among rubbish which had accumulated beneath the wooden stand and, fanned by strong winds, spread with devastating speed. Escape routes were impeded by locked exits at the back of the stand, and many of the dead were crushed by those seeking to escape the inferno by fleeing onto the pitch. The 1986 **Popplewell report** into the disaster made a number of recommendations for the improvement of crowd safety at sports venues.

BRADFORD RIOTS

Disturbances which broke out in the Mannington district of the Yorkshire town in early June 1995. The violent unrest was apparently sparked when the **police** attempted to break up a rowdy game of street football. The incident prompted two nights of clashes between police and predominantly, but by no means exclusively, Asian youths causing over £1,000,000 worth of damage. Community leaders insisted that clumsy policing was largely to blame for the violence, while the police contended that the youths were responsible. The police also claimed that the riots had been the result of a lack of parenting skills in the Asian community. This view was rejected as erroneous and essentially **racist** by many commentators who suggested that the violence was an expression of frustration by youths, socially disadvantaged and faced with the prospect of almost certain long-term **unemployment**, who were angered by the heavy-handed approach of the police.

BRADY, IAN *see* MOORS MURDERS

BRAER OIL SPILL

An oil spill from a Liberian-registered tanker, the *Braer*, which ran aground off Sumburgh Head, the Shetland Isles, on 5 January 1993. The 50,000-ton vessel was en route from Mongstad in Norway to Quebec when its engine failed. Storm-force winds drove it aground, whereupon its 80,000-tonne cargo of Norwegian crude oil began to escape. The ship's 34-member crew was airlifted to safety, but high winds prevented the vessel from being refloated, and it broke up on 12 January, releasing the remainder of its oil. Although it was the largest oil spillage in UK waters since the **Torrey Canyon disaster** of 1967, the dispersant measures undertaken in the clean-up operation were assisted by strong winds in breaking up the oil slick. An inquiry into the disaster was established under the chairmanship of Lord Donaldson of Lymington. Its report, published on 17 May 1994, made 103 recommendations for preventing the pollution of UK waters by merchant shipping.

BRAIN DRAIN

A colloquial term in use since the early 1960s to describe the **emigration** of leading or promising British-trained scientists and academics in order to take up jobs, especially in the USA. They are reportedly lured away by the offer of better facilities and higher pay.

BRENT SPAR

A redundant **North Sea oil** storage platform, the disposal of which was the subject of controversy in mid-1995. *Brent Spar* was decommissioned in 1991, after five years of service as an oil storage buoy. Shell UK decided, with the support of the **UK** government, to scupper the platform in the deep Atlantic, maintaining that this course of action would have very little effect on the marine environment. However, these plans were vigorously opposed by environmentalists. The operation to tow the enormous structure to the dumping ground was persistently hampered by **Greenpeace** activists, who twice boarded the rig. By April 1995 Greenpeace had won the propaganda battle and there was considerable public opposition to Shell's plans not only in the UK but also in Scandinavia, the Netherlands and most clearly in Germany, where Shell petrol stations were attacked. Despite the continuing support of the UK government, faced with a consumer boycott of their goods and increasing pressure from other European governments, on 20 June 1995 Shell unexpectedly announced an abandonment of its plans. Instead the *Brent Spar* was towed to Norway, where it was expected to be dismantled – a process which Shell supporters insisted posed a greater threat to the environment than dumping at sea.

BRETTON WOODS

The conference held in July 1944 in New Hampshire and attended by the UK, which laid the basis for the construction of the post-war financial order. In particular it provided for the establishment of the **IMF** and the World Bank, and the IMF began operating, with some 30 member states, on 1 March 1947. Although the institutions which emerged from Bretton Woods fell far short of John Maynard Keynes's plans for a genuinely independent world central bank with the power to encroach upon the sovereignty of individual states, they did go some way towards addressing the problems of competitive devaluation, exchange and trade restrictions, and a lack of international reserves which had bedeviled the pre-war world.

BRIDGEWATER THREE

Three men found guilty in November 1979 of the murder of Carl Bridgewater, a 13-year-old newspaper boy who had interrupted a burglary at a Shropshire farmhouse on 20 September 1978. The three, James Robinson, Vincent Hickey and Michael Hickey, have persistently protested their innocence and were convicted largely on the basis of the alleged confession of a fourth man, Patrick Molloy. Molloy, who was himself convicted of manslaughter and aggravated burglary for his alleged part in the crime, claimed before his death in 1981 that the confession was false and that he had been beaten by officers of the **West Midlands Serious Crime Squad**.

The three men were allowed to appeal in 1989, but their case was rejected; in February 1993 Kenneth **Clarke**, then Home Secretary, rejected their application for a second appeal to the **Court of Appeal**.

BRIDLINGTON RULES

An accord among trade unions to regulate their spheres of influence. **TUC** unions agreed at Bridlington in 1939 to respect each other's area of organizing competence; where disputes arose they were resolved through the TUC's internal procedures. The Bridlington Rules experienced major crises – such as the **Wapping dispute** – but survived for more than half a century before in 1992 **trade union legislation** empowered any employee to join the union of his or her choice.

BRIGHTON BOMB ATTACK

A spectacular **IRA** bomb attack on the Grand Hotel in Brighton in October 1984, during the annual **Conservative Party** conference. Five people were killed in the explosion, including Sir Anthony Berry, **MP** for Enfield Southgate, and Roberta Wakeham, the wife of John Wakeham, then MP for Colchester South and Maldon and government Chief **Whip**. Norman **Tebbit**, then Trade and Industry Secretary, and his wife Margaretin particular, were seriously injured. Other **Cabinet** members staying at the hotel, including the then **Prime Minister** Margaret **Thatcher**, were deemed to have had a miraculous escape. IRA member Patrick Magee and four others were in June 1986 sentenced to life imprisonment for the attack.

BRINKS MAT ROBBERY

The celebrated raid in which 3.4 tonnes of gold bullion, diamonds and platinum, valued at more than £27,000,000, were stolen on 26 November 1983 from the Brinks Mat security depot at Heathrow Airport. A security guard, Anthony Black, was arrested, confessed to his part in the robbery and was a prosecution witness in the resulting trial at the **Old Bailey**, which ended on 2 December 1984. Two men, Brian Robinson and Michael McAvoy, were convicted and jailed for 25 years and a third alleged associate in the crime was acquitted; Black had earlier been sentenced to six years' imprisonment. Investigators were said to be on course to recover all of the money after one of those convicted of laundering proceeds agreed in 1995 to pay back £3,000,000.

BRITAIN

A term employed loosely to denote either **Great Britain** or the **United Kingdom**. Even in official statements the terms 'Britain' and 'British' are used in such senses, as in 'the British government'.

BRITISH ACADEMY OF SPORT

An initiative launched by **Prime Minister** John **Major** in July 1995 designed to put sport at the centre of school life. The centrepiece of the initiative was a plan to establish a £100 million British Academy of Sport, to be funded by the **national lottery**. The Academy, based on an Australian model, is intended to offer talented youngsters access to the best available coaching. The wider initiative is aimed at improving training and bringing 'every child in every school within reach of adequate sporting facilities by 2000'.

BRITISH AEROSPACE

A company manufacturing aircraft and aerospace components, formed in April 1977 under the Aircraft and Shipbuilding Act 1977 as a publicly owned corporation but privatized in two issues of government shares in 1981 and 1985. It moved into the **motor industry** in July 1988 when it acquired the government's shareholding in the Rover Group (formerly **British Leyland**); in early 1994 it controversially sold this stake to the German company Bayerische Motoren Werke (BMW).

BAe had suffered increasingly severe financial difficulties, forcing the closure of its Hatfield plant in September 1992, and on 24 February 1993 it had revealed a pre-tax deficit of £1,200 million for 1992.

BRITISH COAL

The British Coal Corporation, formerly the National Coal Board. This was the final identity of the publicly owned **coal industry** before it passed into the private sector in December 1994. It had closed 34 pits since 1992, though some of these were re-opened by private operators. Its remaining English coal assets were sold to RJB Mining, while its Scottish assets went to Mining (Scotland) and its Welsh pits to Celtic Energy. After December 1994 British Coal had only non-mining assets to offload before going out of existence.

BRITISH COUNCIL

An independent, non-political organization which promotes the UK abroad. It provides access to British ideas, talents and experience in education, books and periodicals, the English language, the arts, science and technology. The Council was established in 1934 and incorporated by Royal Charter in 1940. It is represented in more than 90 countries and runs libraries and English language schools around the world.

BRITISH ISLES

The geographical entity comprising the **UK**, Ireland, and associated islands including the **Isle of Man** (but not the **Channel Islands**).

BRITISH LEGION

A non-political organization which exists to promote the health and social welfare of British ex-servicemen and their dependants. It was created in 1921 by Field Marshal Earl Haig and in 1971 became known as the Royal British Legion. It operates a network of social clubs throughout the country and each year raises funds by selling poppies to commemorate Remembrance Day.

BRITISH LEYLAND

The partly state-owned car and heavy vehicle manufacturing concern, formed in 1975 from the British Leyland Motor Corporation (BLMC). It was known as BL from 1979 until July 1986 when it was renamed the Rover Group. BLMC itself was formed by the merger in 1968 of British Motor Holdings Ltd (essentially a combination of car manufacturers Austin, Morris and Jaguar) and Leyland Motor Corporation Ltd (Leyland, Triumph and Rover).

British Aerospace (BAe) acquired the government's shareholding in the Rover Group for £150 million in a deal finalized on 14 July 1988. The deal was subsequently the subject of great controversy, because of financial inducements, or **sweeteners**, made available by the government to BAe at the time of the sale.

BRITISH MOVEMENT

An extreme right-wing, racist organization formed by Colin Jordan. Although the BM itself was only formally launched in 1968, it had its roots in the White Defence League, which had played a large part in aggravating the tensions between the black and white communities which led to the **Notting Hill riots** in 1958. Initially BM membership was small, numbering between 50 and 150. However, leadership changes in the mid-1970s and its successful exploitation of potential fascist support created by the disintegration of the **National Front** resulted in something of a renaissance, bringing membership levels to around 3,000, mainly white working-class males. The BM has eschewed participation in elections, concentrating its activities on violence, intimidation and agitation.

BRITISH RAIL

The nationalized rail company. The railways, previously run by several regionally based companies, were nationalized by the **Labour** government under Clement **Attlee** in 1947, placed under the Transport Commission, and from 1962 run by the British Railways Board. The years after the Second World War witnessed a steep decline in rail transport, whether measured by shares of the freight or passenger market, absolute employment, or the extent of the 'permanent way'. High operating costs and losses were partly offset by the public service obligation expressed as a subsidy to passenger travel: enduring difficulties were most dramatically addressed by Richard Beeching, chairman in 1961–5, who sharply reduced the network by means of the so-called **Beeching Axe**. Investment errors such as the replacement of steam by diesel rather than electric locomotives meant a further loss of competitiveness. Even the enthusiastic chairmanship of Sir Peter Parker failed to stem the decline. After 1979 the **Conservative** government at first saw no prospect of **privatization**, modestly introducing operations under market forces only at the margins of what was now British Rail. A structure to permit mainstream privatization was only secured with the passage of the controversial **Railways Act 1993**. Because of this legislation, which envisaged progressive loss of its functions, British Rail played only a secondary role in the 1994 **Railtrack/RMT strike**.

BRITISH SUMMER TIME *see* BST

BRITISH TELECOM *see* BT

BRITTAN, SIR LEON

(b. 1937) The **Conservative** minister who built a second career in Brussels. Brittan entered the **House of Commons** in 1974 and after the Conservative **general election** victory of 1979 rapidly rose to become Chief Secretary to the **Treasury** and then Secretary of State for Trade and Industry. In the 1986 **Westland Affair** Brittan came into conflict with Michael **Heseltine**. Brittan could not convincingly deny his involvement in a leak to discredit Heseltine, who had resigned over Westland, and had to apologize for misleading the House of Commons over another aspect of the affair. He resigned under a cloud. Many observers thought Brittan's resignation had deflected attention from **Prime Minister** Margaret **Thatcher**'s own role in the affair.

In 1988 Thatcher appointed him European Commissioner in place of Lord Cockfield, a move denounced by Sir Edward **Heath**, who complained of the appointment of 'stooges of national governments'. Brittan, however, quickly embraced Europe, energetically pursuing completion of the **Single Market** and advocating **EMU**, especially after he became Vice-President of the **European Commission**, with responsibility for external affairs. His term was renewed in 1994 after a triumph in the **GATT** talks, but his responsibilities in the enlarged Commission appointed in January 1995 were narrowed, a reverse which briefly led him to consider resignation.

BRIXTON RIOTS

Serious inner-city disturbances in south London in 1981. An outbreak of violence on 10–12 April 1981 in the multiracial area of Brixton caused severe damage to property and gave rise to widespread looting. The **Scarman Report**, resulting from a public inquiry into the disorders, made a series of fundamental recommendations both as to the immediate issue and as to more general aspects of the problems facing inner-city areas.

BRIZE NORTON

The RAF base in Oxfordshire notable as the venue for the successful meeting in December 1987 between **Prime Minister** Margaret **Thatcher** and Soviet leader Mikhail Gorbachev, who was stopping over en route for the signing of the INF treaty at a summit meeting in Washington.

BROADCASTING BAN

A ban introduced in October 1988 by Douglas **Hurd**, the then Home Secretary, to prevent the broadcasting of interviews by representatives or supporters of terrorist organizations. It was introduced mainly to deprive terrorist groups of the 'oxygen of publicity'. The ban most notably affected **Sinn Féin**, and led to actors' voices being substituted for those of prominent republican politicians being broadcast on television and radio: although film could be shown, their voices could not be heard. The ban was ended in September 1994, following the announcement of the **IRA ceasefire** in August. The Irish government had ended a similar ban in January 1994 after 21 years.

BROADCASTING COMPLAINTS COMMISSION

The organization which considers and adjudicates on complaints of unjust or unfair treatment in television or sound programmes broadcast by the **BBC** or by any licensee broadcasting under the auspices of the **Independent Television Commission** or the **Radio Authority**. The Commission was created in 1981 under the provisions of the Broadcasting Act 1980, with its powers now being derived from the Broadcasting Act 1990. The Commission's brief is similar to that of the **Broadcasting Standards Council** – created in May 1988 and placed on a statutory basis by the 1990 Act.

BROADCASTING LEGISLATION

A number of pieces of significant post-war legislation which first created and then transformed sound and television broadcasting in the **UK**. Commercial television was given legislative authority under the Television Act of 1954 which created the Independent Television Authority. Under the Sound Broadcasting Act of 1972 this was renamed the **Independent Broadcasting Authority**, which itself was replaced by the **Independent Television Commission** under the radical provisions of the Broadcasting Act of 1990. This act also created the **Radio Authority**, opened up franchises for regional television to competitive bidding, paved the way for a new Channel 5 and provided for some 25 per cent of **BBC** programmes to be made by independent producers under **producer choice**. The Act further provided for the BBC to continue in its role of public service broadcaster.

BROADCASTING STANDARDS COUNCIL

An organization whose purpose is to act as a focus for public concern about television and radio, specifically relating to the portrayal of sex and violence. Its creation was proposed by the government in May 1988 and its statutory basis was confirmed within the provisions of the Broadcasting Act of 1990. The powers of the Council include monitoring domestic programmes and considering public complaints, carrying out research on taste and decency and monitoring broadcasts from overseas **satellite television**. It is also responsible for producing a code of practice on taste and decency. The broadcasting authorities are required to take action to implement such a code, first published in November 1989. The first chair of the Council was Sir William Rees-Mogg; he was replaced in June 1993 by Lady Howe of Aberavon.

BROADSHEETS

A term used to describe that group of daily or Sunday newspapers produced in large-size or 'broadsheet' format. Known also as the 'quality' press, the broadsheets generally provide extensive coverage of politics, economics and current affairs. The *Daily Telegraph*, *Financial Times*, *Guardian*, *Independent* and *The Times* are the national dailies in this group, the Sundays being the *Independent on Sunday*, *Observer*, *Sunday Telegraph* and *Sunday Times*. The quality titles exists in stark contrast to, and with smaller circulations than, their 'popular' counterparts – published as **tabloids** – which present a more limited range of news and stories in a much more compact and populist fashion.

BROADWATER FARM

A council estate in Tottenham, an economically deprived area of north London, and the scene of violent rioting in October 1985 during which a police officer, PC Keith Blakelock, was murdered. The riot followed the death of a local woman, Cynthia Jarrett, when police entered her home. Three young men – Winston Silcott, Mark Braithwaite and Engin Raghip – were subsequently sentenced to life imprisonment for the murder of Blakelock. In November 1991 the Court of Appeal overturned their convictions, finding that police had tampered with confession statements.

BRODRICK REPORT

The Report of the Committee on Death Certification and Coroners under Judge Norman Brodrick released in September 1971, which recommended the abolition of the existing duty on coroners to summon a jury when investigating deaths suspected to be murder, manslaughter or infanticide or to have resulted from road accidents, poisoning or notifiable diseases. The report also suggested that juries should no longer be required to name a person guilty of murder, manslaughter or infanticide, and recommended wider rights of appeal against inquest findings.

BROOKE, GERALD

An anti-**communist** campaigner, Brooke distributed pamphlets attacking the Soviet Union on behalf of emigré organizations during a 1965 holiday there. He was arrested and served four years in labour camps before being repatriated in 1969 in exchange for the Krogers, members (with Gordon **Lonsdale**) of the Portland Spy Ring.

BROOKE, HENRY

(1903–84) A **Conservative** Home Secretary in 1962–64. His period in office was marked most notoriously by the 1963 Enahoro affair, when his decision to order the deportation to Nigeria of Chief Anthony Enahoro to be tried for a political offence in the knowledge, which he did not reveal to the **House of Commons**, that Enahoro would not be allowed to be represented by the counsel of his choice, gave rise to a storm of condemnation from both sides of the House. His position as Home Secretary was severely, and famously, undermined by savage ridiculing on the groundbreaking satirical television show **That Was The Week That Was**. He was given a **life peerage** in 1966.

BROOKE INITIATIVE

An attempt during 1990–2 to initiate talks on **devolution** arrangements in **Northern Ireland**, between the existing constitutional parties there and the British government, as pursued by Peter Brooke, the Secretary of State for Northern Ireland in 1989–92). Brooke had initial discussions throughout the period January–June 1990 with political leaders in the province. A whole series of bilateral talks then took place over the period June 1991–November 1992, but a number of sticking points emerged, including the role of the Irish government in any talks. The Brooke initiative was taken up by his successor, Sir Patrick Mayhew, in April 1992. The process ended in November 1992, when Mayhew informed the **House of Commons** that talks had formally ended because of the failure to agree a settlement for relationships within the province, within the island of Ireland and between the peoples of the **UK** mainland and the island of Ireland.

BROWN, GEORGE

(1914–85) A leading **Labour** politician in the 1960s with a reputation for colourful behaviour. An **MP** since 1945, he was defeated by Harold **Wilson** in the **Labour Party** leadership contest of February 1963, but served as deputy leader of the party from 1960 until 1970. A prominent member of Wilson's **Cabinet** in 1964–8, he served as Secretary of State for Economic Affairs (1964–6) and Foreign Secretary (1966–8). After losing his seat in the **general election** of 1970, he entered the **House of Lords** as a life peer, taking the title Baron George-Brown of Jevington. He resigned from the Labour Party in March 1976 in protest at its support for the **closed shop** in trade unions.

BROWN, GORDON

(b. 1951) The **Labour MP** for Dunfermline East since 1983 and key ally of party leader Tony **Blair**. After graduating from the University of Edinburgh in 1972, Brown had spells as a lecturer at Glasgow College of Technology and a journalist and current affairs editor at Scottish TV before entering Parliament. Since 1987 Brown has served on the **front bench** as **Shadow** Chief Secretary to the Treasury, Shadow Trade and Industry Secretary and Shadow **Chancellor**.

Although initially regarded as the likely successor to John **Smith** as party leader, Brown lost ground to Blair, his friend and fellow **modernizer**, during Smith's tenure. Following Smith's premature death in 1994, in a personal sacrifice widely admired in the party, Brown agreed not to stand against Blair, thus ensuring the success of a modernising candidate in the leadership election of July 1994. Brown and Blair appeared likely to maintain a close working relationship, with Brown being given close control of Labour economic policy.

BRUGES GROUP

An informal Conservative grouping of '**Eurosceptics**'. The title of the group was a reference to a speech made in the Belgian city of Bruges on 20 September 1988 by the then **Prime Minister** Margaret **Thatcher**. In this Thatcher set out a series of five 'guiding principles for the future' of the European Communities (**EC**, later the **EU**), covering willing and active co-operation between independent sovereign states, the need for practical solutions to present problems, the key role of enterprise, the avoidance of protectionism, and the need to maintain a sure defence through **NATO**. The Bruges group sought to perpetuate Thatcher's conviction that the EC should not move in the direction of what it saw as an undue tighter integration of national policies towards the evolution of a 'European' policy, especially in monetary and financial matters, and should oppose any move towards federalism in Europe.

BRUNEI REBELLION

An uprising in December 1962 in the sultanate of Brunei, then a British protectorate, and in parts of Sarawak and North Borneo. The uprising was led by the North Borneo Liberation Army, linked with the Brunei People's Party, which was strongly opposed to the planned entry of Brunei into the Federation of Malaysia. The revolt was suppressed after 10 days with the aid of British forces, and a state of emergency was declared. In the event, the Sultan of Brunei decided in 1963 against joining the Federation. Since the promulgation of the country's first written constitution in 1959 the **UK** had continued to be responsible for Brunei's defence and external affairs until the sultanate's declaration of independence in 1984. Since full internal self-government in 1971 a battalion of Gurkha troops has been stationed in Brunei at the request of the Brunei government, and Britain is committed to keeping the battalion there until 1998.

BRUSSELS

A shorthand term, often with a pejorative connotation, for the bureaucracy and regulations of the **EU**, which has its main headquarters in this medium-sized Belgian city. Brussels is also Belgium's capital, the headquarters of **NATO**, and home of various other European organizations.

BRUSSELS TREATY

The March 1948 treaty creating a military alliance between the UK, France and the Benelux countries, which was later expanded at British instigation to include the former wartime enemies, (West) Germany and Italy, in what became the **WEU**.

BSE

Bovine spongiform encephalopathy, commonly known as 'mad cow disease'. Related to scrapie in sheep, it was believed to have developed in cows fed on infected sheep offal. Research began in 1990 on a possible link between BSE and the human degenerative **Creutzfeld-Jakob Disease**. BSE had first made headlines in the UK in 1988, when farmers were ordered to slaughter all affected cattle, with compensation to farmers concerned. In 1989 the use of all beef offal in human food was banned in the UK, as was, in 1990, the use of certain cattle offal in all animal feed. By mid-1990 over 1,000 cases of BSE were being notified each month, rising to about 3,000 a month over the period 1991–3. In June 1994 Germany disregarded **EU** agricultural policy rules and imposed a unilateral ban on beef imports from the UK, because of consumer fears about the human health implications of BSE.

BSKYB

British Sky Broadcasting, a company launched in November 1990 after a merger between British Satellite Broadcasting (BSB) and **Sky TV**. BSB had launched its five direct broadcasting by satellite channels in April 1990, while Sky TV – its main rival – had been formed in February 1989 by Rupert **Murdoch**, chief executive of **News International**. The new company was owned equally by the shareholders of the two original companies. BSB and Sky TV had sustained heavy financial losses since their creation. This, together with the disappointing sale of **satellite television** dishes, had led to the merger, which created some controversy, the government refusing to refer it to the **Monopolies and Mergers Commission** amid accusations that the move breached the media ownership provisions of the Broadcasting Act 1990.

BST

British summer time, the legal time in the **British Isles** during the summer months – generally from late March to late October each year when the clocks are changed at 1 a.m. on a day specified by the **Home Office**. It is one hour ahead of Greenwich Mean Time (GMT), the time zone marked by the 0 degree meridian (longitude) which passes through Greenwich in south London and which is the legal time in Britain during the winter. The increasing economic unification of Europe has led to calls for British time to be brought in line with Central European time. This would involve the institution of double summer time, with British clocks two hours ahead of GMT in the summer and one hour ahead in the winter. For an experimental period the clocks remained at BST between spring 1968 and autumn 1971. However, at that stage it did not prove popular, with most complaints coming from **Scotland** where day did not break until around 10 a.m. in the dead of winter.

BT

British Telecommunications, a national provider of telecommunications services and a byword for one of the most successful **privatizations** of Margaret **Thatcher**'s second term of office. BT was formally established under the British Telecommunications Act 1981 to run the telecommunications and data-processing services previously undertaken by the Post Office. When BT became a public limited company in 1984 it was the largest ever stock market flotation in the UK. Gross proceeds of the sale, through a share rights issue, amounted to some £3,900 million. The government subsequently disposed of its own 48 per cent shareholding in BT, with some 26 per cent being sold in December 1991 and the remaining 22 per cent in July 1993. The sale was preceded by a massive publicity campaign launched by BT to disseminate information not only about BT itself but also about the nature of the stock market as it applied to a major flotation.

BUCHANAN REPORT

The Buchanan report, *Traffic in Towns*, was published in 1963 by a working group appointed in 1961 by the Ministry of Transport and chaired by Sir Colin Buchanan, an architect and town planner who had worked in the civil service in 1946–63 before taking up an academic post. The report put forward radical proposals on the handling of traffic in towns and cities, including pedestrianization and the separation of slow- and fast-moving traffic. It helped to establish a connection, which hitherto had not been made, between land-use planning and transport planning. Buchanan declared that there needed to be some restriction on road space and that this should be taken into account during the process of urban design. The report noted that there was now in Britain a deterioration in the urban environment due to the motor car generally and more specifically to urban motorways. The report also noted that the British people had become very attached to the car as an 'indispensable' part of everyday life.

BUCKINGHAM PALACE

The London residence of the UK sovereign in the City of Westminster. The Palace was originally Buckingham House, built in 1705 for the Duke of Buckingham. It was bought in 1761 by King George III for his wife, and in 1837 Queen Victoria became the first monarch to live there. By custom, the **Prime Minister** visits the sovereign at Buckingham Palace for a weekly audience when parliament is sitting. The Prime Minister also goes to the Palace to ask the monarch formally for the dissolution of parliament before a **general election**.

BUDGET

The government's statement of the country's financial position for the coming financial year, including the proposals for financing its spending. The budget is presented to the **House of Commons** annually by the **Chancellor of the Exchequer** in a traditionally lengthy speech which reviews the economic background, forecasts future trends, explains monetary and fiscal policy, sets out the state of the public finances and announces specific proposal for changes to taxation. It is preceded by a lengthy lobbying period during which interest groups make policy representations. Great care is, however, taken to ensure that the contents of the Budget Statement remain secret until presented to Parliament, and the Chancellor and all **Treasury** ministers avoid public comment in the immediately preceding weeks, a practice known as 'purdah'. In 1948 an unintentional leakage of a budget detail to a journalist a few minutes before presentation led to the resignation of Chancellor Hugh **Dalton**.

In March 1992 it was announced that presentation of the budget was to be shifted from its traditional March date to November, starting the following year (so that there were two budgets in 1993), in order to synchronize its appearance with publication of the conclusions of the public spending round in the **Autumn Statement**. Nevertheless the tradition of always presenting the budget on a Tuesday was maintained.

BUDGET REBATE

The arrangement, technically known as an 'abatement', under which the UK (or any other member state) gets back a proportion of 'excessive' **EU** budget contributions. A **correcting mechanism** or 'compensatory refund', as it was then known, was first created in 1975 in response to pressure from the UK during its **renegotiation** of **EC** membership. Rebates under this mechanism were to come into play if a state was contributing out of proportion to the size of its economy. On becoming **Prime Minister** in 1979, Margaret **Thatcher** embarked upon an acrimonious confrontation with other member states and extracted much larger rebates, on the rather different grounds that UK contributions greatly exceeded what the UK received from Community expenditure. An agreement in June 1984 confirmed the principle of reducing this 'gap' by 66 per cent, as the basis for the budget rebate system.

BULGER AFFAIR

A high-profile criminal case following the murder on 12 February 1993, of James Bulger, aged two. The child was abducted while shopping with his mother in Bootle, a suburb of Liverpool, and his mutilated body was discovered near a railway line two days later. The shopping precinct's security cameras showed the toddler being led away by two older children and, after huge publicity, two 10-year-old boys were charged with the murder on 22 February. The two were convicted in November and sentenced to be detained at her majesty's pleasure. It was revealed in January 1994 that the trial judge had recommended that they serve a minimum of eight years in detention, although the Lord Chief Justice, Lord Taylor of Gosforth, had recommended a minimum of 10 years. The appalling nature of the crime, and the ages of those involved, meant that the case generated huge public anguish, with concern expressed at the incidence of youth crime and over those factors variously seen as contributing to its causes.

BULLOCK REPORT

The abortive Royal Commission proposing industrial democracy. After two years' consideration the Royal Commission on Industrial Democracy, established under Lord Bullock in 1975, proposed a statutory right of trade union representation on the boards of large private companies. If, by means of a ballot, company employees approved, employee-directors would be given equal representation on the board with shareholders, with the balance in the hands of independent directors. The Bullock proposals drew considerable hostility from employers (though the **CBI** had been represented on the Commission); trades unions, however, were divided, with a minority, strongly supported by the **TUC**, favouring free **collective bargaining**. Eventually the **Labour** government produced a **White Paper**, but this retreated from Bullock, especially by not restricting employee representation to the unions. The proposals lapsed when Labour lost office.

BUREAUCRACY

The system of adminstration of the affairs of state (hence 'bureaucrat' – a functionary of the system). Bureaucracies tend to be highly organized and hierarchical. Although in most cases the bureaucracy is nominally the impartial agent of government, it often behaves as an elite, jealously protective of its own interests, eager to centralise power and unwilling to surrender powers or prerogatives once acquired.

BURGESS, GUY

(1910–63) A flamboyant Soviet spy. Burgess was recruited in the 1930s by Soviet intelligence while at Cambridge, where he was a contemporary of Donald

Maclean and Kim **Philby** and where Anthony **Blunt** was a Fellow. Burgess, openly Marxist when first at university, later followed Soviet advice and broke with the **Communist Party of Great Britain**. During the 1930s he gained access to ruling circles where he professed right-wing views and began occasional work for **MI5**. After spells at the **BBC** and *The Times*, Burgess joined the War Office as a propaganda expert in 1938. From 1941 he again worked for the BBC and also for the Political Warfare Executive and the Ministry of Information. He used each post to widen his circle of contacts and gather information which was relayed to his Soviet spymasters. Three years later (again on Soviet encouragement) he joined the Foreign Office (later the **FCO**), rising to be personal assistant to the Minister of State, Hector McNeil, when the **Labour Party** entered office in 1945. Personal disreputableness led to his transfer to the Far Eastern Department of the FCO in 1948 and then to the post of Second Secretary at the British embassy in Washington; in all capacities he kept up a steady stream of information to the Soviet Union. In 1951 he was dismissed from the Foreign Office for 'unacceptable behaviour'. Warned by Philby that Maclean was about to be interrogated by MI5, Burgess belatedly arranged Maclean's escape in May 1951 and on Soviet advice joined him in exile. The scandal of their defection became a symbol of the laxity of the **Establishment** in security matters.

BUSBY BABES

The youthful Manchester United football team managed by Matt Busby, which won the Football League Championship in 1956 and 1957. In an appalling tragedy seven members of the squad as well as journalists and members of the club's staff were killed in February 1958 when, on the way home from qualifying in Belgrade for the European Cup semi-finals, their plane crashed on take-off from a snow-covered Munich airport. Of the players who were killed, four were full internationals; a fifth international, 21-year-old Duncan Edwards, died a fortnight later of his injuries.

BUTLER, R. A. 'RAB'

(1902–82) A **Conservative** politician who was a member of the government during the Second World War and the post-War years. 'Rab' Butler was elected to parliament in 1929. During the 1930s he worked at the ministries of India, Labour and Foreign Affairs. He became President of the Board of Education during the War and was primarily responsible for the 1944 **Butler Education Act** which shaped the post-War educational system. When the Conservatives were re-elected in 1951, Butler became **Chancellor of the Exchequer**. He vigorously supported government policy during the **Suez Crisis** of 1956. Partly as a result of this he was passed over for leader of the Conservative Party in favour of Harold **Macmillan**. Butler held the posts of **Leader of the House of Commons** (1955–61); Home Secretary 1957–62); and Foreign Secretary (1963–4). He was made Baron Butler of Saffron Walden in 1965 and a Knight of the Garter in 1971.

BUTLER EDUCATION ACT

The 1944 legislation brought about by the **Conservative** President of the Board of Education R. A. **Butler** which laid the foundations of the modern education system. The Act divided primary and secondary education at age 11. Secondary education was to take place in three types of school: **grammar**, technical and **secondary modern**. The minimum **school leaving age** was to be raised from 14 to 15 (this took place in 1947). Fee-paying in maintained schools was abolished and provision was made for free **school milk**, subsidised meals and free medical and dental examinations for pupils. The number of education authorities was reduced and the title of President of the Board of Education was changed to Minister of Education.

BUTSKELLISM

The supposedly shared philosophy behind the policies of the **Conservative** and **Labour** parties in the 1950s. The term, coined by the *Economist* in the mid-1950s, was used later by **Thatcherite** detractors to deride the blandness of compromise and **consensus politics**. It derives from a combination of the names of R. A. **Butler** and Hugh **Gaitskell** (Conservative and

Labour **Chancellors of the Exchequer** in 1950–1 and 1951–5 respectively). Butskellite **Conservatism** accepted the principle of the **welfare state** and the **nationalization** of 'the commanding heights of industry' carried out by the Labour government of Clement **Attlee** in 1945–51. Conversely, a significant element in the attitudes and policies of Gaitskell (leader of his party in 1955–63) was his efforts to eliminate **Clause IV** from the constitution of the Labour Party in the late 1950s.

BUTTER MOUNTAIN

The vast surplus of butter built up in **EC** storage in the 1970s and early 1980s. Agricultural surpluses of this kind were the most visible symbol of problems in the EC's common agricultural policy (**CAP**), as the price support system gave dairy farmers the incentive to produce more than the market required. The problem was compounded by the fact that New Zealand producers had been allowed to go on exporting some of their much cheaper butter to the otherwise highly protected EC market as a special concession after the UK's **accession** to the EC in 1973. In the mid-1980s the butter mountain consisted of over 1,400,000 tonnes of surplus stocks. The CAP also created other 'mountains', notably of beef, as well as a **'wine lake'**. The issue was eventually tackled in two ways: by measures to dispose of surpluses, including controversial cheap sales to the Soviet Union; and by imposing production quotas on farmers.

BY-ELECTION

An election held in order to fill a vacancy in the **House of Commons** during the lifetime of a parliament. A vacancy in a **constituency** may occur through the death, retirement or expulsion of a sitting member. The date of the by-election is fixed by the issue of a writ on the warrant of the **Speaker**. Political parties in government have often found it difficult to win by-elections, and some have had small parliamentary majorities threatened by by-election losses. The **Liberal Democrats** and, before them, the **Liberal Party** have traditionally performed well in by-elections.

CAB

Citizens' Advice Bureaux, a nationwide network of public information offices funded in each area by local authorities. Trained staff offer advice and information, particularly on social security and housing regulations and family and consumer law. Staff are largely volunteers.

The CAB was established in 1939, initially to disseminate knowledge of emergency government regulations in the Second World War. Constraints on public spending since the late 1980s have resulted in the network of offices shrinking. The National Association of Citizens' Advice Bureaux (NACAB), the network's managing body, has increasingly played a campaigning role on matters of social policy.

CABINET

The committee of senior ministers whose functions are the final determination of policy, control of government and co-ordination of government departments. Chosen by and presided over by the **prime minister**, the Cabinet devolved during the eighteenth century as an inner committee of the **Privy Council**, whose role has become mainly formal. Since the Second World War Cabinets have generally comprised between 15 and 25 ministers, including those responsible for each government department. It has also been customary to include at least two non-departmental ministers. The Cabinet usually meets weekly at 10 **Downing Street** while Parliament is sitting. Its proceedings are secret and it is bound by **Cabinet responsibility**, which means that a Cabinet acts unanimously and that if a member strongly opposes a decision he or she must resign.

CABINET COMMITTEES

Committees which allow more detailed consideration of matters within the scope of the **Cabinet**. Some are authorized to take decisions on behalf of the Cabinet while others report back to it. These bodies have traditionally been secret, but in May 1992 the **Conservative** government decided under its **Citizen's Charter** initiative to publish the composition and terms of reference of 26 standing Cabinet committees and sub-committees.

CABINET OFFICE

The government department which provides administrative support to the **Cabinet** and is responsible for running the **civil service**. The Office comprises the Secretariat, which supports ministers collectively in the conduct of Cabinet business, and the Office of Public Service and Science (OPSS), which is responsible for the **Citizen's Charter** initiative, policy on **open government**, senior **civil service** and public appointments, and the management and organization of the civil service and recruitment into it. The OPSS is also responsible for the Civil Service College, the Recruitment and Assessment Agency, the Occupational Health Service, Her Majesty's Stationery Office (**HMSO**), the Central Office of Information (**COI**) and the Office of Science and Technology. The OPSS supports the **Prime Minister** in his capacity as Minister for the Civil Service, with responsibility for the day-to-day supervision delegated to the Chancellor of the **Duchy of Lancaster**.

CABINET RESPONSIBILITY

The doctrine of collective responsibility for government policy and actions shared by all members of the **Cabinet**. Thus the Cabinet is always seen to act unanimously, even when Cabinet ministers do not all agree on a particular subject or policy. Once policy on a matter has been decided, each minister is expected to support it or resign. The December 1985 **Westland affair** exposed the dangers of the Cabinet proceeding without consensus, provoking the resignations of two Cabinet ministers and threatening the survival of the **Thatcher** government.

CABINET SECRETARY

The head civil servant in the **Cabinet Office**, a post at the heart of government. The Secretary to the **Cabinet** is responsible for the Secretariat, which takes charge of all Cabinet papers, prepares agendas for meetings, prepares summaries of evidence, informs ministers of previous Cabinet decisions, records decisions and notifies government departments concerned. The Cabinet Secretary is head of the home **civil service**. The post is currently held by Sir Robin Butler.

CABLE TELEVISION

The transmission of television signals to domestic sets through a network of underground cables. One of the most rapidly expanding areas of television technology, cable TV differs from **satellite television** in that it has the potential to be interactive – messages could be sent to and from the viewer – and encourages extremely localised channels. Compared with the **BBC** or **commercial television**, cable is currently relatively unregulated. The lack of regulation extends to the digging of trenches to house the cables, which does not require local authority permission. The cable companies have come under fire from environmental groups, who claim that the works disturb the roots of trees and will ultimately lead to the destruction of more than one million trees.

CADW *see* ENGLISH HERITAGE

CALCUTT REPORTS ON PRIVACY AND PRESS SELF-REGULATION

A series of reports on aspects of privacy and self-regulation in the press, published in the early 1990s by Sir David Calcutt, Master of Magdalene College, Cambridge. Appointed in July 1989 in response to growing complaints about the intrusive behaviour of the press, the Calcutt Committee published its report in June 1990. It proposed the creation of three new criminal offences: trespass on private property to obtain personal information for publication; planting surveillance devices on private property; and taking photographs or making a voice recording on private property with a view to publication. The report also recommended the replacement of the **Press Council** by the **Press Complaints Commission**, a recommendation which was given effect in January 1991. A second report published in January 1993 was severely critical of the Commission because of its failure to operate a code of practice which commanded the confidence of the public.

CALDER HALL

The first commercial nuclear power station in the UK, which started operating in 1956 at a site in Cumberland near **Sellafield**. Calder Hall A, and Calder Hall B built two years later, were both two-reactor stations. Unlike the subsequent **Magnox** series of gas-cooled reactors, Calder Hall used a graphite-moderated design, as did the nearby **Windscale** reactor (used for producing weapons grade plutonium) which was damaged by fire in October 1957.

CALLAGHAN, JAMES

(b. 1912) The avuncular **Labour** politician who was **Prime Minister** in 1976–79. Callaghan, a former union official and petty officer in the Royal Navy, became an **MP** in 1945 and held minor office in the **Attlee** government. In **opposition** he reached the **Shadow Cabinet**, but stood unsuccessfully for the Labour deputy leadership (in 1960) and later the leadership (in 1963). He became **Chancellor of the Exchequer** in 1964, his tenure marked by economic conservatism and the defence (with Prime Minister Harold **Wilson**) of the value of sterling against the dollar; he also introduced corporation tax and selective employment tax. After currency crises in 1964 and 1966, a third, in November 1967, forced **devaluation** on Callaghan, who felt bound to resign as Chancellor; he became **Home Secretary** until Labour lost office in 1970. In 1969 it was his responsibility to send British troops to **Northern Ireland**.

Devaluation had damaged Callaghan's reputation, but in 1969, after controversially joining unions in opposing **In Place of Strife**, he was credited with embodying centrist Labour opinion. He was the first prominent Labour figure to shift against the **EEC** after 1970; in 1974 he became Foreign Secretary and was the most senior government figure after Wilson. Wilson's sudden resignation in 1976 left Callaghan well-placed to be elected Labour Party leader and Prime Minister.

For three years Callaghan steered a relatively conservative course, acknowledging the profit motive, and presiding over economic recovery. After March 1977 he stayed in office thanks to the **Lib-Lab Pact**, but stumbled in Autumn 1978 by seeking a fourth year of **incomes policy**. His attempt to impose a 5 per cent pay norm encountered widespread industrial action, quickly labelled the **Winter of Discontent**, and his unflappable demeanour was interpreted by the press as complacency. When the government failed to deliver **devolution** Scotland, the minority parties sided with the **Conservatives** to defeat it in a March 1979 confidence vote: Labour lost the following **general election**. Callaghan remained party leader until November 1980, retiring as an MP in 1983 and being made a **life peer** in 1987.

CALVI AFFAIR

The scandal surrounding the mysterious death in London in June 1982 of an Italian, Roberto Calvi – 'God's banker'. A member of the P-2 Masonic lodge, and president of the Italian Banco Ambrosiano (which was closely entwined with the Vatican Bank), Calvi was found hanging under Blackfriars Bridge. A London inquest eventually returned an open verdict, but a court in Milan in 1989 decided that Calvi had been murdered. Banco Ambrosiano's collapse and liquidation had far-reaching repercussions, with fraud and corruption trials stretching into the early 1990s.

CAMBRIDGE MAFIA

A media phrase coined because of the number of Cambridge University graduates in the **Cabinet** in the early 1990s – seven out of 23 as of early 1995 – whereas **Conservative** cabinets were traditionally dominated by Oxford men. Four of the seven (Kenneth **Clarke**, Michael **Howard**, John Gummer and Ian Lang) had been contemporaries – around 1960 – and the first three were all presidents of the Cambridge Union in 1962–3.

CAMELFORD

A country town in Cornwall, south-west England, which was at the centre of public controversy following the supply of contaminated mains water to local residents in July 1988. The water, polluted as the result of an error at the Lowermoor water treatment works, contained copper, lead and concentrations of aluminium 500 times higher than the maximum allowed by regulation. Residents complained of sickness, diarrhoea, skin problems and amnesia, and stocks of fish in the local Allen and Camel rivers were completely wiped out. Public complaints centred on the decision of the local water authority and the Department of Health to advise people in the immediate aftermath of the accident that the contaminated water was not dangerous.

CAMELOT *see* NATIONAL LOTTERY

CAMILLAGATE

The scandal associated with the publication in January 1993 of tape recordings alleged to feature the Prince of Wales and his friend, Camilla Parker-Bowles, in amorous conversation. The scandal further undermined the public popularity of the Prince, who had been accused in Andrew Morton's book, *Diana – Her True Story*, published in 1992, of having conducted an affair with her for several years.

CAMPAIGN FOR PRESS AND BROADCASTING FREEDOM

A pressure group formed in 1979 to campaign for a more democratic, open and accountable media. The group wishes to see a media that is also more accessible, with greater diversification and more choice for the viewer, reader and listener. Its campaigns centre around a radical view of press and broadcasting, involving the introduction of freedom of information legislation and opposition to the monopoly ownership of newspapers. The group organizes events to publicise its cause and publishes a twice-monthly bulletin as well as occasional pamphlets.

CAMPAIGN GROUP

A group of hard-left **Labour MPs**, including Tony **Benn** and Dennis **Skinner**, established in 1982 to rally opposition to the expulsion of members of **Militant Tendency** from the Labour Party. Campaign backs the maintenance of 'umbilical' links with the trade unions and was opposed to the amendment of **Clause IV** of the party's constitution secured by Tony **Blair** in April 1995. The group has become increasingly marginalized since the rise of the **modernizers**.

CAMPSFIELD HOUSE

The UK's largest detention centre for **asylum** seekers, situated near Oxford. The other main detention centres are at Harmondsworth **Immigration** Detention Centre and Haslar Holding Centre, but asylum seekers are also held in prisons. Campsfield was opened in November 1993 with 200 places for asylum seekers, who, under the 1971 Immigration Act, can be detained indefinitely without charge and with little or no recourse to bail. Although the 1993 Immigration and Asylum Appeals Act was intended to speed up the consideration of applications, according to **Amnesty International** the length of time for which applicants are detained has increased. Inmates at Campsfield staged protests and a hunger strike in March 1994 in protest at their detention, the number of asylum seekers detained in the UK having risen in February 1994 as high as 950. In November 1994, 654 asylum seekers were in detention, of whom three-quarters had been detained for over one month; 40 per cent of asylum seekers were being held in prisons.

CANARY WHARF

A prestigious office development in the Docklands area of east London. It become the symbol of urban regeneration financed by private capital in the boom of the mid-1980s, and the victim of the property slump which followed. Canary Wharf was conceived in 1988 but by the time the first phase was finished in 1992 the Canadian-based developers, Olympia and York, had gone into administration in the UK under insolvency procedures after failing to meet repayments on bank loans. The government refused to bale out the project, insisting that the main transport link to the area, the extension to the Jubilee Line underground railway, should be part-financed by the private sector. The distinctive Canary Wharf tower eventually came to house a number of newspaper offices which had re-located from their traditional home in **Fleet Street**.

CAP

The common agricultural policy, a central element in the **EEC** (and thus in the **EC** and now the **EU**) since the 1957 **Treaty of Rome**. It is essentially a single internal market for agricultural produce, with an elaborate system for guaranteeing the incomes of farmers by fixing a minimum Community-wide price for their produce. 'Intervention' then involves buying up surpluses to keep prices from falling, although since the introduction of reforms in March 1984 there has been more emphasis on setting quotas to restrict overproduction. According to the principle of Community preference, farmers are protected against competition from overseas by import levies, a particularly controversial matter for the UK in the 1970s because UK consumers were used to cheaper food, particularly from **Commonwealth** countries such as New Zealand. The CAP is funded through the European Agricultural Guidance and Guarantee Fund (known by its French acronym, **FEOGA**), which consumes the lion's share of the Community budget.

CAPITAL PUNISHMENT

The death penalty imposed by the state. In the UK the death penalty for murder was abolished in 1965, initially for a five-year period; approval for permanent abolition was given in December 1969 by both Houses of Parliament. It is retained for high treason, in **England** and **Wales** for piracy with violence, in Jersey (**Channel Islands**) for murder, and in the **Isle of Man** for murder, treason and genocide. Members of the armed forces may also be sentenced to death for certain crimes in wartime, such as espionage or treason. The Queen can commute such sentences to life imprisonment. The last executions were carried out on 13 August 1964. Murder convictions now carry a mandatory life sentence, with decisions as to if and when prisoners may be released on licence left to the Home Secretary.

CAPPING

The imposition by the government of spending limits on local authorities. The power was introduced under the Rates Act 1984, largely in response to the levying by authorities of high levels of local taxation under the **rates** system. Capping has became increasingly controversial as councils have blamed the spending limits for cut backs in services. In addition, the **Labour Party** has accused **Conservative** central government of bias in its application of the spending limits, citing the fact that the capped councils have most frequently been Labour-controlled, while Conservative councils have been rewarded with government grants. The government retained the power to cap local authority spending after the introduction of the **poll tax**, which replaced the rates, and of the later **council tax**.

CARDIFF AIR CRASH

An air crash on 12 March 1950, in which 80 people were killed. The Tudor V charter airliner was carrying Welsh rugby supporters who had been to a Wales-Ireland international match when it crashed into a field while approaching Cardiff airport in clear weather. At the time, the death toll made it the worst civil air disaster to have occurred anywhere in the world.

CARE IN THE COMMUNITY

The policy on mental health care introduced by the **Conservative** government in the 1990s. The National Health Service and Community Care Act of 1990, implemented in England and Wales on 1 April 1993, was designed ostensibly to improve the quality of life and the chances of recovery of some residents of mental institutions, by enabling them to live instead in their own homes. Specialized assistance was to be provided for this, but critics attacked as inadequate the state assistance which was actually made available, and suggested that the expressed objective of reduced institutionalization was merely an excuse for cost-cutting.

CARLTON CLUB

The exclusive political club for **Conservative Party** grandees, and a pillar of the **Establishment**. Founded in 1832 by opponents of the extension of the franchise under the Great Reform Bill, the Carlton Club performed many of the functions later assumed by **Central Office**. The Club remains influential as a meeting place of the Tory **men in grey suits**, but Conservative **MPs** no longer join as a matter of course.

CARR, L. ROBERT

(b. 1916) Reginald **Maudling**'s successor as **Conservative** Home Secretary in 1972, a post he held until 1974. Before his appointment as Home Secretary he piloted a controversial Industrial Relations Bill through the **House of**

Commons as Minister of Employment (1970–72). He resigned from the Conservative **Shadow Cabinet** in 1975 and was given a **life peerage** in 1976.

CARRINGTON, LORD

(b. 1919) Secretary of State for Foreign and Commonwealth Affairs in 1979–82 in the **Conservative** government of Margaret **Thatcher**. Carrington, who first held government office in the mid-1950s and was widely regarded as the diplomat par excellence, resigned shortly after the April 1982 invasion of the **Falkland Islands** by Argentina; he was replaced by Francis **Pym**. Carrington went on to serve as Secretary-General of **NATO** (1984–89) and acted as an **EC** peace negotiator in former Yugoslavia in 1991–2.

CASH FOR QUESTIONS

A 1994 scandal involving **Conservative MPs** who were prepared to accept money in return for asking parliamentary questions. Acting on information believed to have come from Mohamed al-**Fayed**, a journalist from the *Sunday Times*, posing as a businessman, approached 10 Conservative and 10 **Labour** MPs. Two of the Conservatives, Graham Riddick (MP for Colne Valley) and David Tredinnick (Bosworth), each agreed to accept payment of £1,000 in return for tabling parliamentary questions. The scandal caused a storm of publicity, and was a component of what became widely known as the **sleaze factor** surrounding the government of John **Major**. The **House of Commons**' Committee of Privileges on 5 April 1995 found that the two MPs had been guilty of a 'serious error of judgement', and suspended Tredinnick and Riddick from the chamber for 20 and 10 days, respectively, without pay. It also reprimanded Bill Walker, Conservative MP for Tayside North, for agreeing to ask a question in return for a payment to a charity of his own choosing, and criticized the *Sunday Times* for having used entrapment and deception.

CASTLE, BARBARA

(b. 1910) A spirited **left-wing Labour** politician, Castle had associated with Stafford **Cripps** and Aneurin **Bevan** before the Second World War. She entered Parliament in 1945 and went on to became **PPS** to Harold **Wilson** at the **Board of Trade**, aligning herself with the left of the party. Joining Labour's **NEC** in 1950, she became a flamboyant representative of the **Bevanite** faction and was one of the most popular figures with the constituencies throughout Labour's years in opposition. In government after 1964 she was a consistent ally of Wilson, moving from the Ministry of Overseas Development to the **Department of Transport** in 1965 (when she introduced the 70 mph speed limit and the 'breathalyser' test for drunk drivers), and then to the Department of Employment and Productivity in 1968. The following year she published **In Place of Strife**, a unique attempt by a Labour government to regulate union behaviour. The attempt foundered on party and union opposition and her popularity with the left was never recovered, though she regained some of her proselytizing zeal in campaigns against **EEC** entry in Opposition after 1970. Her final (1974–6) spell as a Minister at Health and Social Security brought the introduction of earnings-related pensions for those without occupational pension schemes. On succeeding Wilson as **Prime Minister**, James **Callaghan** (a longstanding opponent) forced her resignation. On leaving the **House of Commons** in 1979 she was immediately elected to the **European Parliament**, where she became leader of the British Labour Group, retiring in 1984. In 1990 she was created a **life peer** and remains an active member of the **House of Lords**.

CATALYTIC CONVERTER

A device which converts polluting chemicals in the exhaust fumes of petrol-driven vehicles into substances less harmful to the environment and human health. Catalytic converters (which currently have up to 90 per cent efficiency) are inserted between the engine and the exhaust. They contain a honeycomb-like structure, coated with platinum, palladium and rhodium. When exhaust fumes pass through the converter, the metals act as catalysts for chemical reactions which convert carbon monoxide and nitrogen oxides into carbon dioxide, water vapour and nitrogen. In the UK all new cars sold since 1993 have been fitted with catalytic converters.

CATHY COME HOME

A television play directed by Ken Loach about poverty and **homelessness**, broadcast in 1966. It provided a sharp reminder that fundamental social problems continued to exist in so-called prosperous **Britain**. The programme sparked off a national debate on homelessness and led to the formation of the campaigning pressure group, **Shelter**, in 1967.

CBI

The Confederation of British Industry, the main employers' organization in the UK. The CBI was formed in 1965 through the merger of the Federation of British Industries, the British Employers' Confederation and the National Association of British Manufacturers. It is a body with corporate membership from industry, commerce, retailing, finance, mining, construction, transport and the nationalized industries. As a pressure group, it ensures that its members' problems and requirements are fully understood within parliament and government as well as, increasingly, within the **EU**. Under both **Labour** and **Conservative** governments it was represented on a number of official bodies (such as **NEDDY**), although this corporatist function is now less prominent.

CCT

Compulsory competitive tendering of local government services. CCT is the process whereby local authorities in **Great Britain** are required to invite tenders for an increasingly wide range of services hitherto provided by the authorities themselves. The presumption in such tendering exercises is that no barriers should be placed in the way of authorities divesting themselves of the services in question through unfair accounting or other practices. While the process had already been introduced to a limited extent in the early 1980s, the main thrust towards expansion was provided by the Local Government Act 1988.

CEASEFIRE

The voluntary cessation of violence by military organizations, whether temporary or permanent. They have most notably been announced in **Northern Ireland** in August 1994 by the **IRA** and six weeks later by the **Combined Loyalist Military Command**. Both ceasefires arose following initiatives during the early 1990s from the British government, prominent politicians in Northern Ireland – including leaders of **Sinn Féin** (commonly referred to as the IRA's political wing) – and US diplomats. These moves included the **Brooke initiative** of 1990–2 and the joint British-Irish **Downing Street Declaration** of December 1993. Accepting that the intention was to have a permanent ceasefire, representatives of the British government began preliminary talks with *Sinn Féin* and with **loyalist** groups in December 1994.

CEGB

Central Electricity Generating Board, the body created under the Electricity Act of 1957 to maintain and develop the electricity supply industry in England, Wales and Scotland. As a preparatory step towards **privatization**, the Electricity Act of 1989 divided the CEGB's generating capacity into two competing generating companies: the non-nuclear PowerGen would own 30 per cent of the capacity, while National Power would own the remainder including the nuclear power stations. A National Grid Company was established to be jointly owned by the 12 new supply companies created from the area boards of England and Wales. The regional electricity companies were sold by public **flotation** in November 1990, while PowerGen and National Power were sold by the same method in March 1991.

CENSORSHIP

The means by which freedom of expression may be limited on the grounds of immorality, obscenity or libel, and by which the dissemination of information may be limited on the grounds of national interest. The implementation of censorship in the UK takes many shapes and forms. In 1979 the **Williams Committee Report on Obscenity and Film Censorship** recommended that the printed word in pornographic material should not be restricted nor prohibited, but that such material as pornographic films and photographs should be prohibited. The British Board of Film Classification (BBFC), an independent non-statutory body, approves and classifies films for public viewing and in this way adopts a protective role towards children in relation to the kind of films they are able to watch. The **Official Secrets Act** makes it a crime for anyone to obtain and communicate information potentially harmful to the national interest. The UK government in October 1994 lifted its controversial **broadcasting ban**, imposed in 1988, whereby the voices of representatives of proscribed organizations were prevented from being heard on radio or television.

CENTRAL OFFICE

The headquarters of the **Conservative Party** in Westminster's Smith Square. Conservative Central Office was established by Conservative leader Benjamin Disraeli in 1870 to improve party organization and unity. It assumed some of the responsibilities hitherto carried out by members of the **Carlton Club**. Central Office now plays an important role in campaigning, fund raising and policy formulation and is the main conduit between Conservative leaders and the party's rank and file.

CENTRAL OFFICE OF INFORMATION *see* COI

CENTRE FOR POLICY STUDIES

A **think tank** founded in 1974 by Sir Keith **Joseph** to put forward free-market ideas within the **Conservative Party**. Under the direction of Alfred Sherman it effectively eclipsed the official party research department. Responsible for many of the radical economic and other policies carried out after the party took office in 1979, the CPS is closely associated with **Thatcherism**, which the present director Gerald Frost has described as 'a moral as much as a political movement'.

CERTIFICATE OF SIXTH YEAR STUDIES *see* HIGHERS

CFCs

Chlorofluorocarbons, a family of chemicals discovered in 1930 which revolutionised the techniques of refrigeration but were later recognized to be **greenhouse gases** which contribute significantly to the **greenhouse effect**. CFCs are stable gases used widely in refrigeration, in aerosol spray cans and in the production of insulating packaging for convenience foods. The chlorine they contain also damage the **ozone layer**. The 1987 Montreal Protocol aims to halve the use of CFCs by the end of the century.

CHAIRMAN OF WAYS AND MEANS

A member of the **House of Commons** who acts as deputy **Speaker** and chairs committees of the whole House. The Chairman of Ways and Means and the deputy chairman are appointed for the duration of a parliament by a resolution of the House on a government motion. While deputising for the Speaker, the Chairman occupies the Speaker's chair and exercises the powers of that office. While chairing a committee of the House he or she sits at the Table of the House. The title comes from the Committee of Ways and Means, which, before its abolition in 1967, was the means by which all measures for raising government revenue were introduced.

CHAMPAGNE SOCIALISTS

Left-wing members of the fashionable middle and upper classes, whose commitment to socialism is regarded as superficial and hypocritical because of their lifestyle. Champagne socialists are said to be anxious to retain privileges for themselves while arguing for a more equal society; thus for example they support **comprehensive schools** while educating their own children privately.

CHANCELLOR OF THE EXCHEQUER

The chief minister at the **Treasury**, the Chancellor is in day-to-day charge of the running of the department. Formally, he is a member of the Treasury Board, as Second Lord of the Treasury (the First Lord being the **Prime Minister**). The other members of the Board are five junior lords (usually Government **whips**). The Chancellor, a senior member of the **Cabinet**, is responsible for the government's economic policy. He announces the government's taxation and public expenditure plans in the annual **Budget** statement in the **House of Commons**.

See also Appendix III.

CHANCERY

One of three benches of the **High Court** in **England** and **Wales**, with the **Queen's Bench** and the Family Division. Its jurisdiction is primarily in financial matters – for example bankruptcy and taxation – property law and contentious probate cases. Its president is the **Lord Chancellor**, although he or she does not sit in court, which is presided over by the Vice-Chancellor. The court also hears appeals from the county courts in bankruptcy and certain other cases.

CHANNEL ISLANDS

One of the two British **crown dependencies**, they lie in the English Channel off the French coast of Normandy. The Islands, with their own legislative assemblies and legal system, are divided into two Bailiwicks, one comprising Jersey and the other Alderney, Sark, and Guernsey with its dependants Herm and Jethou. Each Bailiwick has a Lieutenant-Governor appointed by the Crown and a Bailiff, also appointed by the Crown, who presides over sittings of the local legislatures, the States. These elected assemblies may initiate legislation which must receive the **Royal Assent**. Acts of the **UK** Parliament do not apply unless by express provision. Proposals for raising revenue made by the States require authorization by Order in Council. The Islands have their own courts of law, but there remains leave to appeal to the Judicial Committee of the **Privy Council**. The Channel Islands were the only part of **Britain** to be invaded by German forces during the Second world War.

CHANNEL TUNNEL *see* CHUNNEL

CHARITY COMMISSION

A **quango** appointed under the Charities Act of 1960 which works in **England** and **Wales** as an advisory and information body for charities and which investigates alleged abuses of charitable status. The London-based Commission also provides advice on the administrative machinery of charities and maintains a full register of such organizations.

CHARLES, PRINCE OF WALES

(b. 1948) The first son of Queen **Elizabeth II** and the Duke of **Edinburgh** and heir to the throne. Charles was educated at Gordonstoun and Cambridge, afterwards serving in the RAF and the Royal Navy in 1971–6. He was invested as Prince of Wales at a ceremony at Caernarvon Castle in 1969. The Prince's marriage to Lady **Diana** Spencer in 1981 was an occasion of national rejoicing focused on a spectacular ceremony at St Paul's Cathedral. There are two sons of the marriage, Prince William and Prince Henry, but the couple's growing estrangement, culminating in formal separation in 1992, was mirrored by the decline in popularity and respect of the **Royal Family**. The constitutional implications of the separation were the subject of much speculation, particularly with regard to the Prince's potential position as **Defender of the Faith**, at the head of the **Church of England**. Debate intensified after Charles effectively admitted to adultery in a television programme, *Charles: the Private Man, the Public Role*, broadcast in June 1994 and seen by millions. It was widely assumed that his liaison had been with Mrs Camilla Parker-Bowles, and when she divorced in January 1995, speculation was rife that Charles would eventually divorce Diana to marry Camilla.

The Prince has taken an active role in charity work, with a particular interest the environment, organic farming and the inner cities. He is seen as a serious and thoughtful man, if somewhat eccentric. His strong views on subjects such as modern architecture sometimes excite controversy, as when he described a proposed extension to the National Gallery as a **'monstrous carbuncle'**.

CHARTER 88

A pressure group which demands a new constitutional settlement guaranteeing political, civil and human rights. Charter 88 was launched with the publication of a statement, signed by some 240 prominent figures, in the 2 December 1988 issue of the magazine *New Statesman and Society*. Its name referred both to Czechoslovakia's dissident Charter 77, and the tercentenary of the British 'Glorious Revolution' of 1688. Its signatories claimed that rights were '. . . being curtailed while the powers of the executive have increased . . . and ought to be diminished'.

CHATHAM HOUSE

The commonly used name for the Royal Institute of International Affairs (RIIA), the central research institute on international affairs and **think tank** for the foreign policy establishment. Chatham House (the name comes from the RIIA's address in St James's Square at what was once the London home of Lord Chatham) was founded in 1920 and was originally closely linked with what is now the Foreign and Commonwealth Office (**FCO**) research department. In the postwar period it has received some FCO grant funding but is primarily dependent on its own resources, mainly from individual and corporate membership subscriptions. Chatham House runs research programmes, publishes policy-oriented studies and hosts regular open meetings centring on talks by experts and visiting foreign politicians. The expression 'Chatham House rules' refers to the understanding that the views and information exchanged at such meetings may not be cited or directly attributed afterwards.

CHATTERING CLASSES

Members of the intelligentsia perceived to set the cultural agenda. The chattering classes' preoccupations, which vary widely from political and moral issues to popular music and fashion, result from the informal conversation said to constitute much of the leisure time of professional people. The media, which employ many members of the chattering classes, often reflect their changing preoccupations.

CHEAP MONEY POLICY

The use of low interest rates to facilitate borrowing and economic revival. Although **Treasury** policy from 1932, it became identified after 1945 with Hugh **Dalton**, **Chancellor of the Exchequer** in the **Attlee** government. It facilitated government policy effectively until the **Winter of '47**, after which **City** fears about **inflation** made it impracticable to continue. Stable low lending rates were formally ended in R. A. **Butler**'s 1952 **budget** which sharply raised the bank rate.

CHEQUERS

The official country residence of the **Prime Minister**. The house and estate of Chequers, in Buckinghamshire, northwest of London, was given to the country by Lord and Lady Lee of Fareham in 1917-21, to serve as the official country home of the Prime Minister of the day (10 **Downing Street** being his or her official London residence).

CHEVALINE

A British upgrade of the submarine-launched **Polaris** nuclear missile. The Chevaline programme was initiated in 1971, but development was slower and more costly than planned. By the time the missile came into service in 1982, the government had already committed itself to buying the US **Trident II** missile as its replacement.

CHEVENING

The official country residence of the Foreign and Commonwealth Secretary, located in Kent.

CHILD BENEFIT *see* FAMILY ALLOWANCE

CHILD POVERTY ACTION GROUP

A non-governmental organization which lobbies for the relief of deprivation among children or families with children. It was founded in 1965 and derived its initial impetus from the pioneering work of Brian Abel-Smith and Peter Townsend on family deprivation. Although in the 1970s its criticisms of the **Labour Party**'s **incomes policy** were contentious, in the 1980s it influenced Labour thinking. The group specializes in welfare advice to low-income claimants and its publications on benefit entitlements are considered authoritative.

CHILD SUPPORT AGENCY *see* CSA

CHILDLINE

A national charity which operates a telephone line for children requiring counselling. ChildLine was launched in 1986 after the need for a dedicated helpline for young people was brought to public attention by TV personality Esther Rantzen. ChildLine offers a free and confidential 24-hour telephone counselling service. While most children using the service are the victims of sexual or physical abuse, other common problems include bullying, drug and alcohol abuse, pregnancy and bereavement. In April 1995 the organization reported that it had counselled 430,581 children and young people and had given advice to 56,117 adults since its launch.

CHILDREN ACT

A piece of legislation representing the most sweeping reform of child law in the century. The Children Act 1989 enshrined five main principles: the child's welfare was paramount; children were best cared for by both parents where possible; the state and the courts should intervene only where this would clearly make things better for the child; delay was not generally in the interest of the child; and the laws and procedures on children should be unified. Under the Act, which came into effect in October 1991, old concepts such as custody, care and control and access were replaced by new, flexible orders: residence, contact and prohibited steps. Parents who separated would both continue to have parental responsibility; children would be granted the right to be heard when legal decisions were made about them; new regulations were brought in for social workers involved in child protection; a new court structure was created to oversee the new uniform child law.

CHILTERN HUNDREDS

The more well-known of the two sinecures for which **MPs** traditionally apply if they wish to give up their seat. In theory they are not allowed simply to resign, but disqualification from membership of the **House of Commons** is automatic for the holder of any of certain specified 'offices of profit under the Crown'. (These offices are now defined in the House of Commons Disqualification Act 1975.) The approved procedure for an MP wishing to quit is thus to apply for, and accept, the nominal office of Bailiff of the three Chiltern Hundreds of Stoke, Desborough and Burnham, in Buckinghamshire, or alternatively the nominal office of Steward of the Manor of Northstead.

CHINGFORD SKINHEAD

One of the many nicknames for Norman **Tebbit**, the **Conservative MP** for Chingford in 1974–92.

CHINOOK HELICOPTER CRASH

The worst-ever civilian helicopter accident, in which 45 people died on 6 November 1986. The Chinook helicopter was carrying Shell oil workers from Brent oil field to Sumburgh airport when it crashed into the North Sea two miles off the Shetland Islands. Despite an immediate air-sea rescue operation, there were only two survivors.

CHOGM

The Commonwealth Heads of Government Meeting, the main policy-making body of the **Commonwealth**. A CHOGM is formally convened every two years. Designed to compensate for the absence of a formal Commonwealth charter or governing structure, it was first assembled in 1935. Since 1965 it has been assisted by the Commonwealth Secretariat, whereas it was previously serviced by the UK Commonwealth Relations Office. In 1989 the CHOGM initiated a high-level appraisal of directions and structure. Major concerns in recent years have included decolonization, economic development and ways of ending apartheid in South Africa, over which **Prime Minister** Margaret **Thatcher** (who with her private secretary allegedly referred privately to CHOGM as 'compulsory handouts to greedy mendicants') was involved in sharp controversies at the 1987 and 1989 CHOGMs.

CHRISTIAN AID

A non-governmental relief and development agency founded in 1948. Christian Aid, backed by the Catholic Church and the **Church of England**, combats poverty in some 70 countries worldwide, including **Britain**. It aims to help communities become self-sufficient and in contrast to many development agencies prefers to channel assistance through local organizations rather than maintain overseas staff. In recent years it has become increasingly critical of the attitude of the West to developing countries and has vocally supported the campaign for Third World debt to be wiped out.

CHUNNEL

A familiar contraction of 'Channel Tunnel'. Plans for a tunnel beneath the Channel between England and France, mooted in the nineteenth century, were resurrected in 1957, but abandoned again in 1975 after lengthy studies, even though the French and UK governments had reached an agreement that the Chunnel could go ahead. The project was once more revived in 1981, and after several years of work, various delays and escalating costs a rail tunnel – constructed by Trans-Manche Link, operated by Eurotunnel, and capable of carrying passengers, cars and freight – was officially opened on 6 May 1994, although a limited commercial London–Paris rail service only began in November 1994, with the Folkestone–Calais shuttle service coming into operation the following month. Completion of the controversial high-speed rail link on the English side of tunnel was not expected to be completed before the end of the century.

CHURCH COMMISSIONERS

Established in 1948, the main task of the Commissioners is the management of the assets of the **Church of England**, the income from which is used for stipends, housing and pensions for the clergy and their widows. The Commissioners became embroiled in controversy during the late 1980s and early 1990s when they came under criticism for approving a number of poor speculative investments in property and land – during 1988–92 the value of the Church's assets fell by £800 million. Altogether there are currently 94 Commissioners, of whom three are the Church Estates Commissioners; the majority of the remainder are ex officio and include, besides the **archbishops of Canterbury** (the chairman of the Commissioners) and of York, such holders of state office as the **Lord Chancellor**, the **Chancellor of the Exchequer** and the **Lord Chief Justice**, and also the Lord Mayors of London and York.

CHURCH OF ENGLAND

The **established church** of **England**. Regarded as a **national church**, it has been 'by law established' since the Second Act of Supremacy of 1559, and was formally united with the state under the Settlement Act of 1701. Its adherents are members of the **Anglican** Communion, of which it is the mother church. It acknowledges the monarch as its head, and is represented in Parliament by bishops nominated by the **Prime Minister** and appointed by the monarch, who sit in the **House of Lords**. The Church has two provinces, Canterbury and York, presided over respectively by the **Archbishop of Canterbury** and the Archbishop of York. There are, in addition, 24 senior bishops.

CHURCH OF SCOTLAND

The **national church** of Scotland, formed in 1560 and Reformed and evangelical in doctrine and presbyterian in constitution. Like the **Church of England**, it is an **established church** whose status was formalized by Parliament under the 1921 Church of Scotland Act which recognized the spiritual freedom of the Church 'to adjudicate finally in all matters of doctrine, worship, government and discipline'. However, unlike the Church of England, the establishment of the Church of Scotland was underlined by a unique ecclesiastical independence. This stemmed partly from its presbyterian constitution, with its emphasis on the over-arching Lordship of Christ, and partly from popular perceptions of the Church as the only surviving testament of a distinct Scottish identity. The Church of Scotland achieved its present form in 1929 when it was rejoined by the Free Church of Scotland.

CHURCHILL, SIR WINSTON

(1874–1965) Statesman and wartime leader. Son of the **Conservative** radical Lord Randolph Churchill, Churchill joined the army in 1895, and was a war correspondent in the Boer War. He entered Parliament as a Conservative in 1900, but joined the **Liberals** in 1906 because of his opposition to tariff reform, and was made President of the **Board of Trade** in 1908, when he was closely identified with the social reforms of Lloyd George. He became First Lord of the Admiralty in 1911 until the formation of the coalition government of 1915. Churchill was strongly criticized for his backing of the disastrous Dardanelles expedition and he resigned to become a colonel in the trenches. Lloyd George brought him back as munitions minister in 1917. He re-joined the Conservative Party in 1924, serving as **Chancellor of the Exchequer** until 1929.

During the 1930s he remained in the political wilderness, isolated from much of his own party through his vigorous opposition to Hitler and to Chamberlain's policy of appeasement. At the outbreak of the Second World War he was brought back to the Admiralty and he replaced Chamberlain at the head of a coalition government in May 1940. Using broadcasting to carry the rhetoric of a former age, he raised the morale of the British people to turn the tide of the War. His strong connections with the USA greatly aided the establishment of the Atlantic Alliance.

The Conservatives lost the 1945 **general election**, and Churchill had little to do with the reconstruction of his party, although he benefited from it with a final period in office in 1951–5. Churchill's funeral, an acknowledgment of his world reputation as an inspiring war leader and great orator and of the vividness of his personality, was one of the great state occasions of the twentieth century.

CHURCHILL PAPERS

The archive of Sir Winston **Churchill** which were controversially purchased for the nation in April 1995 by the National Heritage Memorial Fund, using funds raised by the **National Lottery**. The Fund paid around £12.5 million to a trust representing the Churchill family (including Churchill's grandson and namesake who was a **Conservative** MP) which retained the copyright on all the private papers. The sale was approved by the government, which insisted that no money had changed hands for the public papers of the former **Prime Minister**.

CHUTER EDE, JAMES

(1882–1965) Home Secretary in the 1945–51 **Attlee** governments, during which time he introduced the Criminal Justice Act of 1948 and was involved in a controversy over **capital punishment**. With the defeat of the **Labour Party** in the 1951 general election, Chuter Ede was succeeded as Home Secretary by Sir David **Maxwell Fyfe**. He was awarded a **life peerage** in 1964.

CITIZENS' ADVICE BUREAUX *see* CAB

CITIZEN'S CHARTER

A government 'charter' for the improvement in standards of public services. The basic citizen's charter was an initiative of Prime Minister John **Major** in 1991. It paved the way for a proliferation of subsidiary charters (around 40 by early 1995), covering different aspects of public service. In each case the government or another authority set out standards of services, quality, choice and value for money. In some instances there were guarantees of redress if these standards were not met. The initiative led to hospitals undertaking to see patients within a certain period of their arrival, although these standards were not necessarily met, and British Rail compensating passengers for late running trains.

CITIZENSHIP

Status conferring rights (and obligations) on individuals vis-à-vis the state. Under the 1981 **Nationality** Act only British citizens have right of abode in the UK. Other rights, such as that to vote and to stand for public office, are shared with Irish, **Commonwealth** and, at local level, **EU** citizens.

THE CITY

The historic heart of London, now its financial centre. Within a square mile many important financial institutions – such as the **Bank of England**, the **London Stock Exchange** and the head offices of major banks and insurance companies – are located. The City has its own **police** force and **local government** – the Corporation of the City of London, equivalent in status to London's 32 borough councils.

In the mid-to-late 1980s, the high salaries and extravagant lifestyles of many young City employees, often dubbed **yuppies**, attracted a lot of media attention.

CITY TECHNOLOGY COLLEGES

Independent colleges partly funded by industry providing general secondary education with a technological bias, whose establishment was provided for by the 1988 Education Reform Act. The intention was that running costs would be funded by government, while the capital costs would be provided by the private sponsors. The then Education Secretary, Kenneth **Baker**, officially opened the first City Technology College at Kingshurst, in Solihull, West Midlands, in November 1988. Altogether 15 colleges were established by autumn 1993, a total which had not increased by May 1995.

City technology colleges are not to be confused with **technology colleges**.

CIVIL LIST

Payments by the state to meet the official expenses of certain members of the Royal Family. The present Civil List arrangements date back to the mid-eighteenth century when King George III surrendered hereditary revenues of the Crown. The level of Civil List payments was traditionally fixed at the beginning of each reign, but in 1972 it was decided that it should be revised every 10 years. In 1975 it began to be revised annually because of the effects of inflation, but in 1991 reverted to 10-year revisions. In early 1993 it was confirmed that Civil List payments were in future to be restricted to Queen **Elizabeth**, the Duke of **Edinburgh** and the **Queen Mother**, and moreover that the Queen would pay income tax (on all her personal income) and capital gains tax.

CIVIL RIGHTS

The term used by those who perceive the need to campaign for a set of basic rights in relation to the vote, to freedom of movement, speech and association, to equality of opportunity and the right not to be discriminated against on the grounds of religion, race or gender. **Northern Ireland** saw the emergence of a civil rights movement in Belfast in 1967, some two years before **the troubles** began. The Northern Ireland Civil Rights Association (NICRA) sought a number of reforms, including universal franchise in local government elections in line with the rest of the **UK**, the independent redrawing of electoral boundaries, legislation against discrimination in local government employment, a fair housing allocation system, and the withdrawal of the Public Order (Amendment) Bill (which became law in 1970 to deal with street tactics adopted by civil rights campaigners).

CIVIL SERVICE

Officers of the Crown who work impartially in a civil capacity in a department of government, paid in money voted by Parliament. Until 1968, the **Treasury** was responsible for civil service matters. That year, in response to the recommendations of the Fulton Report, a separate ministry – the Civil Service Department – was created. The reform was partially reversed in 1981 when responsibility for civil service manpower, pay and pensions was transferred back to the Treasury. The other aspects of the civil service, such as organization, management, recruitment, training and personnel, come under the Office of Public Service and Science, attached to the **Cabinet Office**, under the ministerial guidance of the Chancellor of the **Duchy of Lancaster**.

The civil service has undergone continuing reforms in recent years, including the imposition of a unified grading structure in 1984 and the Next Steps programme aimed at streamlining administration by creating separate executive agencies. A government **White Paper** on the future of the civil service was introduced in the **House of Commons** in July 1994. Entitled *Continuity and Change*, it envisaged a reduction of some 50,000 in the number of civil service posts (reducing them from the then current total of 533,000 to 'significantly' below 500,000 over four years), a streamlining of the upper echelons of the civil service, and the adoption of more private-sector practices.

CJD *see* CREUTZFELD-JAKOB DISEASE

CLAPHAM RAIL CRASH

A railway accident which occurred just south of Clapham Junction, in south London, on 12 December 1988. The accident happened at 8.13 a.m., when a stationary Basingstoke to Waterloo passenger train was struck from behind by a passenger train travelling from Bournemouth to Waterloo. The wreckage of the two trains was then hit by an empty southbound train travelling from Waterloo in the opposite direction. A total of 35 people were killed and some 200 injured in the incident. A public inquiry into the disaster, chaired by Sir Anthony Hidden QC, published its findings on 7 November 1989. The report found that faulty rewiring work carried out at a relay room near Clapham on 27 November 1988 had caused a signal failure which led to the crash. A total of 93 recommendations were put forward to improve railway safety. A jury at the inquest of those who died returned verdicts of unlawful killing on 13 September 1990, but the Director of Public Prosecutions chose not to bring manslaughter charges against British Rail or any of its employees.

CLARKE, KENNETH

(b. 1940) **Chancellor of the Exchequer** since 1993 in the **Conservative** government of John **Major**. A member of the **Cambridge Mafia** and president of the Cambridge Union, Clarke graduated and was called to the Bar in 1963. He entered Parliament in 1970, and under Margaret **Thatcher** served as Paymaster-General and Minister for Employment (1985–7) and Secretary of State for Health (1988–90). Under Major, Clarke served as Secretary of State for Education and Science (1990–2) and then as Home Secretary before replacing Norman **Lamont** as Chancellor in May 1993. A stocky, somewhat dishevelled figure with a populist penchant for beer, jazz and football, Clarke is the doyen of the pro-European left wing of the Conservative Party and as such is often spoken of as a future party leader and **Prime Minister**.

CLASS WAR

A contemporary anarchist organization in the UK which takes its name from the most extreme form of class struggle, a fundamental tenet of Marxism. Marxist theory holds that antagonism between classes is intrinsic to non-communist societies and therefore provides the driving force of history; class war is most acute under capitalism, when the emergence of the proletariat ignites a war for control of the means of production which will culminate in the victory of the proletariat over the bourgeoisie, and the establishment of communism.

CLAUSE IV

Clause IV of the **Labour Party** constitution, which sets out the party's basic tenets. Clause IV was 'updated' in 1995. According to the original clause, drawn up in 1918, Labour's goal was 'to secure for the workers by hand or by brain the full fruits of their industry and the most equitable distribution thereof that may be possible upon the basis of the common ownership of the means of production, distribution and exchange, and the best obtainable system of popular administration and control of each industry or service'. Although the Party's left wing regarded the clause as sacrosanct, **modernizers** from Hugh **Gaitskell** onwards have in practice accepted the mixed economy. The Labour Party voted overwhelmingly at a special conference in April 1995 to replace Clause IV with a new statement of Labour values, drafted by new leader Tony **Blair**, committing the party to a mixed economy.

CLAUSE 28

Controversial legislation in the UK outlawing any 'promotion' of homosexuality by local authorities. Clause 28, eventually enacted as Section 28 of the Local Government Act 1988, was fiercely contested in parliament and by campaigners for homosexual and other civil rights. It prohibits local authorities throughout **Great Britain** from intentionally promoting homosexuality, or publishing material with the intention of promoting homosexuality, and from promoting the teaching in any of their own schools of the acceptability of homosexuality as a 'pretended family relationship'.

CLAY CROSS

The local government authority in Derbyshire whose councillors defied central government in 1972 over increases in council house rents. The overwhelmingly Labour-dominated Clay Cross urban district council refused to implement rent increases as required under the **Conservative** government's Housing Finance Act. As a result several Labour councillors were fined, surcharged and disqualified from office. The succeeding Labour government in 1974 lifted the disqualifications, but – in the face of **left-wing** opposition – declined to cancel the surcharges, so that some of the councillors faced bankruptcy. Members of the council were also in dispute with the government over implementation of wages restraint for their local authority employees.

CLEAN AIR LEGISLATION

Legislation passed to reduce air pollution. Legislation was first enacted in response to the rapid deterioration of air quality in London and other urban areas. The Clean Air Act 1993, which consolidated earlier legislation on air pollution including the Clear Air Acts 1956 and 1968, restricts the emission of smoke, grit and dust, and allows local authorities to establish smokeless zones – areas in which the emission of smoke from domestic and industrial users is restricted. Air quality has improved considerably over the past 30 years: total emissions of smoke have fallen by over 85 per cent since 1960 mainly as a result of domestic smoke control, and winter sunshine in central London has increased by about 70 per cent since 1958. However, although there are no more **smog** deaths, an increase in vehicle emissions and volatile organic compounds (**VOCs**) have had an adverse effect on air quality. The worst air pollution incident since the smogs of the 1950s occurred in December 1991 in London, when 150 people died.

CLEAR BLUE WATER

A reference to the **Conservative** right's call to distance the party from the rightward shifting **Labour Party** under Tony **Blair**, by itself moving further to the right. Leading right-winger Michael **Portillo** delivered a speech entitled 'Clear Blue Water' at a fringe meeting organized by the Thatcherite **Conservative Way Forward** group at the 1994 Conservative Party conference. The speech contained Portillo's message that the state apparatus is too big and that young people must make welfare provision for themselves.

CLEGG, PRIVATE LEE

The paratrooper controversially released from prison on licence in July 1995. Private Clegg had been imprisoned in June 1993 for the murder of Karen Reilly, who had been shot in the back of the head in September 1990 after the stolen car in which she was travelling drove through a parachute regiment patrol checkpoint in west Belfast. The driver of the car, Martin Peake, was also shot dead, but no murder charges could be brought on his account because no bullet was recovered. The soldiers at the checkpoint at no point believed that the **joyriders** were terrorists, and also held rowdy celebrations at their barracks after the shootings. At the 1993 trial Mr Justice Campbell found that the fourth shot fired by Clegg at the vehicle (the shot which killed Reilly) had been 'an excessive use of force' because the car had at that point passed the checkpoint. Clegg was sentenced to life imprisonment for the murder of Reilly and to four years in connection with the death of Peake. Another paratrooper, Barry Ainsworth, was sentenced to seven years for the attempted murder of Peake and to five years for attempting to cover up the affair. Four other paratroopers were acquitted. The case attracted relatively little attention in mainland **Britain** until January 1995, when Clegg's appeal reached its final hearing in the **House of Lords** after its rejection by **Northern Ireland**'s appeal court in March 1994. A week after the **Law Lords'** rejection of the appeal, campaigners for Clegg's release managed to invoke a massive public sympathy, putting forward the view that the young soldier had been placed in an intolerable position by having to make a split-second decision. Newspapers led by the **broadsheet** *Daily Telegraph* and **tabloid** *Daily Mail* inspired 2,000,000 letters calling for Clegg's release. In March Northern Ireland Secretary Sir Patrick Mayhew referred the case to the Northern Ireland Life Sentence Review Board in view of 'exceptional mitigating' factors. Ballistic tests were carried out at the behest of Clegg's legal adviser, and at a meeting on June 6 the Board agreed to reconsider Clegg's case, giving rise to the resignation of a senior member of the Board because of what she saw as 'a major deviation' from previous practice and procedure. Clegg was released on July 3 on the order of Sir Patrick Mayhew. It was widely perceived that the exact timing of Clegg's release had been in order to boost **Prime Minister** John **Major** on the eve of the **Conservative Party** leadership election, since, as confirmed by **Downing Street**, Mayhew had reached his decision on June 30. The decision to free Clegg was met with protests from Irish politicians and with widespread violence in Northern Ireland (after nearly a year of relative calm); more than 100 cars were set alight in west Belfast by protestors complaining that neither **republican** nor **loyalist** prisoners could expect such lenient treatment. These views were echoed by the **SDLP**, while Irish Prime Minister John Bruton said that he expected the British government to apply the approach used in the Clegg case to all similar cases. The release of Clegg was also condemned by international human rights groups as an example of political interference in the judicial process. Clegg himself was expected to return to his regiment after refresher training.

CLEVELAND CHILD SEX ABUSE AFFAIR

A controversy over the diagnosis of sexual abuse in a large number of children in Cleveland in 1987. In the space of five months, 121 children were deemed to have suffered abuse and were removed from their families by social workers. The initial diagnoses were carried out by two paediatricians at Cleveland General Hospital, Dr Marietta Higgs and Dr Geoffrey Wyatt. The affair led to widespread controversy, but at the same time focused attention on the problem of child abuse and how to detect it. Within 12 months nearly 100 of the children had been returned to their parents, although some remained on the 'at risk' register.

An official report chaired by Lady Justice Butler-Sloss, published in July 1988, said that the unshakeable convictions of the doctors concerned were largely responsible for unnecessary distress, but also that the agencies responsible for child protection had failed in terms of both internal and external communication and in understanding of each other's functions. Widespread changes in child protection practice were announced by the government as a result.

CLOSED SHOP

Compulsory membership of a trade union. The pre-entry closed shop requires that only members of a specific union be recruited to the workplace; the post-entry variant occurs when a new employee is required to join a certain union. The first rapidly became illegal under **trade union legislation** since 1979; the second has been eroded both by law and by growing employer repugnance.

CLYDE REPORT *see* ORKNEYS CHILD ABUSE AFFAIR

CND

The Campaign for Nuclear Disarmament, an organization which mobilized mass opposition to nuclear weapons in general and the UK's independent nuclear deterrent in particular. Founded in 1958 by a group including Bertrand Russell and Canon John Collins, CND was active in the late 1950s and early 1960s and again in the early 1980s. It organized an annual march to **Aldermaston** for several years and campaigned widely for the adoption of **unilateral nuclear disarmament**. However, it faded after the signing of the Partial Test Ban Treaty in 1963. In the early 1980s, under the leadership of Monsignor Bruce Kent, CND was reactivated in response to the planned deployment of US **cruise** missiles in the UK. During this phase CND organized several massive demonstrations and supported the protest at **Greenham Common**, but failed to prevent the deployment of the missiles. The influence of the organization declined considerably in 1990 with the ending of the **Cold War** and the withdrawal of cruise missiles by the USA in return for the destruction of Soviet SS20s.

COAL INDUSTRY

The industry whose **nationalization** in 1946 was a key achievement of the **Attlee** government and whose return to the private sector was regarded by **Conservatives** as the ultimate **privatization**. Before the Second World War coal was the scene of some of Britain's most bitter industrial relations disputes, most dramatically in 1926 when the resistance of the Miners' Federation of Great Britain (later the National Union of Mineworkers – **NUM**) to cuts in wages precipitated the General Strike. In 1947 all deep coal mining was gathered within the auspices of the National Coal Board (NCB) which reached peak output in 1955. After this date production, the number of pits and employment continually fell as coal was challenged as an energy source by **North Sea Oil**, nuclear power and gas. Major strikes in 1972 and 1974 restored the purchasing power of the miners and the 1974 Plan for Coal envisaged an expanding but more efficient industry. In practice a decade of decline followed and the NCB returned major deficits. The year-long **miners' strike** of 1984–5 failed to prevent run-down, although it cost **British Coal**, the National Coal Board's successor – now chaired by the quixotic Ian MacGregor – £1,750 million. Further decline followed as coal markets faced a new threat presented by a newly privatized electricity generating industry. From the late 1980s Conservative ministers began to promise that coal itself would be privatized. In September 1992 the President of the **Board of Trade**, Michael **Heseltine**, published plans to execute a rapid shrinkage of British Coal from 50 to 31 pits but public outcry forced a partial moratorium and energy review, so that immediate closures were reduced to 10. The review, however, proved to be just a stay of execution; following the publication of its report, which failed to disclose new markets which would offset the imminent loss of much demand from electricity generation, closures continued. By December 1994 BC had shut 34 pits. By January 1995 what remained of BC had been split into a Scottish, a Welsh, and three English regions, with the latter being acquired by a single firm, RJB Mining.

CO-DECISION

A jargon word within the **EU** for the enhanced role of the **European Parliament** under the **Maastricht** Treaty, beyond its original right to be consulted and its right under the **Single European Act** to 'co-operation'. The Parliament still has no right to initiate legislation. Co-decision (with the **Council of Ministers**) applies for legislation on completion of the **single market**, freedom of movement for workers and new initiatives on the environment, consumer protection, public health, culture, Community transport infrastructure, energy and telecommunications.

COD WAR

The general colloquial expression used to dramatise disputes between the UK and Iceland over fishing rights. The 'first cod war' in 1958, over Iceland's extension of its **territorial waters** from six to 12 nautical miles, ended in agreements with the UK, and with West Germany, in 1961. In 1972, however, Iceland announced that it was extending its fishing limits to 50 miles (generally representing the extent of the country's **continental shelf**). This precipitated a 'second cod war' – serious confrontations between British (and West German) fishing vessels and Icelandic gunboats, and direct intervention by the Royal Navy in May 1973. The **ICJ** ruled in July 1974 that Iceland was not entitled to exclude British or West German fishing vessels between the 12-mile and 50-mile limits. A two-year interim fisheries agreement between the UK and Iceland had meanwhile been concluded, however, in November 1973. Its expiry, and Iceland's declaration of a 200-mile fisheries limit with effect from October 1975, was followed by the 'third cod war': Royal Navy frigates, sent in late November to protect British trawlers from warp-cutting and other harassment, became involved in collisions with Icelandic coastguard vessels, and Iceland broke off diplomatic relations with the UK in February 1976, the first such breach between **NATO** member countries. In June 1976 the two sides signed an interim agreement, setting specific limits for a six-month period, after which British trawlers would have only such access rights as Iceland was prepared to allow within its 200-mile zone. Thereafter, with the British long-distance trawler fleets in terminal decline, negotiations on access to Icelandic waters were handed over to the **EC**.

COHESION FUND

A substantial **EU** fund to subsidize projects in poorer member countries, created as part of the package by which Spain, Portugal, Greece and Ireland were won over to support the 1991 **Maastricht** agreement. The fund was formally established on 16 May 1994. It supplements the existing EU structural funds – the agricultural funds under the **CAP**, the European Regional Development Fund

(ERDF) and the European Social Fund (**ESF**). The cohesion fund provides capital for transport infrastructure projects and environmental measures. The UK does not have access to this funding, which is restricted to member countries whose per capita **GDP** is less than 90 per cent of the Community average.

COHSE

The Confederation of Health Service Employees (COHSE), a trade union representing nurses and ancillary health workers. The union dates from 1946. Expelled from the **TUC** in 1972 for failing to de-register under the Industrial Relations Act 1971, it returned in 1974 to become a militant advocate of higher pay. Membership boomed as new campaigns and industrial action dramatized low pay in the **NHS**. COHSE peaked at around 220,000 members in the early 1980s, of whom 80 per cent were women, and rivalled **NUPE**, and the Royal College of Nursing for the allegiance of nurses. In the 1980s new discontent erupted periodically over nurses' pay. COHSE, NUPE and **NALGO** amalgamated to formed **Unison** in 1993.

COI

The Central Office of Information, an executive agency which provides consultancy, design and production facilities for all publicity activities within all fields, while specializing in government organizations. The COI conducts government display advertising, television, film production, exhibitions, marketing, publications, radio, photography and market research.

COLD WAR

A phrase in common usage from 1947, describing the protracted period of postwar antagonism between the communist bloc, particularly the Soviet Union, and the **West**, led by the USA. Sir Winston **Churchill**'s March 1946 speech at Fulton in Missouri, USA, when he warned of the threat of Soviet expansion and of an iron curtain falling across Europe, and the subsequent Soviet imposition of communism in East-Central Europe, are usually offered as starting points of the Cold War. The two blocs fought a vigorous propaganda battle in which each sought to discredit its rival and to gain prestige for itself. The balance of terror which followed the Soviet Union's development of the atomic bomb led the blocs to avoid direct military conflict, although there were several dangerous confrontations, including the 1962 Cuban missile crisis. Much conflict took place by proxy: one bloc funded and trained indigenous military groups to engage opposing forces when it appeared that the rival bloc was likely to extend its sphere of influence, for instance in Afghanistan.

The Cold War forced the two blocs to maintain their readiness for a possible 'hot war'; the expense of the resulting **arms race** eventually helped to bankrupt the Soviet Union. The appointment in 1985 of Mikhail Gorbachev as general secretary of the Communist Party of the Soviet Union marked the beginning of a rapprochement with the West, which was confirmed with the Soviet decision in 1989 not to intervene when the communist regimes in eastern Europe were collapsing. The final dissolution in 1991 of the Warsaw Pact – the military alliance between the former communist bloc countries – provided one of the clearest symbols of the ending of the Cold War.

COLLATERAL DAMAGE

A piece of military jargon widely used during the 1991 **Gulf War** to betoken damage inflicted on non-military targets. Despite the use of **smart weapons**, the US-led air campaign resulted in a widespread loss of civilian life. Little information was released by the allies, but it was acknowledged that some 'collateral damage' had been inflicted.

COLLECTIVE BARGAINING

The setting of workplace wages, conditions and benefits by agreement between employer and employee representatives. Collective bargaining in Britain reached its height in the 1970s, when peak levels of union organization compelled employers to negotiate across most sectors of the economy. Most agreements were negotiated nationally, with some local variation. Since then, successive **recessions**, **trade union legislation**, **privatization**, and the reluctance of employers to engage in negotiations have reduced its scope; collective bargaining continues where union membership persists but is normally now located at the level of the company or the business.

COLLECTIVE SECURITY

A fundamental notion in international relations, that states may act together to ensure conformity with recognized rules and norms of international behaviour. A basic tenet of the League of Nations after the First World War, it failed to develop effectively in the inter-war era, hampered by the League's restricted mandate and limits on its power to use force against aggression. The Second World War alliance against the German-led Axis coalition again encouraged hopes of postwar co-operation to resist threats to peace, and in the Washington Declaration of 1942 the 26 Allied countries laid the foundations of the **UN**, a determined move in this direction. However, the **Cold War**, which had developed by the early 1950s, and the emergence of rival blocs allied to the USA and the Soviet Union, quickly eroded the authority of the UN as an agent of collective security. The UN **Security Council** became locked in stalemate, with its permanent members using their right of veto to prevent action on major issues. The UN General Assembly invoked the principle of collective security to override a Security Council veto under the Uniting for Peace resolutions to oppose aggression in North Korea and Egypt in 1950 and 1956 respectively.

With the passing of the Cold War there has been a gradual revival of emphasis on collective security, although its precise implementation has been fraught with controversy as in the case of the **Gulf War** against Iraq in January–February 1991. Recent trends suggest that the traditional notion of collective security, as embodied in the UN system, may gradually be redefined, with the widening of what were formerly the Western security alliances (principally **NATO**) to include their former Warsaw Pact adversaries, and the enlargement of the security role of newer bodies such as the Organization for Security and Co-operation in Europe (OSCE, formerly the CSCE).

COLONIAL OFFICE

The former government department concerned with British colonies overseas. Its staff was combined with that of the **Commonwealth Relations Office** in 1966 to form the Commonwealth Office. This was then incorporated into the Foreign and Commonwealth Office (**FCO**) in 1968.

COLONIALISM

A term associated chiefly, though not exclusively, with the consequences of Western overseas expansion from the sixteenth century. It involved the taking and the economic exploitation, although not necessarily the settlement, of African, American, Asian and Australasian territories by the British and other Europeans, and was generally supported by a political organization which brought together different cultures, tribes or nationalities under a dominating metropolitan centre. While frequently the outcome of military conquest, colonialism was justified by an elaborate ideology based on the assumption that certain territories and people required domination. This idea, which was subsequently to evolve as the recognizable creed of imperialism, defined by the attitudes of the dominant metropolis, fuelled a cultural discourse among Western colonial powers which justified their control of foreign territories. Among the British, territorial acquisitions fulfilled the inherent responsibilities of the 'White Man's Burden'.

At the end of the Second World War the UK still ruled a vast overseas empire (which included great swathes of Africa and Asia), but successive governments, in response to both nationalist aspirations and world pressure, gradually granted independence to the colonies, beginning with India and Pakistan in 1947. By 1985 more than 30 other former British dependencies had achieved independence, nearly all of them becoming members of the **Commonwealth**.

See also Appendix I.

COMBINED LOYALIST MILITARY COMMAND

An umbrella organization for a number of **loyalist** paramilitary groups in **Northern Ireland**. It includes the **UDA**, the **UVF**, and the **Red Hand Commandos**.

The Military Command announced a **ceasefire** in October 1994, which it declared would be permanent so long as there was a continued cessation of **republican** or **nationalist** violence as announced by the **IRA** in its historic statement of August 1994.

COMET CRASHES

A series of crashes in 1953–4 involving Comet airliners, manufactured by the de Havilland company. Comets crashed near Calcutta on 2 May 1953, killing all 43 people on board, and near Elba on 10 January 1954, with the loss of 35 lives. After another aircraft crashed on April 8 while en route from Rome to Johannesburg, killing 21 passengers and crew, the government grounded all Comets the next day by withdrawing their certificates of airworthiness pending extensive tests. The report of a Court of Inquiry into the disasters, published in February 1955, revealed that lack of experience in designing pressurized cabins had given rise to a structural weakness, rendering the aircraft susceptible to metal fatigue in the cabin roof which could cause part of the roof to disintegrate.

COMMERCIAL RADIO

The network of **UK** commercial radio stations which began broadcasting in the mid-1970s under the Sound Broadcasting Act of 1972, and which generate revenue from advertising. The first franchise had been granted by the **Independent Broadcasting Authority** to the London Broadcasting Company in 1973, with regional stations being established soon afterwards. The **Radio Authority** in the early 1990s awarded franchises to three new national commercial stations, and a further eight for radio broadcasting in London. There are currently almost 150 commercial radio stations, including the all-woman Viva – launched in July 1995 – competing with the BBC's network.

COMMERCIAL TELEVISION

The regional independent television (ITV) broadcasting companies in the **UK** whose programmes were first transmitted in September 1955 and whose funding principally comes from the sale of advertising time. The legislative authority for commercial television came from the Television Act of 1954, which created the Independent Television Authority, renamed in 1972 the **Independent Broadcasting Authority** (IBA) under the Sound Broadcasting Act. The IBA was in 1991 replaced by the **Independent Television Commission**, whose job was to regulate commercial television and to issue licences to the highest bidder by competitive tender according to specific tests of quality. Under new ownership regulations announced by the government in November 1993 and arising from the terms of the Broadcasting Act of 1990, an independent television company could hold a maximum of two regional licences in areas with the largest advertising revenue – except in London. As of mid-1995 there were 15 commercial television broadcasting companies.

COMMISSION

The European Commission, which was formally called the Commission of the European Communities (**EC**) until November 1993. The Commission is the Community body charged with formulating proposals and with managing Community affairs, whereas policy decisions are made by the Council of Ministers. A new 20-member Commission took office for a five-year term in January 1995, headed by Jacques Santer. Currently the commissioners are appointed by the **European Council** (and in effect by the national government of their member state; traditionally one of the two UK commissioners is put forward by the opposition). The whole team must obtain the approval of the European Parliament. Some changes in the appointment procedure are due from 1996 under the **Maastricht** Treaty. Commissioners are not supposed to represent national interests, holding instead a community-wide responsibility for a particular area of policy. Among the most influential British members of the Commission have been Roy (now Lord) **Jenkins**, who was Commission President in 1977–80, and Sir Leon **Brittan**, a Commission vice-president since 1989; the other British member from 1995 is former **Labour Party** leader Neil **Kinnock**.

COMMISSION FOR RACIAL EQUALITY *see* CRE

COMMITTEE OF 100

A more militant offshoot of **CND** in the UK, formed in 1960 as the Committee of 100 for civil disobedience against nuclear weapons, and headed by Bertrand Russell. It undertook a number of forcible 'sit-downs' outside government buildings and at strategic bases, designed to invite confrontation with the police. It also broadened its scope to include other causes, such as opposition to the visit to London in July 1963 of King Paul and Queen Frederika of Greece. However, it gradually lost its leading role to other more specifically targeted organizations, and disbanded in 1968.

COMMITTEE OF THE WHOLE

A procedural device whereby an entire legislative assembly transforms itself into a committee presided over by a chair rather than the **Speaker**. Associated particularly with the **UK**, the USA, Australia and Canada, the device is often used to consider details of financial or constitutional legislation.

COMMITTEE STAGE

Detailed consideration of draft legislation. A bill which has received its **second reading** in the **House of Commons** passes to a committee for close examination. This is usually a committee of the whole house or a **standing committee**; more rarely, the Bill can go before a **select committee**. The bill is considered clause by clause and sometimes largely remodelled. When the committee stage is concluded the Bill goes back to the house for the 'report stage' during which amendments to meet points made in committee are proposed and debated. Procedure in the Lords is similar: bills are normally considered by a committee of the whole house, but there is provision for consideration by a public bill committee, a special standing committee or a select committee.

COMMON FOREIGN AND SECURITY POLICY

The single policy of member states of the **EC** agreed at the December 1991 intergovernmental conference in **Maastricht**. EC member states had been committed to co-operation on foreign policy under the 1985 **Single European Act**.

COMMON HEALTH SERVICES AGENCIES

see NATIONAL BLOOD AUTHORITY

COMMON MARKET

The popular name for the **EEC**, but also a general term applicable to other organizations which implement free trade and other forms of economic co-operation within a geographical area.

COMMONWEALTH

A voluntary association of 50 independent states which evolved from the British Empire, and has latterly been concerned mainly with decolonization, economic development, and white minority rule in southern Africa. Its origin is generally traced back to the 1931 Statute of Westminster which confirmed the sovereignty of the '**White Commonwealth**' countries, namely Australia, Canada, New Zealand and South Africa, while enabling them to retain the British monarch as queen or head of state. A revised formula agreed in 1949 allowed India, and thus other members, to become republics within the Commonwealth while acknowledging the British monarch as symbolic head of state. Of the Commonwealth's current membership, 16 states, including the **UK**, have Queen **Elizabeth** as head of state, five others are national monarchies, and 29 are republics. The organization has no formal charter or governing structure; policy is defined at biennial summits, known as **CHOGMs**, and implemented through the Commonwealth Secretariat, headed by a secretary-general.

See also Appendix I.

COMMONWEALTH DEVELOPMENT CORPORATION

A body which assists in the development of country economies. Its main activity is to provide long-term finance in the form of loans or risk capital for a variety of projects. The Corporation covers British dependent territories and, with ministerial approval, any Commonwealth or other developing country. The Corporation is presently authorized to operate in about 50 countries in addition to British dependent territories.

COMMONWEALTH FOUNDATION

A London-based body established in 1965 to promote professional co-operation within the **Commonwealth**. Its mandate was extended in 1979 to include co-operation with non-governmental organizations (**NGOs**), and its functions widened to include culture, information, the media, rural development and the interests of handicapped groups and women.

COMMONWEALTH IMMIGRANTS ACTS

Legislation dating from 1962 and 1968 designed to limit **immigration** from **Commonwealth** countries. Under this legislation immigration officers could deny admission to the UK to any Commonwealth citizen, unless she/he were born in the UK, held a UK passport, had a parent or grandparent who was born, naturalized or adopted in the UK, was self-supporting or had a work permit. The Home Secretary was given the power to **deport** Commonwealth citizens under the 1962 Act. The 1968 Act made it an offence to land in **Britain** without adhering to immigration regulations. The act was repealed by the 1971 Immigration Act, which itself was amended by the 1981 British **Nationality** Act.

COMMONWEALTH INSTITUTE

The exhibition and resource centre for the **Commonwealth**. The Commonwealth Institute in Kensington, London, has permanent exhibitions on all member countries, other temporary exhibitions and a library and resource centre. There is also an autonomous Scottish Institute in Edinburgh. Traditionally, it has been funded by the **UK** government and other Commonwealth member states. However, in 1993 the UK government announced that grant support, which amounted to around £3,000,000 annually, would from 1996–7 be reduced each year, with a view to being ended by 1999.

COMMONWEALTH PREFERENCE

A preferential system of trade tariffs announced by the UK in July 1971 to safeguard trading relations between itself and its **Commonwealth** partners. Opponents of UK entry into the **EC** had argued strongly that EC membership would adversely affect Commonwealth countries, and in particular that it would shut out their cheap farm produce. The preferential system announced in 1971 provided for continued special access to UK markets for some Commonwealth countries, in particular New Zealand, and made special arrangements for the gradual introduction of external tariffs and levies on goods from Australia and Canada. African, Caribbean and Pacific (ACP) countries within the Commonwealth were allowed to maintain existing trading arrangements until 1975, pending the entry into force of the Lomé Convention.

COMMONWEALTH RELATIONS OFFICE

A former government department responsible for relations with independent **Commonwealth** countries. In 1965 the duties and posts of the Commonwealth Relations Office were combined with those of the foreign service and the trade commissions service to form the diplomatic service. The departments of the **Colonial Office** and the Commonwealth Relations Office were merged in 1966 to form the Commonwealth Office. This in turn was incorporated into the Foreign and Commonwealth Office (**FCO**) in 1968.

COMMUNIST PARTY OF GREAT BRITAIN

see CPGB

COMMUNITY CHARGE

The official name for the controversial 'poll tax' introduced by the **Conservative** government, in **Scotland** in April 1989 and in **England** and **Wales** in April 1990. Local taxes under the previous rates system had been levied according to notional values of homes, but the community charge was based on the number of adults in the household, and for many it represented a considerable increase over the rates. The tax was exceptionally unpopular, provoking nationwide protests including serious rioting in London on March 31, 1990, and demonstrations in normally loyal Conservative areas. Non-payment of the tax was unusually high. The tax was associated closely with Margaret **Thatcher's** administration and was seen in many ways as her nemesis. Her successor, John **Major**, took steps to abolish it soon after coming to office; in March 1991 it was announced that it would be replaced by the **Council Tax** in April 1993.

COMMUNITY OF THE PEACE PEOPLE

Established in 1976 as the Peace Movement – but soon renamed – by a group of women who witnessed the death of three young children struck by a gunman's getaway car after a terrorist incident in Belfast, **Northern Ireland**. In its early stages the group – consisting of Ciaran McKeown, Mairead Corrigan and Betty Williams, of whom the latter two won the Nobel peace prize in 1976 – was able to attract support from a number of well-attended rallies in the province, as well as in the Irish Republic, London and overseas. It also drew financial support from a number of countries. The group's founders announced in 1978 that they were to withdraw to allow the election of a new leadership.

COMMUNITY SERVICE ORDER

A court sentence used in place of imprisonment for more minor offences. It requires convicted offenders aged 16 or over to perform unpaid, disciplined and socially useful work in the local community for a specified period of between 40 and 240 hours. A CSO is made only with the offender's consent and on the basis of a pre-sentence report on the individual submitted by probation officers or social workers.

The Criminal Justice Act 1991 sought to widen the range of community penalties available to courts, and introduced sentencing guidelines requiring judges to imprison offenders only when the offence was so serious that a custodial sentence was the only justifiable one. This was part of a strategy to reduce prison numbers; subsequent Acts, however, have reversed this trend. The 1991 Act introduced a new 'combination order', combining community service with a **probation order** and also a new curfew order, confining people to their homes at certain times and enforced by means of **electronic tagging** to monitor their whereabouts. A Home Office **Green Paper** published in March 1995 included proposals to strip probation officers of the power to decide the nature of non-custodial sentences.

COMPASSION FATIGUE

The phenomenon whereby, in the face of almost continuous demands and with its sympathy exhausted, the public feels unable to give to those in need.

COMPREHENSIVE SCHOOLS

Secondary schools with a non-selective intake which originated in the late 1950s and were introduced widely from the 1960s. Egalitarian and anti-elitist in conception, they replaced the existing tripartite system of **grammar**, **secondary modern** and technical schools in the state sector, to the extent that by 1993 about 85 per cent of local authority maintained secondary schools in England were comprehensive, as were virtually all those in Wales and all those in Scotland, although most of those in Northern Ireland had a selective intake. The **GERBIL** (the Education Reform Act 1988) provided for schools '**opting out**' from local authority control, but stipulated that any **grant-maintained** comprehensive school would need to go through specific procedures if it wished to become selective.

COMPULSORY REPATRIATION

The deportation of refugees to their homeland. In the case of Vietnamese **boat people** in **Hong Kong**, the Hong Kong authorities carried out the first compulsory repatriation of refugees deemed **economic migrants** in December 1989. Vietnamese and US opposition to the policy meant that the next operation was not carried out until mid-1992, when Vietnam and the UK signed an agreement providing for the blanket return to Vietnam of all so-called economic migrants. Since then compulsory repatriation flights from Hong Kong have occurred at regular intervals.

CONCORDE

The only supersonic aircraft in commercial use. Agreement on this Anglo-French venture was announced in November 1962. The development of the delta-winged airliner cost £1,500 million (US$2,250 million) and the maiden flight of the first prototype took place at Toulouse on 2 March 1968. On that occasion

UK Minister of Technology Anthony Wedgwood Benn (now Tony **Benn**) finally ended speculation as to the spelling of the aircraft's name by announcing that it would have the French final 'e', which he said stood 'for excellence, for England, for Europe and for Entente'. The plane went into commercial use on 21 January 1976. The advantage of Concorde's cruising speed – Mach 2 (1,350 mph/2,150 kph) or twice the speed of sound – is offset commercially by the limited seating capacity (100 passengers) and high running costs.

CONES HOTLINE

A notorious initiative generated by the **Citizen's Charter**, launched in December 1992 and intended to relieve drivers frustrated by unnecessary roadway cones. It was reported in mid-1995 that after a total of 17,700 calls to the hotline, a grand total of five sets of cones had been removed. As a result the Highways Agency was said to be relaunching the scheme, which had thus far cost £120,000. However, it was announced at the end of July that the hotline was to be scrapped.

CONFAIT REPORT

A report published in 1977 investigating the case of three youths wrongfully convicted of the murder of a man named Maxwell Confait on the strength of false confessions. The report highlighted errors and oversights in the prosecution of the case, which began with **police** interviews held in the absence of any parent or solicitor. It recommended a code of practice for interviewing juveniles, and people with a mental illness or disability. This included conducting interviews in the presence of an adult who can assist communication and interpretation of answers, except in urgent cases were information is sought to prevent harm to others or serious damage to property.

CONFERENCE SEASON

The annual round of party political conferences, which takes place every September, usually in British seaside resorts such as Brighton, Blackpool and Torquay. Whereas the party conferences of the **Labour Party** and **Liberal Democrats** have a considerable role in policy-making, **Conservative Party** conferences have traditionally been relatively tame affairs closely managed by the party's **men in grey suits**. All the major parties treat the conference season as an opportunity to raise their profile in the media and as an important rallying point for the party faithful.

CONSENSUS POLITICS

The explicit or tacit alignment of the policies of two or more otherwise opposed parties within a legislature or political system. As this course may result in a minimization of confrontation, it may be seen as the converse of the pursuit of **conviction politics**.

CONSERVATISM

A broadly **right-wing** ideology, associated in the UK with the **Conservative Party**, which emphasizes individual responsibility, an appropriate distribution of the rewards of individual enterprise, a minimal role for the state and the rule of law.

There are two contradictory strains of thought within Conservatism: (i) the radical and liberal strain, associated with upwardly mobile social groups, which stresses the centrality of the market and individual responsibility and whose roots are in the government of Sir Robert Peel in the 1840s and culminate in the strongly ideological **Thatcherite** era; and (ii) the traditionalist strain, associated with the **Establishment**, which stresses hierarchy, religion and the family and whose roots are in the **one-nation Toryism** of Benjamin Disraeli and exemplified in contemporary politics by Sir Edward **Heath**'s brand of pragmatism and consensus.

Conservatism's opponents criticize it for perpetuating political and economic inequalities by duping the underprivileged into accepting the status quo.

CONSERVATIVE PARTY

The right-wing party which has been a leading force in British politics since the Victorian era. Formally the National Association of Conservative and Unionist Associations, the Conservative Party grew out of the **Tory** Party in the 1830s, and the word 'Tory' remains a synonym of 'Conservative'. The party is host to both, somewhat contradictory strains of

conservatism, one traditional and backed by the **Establishment**, and the other radical and innovative and backed by upwardly mobile groups; hence (roughly) the division between the **wets** and **dries** of the radical **Thatcherite** era. The party is unified, however, in its emphasis on law and order, **family values**, patriotism, strong national defence and the virtues of free enterprise.

The Conservative Party's support is still essentially middle class, although it has attracted the voting support of up to one-third of the working class. There is little internal democracy in the party and Conservative Party conferences have tended to be comparatively tame affairs. Nevertheless the party is confronted with a widening division over European policy, with a relatively small, but vocal band of **Eurosceptics** having a disproportionate impact on policy.

Conservative Way Forward

The **Thatcherite** pressure group formed by Cecil Parkinson and Norman **Tebbit**. A **Eurosceptic** formation, it nevertheless supported John **Major** against John Redwood in the party leadership election in June–July 1995. Its current members include Kenneth **Baker**, David Amess and Sir George Gardiner.

Constituency

A locality represented by an **MP**. There are currently 651 constituencies, each of which elects an MP to the **House of Commons** at a **general election**. The population, geographical size and social composition of constituencies varies widely. The largest concentration of constituencies are in London (84) and the rest of the south and south-west **England** (177). In the Midlands there are currently 100 constituencies, in the north of England 163, in **Wales** 38, in **Scotland** 72 and in **Northern Ireland** 17. The House of Commons has accepted the report of the **Boundary Commissions** recommending an increase in the number of MPs to 659 at the next general election. For many MPs a large part of their workload concerns issues brought to them by their constituents. Most MPs hold constituency 'surgeries' at weekends, when they make themselves readily available to their constituents.

Constitution

A body of rules concerned with the distribution of power among organs of government. The **UK** is almost alone among sovereign states in having no formal written constitution. Many constitutional principles are contained in statutes such as Magna Carta (1215), the Bill of Rights (1689) and the **Parliament Act 1949**. Others are based on traditional practices and ideas which have evolved through time. One of these customs maintains that issues of constitutional importance cannot be decided without lengthy and detailed consideration, often involving a **general election** to provide the government with a mandate for change or for a **referendum**.

Consumers' Association

The largest independent consumer protection body in **Britain**. Established in 1956, the Association aims to facilitate informed consumer choice and to improve the quality of goods and services provided to the consumer. The publicity function is achieved by media pressure and the publication of a range of *Which?* consumer guides and other well-known titles such as the *Good Food Guide*. In recent years the organization has been attacked for being too concerned with testing appliances and failing to address adequately broad issues such as poverty, the impact on the environment of consumption and the power of advertising. It was thought that the appointment in September 1994 of Sheila McKechnie, hitherto the outspoken director of the housing charity **Shelter**, as the director of the Consumers' Association, would lead to a change in emphasis.

Continental Shelf

The relatively gradual slope of the seabed offshore, before the point where it falls away steeply to the ocean floor. The UK was among the first countries to claim, in the 1940s, exclusive jurisdiction over the fisheries, mineral and other resources of the continental shelf. This concept had gained eventual acceptance by the time of the agreement at the **UN** Conference on the Law of the Sea (UNCLOS) in 1982, when **territorial waters** were deemed to extend 12 nautical miles offshore, the continental shelf was delimited as extending up to 350 miles offshore depending on local geography, and coastal states were accorded jurisdiction within it, in addition to their rights over a 200-mile **EEZ**. The Law of the Sea Convention guaranteeing these rights came into force in November 1994.

CONTRACEPTIVE PILL *see* the PILL

CONVERGENCE

A jargon word much used in the **EU** for the process by which the economies of member countries are to become more closely comparable in terms of their performance. The controversial third stage of economic and monetary union (**EMU**) may only be embarked upon by those states which have achieved the necessary convergence on four key measures – inflation rates, the control of government deficits, currency stability, and interest rates.

CONVERTIBILITY

The policy which permits one currency to be exchanged freely for others. Key **IMF** objectives include establishing a multilateral system of payments, in respect of current transactions between member countries, and eliminating the foreign exchange restrictions which hamper the growth of world trade. By July 1994 a total of 93 IMF members (out of a total membership of 179) had formally accepted the obligations contained in the relevant sections of Article VIII of the Fund's Articles of Agreement; these included undertakings not to engage in discriminatory currency arrangements or multiple currency practices without IMF approval.

CONVICTION POLITICS

The pursuit of political beliefs with little or no concern for opposing points of view. Depending on the standpoint of the observer, conviction politics (one of the catchphrases of **Thatcherism**) may be seen either as stubbornly dogmatic or as intellectually purist. In either case conviction politics make impossible any approach towards **consensus politics**.

THE CONVOY

The convoy of vehicles, also known as the peace convoy or the hippy convoy, driven by **New Age travellers** and others which began descending on the ancient Stonehenge monument on Salisbury Plain in late May 1985 to celebrate the summer solstice, thus defying a **police** cordon of the area. After clashes with police the convoy was halted in a bean field some 10 miles from the monument; the police arrested 520 people, of whom dozens were beaten, and damaged scores of vehicles. The **Police Complaints Authority** subsequently upheld complaints that the police had used excessive force, but failed to identify the officers involved.

There were further clashes in subsequent years as police sought to retain restrictions on access to Stonehenge.

COREPER

The Committee of Permanent Representatives of member states of the **EU**, consisting of government officials at ambassadorial level who are responsible for ensuring the continuity of policy between sessions of the **Council of Ministers**.

CO-RESPONSIBILITY LEVY

A tool to help the reform of common agricultural policy (**CAP**) which gained acceptance in the mid-1980s in the **EC** (later the **EU**) despite resistance from farmers. While guaranteed prices remained the core of the CAP, dairy and cereal producers found themselves obliged to pay the levy as a direct contribution to the cost of buying up and storing their surplus production. British farmers resented paying a penalty for 'overproduction' and argued instead for a policy to discourage the many less efficient farmers on the continent.

CORNISH NATIONALIST MOVEMENT *see* MEBYON KERNOW

CORPORAL PUNISHMENT

Discipline imposed by physical means such as beating, caning or slapping. Corporal punishment was outlawed in state schools in 1986 following a case brought before the **European Court of Human**

Rights. The practice remains legal in **private schools**.

CORPORATISM

A theory criticizing the relationship between government and large industrial and commercial corporations that suggests that the corporations play a significant role in policy making. In part this is said to be because civil servants rely on the business community in a particular sector for the knowledge and expertise necessary to make policy decisions. Industrial concerns, especially internationally operating multinational firms, are often considered to be dictating to democratically elected governments.

CORRECTING MECHANISM

The formula for calculating a **budget rebate** from the **EC**, which was worked out in 1975 as part of the UK's **renegotiation** of its membership terms. The mechanism specified percentages (on a sliding scale) to be repaid from a member state's contributions to the Community budget, when its contributions were disproportionate to its overall share of Community **GNP**. The incoming **Thatcher** government in 1979 dismissed this arrangement as having achieved nothing, and successfully demanded a new system where budget rebates would offset any excessive gap between a state's contributions to and receipts from the Community budget.

CORRIE BILL

The first serious attempt by a **backbencher** to amend the 1967 **Abortion Act**. Put forward in 1979 by **Conservative MP** John Corrie, the bill gained a **second reading** but failed to get past the **committee stage**. A similar attempt to restrict the availability of terminations was later made in the late 1980s by the **Alton Bill**. *See also* Appendix VI.

COUNCIL FOR THE PROTECTION OF RURAL ENGLAND

A prominent countryside conservation group. The Council was founded in 1926 as the Council for the Preservation of Rural England, adopting its present name in 1969, and is often perceived as an **Establishment** countryside organization. With the recent higher profile of **environmentalism**, it has adopted a more campaigning style over such diverse issues such as the erosion of the green belt, motorway building and out-of-town shopping centres. It is a persuasive lobbyist at **Whitehall** and **Westminster** on behalf of the landscape environment.

COUNCIL HOUSING

Accommodation rented to residents by local authorities. Margaret **Thatcher**'s **Conservative** government introduced in the Housing Act 1980 the controversial **right to buy** policy under which council housing tenants were encouraged under the **right-to-buy** scheme to buy their homes by means of discounts and other incentives. This had the effect of reducing the stock of council housing, and was criticized by opponents as contributing to **homelessness**. Under the Housing Act 1988 council tenants could vote to transfer control of their estates from local authorities to newly created Housing Action Trusts.

COUNCIL OF EUROPE

A Strasbourg-based intergovernmental organization founded in May 1949, which had grown to 34 member countries as of May 1995 with a string of recent accessions by eastern European countries. Not to be confused with the **EU**'s intergovernmental **European Council**, it seeks to promote common legal and other standards as the basis of civil society and to protect human rights, particularly through its **European Court of Human Rights** set up under the 1950 **European Convention on Human Rights**.

COUNCIL OF MINISTERS

A term often used for national governments, but also within international organizations, notably for the principal decision-making body in what is now called the European Union (**EU**, formerly the **EC**). Here it consists of ministerial-level representatives of member governments, with the presidency held for six months by each member country in alphabetical rotation. A Council of (Foreign) Ministers meeting usually takes place every month, while ministers responsible for other portfolios have

Council of Ministers meetings of varying frequency.

The possibility that one country can veto decisions in the Council of Ministers has blocked a number of initiatives as well as holding up agreements on such matters as the budget or agricultural prices. Decisions are only taken by simple majority vote on minor procedural matters, and the **Luxembourg compromise** of 1966 restricted the proposed introduction of qualified majority voting to instances where no member state invoked its essential national interest. This began to change in the 1970s, with qualified majority voting on budgetary issues, and under the **Single European Act**, especially for issues relating to creating the **single market**. Even so, two large states and a small state could muster a blocking minority of 23 out of the 76 votes (10 each for France, Germany, Italy and the UK, eight for Spain, five each for Belgium, Greece, the Netherlands and Portugal, three each for Denmark and Ireland, and two for Luxembourg). Efforts by the UK to preserve this position when the Council of Ministers was expanded, to incorporate four new member states from 1995, eventually produced a formula in March 1994 known as the **Ioannina compromise**.

COUNCIL TAX

A local tax introduced by the **Conservative** government in April 1993 to replace the controversial **community charge** or 'poll tax'. Unlike its predecessor, which was a per capita charge, the new system was a property tax related to the value of people's homes, with a reduction for single adult occupiers. The council tax was generally welcomed as a fairer system than the community charge, although there was some opposition to the decision to levy it according to 1991 property values, rather than (lower) 1993 values.

COUNTY COUNCILS

In non-metropolitan areas of **England** and **Wales**, the locally elected bodies which, with **district councils**, perform the functions of **local government**. Each county has its own council, and contains a number of districts, each of which has its own district council. County councils manage the provision of services including education, police, libraries, roads and transport, refuse disposal and social services. Certain services, for example museums and recreation areas, are managed jointly by county and district councils. Nine regional councils perform the same functions in **Scotland**. There are currently 47 county councils in England and Wales. However, following the recommendations of the Local Government Commission made in early 1995, the government decided to abolish four English county councils (Avon, Cleveland, Humberside and Isle of Wight) from April 1996, with at least one (Berkshire) and probably others disappearing in subsequent years. They will be replaced by unitary district councils.

See also map, pp. xii–xiii.

COUNTY COURTS

A network of local courts with jurisdiction over minor civil cases in **England** and **Wales**. A Circuit judge presides, and the court's registrar, a solicitor, keeps its records. Certain disputes involving sums of less than £1,000 may be dealt with by arbitration before the registrar. The courts were established under the County Courts Act 1846 with the intention of making justice available locally and inexpensively. Appeals against decisions can be made to the **Court of Appeal**.

COUNTY HALL

An elegant six-storey building on the south bank of the river Thames in London, the headquarters from 1922 to 1965 of the London County Council (**LCC**) and then, until 1986, of the Greater London Council (**GLC**). The building is at the south end of Westminster Bridge, which leads over the river to the **Palace of Westminster**. Its office space was largely unused after the abolition of the GLC by the **Conservative** government of Margaret **Thatcher** in 1986. Turning down a rival bid from the London School of Economics (LSE), the government controversially gave Shirayama, a Japanese company, clearance to develop the building as a hotel. In March 1995 a leaked **National Audit Office** report revealed that not only had the Cabinet been misinformed about the viability of the LSE bid, but that Shirayama had only paid £50 million of the £60 million sale price, deferring the remaining £10 million until the next century.

COURT OF APPEAL

The court to which appeals may be made against decision in the **High Court** and **county courts**. Located in London's Strand, it has two divisions, civil and criminal. The criminal division was created under the Criminal Appeal Act 1968 to replace the Court of Criminal Appeal. Both divisions have the power to overturn, alter or uphold the decisions of lower courts and to order a fresh trial. Appeals lodged against decisions in the Court of Appeal are heard in the **House of Lords** – the final court of appeal in all civil and criminal cases – by the **Law Lords**.

COURT OF SESSION

The superior civil court under **Scotland**'s separate judicial system. The Court, presided over by the Lord Justice General and the Lord Justice Clerk, is divided into two houses. The Inner House, with two divisions each consisting of four judges, acts mainly as a court of appeal; further appeal can be made to the **House of Lords**. The Outer House is a court of first instance. The judges of the Court of Session are the same as those of the **High Court of the Justiciary** (Scotland's superior criminal court).

CPGB

The Communist Party of Great Britain, founded in 1920 as a revolutionary communist movement dedicated to radical changes in the economic and social system. It was unsuccessful in its attempts throughout the 1930s and 1940s to affiliate to the **Labour Party**, and its own most notable representative in Parliament was Willie Gallagher, who won West Fife for the party in the **general elections** of 1935 and 1945. Following the fall from power of communist parties throughout eastern Europe and the increasing trend towards right-wing governments, the party in 1991 changed its name to **Democratic Left**. A new constitution was adopted which excluded the principles of Marxist-Leninism. The party did not put forward candidates of its own in the 1992 general election, but advocated 'tactical voting' to defeat the incumbent **Conservative** government. The **Morning Star** is the voice of the party.

CPS

The Crown Prosecution Service, a government-funded body of barristers and solicitors which undertakes prosecutions in **England** and **Wales** on behalf of the police. It was introduced under the Prosecution of Offenders Act 1985, implemented in October 1986. Prior to the creation of the service, the police had been responsible for both investigating and prosecuting offenders, but in the wake of some disquiet over police performance the **Royal Commission** on Criminal Procedure (1977–81) recommended a new independent prosecution body. The head of the service is the **DPP** (Director of Public Prosecutions).

CRACK

A highly addictive narcotic which is manufactured by heating cocaine, water and baking powder and breaking the resulting hard substance into small fragments to be inhaled or smoked. Crack can reputedly make its consumers paranoid, hostile and highly aggressive, and is sometimes adulterated with heroin and other dangerous substances. Increasing levels of violent crime in the USA in the 1980s have been blamed on the rise of crack addiction, particularly among the urban poor. Crack has also become available in **Britain's** blighted **inner cities**, particularly London, Manchester and Glasgow, and control of the trade is sometimes associated with **Yardies**.

CRAIG, CHRISTOPHER *see* BENTLEY AND CRAIG

CRE

The Commission for Racial Equality, the body set up under the 1976 **Race Relations** Act which is responsible for the Act's implementation. The CRE, which consists largely of representatives of a broad cross-section of racial minorities, has a chair and not more than 14 members who are appointed by the Home Secretary. It seeks to promote equal opportunities and good relations between different ethnic groups, and conducts investigations into discriminatory practices, in order to work towards the elimination of **racism**. The CRE supports individuals taking up complaints of discrimination, can take action against discriminatory advertisements, and has published a code of practice for employers. However, like the Equal Opportunities Commission (**EOC**), it lacks powers to uncover and eradicate pervasive but hidden forms of discrimination.

CRESSWELL MINE DISASTER

A disaster in which 80 miners were killed in Cresswell colliery, Derbyshire, on 28 September 1950. The dead were among 240 men working underground when a fire broke out on a coal conveyor belt. Trapped by the flames and a roof fall, most of those who died were overcome by fumes. A similar number of miners died less than a year later in the **Easington mine disaster**.

CREUTZFELD-JAKOB DISEASE

A degenerative disease and the so-called human equivalent of **BSE** or 'mad cow disease'. However, a government-funded study released in October 1994 concluded that there was 'no conclusive evidence' that CJD could be directly attributable to BSE. The study said that the apparent increase in CJD since the 1970s had been caused mainly by the fact that the disease was being recognized in people over 75 who would previously have been diagnosed as having senile dementia. The 1994 annual report of the CJD surveillance unit in Edinburgh said that the number of CJD cases in the UK fell from 55 in 1992 to 40 in 1993, after having risen for the three years previous to 1992. Statistical analysis of the cases showed no occupational link; people working with animals were no more likely than others to develop CJD. While CJD victims were more likely than matched control subjects to have been regular eaters of meat, particularly veal, Dr Robert Will, the unit's director, attributed this finding to 'recall bias'.

CRICHEL DOWN

A case of maladministration under the 1951–5 **Conservative** government, and a prime instance of a resignation because of the principle of ministerial responsibility. Three farms at Crichel Down in Dorset had been compulsorily purchased in 1940 for use as a bombing range. At the beginning of the 1950s the land was consolidated into a single farm unit and let to a single tenant, disregarding applicants (including previous owners) who wanted to rent or buy parts of it. A public inquiry criticized the conduct of various civil servants. Although its report in July 1954 attributed no direct blame to Agriculture Minister Sir Thomas Dugdale, he nevertheless resigned (as both his junior ministers also offered to do), accepting full ministerial responsibility for the actions of his officials.

CRICKET TEST

The test of a black British person's loyalty to England devised by **Conservative** politician Norman **Tebbit**. In a US newspaper interview Tebbit declared that although British blacks owed their allegiance to the UK, most, including those born in Britain, would support their country of origin when it played England at cricket. His views were rejected as **racist** by the **Labour Party** and the black community and rekindled, albeit briefly, the political debate about **immigration**.

CRIMINAL INJURIES COMPENSATION SCHEME

A government programme established in 1964 under which ex gratia payments are made to victims of violent crime. A **White Paper** published on 15 December 1993 proposed the replacement of the existing system, under which payments were assessed on the basis of common law damages, with a fixed scale of 25 awards ranging from a minimum of £1,000 to a maximum of £250,000. Without being debated in Parliament, the new scheme was introduced on 1 April 1994, and on 9 November 1994 the **Court of Appeal** ruled that Michael **Howard**, the Home Secretary, had acted unlawfully in introducing the scheme without parliamentary approval.

CRIMINAL JUSTICE SYSTEM

The network of officials and public bodies responsible for enforcing the law and capturing and punishing offenders. In the wake of riots in the **inner cities** in 1981, the Police and Criminal Evidence

Act 1984 widened police powers to stop and search people and vehicles. In the late 1980s and early 1990s the problem of overcrowding in UK prisons received publicity, and government policy, as contained in the Criminal Justice Act 1991, was to attempt to limit the prison population by encouraging the courts' use of non-custodial sentences and fines.

In recent years the government has toughened its stance as a result of controversy surrounding **young offenders**, **raves**, **new age travellers**, **hunt saboteurs** and **squatters**. In a speech to the **Conservative Party** conference on 6 October 1993 Michael Howard, the Home Secretary, said that 'prison works' and that new measures might mean that: 'More people will go to prison. I do not flinch from that.' The Criminal Justice and Public Order Act 1994 introduced limits on a suspect's **right to silence**, tough new penalties for young offenders and new police powers to combat trespass and move on protestors.

See also Appendix VI.

CRIPPS, SIR STAFFORD

(1889–1952) An economist and **Labour** statesman who replaced Hugh **Dalton** as **Chancellor of the Exchequer** in 1947. Noted for his moral and intellectual authority, Cripps introduced three budgets, inaugurating betting tax in his first delivered in April 1947, before resigning because of ill-health brought on by overwork in 1950.

CRISIS? WHAT CRISIS?

The headline in the **Sun** newspaper of 11 January 1979 referring to a tanned and apparently relaxed Jim **Callaghan** (**Sunny Jim**) at London airport on his return home from a seven-country summit in Guadaloupe during the **winter of discontent**. At the airport Callaghan, the **Labour Prime Minister**, answered a question from a journalist about the 'mounting chaos in the country' by stating: 'I don't think that other people in the world would share the view that there is mounting chaos.'

CROCKFORD'S CLERICAL DIRECTORY

A listing of all **Church of England** clergy. Named after John Crockford, its first printer and publisher, the first edition appeared in 1858. Its traditionally anonymous preface comments on the issues currently being addressed by the Church of England, and that of the 1987/88 edition attracted particular public attention, its author – soon revealed to be Gareth **Bennett**, an Oxford academic – heavily criticising the Church's apparent drift towards liberal ideology under the ministry of the then **Archbishop of Canterbury**, Robert Runcie. Bennett's suicide in December 1987, within weeks of his identity being revealed, fuelled intense speculation about disagreements within the Church, and in particular, the growing alienation of the **Anglo-Catholic** movement, of which Bennett was a prominent member.

CROSLAND, ANTHONY

(1918–77) Author of the hugely influential 'revisionist' text *The Future of Socialism* and **Labour** Secretary of State for Foreign and Commonwealth Affairs from April 1976 until his sudden death in February 1977. In *The Future of Socialism* (1957), Crosland argued that it was unnecessary, as well as undesirable, to engage in wholesale **nationalization**; social justice and equality – the central values of his brand of so-called 'revisionist socialism' – could be achieved by the reallocation of wealth and resources. The book not only provided an ideological basis for Hugh **Gaitskell** and his supporters, but had a profound impact on the approach of the Labour governments led by Harold **Wilson** and James **Callaghan**. Prior to his appointment as Foreign Secretary, Crosland had held a number of government posts, including President of the **Board of Trade**. He was replaced as Foreign Secretary by David **Owen**.

CROSSBENCHERS

Peers without party affiliation. Government supporters and opposition peers sit opposite each other in the **House of Lords**, as in the **House of Commons**, but the Lords also has benches ranged across the chamber facing the throne. Independent peers without party ties sit on these 'crossbenches'.

CROSSMAN DIARIES

The memoirs of senior **Labour** politician Richard Crossman, which gave one of the first and most candid accounts of the day-to-day workings of the **Cabinet**. The *Diaries of a Cabinet Minister* were published in three volumes between 1975 and 1977. Crossman was a member of the Labour government between 1964 and 1970 as successively Minister of Housing and Local Government, **Leader of the House of Commons**, and Secretary of State for Social Services.

CROWN COURT

The network of courts which hear the more serious criminal cases in **England** and **Wales**, where trials are heard by **jury**. It also hears appeals from **magistrates' courts**, where less serious criminal cases are heard, and may be requested by magistrates to sentence offenders where sentencing powers in the lower court are considered inadequate. Cases are heard in around 90 centres throughout England and Wales and organized into six 'circuits'. High Court judges, circuit judges or senior barristers who serve as part-time recorders preside. Crown courts in Northern Ireland and the **High Court of the Justiciary** in Scotland perform similar roles.

Appeals against decisions of the Crown Court can be made to the criminal division of the **Court of Appeal** or the **Queen's Bench** division of the **High Court**. If the case is certified by one of these courts to involve a point of law of general public importance, a further appeal may be made to the **House of Lords**.

CROWN DEPENDENCIES

The **Isle of Man** and the **Channel Islands**. Lying off shore from the **UK**, they are not integral parts of the country but are dependencies of the British Crown and have considerable self-government in internal affairs. Crown dependencies are not to be confused with **dependent territories**.

CROWN PROSECUTION SERVICE *see* CPS

CRUISE

US intermediate-range missiles developed in the 1970s and 1980s, designed to fly low over land and read their position from the topography so that, with detailed mapping, they could be guided to their targets. The most famous and controversial cruise missile was the ground-launched version with nuclear warheads, deployed from 1983 in Western Europe, under US sole control, as agreed by **NATO** in the 1979 twin-track decision. Opposition to cruise was the focus of massive peace campaigns and protests. In the UK these centred on **Greenham Common**, the RAF base in Berkshire outside which a women's peace camp had been established by the time the first cruise missile arrived on 14 November 1983. The removal of the nuclear-armed cruise missiles from Europe was agreed between the USA and the Soviet Union in the 1987 INF treaty; the first of them to leave Britain (in September 1988) were the 18 at RAF Molesworth in Cambridgeshire, while the last of the 96 at Greenham left on 5 March 1991.

CS GAS

An irritant (orthochlorobenzylidene malononitrile – its common name derives from US chemists Ben Carson and Roger Staughton) used by UK police as a means of public order control. The gas, as well as **plastic bullets**, was made available to the police in 1981 in response to the **Brixton riots** and other violent disturbances in **inner cities**, but were to be used only as a last resort, where the chief police officer believed that there was a risk of serious injury, loss of life or widespread destruction of property. In March 1995 Home Secretary Michael **Howard** indicated that police officers could be issued with CS gas canisters attached to their belts if trials were successful.

CSA

The Child Support Agency, a highly controversial executive agency designed to collect and enforce child maintenance. The CSA was set up under the Child Support Act 1991 and began operations in April 1993. It took over from the courts the task of assessing child maintenance payments and then collecting and enforcing those payments made by an absent parent. There was sustained criticism of the Agency in its first months of operation on the grounds that it made numerous errors, that it pursued absent fathers with excessive zeal, that it concentrated on absent parents who were already making payments rather than try to trace those who were making none, and that it ignored the needs of second families. Critics also suggested that it appeared that its primary commitment was to benefit the **Treasury** rather than to support children. A campaign against the Agency by fathers' groups resulted in radical changes announced in January 1995. An upper limit was placed on the proportion of net income which could be paid in maintenance, an appeals procedure was introduced, and 'clean-break' settlements would be taken into account in calculating maintenance. In July 1995 the agency came under renewed fire when in emerged that it had failed to collect a large proportion of the total £525 million due from absent parents, and that up to half of its assessments were wrong. A report of the **National Audit Office** found that the CSA, with annual operating costs of around £200 million, collected only £76,400,000 in 1994–5. The report said that staff regularly made faulty assessments even when they had been provided with all the necessary information. It found that only 47.4 per cent of maintenance assessments were correct, with doubts about the accuracy of 16.5 per cent, while the remaining 35.9 per cent of assessments were wrong, invalid, illegal or unenforceable.

CSE
Certificate of Secondary Education examination. The CSE was introduced in 1965 to replace a variety of examinations and qualifications set by local authorities. It was a school-based examination taken at about the age of 16, by pupils who were perceived as being less academically inclined, as an alternative to **O-level** examinations. There were five grades of award, the top one (Grade 1) being the equivalent of an O-level pass. The two examinations were combined in 1988 under the **GCSE**.

CSO
The Central Statistical Office, an executive agency since 1991 which deals with government statistics. The CSO compiles and disseminates statistical information required by the government for central economic management. It also meets the government's obligations to provide information under European Union (**EU**) legislation. Ministerial responsibility for the CSO rests with the **Treasury**.

CULLEN REPORT *see* PIPER ALPHA

CUMMNAN na mBAN
The women's wing of the Provisional **IRA**, used to trap British Army soldiers in lethal ambushes. A proscribed organization, it was in the late 1970s integrated into the existing **republican** military structure.

CURRENT-ACCOUNT BALANCE
A calculation of a country's foreign earnings position. The current-account balance is determined by adding net **invisible earnings** to the net (visible) trade balance. The result may be a positive figure (a surplus) or a negative one (a deficit). The term does not cover transactions on capital account.

CUSTOMS AND EXCISE
A government department responsible for collecting and administering customs and excise duties and value added tax (**VAT**) imposed in the annual Finance Acts or by other legislation. Most revenue is made up of VAT and duties on oil products, tobacco, alcoholic drinks, car tax and betting and gaming tax. The department is also responsible for the control of imported and exported goods, the compilation of trade statistics and preventing the importation of prohibited goods such as firearms, explosives, drugs, diseased plants and animals and pornographic material.

CYBERSPACE
A term offering the analogy of a physical location within which electronic communication takes place. Essentially a 1990s term in **Britain**, it evokes an interconnected world of computerized networks, particularly associated with the growth of the **Internet**, rather than the more traditional 'one-to-one' dial-up links between two individuals or between a user and an information provider.

CYPRUS

The largest island in the eastern Mediterranean, under British rule from 1914 to 1960, the scene of a struggle for independence (and, unsuccessfully, for *enosis* or union with Greece) and a violent confrontation between British forces and **EOKA** guerrillas in 1955–60, and since then a member of the **Commonwealth**. British involvement continues, as **Britain** is one of the guarantors (with Greece and Turkey) of the independence settlement and is the main provider of troops and funds for the UN force (UNFICYP) which has attempted since 1964 to reduce the incidence of intercommunal violence between the majority Greek Cypriots and the minority Turkish Cypriots. A short-lived pro-Greek military coup and then a Turkish invasion in 1974 led to de facto partition, with the establishment of an unrecognized Turkish Cypriot state in the north and east.

The behaviour of British troops came under scrutiny in 1994 following the arrest of three soldiers in connection with the murder of a Danish woman and an attack on her Cypriot boyfriend.

D-NOTICES

A system of voluntary self-censorship by the press and other media, initiated in 1912. The media generally undertook under these arrangements to abide by directions by the Defence (Press and Broadcasting) Committee, to refrain from referring to certain sensitive areas of information without prior sanction. In August 1993 as part of the 'open government' commitment, the name of the committee was changed to the Defence (Press and Broadcasting) Advisory Committee, and the range of topics now covered by DA-Notices was reduced. Publishers, editors and programme editors were asked to approach the Committee before divulging details of defence plans and operations, conventional weapons, nuclear weapons, government cyphers, security and intelligence services, and the identification of certain sensitive installations.

DAHRENDORF REPORT

The report of an eight-member independent group on the **welfare state**, commissioned by **Liberal Democrat** leader Paddy **Ashdown** and chaired by leading academic Lord Dahrendorf. The report, published in July 1995, put forward ambitious proposals for improving the means of wealth creation and for strengthening social cohesion which were welcomed by both the **Labour Party** and the **TUC**. Among specific suggestions were those for compulsory earnings-related second-tier **pensions**, plus an increase in the value of the basic state pension; a **minimum wage** (although the level was unspecified); compulsory employee and employer contributions to 'individual learning accounts', giving people life-long access to learning; reform of the **City** to discourage short-termism; and tax incentives to encourage people to invest in small companies, plus a local network of investment agencies to channel funds specifically to smaller enterprises. The commission, which deliberated for 18 months, also called for 'a vocabulary for change' which would redefine traditional notions of wealth and replace talk of rich and poor with that of those who are included or excluded from full participation in society.

DAILY WORKER *see* MORNING STAR

DALTON, HUGH

(1887–1962) **Chancellor of the Exchequer** during the first three years of Clement **Attlee**'s postwar Labour government and one of the architects of the **Welfare State**. Dalton, an Old Etonian, resigned as Chancellor in November 1947 after he spoke to a journalist about the contents of his fourth **budget** (an 'austerity' package which raised profits tax, purchase tax and alcohol duties) moments before presenting it to the **House of Commons**, thereby gravely violating protocol. He was made a **life peer** in 1960.

DALYELL, TAM

(b. 1932) A Labour **backbench** MP, best known for his vigorous parliamentary campaign during and after the **Falklands conflict** over the **Belgrano** affair.

DANGEROUS DOGS ACT

Legislation hurriedly introduced in June 1991 following a public outcry over a series of savage attacks by dogs on young children and adults. The bill, which required owners of specified breeds of dogs to have them registered and neutered and to keep them muzzled when in public places, was published on 5 June, only 15 days after Home Secretary Kenneth **Baker** had announced that legislation would be brought forward. It followed several conflicting statements by Baker, some of which suggested that as many as 10,000 pit bull terriers – one of the specified breeds – would have to be put down. Debate in the **House of Commons** was restricted to one day under a **guillotine** motion. The rapid drafting and passage of the bill resulted in several areas of ambiguity as well as loopholes in the legislation.

DATA PROTECTION ACT 1984

Legislation designed to 'regulate the use of automatically processed information relating to individuals and the provision of services in respect of such information'. Effectively, the Act gave people the right to know what information was held about them on certain data bases, and to have such information removed in some circumstances. The Act set up the office of the Data Protection Registrar whose functions were to compile a register of data users, to promote the principles of the legislation and deal with complaints from the public.

DE LOREAN AFFAIR

The events leading to the collapse of the De Lorean Motor Company in Northern Ireland. The company had received nearly £80,000,000 from the UK government to establish a plant in an area of high unemployment in Belfast, to build a high-speed car of novel 'gull-wing' design. In early 1982, after only four years, the company went into receivership, amidst allegations of irregularities. Production ceased later that year. After lengthy investigations a warrant was issued in Belfast in mid-1992 for the arrest of the company's founder John De Lorean, a US citizen.

DEARING REPORT

A report on the **national curriculum** in schools in **England** and **Wales**. Following serious teacher disruption to the implementation of the national curriculum – in particular regarding the testing of pupils – Sir Ron Dearing (chair-designate of the School Curriculum and Assessment Authority) was appointed in early 1993 to carry out an urgent review. In his report published in January 1994 Sir Ron recommended a substantial streamlining of the compulsory curriculum (especially outside the core subjects of English, mathematics and a single science) and a simplification of the system of pupil testing. The government accepted Sir Ron's recommendations.

DEATH OF A PRINCESS

The title of an independent television drama-documentary which contained revelations about the Saudi royal family and caused a rift in British-Saudi relations. The programme was made in the late 1970s, but was not transmitted until April 1980. It included the execution of a Saudi Arabian princess supposedly for adultery. The Saudi royal family made a request of the Independent Broadcasting Authority (**IBA**) that the film should not be broadcast, but this was turned down; the IBA argued that the broadcasting institutions in the **UK** were not creatures of the state. The Saudi authorities then proceeded to expel British diplomats from Saudi Arabia and threatened to implement economic sanctions against the UK. In the event, the controversy petered out with no sanctions being applied and no further expulsions being ordered.

DEATH ON THE ROCK *see* SHOOT TO KILL POLICY

DEATH PENALTY *see* CAPITAL PUNISHMENT

DECIMALIZATION

The rebasing of coinage on the decimal system. Until 1971 **sterling** was denominated on the basis of 240 pence to the pound, and 12 pence to the shilling, with subordinate coinage. Decimalization introduced 100 (new) pence to the pound and abolished shillings (thereby rendering obsolete other coins such as the half-crown). The new coinage, introduced on 15 February 1971, was popularly believed to have accelerated **inflation**, as traders 'rounded up' their prices.

DECOLONIZATION

The 'withdrawal from empire' by colonial powers, and the achievement of independence by their colonies and other similar territories. The process of decolonization of what was the British Empire started after the Second World War with the independence of India and Pakistan in 1947, and accelerated from the early 1960s, although most former colonies remained linked to the UK through the **Commonwealth**. By 1995 there were only a few remaining British **dependent territories**, including a few Caribbean islands, Bermuda, British Indian Ocean Territory, the **Falklands**, **Gibraltar**, **Hong Kong**, Montserrat, Pitcairn Islands, St Helena and Dependencies, South Georgia and the South Sandwich Islands, and the Turks and Caicos Islands. These are not to be confused with the **crown dependencies** – the **Isle of Man** and the **Channel Islands**.

See also Appendix I.

DECOMMISSIONING

In the nuclear industry the dismantling of nuclear reactors at the end of their active life. It is a costly and complex procedure that involves the safe removal and disposal of hazardous materials, but it can be delayed for as much as 100 years or more after the plant's closure. It is distinct from the disposal of nuclear waste which is produced by the plant's operations.

DEFENCE COUNCIL

A body within the Ministry of Defence chaired by the Secretary of State for Defence (a post currently held by Michael **Portillo**) with overall responsibility for running the armed forces. Membership of the Council consists of politicians, senior members of the armed forces and a number of advisers.

DEFENCE REVIEW

The government's periodic reassessment of defence capabilities and military support arrangements. The July 1994 defence review known as **Front Line First** concentrated its attention on rationalizing and reducing the cost of administration (cutting 7,100 Ministry of Defence (**MOD**) civil service jobs, 7,500 in the RAF, 2,200 in the Army and 1,900 in the Royal Navy) and of storage arrangements, infrastructure and training, while taking steps to enhance front line capability. One notorious outcome of a defence review was when it was decided in 1981 to withdraw HMS *Endurance* from service, thereby helping to convince the Argentine military junta that the UK government had no real intention to protect the **Falklands** from invasion.

DEFENDER OF THE FAITH

A key component of the coronation oath. It dates back to the Act of Settlement of 1701, which strengthened the links between Church and state by requiring the monarch to be a Protestant and to swear 'to maintain the Protestant Reformed Religion established by law'.

DEFORESTATION

The permanent destruction of forested areas as a result of human activity. Trees are cut down for fuel, cut or burned to clear land for arable use, or removed in commercial logging operations; other contributory factors are overgrazing and consequent soil erosion, and damage from airborne pollutants falling as **acid rain**. Deforestation in turn upsets the carbon balance and leads to further soil erosion, as well as reducing biodiversity as natural habitats are destroyed, and contributing to **global warming**.

DE-INDUSTRIALIZATION

A contentious term signalling structural changes in the economy away from 'smokestack' industries such as **coal**, **shipbuilding** and **steel**. De-industrialization implies variously a shift in the balance of employment away from manufacturing towards services and a decline in the share of **GDP** contributed by the **manufacturing sector**. The process of de-industrialization accelerated in the 1980s under the **Thatcher** government, with supporters of the process arguing that it was a long-term, and even helpful, process which assisted in the expansion of the **services sector**. Critics, however, maintained that the speed with which the process was being carried out had unnecessarily harsh consequences.

DELORS PLAN

The report presented in April 1989 by a group of EU central bank governors headed by **Commission** President Jacques Delors, setting out a three-stage plan for implementing **EMU**. A second set of proposals associated with Delors, dubbed 'Delors II', was presented in February 1992 by the Commission. It envisaged increasing the Community budget by 5 per cent annually from 1993 to 1997, raising more of the money in the form of Community 'own resources' rather than member government contributions, and doubling the **cohesion fund** for spending in the poorer member countries. Delors II was scaled down to a more modest seven-year plan approved by the **European Council** in Edinburgh in December 1992, whereby total expenditure would rise from 66,800 million **ECU** in 1992 to 84,000 million ECU in 1999.

DEMOCRATIC DEFICIT

In the **EU**, the perception that decision-making lacks democratic legitimacy. The issue was addressed in the **Maastricht** treaty, at the insistence of Germany in particular, by increasing the role of the **European Parliament**, giving it certain new **co-decision** powers, and emphasising the principles of **transparency** and **subsidiarity** in Community decision-making.

DEMOCRATIC LEFT

The small successor party to the Communist Party of Great Britain (**CPGB**), created in 1991. The Democratic Left dropped its precursor's commitment to Marxism-Leninism and turned to another, globally oriented, holistic ideology, eschewing the left's preoccupation with class and instead embracing community. Among the values listed in the party's constitution are pluralism, democracy, 'universal human rights and equal life chances for all' and (environmental) sustainability.

DEMOCRATIC UNIONIST PARTY *see* DUP

DEMOS

(Greek, 'people') An independent **think tank** founded in 1993. It has an eclectic approach and very successful media strategy. Although director Geoff Mulgan was a former adviser to **Labour**'s Gordon **Brown** and stresses his links with the Labour Party leadership, the organization also publishes work by **Conservative** thinkers. Its most important research to date is an examination of the values of 18- to 34-year-olds, the so-called disgruntled and disconnected 'Generation X'.

DENNING, LORD

(b. 1899) The judge who was **Master of the Rolls** in 1962–82, when he was generally considered to have a profound regard for justice but was responsible for a number of controversial decisions. In 1963 he held the official inquiry into security issues raised by the **Profumo affair**, and his report cleared John Profumo of having compromised national security while Secretary of State for War. In August 1990, when the conviction of the **Birmingham Six** for terrorist offences was being re-examined following public pressure, he was at the centre of bitter controversy after he said in an interview published in the *Spectator* magazine that the Six 'would have been forgotten' if they had been hanged rather than imprisoned, and then 'we shouldn't have had all these campaigns to get them released'. After a brilliant academic career at Oxford he was called to the Bar in 1923 and became a **High Court** judge in 1944. He was made a **life peer** in 1957.

DEPARTMENT OF EMPLOYMENT *see* DOE

DEPARTMENT OF NATIONAL HERITAGE

A government department dealing with miscellaneous national issues. It was created in April 1992 and took over several functions from the **Home Office** and the **Department of the Environment**. Its responsibilities are the arts and libraries, broadcasting and press issues, sport, tourism and heritage, film policy, export licensing of antiquities, the **national lottery** and the Millennium Fund. The first Minister of National Heritage was David Mellor, whose enthusiasm for the job earned him the title 'minister of fun'. The epithet came to haunt him, however, as the **tabloid** press disclosed details of his sex life, precipitating his resignation in September 1992.

DEPENDENCY CULTURE

A term first coined by sociologists in the late 1970s, to describe a condition affecting those members of society who are entirely dependent on welfare benefits and other forms of public assistance. The theory asserts that in time they become habituated to **unemployment** and lose hope of, or desire for, any other source of income.

DEPENDENT TERRITORIES

The remains of the formerly extensive British Empire. In 1995 British dependent territories consisted only of **Hong Kong** (to be returned to Chinese rule in 1997); Bermuda; a handful of Caribbean islands (Anguilla, the British Virgin Islands, the Cayman Islands, Montserrat and the Turks and Caicos); **Gibraltar**; the **Falkland Islands**, South Georgia and the South Sandwich Islands; St Helena, Ascension and Tristan da Cunha; Pitcairn; the British Indian Ocean Territory; and the British Antarctic Territory. Hong Kong has nearly 6,000,000 inhabitants, the rest under 200,000 put together.

DEPORTATION

Expulsion from a country. The Home Secretary has the authority to order the deportation of individuals who are not British citizens but who have entered the UK lawfully, under specific categories: where someone has entered with limited leave to remain but overstays or breaks his/her conditions of entry; if deportation is deemed to be 'conducive to the public good'; or if an adult is convicted of an imprisonable offence and the judge has recommended deportation. The Home Secretary may also order the deportation of the spouse and/or dependent children of a deportee, although this power has not been used since 1983. Powers of deportation are granted under various **immigration** and **nationality** acts, although the Home Secretary retains discretionary powers. **Asylum** seekers entering the country illegally, who are not granted either **exceptional leave to remain** or **refugee** status, face deportation.

In 1991 the case of a Zaïrean teacher, who had been refused asylum and was deported in May before his appeal was heard, resulted in Kenneth Baker, the then Home Secretary,being found in contempt of court for cancelling the teacher's return flight to the UK in contravention of a **High Court** order that he be returned safely to the UK. A year later the **House of Lords** upheld the ruling. The number of deportations and 'departures under supervision' increased from 818 in 1986 to 2,406 in 1991, to 2,475 in 1992, but fell to 2,068 in 1993.

DEPUTY PRIME MINISTER

A seldom used position in the **UK** government structure. With the exception of Herbert **Morrison**, Deputy Prime Minister in the **Attlee** government, all postwar holders of the post have been **Conservative**. The position is ill-defined, and many holders, most notably Sir Geoffrey **Howe**, have had little effective power. On his appointment as First Secretary of State and Deputy Prime Minister in July 1995, Michael **Heseltine** made it clear that he would wield considerable authority over the government. He is based in the **Cabinet Office**, with staff, and as chair of 10 **Cabinet committees** formerly chaired by the Chancellor of the **Duchy of Lancaster** as well as that on science previously headed by the Prime Minister, he has influence over policy extending across all **Whitehall**.

See also Appendix III.

DEREGULATION

The removal of governmental and similar regulations on business activities, which began in 1993. Some 7,000 regulations, built up over a lengthy period of time, had come to be seen by the **Conservative** government as anachronistic, stultifying and inimical to enterprise, and task forces set up in 1993 put forward several hundred recommendations, most of which were accepted. A Deregulation and Contracting Out Act, introduced in early 1994 and enacted in November of that year, provided for further deregulation and contracting out of various functions vested in ministers, local authorities, certain government bodies and the holders of certain offices. As a result, a new **select committee**, the deregulation committee, was set up on 24 November.

DERIVATIVES

The general term for various financial instruments whose value is entirely speculative. Derivatives range from commodity futures contracts to currency swaps, stock options and 'contracts for difference' of various kinds. Firms which write – or buy – derivatives contracts in a given market are backing their judgement of the likely movement of that market between the purchase date and the date at which the contract matures. The great majority of financial companies in the **City** claim to use derivatives only to 'hedge' or minimize their exposure to a given movement in the market. The lure of the derivatives markets for speculators, however, is magnified because the buyer is typically required to put up in cash only a small percentage of the purchase price (the 'margin'). In a regulated market, a firm may face a 'margin call', requiring that it put up more cash against its contracts, if the authorities consider that it has become overexposed. However, the issue of regulation of derivatives trading remains controversial. Critics point to the rapid growth of derivatives as contributing greatly to the volatility of financial markets, particularly since the 1987 **Black Monday** equity market crash. The pressure for tighter controls intensified in 1994, as a string of companies and public authorities worldwide incurred major losses on derivatives trading. Most spectacular were losses of some £1.5 billion, on the US oil futures market, admitted in January 1994 by the German engineering group Metallgesellschaft; similar-scale losses which forced Orange County in California to file for bankruptcy in December; and, above all, the collapse in February 1995 of **Barings Bank** as a result of a trader's uncontrolled activity in Far Eastern markets. This debacle called into question the stance of the **Bank of England**, which had advocated minimum regulation, but then had to admit its inability to bail Barings out.

DEROGATION

A term used in international agreements when a country is exempted, usually temporarily, from having to apply a law or ruling. In the **EU** new member countries sometimes obtain protection for particularly vulnerable industries by obtaining a derogation in order to avoid applying a common policy regime during a transitional period. An existing member country may also seek derogations to delay the introduction of new Community regulations there. In national law, the maxim that 'no-one can derogate from his own grant' means that someone contracting to sell a property cannot then do anything which reduces its value before the conveyance takes place.

DERRY

The name by which the nationalist community in **Northern Ireland** refers to the City of Londonderry. A dispute broke out in 1984 over a request by the **SDLP**-controlled Londonderry City Council to change its name to Derry City Council. The request was granted by the **Northern Ireland Office**, giving rise to **loyalist** protest. However, the name of the city would remain officially Londonderry, the form specified in its Royal Charter of 1613, because of the unwillingness of the council to make a 'humble petition' to Queen **Elizabeth** for the granting of such a change. Since it is frequently referred to as 'Derry/Londonderry', locals have taken to calling it 'stroke city'.

DES

Department of Education and Science. The DES was set up in 1964, combining the Ministry of Education and the office of the Minister of Science. Responsibility for science policy was transferred to the **Cabinet Office** in July 1992 and the ministry was renamed the **DFE**, Department for Education.

DESELECTION

The procedure whereby a party may refuse to select a sitting member of parliament as its candidate for a further term of office. The requirement for a process of 'mandatory **reselection**' was introduced by the **Labour Party** in 1979–80, largely at **left-wing** initiative. In practice only a handful of Labour **MPs** were deselected at each of the three succeeding **general elections**, although a number of others withdrew or declined to undergo a potentially hazardous reselection procedure. In the less formalized process of reselection of Conservative candidates, a few MPs were also not chosen.

DESERT SHIELD

The code name given to the US-led multinational force whose establishment was formally announced on 9 November 1990, which was aimed at securing the withdrawal of Iraqi forces from Kuwait, which had been invaded in August 1990. Its active deployment began in January 1991 with the launch of Operation **Desert Storm**, and the total number of forces in the Gulf by the end that month was estimated at 705,000. The size of the UK's involvement, including 35,000 UK personnel already in the Gulf by the outbreak of hostilities – comprising the main 1st Armoured Division and support, and naval and air units – totalled 42,000 troops; there were also 7,500 UK troops based in the Mediterranean and in the near east.

DESERT STORM

The code name given to the air offensive launched by US-led allied forces on the night of 16–17 January 1991 against targets in Iraq and Iraqi-occupied Kuwait. The campaign, which was due to achieve its objectives in a matter of days, went on until 27 February, when the Iraqi forces were defeated. By contrast, the ground war launched on 24 February, codenamed 'Desert Sabre', which was expected to last longer, ended in just four days. The war resulted in fewer than 500 casualties on the allied side, while Iraqi military casualties were estimated at between 50,000 and 100,000; Iraqi civilian casualties were thought to have numbered at least 10,000, mostly due to the air war.

DESIGNER SOCIALISTS *see* CHAMPAGNE SOCIALISTS

DETERRENCE

The attempt to prevent an attack from taking place by signalling the determination to respond with such force that the attack could gain no advantage. Deterrence may, in theory, be achieved by building alliances or by developing a collective security system, but in the post-war world it has been used mainly as the rationale for an individual state to build up its own military strength. Although defensive in posture, the strategy relies in the first instance on credible offensive weapon technology and, in an atmosphere of mutual mistrust, is likely to stimulate an arms race. Nuclear deterrence was the central US strategy of the **Cold War** and has been used consistently by UK governments to justify the continued existence of an **independent nuclear deterrent**.

DEVALUATION

The formal, unilateral reduction in the value of a national currency compared with the dominant currency of the time. Since entering the Bretton Woods system of world monetary structure in 1944 at an exchange rate of US$4.03 to the pound, there have been four devaluations of **sterling**. That of 1949 was intended to cut domestic demand at a time when the current account needed to be improved by greater exports: sterling was devalued by 30 per cent to $2.80 to the pound. A devaluation in 1967 was also provoked by attempts to improve the current account; against a background of weakness and speculation the pound was cut in value by 14 per cent to $2.40 to the pound. By 1976 sterling had, like other currencies, been floating for four years and it had steadily depreciated to a rate of $1.60 to the pound, some 20 per cent of its value having being lost in the two years 1974–6. This 'managed' depreciation was accompanied by a resort to standby credits from the **IMF**. 1992 saw the first devaluation by a **Conservative** government, on September 16 – now known as **Black Wednesday**. On this occasion the pound was the victim of intense speculation on the **foreign exchanges** by dealers convinced that it could not maintain its parity of DM 2.95 to the pound in the exchange rate mechanism (**ERM**) of the European Monetary System (**EMS**). After the failure of **Bank of England** intervention and interest rate hikes to protect the pound, sterling was 'suspended' from the ERM and left to float; within a month it had fallen to DM 2.50 to the pound.

See also Appendix V.

DEVLIN, BERNADETTE

(b. 1947) A radical **republican** activist in **Northern Ireland** at the outset of the

Troubles in 1968. At 21 she was the youngest member of the **House of Commons** when she was elected in April 1969 to represent Mid Ulster for the Independent Unity Party. In 1971 she lost **Roman Catholic** support when she gave birth to an illegitimate child; she married in 1973, becoming Bernadette McAliskey, and unsuccessfully contested the February 1974 **general election**. She founded the Irish Republican Socialist Party in 1975, and unsuccessfully contested the 1979 elections to the **European Parliament** as an independent. She is no longer active in national politics, but was notable in her day for her youth, her energy and a fiery commitment to her cause. On one occasion in January 1972 she stormed across the floor of the Commons and physically attacked Home Secretary Reginald **Maudling**, the day after the **Bloody Sunday** killing of 13 Catholics in **Bogside**. In 1981 she actively supported the **IRA** hunger strikers, surviving an assassination attempt in that year.

DEVOLUTION

The diffusion of powers – constitutional or other – from a central authority to regional or other lower levels. In the UK this term has been used especially to apply to the relationship between the central government on the one hand and **Scotland**, **Wales** and **Northern Ireland** on the other. Proposals to devolve large areas of responsibility were, however, decisively defeated in March 1979 in a **referendum** in Wales and withdrawn after only narrow acceptance in a referendum in Scotland. In Northern Ireland there was a short-lived **power-sharing** experiment with a devolved assembly and executive in 1973–4 and ideas for a devolution of powers were also proposed in the February 1995 **framework document**. At the European level the concept of **subsidiarity** has been favoured by those seeking the devolution of decision-making powers to the lowest appropriate level.

DFE

The Department for Education – the government department responsible for education policy in **England**, including the organization of schools, funding, the **national curriculum**, examinations and religious education. The DFE also deals with higher education including relations with **universities** in England, **Wales** and **Scotland**. In the July 1995 government reshuffle the DFE was unexpectedly given most of the responsibilities, in particular training, of the now abolished **DOE**, and renamed the Department for Education and Employment.

DHSS

The Department of Health and Social Security, established in 1968 and abolished in 1988. Its functions were split between two new departments, the **Department of Health** and the **Department of Social Security**. The DHSS had previously been responsible for the **NHS** and personal social services.

DIANA, PRINCESS OF WALES

(b. 1961) The estranged wife of the heir to the British throne, **Charles**, the Prince of Wales. Born Lady Diana Spencer, at the age of 20 she married Prince Charles on 29 July 1981; she gave birth to two sons, William in June 1982 and Henry (known as Harry) in September 1984. From 1987 there were persistent rumours that the couple were unhappy and that Princess Diana suffered from bulimia and other eating disorders. The couple separated in 1992, but it was maintained that there was no reason why she should not become queen. The **Camillagate** scandal in January 1993 and the January 1995 announcement of the divorce of the Prince of Wales's friend Camilla Parker-Bowles renewed speculation that Diana and Charles might themselves divorce so that the Prince could remarry.

Princess Diana has won warm and genuine admiration from many quarters for her commitment to charity work, in particular from homosexual men and women for her work with **AIDS** charities and sufferers.

DIEGO GARCIA

The principal island of the Chagos archipelago in the Indian Ocean, administered from 1965 as part of the British Indian Ocean Territory, but over which Mauritius claims sovereignty. The sovereignty dispute, pursued by Mauritius from 1980, was exacerbated by protests over the British having let the island to the

USA as a military base, and by a dispute over compensation for islanders resettled when the copra plantations were closed in 1971. The Mauritian campaign over Diego Garcia was renewed in the early 1990s. In 1991 the USA used B–52 bombers from the base on Diego Garcia during the **Gulf War**.

DIKKO AFFAIR

A bizarre diplomatic incident between the UK and Nigeria. UK customs found the Nigerian politician Umaru Dikko drugged in a crate at London's Stansted Airport on 5 July 1984. With him, in other crates, were three Israelis and a Nigerian diplomat, who were later charged with kidnapping and administering drugs. Dikko had been Minister of Transport under the civilian government of President Shehu Shagari, and had fled to London following the coup in December 1983. The new regime expressed a desire for him to return to face corruption charges, but made no formal extradition request. His abduction was apparently the work of Nigerian intelligence agents who had planned to send him home as a secure consignment of diplomatic baggage. The UK government protested at the violation of its sovereignty and the incident led to a period of poor relations between the two countries, exemplified by a series of tit-for-tat diplomatic expulsions.

DIPLOCK COURTS

The practice adopted in **Northern Ireland** since the 1970s whereby those accused of terrorist offences appear in court before a judge but without a **jury**. Lord Diplock had recommended this solution in 1975 when he chaired a commission to examine 'legal procedures to deal with terrorist activities'. With the Diplock courts in operation, the previous policy of **internment** – imprisonment without trial – was phased out. The administration of justice in the province had become a serious problem at this time because juries and witnesses were either influenced by their religious or political bias or were open to threats of coercion.

DIRECT GRANT SCHOOLS

Mainly fee-paying **grammar schools** which were directly funded by central government rather than locally. Such institutions in **England** and **Wales** were not maintained by the local education authority, but received funds direct from the **Department of Education and Science** or the Welsh Office, in return for which up to half its places ('free places') were offered to pupils who had attended a maintained primary school. The Scottish equivalent was grant-aided schools. The direct-grant system was phased out from 1976, when direct grant schools had to decide whether to become independent or fully maintained.

DIRECT RULE

The exercise by the **UK** government of direct responsibility for the government of **Northern Ireland**. Following the breakdown of talks in early 1972 on a solution for the problems of Northern Ireland, the UK government in March of that year took responsibility for all legislative and executive powers, with the new **Secretary of State** for Northern Ireland being made answerable to the House of Commons. A **Northern Ireland Assembly** was elected in June 1973, but the short-lived **power-sharing** Northern Ireland Executive collapsed in May 1974 in the face of massive industrial action by Protestant trade unionists opposed to the December 1973 **Sunningdale Agreement**. Under the Northern Ireland Act 1974 (subsequently renewed annually by parliamentary order) direct rule was once more exercised by the Secretary of State. A largely consultative Assembly was set up in 1982, but this was dissolved in June 1986 after it had been boycotted by many of its members in protest at the conclusion of the **Anglo-Irish Agreement** the previous November. Lengthy, but so far inconclusive, discussions have been held in recent years for the establishment of some form of devolved government in Northern Ireland.

DIRECTOR-GENERAL OF THE BBC

The chief executive officer of the British Broadcasting Corporation (**BBC**), appointed by the **Board of Governors** to head the BBC's board of management which is the body in charge of the day-to-day running of the Corporation. The Director-General in 1995, John **Birt**, appointed in December 1992, is eager to develop the BBC as an innovative and challenging service at a time of radical change partly arising from the government's **broadcasting legislation**.

DIRTY PROTEST

The protest in **Northern Ireland** of those **IRA republican** prisoners convicted in **Diplock courts** in the late 1970s, who refused to accept their ordinary criminal status in prison; the status of special category prisoner had been abolished in 1975. Denied their own clothes and other facilities by the prison authorities, the prisoners responded by spreading excrement and food over the cell walls. By mid-1978 nearly 300 prisoners were participating in the 'dirty protest'. Lack of success led many of them to resort to hunger strikes, and 10 hunger strikers died during 1981, causing widespread international criticism of the **UK** government's handling of the situation. One of the dead men was Bobby Sands, who was elected to the UK Parliament in an April 1981 **by-election** in Fermanagh and South Tyrone. The dirty protest ended in October 1981, when a package of reforms was introduced in Northern Ireland prisons, only one of which, the right to wear their own clothes, was among the original demands of the protesters.

In 1995 republican prisoners at Whitemoor Prison in mainland Britain began a dirty protest in support of their demands for their transfer to prisons in Northern Ireland.

DISABLED RIGHTS

In the absence of a **bill of rights** which would set out the fundamental rights of all, the rights of people with disabilities are protected under individual acts passed over more than 50 years. These include 1944 legislation requiring employers of more than 25 people to ensure that at least 3 per cent of their staff complement are registered disabled (concern at that time centring on those disabled as a result of the Second World War). Furthermore, services which the state is obliged to provide for the disabled were set out in legislation passed in 1970. State disability allowances which can be paid to the registered disabled include a severe disablement allowance, a disability living allowance (which has a care and a mobility component), a disability working allowance, and a war disablement pension. Unsuccessful attempts to extend the rights of the disabled were made in 1991 and 1993 in two **private member's bills** introduced by **Labour MPs**. When the later bill was controversially talked out with the connivance of the Minister for Social Security and Disabled People, Nicholas Scott, there was an angry reaction from the disabled community, prompting a series of demonstrations at the **Palace of Westminster**. In November 1994, the **Conservative** government introduced the Disability Discrimination Bill. This envisaged an end to the quota system, which was perceived as 'outdated and unworkable', instead giving disabled people a statutory right of non-discrimination in employment as well as new rights of access to goods and services. It provided for the creation of a National Disability Council which would inform and advise the government on how to end discrimination against disabled people. However, the Council would not have the powers of enforcement enjoyed by the Commission for Racial Equality (**CRE**) provided for by the **Race Relations** Act or the Equal Opportunities Commission (**EOC**) established under the **Sex Discrimination Act**. As of mid-1995 parliamentary approval of the bill had still to be completed.

Pressure groups and charities which seek to empower people with disabilities, promote their rights and conduct research into preventive measures include Radar (the Royal Association for Disability and Rehabilitation), Mencap (the Royal Society for Mentally Handicapped Children and Adults), **MIND** (National Association for Mental Health) and SCOPE (formerly the Spastics Society).

DISCOUNT HOUSES

Institutions peculiar to the **City** of London which developed there in the nineteenth century as bill brokers for industrialists, but which now act as intermediaries between the **Bank of England** and the rest of the banking sector. They do this by helping to promote an orderly flow of short-term funds between the government and the banks, enabling the Bank of England to keep short-term interest rates within a certain band.

DISCRETIONARY SOCIAL FUND *see* SOCIAL FUND

DISESTABLISHMENT

The deprivation of the status and privileges of being an **established church**. The issue of the possible disestablishment of the **Church of England** may be traced back to Parliament's refusal to sanction the use of the Revised Prayer Book in 1927, and has since been raised from time to time; it became the subject of keen public debate only after the separation in 1992 of **Charles**, the Prince of Wales, and his wife Princess **Diana**. This event, which raised questions about an eventual royal divorce, also triggered speculation about Prince Charles' fitness thereafter to act as Supreme Governor of the Church of England and **Defender of the Faith**. Constitutionally, disestablishment would entail the abolition of the coronation oath pertaining to the monarch's obligation to lead the Church of England and uphold the Protestant faith, and would result in the suspension of the monarch's right to appoint deans and bishops. Whether or not a divorced monarch could assume the position of the Supreme Governor of the Church of England remains, however, a moot point.

DISTRICT COUNCILS

In non-metropolitan areas of **England** and **Wales**, the locally elected bodies which with **county councils** manage the provision of specified local services. District councils are drawn from smaller areas within counties. Under the Local Government Act 1972, effective April 1974, there are 304 district councils in England and Wales. There are also 36 **metropolitan district councils** in city areas of England outside London (and 32 borough councils and the Corporation of the **City** of London in Greater London). District and metropolitan district councils manage services including housing, local planning and building regulations, cemeteries and refuse collection. In **Scotland**, there are 53 districts while in **Northern Ireland** there are 26 district councils responsible for local environmental and certain other services.

Following the report of the Local Government Commission in 1995, the government decided to create 14 unitary district councils to replace from April 1996 four county councils (Avon, Cleveland, Isle of Wight and Humberside). Other changes to the number and responsibilities of district councils as a result of the Commission's report were likely, but as of mid-1995 had not been resolved.

DIVIS

An infamous block of flats in the Catholic **Falls Road** area of Belfast, scene of many incidents of murder and violence. One of the most notorious occurred in August 1969, at the start of **the troubles**, when the **RUC** fired a Browning machine gun into the Divis flats. A tribunal of inquiry into the riots was established in the same month under Mr Justice Scarman. Its report, published in April 1972, concluded that 'undoubtedly mistakes were made [by the police] and certain officers acted wrongly on occasions'. It drew particular attention to the use of the machine gun, and on one occasion described its use as 'wholly unjustifiable'. However, the tribunal rejected the general case of 'a partisan force co-operating with Protestant mobs to attack Catholic people' as 'devoid of substance'.

DIVORCE RATE

The proportion of married couples legally separating and dissolving their marriage, whose steady rise in the decades since the Second World War has been seen in some quarters as indicative of social crisis. Figures of divorce decrees made absolute rose from 8,396 in 1940 to 32,516 in 1950 and 165,658 in 1990. In this period it became easier to get a divorce as the law in **England** and **Wales** was relaxed under the Matrimonial Causes Acts 1950 and 1967 and the Divorce Reform Act 1969. At the same time women became more economically independent, making divorce a more realistic option for them. Under the Matrimonial Causes Act 1973, applicants in England and Wales must prove that a marriage has broken down irretrievably.

See also Appendix VI.

DNA

Deoxyribo-nucleic acid, the molecule which forms chromosomes and which contains the blueprint of the genetic make-up of the individual. The double helix structure of the molecule was first determined in 1953 by Francis Crick and James Watson who, with Maurice Wilkins, were awarded the 1962 Nobel Prize for medicine and physiology for their achievement. Since each act of sexual reproduction produces a unique recombination of DNA, individuals (except for identical twins) may be identified by their DNA, a technique known as DNA fingerprinting or **genetic fingerprinting**. DNA examination procedures are also being perfected to identify genetically inherited diseases and conditions. The **Criminal Justice** and Public Order Act 1994 allowed the **police** to take DNA samples from suspects to build up a **DNA database**.

DNA DATABASE

The world's first **DNA** database established in Birmingham in April 1995. The **Criminal Justice** and Public Order Act which came into force in April 1994 allowed the **police** to take saliva swabs, deemed 'non-intimate', from suspects. If the suspect is subsequently convicted or cautioned for a recordable offence, the DNA information contained in the swabs is then recorded in the database. The police anticipated that 135,000 samples would be stored in the first year, with five million to be recorded by the end of the century. The first use of the new powers took place in early May 1995 when samples were taken from among 911 people arrested during an anti-burglary operation.

DOCKWORKERS

The perennially militant ports' workforce. Despite the establishment of a Dock Labour Board (under the Dock Workers (Regulation of Employment) Act 1946) to regulate labour on the docks, industrial unrest was endemic in the late 1940s and 1950s. The 1965 Devlin Report addressed a longstanding grievance by proposing that the system of casual dock labour be replaced by regular employment and that measures be taken to hasten productivity growth. Many of its recommendations were implemented in the Docks and Harbours Act 1966, which established a national dock labour scheme requiring work at all ports within the scheme to be undertaken solely by registered dockworkers. This effectively killed casual dock labour, but there were further major disputes in 1967, when a London and Liverpool stoppage was associated with a national **balance of payments** crisis, in 1972, when London dock leaders were imprisoned for defiance of the law, and in 1984. However, port employment declined from the 1970s as newer and more competitive non-scheme ports expanded their share of trade. In July 1989 the **Conservative** government abolished the Scheme, provoking the last national docks stoppage, ostensibly over a trade dispute. On this occasion, however, solidarity was weak and the strike was abandoned on 1 August, to be followed by many redundancies.

DOE

The Department of Employment, the government department with responsibility for labour affairs until July 1995, when it was abolished. The DOE (formerly the Department of Employment and Productivity, DEP) was fashioned in 1968 from the Ministry of Labour (itself established in 1916), reaching a peak of influence in the 1970s. In the 1980s, under successive **Conservative** governments, it put forward anti-**trade union legislation** almost annually, requiring strike ballots, restricting picketing and banning the **closed shop**. At the same time many functions were stripped away, with unemployment statistics being compiled by the **DSS** and training increasingly falling under the control of the **DFE**; however, the department remained under the direction of a Minister of **Cabinet** rank. In an unexpected move in July 1995 **Prime Minister** John **Major** abolished the department, assigning the bulk of its remaining responsibilities to the **DFE**, which was renamed the Department for Education and Employment. The move was condemned by the **Labour Party** and the **TUC** as symptomatic of **Tory** complacency about unemployment.

DOE

The Department of the Environment, the government department responsible for the environment and for housing and local government in **England** and **Wales**. It was formed in 1970, and its responsibilities for Transport were hived off in 1976.

DOH

The Department of Health, the government department responsible for the **NHS** in **England**. The department is also concerned with personal social services run by local authorities in England for children, the elderly, the infirm, the handicapped and other people in need. It has responsibilities in the field of food hygiene, and the ambulance and first aid services. It is one of the biggest-spending government departments, and successive governments have sought to control its expenditure.

D'OLIVEIRA AFFAIR

A controversy in August and September 1968 which ended by increasing the isolation of South Africa over apartheid in sport. Basil D'Oliveira was a South African-born Coloured who had come to England in 1960, since in his native country his career as a professional cricketer was effectively prohibited by apartheid. He had played many times for England, and distinguished himself in the final international match of the summer of 1968. The MCC (England) cricket team, due to make a winter tour to South Africa, was then announced, without including his name, a decision for which sporting reasons were advanced but which was criticized as an attempt to avoid a widely predicted confrontation with the South African authorities. However, on 16 September one of those who had been selected, Tom Cartwright, withdrew because of injury and the selectors chose D'Oliveira to replace him. The South African authorities thereupon declared that the team was unacceptable, with South African Prime Minister J. B. Vorster claiming that it was 'no longer a cricket team but a team of troublemakers for South Africa's separate development policies'. On 24 September the tour was cancelled, and there were no further official internationals between England and South Africa until 1994, after the end of the apartheid regime.

DONALDSON REPORT *see* BRAER TANKER DISASTER

DOT

The Department of Transport, a government department represented in the **Cabinet** by a Secretary of State. The department is responsible for all land, sea and air transport (including domestic as well as international civil aviation), international transport agreements, shipping and ports, HM Coastguard and marine pollution. It oversees all road transport including motorways and other trunk roads, and has responsibility for local authority transport, road safety, vehicle standards, registration and licensing of vehicles, and the regulation of private car hire and taxi cabs, and of the road haulage industry. Its responsibilities also include supervision of **London Transport**, **British Rail** and the Civil Aviation Authority.

DOUGLAS-HOME, SIR ALEC

(b. 1903) The diffident, aristocratic **Conservative Prime Minister** in 1963–4. Before the Second World War, Home (as Lord Dunglass) had acted as **PPS** to Neville Chamberlain. Succeeding to his father's earldom in 1951, he was later incapacitated by polio, but in 1958 took office as Lord President of the Council in the **Cabinet** of Harold **Macmillan**. In 1960 he became the first Foreign Secretary in 20 years to sit in the **House of Lords** and in 1963 represented Britain at the negotiations leading to the Test Ban Treaty. When illness forced Macmillan's resignation later that year the so-called **magic circle** ensured that Macmillan controversially recommended to the Queen that she invite Home, rather than R. A. **Butler** or Lord **Hailsham**, to form a government, a feasible step following recent legislation permitting hereditary peers to renounce their peerages. He gave up his title to enter the Commons as Sir Alec Douglas-Home.

Douglas-Home had been put forward in an effort to unite the Conservatives, though several prominent figures (including Enoch **Powell** and Iain **MacLeod**) were affronted by his undemocratic selection and refused to serve under him. He was able to form an administration but it lasted for only a year until Labour's narrow **general election** victory in October 1964; he was throughout handicapped in debate against the much younger Harold **Wilson** who mocked his aristocratic background. Ten months after this defeat he resigned the Conservative leadership but remained prominent in the party's councils. He returned to the Foreign Office, serving under Edward **Heath** in 1970–4 and was at the Prime Minister's side during the successful negotiations to enter the **EEC**. After retirement from the Commons in 1974 he again returned to the Lords, this time as a **life peer**.

DOUNREAY

A nuclear power centre in Caithness (northern **Scotland**), until 1994 home to the government-funded prototype of the experimental fast-breeder nuclear reactor. The fast-breeder reactor, which is fuelled by plutonium produced by the reprocessing of the fuel used in conventional thermal reactors, was considered in the late 1950s to represent the future of electricity generation using nuclear power and attracted substantial official funding. However, the programme did not prove successful and the government announced on 21 July 1988 an end to research funding for fast-breeder reactors from 1994. The prototype reactor closed on 31 March 1994.

On 19 November 1992 the government announced it would also withdraw its share of the funding for the European Fast Reactor, a joint research project with France and Germany agreed in 1989.

DOWNING STREET

The street where the **Prime Minister's** London residence is situated, at Number 10. The term Downing Street is commonly used to denote the Prime Minister's office, and is also employed in the supposedly non-specific attribution of views and comments, as in the expression 'according to Downing Street sources'. The street is now composed of just three houses: 11 Downing Street is the official residence of the **Chancellor of the Exchequer**, while 12 Downing Street serves as the Chief **Whip's** office. Since October 1989, when gates were erected at the entrance to the street (which is a cul-de-sac), the public has been denied access.

DOWNING STREET DECLARATION

A joint **UK**–Irish peace declaration on the future of **Northern Ireland** issued in December 1993. The declaration was drawn up by Prime Minister John **Major** and Albert Reynolds, his Irish counterpart, at a meeting at Major's **Downing Street** office on 15 December 1993. It reaffirmed the UK government's commitment to a constitutional guarantee for Northern Ireland, emphasized that it was for the people of the island of Ireland alone to exercise their right to self-determination, and contained a UK undertaking to legislate for a united Ireland if that were clearly desired by a majority in the province. This declaration was followed by an **IRA ceasefire**, announced on 31 August 1994, and a **loyalist** paramilitary one, announced on 13 October. The Irish and UK governments subsequently presented a joint **framework document** for all-party constitutional talks on a durable settlement for Northern Ireland on 22 February 1995.

DPP

The Director of Public Prosecutions, the head of the **CPS**, responsible for criminal proceedings brought on behalf of the **police** in **England** and **Wales**. The holder of the office is appointed and supervised by the **Attorney General**. Since 1992 the DPP has been Barbara Mills, the first woman to be appointed to the position.

DREAM TICKET

A supposedly ideal combination of candidates for an election. In the UK, the expression became current in 1983, when Neil **Kinnock** defeated Roy **Hattersley** to win the leadership of the Labour Party; Hattersley then pledged his support and was elected deputy leader to complete the 'dream ticket'.

DRIES

Right-wing, **Thatcherite** Conservatives, dubbed 'dries' in contrast to the Thatcher **Cabinet**'s more pragmatic **wets**. The dries, who included Norman **Tebbit** and Sir Keith **Joseph**, espoused **monetarist** economics and a tough line on the **EC**, emphasized the virtues of the market and argued for a minimal state. Since Thatcher's downfall some have been associated with the **No Turning Back** group.

DRIFT NETS

Long fishing nets which catch not only the fish intended but also anything else nearby. In the 1950s the original material for drift nets – cotton, hemp or flax – was replaced by cheaper plastics. Unlike the natural fibres previously in use, these plastics were not detectable by marine mammals, either acoustically or visibly. Moreover, it is estimated that 1,200 metric tons of drift nets are annually lost or discarded at sea, becoming death traps for turtles, dolphins and porpoises. In 1989 the **UN** General Assembly called for the banning of ocean drift nets. **EC** law bans nets longer than 2.5 km, but the use of drift nets was a key issue in the so-called **tuna war** in mid-1994. In the Pacific nets up to 25 miles (40 km) long, colloquially termed 'walls of death', are still used mainly by fishing fleets from Japan, Taiwan and Korea.

DSF *see* SOCIAL FUND

DSS

The Department of Social Security, the government department responsible for all matters concerning social security. Its precursor was the Ministry of Social Security set up in 1966, combining responsibilities for pensions and national insurance with those of the National Assistance Board. A merger in 1968 with the Ministry of Health formed the Ministry of Health and Social Security, later the **DHSS**, but health and social security were once more separated in 1988. Many of the DSS's responsibilities are being transferred to **executive agencies**.

DTI

The Department of Trade and Industry, a government department formally established in 1983. Its ministerial head carries the vestigial title of President of the **Board of Trade**, which dates back to 1786, and on being appointed in 1992 Michael Heseltine chose to use this in preference to the title of **Secretary of State** for Trade and Industry. The DTI is responsible for international trade policy, the promotion of exports, policy in relation to industry and commerce, competition, consumer protection and deregulation, policy on science and technology research and development, and company legislation. In 1992 it also subsumed the Department of Energy.

DUAL KEY

The requirement that both the UK **Prime Minister** and the US President should give consent before the firing of any of the US nuclear–armed **cruise** missiles based in **Britain** from 1983 to 1991. Controversy turned in 1983 on the difference between a procedural understanding and a physical dual–key system, which the USA had offered if the UK would meet the costs, estimated by the UK government to be £1 billion. Prime Minister Margaret **Thatcher** said on 18 January 1983 that 'the use of US bases in the UK in an emergency would be for joint decision by [the UK] government and the US government in the light of the circumstances prevailing at that time', and stressed that this rule had existed for 30 years – a reference to the **Attlee**–Truman agreement of 1951 and the **Churchill**–Truman communiqué of 1952.

DUAL-USE TECHNOLOGY

Machinery, electronic equipment or industrial plant which can be used for chemical or nuclear weapons production or other military purposes, but is ostensibly intended for non-military use. During the **Cold War** efforts to control Western technology transfer to the communist bloc centred on COCOM, which was bedevilled by the difficulty of identifying and controlling dual-use technology. In the early 1980s in particular, the USA frequently pressed its allies to support tighter regulations.

DUBLIN CONVENTION

A convention with the full title of the Convention Determining the State Responsible for Examining Applications for **Asylum** Lodged in One of the Member States of the European Community. The Convention was signed by 11 of the then 12 **EC** member states in June 1990 and by Denmark a year later. Ratified by the **UK** in June 1992, by June 1995 the Convention, pending ratification by Belgium, Ireland and the Netherlands, had yet to enter into force. It sets out a framework for co-ordinating policy on asylum and **immigration**, detailing the criteria for establishing which signatory state is responsible for considering an asylum application. It seeks thereby to end the phenomenon of '**refugees** in orbit' whereby asylum seekers find themselves transferred from one **EU** state to another with none willing to consider their application. (The Convention complements the **Schengen Convention** on the removal of internal border controls. Both are intergovernmental treaties and come under the third pillar of the **Maastricht** Treaty on European Union.)

DUCHY OF CORNWALL

An estate providing Crown revenue. The Duchy was instituted by Edward III in 1337 to provide revenue to the heir to the throne as the Duke of Cornwall, a title currently held by Prince **Charles**. The Duchy is a private estate regulated by Acts of Parliament comprising mainly agricultural land in south-west England, with a small area in London which includes the Oval cricket ground.

DUCHY OF LANCASTER

Crown land and estates. The Duchy and County Palatine of Lancaster have been attached to the Crown since 1399, when John of Gaunt's son came to the throne as Henry IV. As the Lancaster inheritance it goes back to 1265. Edward III elevated Lancashire into a County Palatine in 1351. The Chancellor of the Duchy of Lancaster is responsible to the monarch for the general administration of the Duchy. As a member of the **Cabinet**, the Chancellor is also responsible to the **Prime Minister** for other duties.

DUMBARTON OAKS CONFERENCE

A conference involving the USA, the UK, the Soviet Union and China, held in a mansion of that name in Washington DC in August–October 1944, which agreed the basic structure for the **UN**.

DUNCAN REPORT

The second of two major reports in the 1960s on the UK's foreign policy machinery. The Duncan report in 1969, by contrast with the **Plowden report** of 1964, stressed the need to relinquish the pretension to being a world power, and to maintain a more modest foreign service as appropriate to 'a major power of the second order'.

DUNKIRK TREATY

A military treaty signed in March 1947 by France and the UK committing each side to support the other militarily in the event of an attack by Germany. One year later, the **Brussels Treaty** extended this commitment to the defence of the **Benelux** countries. The latter treaty, however, did not mention Germany, and was assumed to apply equally to the **Soviet Union** which by then posed the more likely military threat.

DUP

The Democratic Unionist Party, founded by the Rev. Ian **Paisley** in 1971, and representing the more extreme form of **unionist** politics. The DUP co-operates with James **Molyneaux**'s (Official) Ulster Unionist Party (**UUP**) party in an attempt to protect and promote unionist interests in **Northern Ireland**. However, it has on occasions taken its own distinct line or adopted its own – often risky – tactics, largely because of Paisley's maverick temperament. Through its leader, the party has consistently called for the Irish Republic to renounce its claim to the north and Paisley himself has gained dubious publicity for the DUP by – for example – branding the British government as 'treacherous' following the December 1993 **Downing Street Declaration**.

E-NUMBERS

A codification system used in **EU** member countries for substances added to food during processing. E-numbers cover various preservatives, colourings, emulsifiers and stabilizers, antioxidants, sweeteners, and other miscellaneous additives and are applied to substances which have been tested, pronounced safe and approved by all EU member countries. Concern over food additives has centred on their putative links with symptoms such as hyperactivity in children, asthma, eczema and migraine.

EARLY DAY MOTION

A parliamentary device to publicize an opinion. The majority of motions tabled in the **House of Commons** are put down 'for an early day'. In doing so, the **MP** tabling the motion implicitly accepts that the motion will not be debated. Nevertheless, it permits the MP to express an opinion on an issue with the protection of parliamentary privilege. It also allows an MP to gauge the popularity of a particular view by the number of signatures of other MPs which the motion attracts.

EASINGTON MINE DISASTER

An explosion at Easington Colliery, Durham, which killed more than 80 miners on 29 May 1951. The incident occurred less than a year after the **Cresswell mine disaster** had killed a similar number of miners.

EAST COAST FLOODS

Widespread flooding which devastated the east coast of England on 3 February 1953. Hurricane–force winds and high tides breached sea defences from Lincolnshire to Kent. Several hundred people were drowned and many thousands left homeless by the disaster which was estimated to have caused damage worth £40 million. The incident occurred within six months of the **Lynmouth floods**.

EAST OF SUEZ

The defence commitments outside Europe, particularly in Singapore and the Gulf, which sustained the image of the UK as a **first–rank power**, but which the Ministry of Defence (**MOD**) in the mid–1960s began to see as incompatible with the **Labour** government's efforts to hold down expenditure. Although **Prime Minister** Harold **Wilson** continued to proclaim an East of Suez policy well into 1967, its abandonment was prompted by the November 1967 **sterling crisis**. On 16 January 1968 Wilson announced the decision to withdraw by the end of 1971 from defence commitments East of Suez; the process was delayed, but in the end seen through, by the incoming **Conservative** government in 1970.

EBRD

The London-based European Bank for Reconstruction and Development, set up in May 1990 and inaugurated formally in April of the following year with a brief to promote the development of market economies in central and Eastern Europe. Its first president, Jacques Attali, departed in 1993 amid recriminations over the extravagant fitting-out of the headquarters building. By 1995 the EBRD's lending operations (mainly to the private sector) had developed to the extent that Attali's successor, Jacques de Larosière, predicted the need for a capital replenishment by the end of 1997. The Bank approved 109 projects worth over £1.5 billion in 1994, and made net project disbursements of over £400 million.

EC

The European Communities, more generally referred to as the **EU** since 1 November 1993, the date on which the **Maastricht** Treaty on European Union took effect. The three European Communities were the **EEC**, the **ECSC** and **Euratom**. After the Merger Treaty (signed in 1965 and in force from July 1967) the proper collective term for them was the EC (as indeed it remains in legal terms even since the introduction of 'EU'). However, the acronym EC was much more often expanded as 'European Community' than as the officially correct 'European Communities'. The picture was made more confused in 1993 when, under the **Maastricht** Treaty, the European Economic Community (EEC) was expressly renamed the European Community.

ECJ

The European Court of Justice, set up under the 1957 **Treaty of Rome** and responsible for ruling on whether **EU** member countries (and institutions) are acting in accordance with Community law. Matters are referred to the ECJ by the EU **Commission** and by individual appellants. It is sometimes confused with a quite separate body under the **Council of Europe**, namely the **European Court of Human Rights**.

ECONOMIC MIGRANT

A non-political refugee. The term has been used by the **Hong Kong** authorities to classify the majority of Vietnamese **boat people** living in camps in the colony. Those screened out by the authorities as economic migrants are deemed to have fled Vietnam for largely economic reasons (i.e. to better themselves materially) and are therefore liable to compulsory repatriation. A much smaller number were deemed genuine 'political refugees', judged to have fled their homeland because of persecution, and were therefore eligible for resettlement in third countries. The term is increasingly being used to describe people from the former Soviet bloc who have left home in search of work, mainly in western Europe.

ECSC

The European Coal and Steel Community, which the UK did not join when it was first set up by the **Inner Six** in April 1951. The ECSC treaty entered into force on 25 July 1952 and was a model for further functional integration between the Six in the **EEC**. The UK did sign an association agreement with the ECSC in December 1954, but only became a full participant in January 1973 by virtue of **accession** to the European Communities (the **EC**, formed in 1967 by the merger of the ECSC, EEC and Euratom).

ECU

The European Currency Unit, the notional monetary unit used in **EU** budgeting, and the benchmark against which the values of member states' currencies are expressed in the **EMS**. The value of the ECU is calculated periodically according to a weighted 'basket' of national currencies. The ECU replaced the European unit of account (EUA) in Community budgeting in 1979. It is now also used as the denomination for **Eurocurrency** bonds and even travellers' cheques. When European monetary union (**EMU**) is completed, the EU will need to agree on (among other things) a name for a single currency (Germany favours 'Franken'), but the retention of ECU would be certain to inflame **Eurosceptics** as a symbolic sell-out.

EDEN, SIR ANTHONY

(1897–1977) A **Conservative** statesman. Eden served as Foreign Secretary from 1935–8, resigning over his opposition to appeasement. He returned to government as Foreign Secretary throughout the Second World War and took up the post again when the **Conservative Party** regained power in 1951–5. Eden became **Prime Minister** after the Conservative **general election** triumph of 1955 but his premiership foundered in the **Suez Crisis** of the following year. Dogged by ill-health and battered by events, he resigned. He was created Earl of Avon in 1961.

EDINBURGH, DUKE OF

(b. 1921) Prince Philip, the husband and consort of Queen **Elizabeth II**. Born in Corfu into the Greek Royal Family, he is related by blood to the British, Danish and Russian royal families. His family was forced to flee Greece and he was brought up in London and Paris. He joined the Royal Navy in 1939, seeing action in the Second World War. He became a naturalized British subject in 1947, taking the name of Philip Mountbatten, and was created Duke of Edinburgh in the same year, on the eve of his marriage to the then Princess Elizabeth. The Duke has adopted an active role as consort, showing a keen interest in, among other things, housing and industry and science. He sponsors the Duke of Edinburgh awards for young people, and his love of blood sports has not prevented him from taking a prominent role in wildlife conservation. He has, however, been the centre of controversy on a number of occasions, including a visit to China, when in an aside he referred to the Chinese as 'slitty eyed'.

EDUCATIONAL REFORM

Modifications to the education system through legislation. The postwar era has seen widespread reforms to the education system, notably: the **Butler Education Act 1944**, establishing a tripartite system of secondary education; the Education Act 1980, giving parents the statutory right to express a preference about their child's school; the Education Reform Act 1988, introducing the **national curriculum** and **grant maintained schools**; and the Education (Student Loans) Act 1990, partially replacing **student grants** with **student loans**.

EEA

The European Economic Area, the world's largest free trade area, which came into existence with effect from January 1994 and comprised members of

EFTA and the **EU**. The EEA agreement had actually been completed in October 1991 at the end of lengthy negotiations (during most of which it was referred to as the EES, the European Economic Space). It embodied the principles of free movement of goods, services, people and capital, and required the EFTA countries to adopt the EU's **acquis communautaire**, by passing some 1,500 acts into national law, although they would not apply the EU's common agricultural, fisheries or coal and steel policy. The EEA also required new institutions – a ministerial council, courts to arbitrate in disputes, a consultative committee and a joint parliamentary committee.

However, the apparent significance of the achievement of the EEA was diminished, first by the fact that a Swiss **referendum** in December 1992 voted against joining the EEA, which at that stage had the effect of keeping out Liechtenstein too, because of its close customs union with Switzerland. Secondly, the accession of EFTA members Austria, Finland and Sweden to the EU in January 1995 meant that only Iceland and Norway of the EFTA countries were non-EU EEA members. On 9 April 1995 voters in a referendum in Liechtenstein voted in favour of Liechtenstein joining the EEA from 1 May 1995.

EEC

The European Economic Community, a term often loosely used to refer to the whole edifice of European regional integration of which the EEC was the most important element. Strictly speaking, the EEC and **Euratom** were founded under the Treaties of Rome, which were signed in March 1957 by the six member countries of the existing **ECSC** (France, Germany, Italy and the **Benelux** countries) and which came into effect in January 1958. The task of the EEC was to create a **common market**, and to go beyond that in integrating economic policies among its members. After the Merger Treaty (signed in 1965 and in force from July 1967) the proper collective term for the ECSC, EEC and Euratom was the **EC**, standing for European Communities. The picture was made more confused in 1993 when, under the **Maastricht** Treaty, the word Economic was deleted from the EEC's name, changing it to the European Community.

EETPU

The Electrical, Electronic, Telecommunications and Plumbing Union, a right-wing union which vigorously represents electrical craftsmen. Formerly under communist leadership, it was expelled in 1961 from the **TUC** for ballot-rigging. The scandal catapulted the union to the political right under a series of uncompromising leaders: Les Cannon, Frank Chapple and Eric Hammond. Restored to the TUC, it became a principal practitioner of the new realism and its disregard for recruitment boundaries alarmed other unions. Its members sustained **News International** during the **Wapping dispute**, and revelations about its conduct led to a second expulsion (this time for breaking TUC rules) in 1988. In 1992 it merged with the politically sympathetic **AUEW** to form the Amalgamated Engineering and Electrical Union (AEEU) but its re-entry to the TUC in this guise proved controversial at the 1993 Congress.

EEZ

Exclusive economic zone – the offshore area extending for 200 nautical miles within which a coastal state has control over all economic resources. The EEZ concept was incorporated in the convention known as UNCLOS III concluded in 1982 at the UN Conference on the Law of the Sea. The UK did not sign the convention (principally because of concern about other provisions concerning seabed mining), but does effectively subscribe to the broad consensus on a 200-mile EEZ. In its own case, however, the formal claim to a 200-mile exclusive fisheries area is greatly modified by UK participation in the **EU's** common fisheries policy.

EFTA

The European Free Trade Association, which was set up in 1960 under the Stockholm Convention. Its seven original members were the **UK** and Denmark (which both left in 1973 to join the **EC**), Portugal (which left for the same reason in 1986), Austria, Switzerland, Norway and Sweden. These were the **Outer**

Seven, brought together in what was essentially a British initiative for a less integrationist conception of co-operation than that being pursued by the **Inner Six** countries then setting up the **EEC**. By 1967 EFTA had achieved its main objective, the elimination of internal trade barriers (although not in agricultural trade). Iceland joined in 1970 and Finland and Liechtenstein moved from associate to full membership in 1986 and 1991 respectively. EFTA's main preoccupation in the early 1990s was defining a more structured relationship with the EC, a process which led to the creation of the 17-country **EEA** in 1994. Within a year, however, the EEA became largely irrelevant, as Austria, Finland and Sweden all joined the **EU** proper in January 1995.

ELDO *see* ESA

ELECTORAL REFORM

The goal of pressure groups and campaign organizations who wish to bring about fundamental changes in the organization of representative democracy in the **UK**. The current **first-past-the-post** electoral system for the **House of Commons** is based on voters simply indicating on the ballot paper a first preference only, so that a candidate will be elected on a simple, or relative, majority. The result is a House of Commons in which the two main parties, **Conservative** and **Labour**, are over-represented, while the **Liberal Democrats** and other smaller parties are seriously under-represented. Suggestions for electoral reform are often based on variations of **proportional representation**, whereby the distribution of a party's seats in the legislature compares more exactly with the proportion of votes cast at the poll for that party.

ELECTORATE

Those entitled to vote in local or parliamentary elections. The names of eligible voters are entered onto an electoral register drawn up by each local authority every 12 months. In a **general election** all **UK** citizens as well as citizens of other **Commonwealth** countries and the Republic of Ireland aged 18 or over who are resident in the UK on the qualifying date (10 October each year) may vote. Certain categories of people are disqualified: peers, felons (those serving a prison sentence of one year or more), people of unsound mind and people convicted of corrupt electoral practices within the preceding five years. In local elections **EU** citizens resident in the UK may also vote. The total UK electorate in the 1992 general election was 43,725,003.

See also Appendix II.

ELECTRONIC TAGGING

A means of enforcing community sentences and bail conditions by requiring defendants to wear electronic bracelets which set off an alarm if the defendant breaks a curfew order. Tagging orders are used only with the defendant's consent. Experimental schemes were carried out in 1989–90, but were abandoned after tagged offenders absconded or committed further offences; the experiment was also dogged by mechanical failures. The **Criminal Justice** and Public Order Act 1994 provided for fresh trials of tagging devices in Manchester and Norfolk, which, beginning in July 1995, were to last for six months. They were to be conducted by the private security firm Securicor at a cost of £1,300,000. Two weeks into the trials the courts had not ordered a single offender to be tagged, and, describing the trials as an 'expensive fiasco', the National Association of Offenders commented that the chances of **magistrates** agreeing to any more than a handful of offenders being tagged was 'virtually nil'. The Association reported that although more than 1,500 petty offenders meeting Home Office tagging criteria had been through the courts in Manchester and Norfolk during the two weeks, a pre-sentence report was prepared in just one case. Despite the poor start to the pilot project, courts in Reading were also given the power to tag in mid-July 1995.

ELEVEN-PLUS

A public examination to select pupils for secondary education at the age of 11. Introduced through the landmark **Butler Education Act** 1944 as a means of placing children according to their perceived academic ability within one of three bands of secondary education (**grammar school**, technical school or **secondary modern school**), the 11-plus came to be criticized as intellectually flawed and socially divisive. The **Labour** government in 1965 instructed local authorities to phase out selection, but this policy was reversed by the **Conservative** government in 1970. When Labour regained power their Education Act 1976 required local authorities to draw up plans for a **comprehensive system** of education. Nevertheless, some Conservative authorities retained state-run grammar schools and a form of 11-plus into the 1980s.

ELGIN MARBLES

Marble sculptures from the Parthenon in Athens, obtained cheaply from the occupying Turks by the British ambassador Lord Elgin in 1801 and later sold by him to the British Museum. A Greek campaign for their return was spearheaded by Melina Mercouri as Minister of Culture in the 1980s. The Elgin marbles issue is the most celebrated of many disputes about the ownership of cultural treasures removed from their country of origin in wartime, under colonial rule or in circumstances of dubious legality.

ELIZABETH, QUEEN MOTHER

(b. 1900) The mother of the current sovereign, Queen **Elizabeth II**. As the Lady Elizabeth Bowes-Lyon she married the future King **George VI** in 1923. During the Second World War she endeared herself to the people of London by continuing to live at **Buckingham Palace** and touring bomb-damaged areas of the East End to raise morale. Since her husband's death in 1952 she has become perhaps the most popular member of the **Royal Family** in her role as the Queen Mother.

ELIZABETH II, QUEEN

(b. 1926) The reigning sovereign. The daughter of King George VI, she married the Duke of **Edinburgh** in November 1947 and ascended the throne in February 1952 on the death of her father. Her coronation in Westminster Abbey in June 1953, one of the first state ceremonies to be televised, was one of the great state occasions of the century, and marked the start of a period of high popularity for the monarchy which was to last until around the time of the **Silver Jubilee** in 1977. The Queen then had to face the challenge of a decline in the public esteem of the **Royal Family**. The marriages of three of her children failed, culminating in the separation of the Prince and Princess of Wales in 1992, a year described by the Queen as her **'annus horribilis'**. A country hit by economic recession seemed less willing to devote resources to the monarchy, leading to the Queen's declaration, also in 1992, of her readiness to pay tax on her personal income and to agree to a scaling down of the **civil list**. However, her dignity and obvious devotion to duty, and the enthusiasm with which she represents Britain abroad, appears to have maintained her personal standing with her subjects.

ELLIS, RUTH

The last woman to be executed in the UK. Ruth Ellis was found guilty in June 1955 of the murder of her lover, David Blakely, outside a Hampstead pub. She was sentenced to death and hanged on 13 July within the confines of Holloway Prison.

EMERGENCY BUDGET

The expansionist **budget** presented by **Conservative Chancellor of the Exchequer** Reginald **Maudling** in 1963. His first budget, it was organized around the theme 'expansion without inflation' to revive the economy after the 1962 **recession**. It included tax cuts of £300 million and proposals to revive the depressed areas but later attracted criticism for preparing the over-heating of the economy the following year.

EMERGENCY PROTECTION ORDER

An order providing for a child to be removed to accommodation provided by the applicant or for a child to be taken into care. Such orders are issued under the **Children Act** 1989 and have received controversial publicity in cases of suspected child abuse, such as in the **Cleveland** and **Orkneys** affairs.

EMERGENCY PROVISIONS

Measures under which the government has taken special powers since 1973 to deal with the internal security situation in **Northern Ireland**. The Northern Ireland (Emergency Provisions) Act 1991 brought together various earlier enactments, including the relevant sections of the **Prevention of Terrorism (Temporary Provisions) Act** 1989. The Emergency Provisions Act is subject to annual renewal by order in parliament. Following its August 1994 declaration of a **ceasefire**, the **IRA** has stepped up its campaign for the measures to be revoked.

EMIGRATION

The departure of a country's citizens to live and work in another country, driven either by economic necessity or by the need to escape political or religious persecution. In the UK there was a boom in emigration in the immediate post-war years, as Britons left in search of economic prosperity, especially in Canada and Australia. However, numbers have fallen off sharply since 1970, partly because of stricter **immigration** controls in other countries. Nevertheless official figures indicate that the number of emigrants from the UK exceeds the number entering the country each year.

EMILY'S LIST

An initiative launched in February 1994 by Barbara Follet to get more women elected as **Labour MPs**. The name derives from Emily Pankhurst, a leading suffragette, as well as the curious acronym Early Money is Like Yeast. Its principal activity centres on fund-raising to assist female prospective Labour Party parliamentary candidates.

EMPIRE WINDRUSH

The name of the ship that left Kingston, Jamaica, on 8 June 1948, carrying 492 migrants from the West Indies to the UK, whose voyage is taken as the starting point for the wave of West Indian **immigration** to the UK in the 1950s and 1960s. Immigration from the West Indies was encouraged by the British government, which was keenly aware of the employment needs of the newly founded **NHS** as well as of the public sector and public transport. Under the Nationality Act 1948 West Indians were granted the right of free entry to the UK and many came seeking work – particularly in the wake of USA legislation in 1952 limiting West Indian immigration to that country. The high numbers of immigrants led to tensions in **race relations**, and many, including Enoch **Powell**, campaigned for limits on immigration. The **Commonwealth Immigrants Acts** 1962 and 1968 and the Immigration Act 1971 introduced new rules limiting the right of entry to and abode in the UK.

EMS

The European Monetary System, an arrangement for closer monetary co-operation within the **EU**. Put forward by Germany and France in 1978, and operational from March 1979, it was designed as an interim measure, pending decisions on creating an economic and monetary union (eventually agreed at **Maastricht** in 1991). The inner core of the EMS is the **ERM** (Exchange Rate Mechanism), in which the **UK** participated only from October 1990 until **Black Wednesday** in September 1992.

EMU

European monetary union within the **EU** framework. EMU is a long-standing project, dating back to the early 1970s. Some of its elements were contained within the **EMS** as established in 1979, but a renewed impetus to create a full union came from the **Delors plan** of April 1989. Stage one of a three-stage process, strengthening policies through existing institutions and participation in the EMS, came into effect in July 1990, when remaining constraints on capital movement were lifted for most member countries. Stages two and three, for completion by 1999, were laid down at **Maastricht** in 1991. Stage two was implemented with the establishment of a European Monetary Institute in Frankfurt on 1 January 1994. Stage three, the most significant step, involves transforming this institute into a fully fledged **European central bank** by July 1998 at the latest, and accepting legally binding policy guidelines, with irrevocably fixed currency rates against a single European currency which is to be established by 1 January 1999. At Maastricht, however, John **Major's** government insisted on a special provision for member countries **opting out** of stage three.

It became clear in mid-1995 that stages two and three were well behind schedule and that a single currency was unlikely to be introduced before 2002.

ENEMY WITHIN

Clandestine and subversive elements working to undermine the state or other organizations. The controversial use of this term by **Prime Minister** Margaret **Thatcher** at the time of the 1984–5 **miners' strike** implied the existence of a 'hidden agenda' behind the activities of **NUM** president Arthur **Scargill**. Critics accused her of somehow equating this 'enemy within' and the 'enemy without' in an effort to reinvoke the **Falklands factor**.

ENERGY CRISIS

The severe shortage of non-renewable sources of energy. The term was first used in the 1970s when sudden oil price rises forced a re-evaluation of the use of oil, leading to changes in the automotive industry to make cars more energy-efficient, and an increase in general awareness of the use of finite sources of energy.

ENERGY SOURCES

The natural resources and processes that can be transformed by technology into the energy needed to meet human needs. Traditional energy sources are the fossil fuels coal, oil and natural gas but in the second half of the twentieth century it has become clear that world supplies are dwindling and alternative sources must be found. In the same period, nuclear power stations – which generate heat and thereby electricity from controlled nuclear fission – have proliferated. The nuclear energy industry has absorbed large amounts of public money in start-up costs and subsidy. Public concern has persisted over possible accidents and the difficulties of **decommissioning** reactors and disposing of **hazardous waste**. However, supporters argue that, unlike power stations burning fossil fuels, nuclear power installations emit no harmful side products such as carbon dioxide, and they claim that difficulties of disposal and shutdown have been exaggerated.

Technology also exists to use naturally occurring renewable sources of energy. Large-scale hydroelectric power stations which produce electricity from the energy of falling water have generally involved the construction of vast dams and considerable environmental disruption, and have become increasingly controversial in the 1980s and 1990s. Other schemes harnessing wave and tidal energy, wind energy and solar energy have attracted comparatively little official interest in the UK. Some 'wind farms' of large windmill-like generators have been built. A government-funded research programme into wave energy ran for several years but was cancelled in the 1980s.

Supporters of renewable energy sources have argued that official reluctance to develop such projects derives from a desire to protect the very expensive nuclear energy industry from competition. Other groups have used the same argument to explain the government's policy with regard to the **coal industry**.

ENERGY TAX

An environment protection proposal. Energy tax proposals usually centre on the concept of a levy on the carbon content of fuels. This is intended to reduce the rate of accumulation of carbon dioxide in the atmosphere, thus slowing **global warming**. Energy taxes could cut the cost of environmental regulation but would raise energy costs. Since energy costs currently tend to be hidden, this is politically hazardous. US President Bill Clinton introduced an Energy Bill in 1993; that same year saw **VAT** extended to domestic fuel costs in the UK at a rate of 8.5 per cent, a move which the **Major** government rather belatedly sought to present as an environment-friendly move when the scale of opposition to the measure became apparent.

ENGLAND

The southern and largest country of the **UK**. England is historically that part of **Britain** governed by English law (which also pertains in **Wales**). England was a separate kingdom until 1707 when, during the reign of Queen Anne (1702–14), the English and Scottish parliaments both passed an Act of Union. No government minister or department is exclusively responsible for matters in England, in contrast to the arrangements for **Scotland**, Wales and **Northern Ireland**.

ENGLISH HERITAGE

The principal organization responsible for the conservation of the built heritage (which includes archaeological remains) in **England**. Set up under the National Heritage Act of 1983, English Heritage is a government-funded **quango** which is the government's official adviser on the conservation of the historic environment, and is the major conduit for public funding for rescue archaeology and for repairs to historic buildings and ancient monuments. It advises the **Department of National Heritage** on the listing of buildings and scheduling of archaeological sites considered worth protecting, and itself maintains approximately 400 historic properties owned by the state and accessible to the public. Historic Scotland and CADW perform similar functions for **Scotland** and **Wales** respectively.

ENNISKILLEN

Site of an **IRA** bomb explosion in **Northern Ireland** in 1987. The explosion, which aroused particularly strong revulsion, occurred on 8 November 1987, as crowds were gathering for a Remembrance Day Service at Enniskillen, County Fermanagh; 11 people were killed and more than 60 injured. The IRA acknowledged responsibility, but claimed that the bomb had been intended for army personnel rather than civilians and that it had exploded accidentally.

ENTERPRISE CULTURE

A term used in the 1980s to define the social ethos promoted by the **Conservative** government of Margaret **Thatcher**, in particular through the commitment to the free operation of market forces, **privatization** and the spread of share ownership, and a growth in home ownership through the sale of **council housing**.

ENVIRONMENTAL AUDIT

An assessment of the true costs of products and services by taking into account the hitherto uncalculated cost of their impact on the environment. Environmental audits are closely linked to the principle of 'polluter pays'. In March 1993 the **EC** announced a voluntary scheme for industry, according to which participating companies would carry out a thorough environmental assessment every three years.

ENVIRONMENTAL POLLUTION, ROYAL COMMISSION ON

The body established in 1970 to advise the **UK** government on issues connected with the pollution of the environment, which in a report published on 26 October 1994 recommended far-reaching changes to official transport policy. The report proposed a series of targets including a 20 per cent cut in the vehicle emissions of the environmentally harmful gas carbon dioxide by 2020, and an increase in the number of journeys made on public transport from 12 per cent of the total to 20 per cent by 2005 and 30 per cent by 2020. It also suggested a series of policy measures including cutting planned expenditure on major highways by 50 per cent, increasing subsidies for public transport and doubling the UK government duty on fuel in real terms by 2005.

ENVIRONMENTALLY FRIENDLY

A term for brands of products which have a less harmful impact on the environment than their standard equivalents. Products which may be recycled, which are produced without depleting scarce resources, which do not contain ozone-damaging **CFCs**, or which are energy efficient may be described as environmentally friendly. Government schemes, such as the EU's **eco-labelling**, are designed to help consumers identify such products and are leading to increased **green consumerism**.

ENVIRONMENTALLY SENSITIVE AREA *see* ESA

EOC

The Equal Opportunities Commission, established in the UK in 1975 under the **Sex Discrimination Act**. Its role is to work towards the elimination of discrimination on the grounds of sex or marital status, and to promote equality of opportunity between men and women generally. In recent years it has instigated or supported several cases before the European Court of Justice (**ECJ**) which have resulted in the UK government being obliged to amend domestic legislation so as to eliminate discrimination. There is a separate Equal Opportunities Commission for **Northern Ireland**.

EOKA

An acronym of the Greek *Ethniki Organosis Kyprion Agoniston* – National Organization of Cypriot Fighters – the guerrilla group unsuccessfully demanding union with Greece which fought the British in the late 1950s in **Cyprus**. After independence in 1960 EOKA, led by Gen. George Grivas, spearheaded continuing violence against Turkish Cypriots (and increasingly against the Cyprus government led by Archbishop Makarios); its successor, EOKA B, took part in the short-lived military coup of 1974.

EPU *see* EUROPEAN POLITICAL UNION

EQUAL PAY ACT

The first primary statute seeking to harmonize male and female wage levels. The **Labour** government's Equal Pay Act 1970 applies to men and women under virtually all circumstances, and without a minimum period of employment. It was limited in its application because comparisons had to be made with broadly similar work by another individual for the same employer. The Equal Pay (Amendment) Act 1983 partially addressed this limitation by permitting claims for equal pay based on work of equal value; its introduction by a reluctant **Conservative** government only came after pressure from the European **Commission**.

Soon after passage of the 1970 Act differentials narrowed substantially. Thereafter, however, change was slow, and in 1992 female employees on average earnings still received only 79 per cent of the average hourly earnings of their male equivalents.

See also Appendix V.

ERM

The Exchange Rate Mechanism, regarded as the core of the **EMS** (European Monetary System), but badly damaged by the ERM crisis of **Black Wednesday** in September 1992 and the withdrawal of the UK (which had joined only in October 1990) and Italy. The principle of the ERM was that the central rate of exchange for a participating currency was fixed against the **ECU**, and the authorities of the country concerned were required to keep any fluctuations within a 'band' normally of 2.25 per cent above or below this rate. The weakness of the system after the 1992 crisis was reflected in the widening of fluctuation bands to 15 per cent in August 1993. Under the **EMU** process the ERM is intended to be superseded by a single EU currency.

ESA

An environmentally sensitive area, the official designation for land in **England**, **Scotland** and **Wales** that is being used and managed in a manner that is not damaging to the environment. Farmers who choose to enter such schemes are offered by the state a standard level of payment for those who make modifications to accepted techniques and a higher one for those who reintroduce traditional practices.

ESA

The European Space Agency, formed in 1973 as the result of the merger of the European Space Research Organization (ESRO) and the European Launcher Development Organization (ELDO). ESA's convention instructed it to provide for and promote, for exclusively peaceful purposes, co-operation among European states in space research and technology and their space applications. This envisaged the elaboration and implementation of a long-term European space policy linked to a coherent industrial strategy which would encourage member states progressively to integrate national programmes into a common one, particularly the development of and applications of satellites. In the mid-1970s, France was the driving force behind the new Ariane rocket programme for which the ESA took responsibility. In 1984 it passed this to Arianespace, a semi-private body dominated by the French National Space Agency (CNES) and French private companies. The current ESA member states are Austria, Belgium, Denmark, France, Germany, Ireland, Italy, Netherlands, Norway, Spain, Sweden, Switzerland and the UK. Finland is an associate member and Canada is a co-operating state.

ESF

The European Social Fund, one of the **EU's** so-called 'structural funds'. Unlike the European Regional Development Fund and the **cohesion fund**, the ESF may support projects anywhere in the EU, usually on the basis of providing 'matching funds' in partnership with local or national funding bodies. Some organizations in the UK rely quite heavily on ESF funding, particularly for projects to tackle youth **unemployment**, although the process of applying for grants and the timetable of disbursements can cause headaches.

ESSEX MAN

A colloquial and humorous term for a type of right-wing voter, a working-class man who has become wealthy and successful despite poor education, who shows little respect for middle-class notions of taste and respectability and is liable to have outspoken opinions. The term was apparently coined in 1990 by political columnist Simon Heffer, himself a native of the county of Essex. It is also used to describe a constituency of voters whose support a prospective government must win and which made a decisive contribution to John **Major**'s **general election** victory in April 1992.

ESTABLISHED CHURCH

A church recognized by law as the official church of a nation or state and supported by civil authority. In Britain the two established churches are the **Church of England** and the **Church of Scotland**, the Church of Wales having been disestablished in 1920. In **England**, the Church and the state were formally united under the Second Act of Supremacy promulgated by Queen Elizabeth I in 1559, which decreed that the Church of England was 'by law established'. A consequence of the enactment was the adoption by the sovereign of the title Supreme Governor of the Church of England and the acknowledgement of the authority of Parliament in areas where secular authority was competent to exercise control. Links between the Church of England and the crown were finally sealed under the Settlement Act of 1701 which required the monarch to be a Protestant and to swear 'to maintain the Protestant Reformed Religion established by law'. In practical terms, establishment has also meant that senior ecclesiastical office-holders, notably the **Archbishop of Canterbury**, are appointed by the Crown.

In **Scotland** the establishment of the Church of Scotland was confirmed by the Church of Scotland Act of 1921. However, establishment has little practical significance, in that, the acknowledged head of the Church is God and not the monarch; nor does the monarch exercise a prerogative in matters pertaining to Church legislation and patronage. However, establishment has immense symbolic value not only as a recognition of the national importance of Christianity in Scotland, but also as the means of reaffirming a distinct Scottish national identity.

THE ESTABLISHMENT

The network of holders of influence unified by common social background and attitudes. Although used throughout the twentieth century, the term 'Establishment' gained in credibility after a seminal *Spectator* article of 1955 in which the journalist Henry Fairlie alleged a cover-up of the **Burgess** and **Maclean** affair by the social elite. Fairlie extended the term to embrace all those who enjoyed influence because of their position in society. Members of the Establishment will normally have had a **public school** education, be **Oxbridge** graduates, and hold positions of influence in prominent British institutions. These Establishment-led institutions are usually taken to include the higher echelons of the **civil service**, the **judiciary**, the **established church** and the **BBC**. Members of the Establishment are also present in great numbers in Parliament and on the boards of major companies. They are frequently appointed to public boards and committees from a list (kept in **Whitehall**) of the **Great and Good**.

ETHNIC MINORITIES

The term used to describe those communities in the UK, such as Afro-Caribbeans and Asians, who have different ethnic or racial origins from the majority of the indigenous population. While the UK has been home to people of different ethnic backgrounds for hundreds of years, and there are long-established black communities in a number of areas (such as Liverpool and Cardiff's Tiger Bay), the ethnic make-up of the UK population has only really diversified in the postwar period. Since 1945 successive waves of **immigration** have brought relatively large numbers of people from the **New Commonwealth**, as well as **refugees** from Cyprus (both Greek and Turkish), Vietnamese **boat people** and most recently Kurds. In the mid-1990s ethnic minorities accounted for around 5 per cent of the population, of whom over 50 per cent had been born in the UK. Members of ethnic minorities are concentrated in the **inner cities**, where they tend to suffer higher rates of **unemployment**, greater social deprivation and frequent **racist** attacks from groups like the **BNP**.

See also Appendix IV.

EU

The European Union, the most highly developed organization of regional integration in the world, which currently consists of 15 member states: the original **Six** (France, Germany, Italy and the **Benelux** countries), joined in 1973 by Denmark, Ireland and the UK, in 1981 by Portugal and Spain, in 1986 by Greece and in 1995 by Austria, Finland and Sweden.

In general usage the term EU replaced European Community (**EC**) from 1 November 1993, the date on which the **Maastricht** Treaty on European Union took effect. The EC **Council of Ministers** decided on 8 November to call itself the Council of the European Union, or EU Council. Strictly speaking the term EU is a concept which does not have any formal existence in law. It embraces what had been designated since 1967 the European Communities (the **EEC**, the **ECSC** and **Euratom**), other activities incorporated through the **Single European Act**, and also the two 'pillars' of intergovernmental co-operation under the Maastricht treaty, on foreign and security policy and on justice and home affairs.

EURATOM

The European Atomic Energy Community, part of the **EU** and originally one of the three European Communities, whose institutions were merged from 1967 in the **EC**. **Euratom** first came into existence in 1958, simultaneously with the **EEC**, both these organizations having been established under the Treaties of Rome signed in March 1957. Its stated purpose was to promote the nuclear industry in member countries and to foster co-operation between them.

EUROCRAT

A common colloquial term for a European **bureaucrat**. Like many other words coined with Euro- as their prefix, it is often used in a hostile tone, to convey the sense that Eurocrats are meddlesome, distant (in **Brussels**) and devoid of common sense.

EUROELECTIONS

Media shorthand for direct elections to the **European Parliament**, which have been held every five years since 1979 (the Parliament having previously consisted of members chosen by national parliaments). The use of the **first past the post** system in **Great Britain**, rather than proportional representation as elsewhere in the **EU**, has tended to mean that almost all the UK **MEPs** are either **Conservative** or **Labour**, although Euroelections have produced some striking results for fringe parties, in particular when the **Green Party** won 15 per cent in June 1989. That poll marked the first defeat for the Conservatives in a nationwide election since 1974, while the June 1994 Euroelections, in which the Conservatives won only 27.8 per cent of the vote, was their worst result in the twentieth century.

EUROFIGHTER

The Eurofighter 2000 aircraft, jointly developed by the **UK** (by **British Aerospace**), Germany, Spain and Italy, which made its maiden flight on 27 March 1994, after serious delays over technical problems and political and financial disputes.

EUROPE A LA CARTE

The notion that **EU** member states could pick and choose, as if from a menu, those elements of the integration process in which they wished to participate. The phrase was used disparagingly to describe the attitude of the UK government under John **Major**, **opting out** from the

social charter in 1989, opposing the inclusion of the **social chapter** in the **Maastricht** Treaty and reserving the right to opt out from monetary union (**EMU**). In the UK government's view, however, Europe à la carte was preferable either to embracing **federalist** enthusiasms or to secondary membership status in a **two-speed Europe**.

EUROPE OF THE REGIONS

One of the initiatives to develop the **EU** under the **Maastricht** Treaty, designed specifically to help 'close the gap between the EU and its citizens' and to promote the concept of **subsidiarity**. It involves the creation of a 189-member EU Committee of the Regions, which met for the first time in Brussels in March 1994. The Committee has an advisory role on EU social and regional legislation.

EUROPEAN CENTRAL BANK

The institution which is to be created, as the cornerstone of monetary union (**EMU**) in the **EU**, under the **Maastricht** Treaty. It is intended to be a supranational body with an independent president, and is widely expected to be modelled on the German Bundesbank. Its creation (to supersede a Frankfurt-based interim European Monetary Institute) is scheduled to precede the final stage three of EMU.

EUROPEAN COMMISSION *see* COMMISSION

EUROPEAN CONVENTION ON HUMAN RIGHTS

A multilateral treaty of the **Council of Europe** guaranteeing civil liberties. Its full title is the European Convention for the Protection of Human Rights and Fundamental Freedoms. It was adopted on 4 November 1950 and came into effect on 3 September 1953. In contrast with most international instruments, the Convention has effective enforcement mechanisms, namely the European Commission of Human Rights and the **European Court of Human Rights**. Since 1966 people in the **UK** have been able to make use of the Convention's individual complaints procedure. However, the Convention has not been incorporated into British law and individuals must exhaust national remedies before they can have recourse to the European Court of Human Rights – a time-consuming and costly process. The Convention has nevertheless provided much of the impetus for liberalizing British law with respect to individuals' rights and freedoms.

EUROPEAN COUNCIL

The meetings of **EC** heads of state and government and the President of the **Commission**. The European Council (not to be confused with the **Council of Europe**) became a regular forum in 1974, after a series of ad hoc summit meetings had helped to revive the process of integration in the EC. It is now normally held three times a year. In November 1993, after the **Maastricht** Treaty on European Union had come into force and the term **EU** was being adopted widely to describe what had been called the EC, the European Council decided to rename itself the EU Council or the Council of the European Union.

EUROPEAN COURT OF HUMAN RIGHTS

The Strasbourg-based court, not related to the **EU**, which considers cases referred to it either by governments or individuals under the 1953 European Convention for the Protection of Human Rights and Fundamental Freedoms. The Convention was developed under the **Council of Europe**, and countries joining the Council accede separately to this and the various other conventions.

EUROPEAN COURT OF JUSTICE *see* ECJ

EUROPEAN MONETARY UNION *see* EMU

EUROPEAN PARLIAMENT

One of the three principal institutions of the **EU**, with the **Council of Ministers** and the European **Commission** The weakness of the parliament has given rise to the complaint that the EU suffers a **democratic deficit**, although the **Maastricht** Treaty does increase its role, particularly by giving it powers of **co-decision** with the council in certain areas and a say in Commission appointments. Previously it was basically only consultative, although from 1975 it had powers to influence the Community budget. Moreover, it was not until 1979 that it was elected directly, rather than appointed by the parliaments of member states. The European Parliament meets in Strasbourg, with committee sessions in Brussels and a secretariat in Luxembourg. It is in the committees that members (**MEPs**) do their main work, considering Commission proposals en route to the Council of Ministers.

Elections are held every five years, the most recent in June 1994. By that stage the number of MEPs had reached 567, of which the **UK** had 87. These seats were won as follows: **Labour Party** 62, **Conservative Party** 18, **Liberal Democrats** 2, **Scottish National Party** 2, with the **DUP, SDLP** and **OUP** each winning a single seat.

EUROPEAN POLITICAL UNION

One of the two integral parts of the **Maastricht** Treaty as concluded in December 1991 by the **EU** member countries, and sometimes abbreviated as EPU since the other part is **EMU** or economic and monetary union. According to the approved text, the Treaty marked a new stage in 'creating an ever closer union'. In the UK, the **Major** government has been at some pains not to specify whether EMU and political union are inextricably linked. It prefers to stress the notion of **subsidiarity**, the Maastricht commitment that action at the EU level would only be taken 'if and in so far as the objectives . . . cannot be sufficiently achieved [individually] by the member states'. New areas of EU competence under the Treaty include 'union citizenship', and there is an increased role for the **European Parliament**, but the formulation of common foreign and security policies, and co-operation on judicial and home affairs, are defined as separate 'pillars' outside the EU's decision-making machinery.

EUROPOL

A new **EU** agency for co-ordination of policing, created under the **Maastricht** Treaty but still not yet functioning as of May 1995, although its Drugs Unit was operational in The Hague. Europol's brief overlaps with that being pursued under the **Schengen Convention** by a smaller group of member states within the EU.

EURO-REBELS

Some 40 **Eurosceptic Conservative MPs** (with a hard core of about 26) who on various occasions voted against or failed to support the government in votes on legislation relating to Europe. In particular the term is applied to the eight MPs (Nicholas Budgen, Michael Cartiss, Christopher Gill, Teresa Gorman, Tony Marlow, Richard Shepherd, Sir Teddy Taylor and John Wilkinson) who abstained in a key parliamentary vote on the European Communities (Finance) Bill in November 1994 and consequently had the **whip** withdrawn, along with Sir Richard Body who resigned the whip in solidarity. The government was effectively left in a minority of five. With the exception of Sir Richard Body they returned to the party fold in late April 1995, on the eve of the local government elections, on what appeared to be their own terms, and their loyalty to **Prime Minister** John **Major** remained in some doubt.

EUROSCEPTICS

A term increasingly current in the 1990s in the debate about the **Maastricht** Treaty and the future development of the **EU**. It is loosely applied to those who regard closer integration as inimical to national interests. More specifically it refers to those (mostly right-wingers) within the **Conservative Party** who voted against ratification of Maastricht in November 1992, failed to defeat the Major government on that occasion, but thereafter appeared to exercise a growing influence over the party's rhetoric on European issues.

EUROSTAR

The train, capable of travelling at 186 mph, which carries passengers and freight through the Channel Tunnel in a shuttle service from London to Paris or Brussels, via Folkestone and Calais (and connecting at Lille with the main European rail services). Operated by **Eurotunnel**, the Anglo-French builders of the tunnel, the trains began operating in September 1994. Only a limited service initially became available in a project which was severely behind schedule and continued to be dogged by delays, due principally to a multitude of government inspections and trials which unearthed many problems of a technical and health and safety nature.

EUROTUNNEL

A private-sector Anglo-French consortium responsible for financing, building and operating the Channel Tunnel (**Chunnel**). The consortium had been granted its concession for the project under the Channel Tunnel Act of 1987, and announced its first share rights issue in November of that year, with further issues in November 1990 and May 1994. In April 1994 the group settled a longstanding financial conflict with its French partner Transmanche-Link, the tunnel contractors, but the project continued to experience financial and technical problems. Although the tunnel was officially opened by Queen **Elizabeth II**and President François Mitterrand of France in May 1994, it was by September of that year only able to operate limited freight and passenger services. The delay added to the company's already huge financial problems, and even after the establishment of a full service in 1995, in the middle of the year the company was said to be losing £2,000,000 per day.

EUTHANASIA

Death caused deliberately in the interests of the person who is killed. Although suicide was decriminalized in 1961, anyone 'who aids, abets, counsels or procures the suicide of another or an attempt by another to commit suicide' may be punished under the Suicide Act of that year. Doctors who, by request, shorten the life of a dying patient are thus technically guilty of murder, although prosecutions are infrequent. Pressure groups such as the Hemlock Society, the Voluntary Euthanasia Society and Exit have campaigned to make euthanasia or 'mercy killing' lawful in certain situations. These include that of severely disabled infants who have a short life expectancy, and of old people who are suffering from terminal illness and have asked in advance to be assisted to die. Medical advances enabling individuals to be kept alive but in a 'persistent vegetative state' have rendered the question more difficult.

The situation was highlighted by the case of Tony Bland, who was crushed in the 1989 **Hillsborough football stadium disaster**. Although all cerebral activity had ceased, his parents' wish that he be allowed to die was only granted four years later after the **House of Lords** ruled that medical staff could stop giving him medical treatment and intravenous nourishment.

EXCEPTIONAL LEAVE TO REMAIN

Permission to remain in the **UK** sometimes granted to **asylum** seekers who are not granted **refugee** status and would otherwise face **deportation**. Exceptional leave to remain is entirely discretionary and is seen by pressure groups such as the **Joint Council for the Welfare of Immigrants** as a way of treating a growing number of asylum seekers as second class refugees.

Although the number of asylum seekers granted formal refugee status has fallen in recent years, the number of applicants granted exceptional leave to remain rose from just over 2,000 in 1990 to 15,325 in 1992. However, the entry into force of the Asylum and **Immigration** Appeals Act in July 1993 has resulted in a severe reduction in numbers granted exceptional leave to remain. In 1993, 16 per cent of asylum seekers' applications were refused, 77 per cent were given exceptional leave to remain and 7 per cent were granted refugee status. In 1994, 74 per cent were refused, 21 per cent given exceptional leave to remain and 5 per cent granted refugee status.

EXCHANGE RATE

The value of a currency as expressed in other leading currencies. Traditionally a high exchange rate was invariably taken as an index of economic strength. As a result the efforts of most UK governments have been bent towards maintaining sterling's value by intervention by the **Bank of England** in the foreign exchange markets and manipulation of **interest rates**. Anguish when these efforts have failed to forestall a **devaluation** has been correspondingly great, although the effect has normally been to boost competitiveness. In the modern era a robust exchange rate has been used in order to bear down upon **inflation** but an unrealistic value for sterling (as many believe was the case during **Britain's** membership of the **ERM**) may lead to penal interest rates and/or ultimately to devaluation. International attempts to 'manage' the exchange rate by some kind of fixed system of parities are usually followed by a period of floating currencies.

See also Appendix V.

EXECUTIVE

The constitutional term for the government, the first branch of the constitutional division of powers, together with the **legislature** and **judiciary**. In **Britain** the term refers specifically to the **Prime Minister**, the **Cabinet** and the **civil service**.

EXOCET

The French-made air-to-ship (AM-39) and ship-to-ship (MM-38) missiles which became famous when used by Argentina in the 1982 **Falklands conflict**. The word Exocet came into vogue to convey the impression of a lightning and devastating attack.

EXECUTIVE AGENCIES

Agencies which operate under the overall supervision of government departments, but whose chief executives have day-to-day responsibility. It was announced in February 1988 that the executive functions of government (as opposed to policy advice) should be carried out by such agencies as far as was practicable. By mid-1995 there were over 90 executive agencies, together with over 30 executive units of **Customs and Excise** and a similar number of executive offices of Inland Revenue.

EXPULSION *see* DEPORTATION

EXTRADITION

The act of physical removal by one country to another, under mutual legislative authority or agreement by treaty, of a person or persons suspected or convicted of criminal offenses in the country making the request for such an extradition. The practice of extradition has been most notably controversial between the governments of the **UK** and the Republic of Ireland. In a number of cases in 1988–90, Irish courts failed to extradite a number of suspected republican terrorists to the UK. This state of affairs resulted from a lack of clarity between the two governments over extradition procedures and problems arising from the (Irish) Extradition Act of 1987, which prevented extradition for crimes deemed to have political motivation.

FABIAN SOCIETY

A moderate socialist society founded in 1883–4 and a co-founder of the **Labour Party**, to which it is now affiliated. The Fabians eschew revolutionary change in favour of an evolutionary and democratic advance to socialism. Among its founders were three architects of the modern Labour movement, George Bernard Shaw and Sidney and Beatrice Webb. The Society opened dozens of local branches and still organizes meetings, lectures, conferences and summer schools. The Fabians now back reform of **Clause IV** of the Labour constitution, a reduction in the strength of the trade union **block vote** at party conferences and the election of the party leadership by the **PLP**.

FAIR EMPLOYMENT COMMISSION

An organization established under the terms of the Fair Employment (**Northern Ireland**) Act 1989. It replaced the Fair Employment Agency, and its main purpose is to encourage employers to review their employment practices, a source of extreme sectarian friction in Northern Ireland. The Commission carries out this function through a variety of monitoring and persuasive procedures. It was sharply criticized by the Democratic Unionist Party **DUP** during the 1992 **general election** campaign for being a 'self-confessed religiously unbalanced body'.

FAITH IN THE CITY

A controversial **Church of England** report published in December 1985. An inquiry was set up in 1983 by the then **Archbishop of Canterbury**, Robert Runcie, following outbreaks of rioting in several **inner city** areas. Its report questioned the morality of government policy on home ownership and called for an end to mortgage tax relief so that more public money would be available to relieve urban deprivation. The report was strongly criticized by the **Conservative** government, some members of which saw it as inspired by the extreme left. One unnamed **Cabinet** minister was quoted as calling the document 'pure Marxist theology'.

FALKLANDS CONFLICT

A conflict between the **UK** and Argentina in 1982 over the Falkland/Malvinas islands, a British dependency in the South Atlantic which Argentina had long claimed. The Argentine military junta launched an invasion of the islands on 2 April 1982, prefaced by the occupation of the British protectorate of South Georgia, largely to restore its domestic standing but also as dramatic gamble to advance its sovereignty claims, since bilateral negotiations had apparently reached stalemate. Efforts to mediate were undertaken variously by **UN**, US and Peruvian diplomats. The UK government, armed with UN **Security Council** resolution 502 demanding an immediate Argentine withdrawal, responded by sending a naval **Task Force** to recapture the Falklands. Notable incidents included the sinking of the **Belgrano** (2 May), the **Exocet** attack on HMS *Sheffield* (4 May), the battles at Goose Green and Mount Longdon (29 May; 11–12 June) and the final capture of Port Stanley (14 June). There were a total of 255 British and 655 Argentinean casualties. The defeat spelled the end of the military dictatorship in Argentina, but gave rise to the so-called **Falklands factor** in the UK.

FALKLANDS FACTOR

The reason given for the revival in the political fortunes of the hitherto unpopular **Conservative** government, and especially of Prime Minister Margaret **Thatcher**, after the 1982 **Falklands conflict**. An upsurge of patriotic feeling was generally considered to have helped them win a landslide victory at the **general election** called by Thatcher in June 1983, a year before the end of the parliamentary term.

FALLS ROAD

A **Roman Catholic** district of Belfast in **Northern Ireland**, running west from the city and parallel to the Protestant **Shankill** Road area. The roads are separated by a **peace wall**, built in 1969 after scenes of severe rioting and house-burning. The Falls Road area, which includes the Milltown cemetery, was the scene of murder and violence in March 1988 when mourners attending the funeral of three **IRA** members killed in Gibraltar by British security forces (in an incident reported as part of their alleged **shoot to kill** policy) were attacked by loyalist gunmen. Three people were killed and 68 injured in what became known as the **Milltown murders**. Three days later, during the funeral of one of the civilians, mourners attacked and killed two British army soldiers whose private vehicle had been passing through the Falls Road area.

FAMILY ALLOWANCE

The weekly payment made to the mother of a family with two or more children for all children save the eldest. Family allowances were introduced in 1946 under the Family Allowances Act 1945 and replaced in 1975 under the Child Benefits Act 1975. They were not related to **national insurance** contributions, and were paid to mothers when there were at least two children under age 18 or in full-time instruction.

Child benefit is paid to the mother, or prime carer, for each child at a rate set each tax year (in 1995–6 £10.40 a week for the eldest child and £8.45 a week for each subsequent child) for those under 16 or those under 19 in full-time secondary education. Like family allowances, child benefit is non-contributory and is not means-tested, being paid to all mothers regardless of income. The universal nature of the benefit makes it vulnerable to attack by those advocating public expenditure cuts. Since 1979 there have been persistent rumours that child benefit is under threat from the **Conservatives**.

FAMILY VALUES

A Christian-influenced ethical creed which emphasizes the moral and social centrality of the family and its needs in assessing both individual action and public policy. Exponents of family values therefore tend to abhor divorce, adultery and **single parenthood**, which they regard as the harbingers of crime, anomie and social irresponsibility, and to support increased spending on education.

Family values were once the provenance of the right and are therefore associated with opponents or critics of **abortion** and **sex education**. The **Conservative Party** has placed family values firmly on the agenda in the 1990s, creating, for example the **Child Support Agency** in 1991, although the strategy backfired in the **Back to Basics** campaign. **Labour Party** leader Tony **Blair**, as part of his mission to appeal to **middle England**, has also embraced family values.

FARNBOROUGH AIR DISASTER

A disaster which occurred on 6 September 1952 at the Farnborough air show, when a prototype jet crashed among the 150,000 spectators. Twenty-six people were killed and 65 injured as debris from the de Havilland 110 fighter, including one of its engines, fell into spectators' stands and a car park. The aircraft's test pilot and his observer were also killed in the accident.

FAST BREEDER REACTOR

A type of nuclear reactor which produces plutonium from Uranium-238 while generating nuclear power. FBRs have no moderator, such as water as in the **PWR**, to slow down the neutrons generated in the controlled chain reaction which produces nuclear energy. Some of these neutrons collide with atoms of uranium-238 (a non-fissile form of Uranium), to form plutonium, a fissile and highly toxic material, which may be extracted by **nuclear reprocessing**.

FATHER OF THE HOUSE

The member of the **House of Commons** with the greatest seniority of service. In this capacity Sir Bernard Braine (Father since 1987) was succeeded in April 1992 by Sir Edward **Heath**, an **MP** since 1950 and **Prime Minister** in 1970–4.

FATWA

(Arabic, 'edict') A published opinion or decision regarding religious doctrine. Traditionally the preserve of a recognized religious authority, it is a common feature of Islamic law, Current familiarity with the term dates mainly from February 1989 when Iran's spiritual leader, the late Ayatollah Ruhollah Khomeini, passed a death sentence on the Muslim-born British author, Salman Rushdie, who was judged to have committed apostasy and blasphemy in his novel, **The Satanic Verses**. The controversial ruling, questioned by many Muslims, spawned similar pronouncements by lesser religious figures, most recently against the Bangladeshi author, Taslima Nasreen, who was accused of blasphemy in her novel *Lajja*.

FAYED, MOHAMED AL-

(b. 1933) A businessman who, together with his brothers Ali and Saleh, won a bitter fight in the 1980s against Roland 'Tiny' **Rowland**, the chief executive of **Lonhro**, for control of House of Fraser and the prestigious Harrods store in London. A **DTI** report, strongly critical of the al-Fayeds, was released in March 1990, but no official action was taken against them and a series of legal suits by Lonhro failed or were dropped. On 22 October 1993 Mohamed al-Fayed and Tiny Rowland announced an end to their feud.

On 20 October 1994 the *Guardian* newspaper alleged that two junior ministers, Tim Smith and Neil Hamilton, had, prior to their appointment to office, accepted payments to table parliamentary questions on behalf of al-Fayed. It was also reported that Hamilton had enjoyed free accommodation and other services at the Ritz hotel in Paris – controlled by al-Fayed – which had not been declared in the members' interests register. A report by **Cabinet Secretary** Sir Robin Butler later stated that the affair had become public after Mohamed al-Fayed had unsuccessfully approached the government in an attempt to have the DTI report revised or withdrawn in return for not making public allegations against government members. Smith resigned immediately after the scandal broke, and Hamilton, after struggling to retain office, eventually followed his example. On 25 October, the day of Hamilton's resignation, **Prime Minister** John **Major** announced the establishment of the **Nolan Committee** to combat the **sleaze factor** affecting his government by examining the conduct of public life. Also investigated by Butler was Jonathan Aitken, Chief Secretary to the **Treasury**. The *Guardian* in late October made allegations concerning his stay in the Paris Ritz in September 1993 (when he had been Minister for Defence Procurement), and the source of the funds used to pay his hotel bill. It was later revealed that the newspaper had obtained a copy of Aitken's bill by using House of Commons' notepaper purporting to have been signed by his private secretary. This deception was widely condemned in Parliament, and was the subject of an inquiry by the Commons Committee of Privileges.

FCO

The Foreign and Commonwealth Office, the government department responsible for external relations and representation. The **Secretary of State** for Foreign and Commonwealth Affairs is often popularly referred to simply as the Foreign Secretary. The FCO was created in 1968 through the merger of the original Foreign Office (formed in 1782) and the Commonwealth Office, the latter having itself been formed only in 1966 by the absorbtion of the Colonial Office (formed in 1854) into what had once been the Dominions Office (formed in 1925 and renamed as the Commonwealth Relations Office in 1947).

FEARLESS TALKS

The second and final round of negotiations on 9-13 October 1968 between **Prime Minister** Harold **Wilson** and Rhodesian leader Ian Smith to persuade Smith to end **UDI**. The two leaders met two years after the abortive **Tiger Talks**, aboard HMS Fearless off Gibraltar on 9–13 October 1968. No agreement was reached on either occasion. The next attempt to resolve the dispute was the 1971 **Pearce Commission**.

FEDERALIST

An advocate of federal arrangements. In the context of the **EU**, federalists argue the need for decision-making powers to be given to supranational EU bodies, and for policy implementation on certain issues to be Community-wide rather than determined at individual national level. Federalism was part of the early inspiration behind the **EC**, and came to the forefront again with its development from the **Single European Act** to **Maastricht** and beyond. The concept of federalism is anathema to the defenders of national sovereignty; any positive use of 'the f-word' is therefore guaranteed to arouse the wrath of the **Eurosceptics**.

FEEL-GOOD FACTOR

A term first used in US popular psychology, which began creeping into economic journalism in the 1990s, meaning an imprecisely defined sense of well-being and confidence. There is an overlap with the expression 'business confidence', a state widely researched in attempts to analyze investment trends. The sloppier usage 'feel-good factor' is used more for the attitude of individuals towards consumer spending, saving and borrowing, and even their voting behaviour. The expression enjoyed a particular vogue in the early part of 1995 when **Chancellor of the Exchequer** Kenneth **Clarke** argued that economic trends would justify greater consumer confidence – but that the 'feel-good factor' was lagging far behind, and might not come right in time for the government at the next **general election**.

FELLOW-TRAVELLER

One who sympathizes with the aims of a political party (usually the Communist Party) but is not a member. The term gained currency during the late 1940s and 1950s when concern over the spread of communism was at its height.

FEMINISM

The ideology which advocates the rights of women and their political, social and economic equality with men. The roots of modern feminist thought are conventionally traced back to the late eighteenth century and the works of Mary Wollstonecraft. The first so-called 'wave' of feminism is most often located between the mid-nineteenth and early twentieth centuries and is associated with groups such as the suffragettes demanding votes for women, and those demanding birth control. A second 'wave' has been identified with the **women's lib** movement of the late 1960s and has persisted as a social and political concept since then.

Although there are different tendencies within feminism, in broad terms it argues that the rights currently allowed to women are inferior to those of men and that in all social relations their status is either implicitly or explicitly inferior, allowing them to be dominated by men. Feminists argue that biological differences between the sexes do not explain all the observed differences in their social status, roles and behaviour, and that women should not therefore be denied political, social or economic advancement on the basis of their gender. Feminists also advocate that a lower value should not be placed on so-called 'feminine' attributes, such as compassion, as opposed to 'masculine' ones, such as aggression, and that women should not be urged to think that fulfilment is only possible in relation to men.

FEOGA

(French acronym for *Fonds Européen d'Orientation et de Garantie Agricole* – European Agricultural Guidance and Guarantee Fund) The largest fund by far under the **EC** budget, used to finance the common agricultural policy (**CAP**). Most of its money, despite the recent emphasis on reforming the CAP, still goes on price support (the 'guarantee' aspect) rather than on structural policies ('guidance').

FESTIVAL OF BRITAIN

The arts and cultural festival which opened in London in May 1951. The Festival, which took place 100 years after the Great Exhibition, was proposed as a way of 'patting Britain on the back' after the years of war and deprivation. It centred on London's South Bank of the Thames between Waterloo and Blackfriars Bridges, an area which had been badly bomb damaged and which was rebuilt by a team of architects headed by Sir Hugh Casson especially for the Festival, with the Royal Festival Hall as the centrepiece. The cost of the Festival was estimated at £8,000,000 and was criticized by **Conservative** politicians who dubbed it '**Morrison's** folly'. However, it proved very popular and contributed to the feeling of well-being which characterized the 1950s.

FIANN Na hEIREANN

A proscribed **IRA** youth organization.Traditionally, members assisted IRA units as look-outs and stage-managed incidents designed to trap members of the security forces. Analysts believe that the group's influence and membership declined markedly in the 1980s as the **IRA** began regularly using active service units.

FIMBRA

The Financial Intermediaries, Managers and Brokers Regulatory Association. FIMBRA is one of the financial self-regulatory organizations in the UK, formed originally in 1979 and taking its present name in 1986. Under the Financial Services Act 1986 it regulates firms providing independent financial advice and services to members of the general public, under the umbrella supervision of the Securities and Investments Board. In 1992 it was proposed that a new Personal Investment Authority should effectively supersede both FIMBRA and various other self-regulatory organizations.

FINANCIAL SERVICES ACT 1986

Legislation creating a new regulatory framework for financial markets. The Act came into force in April 1988, when it became a criminal offence to conduct investment business without authorization. Such business now has to be done through a recognized investment exchange and governed by an approved self-regulatory organization. The **Securities and Investment Board** was set up to oversee investment business.

FIRST PAST THE POST

A method of electing a candidate in a **single-member constituency** system in which the winner is the candidate with a simple plurality, i.e. the highest vote. It is used for elections to the **House of Commons** but is much criticized by advocates of **proportional representation**.

FIRST-RANK POWER

The status to which the UK continued to aspire in the post-1945 period, placing itself alongside the USA and the Soviet Union as one of the **Big Three** wartime allies and holding one of the five permanent seats on the UN **Security Council**.

The notion became increasingly hard to sustain with the ending of the British imperial role worldwide, and the emergence of Japan, Germany, France and by some accounts even Italy as economies outstripping the UK. Reluctant to accept second-rank status, figures such as Harold **Macmillan** and Harold **Wilson** in the 1960s and Margaret **Thatcher** in the 1980s made much of the idea that the UK had a special global influence in its **special relationship** with the USA. In practice, however – at least since the withdrawal from defence commitments **East of Suez** announced in 1968, the **Duncan report** of 1969 and UK **accession** to the European Communities in 1973 – most UK foreign policy has been conducted on the basis that it is a 'major power of the second order'.

FIRST READING

The introduction of draft legislation into Parliament. Bills may be introduced in the **House of Commons** by three methods: first, any **MP** may present a bill through a short formal procedure having given a day's notice; secondly, bills may be introduced by 'Order of the House', although this is uncommon except with major financial measures or **ten minute rule** bills; thirdly, bills may be brought from the **House of Lords** when their passage there is complete. After first reading, the Bill is printed and a date is fixed for **second reading**. Similar procedures apply to first reading in the Lords.

FLEET STREET

A term used to signify the national press as a whole, and the influence which it has exerted. Fleet Street in central London was traditionally the location of the head offices of the main national newspapers, but in the 1980s they started moving out of the **City** of London, with its geographical constraints, and the phrase is no longer logically applicable. The homogeneity implied by the phrase 'Fleet Street' has moreover been broken by the ramifications of new technology, whose introduction by the Times group of newspapers (**News International**) sparked off the lengthy **Wapping dispute** in 1986–7.

FLETCHER, WPC YVONNE

The police officer whose killing in April 1984 prompted the **Libyan embassy siege**. WPC Fletcher was shot outside the Libyan embassy or 'people's bureau' in London on 17 April, apparently in a burst of gunfire directed from within the embassy against a demonstration by opponents of the Kadhafi regime. Libya denied the British claim that WPC Fletcher had been shot from inside the embassy. The UK government, however, demanded that the Libyans bring the killers to justice, and broke off diplomatic relations with Libya.

FLEXIBLE RESPONSE

The doctrine of **deterrence** which supplanted MAD (mutually assured destruction) among **NATO** planners, and was formally adopted by the NATO Defence Planning Committee in December 1967. NATO defence would be based on a mixture of conventional weapons, theatre nuclear weapons, and strategic weapons. It was made explicit that nuclear weapons might be used in response to a Soviet non-nuclear attack in Europe, even before NATO's conventional defences had been defeated, but an aggressor would be uncertain as to the level and timing of any response. NATO commanders were supposed to judge the appropriate level, and be prepared to escalate deliberately, in theory in a carefully controlled process, if one level of defence were proving inadequate. 'Thinking about the unthinkable' use of nuclear weapons was opened up under this doctrine, which was seen by its detractors as a recipe for disastrous instability.

FLIXBOROUGH CHEMICALS DISASTER

A huge explosion at the Flixborough chemicals plant on Humberside on 2 June 1974. The explosion, which occurred at 4.35 p.m., killed 29 people and wrecked some 100 nearby houses. The blast was blamed on a build-up of inflammable gases.

FLOODS OF 1947

Severe flooding in March–April 1947. The floods were greatly exacerbated by melting snow after one of the most severe winters on record. They killed 2,000,000 sheep and damaged 500,000 acres of wheat, greatly adding to the misery of a post-war Britain which was still enduring strict **rationing**.

FLOTATION

The practice of raising new capital funding for a company by the issue of subscriptions, or shares, to the public for the first time, known as a 'public flotation'. This has generally been the means by which the **Conservative** government since the early 1980s has implemented the **privatization** of many former state-owned assets and public utilities, most notably **British Aerospace**, **BT** and the water, gas and electricity industries.

FLOWER POWER

A term associated with the youth culture of the 1960s, particularly the hippy movement. It encapsulated the belief in the superiority of 'alternative' values such as love, peace and expanded self-awareness through meditation and drug use.

FLYING PICKET

A mobile group of trade unionists which can be deployed at a range of locations in support of industrial action. In the UK the use of flying pickets became increasingly widespread in the 1970s, and caused considerable disruption of industry. Under the **Thatcher** government (1979–90) the powers and rights of trade unions were progressively whittled away. The Employment Act 1980 provided that a worker might generally picket only at his or her own place of work (and thus forbade **secondary picketing**); moreover, the code of conduct issued under this Act laid down that the number of members of a picket should not normally exceed six. During the 1984–5 **miners' strike**, attempts to use flying pickets and mass pickets were thwarted by the police using existing powers to prevent obstruction or intimidation.

FOOT, MICHAEL

(b. 1913) The fiery **left-wing** orator, former leader of the **Labour Party** and distinguished journalist and author. Foot first stood for Parliament in 1935 and was MP for Plymouth Devonport in 1945–55, during which period he became the closest associate of Aneurin **Bevan**. He became editor of **Tribune**, which he made a **Bevanite** organ, and a scourge of the Labour right then centred around Hugh **Gaitskell**. Though he had differed from Bevan in his advocacy of **unilateralism**, Foot was a natural choice to succeed him in 1960 as MP for the Welsh seat of Ebbw Vale. Thereafter he combined the *Tribune* editorship with resumption of his radical parliamentary role, gaining public prominence as a tireless **CND** campaigner. After 1970 he occupied a more central place in the party; in the government of Harold **Wilson** he took office in 1974 for the first time as Employment Secretary, overseeing repeal of **Conservative** industrial relations legislation and the introduction of new employment laws more congenial to the trade unions. Though defeated by James **Callaghan** in the 1976 contest for the succession to Wilson as **Prime Minister**, Foot became **Leader of the House of Commons** and **Lord President of the Council**, staying until Labour lost office in 1979. In 1980 he won a surprise victory over Denis **Healey** for the party leadership and promised to lead a great crusade against **unemployment**. However, his time as **Leader of the Opposition** was marred by party splits, the defection of the **SDP**, and the bitter contest between Tony **Benn** and Healey for the deputy leadership, and the recovery of Conservative fortunes after the **Falklands conflict**. He also came under attack for his personal appearance, the press having a field day after he attended the 1982 armistice memorial ceremony at the Cenotaph apparently wearing a donkey-jacket. The 1983 **general election** was a disaster for Labour and Foot resigned soon after, the leadership passing to Neil **Kinnock**. However he remained in the **House of Commons**, only retiring at the 1992 **general election**. In July 1995 he won a notable legal victory when he sued the *Sunday Times* and its proprietor Rupert **Murdoch** for libel. The *Sunday Times* apologised in court and paid him substantial damages for publishing in February three pages of articles under the headline 'KGB: Michael Foot was our agent'. The allegations were greeted with widespread disbelief and ridicule; even Foot's most ardent political opponents acknowledge his integrity and that he is motivated equally by socialism and patriotism.

FORD WORKERS' STRIKE

A rare example of successful industrial action during the **Thatcher** years, when 32,000 Ford (UK) car workers struck for nine days in February 1988 against the imposition of new working practices. The strike ended when management conceded a 14 per cent wage increase, agreed that all changes would be negotiated at plant level, and foreswore compulsory redundancies; management also promised that within two years there would be harmonization of blue- and white-collar pay. This conclusion was, however, followed by a decision of Ford of America not to build a high-tech plant in Dundee where a bitter dispute had arisen between the **TGWU** and the **AUEW** (which had been granted negotiating rights).

FOREIGN EXCHANGE CONTROLS

Government restrictions on the mobilization of private gold and foreign currency assets. Introduced as an emergency measure in 1939, exchange controls were abolished in stages between June and October 1979 – their abolition represented one of the first steps by the new **Thatcher** government to promote economic freedom and market forces.

FOREIGN OFFICE see FCO

FORESTRY COMMISSION

A body established in 1919 to promote the interests of forestry, the development of afforestation and the production and supply of timber in the UK. In pursuance of its policy of a greater role for the private sector, the **Conservative** government's Forestry Act 1981 reduced the Commissions's grant in aid which financed forestry enterprise. The Act also allowed private investment in those assets through sale and lease-back of a proportion of the Commission's woodlands and land awaiting plantation. The disposals programme had grown from some 400 hectares in 1979–81 to 15,000 hectares over the period 1993–6. The government announced in July 1994 that the forest management element of the Forestry Commission – Forest Enterprise – was to become an **executive agency**.

FORTRESS EUROPE

A term originally used in connection with the trade barriers erected around **EU** countries but now also used to refer to restrictions on entry imposed on non-EU citizens. In international trade terms, the introduction of the **single market** within the EU was contrasted with an apparent increase in protectionism towards other trading blocs and countries. The term has also come to refer to the obstacles in place preventing such groups as migrants, **refugees** and **asylum** seekers entering the EU.

FORUM FOR PEACE AND RECONCILIATION

A body established by the Irish government under the auspices of the joint British-Irish **Downing Street Declaration** of December 1993, with the aim of advancing the peace process in **Northern Ireland**. Its first meeting was held in Dublin in October 1994, attended by the then Irish Prime Minister Albert Reynolds, the Irish Foreign Affairs Minister Dick Spring and **Sinn Féin** president Gerry **Adams**. With the aim of enabling Sinn Féin to participate in the forum, it was intended that the **UK** government would play no formal part in its proceedings, while the Northern Ireland **unionists** boycotted the event because of Adams's involvement.

FOUR-MINUTE WARNING

The expected length of time between the first warning and the arrival of nuclear bombs or missiles at targets in the UK, in the event of a Soviet attack. The phrase was current from the 1950s and remained part of the popular consciousness throughout the **Cold War**, without anyone feeling the need to make it more precise in relation to changes in missile detection or Soviet offensive capability.

FOUR-POWER AGREEMENT

The September 1971 agreement on Berlin, reached between the USA, the UK, France and the Soviet Union, the four powers which had been **Allies** in the Second World War. The final protocol was signed on 3 June 1972. It relaxed the segregation of West Berlin (administered by the **Western Allies**) from the eastern sector (designated the capital of

East Germany and under Soviet administration), providing for improved access to West Berlin from the DDR, and stronger ties (but not integration) between West Berlin and the Federal Republic of Germany. The settlement formed part of the West German policy of detente with the East known as Ostpolitik.

FOURTH ESTATE

A term used to indicate the power of the press. The first three 'estates' (traditionally used with reference to France and England) were deemed to be the nobility, the church (clergy) and the commons (citizens), each of which enjoyed and exercised certain rights and powers. By extension, the term fourth estate became employed in the nineteenth century to indicate the countervailing importance of newspapers. The term has tended to drop out of use with the increasing influence of radio and then television.

FRAMEWORK DOCUMENT

The joint proposals put forward on 22 February 1985 by the **UK** and Irish **Prime Ministers**, John **Major** and John Bruton, for conducting all-party constitutional talks on the future of **Northern Ireland**. A stage in the peace process stemming from the 1993 **Downing Street Declaration**, the document was designed to allow for both **Sinn Féin** and the former **loyalist** paramilitaries to participate in the political process now that both had declared and maintained their cessation of violence. Its key provisions included creating a Northern Ireland assembly and an accountable executive, a north-south body with 'executive, harmonizing or consultative functions', a parliamentary forum including members of the Irish parliament, and a standing UK-Irish intergovernmental conference and secretariat. The Irish and British governments also promised constitutional legislation, on the one hand removing any Irish territorial claim to 'jurisdiction over Northern Ireland contrary to the will of a majority of its people', and on the other hand committing the British government to 'uphold the democratic wish of a greater number of the people of Northern Ireland on the issue of whether they prefer to support the Union or a sovereign united Ireland'.

FRANKS REPORT

The official UK report on the circumstances leading up to the 1982 **Falklands conflict**. Shortly after the end of hostilities, a board of inquiry was set up in July 1982 under the chairmanship of Lord Franks, a distinguished former diplomat, banker and academic. Its report was published on 18 January 1983. It cleared government ministers of blame for the Argentine invasion, but criticized the government's intelligence gathering process; in particular it recommended closer liaison between the intelligence assessment staffs, the Foreign and Commonwealth Office (**FCO**) and the Ministry of Defence (**MOD**), and the transfer of chairmanship of the joint intelligence committee from the FCO to the Cabinet Office.

FREE CHURCHES

Protestant churches other than the **established church**. They emerged as a force in the late 19th century following the extension of the franchise and the spread of democratic ideas which, it was believed, would significantly weaken the privileges of the established church. The main free churches in England and Wales are the **Methodists**, Congregationalists, Baptists and Presbyterians; in Scotland the most prominent free church is the **Free Presbyterian Church of Scotland**. The identity of the free churches has generally tended to rest on their ecclesiastical non-conformism and their association with political liberalism.

FREE PRESBYTERIAN CHURCH OF SCOTLAND

A faction of the **Church of Scotland**, which broke away in 1893 and is informally known as the 'wee frees'. Calvinistic in doctrine, in May 1989 it received wide publicity after its Synod disciplined and suspended one of the church's most prominent elders, the Lord Chancellor, Lord Mackay of Clashfern, for attending Roman Catholic requiem masses for two colleagues; the church considered the Catholic service to be idolatrous. Supporters of Lord Mackay, who formed a minority within the church, eventually broke away to form the Presbytery of the Associated Presbyterian Churches.

FREE WORLD

A Western **Cold War** term referring to Western-style democracies with a market economy, and excluding the world's dictatorships, particularly those of the left.

FREEDOM AND FAIRNESS CAMPAIGN

A media campaign launched by the **Labour Party** in April 1986 in an attempt to change its image. The campaign opened with a slick, US-style party political broadcast, the first fruit of the appointment to **Walworth Road** of Peter Mandelson to be director of campaigns and communications. The campaign also introduced the red rose as the party's emblem.

FREEDOM ASSOCIATION

A right-wing pressure group. Originally known as the National Association for Freedom (NAFF), the Freedom Association made its name by backing and funding court actions by individuals dismissed for refusing to join a **closed shop**. A prominent member was George Ward, the controversial employer involved in the **Grunwick dispute**. After enactment of the **trade union legislation** under the **Conservatives** in 1980s, the Association reverted to a more propagandist role.

FREEDOM OF INFORMATION

The basis for legislation guaranteeing citizens access to bureaucratic records with certain restrictions. Such legislation exists in most Western democracies but not in the **UK**. A freedom of information campaign was launched in 1984 but has thus far had no success in securing the passage of a Freedom of Information Act, although the government was persuaded to introduce a freedom of information code in April 1994. Under this code public bodies are expected to answer a request for information from members of the public within six weeks. If they are not satisfied with their response they may complain to an **ombudsman**.

FREEDOM OF SPEECH

The right to speak or write freely on any issue without **censorship**. This fundamental right, which is ultimately guaranteed in the **UK** by the **European Convention on Human Rights**, is limited by legislation against libel, **blasphemy**, **obscenity**, breach of confidence and copyright and by the **Official Secrets Act** 1988. The **Public Order Act** 1986 also allows prosecution of those 'stirring up racial hatred', as does the Football Offences Act 1991 of those chanting in an indecent or **racist** manner at football matches.

FREEMASONS

A worldwide secret society for men, believed to have grown from the medieval stonemasons' guilds. The modern freemasons' movement, the Society of Free and Accepted Masons, developed particularly in the seventeenth and eighteenth centuries. Members, organized in lodges, hold regular meetings, with arcane ceremonies and dress. Membership is by invitation only and an oath of secrecy is sworn by all members. The Duke of Kent is the Grand Master of the United Grand Lodge of England. The police force, lawyers and public servants are reputed to be well represented, and there have been persistent allegations that freemasons in public life look after each other's interests in a clandestine manner and moreover that in order to advance in certain professions, membership of the organization is an unspoken requirement. The movement has encountered strong opposition in many countries from the Roman Catholic Church.

FRESH START GROUP

A **Eurosceptic** group within the **Conservative Party**, made up of around 60 **MPs** who called for a 'fresh start' on Europe in a parliamentary motion after the Danish electorate rejected the **Maastricht** treaty in a referendum in May 1992. An amorphous grouping, it meets weekly and only discusses Europe, the sole topic on which all members agree. Its members include Nicholas Budgen and Michael Spicer. It was after a heated meeting with the group in June 1995 that **Prime Minister** John **Major** made his dramatic '**put up or shut up**' declaration and resigned the party leadership.

FRIEDMANITE

An adherent of the Chicago school of economic theory, which emphasizes the money supply as a main determinant of aggregate demand. The foremost exponent of this **monetarist** school, Milton Friedman (born 1912), was professor of economics at the University of Chicago in 1948–83, and Friedmanite theories underlay much free-market economic philosophy, including **Thatcherism**.

FRIENDLY FIRE

A term used when wartime casualties are accidentally inflicted by forces on the same side as the victims. Like **collateral damage**, the term was used extensively during the 1990–1 **Gulf War**, particularly in relation to an incident on 26 February 1991, when nine British soldiers were killed in an attack by US warplanes.

FRIENDS OF THE EARTH

In the **UK**, an environmental campaigning group which conducts issue-based public campaigns on a range of **green** issues such as the exploitation of renewable **energy sources**, waste recycling and air pollution. Its approach is generally less physically confrontational than that of fellow environmental group **Greenpeace**. Jonathon **Porritt**, its director from 1984 to 1990, proved a successful publicist and significantly raised the group's public profile. The UK group is part of an international network of Friends of the Earth organizations which has its headquarters in Amsterdam.

FRONT BENCHES

That area in both the **House of Commons** and the **House of Lords** where government and opposition spokespersons sit. Seating in both the Commons and the Lords is arranged so that the Government benches face those of Her Majesty's Opposition. Members sitting on the front benches are official party spokespersons: in the case of the government side, they are ministers, on the opposition side, they are members of the **Shadow Cabinet**. In the Commons, the government front bench is also known as the Treasury Bench.

FRONT LINE FIRST

The title given to the July 1994 **defence review**, signalling that front line capability would be given top priority, while giving increased emphasis to conducting military operations on a joint service basis. Against a background of cuts in support and administration, the Navy would get two new assault ships and a new class of nuclear-powered submarines, and the Army would move to a tank fleet consisting entirely of Challenger 2s.

FTSE-100 INDEX

The Financial Times Stock Exchange index, the most avidly followed measure of share prices in the UK. It charts movements in the weighted valuation of shares in the 100 largest UK companies in terms of market value. The FTSE-100 was introduced by the **London Stock Exchange** at the beginning of 1984, with the base of 1000 as of 30 December 1983. The main share indexes in other key trading markets are the Dow Jones index in the United States, the Nikkei index in Japan and the Hang Seng index in Hong Kong.

FULL EMPLOYMENT

An ill-defined term often understood to signal the availability of jobs for all those wishing to work. Advocates of full employment frequently refer to the acceptance in the 1944 **White Paper** on Employment of the state's responsibility to achieve a 'high and sustainable level of employment'. This implied economic intervention (by **nationalization**, subsidy, or some other means) to secure jobs – a sharp contrast to the more narrow view of legitimate state involvement which had prevailed before the Second World War. Governments of both parties pursued full employment policies, and at times after the war Britain experienced labour shortages. This commitment, however, implied higher public spending. From the later 1960s each successive nadir of the economic cycle brought higher rates of unemployment, and politicians began to lose confidence in the full employment commitment. On assuming power in 1979, the **Conservative Party** signalled that its principal economic objective was a low rate of **inflation**. This suggested that unemployment would be allowed to rise as market forces determined, since government would no longer mount expensive counter-cyclical activity.

FUNDAMENTALIST

A currently controversial term which is loosely applied to describe persons or groups professing ideas drawn from a narrow interpretation of religion and which is deemed by some commentators to be intrinsically derogatory. It is generally regarded as antithetical to the modern preference for secular rationality, the adoption of religious tolerance with accompanying tendencies towards relativism, and individualism. Although its current usage has tended most widely to refer to religious extremists in contemporary Muslim societies, the term is being used increasingly to characterize revivalist Christian movements.

FYLINGDALES

The site of the radar installation in North Yorkshire which is designed to give warning of missile or aircraft attack.

G-5

Finance ministers of France, Germany, Japan, the **UK** and the USA, who convene informally to discuss international monetary matters and to establish the agenda for wider formal meetings of the **G-7**.

G-7

The Group of Seven most powerful industrialized countries – Canada, France, Germany, Italy, Japan, the **UK** and the USA – whose heads of state and government have met for annual summits since the mid-1970s (although Canada was not included in the first such summit, at Rambouillet, France, in November 1975). Also present at all the summits since 1977 has been the president of the European **Commission**. G-7 finance ministers and central bank governors and the heads of the World Bank and the **IMF** also meet annually in a process formalized at the Tokyo Economic Summit of May 1986. In recent years G-7 summits have tended increasingly to concentrate on political issues, notably on proposals for a collective strategy for the economic and social reconstruction of the newly independent states which were the former Soviet Union. G-7 ministerial meetings, often preceded by consultations shrouded in secrecy, have in turn fuelled speculation of divisions over the co-ordination of economic and fiscal policies.

G-10

The Group of 10 leading industrialized countries. Formally established in 1962, the group now consists of 11 members – Belgium, Canada, France, Germany, Italy, Japan, the Netherlands, Sweden, the **UK**, the USA and Switzerland, previously an associate member. In 1962 the group agreed to lend funds in their own currencies to the **IMF** under the General Arrangements to Borrow. G-10 ministers and central bank governors meet regularly to discuss international monetary issues.

G-24

The Group of 24. The term used within the **IMF** to refer to the group, which includes the **UK**, established to represent the interests of developing countries. Confusingly, 24 was also the number of member countries of the Organization for Economic Co-operation and Development (OECD) (until Mexico joined in 1994) and the term Group of 24 was used for these countries in the early 1990s in respect of an initiative co-ordinated by the **EU** to raise funds to help build market economies in former communist countries.

GAELIC

A celtic language two distinct varieties of which are spoken in Ireland and **Scotland**, the distinctions being great enough so that the word Gaelic itself is pronounced differently in the two countries. While Irish Gaelic is an official language of the Republic of Ireland, it is not spoken in **Northern Ireland**. Scottish Gaelic does not have official status and according to the 1991 census there were just 69,510 people in Scotland aged three and over who could speak, read and/or write it, the equivalent of 1.4 per cent of the Scottish population in that age group.

GAGGING ORDER

The popular term used in the **UK** to denote public interest immunity certificates (PIIs). These certificates, signed by government ministers, prevent information contained in the documents covered by them from being released in court and other proceedings, on the grounds that such disclosure would be detrimental to the public interest. Little attention had been paid to these procedures until 1992 when a number of ministers signed PIIs relating to the trial of three **Matrix Churchill** executives. The subject was closely examined by the **Scott inquiry**, and during the inquiry's hearings in early 1994 Lord Justice Scott appeared to express disquiet over the apparent use of such certificates by ministers to prevent uncomfortable information being made public, even though such actions could prejudice the defendants' fair trial.

GAIA

The Greek goddess of the Earth, and hence a potent image underpinning the ecological movement. The 'Gaia hypothesis' as expounded in James Lovelock's 1979 book *Gaia: A New Look at Life on Earth* sees all living things as part of a whole rather than as subordinate to humankind. Lovelock states that the Earth is 'a single system made and managed to their own convenience by living organisms', and argues for a biocentric view which respects all living things, including the human race, as parts of a single complex system.

GAITSKELL, HUGH

(1906–63) The cerebral right-wing **Labour Party** leader. Gaitskell, an economist and former **civil servant**, entered Parliament in 1945 and went on to become Minister of Fuel and Power, Minister for Economic Affairs (assisting Sir Stafford **Cripps**) and in 1950 succeeded Cripps as **Chancellor of the Exchequer**. His cautious approach at the **Treasury** was subsequently pursued by the **Conservative** R. A. **Butler** leading to a period of **consensus politics** known as **Butskellism**. His sole budget, produced in 1951 under the shadow of rearmament, was generally well-received, but the imposition of certain health charges provoked dramatic resignations by Aneurin **Bevan**, Harold **Wilson** and John Freeman. This hastened the end of the **Attlee** government and personalized the rivalry between Gaitskell and Bevan which eventually split Labour while in opposition. Gaitskell defeated Bevan for the post of party treasurer in 1954, and when Attlee retired the following year the **PLP** elected him as leader with 157 votes compared with 70 for Bevan and 40 for Herbert **Morrison**. Partial reconciliation came when Bevan joined him in opposing **unilateralism** and agreed to become Labour's deputy leader. Gaitskell, however, continued to be embroiled in party conflict. In the aftermath of Labour's heavy 1959 **general election** defeat he unsuccessfully sought the amendment of **Clause IV** of the party's constitution to remove its commitment to **nationalization** . The following year Labour's conference voted for nuclear disarmament despite Gaitskell's powerful and defiant speech in which he vowed to 'fight and fight and fight again to save the party we love'; in 1961 the decision was reversed. In 1962 Gaitskell healed old wounds with his opposition to the **Conservative** bid to enter the **EEC**, although this alienated longstanding supporters on the Labour right. In January 1963 he died of a rare immunological complaint.

GALLUP POLL

A method of assessing public opinion by questioning a representative sample of the population. It was devised by George Horace Gallup, a US journalist and statistician. He founded the American Institute of Public Opinion in 1935 and used his method to forecast **elections**, with only narrow marginal errors in each case (although in 1948 the poll wrongly predicted that Dewey would beat Truman in the US presidential election). The practice was adopted in the UK in the 1960s. One of the most notable exceptions to the reliability of the Gallup poll in the UK proved to be the 1970 **general election**. With Gallup giving the **Labour Party** a 7 per cent lead during the last week of the campaign, the outcome of a **Conservative Party** victory highlighted the marked discrepancy between opinion poll findings during the contest and actual voting intentions.

GANG OF FOUR

The popular name for the four senior **Labour Party** members, who had all served as **Cabinet** ministers in the **Labour** government of 1974–9, who defected in 1981 to form the **SDP**: Roy **Jenkins** (former Home Secretary); David **Owen** (Foreign Affairs); William Rodgers (Transport) and Shirley Williams (Education and Science).

GARDNER, JOY

(1953–93) A Jamaican-born woman who collapsed and died after **police** sought to enforce a **deportation** order in July 1993. Gardner had entered the **UK** on a six-month visitor's permit in 1987 and had a son the same year. She collapsed at her North London home on 28 July 1993 during a struggle with five police officers during which she was gagged and bound; she died four days later. Three of the officers (Det.-Sgt. Linda Evans, PC Colin Whitby and PC John Burrell) were subsequently charged with manslaughter. Their trial began in May 1995 and with the **jury** directed by the judge to acquit Burrell early in proceedings. The trial ended the following month when Evans and Whitby were found not guilty; they immediately returned to duty and were not subject to police disciplinary procedures. However, one of their senior officers was suspended pending disciplinary charges relating to a lack of supervision.

Gardner's family continued to demand a public inquiry into the circumstances surrounding her death, and indicated that they would take civil action against the police.

GATT

The General Agreement on Tariffs and Trade – the international organization within the **UN** framework which is supposed to improve the conditions of international trade, through the reduction of tariffs and similar barriers and through the elimination of discriminatory trading practices. GATT was established effective 1 January 1948 after a proposed International Trade Organization had failed to secure the necessary backing. It operates in various ways. It encourages most-favoured-nation (MFN) treatment and the elimination of a range of potentially discriminatory measures; it examines trade disputes between member countries; it reviews the trading policies of individual member countries; and it has held a series of major global multilateral trade negotiations such as the Kennedy Round, the Tokyo Round and the Uruguay Round. At the conclusion of the Uruguay Round, in December 1993, the participants agreed to establish a World Trade Organization (WTO), encompassing GATT itself, which finally entered into force on 1 January 1995.

GAY PRIDE TRUST

A voluntary organization which organizes events to celebrate the pride of homosexual men and women in their sexuality, principally the Lesbian and Gay Pride March and Festival which takes place in London in June of each year. The history of the Trust goes back to 1972 when the first Gay Pride March was held.

GCE

The General Certificate of Education. The GCE qualifications were established with effect from 1951 as the basic certificates of achievement for pupils at schools in **England** and **Wales**. These replaced the former School Certificate and Higher School Certificate, and there were initially two levels of examination: Ordinary or O-level taken generally at age 16 and Advanced or **A-level** taken generally at age 18. However, both O- and A-level examinations could be taken at any age and were not restricted to those at school. GCE O-level examinations were supplemented by **CSE** (Certificate of Secondary Education) examinations in 1965 and both levels were superseded in 1988 by **GCSE** qualifications.

GCHQ

The Government Communications Headquarters, part of the UK intelligence machinery which provides government departments and military commands with signals intelligence. Established in 1946 as the successor to the Government Code and Cipher School, it was officially acknowledged as an intelligence service in 1983, and placed on a statutory basis in 1994. Controversy over GCHQ arose in January 1984 when the Thatcher government announced that employees there were to be forbidden to belong to trade unions; the few employees who refused to observe this instruction were eventually dismissed in 1988–9. The Council of Civil Service Unions has refused to accept affiliation to the government-approved 'Government Communications Staff Federation'. In mid-1995 the government threatened to withdraw from the International Labour Organization as that organization continued to put pressure on the government to allow trade union activity at GCHQ.

GCSE

General Certificate of Secondary Education. The GCSE qualification was introduced in 1988 as the main certificate of achievement for pupils at schools in **England** and **Wales** at age 16, in succession to the former **GCE** O level and **CSE** (Certificate of Secondary Education) examinations. However, GCSE examinations may be taken at any age and are not restricted to those at school.

GDP

The gross domestic product, one of the two common measures of the size of a national economy. GDP is an aggregate measure of economic activity. It represents the value of all goods and services produced domestically. However, it excludes net property income from abroad, which is included in **GNP**. It may be measured in terms of either constant factor cost or market prices. In 1994 the **UK's** GDP at market prices was £668.085 billion, representing an increase of 3.9 per cent in real terms over 1993 and the UK's best year of growth since 1988.

GENERAL ELECTION

The means by which the members of a new Parliament are elected to the **House of Commons**. Elections are by secret ballot with each elector casting one vote. The candidate receiving the most votes in a parliamentary **constituency** is elected as **MP** for that constituency. The maximum life of a Parliament (and therefore the maximum time between general elections) is five years, but the sovereign may dissolve Parliament at the request of the **Prime Minister** before that time. The date, customarily a Thursday, must be announced a minimum of three weeks before the general election is held. There is extensive legislation controlling the conduct of elections, including the limit of candidates' expenses, polling hours and the content of broadcasting during election periods.

See also Appendix II.

GENERAL SYNOD

The governing body of the **Church of England**. It was established in 1970 under the 1969 Synodical Government Measure and replaced the Church Assembly. It has the power to make canons and to frame statute law, while recognizing Parliament's final authority to decide on changes in worship and doctrine. Jointly presided over by the **Archbishop of Canterbury** and the Archbishop of York, it meets twice a year. It has 574 members in total, divided between three houses: the House of Bishops, the House of Clergy and the House of Laity (almost all of whom are representatives of the dioceses elected by the deanery synods). With the advent of the **ordination of women** there has been a shift of emphasis in the House of Clergy which currently contains 25 women deacons.

GENETIC FINGERPRINTING

The recording of characteristics of the **DNA** of an individual. The use of the procedure for forensic purposes has increased dramatically in recent years. Only a tiny sample of blood, semen or any body tissue is required to establish identification, and genetic fingerprinting evidence has been used extensively. Since April 1994 the British police have been permitted to store DNA samples from suspects in a national **DNA database**.

GEORGE VI, KING

(1895–1952)The sovereign from 1936 until his death in 1952. The modest George, Duke of York, was the second son of George V who succeeded his brother Edward on the latter's abdication in 1936. Although the abdication crisis had damaged the monarchy, George and his consort Queen **Elizabeth** (later Queen Mother) quietly restored its prestige with their more open and democratic style. His personal awkwardness did not diminish the impact of his uniformed visits to bomb sites during the Second World War, and the perception that the **Royal Family** shared in the privations of the postwar era. On his death he was succeeded by his daughter **Elizabeth**.

GERBIL

The Great Education Reform Bill, the generally pejorative title attributed to the Education Reform Act 1988. This wide-ranging legislation, relating to **England** and **Wales**, in particular introduced the **national curriculum**, provided for the **grant-maintained schools** which have opted out of local education authority control, devolved budgetary control to individual schools, and established **city technology colleges**.

GERRYMANDER

The manipulation of electoral constituency boundaries to include or exclude groups of votes according to the interests of a particular party or candidate. The portmanteau word comes from combining the name of Massachusetts Governor Elbridge Gerry (1744–1814) and the word 'salamander', because the 1811 gerrymandered map of Massachusetts was thought to resemble a salamander. More recently, **Conservative** leaders of the flagship **Westminster council** have been accused of gerrymandering in 1987–9 by allegedly targeting marginal wards and selling off council flats there, thus replacing notionally Labour-voting council tenants with notionally Conservative-voting home owners.

GENEVA SUMMIT 1955

A summit meeting in July between the Soviet Union and the three main **Western Allies**, and the first real occasion on which the respective leaders (including Bulganin and Khrushchev on the Soviet side) had come together to make declaratory statements about ending the **Cold War** since Stalin's death in March 1953. Substantive discussions between foreign ministers, however, achieved nothing, and the thaw ended the following year with the Soviet suppression of the Hungarian uprising.

GIBRALTAR

A UK **dependent territory**, on a rocky peninsula on the south coast of Spain overlooking the entrance to the Mediterranean, whose 30,000 inhabitants have internal self-government under the 1969 Constitution, having rejected independence in a 1967 referendum. The substantial British naval presence was much reduced in 1984. Spain contests the British claim to Gibraltar, which dates from the occupation of 1704 and the Treaty of Utrecht in 1713. After unsuccessful negotiations in the late 1960s Spain closed the border in 1969, but reopened it in 1985 following a British undertaking (in the 1984 Brussels agreement) to discuss the sovereignty issue.

GLASS CEILING

A metaphor for the invisible barriers to personal progress encountered particularly by women and members of ethnic minorities. The term, which implies the existence of ingrained prejudices, is employed to explain why, despite equal opportunities legislation, proportionally very few members of such disadvantaged groups occupy leadership positions. The use of **positive discrimination** is advocated as a means of breaking through the glass ceiling.

GLASTONBURY

An annual music and arts festival held near Glastonbury, Somerset, since 1970. The largest and most well-established of the country's annual pop festivals, Glastonbury attracts some 100,000 people and boasts appearances from internationally renowned artists and performers.

GLC

The Greater London Council, the elected local government authority for London from 1965 to 1986. The GLC principally succeeded the former London and Middlesex County Councils and their component metropolitan boroughs, county and municipal boroughs and urban districts. Within the GLC area were 32 London boroughs and the **City** of London. The GLC's responsibilities included education in the centre of Greater London (through the Inner London Education Authority), housing (shared with the boroughs), planning, highways and transport, parks, and fire services. From 1981 under Labour control (led by Ken Livingstone), it came into sharp conflict with **Prime Minister** Margaret **Thatcher**'s **Conservative** government. It was abolished (along with the six metropolitan counties elsewhere in England) in 1986, when its remaining powers were devolved generally to the London boroughs and to the City of London.

GLENEAGLES AGREEMENT

The 1977 decision by **Commonwealth** Heads of Government to ban official sporting links with South Africa until the dismantling of apartheid. The Agreement, named after the venue of the meeting (the Gleneagles Golf Club in Scotland), was part of the sanctions programme launched against the South African apartheid regime.

GLOBAL WARMING

The progressive gradual rise of the earth's surface temperature thought to be being brought about by the **greenhouse effect** and to be responsible for changes in global climate patterns. Some researchers warn of apocalyptic consequences for human civilization if global warming is not brought under control; its effects seem to include such phenomena as an increase in the frequency and severity of storms, rising sea levels and changes in temperature and rainfall affecting agriculture. A long-term project to determine global temperature by taking underground measurements found a total rise of 0.041° C in average temperature between 1963 and 1990. The second World Climate Conference held in Geneva on 5–7 November 1990 recognized global warming as a reality, despite the continuing scepticism of some scientists. Debates at the 1992 Earth Summit held in Brazil addressed ways to control as well as respond to global warming, and over 160 countries signed the Framework Convention on Climate Change aimed at reducing emissions of greenhouse gases.

GMB

The General, Municipal and Boilermakers' Union – a large, moderate general trade union. For many years one of the **TUC's** 'big three', the GMB traces itself to the 1924 merger of three nineteenth century unions. Membership expanded after the Second World War through public service expansion and mergers with the Boilermakers (1982), APEX (1989), the Garment Workers (1991), and the Furniture Workers (1993). GMB general secretaries such as Tom Williamson, Jack Cooper, and David Basnett influenced **TUC** policy and reliably supported **Labour Party** leaders. Their successor John Edmonds repositioned the union in the political centre, although most of the GMB's 16 sponsored **MPs** are on the right. With some 830,000 members, the GMB remains Britain's third largest union, representing one in 20 British workers and organizing in 34 of the top 50 companies. It voted in favour of the amendment of **Clause IV** of the Labour Party's constitution in April 1995.

GMT

Greenwich Mean Time, the time zone marked by the 0° meridian of longitude which passes through Greenwich in south-east London. It serves as the basis for standard time zones throughout the world. In the UK GMT is employed from autumn to spring, but is replaced during the summer by British Summer Time (BST). The dates on which the changes take place are specified by the **Home Office**. Generally, at 2 a.m. on the third Sunday in March (unless this is Easter Day, when it happens on the second Sunday) legal time is set one hour in advance of GMT; at 2 a.m. on the fourth Sunday in October it reverts to GMT. Campaigners have called periodically for changes, resulting in a three-year experiment in 1968–71 during which BST was kept all year round (and known as British Standard Time). The suggested advantage of the extra hour of daylight in winter evenings were less crime, a saving in electricity and a boost to tourism. However, the experiment was abandoned after reports of accidents involving children on the way to school, particularly in Scotland.

GNP

The gross national product, one of the two common measures of the size of a country's economy. GNP is a measure of economic output which includes certain components not covered by **GDP**. It may be measured equally from the supply side or from the demand side. GNP is widely employed as an international basis of comparison. It has also been used as a base for the calculation of the target of 0.7 per cent of income which developed countries were urged to devote to overseas aid, as set out in the report of the Pearson Commission in 1969. In 1994 the UK's GNP was £679.305 billion as against £632.427 billion in 1993. Between 1985 and 1993 the real growth rate of UK's GNP per capita was 1.3 per cent.

GOLD STANDARD

A monetary convention, now obsolete, whereby a currency's value is denominated in terms of a given weight of gold. From January 1934 until the **Smithsonian agreement** of December 1971 the US dollar's value was defined as being $35 per fine ounce of gold. This value was changed to $38 at the end of 1971, and to $42.22 in 1972. Meanwhile, the dollar's actual convertibility into gold had been suspended, in August 1971. Parities of the currencies of other **IMF** countries, also originally defined in terms of gold or of the US dollar, were gradually delinked from the gold/dollar standard as a result of the monetary turmoil in the 1970s, and there was a switch to defining currencies in terms of the IMF special drawing right (SDR), based on the value of a 'basket of currencies'. From the end of 1980 the value of the SDR itself was formally delinked from gold (this link having effectively been discontinued in 1974). Gold thereafter became purely a commodity, whose price fluctuates according to market conditions.

GORBALS

The **inner city** area of Glasgow, **Scotland**, very densely populated in the nineteenth and first half of the twentieth centuries, when its name conjured images of families surviving in squalid housing and grinding poverty. Its notorious tenements were mostly demolished in the 1950s to 1970s and the area has since been redeveloped. Gorbals residents were moved out to large housing estates such as Easterhouse, Castlemilk and Drumchapel on the city outskirts.

GORDON WALKER, PATRICK

(1906–80) Briefly Secretary of State for Foreign Affairs in Harold **Wilson's** first **Labour** government. Defeated in the 1964 **general election** as Labour **MP** for Smethwick, a seat he had held since 1945, Gordon Walker was nevertheless appointed as Foreign Secretary in October 1964. He had been defeated in Smethwick by the Conservative Peter Griffiths in a campaign tainted by explicitly racist remarks. When the **House of Commons** met after the elections, Wilson denounced Griffiths as a 'parliamentary leper' in a speech widely regarded as the first explicit indication of official prime ministerial disapproval of **racism** in parliamentary politics. In January 1965, Gordon Walker fought and lost Leyton, a seat which had become vacant on the creation of a **life peerage** for its Labour MP; he was immediately replaced as Foreign Secretary by Michael **Stewart**. Gordon Walker went on to win Leyton in 1966 and he served as Minister without Portfolio and Secretary for Education and Science in the second Wilson government. He was made a life peer in 1974.

GRAMMAR SCHOOL

A secondary school which offers an academic education from age 11 to 18 for children selected by the **11-plus** examination. Although they have been widely replaced under the **comprehensive system**, some localities have retained a system of grammar and **secondary modern** schools.

GRANT-MAINTAINED SCHOOLS

The term describing schools in **England** and **Wales opting out** of local education authority control and receiving funding directly from the central government. Provision for such status was contained in the Education Reform Act 1988 (**GERBIL**); similar but separate provisions apply to **Scotland**. For a school to apply to become grant-maintained, a ballot has to be held of parents of children or students currently at the school. By mid-1994 the number of grant-maintained schools had risen to around 1,000. Education at a grant-maintained school remains free.

Until mid-1995 the **Labour Party** had officially opposed the opting-out of schools from local authority control, and the decision in late 1994 of Labour leader Tony **Blair** to send one of his children to such a school was met with **Tory** derision, as well as condemnation by elements in his own party. In June 1995 Labour effectively abandoned its position when it accepted the principle of grant-maintained schools, but it insisted on greater accountability by calling for local authorities to be represented on all school governing bodies.

GREAT AND GOOD

The informal name of the officially maintained list of those eligible for public appointments. This facetious term, coined by Anthony Sampson in 1965, connotes those (usually members of the **Establishment**) thought suitable to be selected to serve on **royal commissions**, committees of inquiry or **quangos**. The Great and Good may be of the social elite but do not necessarily hold **Conservative** views. The list has therefore also been employed under **Labour** governments.

GREAT BRITAIN

Great Britain, comprising **England**, **Wales** and **Scotland**, was formed as a result of the 1707 Act of Union when England and Scotland were united, although the crowns of the two countries had already been united in the person of the monarch in 1603 when James VI of Scotland became also James I of England. England and Wales on the one hand and Scotland on the other have separate legal systems, and legislation passed by Parliament may relate to England and Wales, to Scotland or to all three territories, or to the whole of the **UK**, including **Northern Ireland**. The term Britain is frequently used loosely to denote the UK as the sovereign state.

GREAT DEBATE

The six-day **House of Commons** debate on 21–28 October 1971, which ended by approving, without recourse to a **referendum**, the decision of the government of Edward **Heath** to join the **EC**. The debate was the longest in parliament since the Second World War. **Conservative** MPs were allowed a free vote (39 of them voting against the government motion), whereas a **three-line whip** was imposed for **Labour** members, 69 of whom nevertheless defied the whip to vote in favour.

THE GREAT STORM *see* HURRICANE, THE

GREAT TRAIN ROBBERY

The dramatic robbery of a mail train near Cheddington, Buckinghamshire, on 8 August 1963. It was carried out by an armed gang who escaped with an estimated £2,500,000 from 120 mailbags. Twelve members of the gang were later captured and tried. They were convicted in April 1964 and received a total of 307 years imprisonment, with seven members jailed for 30 years. Charlie Wilson escaped from prison in August 1964 while the most notorious gang member Ronald Biggs escaped with three others (Eric Flower, Robert Anderson and Patrick Doyle (aka Anthony Jenkins)) in July 1965. Biggs fled to Brazil and is still at large, remaining something of a folk hero.

GREEN

A party, or a party member or supporter, committed to environmentalist issues in a political context. The term green was first applied to the environmentalist lobby in Europe in the 1970s, particularly to West German activists who were mainly concerned with anti-nuclear campaigning and in 1979 formed their own national party, which won seats in the federal parliament for the first time in 1983 and has now become an accepted part of German politics. In the **UK**, however, the **Green Party** has had limited electoral success, not least because of the **first past the post** electoral system. Instead, pressure groups such as **Greenpeace** and **Friends of the Earth** have had more impact on UK politics. The term green is also applied as a qualifying adjective to personal behaviour which attempts to minimize the impact of an industrialized society on the environment, as in **green consumerism**.

GREEN BELT

The areas around cities and towns in the **UK** in which building development is prohibited. The designation of green belt areas, an initiative dating from the 1950s, is intended to protect the countryside from the sprawling growth of cities, to prevent neighbouring towns from expanding until they meet, to preserve the special character of historic towns and to assist in urban regeneration. As of 1995 some 1,500,000 million hectares in **England** and **Wales** had been designated as green belt, with around 200,000 hectares in **Scotland**.

GREEN CONSUMERISM

The purchase of products regarded as having a less negative impact on the environment than others on the market. The phenomenon developed in the **UK** in the late 1980s as a consequence of the spread of **green** politics and increasing concern for the environment. Since then there has been a proliferation of products claiming to be 'environmentally friendly' and 'green', particularly cleaning products, but also other items such as tuna fish caught by a pole and line rather than by net to avoid dolphin deaths. Public concern about the rain forest has also prompted a decline in the use of woods such as mahogany in favour of timber from 'sustained' forests.

GREEN GODDESSES

The name given to the fire engines held in reserve by the armed forces to maintain services during the 1977–8 fire fighters' strike.

GREEN PAPER

A consultative document issued by the government. A Green Paper generally sets out policy proposals, often including alternative courses of action, on which representations and expressions of view are invited. As appropriate, such a document may be followed after the end of the consultation period by a **White Paper** containing the government's conclusions and firm decisions on legislative or other similar action.

GREEN PARTY

A minor British party specializing in **green** issues. The party was founded in 1973 as People, and known as the Ecology Party between 1975 and 1985. On the back of a wave of interest and concern among the media and public in environmental issues, the party achieved a startling success in the European elections of 1989, winning 15 per cent of the vote – the European green movement's best result. However, even as their popularity peaked the Greens, which had always included a diverse collection of groups, became divided. The party gained a reputation, fuelled by the tabloid press, for radical and bizarre policies. An acrimonious personal row between senior members Jonathon **Porritt** and Sarah Parkin further damaged the party. With the country plunging into recession from 1990, the electorate returned to more traditional political preoccupations in the 1992 **general election**, when the Green Party scored only 0.51 per cent of the vote.

GREEN POUND

The special fixed (rather than fluctuating) valuation of the pound used in determining the prices paid to UK farmers for their agricultural produce under the **CAP**. Each **EU** member country has a corresponding 'green currency'. A further layer of complexity was created by the introduction of 'monetary compensatory amounts', or MCAs, which were applied to agricultural trade between member states so as to preserve the artificial green currency system. A decision to phase out MCAs was part of the 1984 CAP reform agreement.

GREEN SHOOTS OF RECOVERY

The phrase used by **Chancellor of the Exchequer** Norman **Lamont** in October 1981 for the first signs of the ending of the **recession**. The phrase came to haunt him and the **Conservative** government when the following year the economy suffered a further sharp downturn.

GREENHAM COMMON

The site of a US Air Force base in Berkshire, in the UK. With the news that **cruise** missiles would be deployed at the base, the site became the focus of anti-nuclear protests, and in September 1981 a group of women established a permanent peace camp outside the base. Supported by **CND**, their demonstrations included almost daily breaches in the perimeter fences and the constant harassment of military convoys, although the missiles nevertheless arrived on schedule in 1983. The last missiles were removed on 5 March 1991 as a result of the 1987 Intermediate-Range Nuclear Forces (INF) Treaty between the superpowers; the closure of the camp had been announced in 1990.

GREENHOUSE EFFECT

The progressive, gradual warming of the earth's atmospheric temperature, caused by the insulating effect of carbon dioxide and other **greenhouse gases** as their proportion in the atmosphere has increased. The greenhouse effect occurs because greenhouse gases allow short-wave radiation from the sun to penetrate through to warm the earth, but prevent the resulting long-wave radiation from escaping back into the atmosphere, trapping it beneath an insulating gaseous layer. There is concern that the greenhouse effect may have a devastating impact on human civilization in future through rising sea levels, desertification and climatic change. In an effort to combat the greenhouse effect, over 160 governments signed at the World Climate Convention at the 1992 Earth Summit.

GREENHOUSE GASES

Gases which, because of their properties relating to the transmission or reflection of different types of radiation, may raise the earth's atmospheric temperature and thereby contribute to the **greenhouse effect** and **global warming**. Greenhouse gases include the common gases carbon dioxide and water vapour, and also gases such as methane and **CFCs** which are rarer but whose effect is much greater. The increase in such gases in the atmosphere has come about largely because of human activity such as the burning of fossil fuels, the emission of pollutants into the atmosphere, and **deforestation**.

GREENPEACE

One of the first and best-known environmental pressure groups, whose members, now organized internationally with a headquarters in Amsterdam, engage in non-violent action to disrupt environmentally damaging projects. Greenpeace's undertakings, which are backed by scientific research, have been effective in raising public awareness of environmental issues. The group began in 1971 when a group of Canadian and US activists successfully interrupted planned nuclear tests on Amchitka Island, Alaska. Greenpeace's activities often involve a level of personal danger for their participants, as was most notably demonstrated in 1985, when its ship *Rainbow Warrior* was sunk in Auckland harbour by French secret agents and a crew member was killed. Among its successes have been campaigns against whaling, seal culling, dumping nuclear waste at sea, and the disposal of the **Brent Spar** oil rig.

GRIFFITHS REPORT *see* CARE IN THE COMMUNITY

GRIMOND, JO

(1913–93) The colourful **Liberal Party** leader from 1956 to 1967. Grimond was educated at Eton and Oxford before serving in the Second World War. He first contested the Orkney and Shetland seat in 1945 and was finally elected in 1950. He rose quickly through Liberal Party ranks to become leader in 1956 after which he used his position to reposition his party as a radical non-socialist left-of-centre force. Energetic and a powerful speaker, Grimond was rewarded with significant **by-election** successes at the expense of the **Conservatives**, notably at Torrington in 1958 and in 1962 at Orpington. Grimond's aim was to displace the **Labour Party** as the home for radicals. Though he raised the party's popular vote and the number of its **MPs** (by 1966 there were 12), he did not lead a decisive break-out from the party's Celtic strongholds and only proved able to capture Conservative seats. He retired in 1967, returning briefly as joint leader with David Steel during the crisis following the resignation of his successor in the **Thorpe case**. He retired from the **House of Commons** in 1983 when he was made a **life peer**.

GROCER

The nickname given to Edward **Heath** while **Prime Minister** by the satirical magazine **Private Eye**.

GROSVENOR SQUARE

The site of the US embassy in London and the venue of a mass demonstration against the Vietnam War on 27 October 1968. Although the actions of the 30,000 protestors did not compare with the revolutionary activity seen on the streets of Paris in **1968**, the demonstration was a strong indication of local popular disapproval of US policy in Vietnam.

GROUNDNUTS SCHEME

A maladministration scandal of the **Labour** government of Clement **Attlee**, which in 1946 was committed to rapid expansion of agricultural production in the colonies. To this end two public corporations were established in East Africa, one of which, the Overseas Food Corporation (OFC) was to run a groundnut scheme in Tanganika (now mainland Tanzania). By 1949 the OFC was behind schedule, having experienced technical, climatic and management difficulties. Adverse press comment mounted, but by the time it was abandoned the following year the scheme had cost the taxpayer £30,000,000. Labour beat off demands from the opposition for a public inquiry but the affair caused lasting damage to the reputation of John Strachey, the Minister of Food.

GRUINARD

An island off the north-west coast of **Scotland** which was used by the government during the Second World War to conduct research into biological warfare. The island, which became contaminated with anthrax for many years, has now been declared safe following an intensive decontamination programme.

GRUNWICK DISPUTE

The bitter 1977 recognition dispute dramatized by mass picketing. Grunwick was a North London photo-processing plant, the head of which, George Ward, dismissed his staff who had joined the white-collar union APEX. The sacked workers enjoyed widespread support, and when post office workers decided to stop delivering mail to the factory, the right-wing National Association for Freedom (NAFF, the forerunner of the **Freedom Association**) took successful court action forcing them to reverse the decision. Heartened by this victory, Ward became more determined. Despite massive picketing support by other unions and the recommendation by **ACAS** that Ward recognize the union, he refused to concede and none of the workers were reinstated. Nonetheless the dispute was a potent symbol of contemporary union strength.

GUILDFORD FOUR

A group wrongly imprisoned in the UK for alleged **IRA** activities. Patrick Armstrong, Gerard Conlon, Carole Richardson and Paul Hill were sentenced to life imprisonment in September 1975 for the murder of all or some of the seven victims of the 1974 **IRA** bombing of two public houses in Guildford and at Woolwich. Campaigns for a review of their case eventually led in October 1989 to their release on appeal, and their convictions were overturned as unsafe and unsatisfactory after new investigations had revealed that misleading evidence had been given at their trial by police officers. Three of these officers were in May 1993 acquitted of conspiring to pervert the course of justice at the 1975 trial. The release of the Guildford Four was followed 15 months later by that of the **Birmingham Six**.

GUILLOTINE

A parliamentary procedure in the **House of Commons** designed to curtail debate. The guillotine takes the form of a 'timetable motion' introduced by the government, laying down a strict schedule for consideration of the different stages of contentious legislation on which the opposition parties have taken, or threaten to take, delaying action. The guillotine procedure does not apply in the **House of Lords**.

GUINNESS SCANDAL

A **City** takeover battle which led to fraud convictions for a number of high-flying financial figures. In April 1986 the Guinness group won a battle to take over the Distillers Company, beating off a challenge from the Argyll supermarket group. A **DTI** inquiry found that irregularities had taken place, and an investigation by the **Serious Fraud Office** resulted in a criminal trial in 1990. The prosecution contended that an illegal operation had been mounted to support the Guinness share price during the takeover. Four defendants were found guilty: Ernest Saunders – the former Guinness chief executive, Gerald Ronson – an entrepreneur – and Anthony Parnes, a stockbroker, were imprisoned; Jack Lyons, a financier, was spared prison because of ill-health, but was later stripped of his knighthood.

The sending of Saunders to an open prison caused considerable public disquiet. This intensified when he was released early, apparently because he was suffering from Altzheimer's disease. Despite the degenerative effects of this disease Saunders appeared able to resume a normal active life. It was announced in December 1994 that the cases of the 'Guinness four' were to be referred back to the Court of Appeal in the light of the emergence of new evidence.

GULF CRISIS

A phrase which, in its most common usage, covers the period of confrontation and diplomatic and military manoeuvring between Iraq and a US-led international coalition, which began with the Iraqi invasion of Kuwait on 2 August 1990 and culminated in the 'Gulf conflict' or '(second) **Gulf War**' of January–February 1991.

GULF WAR

An alternative name for the protracted and immensely destructive Iran-Iraq war of 1980–90. The same phrase (or the variant 'Gulf conflict') is also used, confusingly, for the major conflict between forces of the US-led coalition (code-named **Desert Shield**) and Iraqi forces between 16 January and 28 February 1991, in which Iraqi forces were badly defeated and driven out of Kuwait. A careful distinction between the 'first Gulf War' and the 'second Gulf War' is not generally made.

GULF WAR SYNDROME

A debilitating medical condition suffered by many Allied service personnel who had served in the 1991 **Gulf War** against Iraq. Symptoms include chronic fatigue, hair loss, memory loss, depression, nausea, headaches, and birth defects among the offspring of Gulf veterans. In the UK, more than 500 Gulf veterans – more than 1 per cent of the entire British force – had complained of Gulf War syndrome, and legal suits were in progress on both sides of the Atlantic in an attempt to secure compensation. Although the US Defence Department has recognized the condition, the UK Ministry of Defence has so far refused to do so. A wide variety of explanations was offered as to the cause of the illness, including the use by Iraqi forces of chemical or biological weapons. However, in April 1995 it emerged that independent research, supported by tests done by the US defence establishment, had produced strong evidence that the syndrome was a result of the combination of insect repellant used by troops and the cocktail of medication given to them as a precaution against attacks by chemical and biological weapons.

GURKHAS

A group of people inhabiting the Nepal mountains, from whom men have been recruited into the British army since 1815. The cuts in defence spending by the UK government as announced in 1991 was intended to reduce the number of Gurkha regiments within the army from five to two by 1996. It was intended, however, that a Gurkha brigade would be retained in **Hong Kong** following the return of the colony to China in 1997.

GUTTER PRESS

A derogatory term used to describe those **tabloid** newspapers which thrive on aggressive human interest stories centred around sex and sensationalism. Such stories typically involve 'exclusive' details, on occasions invented, of the private lives and personal relationships of those in the world of television and entertainment in general, as well as in more recent years of the **Royal Family**. The 'gutter press' stand accused of being willing to indulge in any form of intrusive activity to produce their particular brand of journalistic copy. Stories are often provided by those close to the subject of the article, encouraged by financial reward from the newspaper in what has become known as 'cheque-book journalism'.

GYPSIES

The Gypsy or Romany community is descended from a Caucasian people who came originally from India to Europe in the fourteenth or fifteenth century and have maintained a migratory way of life. There is a history of friction between Romanies and various majority communities, who have sometimes blamed them for crime and creating a nuisance. The 1968 Caravan Sites Act gave Romanies legal sites and access to health, education and welfare services. The duty of local authorities to provide sites was removed by the **Criminal Justice** and Public Order Act 1994, which also increased the powers of councils to move on unauthorized campers.

H-BLOCK

The accommodation blocks of the **Maze prison** near in Belfast, **Northern Ireland**, so named because of their layout, in which convicted **loyalist** and **republican** prisoners serving sentences for terrorism-related offences are held. In the late 1970s and early 1980s **IRA** prisoners staged protests in support of their claim for special political status, by refusing to wear prison clothes and by smearing excrement and food on the walls of their cells (the **dirty protest**). In late 1980 and early 1981 groups of IRA prisoners went on hunger strike; one of these, Bobby Sands, was elected to the UK House of Commons in April 1981, narrowly defeating his **unionist** opponent, but died as a result of his hunger strike less than a month later. Two H-Block prisoners were elected to the Irish *Dáil* (legislature) in 1981; one died shortly after election.

H-BOMB

The hydrogen bomb, the second generation of nuclear weapons, whose development, testing and unprecedented menace overshadowed the 1950s. First the USA (on 1 November 1952) and then the Soviet Union (in August 1953) tested H-bombs and brought them into their arsenals, giving them (and later the other nuclear powers) a global destructive capacity greatly outweighing even that which they already had with the atom bomb. The H-bomb is a thermonuclear device; its immense power comes from nuclear fusion reactions, which are set off by the heat from an initial nuclear fission.

HABEAS CORPUS

A legal writ demanding that a person holding another in custody should produce the detainee in court and give the court reason for the detention. If no good reason is given, the court may order release of the detainee. The writ is issued by the Divisional Court of the **Queen's Bench** Division of the **High Court** or when the court is not sitting by a High Court judge. In **England** and **Wales** the writ dates back to the thirteenth century and enshrines a central principle of English law, that a person may not be indefinitely detained without being charged with an offence. The writ is not used in Scottish law.

HAGUE, WILLIAM

(b. 1961) **Conservative** wonder child appointed **Secretary of State** for **Wales** in July 1995 at the tender age of 34 – the youngest **Cabinet** minister since Harold **Wilson** was appointed President of the **Board of Trade** in 1947 at the age of 31. At 13 Hague was ordering **Hansard** from the local newsagent and learning by heart the speeches of Sir Winston **Churchill** and Iain **Macleod**. He first came to public attention as a precocious 16-year-old when he spoke at the 1977 **Tory** conference, declaring that it was time to 'roll back the frontiers of the state'. His political career then soared: President of the Oxford Union, speech writer for Sir Geoffrey **Howe**, **MP** for Richmond, North Yorkshire, **PPS** to Norman **Lamont** when **Chancellor of the Exchequer**, and then junior minister at the **DSS**, before his appointment to the Welsh Office.

HAILSHAM, LORD

(b. 1907) The excitable **One Nation Tory** and barrister. As Quintin Hogg, Hailsham had been elected **Conservative MP** for Oxford in a famous 1938 **by-election**. Having succeed to the family title, he became active in the **House of Lords** after the Second World War. He was appointed First Lord of the Admiralty in 1956 and Minister of Education and party chairman (under **Prime Minister** Harold **Macmillan**) the following year. He presided over the great Conservative **general election** victory in 1959 but was then replaced by Macmillan, who had found him an unsafe appointment as chairman, and made Minister of Science. During the 1963 **recession** he became Minister for the North-East, charged with leading a recovery for the region. When Macmillan fell ill that autumn Hailsham flamboyantly renounced his peerage to make himself eligible for the succession, but his highly publicized ebullience deterred the Prime Minister from proposing his name to the Queen. Though disappointed he agreed to serve under Sir Alec **Douglas-Home** (who had likewise renounced his peerage) and remained part of the leadership during the opposition years which opened up in 1964. In 1970 he returned as a **life peer** to the Lords, becoming **Lord Chancellor** and remaining at that post until Edward **Heath** lost office in 1974, although he returned to the post for two years under Margaret **Thatcher**. After retiring from government he continued to make speeches in the Lords and to defend the constitution of the **judiciary**.

HANDBAGGING

A colloquial term to describe Margaret **Thatcher's** habit of dealing peremptorily with members of her own **Cabinet**. Ministers who displeased Thatcher would often be publicly snubbed, contradicted or dismissed; satirists compared the experience of such ministers to being struck by Thatcher's handbag. In a notable case of handbagging, Thatcher notoriously interrupted Foreign Secretary Francis **Pym** during a press conference at the height of the 1983 election campaign, openly to contradict his view that a government with a large majority in the **House of Commons** was potentially too powerful.

HANSARD

The official report of proceedings in Parliament. Originally initiated unofficially in 1803, *Hansard* is now published by **HMSO** daily during parliamentary sittings, and covers proceedings on the floor of each House of Parliament and (separately) in standing committees. Although widely assumed to be a verbatim account of proceedings, the *Hansard* recorders are given discretion to 'tidy up' **MPs**' spoken English.

HARMONIZATION

A bureaucrat's word for making one set of rules compatible with (or identical with) another. The heyday of harmonization in the **EU** (then the **EC**) was the latter part of the 1980s, when hundreds of harmonization directives were adopted, ranging from **VAT** rates and tax regimes to environmental protection standards, and had to be incorporated in legislation in member countries, in the process of creating the **single market** by **1992**.

HARRODS

The prestigious department store located in central London. It is owned by the Al **Fayed** Investment Trust (UK), which acquired the Harrods parent company – House of Fraser Holdings plc – in 1985. The acquisition was followed by years of controversy during which the al-Fayed brothers – Mohamed and Ali – were criticized in a **DTI** report, and they became involved in a public row with **Lonrho** chief executive Tiny **Rowland**, who had wanted Lonrho to take over House of Fraser. The report, published in March 1990, declared that the brothers had dishonestly misrepresented their origins and wealth in persuading the department not to refer the acquisition to the **Monopolies and Mergers Commission**. It concluded that the responsibilities of advisers to companies needed to be clarified, and that the **City** takeover code required tightening. For his part, Rowland argued in public with Mohamed al-Fayed – largely through the *Observer* newspaper, which he then owned – about the ownership and control of Fraser, but they announced in October 1993 that they had resolved their longstanding dispute.

HARRODS BOMB

An **IRA** explosion in London during the busy Christmas shopping season in 1984. A car bomb exploded on 17 December outside the Harrods department store in Knightsbridge. Two police officers and three civilians were killed and nearly 100 others were injured. The IRA admitted responsibility, but said that the explosion had been 'unauthorized'.

HARROW TRAIN CRASH

A rail disaster just north of London on 8 October 1952, which killed 112 people. The multiple train accident, the worst since 1915, happened when a 7.31 a.m. commuter train to London was about to leave Harrow and Wealdstone station. It was hit from behind by an express train from Perth. Moments later a third train, travelling north from Euston, smashed into the wreckage.

HATTERSLEY, ROY

(b. 1932) The deputy leader of the **Labour Party** in 1983–92. Hattersley, a Yorkshireman, entered the **House of Commons** as

MP for Sparkbrook in 1964, and was for some time associated with a group which pressed the claims of Roy **Jenkins** to replace Harold **Wilson** as **Prime Minister**. In opposition he sat on the **front bench**, but was one of those who rebelled against the **whips** to support entry into the **Common Market** in 1972. Taking junior office in 1974 Hattersley rose to join the **Cabinet** as Prices and Consumer Affairs Minister in 1976. When many former party allies later defected to form the **SDP** Hattersley declined to join them, preferring to fight the left from within. In 1983 the resignation of Michael **Foot** opened up a four-way contest for the party leadership. Hattersley lost decisively to Neil **Kinnock**, but was elected deputy leader in what was claimed as the **dream ticket**. He was perceived thereafter as a liberal centrist rather than right-wing figure. In the Commons, Hattersley acted as **Shadow Chancellor of the Exchequer** and later as Shadow Home Affairs spokesman. After Labour's 1992 defeat he resigned to become a **backbencher**. He has written several books and is a regular newspaper columnist.

HATTON, DEREK

(b. 1948) A radical leftist **Labour** councillor in Liverpool who rose to national prominence in 1984–5 during the campaign against **rate-capping**. Hatton was linked to the hard-left **Militant Tendency**. In contrast to the more moderate **left-wing** councils in London and Sheffield, led respectively by Ken **Livingstone** and David **Blunkett**, Liverpool councillors deliberately set an illegal rate in 1985. Although Hatton's brand of charismatic populism won support in Merseyside and elsewhere he was denounced by the Labour leadership as a demagogue and an opportunist. The leadership swung firmly against *Militant Tendency*, and Neil **Kinnock** spoke scornfully at the 1985 Labour Party conference of 'the grotesque chaos of a Labour council . . . hiring taxis to scuttle around a city handing out redundancy notices to its own workers'. In a clear snub, Hatton addressed a high-profile Militant rally in the Royal Albert Hall in London in November 1985. The **NEC** suspended the Liverpool Labour Party the same month and in June 1986 voted to expel Hatton from the national party. Hatton eventually resigned as Liverpool Council deputy leader in December 1986, having been disqualified by the courts from serving on the council because of unjustified spending, since when he has pursued a business and modelling career. Hatton was acquitted in March 1993 of having conspired, when deputy leader, to defraud the council, after police investigations into allegedly corrupt land deals involving a construction company.

HAYEK, FRIEDRICH VON

(b. 1899) The Austrian-born British political economist and early influence on the **New Right**. Hayek held professorships from 1931 at the London School of Economics and at the Universities of Chicago and Freiburg, and was jointly awarded the Nobel Prize for Economic Science in 1974. His *Road to Serfdom* (1944) was an early critique of **Keynesian** economics and argued for limits on the role of the state, whose increasing power he regarded as a grave threat to individual freedom. Hayek's thought influenced the **Thatcherite** 'revolution' of the 1980s.

HAZARDOUS WASTE

The byproducts of the nuclear energy industry and of industrial chemical processes, whose transport and disposal is covered by international agreements. The dumping of nuclear waste at sea is covered by a moratorium under the 1972 **London Dumping Conventions** (LDC) effective 1975, but the UK continued to dump nuclear waste until 1984. An LDC meeting in London in October–November 1990 agreed, against the wishes of the UK, a blanket ban from 1995 of all dumping of industrial waste in international waters – including sub-seabed disposal of nuclear waste. There has been continuing controversy surrounding the UK's expanding facilities for reprocessing waste, including nuclear waste.

HEALEY, DENIS

(b. 1917) A dominant **Labour** figure in Parliament over three decades, Healey was **Chancellor of the Exchequer** in 1974–9 and deputy party leader in 1981–3. After service in the Second World War Healey, a prewar Communist, became head of Labour's International

Department and entered Parliament in 1952. Noted for a sharp intellect and bellicose manner, he gained a reputation for toughness in Labour's internal battles, especially over defence and international affairs. During 1964–70 he was Minister of Defence, achieving agreement to the withdrawal of British forces from **East of Suez** by means of a seminal **White Paper** of 1966. In 1974, after warning in opposition that his policies would bring 'howls of anguish' from the rich, he took office as Chancellor of the Exchequer, raising the basic rate of income tax. He was to present no less than 15 budgets in the next five years. After 1975 he shifted Labour's policies towards cuts in public expenditure and became a demonic figure for the left, attracting little support from the **PLP** for his leadership bid in the wake of Harold **Wilson's** 1976 resignation.

That autumn sterling's weakness compelled negotiations with the **IMF**, and it fell to Healey to force through consequent public expenditure cuts. This, his truculent style, and the decision to persist with an **incomes policy** drew considerable party hostility. In 1980 he was comfortably defeated by Michael **Foot** in the election for a successor to James **Callaghan**. The next year he was elected deputy leader by the party's new electoral college but only by the narrowest of margins against Tony **Benn**. He continued as **Shadow** Chancellor, and after 1983 (when he and Foot resigned their party positions) as Shadow Spokesman on Foreign Affairs until 1987. He was created a **life peer** in 1992.

HEALTH AND SAFETY EXECUTIVE *see* HSE

HEALTH OF THE NATION

A 1991 **White Paper** setting out targets for improved health care. Published in July 1992, it set out five key areas for action in preventative medicine: coronary heart disease and strokes, cancers, mental illness, sexual health and accidents. Targets were set for the reduction of deaths in each area, the White Paper committed the government to a comprehensive strategy to cut tobacco consumption, and resources were promised to local authorities to help them with new responsibilities in caring for the mentally ill.

HEALTH WHITE PAPER 1989 *see* WORKING FOR PATIENTS

HEATH, EDWARD

(b. 1916) The Europhile **one nation Conservative Prime Minister** in 1970–4. Heath became an **MP** in 1950, becoming chief **whip** by 1955 and Minister of Labour four years later. As number two to Sir Alec **Douglas-Home** at the Foreign Office as well as **Lord Privy Seal**, with responsibility for European Affairs, he negotiated Harold **Macmillan's** abortive 1963 bid to enter the **Common Market**. In 1964, as Trade and Industry Secretary, he enacted the abolition of retail price maintenance just before the Conservatives lost office.

In 1965 Heath successfully stood in the party's first elections for the leadership (under the **Berkeley rules**). Until 1970 his stiff public manner rendered him less popular than his party but **general election** victory that year made him **Prime Minister**. His government encountered severe economic difficulties. Until the end of 1971 it steered towards market forces, declining to subsidize and legislating to restrain industrial action; after this, spiralling **unemployment** forced a policy reversal – the celebrated 'U-turn'. The introduction of an **incomes policy** (long scorned by the Conservatives) led to major conflict with the unions, and mounting inflation was further fuelled by the oil crisis.

In 1973 Heath achieved British entry into Europe, but in February 1974 he felt impelled to call an election amid an energy crisis and the **three-day week**, caused by rising oil prices and a prolonged **NUM** strike. The Conservatives were narrowly defeated and lost again in October. This third defeat in four general elections produced a 1975 leadership challenge from Margaret **Thatcher**, who unexpectedly led him even on the first ballot, forcing his resignation.

Heath was co-leader of the 'yes' campaign in the 1975 EEC **referendum**, but his bitterness at losing office was undisguised. After 1979 he periodically voiced opposition to his successor's increasingly right-wing policies and improved as a public speaker, especially in the Commons. After the 1992 general election which left him **Father of the House**, he was knighted; he has continued to combat **Euroscepticism**.

HEATHCOAT-AMORY, DERICK

(1899–1981) The **Conservative Chancellor of the Exchequer** who replaced Peter **Thorneycroft** in 1958. Heathcoat-Amory delivered two budgets before he resigned in mid-1960 and was replaced by Selwyn **Lloyd**. After his resignation he was made First Viscount Amory and served as high commissioner in Canada until 1963.

HERALD OF FREE ENTERPRISE

The British car ferry which overturned and sank off the Belgian coast in 1987 with the loss of 193 lives. Owned by Townsend Thoresen (a subsidiary of the P&O shipping group), the roll-on-roll-off *Herald of Free Enterprise* left the port of Zeebrugge, Belgium, on 6 March 1987 with its bow doors still open, allowing water to rush in and fatally upset the balance of the vessel. The disaster was a contributory factor leading to a tightening of regulations covering the design and operation of passenger ferries and other sea-going vessels.

HESELTINE, MICHAEL

(b. 1933) The charismatic **Conservative** politician. Heseltine, nicknamed **Tarzan**, entered the **House of Commons** in 1959 after a very successful business career, joining the **front bench** six years later. In 1970–4 he held junior posts at the **DoT** and the **DTI**. In opposition he was combative, rebuked for angrily waving the Mace during a debate (when he gained the nickname **Tarzan**). In 1979 he became Environment Secretary under Margaret **Thatcher**, enacting the controversial **right to buy** policy. Both at the **DOE** and later, at the DTI, Heseltine oversaw at the introduction of professional management systems into the **civil service**. He was appointed Defence Secretary after the **Falklands conflict**, and in 1986 was the principal protagonist in the **Westland affair**, dramatically resigning in protest at Thatcher's handling of it.

From the **backbenches** Heseltine published ideas on industrial strategy, built a growing reputation as the Conservative Party's most popular orator, and became a focus for party dissidents. In the crisis following Sir Geoffrey **Howe's** 1990 resignation speech, despite having earlier said that he could foresee no circumstances under which he would stand against her, Heseltine opposed Thatcher for the party leadership. His 152 votes deprived her of a first-round victory and led directly to her decision to resign. In the second (three-way) ballot, he was runner-up to John **Major** and returned to the DOE, with responsibility for replacing the discredited **poll tax**. After the 1992 **general election** he was appointed **Secretary of State** for Trade and Industry, although he chose to be know as President of the **Board of Trade**. His reputation for competence was damaged by his handling of that year's **coal industry** crisis. A heart attack in 1993 interrupted an energetic career, but only temporarily. He went on to rebuild his standing with Conservative activists resentful of his role in toppling Thatcher, renewing speculation that he still harboured hopes of the premiership. However, following Major's June 1995 **'put up or shut up'** challenge, Heseltine placed himself firmly in the Major camp. He expressed his backing for the Prime Minister at every opportunity, although his supporters indicated that Heseltine would enter the leadership race in the event of Major standing down. His loyalty was rewarded by Major, who named him as **Deputy Prime Minister** and First Secretary of State in the reshuffle that followed his leadership victory. This gave Heseltine a key role in the formulation and presentation of all aspects of government policy.

HEYSEL STADIUM DISASTER

The death of 39 spectators and the injuring of some 400 others at the final of the 1985 European Cup football competition between Liverpool FC (England) and Juventus (Turin, Italy) in Belgium's Heysel Stadium on 29 May. Most deaths occurred when part of the stadium collapsed as spectators tried to escape charging Liverpool supporters. As punishment, Liverpool FC was banned from playing in European competitions until 1991.

HIGH CHURCH

A term commonly denoting adherence to the elaborate ritual practices associated with the **Anglo-Catholic** movement of the **Church of England**. Although historically a well-established part of the Church of England, it assumed political significance during the **Thatcher** years when senior government ministers who were known to be High Churchmen, most notably John Selwyn Gummer, launched vigorous attacks against populist tendencies within the Church of England which they regarded as antithetical to the values of the ruling **Conservative** party.

HIGH COURT

The superior civil court in **England** and **Wales**. Its full title is the High Court of Justice and it is located in the Strand in London. It is divided into three parts: the **Queen's Bench** Division presided over by the **Lord Chief Justice**, the **Chancery** Division under the **Lord Chancellor** and the Family Division headed by its President. With the **Court of Appeal** and the **Crown Court**, it makes up the Supreme Court of Judicature.

HIGH COURT OF THE JUSTICIARY

The supreme criminal court under **Scotland's** separate judicial system. It is both a trial court and an appeal court, and its 26 judges or Lords Commissioners of Justiciary, who are presided over by the Lord Justice General and the Lord Justice Clerk, are the same as those of the **Court of Session** (Scotland's supreme civil court). There is no appeal to the **House of Lords** from the High Court of the Justiciary as there is from the Court of Session.

HIGHERS

The common name for the Higher Grade Scottish Certificate of Education examination taken by Scottish pupils after the age of 16. Regarded as more academically demanding than **GCSEs**, passes at this grade are the basis for entry to higher education or professional training. Pupils who have completed their highers may also sit for the Certificate of Sixth Year Studies (CSYS).

HILLSBOROUGH DISASTER

The worst disaster in UK sporting history, in which 95 football supporters were crushed to death in the stadium of Sheffield Wednesday Football Club on 15 April 1989 during an FA Cup semi-final match. The game between Liverpool and Nottingham Forest had already begun when a surge of Liverpool supporters trying to enter the ground was funnelled into a section of the terraces which was already full. An inquiry into the disaster led to the 1990 **Taylor Report** which contained numerous recommendations for the improvement of safety at football grounds. Following the strong criticism of the police operation contained in Taylor's interim report, and in the face of legal action by those injured or bereaved in the tragedy, it was announced on 30 November 1989 that the South Yorkshire police had agreed to make compensation payments totalling up to £50 million to victims of the disaster.

HINDLEY, MYRA *see* MOORS MURDERS

HINKLEY POINT

The Somerset site of a proposed new pressurized water reactor (PWR) nuclear power station. Its construction was given formal approval by John Wakeham, Secretary of State for Energy, on 6 September 1990, but it was not begun because in November 1989 the government had postponed the construction of new PWRs for five years pending the results of a review of its nuclear programme. The Central Electricity Generating Board had initially proposed the construction of two PWRs at the **Sizewell** nuclear plant in Suffolk, one at Hinkley Point and one at Wylfa in Anglesey, but following the five-year freeze it abandoned plans for one of the Sizewell plants and the one at Wylfa.

HIPPIES

Those young men and women who in the late 1960s escaped the constraints and responsibilities of conventional society in pursuit of an idealistic alternative. Onlookers tended to focus on their long hair, colourful clothes, sexual promiscuity and use of illegal drugs. The movement originated on the West Coast of the USA and spread across the USA and to Europe in the years after 1967.

New age travellers' interest in **green** politics and alternative religion in recent years have been seen by many as mirroring hippy concerns.

HISTORIC SCOTLAND *see* ENGLISH HERITAGE

HITHER GREEN TRAIN CRASH

A rail crash in south-east London on 5 November 1967. More than 50 people were killed and 90 injured in the accident.

HIV

The human immunodeficiency virus, the agent responsible for the fatal disease **AIDS**. First discovered by a French team in 1983 and subsequently confirmed by US researchers in 1984, HIV is transmitted by the exchange of bodily fluids, most commonly through sexual intercourse, by blood transfusion, by contamination of needles among intravenous drug abusers, or from mother to infant during pregnancy and birth. The virus is slow-acting with an incubation period of up to 10 years, and works by damaging the body's defences against other diseases. According to official **UK** figures released in January 1995 there were 23,104 registered cases of HIV infection at the end of 1994, of which 3,201 (13.9 per cent) were women. The figures showed a relative decline in the spread of HIV through homosexual sex while the number of people infected as a result of heterosexual sex increased.

HIZB UL TAHRIR

(Arabic, 'Party of Liberation') A militant Islamic party. Allegedly an offshoot of the proscribed Jordanian-based *Hizb al-Tahrir al-Islami* (Islamic Liberation Party) founded in 1953, it is currently active among Muslim students on some British university campuses. It is committed to the establishment of a transnational Islamic state, *khilafah*, and has been widely associated with the dissemination of anti-Semitic and homophobic literature. Although banned by many student unions, it continues to gain access to a wider audience through small college societies, including the 1924 committee (named after the date when the Islamic Ottoman state was abolished) of the School of Oriental and African Studies in London.

HMSO

Her Majesty's Stationery Office, an **executive agency** based in Norwich, which provides printing, binding and office supplies to government departments and publicly funded organizations. Established in 1786, HMSO also serves as the government's publisher; 20 per cent of its printing requirement, such as **Hansard**, and Bills and Acts of Parliament, are produced in its own printing works, while the remainder is obtained by competitive tender. Ministerial responsibility rests with the Chancellor of the **Duchy of Lancaster**.

HOLLIS AFFAIR

The scandal precipitated by allegations that a former **MI5** head was a Soviet **mole**. Sir Roger Hollis, head of MI5 in 1956–65, was posthumously accused of being a Soviet agent by the writer Chapman Pincher in his 1981 book *Their Trade is Treachery*. The charge was repeated in the notorious **Spycatcher**, where Peter Wright voiced the longstanding suspicions of a faction in the intelligence community. Pincher's allegations prompted the establishment of a Security Commission under Lord Diplock. However, only the part of its 1982 report relating to **positive vetting** was ever published. No official statements were made about Hollis, though the suspicion that he was the 'Fifth Man' (after **Burgess**, **Maclean**, **Philby** and **Blunt**) persisted. Later hostile accounts have failed to establish definitively whether he was a spy. In 1994 **MI5** head Stella **Rimington** sought to put an end to the debate by declaring publicly that Hollis was not a Soviet spy.

HOLY LOCH

The US nuclear submarine base on the west coast of **Scotland**, whose closure was announced in February 1991 and completed the following year. The closure of Holy Loch was part of the process of the removal of US missiles from the UK and the withdrawal from service of the US Poseidon nuclear submarines.

HOME OFFICE

The government department responsible for internal affairs in **England** and **Wales**. The Home Secretary is concerned with the criminal law, the administration of justice, the prison and probation services, immigration and nationality, community relations, fire and civil emergency services, electoral arrangements, ceremonial and formal business concerning honours, theatre and cinema licensing, general policy relating to shops, the granting of licences for scientific experiments on animals, and firearms and dangerous drugs and poisons. He exercises certain powers on behalf of the monarch such as the Royal Pardon. The Home Secretary is also the link between the **UK** government and the governments of the **crown dependencies** – the **Channel Islands** and the **Isle of Man**.

HOME REPOSSESSIONS *see* REPOSSESSIONS

HOME RULE

A term used to describe the principal aim of those political parties and campaigning groups which seek autonomous self-government for their country or nation-state. The term was used in the period up to the establishment of the Irish Free State in 1922 by those calling for Irish independence. It has also been used by the **Scottish National Party**, whose current declared policy is that of self-government for **Scotland** as an independent member state of the **EU**.

HOME SERVICE

The domestic television and radio broadcasting service of the **BBC**. The title 'Home Service' was initially given to the BBC radio station founded in 1939, whose name was changed to Radio 4 in 1967, when the Light Programme became Radio 2 and the Third Programme Radio 3. Radio 1 was added in 1967. The term can also be applied to the BBC's two national domestic television channels, BBC1 and BBC2, the new Radio 5 Live, its teletext service (Ceefax) and the local and regional radio stations throughout the country. The home service exists in contrast to the **BBC World Service**.

HOMELESSNESS

The condition endured by individuals and families who have no permanent housing and are forced to occupy temporary hostel or bed and breakfast accommodation, or to sleep 'rough' outdoors. It is a persistent social problem in the **UK**, intermittently the subject of public concern. In the early 1990s there was a surge in homelessness following a rise in the number of home **repossessions** by mortgage lenders. Record homelessness figures for families were reported in 1992 and there was also increasing public concern at the very visible numbers of often young single people sleeping rough on the streets of UK cities. Mortgage rescue schemes, agreed by the government and lenders, in 1991–2 and a government initiative providing hostel places and permanent housing for rough sleepers had some success but failed to solve the problem. **Shelter** reported that in September 1994 a total of 49,330 families lived in temporary accommodation nationwide, while 4,740 households were in bed and breakfast hotels. In March 1995 the organization estimated that 8,600 people were sleeping on the country's streets.

HOME-OWNING DEMOCRACY

The expression of **Conservative** policy, particularly in the **Thatcherite** era, to encourage home ownership as a means of counteracting the dependency culture and sponsoring middle-class aspirations and the values of individual enterprise among the working class. The key legislation in this area was the Housing Act of 1980, which conferred on council tenants the **right to buy** their council flats or houses, and by 1983 some half a million such properties had been sold. The home-owning democracy policy proved extremely popular as the housing boom gathered pace in the 1980s, and dovetailed neatly with the related policy of the **share-owning democracy**, but the collapse of the housing market in the late 1980s left many home owners facing high mortgage repayments and **negative equity** – particularly those who had bought their own council homes.

HOMEWORKING

Paid work undertaken from or at home. Traditionally low-paid piece work for the textile and light manufacturing industries, homeworking is most often associated with women with childcare responsibilities. However, the advent of new technology, with innovations such as **telecommuting**, has changed the face of homeworking.

HONG KONG

A British **dependent territory** comprising part of mainland China and a number of islands, which is due to be returned to China by 30 June 1997. Recent developments in the difficult relationship between China and the **UK** have centred around the scheduled 1997 transfer. In May 1986 the UK Parliament approved the Hong Kong (British Nationality) Order 1986, giving effect to the nationality provisions of the Sino-British **joint declaration** of 1984. The Order created a new status of British Nationality (Overseas) for the 3,250,000 people who held British Dependent Territories Citizen status in Hong Kong. They would not require a visa or entry visa to visit the UK, and would have visiting as opposed to residency rights following the transfer. After the Chinese military suppression of the pro-democracy movement in mid-1989, the UK government passed the British Nationality (Hong Kong) Act of 1990, which secured British citizenship for up to 50,000 heads of households and their families.

HONOURABLE SOCIETY OF THE INN OF COURT OF NORTHERN IRELAND *see* BAR COUNCIL

HONOURS SYSTEM

The award of honours and titles as recognition of public service. An estimated 3,000 honours and titles ranging from life peerages and knighthoods to military honours to membership of the Order of the British Empire are awarded each year by the sovereign, usually on the formal recommendation of the **Prime Minister**. In the case of awards for political service, a committee of the **Cabinet Office** inquires into the names of those put forward for such awards and reports to the Prime Minister. A high proportion of honours have traditionally been awarded to civil servants and the military, although the **Conservative** Prime Minister, John **Major** announced in March 1993 that there would henceforth be more awards for 'ordinary' citizens for service to the community. Consequently large numbers of honours have been conferred on a wide range of people, from school caretakers to road sweepers.

HOSTAGES

The term used to describe the diverse international group of mainly US and British people who were seized and held captive in Lebanon by various factions of the militant pro-Iranian organization *Hezbollah* ('the Party of God') from 1985 on. The group included **Church of England** envoy Terry **Waite** and journalist John **McCarthy**. A series of internationally brokered deals had won the release of the majority of the hostages by the end of 1991.

HOUSE OF COMMONS

The lower, and principal, chamber of parliament. It currently has 651 members (**MPs**): 524 for **England**, 72 for **Scotland**, 38 for **Wales** and 17 for **Northern Ireland**). However, should the recommendations of the 1995 report of the **Boundary Commission** be implemented this number could rise to 659 with five extra English seats, two extra to Wales and a single additional seat for Northern Ireland. Its members are directly elected for a maximum of five years and the House generally sits from November to November, with a three-month break from August to October and brief recesses for Christmas, Easter and Whitsun. Its main functions are to pass legislation, authorize government expenditure, scrutinize government policy and debate political issues. Although the effectiveness of its control over the **executive** has been questioned, it remains a powerful instrument, thanks largely to the process of **question time** and the system of **select committees**.

HOUSE OF LORDS

The upper chamber of Parliament. Its composition as at mid-1994 was 1,194, of whom 773 were hereditary peers, 374 **life peers**, 21 **law lords** and 26 bishops and archbishops of the **Church of England**. In practice only a small percentage of members attend; in 1992–3, average daily attendance was 379.

The legislative powers of the Lords have been greatly limited by the Parliament Acts of 1911 and 1949. A bill which has been endorsed by the Speaker of the House of Commons as a money bill can become law without the consent of the Lords, and any other public bill passed by the Commons, if rejected by the Lords, becomes law 13 months after its first **second reading** by the Commons. The House has judicial powers: it is the ultimate Court of Appeal for the courts of **Great Britain** and **Northern Ireland**, except for criminal cases in **Scotland**.

The **Labour Party** has said that, once in power, it would replace the House of Lords with a new elected Second Chamber which would have the power to delay, for the lifetime of a parliament, change to designated legislation reducing individual or constitutional rights.

HOUSES OF PARLIAMENT

The **House of Commons** and the **House of Lords**, accommodated in the **Palace of Westminster**, where all the principal work of the **legislature** takes place.

HOUSING BENEFIT

A government **welfare benefit**, which provides help with rent costs for those who are **unemployed** or in low-paid work. Under the original scheme 100 per cent of rent was paid to recipients, as long as rent officers approved the amount as within reasonable market levels. However, the **Social Security** Secretary Peter Lilley announced a significant change on 30 November 1994 when he said that from October 1995 benefit would cover a claimant's full rent only up to the average rent for similar properties in the area, and would pay 50 per cent of rent above that limit. Further restrictions on housing benefit were imposed in October 1994, when the limiting of payments covering mortgage interest to the unemployed was announced, effective from October 1995. Despite the protests from building societies and housing groups that such a move would only prolong the recession in the housing market, the government appeared determined to press ahead with the reform, insisting that those taking out new mortgages should take out private insurance to guard against unemployment.

HOWARD, MICHAEL

(b. 1941) **Conservative** Home Secretary since May 1993 and a member of the so-called **Cambridge Mafia**. An **MP** since 1983, Howard served as Secretary of State for Employment in 1990–93.

HOWE, SIR GEOFFREY

(b. 1926) A long-serving **Conservative Cabinet** minister. After Winchester, Cambridge, the army and a successful career as a barrister, Welsh-born Howe entered Parliament in 1964, becoming Solicitor General in 1970. During the next 20 years he was to serve in a variety of senior posts, notably as **Chancellor of the Exchequer** (1979–83), Foreign Secretary (1983–9) and **Leader of the House** and **Deputy Prime Minister** (1989–90). He gained the reputation of a faithful lieutenant of Margaret **Thatcher**, moderating what some saw as her greatest excesses. But their relationship turned sour over the issue of Europe, and a year after his removal from the Foreign Office he resigned from the government, delivering a devastating indictment of her leadership in a personal statement to the **House of Commons** on 13 November 1990, which set in train her downfall as leader a week later. Knighted in 1970, Howe was created a **life peer** in 1992.

HSE

The Health and Safety Executive, a rare tripartite survivor from the 1970s. The HSE, the operating arm of the Health and Safety Commission, was established under the Health and Safety at Work etc. Act 1974. It groups various longstanding workplace inspectorates and extends their activities to advisory, investigatory and legal enforcement functions as well as the remedy of complaints. It is also the licensing authority for nuclear installations and the reporting officer on the severity of nuclear incidents in Britain.

HUMAN SHIELD

A term which became current following Iraq's occupation of Kuwait in August 1990 to describe its use of Western nationals as a defence against possible action by the US-led military coalition

(**Desert Shield**). The policy, which was never officially acknowledged by Iraq, followed an Iraqi order issued on 9 August 1990 closing its borders to foreigners trying to leave Iraq or Kuwait and reportedly authorizing the transfer of some 500 Western nationals to sensitive military installations to deter an allied attack. The resulting international outrage forced Iraqi President Saddam Hussein on 6 December to order the release of all foreign hostages held in Iraq and Kuwait.

HUME, CARDINAL BASIL

(b. 1923) Archbishop of Westminster and leading **Roman Catholic** prelate in Britain. Educated at Ampleforth College, St Benet's Hall, Oxford, and Fribourg University, Switzerland, he was ordained as a priest in 1950. From 1957 he was magister scholarum of the English Benedictine Congregation until 1963, when he was elected Abbot of Ampleforth. In 1976 he was created archbishop of Westminster and then a cardinal by Pope Paul VI. His commitment to closer ecumenical relations has won him wide respect among followers of different denominations, while his concern for human rights was recently manifested in his involvement in securing the freedom of the **Guildford Four**.

HUME, JOHN

(b. 1937) The leader of **Northern Ireland's** (Catholic) Social Democratic and Labour Party (**SDLP**), and member of the **European Parliament** since 1979. After an academic career, he became active in politics, holding positions in the province's Parliament, Assembly and Constitutional Convention over the period 1969–86. He entered the **UK** Parliament as SDLP **MP** for Foyle in 1983, and became prominent in the early 1990s for his attempts to secure progress towards lasting peace in the province. His political work has been marked by a tireless effort to persuade the **IRA**, through its political wing **Sinn Féin**, to renounce violence and embrace the democratic process. Hume held secret talks with Sinn Féin throughout 1993 and was widely credited with having made a significant contribution towards the IRA **ceasefire** declaration of August 1994.

HUME–ADAMS INITIATIVE

A description of a joint peace initiative in **Northern Ireland** which took the form of a number of secret meetings held throughout 1993 between John **Hume**, leader of the (Catholic) **SDLP**, and (republican) **Sinn Féin** president Gerry **Adams**. Details of the discussions were never released, although a joint statement in September 1993 declared they had made considerable progress and believed a process could be devised to allow the divided people of the island of Ireland to move towards a lasting peace. This peace initiative was seen as one of the significant political events culminating in the declaration of a permanent **ceasefire** by the **IRA** in August 1994.

HUNG PARLIAMENT

A **House of Commons** in which no political party has an overall majority. This state of affairs could result from a **general election** in which the governing party has lost its majority, or from **by-election** losses or defections during the term of a Parliament. In February 1974 the **Conservative** government lost its majority at a general election and the **Prime Minister**, Edward **Heath**, attempted unsuccessfully to form a government with the support of the **Liberals** before resigning three days later. In the mid-1970s the **Labour** Government lost its majority through by-elections and defections and continued in power by means of the **Lib-Lab pact**. In May 1995 the **Liberal Democrats** abandoned their policy of maintaining 'equidistance' between the two larger parties, declaring that, in the event of a hung parliament, the party would not be prepared to support a minority Conservative government.

HUNGER STRIKERS *see* DIRTY PROTEST

HUNGERFORD MASSACRE

An incident on 20 August 1987, when a deranged gunman killed 16 people and wounded 14 others in the town of Hungerford. After shooting his first victim, apparently at random, Michael Ryan killed his mother and one of his neighbours before going on an indiscriminate shooting spree. Ryan eventually shot himself dead after being cornered in a local school. It later transpired that he had possessed a large collection of firearms, and on 22 September the government banned automatic weapons of the type used in the massacre.

HUNT SABOTEURS

Those groups of protestors gathering on land used by groups engaged in fox-hunting or other blood sports with the aim of disrupting and preventing the hunt. The growth in this sabotage, together with the actions of **new age travellers** and those attending **raves**, received much publicity in the early 1990s and led to calls for tougher laws to limit such activities. The **Criminal Justice** and Public Order Act 1994 created a new criminal offence of disrupting a lawful activity and gave **police** new powers to direct trespassers they believed were planning such disruption to leave a piece of land.

HURD, DOUGLAS

(b. 1930) Secretary of State for Foreign and Commonwealth Affairs, from 1989 until July 1995, serving in the **Conservative** governments of Margaret **Thatcher** and John **Major**. Educated at Eton and Cambridge, Hurd joined the diplomatic service and was then political secretary to Edward **Heath** before entering Parliament in 1974. After a brief spell as Secretary of State for Northern Ireland (1984–5), Hurd served as Home Secretary in 1985–9 before being appointed Foreign Secretary. He entered the Conservative leadership contest in 1990, but finished last and was quickly confirmed as Foreign Secretary by Major. His firm, measured handling of the 1990–1 **Gulf crisis** won him support from government and opposition alike. He played a central role in redefining the **UK's** role in the **EU**, but, especially during the latter period of his tenure of the post, he was portrayed by **Eurosceptics** as a puppet of **Brussels** and came under considerable pressure from them to resign. During the 1995 party leadership contest Hurd announced his intention to step down as Foreign Secretary. Speaking on 23 June, the day after Major made his astonishing announcement that he was calling a leadership election, Hurd added that his decision had been made some time before; it was widely assumed that in choosing to make the decision public at that time Hurd was seeking to strengthen Major's candidacy. A few days later he announced that he would not stand in the next **general election**, possibly with the intention of resuming his successful second career as a writer of political thrillers. He was replaced as Foreign Secretary in the July reshuffle by Malcom **Rifkind**.

THE HURRICANE

A popularly used term to describe a storm which ravaged southern Britain during the night of 16–17 October 1987. The episode, also known as the Great Storm, involved winds of up to 110 mph and left a £300 million swathe of destruction from Cornwall to East Anglia. At least 17 people were killed in the storm, and there was widespread criticism of the authorities for failing to provide advance warning of the disaster.

IBA *see* INDEPENDENT BROADCASTING AUTHORITY

IBROX

A disaster which occurred at the home ground of Glasgow Rangers Football Club on 2 January 1971. Elated fans surged forward after the home team equalized in the fiercely contested 'old firm' derby match with Glasgow Celtic. Crowd barriers collapsed and 66 people were crushed to death. The recommendations of a committee of inquiry into the incident, conducted by Lord Wheatley, were incorporated into the 1975 Safety of Sports Grounds Act.

ICI

The **UK** chemicals multinational. Imperial Chemicals Industries emerged in the 1930s as a state-encouraged chemicals firm based on Teesside. It grew to be one of the UK's top 10 companies and a global force holding key brands such as Dulux paints. In 1993 ICI's bioscience business was separated off as Zeneca, leaving the parent company in paints, materials, explosives, chemicals and polymers, and tioxide, and still the fifth largest in the UK.

ICJ

The International Court of Justice, based at The Hague and founded in 1946 under a Statute which is an integral part of the **UN** Charter. The ICJ is the principal judicial organ of the UN and is authorized to resolve disputes between UN member states. It is assisted by a governing body composed of 15 judges (including the President), each of a different nationality, who are elected by the **UN General Assembly** and the **UN Security Council** for a nine-year term of office.

IDENTITY CARDS

The official documents issued in some countries to all citizens. Such documents are not issued in the **UK** where they do not enjoy popular support. The carrying of cards has been categorically rejected by rights groups such as **Liberty** as an infringement of civil liberties open to abuse by the **police**. In May 1995 the government published a **Green Paper** setting out various options ranging from maintaining the status quo to the compulsory carrying of cards by all; it was thought that **Conservative** Home Secretary Michael **Howard** would press initially for a voluntary system.

IISS

The International Institute for Strategic Studies, set up in London in 1958 originally on a proposal from the British Council of Churches to broaden the scope of debate on strategic defence issues beyond the military establishment and the **RUSI**. The IISS was soon perceived (especially under the new **Labour** government from 1964) as forming part of the inner circle of 'informed opinion', and thus as having some influence on how foreign and defence policy was made and discussed.

ILLITERACY

A relative term denoting a level of scholarship and reading skill below what is regarded as normal. An adult whose reading level is below that expected of a seven-year-old is regarded as illiterate. The level of illiteracy in modern Britain is hard to assess; in November 1992, some 128,000 people in England and Wales were seeking tuition from the Adult Literacy and Basic Skills Unit.

IMF

The International Monetary Fund, one of the specialized agencies of the **UN**. The IMF was established at the 1944 **Bretton Woods** conference, with the general aims of promoting international monetary co-operation, assisting the growth of international trade, promoting exchange stability and helping to establish a multilateral system of payments for current transactions. The UK was a founder member. In 1964–5, when there was a severe deficit in total currency flow and heavy speculation against **sterling**, the **Labour** government borrowed from the IMF over £850 million. In this way the government managed to ride out crises of confidence in sterling without a severe loss of reserves.

IMMIGRATION

The arrival and settlement of foreigners in a country – a major political concern in the **UK** in recent years, even though official figures have consistently indicated that annual levels of **emigration** from the UK exceed the number of migrants entering the country. In 1948 British **nationality** was conferred on those born in both the UK and the colonies. However, since then immigration to the UK itself has been increasingly restricted from British colonies in covertly **racist** ways. The **Commonwealth** Immigrants Act 1962 controlled the entry of people from Commonwealth countries to the UK for the first time. This was followed by the **Commonwealth Immigrants Act of 1968** and the Immigration Acts of 1971 and 1988. The latter removed the last remaining rights to family reunion in the UK for long-settled Commonwealth citizens. The imposition of visa requirements has also been used to restrict access to the UK. Since 1987 fines of £1,000 per person have been imposed on airlines for each passenger brought to the UK with forged or inadequate travel documents.

The introduction of freedom of movement in the area covered by the European **single market** has given rise to fears expressed by **Eurosceptics** of an uncontrolled influx of immigrants and **asylum** seekers seeking to exploit the UK's social welfare system, if passport checks at borders are dropped completely as provided for under the **Schengen Convention**.

In July 1995 Home Secretary Michael **Howard** announced a crackdown on illegal immigration as part of a drive to reduce fraudulent welfare claims, with staff in benefit offices, hospital and schools and colleges being trained to spot illegal immigrants. Organizations representing public servants expressed strong reservations about their members acting as immigration officers.

IMO

The International Maritime Organization, a **UN** specialized agency based in London, which aims to ensure maritime safety and the prevention of pollution from ships. The IMO was originally founded in 1959 as the Intergovernmental Maritime Consultative Organization, changing its name and status in 1982. Its governing body is the 32-member Council elected by the IMO Assembly. It had 149 member countries as of April 1994.

IN PLACE OF STRIFE

A document published by the **Labour** government on 17 January 1969 setting out its policy for industrial relations, collective bargaining and trade union reform. Among its main proposals were the establishment of a Commission on Industrial Relations, and powers for the government to order a 28-day 'conciliation pause' before strike action was taken and to require compulsory strike ballots. The proposals caused serious dissension within the Labour Party and the trade union movement, and although legislation was introduced it was abandoned by the government in June 1969 after the **TUC** had given a binding undertaking to intervene in serious unconstitutional stoppages.

IN VITRO FERTILIZATION *see* IVF

INCOME SUPPORT

A social security means-tested benefit. It is paid to individuals who are **unemployed** and, if in a couple, whose partners also do not work, and who are not in full-time education, and are available for and actively seeking work. Those who are not required to seek work such as the sick and **single parents** are also eligible. Applicants who have paid sufficient **national insurance** contributions are entitled to the non-means-tested unemployment benefit for the first 12 months of their claim. In a **White Paper** of October 1994 the government proposed the creation of a new single benefit for the unemployed – the job seeker's allowance – to replace Income Support and Unemployment Benefit from April 1996. The proposed allowance would have a single set of rates and be income-related, although applicants with sufficient national insurance contributions would receive a personal non-means-tested rate for the first six months of their claim.

Figures released by the **DSS** in August 1994 revealed that 5,643,000 people, around 10 per cent of the total UK population, were claiming income support, compared to around 4,100,000 claimants in 1989.

INCOME TAX

A direct state tax on earnings from employment and/or from investments. Income tax has its origins in the nineteenth century and remains the principal source of government revenue in the twentieth century. Rates of income tax vary according to the burden of public spending and reached a peak in the 1970s when the **Labour Party** raised the basic rate to 35 per cent and the top rate to 83 per cent. **Conservative** economic policy after 1979 was associated with cuts in the basic rate and a shift to indirect taxation, principally **VAT**. The 1988 **budget** reduced the basic rate to 25 per cent while subsequent budgets gradually widened the coverage of a threshold rate of 20 per cent.

INCOMES POLICY

A government-originated policy seeking to ensure non-**inflationary** growth of incomes within a stable economic framework. The issue of an incomes policy had a particular political importance in the 1970s. The **Conservative** government introduced a 90-day wage/price freeze in November 1972, which was followed by a lengthy period of **wage restraint** under a price and pay code. The breach of this policy by the National Union of Mineworkers (**NUM**) led to industrial action and the imposition of the **three-day week**. The **TUC** in May 1976 agreed new voluntary restraint guidelines with the now Labour government and in July 1976 a new **social contract** was agreed by the **Labour Party** and the TUC. The situation continued to be uneasy, however, and culminated in the 1978–9 **winter of discontent**, as wage demands were sought in excess of the government's 5 per cent guideline.

INDEPENDENT BROADCASTING AUTHORITY

The organization which, as the successor to the Independent Television Authority under the Sound Broadcasting Act of 1972, regulated the output of, and awarded licences to, the independent television contracting companies. The powers of the IBA were expanded in the early 1970s to include local **commercial radio**. It was under the IBA that Channel 4 began broadcasting in 1982, together with its corresponding service in **Wales** – Sianel Pedwar Cymru (SC4). The IBA was replaced by the **Independent Television Commission** in January 1991.

INDEPENDENT LOCAL RADIO

The system of local **commercial radio** stations throughout the **UK** which provide a 24-hour comprehensive service of local news, regular travel and weather information, music, consumer advice, reporting of local events and phone-in programmes. The stations are regulated and their licences are awarded by the **Radio Authority**, which was established in January 1991 under radical **broadcasting legislation** in 1990. The oldest independent local radio company was the London Broadcasting Company (LBC), which in September 1993 lost its two licences to London Radio News. The commercial stations compete with a network of 38 **BBC** local radio stations.

INDEPENDENT NUCLEAR DETERRENT

The capability which the UK developed in the 1950s as a nuclear weapons power, and the defence doctrine that a nuclear attack against the UK (presumptively from the Soviet Union) would more surely be deterred by a UK nuclear capability than by reliance on the US 'nuclear umbrella' within the **NATO** alliance. Significantly, from the time of the 1962 **Nassau Conference** the UK's strategic nuclear capability was dependent on missiles developed by the USA (**Polaris** and then **Trident**). The need to take account of the cherished independence of the British (and French) deterrents proved a significant complicating factor in the nuclear arms control and reduction talks of the late 1980s and 1990s.

INDEPENDENT RADIO NEWS *see* IRN

INDEPENDENT SCHOOLS

Schools which receive no grants from public funds. They charge fees and are owned and managed under special trusts. There is a wide variety of different types of school, from kindergartens to large day and boarding schools and from experimental schools to those established by religious communities. A certain proportion come under the heading, somewhat confusingly, of **public schools**. All independent schools must be registered with the appropriate government department and are subject to inspection. Most independent schools offer a range of subjects similar to state schools, although there is no compulsion for them to adopt the **national curriculum**.

INDEPENDENT TELEVISION COMMISSION

An organization established under the terms of the Broadcasting Act 1990, a radical piece of **broadcasting legislation** aimed at the wholesale reform of British television and radio. The Commission began working in January 1991. It assumed the roles of both the **Independent Broadcasting Authority** and the Cable Authority, becoming responsible as a licensing body for the 16 **ITV** franchises required to broadcast on the new Channel 3 (launched in June 1993), the **current** Channel 4, a new Channel 5, a possible sixth channel, and **cable television** as well as **satellite television**. It became most prominent in October 1991 for its awarding of bids for the 16 independent television franchises, with existing license holders TV-am, Thames Television, TVS and TSW each losing their franchises. Other Commission powers include the issuing of codes of practice on how impartiality requirements are to be applied, on the general standard of programmes, on advertising and sponsorship and on school programmes.

INDEPENDENT TELEVISION NEWS *see* ITN

INDUSTRIAL SECTOR
A broadly defined basic economic activity. In statistical terms the industrial sector seems to imply the production industries, i.e. not only the **manufacturing sector** but also extractive industries like **coal mining** as well as the public utilities. It remains the largest sector in the **UK** economy, although its importance has declined as the **services** and energy sectors have expanded.

INDUSTRIAL SOCIETY
A voluntary body founded in 1918 which by 1993 had more than 10,000 members. Its traditional role was to advocate training but it has broadened its activities and aspires to be the leading **UK** authority on management practices.

INDUSTRIAL TRIBUNALS
Independent judicial bodies which hear employment-related disputes. The competence of tribunals was extended in the 1970s to a range of employment grievances legitimized by the industrial relations legislation of the **Labour** government. Most cases concern unfair dismissal and are brought under the Employment Protection (Consolidation) Act 1978; **trade union legislation** of 1993 extended the scope of unfair dismissal but strengthened incentives to resolve disputes at the pre-tribunal stage.

INFLATION
The rate of price increases. Inflation, measured by the **RPI**, incrementally rose after the Second World War reflecting the impact of rising government spending, **devaluations**, and external shocks such as the 1973 oil price rise. Its monthly peak – 25.9 per cent – came in August 1975. Successive **Thatcher** administrations specified the overcoming of inflation as their principal economic objective, and subordinated other aims (including **full employment**) to this. The annual rate of inflation fell to 3 per cent in the mid-1980s and, after a short period when it exceeded 10 per cent, to around 2 per cent in the mid-1990s.

INLA
The Irish National Liberation Army, the military wing of the Irish Republican Socialist Party. The INLA was founded in 1974 in a protest by republicans against the 1972 **IRA ceasefire**. Its notorious reputation was based on sporadic outbursts of killing, both in the province and on the **UK** mainland. Notable incidents include its claim that it killed **Conservative MP** Airey Neave, the government's then Northern Ireland spokesperson, at the **Houses of Parliament** in 1979, and its attempt in November 1991 to assassinate Laurence Kennedy, a prominent Conservative politician in the province. A lethal internal conflict in 1986–7 led to the death of 12 members and supporters, including Mary McGlinchey. She had been married to the former INLA leader, Dominic 'Mad Dog' McGlinchey, who was killed in the Irish Republic in February 1994.

INLAND REVENUE
The government department, correctly called the Board of the Inland Revenue, responsible for administering and collecting direct taxes – mainly **income tax**, corporation tax, capital gains tax, **stamp duty** and petrol revenue tax. It also advises the **Chancellor of the Exchequer** on policy questions involving them. Routine operations are carried out by more than 30 executive offices. Its Valuation Office is an executive agency responsible for valuing property for tax purposes, for compensation for compulsory purchase, and (in **England** and **Wales**) for local rating purposes.

INNER CITIES
The depressed areas of many large cities, characterized by poverty, high rates of crime and **unemployment** among their inhabitants and by run-down **council housing** estates. The areas are not necessarily at the heart of the city, but are within the ring of more affluent suburbs. Highly concentrated populations and large numbers of **ethnic minorities** have often led to racial tension, and clashes with the **police** have resulted in rioting. Since the late 1980s the government has launched a series of schemes aimed at redeveloping these areas.

THE INNER SIX

The six original founding members of the European Community, namely Belgium, the Netherlands, Luxembourg, France, (West) Germany and Italy. The term 'inner six', or just 'the six', became current in the late 1950s in contrast to the **outer seven EFTA** member countries. It was to some extent revived in the 1980s, to suggest that within the **EC** these countries remained the core and motor of European union, despite the growth of total membership to the **nine**, the **twelve** and beyond.

INSIDER TRADING

The use of privileged information in the financial markets to secure undue personal benefit. The term applies especially to buying or selling securities with inside knowledge that their price is about to be affected (for example, by an imminent takeover bid or by especially favourable or unfavourable financial results). Insider trading became a source of great concern to governments and authorities in the UK and other major trading countries in the 1970s and 1980s, and various pieces of legislation were introduced to criminalize it or to intensify countermeasures and to increase penalties for contravention.

INSTITUTE FOR PUBLIC POLICY RESEARCH

A **think tank** associated with the **Labour Party**. Established in 1988 to help modernize the party following its 1987 electoral defeat, with the election of the modernizing Tony **Blair** as party leader the IPPR has had to look for a new raison d'être and is now concentrating on policy development work. Several IPPR staff have moved to Labour Party headquarters, most notably IPPR leading light David Milliband, who left to head Blair's policy team.

INSTITUTE OF DIRECTORS

A free-market interest group consisting of individual members. It achieved a degree of prominence after 1979, when the **Thatcher** government began to dismantle the network of **corporatism**. Its leaders were appointed to official positions and it sometimes acted as a counterweight to the **CBI** which tended to reflect industrial discontent. In the 1990s the Institute and its director-general emerged as fierce advocates of **deregulation** and **Euroscepticism**.

INSTITUTE OF ECONOMIC AFFAIRS

A **right-wing think tank** created in 1955 by Arthur Seldon and Lord Harris of High Cross to expound the ideas of free-market economics. The Institute, once the main powerhouse of **Hayek**-influenced **monetarist** thinking, was joined on the right in the 1970s and 1980s by the **Centre for Policy Studies** and the **Adam Smith Institute**. The Institute's health and welfare unit remains an influential right-wing force.

INSTITUTE OF FISCAL STUDIES

The independent **think tank** which, as its names suggests, specializes in taxation policy. It has a high profile thanks largely to the almost constant media presence of its director Andrew Dilnot and because its fiercely guarded political neutrality carries considerable weight.

INTEGRATED EDUCATION

An educational policy, practised most notably in **Northern Ireland**, of giving children of different religious and social groups an awareness and tolerance of other cultures and backgrounds. In the province, where conflict between the **Protestant majority** and the **Roman Catholic** minority has been the underlying source of **the Troubles**, in addition to the implementation of the **national curriculum**, integrated education is put into practice, based upon a number of compulsory inter-disciplinary themes, including cultural heritage, education for mutual understanding, health education, information technology, economic awareness and careers education. Cultural heritage helps to break down barriers between the people of the province, while education for mutual understanding enables students to appreciate other people's opinions and see the advantages of resolving conflict by means other than violence.

INTERCEPTION OF COMMUNICATIONS ACT

The 1985 legislation creating a statutory framework to cover the interception of postal and telephone messages. It followed a period of concern among **MPs** about the activities in this area of the security services, **police** and customs staff, who were entitled to listen in on telephone messages or open post on the authority of the Home Secretary (or where appropriate the Secretary of State for **Scotland** or **Northern Ireland** or the Foreign and Commonwealth Secretary). The Act created a new criminal offence of unlawful interception and specified that the Home Secretary or other minister might only authorize interception in the interests of national security, the prevention or detection of serious crime, or safeguarding the **UK's** economic well-being.

INTEREST RATES

The charge on borrowing used to regulate the economy. Manipulation of interest rates was a key instrument of economic management after the Second World War, facilitated by the influence of successive governments over the **Bank of England**. Shifts in the Bank's rate no longer force changes by the financial institutions but are likely to influence them. Governments wishing to damp down **inflationary** growth could raise interest rates and thus cut borrowing: the boom of 1986–9 was ended in this fashion. Governments desiring economic revival after a **recession** could cut interest rates – an option followed by the **Conservative** government from 1992. Raising rates may be politically hazardous, since although savers may be gladdened, borrowers (more numerous since the **right to buy** legislation) are disgruntled. Cutting rates carries the opposite risks.

A depreciating currency can be strengthened by higher rates, making it more profitable for foreign exchange holders to buy sterling. In 1976 the **Labour** government raised rates to 15 per cent for this reason. In theory governments seeking short-term popularity may cut rates. Fear of abuse of this instrument leads critics to propose that the Bank of England should be made independent.

INTERNET

The decentralised linkage arrangements between computers and computer networks around the world, whose potential as a vehicle for electronic communications began catching on rapidly in **Britain** in the 1990s. The original basis of the Internet lay in defence planning in the United States in the 1960s. Links were created such that essential computerized information could be accessed via alternative routes if particular computing centres were damaged by enemy action. Development in subsequent decades was driven largely by academic organizations which saw the potential for joint research and data sharing. The academic network also began being used for electronic mail (email) and electronic conferencing, as were other networks within non-academic organizations. The essence of the Internet (increasingly now known just as 'the Net') is the interconnection of these networks, with the evolution of common conventions and software protocols. Arrangements for dial-up access by personal computer spawned a proliferation of commercial 'Internet access providers' in Britain in the early to mid-1990s, and the new **World Wide Web** application gave a fresh incentive for users to try **surfing** the Internet for information and entertainment. By 1995 the popular image of the Internet as an 'information superhighway' had been tarnished by 'pornography on the Net' exposés, and by the recognition that it was especially difficult to police against use by paedophile or any other groups.

INTERNMENT

The policy, pursued in **Northern Ireland** for a number of years in the 1970s, of interning without trial those suspected of belonging to terrorist organizations. It was first introduced by the Northern Ireland government in August 1971 under the Civil Authorities (Special Powers) Acts 1922–43, providing for arrest, interrogation, and in some circumstances indefinite internment. Following the introduction of **direct rule** in March 1972 these arrangements effectively continued. There was continued argument as to the efficacy of the policy, and there ensued a progressive release of internees and detainees between 1973 and 1975 (when the last were released); the total number so held over the period 1971–5 was nearly 2,000, of whom just over 100 were **loyalists**. Although internment was officially ended in December 1975 by Merlyn **Rees**, the then Secretary of State for Northern Ireland, provision for it remains on the statute book.

INVISIBLE EARNINGS

The elements in a country's **current-account balance** which do not relate to visible (merchandise) trade. Invisible earnings include receipts for international transportation, freight, insurance, travel and tourism, and financial and other services; interest, profits and dividends; receipts from certain government transactions; and certain other transfers (including, in the case of the UK, **EU** transactions). Net invisible earnings are calculated by totalling these earnings, and subtracting the payments made in these same categories.

IOANNINA COMPROMISE

A formula on decision-making within the **EU**, devised at a meeting of the EU's **Council of Ministers** in Ioannina, Greece, in March 1994. Negotiations had just been concluded for the enlargement of the EU, with four new members from January 1995, when the UK took a stand against proposals defining the number of votes needed for qualified majority decision-making. In an expanded Council of Ministers, the overall number of votes was to rise from 76 to 90, and the UK eventually accepted that the minimum 'blocking minority' should also rise, from 23 to 27 (i.e. requiring a larger opposing coalition than the current total of two large states and one small state). In return, the compromise formula stated that 23 opposing votes would be enough to hold up a decision for 'a reasonable period', while member states sought consensus.

IRA

The Irish Republican Army, currently the main militant republican movement in **Northern Ireland**. The IRA was originally formed in the early part of the twentieth century to fight for Irish **home rule**, and represented the military wing of **Sinn Féin**. Following the 1969–70 split in *Sinn Féin* the 'Official IRA' was allied with *Sinn Féin*–The Workers' Party (later just Workers' Party) but ceased activity in 1972. The military wing of the party retaining the name *Sinn Féin* was known as the Provisional IRA, although latterly it has generally dropped the prefix. Proscribed in Northern Ireland in 1974, the IRA also operates in Ireland and on the mainland of **Great Britain**. Its main attacks have been on the security forces, government targets, and 'soft' targets of propaganda value, most notably including the **Enniskillen**, **Brighton** and **Bishopsgate bombs**. Its members have participated in sectarian violence against the Protestant community, particularly where individuals are thought to have connections with the security forces. It also dispenses 'justice' in the Catholic community, its members beating or **kneecapping** those considered guilty of such offences as vandalism, **joyriding**, burglary or drug dealing.

On 31 August 1994 the IRA declared a 'complete cessation of military operations', apparently satisfied by various 'clarifications' of the **Downing Street Declaration** of December 1993. The effective ceasefire paved the way for the first public talks between *Sinn Féin* and the **UK** government in December 1994 in which the government was represented by senior civil servants. Direct talks between the party and ministers were stalled over the timing of the disarming of the IRA but eventually began in May 1995.

IRANIAN EMBASSY SIEGE

The 1980 siege and forcible storming of the Iranian embassy in London. The embassy was seized on 30 April 1980 (a year after the Islamic revolution in Iran) by a group of Iranian dissidents seeking to draw attention to the plight of the Arab minority in Iran and demanding the release of 91 of their comrades imprisoned in Khuzistan. Of the 26 hostages taken in the embassy, five were released before negotiations failed. After two hostages were shot dead, the building was recaptured in a dramatic operation by the Special Air Service (**SAS**). The embassy was gutted by fire, and all but one of the six men who had occupied it were killed in the raid.

IRELAND ACT 1949

The legislative response of the **UK** Parliament to the adoption by the Irish Free State of a separate constitution in 1937 and its becoming a full republic outside the British **Commonwealth** in 1949. The Act declared that in no event would **Northern Ireland** or any part of it cease to be a part of the UK without the consent of the Northern Ireland Parliament (**Stormont**). It was this principle which was upheld within the terms of the **Downing Street Declaration** of December 1993.

IRISH-AMERICAN LOBBY

A term used to denote those American politicians, diplomats and Irish activists in the USA who have attempted to exert a considerable influence over the direction of British government policy towards **Northern Ireland**. For its part, the British government has over the years depended upon its **'special relationship'** with the USA for support from the US government for its bipartisan approach – though tempered by unionist leanings – to the politics of the province. On the other hand, **republican Sinn Féin** has utilised its own financial and political support in the USA, principally through the Irish Northern Aid Committee, commonly known as **NORAID**.

IRN

Independent Radio News, the provider of national and international news services to the **UK** commercial radio network. IRN was established in 1973 as a private limited company and was a subsidiary of the London Broadcasting Company (LBC), with the latter providing the news service. In 1992 IRN awarded its contract for the supply of news to **ITN**. Its principal rivals include Network News, which in 1993 beat IRN to win the contract to supply news to the new national radio station Virgin 1215.

IRON LADY

A term, used either as a compliment or in a derogatory manner, to describe the character of Margaret **Thatcher** during her term of office as UK **Prime Minister** in 1979–90. The term was coined by *Red Star*, the Soviet Union Defence Ministry newspaper, on 24 January 1976.

IRRADIATION OF FOOD

The use of low doses of ionising radiation to kill naturally occurring bacteria in food and thus prolong its shelf-life. The process has been approved in many countries and it was declared safe by a World Health Organization report in December 1988. Government ministers were given powers to license the process under the Food Safety Act 1990. There was some controversy over its introduction, with opponents arguing that the process could not be effectively controlled since irradiation cannot be detected in a batch of food.

ISLAMIC FOUNDATION

A Leicester-based research and publishing body. Since its creation in 1973, it has been the source of a wide range of publications on Islamic theory and practice. Although ostensibly non-political, it is alleged to maintain close links with Muslim fundamentalist groups, including the Pakistan-based *Jamaat-i-Islami*, whose founder, the late Abul Ala Mawdudi, was an adviser to the foundation's first director-general, Khurshid Ahmed. In October 1988 the Foundation was implicated in the distribution to Muslim embassies in the UK of allegedly blasphemous extracts from **The Satanic Verses** by Salman Rushdie to mobilize opinion in favour of a ban on its publication.

ISLAMIC PARTY OF BRITAIN

A pro-Islamic political organization based in Bradford. It was founded in 1989 with the objective of representing British Muslims and lobbying for the introduction of Islamic policies such as interest-free home loans through shared equity. Despite its pro-Islamic orientation, however, the party favours the suspension of the **fatwa** against Salman Rushdie, the author of **The Satanic Verses**. Current membership is estimated at around 1,000, although the party claims to represent the views of all UK Muslims. Five candidates from the party unsuccessfully contested seats in Bradford and London in the 1992 **general election**.

ISLAMIC SOCIETY FOR THE PROMOTION OF RELIGIOUS TOLERANCE

A liberal Muslim organization which emerged in 1989 as one of the few Muslim bodies opposed to the **fatwa** imposed by the late Ayatollah Khomeini on Salman Rushdie, author of **The Satanic Verses**. It was, however, among the first to identify the book with **blasphemy** and supported other Muslim groups in condemning the government's refusal to ban the title. Its leader, Hesham al Essawy, although isolated by most other mainstream Muslim organizations for his strongly stated opposition to the death sentence, continues to speak out in favour of extending the UK's law of **blasphemy** to Islam and other non-Christian religions.

ISLE OF MAN

The small island in the Irish Sea off the coast of Lancashire, which although part of the **British Isles** is not part of the **UK**, but is a **crown dependency**. The Isle of Man was under the nominal sovereignty of Norway until 1266 and eventually came under the control of the British Crown in 1765. Its parliament, the **Tynwald**, celebrated its millennium in 1979.

ITN

Independent Television News, the company which provides national and international news for the whole of the independent **commercial television** Channel 3 network. ITN's main evening news bulletin is *News at Ten*, which became the centre of controversy in mid-1993. Independent television announced its intention to move the programme from its 10 p.m. slot to earlier in the evening, to enable major feature films to be broadcast uninterrupted from 9 p.m. onwards, attracting extra revenue from advertising and allowing the sector to compete better with the **BBC** in showing films at peak viewing time. Immediate protests from Parliament, including that of the **Prime Minister**, caused ITN to change its mind. ITN's proposal served to illustrate the changes and the innovations possible under the new television regime arising from the **Conservative** government's radical **broadcasting legislation**. ITN was taken over in March 1993 by a consortium of television interests, including Carlton Communications.

IVF

In vitro fertilization, the medical technique in which an egg (ovum) is fertilized outside the body and the embryo is transferred to the uterus. The procedure involves mixing the ovum with sperm in a glass receptacle, hence *in vitro* as well as the colloquial expression 'test tube babies'. The procedure was perfected by Patrick Steptoe and Robert Edwards who achieved the first successful human pregnancy by IVF, resulting in the birth of Louise Brown on 26 July 1978 in Oldham. The technique has raised a number of **bio-ethics** questions.

JE NE REGRETTE RIEN

(French, 'I have no regrets'). The response (from a song popularized by Edith Piaf) given by **Chancellor of the Exchequer** Norman **Lamont** in answer to a question about his handling of the economy asked in April 1993 during the Newbury **by-election** campaign. Given the debacle of **Black Wednesday** and successive poor economic indicators, his response was considered extraordinary. The gaffe, coming after a series of critical press reports about his conduct, was perhaps the last nail in Lamont's political coffin, and the following month he was sacked.

JENKINS, DAVID

(b. 1925) The English theologian and prelate who was Bishop of Durham in 1984–94. Ordained in 1954, he was professor of theology at Leeds University from 1979 until his appointment as Bishop of Durham. This was made amid controversy over his interpretations of the Virgin Birth and the Resurrection, which apparently cast doubt on their veracity and suggested that neither were integral to the Christian faith. Widely accused by his critics and sections of the media of betraying his calling by spreading doubt among Christian believers, he is nevertheless widely respected as one of a handful of bishops noted for their theological scholarship.

JENKINS, ROY

(b. 1920) The **Labour** minister, **SDP** leader and European statesman. Jenkins, the son of a mining Labour **MP**, entered the **House of Commons** after a 1948 **by-election**. Despite his close association with Hugh **Gaitskell**, he became Minister of Aviation on the formation of the first **Wilson** government. In 1965 he joined the **Cabinet** as **Home Secretary**, when he oversaw significant liberal legislation on homosexuality, abortion and divorce. As Harold Wilson's unexpected choice to succeed James **Callaghan** at the **Exchequer**, he so cut consumption that the trade figures dramatically recovered. His 1970 **budget** was cautious and later blamed by critics for costing Labour that year's **general election**. Despite rivalry with Wilson (against whom he had conspired in 1968), he became deputy leader of the party, but in 1971 he led 69 Labour MPs voting for **EEC** entry in defiance of the **whip**. The next year he resigned the deputy leadership, but rejoined the **Shadow Cabinet** in 1973 and on Labour's return to power in 1974 again became Home Secretary. He had been a leading figure campaigning for a 'yes' vote in the 1975 **referendum** on membership of the **EEC** and became President of the European **Commission** in 1977–81.

As his term of European office drew to an end Jenkins held private discussions with three Labour figures disenchanted with their Party's leftward drift – David **Owen**, William Rodgers and Shirley Williams – on a new centrist political initiative. The **Gang of Four** launched the SDP in 1981 with Jenkins as leader. He returned to Parliament in 1982, having been triumphantly elected at the Glasgow Hillhead by-election; he had narrowly failed to overcome Labour's majority at the Warrington by-election the previous year. After the 1983 **general election** he yielded the SDP leadership to Owen (referring to him Jenkins said: 'I was more of a Garibaldi – he was more of a Tito'). He lost his parliamentary seat in the 1987 general election, but was immediately created a **life peer** (taking the title Lord Jenkins of Hillhead). A strong advocate of the fusion of the SDP and Liberals, in 1988 he became leader of the Social and **Liberal Democratic** Party Peers in the **House of Lords**.

JENNIFER'S EAR

The subject of a controversial **Labour Party** election broadcast during the 1992 **general election** campaign. The broadcast, on 24 March, featured the plight of a young girl who needed specialist hospital treatment for an ear condition. The broadcast implied that this had been precluded by **NHS** cuts. Considerable controversy arose over the accuracy of the claims (with the **Conservative Party** insisting that she had not been denied treatment), over the identity of the child – whom the media soon revealed to be Jennifer Bennett – and over the fact that the specific purpose of the broadcast was not known beforehand to her immediate family, some of whom were Conservative Party supporters.

JEWISH CHRONICLE

The Jewish weekly founded in 1841. It is the only national and currently the highest-circulating publication on Jewish affairs in the UK. It professes to represent the views of British Jewry as a whole. In recent years it has played an important role in exposing currents of **anti-Semitism** in the UK, including the desecration of graves at Jewish cemeteries across the country.

JOB SEEKER'S ALLOWANCE *see* INCOME SUPPORT

JOINT COUNCIL FOR THE WELFARE OF IMMIGRANTS

An independent pressure group working in the field of **immigration, nationality** and **refugee** law and practice. Founded in 1967 on the initiative of immigrant and multi-racial organizations, the Council advises and represents individuals and families on immigration, nationality and refugee law matters. It also campaigns and lobbies for changes in law and practice, and trains and advises lawyers and others about these laws. The **UKIAS** (United Kingdom Immigrants' Advisory Service) is, by contrast, a government-funded body.

JOINT DECLARATION

The 1984 Sino-British agreement which enshrined the British acceptance that **Hong Kong** should revert to Chinese sovereignty on 1 July 1997. The declaration provided that at that date not only the New Territories should revert to China (having hitherto been held on a 99-year lease) but also Hong Kong Island, which had been ceded to Britain in 1842. The whole territory would comprise a Chinese 'special administrative region' which would have a high degree of autonomy and in which Hong Kong's capitalist system and lifestyle should remain unchanged for 50 years from 1997.

JOINT FRAMEWORK DOCUMENT *see* FRAMEWORK DOCUMENT

JOINT LIAISON GROUP

The joint Sino-British liaison group set up to discuss matters arising from the planned transition of **Hong Kong** to Chinese sovereignty in 1997 under the 1984 **Joint Declaration**. The work of the Joint Liaison Group was thrown into some disarray by Governor Chris Patten's announcement in November 1992 of proposed moves towards democracy in Hong Kong in advance of the 1997 handover.

JOSEPH, SIR KEITH

(1918–94) A **Conservative** Cabinet minister and leading right-wing intellectual. Joseph served as a captain in the Royal Artillery in the Second World War and was a barrister before becoming **MP** for Leeds North East from 1956 to 1987. He held the Cabinet posts of Social Security Secretary (1970–4), Industry Secretary (1979–81) and Education Secretary (1981–6) before being made a **life peer** in 1987.

Joseph's air of aloofness often made him seem ill at ease in the hurly-burly of day-to-day **Westminster** life. Nevertheless, he is credited with being the intellectual father of **Thatcherism**, having devised much of the theoretical framework behind the policies followed by Margaret **Thatcher** in her early years in power.

JOYRIDER

A person who steals a car to drive it fast and recklessly for pleasure. Most frequently bored male unemployed youths, joyriders are often associated with **ram-raiding** and other criminal activity. Increasing concern about the number of vehicle thefts, deaths and damage to property attributed to joyriders was reflected in the Aggravated Vehicle-Taking Act 1992 which increased the maximum penalty for joyriding to five years' imprisonment.

JP

A Justice of the Peace (also known as a lay **magistrate**), an unpaid non-lawyer appointed by the **Lord Chancellor** to preside in a magistrate's court. They sit with at least one and usually two colleagues and are advised on points of law by a legally qualified clerk. A stipendiary magistrate – a full-time, paid lawyer – sits alone in place of JPs in certain busy city courts.

JUDICIARY

The collective term for senior judges in the higher courts, the third and subordinate branch of the constitutional division of powers together with the **executive** and **legislature**. The judiciary applies the law and interprets legislation.

JURY TRIAL

A judicial process in which a judge decides questions of law and members of the public selected at random from the electoral register decide questions of fact and deliver a verdict. In **England**, **Wales** and **Northern Ireland**, the 12-member jury may deliver a verdict of 'guilty' or 'not guilty'. If the jury cannot reach a unanimous decision, the judge may allow a majority verdict provided there are no more than two dissenters. Under the separate judicial system in **Scotland**, the jury consists of 15 members who may deliver three verdicts: 'guilty', 'not guilty' and 'not proven', with the accused being acquitted if either of the last two is given. At least eight members of the jury must support a majority verdict.

An accused person's right to trial by jury is long established and was incorporated in the Magna Carta of 1215. In cases of medium seriousness (such as less serious cases of burglary and some assaults) that may be tried either in **Crown Court** or in **magistrates'** courts, defendants may elect to face a jury at the Crown Court, but the **Runciman Report** on Criminal Justice published in July 1993 controversially recommended the abolition of this right.

JUSTICE OF THE PEACE *see* JP

K4 COMMITTEE

A committee established under the **Maastricht** Treaty on European Union to co-ordinate **EU** policy on matters such as policing, the law, **immigration**, **asylum**, measures to combat drug trafficking and terrorism, and preparatory work to establish **Europol**. The K4 Committee replaced the **Trevi Group** and was established under Title K of the Maastricht Treaty which deals with intergovernmental co-operation in justice and home affairs matters. It derives its name from Article K.4 establishing a co-ordinating committee of senior officials from each EU state which reports to the Council of (Justice and Interior) Ministers. The committee has three senior steering groups dealing with immigration and asylum, security and law enforcement, police and customs co-operation, and judicial co-operation.

KEGWORTH AIR CRASH *see* M1 AIR CRASH

KENYAN ASIANS

An estimated 120,000 people in Kenya of Asian ethnic origin who (like the **Ugandan Asians** and smaller numbers in Tanzania, Malawi and Zambia) held British passports, but who were made the subject of strict quota restrictions under the 1968 **Commonwealth Immigrants Act**. The UK **Labour** government acted swiftly to introduce these quotas (a ceiling of 1,500 per year for all East African Asians) because of fears of a rapid influx of **immigrants**, when the policy of Africanization of business and commerce in their countries of current residence threatened the livelihood of the many Asians in the shopkeeping and small business sector.

KEYNESIAN

An exponent of the highly influential branch of economic theory developed by British economist John Maynard Keynes (1883–1946), which challenged the classical economic assumption that capitalism inevitably involved a cycle of booms and slumps. Keynes argued in his *General Theory of Employment, Interest and Money* (1936) that the level of employment was determined by demand, rather than by wages. Therefore, non-inflationary growth could be achieved and full employment maintained by increasing aggregate demand, particularly through government intervention in the form of public works programmes, even at the risk of running a budget deficit. Keynesian theory was first applied in the USA as the basis for F. D. Roosevelt's New Deal. In the UK the **Attlee** government embraced Keynesianism, which then became a pillar of the cross-party **consensus** of the 1950s and the prevailing economic orthodoxy in the postwar USA and Western Europe. However, stagflation in the 1970s destroyed the Keynesian consensus and **monetarism**, focusing on policies to affect the **supply side** rather than the demand side, was adopted by the **new right**, notably radicals in the **Conservative Party** such as Sir Keith **Joseph** (who was arguably the first **Thatcherite**).

KINCORA

A reference to serious allegations which arose throughout 1989 and 1990 concerning incidents of child sexual abuse occurring during the 1970s, at the Kincora boys' home in Belfast, **Northern Ireland**. An Irish newspaper had initially exposed the allegations in 1980, following which two inquiries had been held. Fresh controversy about Kincora emerged early in 1990 when former British intelligence officer Colin Wallace, who claimed that a 'dirty tricks' campaign of smear and subversion against senior politicians had existed in the 1970s, further alleged that boys at the home were used by British army intelligence as 'pawns' for blackmail purposes, and that the intelligence services were covering up their role in the whole affair.

KING'S CROSS FIRE

A disaster at King's Cross underground station in London on 18 November 1987, in which 31 people, including one firefighter, died. The fire began on a wooden escalator and flashed through the main ticket hall, producing intense heat and thick smoke. An inquiry into the disaster, which published its findings on 10 November 1988, concluded that the fire had been caused by a match or cigarette having ignited accumulated grease and debris on the escalator track. The report also made more than 150 recommendations to improve safety on the underground.

KINNOCK, NEIL

(b. 1942) The **left-wing Labour Party MP** who moved rightwards as party leader in 1983–92. Kinnock was first elected in 1970 as MP for a safe South **Wales** constituency, and initially made his reputation as a fiery but humorous left-wing orator. His call for abstention in Labour's 1981 deputy leadership vote widened an already perceptible distance from the left, and in 1983 he drew support from all sections of the party to become the first leader elected by its electoral college. As leader he increasingly confronted the so-called **militant tendency** in the unions; he refused to endorse the strike tactics of Arthur **Scargill** and opposed unlawful defiance of **rate-capping**. Although his authority increased in the party, at critical moments such as the **Westland affair** he failed to take advantage of weaknesses in the **Conservative Party**. After the 1987 **general election** defeat he accelerated the revision of party policy, dropping commitments to **EC** withdrawal, **unilateralism** and re-**nationalization**. Attacks on Kinnock's personality and lack of experience of government were key features of the Conservatives' unexpected 1992 general election victory. He resigned the party leadership immediately and returned to the **backbenches** until taking up the post of **EU** Commissioner for Transport in 1995.

KITCHEN CABINET

The term commonly used for a small informal grouping of close friends and confidants of the **Prime Minister**. Often meeting with the PM at 10 **Downing Street** at the end of a long day, they provide much-needed support and companionship, usually through the interchange of policy ideas, information of supposed significance and mere gossip. While it is difficult to assess a kitchen cabinet's actual influence on the policy direction of a government, there is little doubt that some prime ministerial friends have enjoyed considerable influence at crucial times. More notable members of recent 'kitchen cabinets' have included Marcia Williams, Gerald Kaufman and Joe Haines (who were close to Harold **Wilson**), and Charles Powell and Bernard Ingham (who were close to Margaret **Thatcher**).

KITH AND KIN

A slogan adopted by British supporters of Ian Smith's declaration of **UDI** in **Rhodesia** in 1965. The slogan was based on the belief that the British government would have neither the political will nor the desire to act against 'white Rhodesians' because of their kinship ties with people in the UK.

KNEECAPPING

A form of punishment carried out particularly by the **IRA** and other paramilitary organizations in **Northern Ireland**. Kneecapping – shooting victims in the knee, often crippling them, or in extreme cases, shooting them in the knees, ankles and elbows, known as a 'six-pack' – has generally been performed less on political opponents than upon those who have brought the organization into disrepute, frequently supporters or former supporters whose behaviour has been condemned by the leaders. More recently those deemed to have committed 'anti-social' crimes such as **joy riding**, mugging or drug dealing have also been kneecapped.

KNOW-HOW FUND

A fund created in 1989 to provide **overseas aid** to support countries in Eastern Europe and the former Soviet Union in transition from communism to pluralism and a market economy. Its specific task is to finance the training of key professionals such as bankers, lawyers and journalists, either in the **UK** or in their home countries. It disbursed £59,000,000 in 1993–4.

KÖNIGSWINTER CONFERENCES

Annual conferences organized since 1949 by the Deutsche-Englische Gesellschaft to promote a broad Anglo-German dialogue. Participants include ministers, officials, parliamentarians, academics and media commentators. Königswinter is a conference centre in a castle on the Rhine near Cologne, but the annual meetings are now hosted alternately by the British and German sides. Heads of government sometimes take part, providing an indicator of the perceived significance of Anglo-German relations.

KOREAN WAR

The war in 1950–3 between communist North Korea (supported by the Soviet Union and China) and South Korea (supported by the USA and the **UN**). From early 1951 onwards it became a static attritional conflict which ended with the signing of an armistice agreement on 27 July 1953. The **Attlee** government reasserted the **special relationship** by supporting the US-dominated UN force. However, the later consequences of British involvement in Korea were increased defence spending and cuts in other areas imposed in the 1951 **budget**, and growing reservations were expressed over US foreign policy, which was seen to be increasingly bellicose.

THE KRAYS

Britain's best-known criminal partnership. Twins Ronnie and Reggie Kray were gangsters in London's East End during the 1960s. Thought to be responsible for the murder of several gangland rivals, their reign of terror was finally brought to an end by **Scotland Yard** detective Leonard 'Nipper' Read who brought them to trial at the **Old Bailey** in 1969. Ronnie was jailed for the killing of fellow gangster George Cornell at the Blind Beggar pub in 1966, while Reggie was given a life term for the murder of Jack 'The Hat' McVitie. After his conviction Ronnie had been certified insane and was committed indefinitely to Broadmoor prison; he died in March 1995 aged 61. Reggie remained in Maidstone prison in the hope of being released after serving 30 years, the minimum term recommended at his trial.

KUWAIT CRISIS

The threat to the former British protectorate of Kuwait from neighbouring Iraq in 1961 and harbinger of the full-blown 1990–1 **Gulf crisis**. Kuwait, a small state at the head of the Persian Gulf, was granted independence from Britain in 1961, having been a protectorate since 1899. Three days after Kuwait's independence, the Iraqi leader, Gen. Kassem, revived his country's claim to Kuwait. Shortly afterwards, Britain signed a defensive pact with Kuwait, and British and Saudi Arabian forces were sent there to forestall any military threat. These forces were later replaced by those of the Arab League, which had admitted Kuwait as a member. When Gen. Kassem was overthrown in 1963 his successor withdrew the territorial claim and recognized Kuwait; the claim was resurrected by Iraqi President Saddam Hussein in 1990, when he invaded Kuwait, precipitating the **Gulf crisis**.

LA FONTAINE REPORT

A June 1994 report into allegations of ritual or 'satanic' abuse of children. The inquiry, chaired by Professor Jean La Fontaine, found no evidence that 'satanic' abuse had taken place in any of the 84 cases it considered. Ritual abuse was substantiated in only three cases, and there was criticism of the methods of some social workers who had investigated the cases. The inquiry was set up by the government after a number of highly publicised cases in the late 1980s and early 1990s, notably the **Orkney child abuse affair**.

LABOUR PARTY

A **left-wing** party formed in 1906 by an alliance of leftist groups, including the **TUC**, the **Fabian Society** and the Independent Labour Party. Although notionally a socialist party, advocating state control of industry – as evidenced by the pre-1995 **Clause IV** of the party constitution – the Labour Party has always been a broad church, comprising both the hard left and social democrats, with the latter almost always in the ascendency. The party's most successful term in office was that led by Clement **Attlee** in the immediate postwar period, which founded the **NHS** and **nationalized** strategic sectors of the economy. Labour's drift to the left in the late 1970s prompted a split in 1981 when several senior members formed the rival centre-left **SDP**. The election of the **modernizer** Tony **Blair** as Labour leader in 1994 confirmed the return to social democracy heralded by Neil **Kinnock**, with consequent significant change within the party (increasingly described as **new Labour**), and appeared likely to return Labour to government after years in opposition.

LADY CHATTERLEY TRIAL

The celebrated proceedings at the **Old Bailey** in October–November 1960 in which the banned novel *Lady Chatterley's Lover* by D. H. Lawrence was declared not to be obscene. The publisher, Penguin Books, had been prosecuted under the **Obscene Publications Act** 1959 for preparing an edition of the novel, which had been banned in the UK for 30 years. The book, first published in Italy and France in 1928, contained frank descriptions of sexual activity and a number of common swear words in detailing the affair between a wealthy woman and the gamekeeper on her husband's estate.

The trial was the first test for the new Act and the verdict was a landmark decision, protecting works of serious literature from similar prosecution in the future. At a time of rapid social change, it was also widely seen as a victory for a new moral consensus of the **permissive society** over more traditional values highlighted by the prosecuting lawyer's words to the jury, 'Is it a book you would wish your wife or servants to read?'. A week after the trial all the 200,000 copies of the first printing run sold out on the first day of publication.

THE LADY'S NOT FOR TURNING *see* U-TURN

LAMB WAR

A confrontation in June–September 1990, when French farmers took violent action to try to stop imports of foreign lamb and beef, attacking lorries carrying live animals mainly from the UK, and in a few cases slaughtering the animals or burning them alive. After diplomatic protests and a threat that the UK might take France to the European Court of Justice (**ECJ**) if the attacks continued, the French government apologized and promised that affected lorry drivers would be compensated.

LAMBETH PALACE

The official London residence of the **Archbishop of Canterbury**, situated in the southern metropolitan borough of Lambeth. Although acquired by the See of Canterbury in the twelfth century, the portion inhabited by the archbishops was erected in 1834. Since 1878 a Conference of the Bishops of the **Anglican** Communion (ecclesiastical bodies in communion with the **Church of England**) has been called once every 10 years to attend the Lambeth Conference.

LAMONT, NORMAN

(b. 1942) **Chancellor of the Exchequer** in John **Major's Conservative** government in 1990–3. One of the **Cambridge mafia** (other future **Tory** luminaries being Norman Fowler, Michael **Howard** and Kenneth **Clarke**), Lamont was elected to Parliament in 1972. After several years as a junior minister, he became Chief Secretary to the **Treasury** in 1989. In 1990 he led John Major's leadership campaign and was rewarded with promotion to the Chancellor's post. Despite a series of gaffes, including his famous '**green shoots of recovery**' speech, he remained Chancellor until May 1993 when he was replaced by Clarke. Speculation about Lamont's replacement had been rife since **Black Wednesday** in September 1992 when he had been forced to suspend sterling from the exchange rate mechanism (**ERM**) of the European Monetary System (**EMS**). An obviously embittered Lamont returned to the **backbenches** from where, in June 1993, he stoutly defended his economic record and delivered a stinging attack on the Prime Minister, accusing the government of 'short-termism'.

LANCASTER HOUSE

The venue in London for the conference which framed the constitution for an independent Zimbabwe and defined how the transition would be achieved. The term Lancaster House also applies to the agreement itself, signed on 21 December 1979 after months of negotiation brokered by Foreign and Commonwealth Secretary Lord **Carrington**. Lancaster House had previously been the venue for several of the constitutional conferences as the UK prepared to grant independence to African colonies – notably the Kenya conferences of 1960 and 1962, and the Central African Federation conference of 1961.

LANCASTER HOUSE AGREEMENT

The agreement brokered by UK Foreign and Commonwealth Secretary Lord Carrington, ending **UDI** and heralding the independence of Zimbabwe. After months of tense negotiations at Lancaster House in London, the agreement was signed on 21 December 1979 by former Rhodesian leader Ian Smith, the then Prime Minister Bishop Abel Muzorewa, Robert Mugabe and Joshua Nkomo, the two main nationalist leaders, and Lord Carrington and Sir Ian Gilmour, representing the British delegation. It provided for a new constitution, under which white minority rights were safeguarded, and instituted special legislative representation for whites for seven years. It also specified a short transition period, during which British sovereignty over the country would be re-established and would be exercised by a Governor (Lord Soames). During the transition the opposing forces were demobilized and a Commonwealth peacekeeping force was deployed. Democratic elections under the new Constitution were held on 27–29 February 1980 and independence was declared on 18 April 1980.

LANDFILL SITES

Those areas used for the disposal of domestic and industrial waste. Both specially prepared holes and existing sites – such as abandoned mines and quarries – are used. It was initially believed that poisons washed from the waste by rainwater would disperse naturally in the surrounding soil, but research has shown that they pollute underground water supplies. Many countries have limited dumping of **hazardous waste** to sites lined with impermeable materials such as plastics, but these sites too have been found to leak.

LAW COMMISSION

A full-time government-appointed body that reviews the law in **England** and **Wales** and makes recommendations on legal reform. The **Lord Chancellor** is responsible for appointing the five commissioners and their legal staff. The commission, established under the Law Commissions Act 1965, presents an annual report to Parliament. A separate commission based in Edinburgh performs the same task for **Scotland**.

LAW LORDS

The Lords of Appeal in Ordinary, who with the **Lord Chancellor** sit in the **House of Lords** as the final court of appeal for all civil and criminal cases in **England**, **Wales** and **Northern Ireland** and in civil cases from **Scotland**. A minimum of three must sit to constitute the court. They deliver a majority verdict and may each give a separate speech.

LAW OFFICERS' DEPARTMENTS

The **Treasury** Solicitor's Department, the **CPS**, the **SFO** and the Legal Secretariat to the Law Officers. Overall responsibility for the work of the departments is in the hands of the **Attorney General**. In **Scotland** similar duties are undertaken by the Lord Advocate's Department.

LAW SOCIETY

The body representing solicitors in **England** and **Wales**. The society controls the examination of applicants to the profession and has powers to discipline practising solicitors for misconduct. Together with the **Bar Council** representing barristers, the Law Society takes a prominent role in public debate about changes to the law. There are separate Law Societies for **Scotland** and **Northern Ireland**.

LAWSON, NIGEL

(b.1932) The pugnacious **Conservative Chancellor of the Exchequer** in 1983–9. Lawson, a former financial journalist and editor of the *Spectator*, entered the **House of Commons** in 1974 and wrote that year's Conservative election manifesto. After the 1979 Conservative **general election** victory he served as Financial Secretary to the **Treasury** and Energy Secretary, and in 1983 was appointed Chancellor. His tenure saw the first major **privatizations** – of **BT** and British Gas – and in 1987 the defence of the economy against the impact of **Black Monday**. In his triumphant 1988 **budget**, higher rate income tax was rationalized at a single rate of 40 per cent and the lower rate cut to 25 per cent. Moreover, with a budget surplus he could make repayments of the National Debt.

By then however, an inflationary boom was causing concern. Lawson, formerly an aggressive advocate of free markets, had begun to differ with **Prime Minister** Margaret **Thatcher** over the significance of the **exchange rate** for monetary policy. In 1988 she appointed Sir Alan Walters as her (part-time) personal economic adviser; he openly advocated that markets alone should determine the value of sterling. Lawson, however, had 'shadowed' the deutschmark to bear down upon inflation. Believing his own position undermined by Walters's contrary advice, Lawson in October 1989 demanded his dismissal, and when Mrs Thatcher refused, he resigned. He left the Commons in 1992 and was created a **life peer**.

LCC

The London County Council, a locally elected body that governed London from 1889 until it was replaced by the **GLC** in 1965. It was established under the London Government Act of 1888 to succeed the Metropolitan Board of Works, and at various times was responsible for the city's drainage, fire service, schools and trams. It had jurisdiction over an area of 117 square miles, now corresponding to Inner London. In 1938 it proposed the London **Green Belt**. Its headquarters were in **County Hall**, at the south end of Westminster Bridge over the River Thames.

LEADER OF THE HOUSE

The two ministers who plan the government's legislative programme: a member of the **House of Commons** and of the **House of Lords** plans and supervises the government's programme in each chamber. The Leader of the House also has the duty of upholding the rights and privileges of the House as a whole, and in this capacity of moving motions relating to the procedure of the House. The position of Leader of the House of Commons is often combined with that of **Lord President of the Council**; similarly the Leader of the House of Lords is often the **Lord Privy Seal**.

LEADER OF THE OPPOSITION

The leader of what is normally the second-largest party in the **House of Commons** and thereby of the **Shadow Cabinet** – the **front bench** of Her Majesty's Opposition – which performs the function of a government in waiting, ready to take over the reins of power. The office of Leader of the Opposition was officially recognized in 1937, and the holder is accorded a salary and membership of the **Privy Council**. The Leader of the Opposition is his or her party's chief spokesperson as well as the Shadow **Prime Minister**. The post is currently held by Tony **Blair**, leader of the **Labour Party**.

THE LEADERENE

One of the many nicknames given to Margaret **Thatcher** during her years as **Prime Minister**; it was intended to convey the idea of an all-powerful leader.

LEAGUE AGAINST CRUEL SPORTS

An anti-bloodsports campaigning group. The League lobbies for legislation to protect wildlife and in particular to abolish hunting and hare-coursing. It also owns land on which hunting is banned.

LEAGUE TABLES

Comparative information on schools. The publication of school league tables by local education authorities was announced in the **Parent's Charter** in 1991. The tables include information on the examination results achieved by schools and on truancy rates and are published in order to help parents to make informed choices concerning the education of their child. A proposal to include the results of **national curriculum** tests was dropped in 1994.

LEASEBACK

An arrangement under which one country may administer and govern a territory while another country holds sovereignty. A leaseback arrangement for the Falkland/Malvinas islands, whereby the islands would continue to be under UK government but with a transfer of sovereignty to Argentina, was one of various formulas put forward prior to the 1982 **Falklands conflict** to settle the long-running dispute between the UK and Argentina. It was rejected by the islanders, who wanted a 25-year freeze on sovereignty negotiations.

LEFT-WING

An umbrella term describing communist, socialist or social democratic ideologies or their adherents. The use of 'left-wing' and '**right-wing**' to describe political ideologies dates back to the National Assembly of Revolutionary France, in which the delegates seated on the left were the most radical, and those on the right the more conservative.

LEGAL AID

The scheme under which funding is provided for those who could not otherwise meet the costs of legal proceedings in **England** and **Wales**. Legal aid dates from 1949 and was intended as a complement to the **NHS**, giving ordinary people access to the legal system. There are three types: Legal Advice and Assistance (LAA, also known as the Green Form scheme), criminal legal aid and civil legal aid. Under the Legal Aid Act 1988, LAA and civil legal aid are administered by the Legal Aid Board under the general guidance of the **Lord Chancellor**, while the Lord Chancellor himself administers criminal legal aid. Applicants are subjected to a means test and also generally to a 'merits test' to assess whether it would be reasonable to grant aid and whether there are reasonable grounds for court action. New regulations introduced in 1993 lowered qualification thresholds and as a result significant numbers were excluded because they earned too much to qualify. There is a separate scheme in operation in **Scotland**.

LEGISLATURE

The second branch of the constitutional division of power, the supreme law-making body which also checks the authority of the **executive**. In Britain the legislature consists collectively of the **House of Lords, House of Commons** and the monarch, although some legislative powers have been imparted to the institutions of the **EU**.

LEND LEASE

The assistance given to Britain by the USA during the Second World War. This involved lending weaponry, warships and other equipment, on the basis that it would be returned after use, even though this was unlikely in practice. The policy was authorized by the Lend-Lease Act passed by the US Congress in March 1941. It began with 50 destroyers being sent to Britain in return for the USA being granted bases in Britain and its empire. By the time Lend-Lease ended in 1945 the USA had received back less than one-sixth of the US$50 billion-worth of equipment it had lent.

LEWISHAM TRAIN CRASH

A rail disaster on 4 December 1957, which killed 92 people. The accident occurred in thick fog as a steam train from Cannon Street to Ramsgate ran into the back of a stationary electric locomotive beneath a bridge at Lewisham station, south London. The bridge then collapsed onto the wreckage, burying many passengers and exacerbating the difficulties of the rescuers. It was the worst rail accident since the **Harrow train crash**.

LEYLAND DAF

The UK's leading truck manufacturer, which went into receivership on 3 February 1993 after the financial collapse of its parent company, the Netherlands-based DAF NV. Leyland DAF was formed in 1987 following the purchase by DAF NV of a 60 per cent holding in Leyland Trucks and Freight Rover – both parts of the then almost wholly UK state-owned Rover Group (until July 1986 known as **British Leyland** or BL).

A rescue package partially funded by the Dutch government and Flemish regional authorities created a new DAF Trucks NV, which no longer included Leyland DAF. This provoked a political storm in the UK, where the government was accused of having caused Leyland DAF's exclusion from the deal by refusing to provide capital. Management buyouts agreed in April and June 1993 ensured the future of Leyland DAF's principal operations, a van manufacturing factory in Birmingham and a truck assembly works at Leyland in Lancashire.

LIBERAL DEMOCRATS

The political party, known initially as the Social and Liberal Democrats, which was formed in 1988 in a merger of the **Liberal Party** and the **SDP**. Although a ballot of the parties' members showed strong support for the merger, 50 per cent failed to vote. The new party began life with considerable grassroots support, with 100,000 members and 3,500 elected councillors. Under Paddy **Ashdown**'s leadership since July 1988 the party has firmly established its position on the centre-left, backing a mixed economy but also a strong **welfare state**, and advocating tax rises to fund improved education. However, despite notable **by-election** victories and the unpopularity of the **Conservative** government, it has struggled to maintain support, and is increasingly in competition in the south with the **Labour Party**, as Labour reclaims the political centre ground.

In a significant change of policy in May 1995, the party decided to abandon its policy of 'equidistance' between the two major parties, announcing that it would not support a future Conservative government in the event of a **hung parliament**.

LIBERAL INTERNATIONAL

A UK-based international organization founded in 1947 in Oxford, with a permanent secretariat in London, which holds annual conferences involving **liberal** parties from approximately 25 countries worldwide.

LIBERAL PARTY

A centre party which played a key political role in the Victorian era and which achieved a modest revival in the 1980s before its effective dissolution in 1988. Although the Liberal Party was almost wiped out in the **general election** of 1950, effective leadership and a strategy of concentrating on local politics contributed to the party's revival by the 1970s (the Liberals gained 18.3 per cent of the vote in the general election of October 1974). This placed the party in a crucial position to influence the **Labour** government in 1977, when its already slim majority had been wiped out, and in March of that year settled the **Lib-Lab Pact** with the government. After losing ground in the 1979 general election the Liberals gradually moved into the centre-left territory vacated by an increasingly radical Labour Party. The party contested the 1983 general election in **Alliance** with the **SDP** and won over one-quarter of the vote. A less impressive performance for the Alliance in the 1987 general election led to a 1988 merger of the Liberal Party and the SDP to form the Social and Liberal Democrats (later the **Liberal Democrats**).

LIBERTY

A pressure group campaigning for personal freedom founded in 1934 as the National Council for Civil Liberties (NCCL). Although it has no political affiliation, in 1975 it was reclassified by the **MI5** as a subversive organization, and files were opened on two of its prominent figures, Patricia Hewitt and Harriet Harman. Knowledge of this came into the public domain courtesy of a former MI5 agent, Cathy Massiter, who made the disclosures in a television documentary. Renamed Liberty in 1991, the organization strongly advocates a **Freedom of Information Act**. Although Liberty favours promulgation of positive human rights, it would prefer that the conferring of undue consequential powers on the **judiciary** were avoided.

LIB-LAB PACT

The parliamentary agreement between the **Labour** and **Liberal** parties in 1977–8. The Labour Party's narrow parliamentary majority following the October 1974 **general election** was whittled away through by-election losses and defections, so that by March 1977 there was an effective majority against the government in the **House of Commons**. Agreement was reached in that month between Labour and the Liberal Party whereby the latter would support the government 'in the pursuit of economic recovery'. This pact was continued until the end of the 1977–8 parliamentary session (in the autumn of 1978). The Labour Party then experienced the **winter of discontent**, involving serious industrial unrest, and was defeated at the general election in May 1979, when the Liberal Party also lost ground.

LIBOR

The London inter-bank offered rate, a rate of interest paid by commercial banks in London for loans between themselves. Libor is generally used as a benchmark for rates charged on other loans, often quoted as a given percentage over (above) Libor.

LIBYAN EMBASSY SIEGE

The events surrounding the shooting of a female police officer outside the Libyan embassy in London in April 1984. Relations between Libya and the UK were tense during early 1984 as a result of a series of bomb attacks aimed at exiled Libyan opponents of the regime of Col. Moamer al Kadhafi. The attacks culminated on 17 April in a gun attack on a demonstration being staged by anti-Kadhafi activists outside the Libyan People's Bureau (embassy) in London. WPC Yvonne **Fletcher** was killed in the shooting, which was apparently directed from inside the bureau. The building was consequently surrounded by security forces demanding the surrender of those responsible for the shooting. After the failure of negotiations aimed at finding a mutually acceptable solution to the resulting crisis, the UK on 22 April severed diplomatic relations and all embassy staff were withdrawn.

LICENCE FEE

A levy imposed by the **BBC** on those operating television sets. At a time of rapid change in the broadcasting world, the principle of a universal licence fee has been criticized, particularly by the **right**. The **Conservative** government indicated in its **Green Paper** of November 1992 that the licence fee would continue, but only because a better idea for funding the corporation had not yet been formulated.

LIFE

The pressure group, also known as Save the Unborn Child, which campaigns nationally and locally to outlaw direct abortion and to establish rights for the unborn foetus from conception onwards. It was established in 1970 largely in response to the **Abortion Act 1967** which legalized abortion up to 28 weeks into a pregnancy. *See also* Appendix VI.

LIFE PEERS

Those created members of the **House of Lords** for their lifetime. Non-hereditary peerages, with the rank of baron or baroness, have been conferred by the Crown since 1876 on eminent judges – the Lords of Appeal in Ordinary, or law lords – to enable them to carry out the judicial functions of the House of Lords. The Life Peerages Act 1958 made it possible for men and women of distinction in public life also to become life peers.

LIFFE

The London International Financial Futures and Options Exchange based in the **City**. LIFFE was created by the merger of the London International Financial Futures Exchange (hence the acronym) and the London Traded Options Market in March 1992. It is Europe's leading futures and options exchange and the third largest in the world.

LIMEHOUSE DECLARATION

The political statement issued on 25 January 1981 by four senior members of the British Labour Party, Roy **Jenkins**, David **Owen**, William Rodgers and Shirley Williams, who became popularly known as the **Gang of Four**, effectively launching the Social Democratic Party (**SDP**). The declaration, made outside Owen's east London home, was a response to the perceived leftwards move of the **Labour Party**, and over the succeeding months the SDP gained the allegiance of increasing numbers of disaffected Labour **MPs**. The SDP subsequently merged with the **Liberal Party** to form the **Liberal Democrats.**

LINE OF SUCCESSION

The official order of succession to the throne, determined by primogeniture. In the **Royal Family** the sons of the sovereign and their descendants have precedence over the daughters, so that **Prince Charles** is in line to succeed his mother **Queen Elizabeth II** as sovereign. The daughters and their descendants have precedence over the lateral lines.

LITTLE ENGLANDER

A derogatory term adopted by pro-European Conservatives in the 1980s to disparage their more **Eurosceptic** colleagues for insularity. There was some irony in this usage, since the term was originally directed against opponents of British imperial expansion in the late nineteenth century.

LIVE AID

The pop concerts organized by the **Band Aid** charity and held simultaneously in venues throughout the world on 13 July 1984. The two main events were in Wembley Stadium in London and JFK Stadium in Philadelphia, where a host of musicians performed, donating their services free, as did everyone else involved in the event. The concerts were televised and broadcast worldwide. All proceeds from the concerts (including ticket receipts, record sales and television fees) went to **Band Aid** to support its relief work in Ethiopia. By 17 July £50 million had been raised.

LIVE EXPORTS

The short-hand term for the export of live animals for slaughter. Live exports, particularly of veal calves, became a highly contentious issue in the 1990s with protests against the trade coming to national prominence in early 1995. The protests brought together supporters of the **RSPCA** and animal rights activists, **new age travellers** and people from **middle England** outraged by what they regarded as the immoral trade. Demonstrations at south coast ports, such as Shoreham and Brightlingsea as well as Dover, frequently prevented lorries embarking on ferries and often brought the demonstrators into conflict with the **police** and port authorities. Protestors also attempted to prevent live exports by air and during a demonstration at Coventry airport in February 1995 a protestor, Jill Phipps, was killed when she fell under the wheels of a lorry. Phipps was subsequently claimed as a martyr for the cause.

LIVINGSTONE, KEN

(b. 1945) The **Labour** politician who was the hard left leader of the Greater London Council (**GLC**) from 1981 until it was abolished in 1986. The radical policies of the GLC under his leadership, particularly on racial matters and transport, brought it into direct conflict with the **Conservative** government of Margaret **Thatcher** and were derided by opponents as being the work of the **loony left**. They also earned him the nickname 'Red Ken'. He countered vitriolic attacks by the **tabloid** press by presenting himself as a self-deprecating type whose great love was his tank of newts and salamanders. In 1987 he became a more moderate **MP** for Brent East.

LLOYD, SELWYN

(1904–78) A **Conservative** Foreign Secretary and **Chancellor of the Exchequer**. Appointed as Foreign Secretary in 1955 by Sir Anthony **Eden**, he managed to survive the political fiasco of **Suez** in 1956. In mid-1960, Eden's successor, Harold **Macmillan**, appointed Lloyd as Chancellor in place of **Derick Heathcoat-Amory**. Lloyd's 1961 emergency economic package aimed to rectify the country's **balance of payments** difficulties through a 'pay pause' and government spending cuts. The package proved highly unpopular, and in July 1962 Lloyd was one of seven Cabinet members replaced by Macmillan in the **'night of the long knives'**. He served as **Speaker** of the **House of Commons** in 1970–6 and was created a **life peer** at the end of his term.

LLOYD-GEORGE, MAJ. GWILYM

(1894–1967) **Conservative** Home Secretary in 1954–57. On leaving the Home Office he was created Viscount Tenby of Bulford.

LLOYD'S OF LONDON

Society of private underwriters providing an international insurance market. Lloyd's has a 300-year history of offering nearly all types of insurance policies underwritten by private individuals with unlimited liability, known as **Names**, who are grouped in syndicates. The premiums, many from abroad, make a contribution worth billions of pounds a year to Britain's **balance of payments**. The tradition of high profits came to an end in the late 1980s, mainly due to claims arising from pollution and natural disasters. Heavy losses resulted in financial ruin for thousands of investors and prompted widespread litigation. Radical reforms were announced in 1993, including the admission of corporate capital into the market for the first time.

LME

The London Metal Exchange, the London-based trade and investment market. Established in 1877, the LME deals in the main industrially used non-ferrous metals: copper, primary aluminium, aluminium alloy, lead, nickel, tin and zinc. LME trading establishes reference prices which are used in metals-related business activities worldwide. The LME provides opportunities to hedge against risks arising from base metals price fluctuations; it also makes storage facilities available, so that participants in the market can make or take physical delivery of approved brands of non-ferrous base metals. It currently lists material from around 50 countries and stores it in warehouses in a dozen of them.

LOADSAMONEY

A fictional character and media phenomenon created by comedian Harry Enfield at the height of the economic boom of 1987–8. Enfield's intention was to satirize **Essex man** as ignorant, selfish, greedy and arrogant, but he dropped the character when he detected approbation of Loadsamoney's values amid the enormous public reaction. Labour leader Neil **Kinnock** derided the **Conservative** government in 1988 for having created a 'Loadsamoney economy'.

LOBBY SYSTEM

The system whereby journalists and others are enabled to meet members of either house of parliament on an 'informal' basis. The phrase derives from the habit of holding such meetings in the busy antechambers or lobbies around the **Palace of Westminster**, many of which are accessible to representatives of the media and invited guests. Information given on lobby terms is generally not attributable to an identified source; instead journalists may for instance ascribe quotes or information to 'sources'. Delegations and others also 'lobby' **MPs** in Parliament, presenting petitions or grievances on a more public basis, sometimes backed by demonstrations in Parliament Square. The lobby system has been criticized by proponents of **open government**, and by both ministers and journalists, each of which groups have argued that the system gives the other undue influence.

LOCAL GOVERNMENT

The set of locally elected bodies that manage the provision of specified services in local areas, such as education and health, with authority delegated by the national government. They are funded by a combination of locally levied taxes, since 1993 known as the **council tax**, and government grants. Local government spending is controlled by central government through its application of grants and by **capping**, the imposition of spending restrictions.

In **England** and **Wales** under the Local Government Act 1972, which took effect in April 1974, local government outside Greater London is exercised by counties and, within these, by districts. As of 1995 there were are 39 **county councils** and 296 district councils in England and eight county councils and 37 district councils in Wales. There are also 32 borough councils and the Corporation of the City of London in Greater London and 36 **metropolitan district councils** in other city areas of England. On mainland **Scotland**, local government is currently on a two-tier basis with nine regions divided into 53 districts, while there are three virtually all-purpose authorities for Orkney, Shetland and the Western Isles. **Northern Ireland** is divided into 26 district councils which have limited powers, with most services provided by statutory bodies and area boards responsible to central government.

Following the Local Government Commission recommendations made in early 1995, the government decided to abolish four English county councils (Avon, Cleveland, Humberside and Isle of Wight), in April 1996 with at least one other county (Berkshire) and probably others disappearing in subsequent years. These would be replaced by unitary district councils. Other changes to local government structure expected to be made were the institution of unitary councils for a number of major towns which would have control without reference to county councils. However, final decisions had yet to be made by mid-1995.

LOCAL GOVERNMENT CAPPING *see* CAPPING

LOCKERBIE

The Scottish town on which a Pan Am airliner – flight PA103, en route from London to New York – crashed after an explosion on board in December 1988. All 259 passengers and crew were killed, as well as 11 people in the town. Mandatory air, arms and diplomatic sanctions were imposed by the **UN** against Libya in April 1992 when the Libyan authorities refused to extradite to the UK or the USA two Libyans (Abdelbaset Ali Mohamed al-Megrahi and Al-Amin Khalifa Fhimah) accused of organizing the bombing of the airliner. In November 1993 the UN approved a stricter package of sanctions against Libya, but stopped short of banning the sale of Libyan oil exports. Despite the imposition of the new sanctions, doubts were widely expressed over the attachment of sole blame to Libya. Some reports proclaimed the involvement of Iran and radical Palestinian factions in the bombing.

LONDON CENTRAL MOSQUE

The UK's main mosque, also known as the Regent's Park mosque. Completed at a site near Regent's Park in London in 1977, it is adjacent to the Islamic Cultural Centre which was inaugurated by King **George VI** in 1944. The mosque, which was founded with the intention of serving the needs of UK Muslims as well as the international Muslim community based in London, is run by a trusteeship of ambassadors of all Muslim countries known as the Central Mosque Trust.

LONDON CLUB

The informal grouping of commercial external creditors from developed countries. The London Club meets frequently to discuss commercial debts outstanding to its members from developing countries which are experiencing severe repayment problems. Its role has been to arrange consolidation and **debt rescheduling** as appropriate in such cases. The corresponding grouping of official creditors is the **Paris Club**.

LONDON DUMPING CONVENTION

The Convention on the Prevention of Marine Pollution by Dumping of Wastes and Other Matter, adopted at a conference in London in December 1972 and in force since 30 August 1975. The convention aims to control the discharging of hazardous waste into the world's oceans from ships and aircraft. Among the substances considered most damaging are mercury, cadmium, plastics, oils, and materials produced for chemical and **biological warfare**. In November 1993 parties to the convention agreed a definitive ban on the dumping of nuclear waste at sea, replacing the moratorium in force since 1983.

LONDON ERUV

A Jewish religious enclave. The establishment of the first such area in the UK was approved in September 1994. Designated for the north London borough of Barnet over an expanse of six square miles covering the neighbourhoods of Golders Green, Hampstead and Hendon, the project aroused fierce local opposition. It was originally refused planning permission when it emerged that part of the boundary would comprise 85 poles connected by wires. The eruv was first proposed in November 1993 by the Jewish United Synagogue and was vigorously supported by the Chief Rabbi, Jonathan **Sacks**. A symbolic enclosure derived from Jewish laws, the purpose of the eruv is to allow Orthodox Jews, especially the disabled and mothers of young children, to attend synagogue or visit their families within a zone where Jewish Sabbath rules, including a ban on driving or pushing prams, could legitimately be relaxed.

LONDON OLYMPICS

The first postwar Olympic Games, held in London in 1948. The London Games (known as the Austerity Games) were the 14th modern Olympiad and the first to be held since the infamous Berlin Games in 1936. Invitations were sent to all countries except Germany and Japan, and some 6,000 competitors from 54 countries took part.

LONDON STOCK EXCHANGE

The **UK** securities market. The London Stock Exchange, located in the **City**, was created in 1973 by the merger of a number of hitherto independent exchanges in London, provincial cities and the Republic of Ireland. It meets the needs of government, industry and investors by providing facilities for raising capital and a central market place for securities trading. Members buy and sell shares on behalf of the public as well as institutions such as insurance companies and pension funds. During 1986 the Exchange went through a period of widespread change, admitting corporate capital for the first time and enacting a series of organizational reforms known as the **Big Bang**.

LONDON TRANSPORT

Established under the London Passenger Transport Act of 1933, which brought together a wide range of public and private transport undertakings, such as underground and surface railways, buses and coaches, and the then existing trams and trolleybuses operating in greater London and its surrounding areas. With millions of journeys per year taken on its buses and underground trains (the tube), LT provided a vital service to the capital. In the early 1980s, when LT was controlled by the **GLC** under the leadership of Ken **Livingstone**, fares were slashed in a successful effort to encourage more people to abandon theirs cars in favour of public transport. However, this move was opposed for ideological reasons by the **Conservative** central government, and in 1984 London Transport's assets and businesses were transferred to London Regional Transport (LRT) under the London Regional Transport Act of that year. In line with the trend towards the increasing **privatization** of public utilities in the 1980s and the **deregulation** of the bus companies in 1986, LRT had by December 1994 sold all 10 subsidiary companies of London Buses, itself an LRT subsidiary.

LONDONDERRY *see* DERRY

LONG KESH *see* MAZE PRISON

LONRHO

The international trading and investment group with widespread interests, including many in Africa (where its operations originated in Rhodesia). The group has long had a high profile and in 1973, amid an internal struggle for control of the company, the **Conservative Prime Minister** Edward **Heath** described that affair as representing the 'unpleasant and unacceptable face of capitalism'. Lonrho, under chief executive Roland 'Tiny' Rowland, was subsequently involved in a lengthy battle with the **Fayed** family over control of the House of Fraser group of stores and in particular of Harrods. In 1994 a new round of boardroom battles led to the ousting of Rowland.

LONSDALE, GORDON

A Soviet intelligence agent. Lonsdale, ostensibly Canadian but almost certainly Russian-born, was a figure in the Portland spy ring which had supplied information to the Soviet Union from the Underwater Weapons Establishment. In January 1961 he was arrested in the UK, along with Peter and Helen Kroger, following information received from a Soviet defector and in March received a long prison sentence. He served three years before being exchanged for Greville Wynne, who had acted as a courier to Oleg **Penkovsky**.

LOONY LEFT

The phrase which achieved wide currency in the early 1980s, particularly in the tabloid press, to describe hard-left activists. The high-spending, **Labour**-controlled **GLC**, Liverpool city council and the London borough of Lambeth, some of whose leaders were linked to the Trotskyite **Militant Tendency**, were accused of wasting ratepayers' money on ideological projects and of an early form of **political correctness** in being preoccupied with minority issues such as gay rights. Other parties dubbed 'loony left' included the **Socialist Workers' Party**.

LORD ADVOCATE'S DEPARTMENT

Responsible for administering the legal system in **Scotland**. The Department drafts Scottish legislation, provides legal advice to other departments on Scottish questions and assists the law officers of Scotland in their duties.

LORD CHAMBERLAIN

The officer dealing with ceremonial matters and functions of the **Royal Family**. The Lord Chamberlain's Office is a department of the Queen's Household and is based at **Buckingham Palace**. The post has been held since 1984 by the Earl of Airlie.

LORD CHANCELLOR'S DEPARTMENT

The department responsible for promoting general reforms in the civil law and administering the courts in **England** and **Wales**. The Lord Chancellor (a post currently held by Lord Mackay of Clashfern) is a government minister dealing with the procedure of the civil courts and the administration of the Court of Appeal, the High Court, the Crown Courts and county courts. He or she also holds ministerial responsibility for the locally run magistrates' courts. The Lord Chancellor is responsible for advising the Crown on the appointment of judges and is himself responsible for the appointment of other members of the judiciary. He is also responsible for the administration of **legal aid** schemes.

LORD CHIEF JUSTICE

The president of the criminal division of the **Court of Appeal** and of the **Queen's Bench** division of the **High Court** in **England** and **Wales**. The holder of the post is second to the **Lord Chancellor** in the judicial hierarchy. Since 1992 the post has been filled by Lord Taylor of Gosforth.

LORD LIEUTENANT

The permanent local representative of the Crown in a county. The title was created in the sixteenth century, and originally carried many responsibilities. The position is now mainly ceremonial, although as head of the county's commission of the peace the holder does make recommendations for the appointment of magistrates.

LORD PRESIDENT OF THE COUNCIL

The Cabinet minister responsible for running the **Privy Council** Office and fulfilling the duties of **Leader of the House**. In that capacity he or she plans and supervises the government's legislative programme in the **House of Commons**, upholds the rights and privileges of the House as a whole, and moves motions about the procedure of the House.

LORD PRIVY SEAL

The Cabinet minister who often acts as **Leader** of the **House of Lords**. The minister is responsible for the progress of government business in the House and for ensuring that the House runs smoothly and efficiently in the interests of all its members. The Lord Privy Seal works from the **Privy Council** Office.

LORD'S DAY OBSERVANCE SOCIETY

A long-established campaign group opposed to commercial and frivolous activity on Sundays. The Society seeks to protect the traditional character of British Sundays on religious grounds and was active in the unsuccessful campaign to prevent **Sunday trading**.

LORDS-IN-WAITING

Members of the royal household attached to the **Lord Chamberlain's** Office. The holders of the office – all peers – advise the sovereign and perform ceremonial functions. They are government **whips** in the **House of Lords**. The female equivalent is Baroness-in-Waiting.

LOUVRE ACCORD

An agreement designed to reduce monetary and economic instability, reached on 21 February 1987 in Paris by finance ministers and central bank governors of Canada, France, West Germany, Japan, the **UK** and the USA. The meeting was held amidst some turmoil in the exchange markets. The participants undertook to intensify their efforts to co-ordinate economic policy, so as to promote more balanced economic growth and to reduce existing imbalances. The countries running big surpluses on their balance of payments undertook to strengthen domestic demand and to reduce external surpluses while maintaining price stability. Countries with balance-of-payments deficits undertook, conversely, to encourage steady, low-inflation growth while reducing their domestic imbalances and external deficits. On exchange rates, the participants expressed their intention of fostering stability around the levels which were then current – a substantial realignment having already taken place since the Plaza Accord of January 1985.

LOYALISTS

The supporters of the closest of links between **Northern Ireland** and the **UK**. It is frequently used to denote the most fervent **unionists** among the Protestant majority population. Some of the more militant groups of loyalists such as the **UDA**, the **UFF** and the **UVF** are banned in Northern Ireland. The 'loyalist' strike of 1974 was instrumental in causing the collapse of the short-lived **power sharing** Northern Ireland assembly and executive. In October 1994 the **Combined Loyalist Military Command** announced that it would 'universally cease all operational hostilities' although it added that the **ceasefire** was 'completely dependent' on the maintenance of the **IRA** ceasefire. The cease-fire was declared in the expectation of loyalist inclusion in multiparty negotiations on the future of Northern Ireland.

LUCAN, LORD

(b. 1934) Richard John Bingham, the seventh Earl of Lucan – an English peer who disappeared in 1974. An unknown assailant entered the home of Lucan's estranged wife on 12 November 1974 and murdered the children's nanny, Sandra Rivett, before attacking Lady Lucan who, convinced that she had been attacked by her husband, staggered into the street suffering from severe head wounds. Lord Lucan, who claimed to have been passing at the time of the attack and to have entered the house and driven off the mystery intruder, disappeared immediately after the incident. He was widely thought to have either commissioned or committed the crime as a bungled attempt to rid himself of his wife, a view confirmed by the jury at Rivett's inquest which named him as the murderer on 19 June 1975. Although since his disappearance there have been regular sightings of Lucan throughout the world, none has been confirmed, and his friends have consistently stated their belief that he committed suicide shortly after the crime.

LUVVIES FOR LABOUR

The disparaging term, used by the left wing and the popular press, for Labour-supporting actors and media personalities who have publicly campaigned on behalf of the **Labour Party**. The 'luvvies' (a slang term for actors) have included film director and actor Sir Richard Attenborough, thriller writer Ken Follett, broadcaster and writer Melvyn Bragg and Oscar-winning actress Glenda Jackson, who was elected in 1992 as Labour MP for the prosperous Hampstead and Highgate constituency in north London. They have also been derided as Hampstead or **champagne socialists** by those who regard their political loyalties as superficial and hypocritical.

LUXEMBOURG COMPROMISE

An agreement among **EC** leaders reached informally in 1966, providing guidelines on the vexed question of whether a member country could veto a decision by the **Council of Ministers**. It became the working practice that unanimity was required, despite the formal rules allowing decisions by **qualified majority voting**, if a member country considered that its vital interests were at stake.

LYNMOUTH FLOODS

A disastrous freak flood which devastated northern Devon in the early hours of 16 August 1952. Several rivers burst their banks after nine inches of rain had fallen on the previous day submerging an area of some 250 square miles. The affected area included the resort town of Lynmouth, where 36 people died and many thousands were left homeless. Within six months, the **East Coast floods** were to produce a considerably higher death toll.

LYNSKEY TRIBUNAL

The tribunal established in 1948 by Clement **Attlee** under Mr Justice Lynskey to investigate allegations at the **Board of Trade** that ministers and government officials had been taking bribes. John Belcher, a junior minister, resigned after admitting receiving small gifts from Sidney Stanley, a confidence trickster who had sought to influence several public figures. During Lynskey's public proceedings it was disclosed that prominent ministers, including Hugh **Dalton**, had had contact with Stanley, although there had been no impropriety on their part.

M1 AIR CRASH

An accident in which a Boeing 737-400 airliner crashed into an embankment of the M1 motorway near Kegworth, Leicestershire, on 8 January 1989. Of the 126 passengers and crew on board the airliner, 44 were killed immediately, and a further three died later in hospital. The crash happened as the aircraft, en route from Heathrow to Belfast, was attempting to make an emergency landing at East Midlands Airport having reported a fire in its starboard engine. However, initial examinations of the wreckage found evidence of a fire in the port engine, leading to the widespread view that the aircraft's crew had caused the crash by closing down the wrong engine. An inquest returned verdicts of accidental death on 22 May 1990. A report by the Accident Investigation Branch of the Department of Transport, published on 18 October 1990, blamed the crash principally on pilot error, and made more than 30 recommendations for the improvement of air safety.

MAASTRICHT

Shorthand for the development of the European Union (**EU**), in the furious debate between Europhiles and **Eurosceptics** in **UK** politics in the 1990s. Maastricht, in the southern Netherlands, is where the 12 EU member states met in December 1991 for the summit which concluded the Treaty on European Union. They returned on 7 February 1992 for the formal signing. After a long process of ratification by member states, what is commonly called the Maastricht Treaty came into force in November 1993. A review conference, scheduled for 1996, will again direct the spotlight on both the principles and the practice of UK participation in the EU. Maastricht, which incorporated two central agreements on **European Political Union** and on **EMU**, also committed the member states to implement two 'intergovernmental pillars' of co-operation, outside the Community's decision-making machinery, covering the development of common foreign and security policy, and co-operation on judicial and home affairs.

McALISKEY, BERNADETTE *see* DEVLIN, BERNADETTE

McCARTHY, JOHN

The British **hostage** held in Lebanon from 1986–91 by pro-Iranian militants. McCarthy, a journalist, was kidnapped in Beirut in April 1986 by members of the Islamic *Jihad*, a faction of the radical pro-Iranian group *Hezbollah* ('the Party of God'). He was released on 8 August 1991, carrying a message to the **UN** Secretary General, Javier Pérez de Cuéllar, which began negotiations that resulted in the release of other hostages in Lebanon, including Terry **Waite**.

McCarthy and Irish hostage Brian Keenan achieved some celebrity in the UK and both they and the already renowned Waite published best-selling books describing their ordeals.

MACGREGOR REPORT

The report of a Royal Commission on the press, established in 1974 by the **Labour** government. Its interim report in 1976 concentrated on the parlous financial situation of British newspapers, and recommended that the government should give interest relief on loans to enable the industry to modernise. In its final report in 1977, the Commission criticized the level of hostility towards the Labour Party to be found in most newspapers, but proposed no particular solutions, other than that the **TUC** ought to have a paper of its own. The Commission was emphatic that the press ought to be left free to be partisan and unrestrained.

McKENZIE ADVISER

Someone entitled to assist the defence of a defendant in court if that person is defending him/herself or has been refused **legal aid** and cannot afford to pay privately. Although not permitted to speak to the court, a McKenzie adviser may sit with the defendant to take notes and give advice.

MACLEAN, DONALD

(1913–83) The high-flying diplomat who was a Soviet spy. Maclean, son of Sir Donald Maclean who led the National **Liberal Party** up to 1932, was at Cambridge where he was one of the **Apostles** along with his contemporaries Guy

Burgess and Kim **Philby** and his senior Anthony **Blunt**. Maclean was bisexual and serious (though later prone to drunkenness) but, like other 'sleepers', renounced his undergraduate Marxism after his recruitment as a Soviet spy in 1933. Shortly afterwards he entered the Foreign Office (later the **FCO**) and began a conventional diplomatic career. Early in the Second World War he was stationed at the British Embassy in Paris. In 1944 he was appointed First Secretary at the British Embassy in Washington where he was part of a network which leaked the secrets of the development of atomic weaponry to the Soviet Union. Four years later he was recalled to a new post as Head of Chancery at the Cairo Embassy but not before the CIA became aware that secret telegrams between the US President and the British **Prime Minister** had been reaching the Soviets. He was recalled in 1950 in a state of mental collapse probably brought on by his double life and excessive drinking. In 1951, warned by Philby, the so-called **Third Man**, he defected to the Soviet Union with Burgess just days before the Security Services, now certain he was a spy, were to draw him in for questioning.

MACLEOD, IAIN

(1913–70) The influential **Conservative** politician who died prematurely shortly after reaching high office. Macleod was educated at Cambridge and fought with the British Army in France during the Second World War before entering Parliament as Conservative member for Enfield in 1950. He held the Health and Labour portfolios from 1952, before his appointment in 1959 as **Secretary of State** for the Colonies, in which capacity he was responsible for the granting of independence to several African countries. Macleod was appointed Party Chairman in 1961, and moved on to edit the *Spectator* in 1963–5. Widely regarded as a possible future leader of the party who influenced a whole generation of Conservative politicians, Macleod died shortly after his appointment as **Chancellor of the Exchequer** in 1970.

MACMILLAN, HAROLD

(1894–1986) The unflappable **Conservative One Nation Prime Minister** 1957–63. A pre-war Stockton-on-Tees **MP** and wartime diplomat, Macmillan represented Bromley after a 1945 **by-election**. As Housing Minister in Winston **Churchill's** 1951 administration he fulfilled a pledge to build 300,000 homes. After a brief spell at Defence he became Foreign Secretary under Anthony **Eden**, attending the Geneva Conference. As **Chancellor of the Exchequer** from 1955 he retrenched, innovating only with **Premium Bonds**. When the **Suez crisis** precipitated Eden's 1957 resignation, the **magic circle** chose Macmillan as **Prime Minister**, becoming the first in that office to master television.

Instinctively expansionist, he relinquished the entire Treasury team in 1958 in preference to large spending cuts – a move he described as 'a little local difficulty'. The 1959 general election was comfortably won by '**Supermac**' on rising living standards (his earlier phrase '**you've never had it so good**' now gained currency). Abroad, he accelerated decolonization, memorably acknowledging African national consciousness in his 1960 **wind of change** speech, and strengthened the special relationship by courting the newly elected President John F. Kennedy.

In 1961, however, pay restraint was unpopularly introduced in order to curb **inflation**. By-election reverses, notably at Orpington in 1962, led Macmillan to change course, dismissing one-third of his **Cabinet** in 24 hours (the **Night of the Long Knives**). However, Reginald **Maudling's Emergency Budget** brought no immediate relief, and the next year Macmillan, now matched against the nimble Harold **Wilson**, saw Britain's application for **EEC** membership blocked by De Gaulle's famous **non**. The **Profumo** and **Vassall affairs** and other scandals deepened the sense of decline. During the 1963 Conservative conference he fell ill, was advised to retire, and recommended Sir Alec **Douglas-Home** as his successor. An earldom was bestowed on him on his 90th birthday in 1984, and he took the opportunity during his time in the **House of Lords** to pillory the **Thatcher** government, most famously comparing **privatization** to 'selling off the family silver'.

MAD COW DISEASE *see* BSE

MAFF

The Ministry of Agriculture, Fisheries and Food. The department is responsible for government policies on agriculture, horticulture and fisheries in **England** and for policies relating to safety and quality of food in the **UK**, including composition, labelling, additives and new production processes. It is also responsible for the protection of the rural and marine environments and for flood defence, is the licensing authority for veterinary medicines and the registration authority for pesticides, and administers policies on the control of animal, plant and fish diseases. As a member of the **EU Council of (Agriculture) Ministers**, the minister negotiates the **common agricultural policy** and the common fisheries policy.

MAGIC CIRCLE

The term coined in 1963 by Iain **Macleod** to describe the 'inner circle' of the **Conservative Party**. This grouping, comprising certain members of the **Cabinet** (or **Shadow Cabinet**) together with influential 'elder statesmen' held supreme sway over the party. In particular, it was instrumental in securing the 'emergence' of a leader who it was deemed could be relied on to uphold the party's traditions. The machinations of the circle can be best seen in the selection of Sir Alec **Douglas-Home** over R. A. **Butler** after the resignation of Harold **Macmillan**. After the Conservatives' loss of office in 1964 and the adoption of rules for formal leadership contests in 1965, the power of the circle was effectively broken.

MAGISTRATES' COURTS

A network of courts that hear less serious criminal cases, undertake preliminary investigation of cases to decide whether they should be referred to **Crown Court** and make local licensing decisions. **JPs** – part-time unpaid non-lawyers – usually preside, although stipendiary magistrates – full-time salaried lawyers – are appointed to certain busy city courts. Appeals may be made to the Crown Court or on a point of law to the **High Court**.

The courts were at the centre of some controversy in 1992–3 because of a system of means-related **unit fines** introduced under the **Criminal Justice** Act 1991. This resulted in a series of highly publicized cases in which offenders received widely differing fines for similar offences. The fines system was withdrawn in 1993.

MAGNOX

A type of gas-cooled nuclear reactor in which a magnesium alloy called Magnox shields the uranium fuel rods. Magnox reactors were built in the UK as the generation of nuclear plant preceding the **AGR**, and are now at the end of their planned life-span. The problem of the immense and imminent cost of decommissioning them was a key element in the UK government's decision that nuclear power generation could not be privatized along with the rest of the electricity supply industry.

MAGUIRE SEVEN

A family from **Northern Ireland** imprisoned in 1976 after being found guilty of handling explosives used in the 1974 Guildford and Woolwich public house bombings, and whose convictions were then quashed as being 'unsafe and unsatisfactory' by the **Court of Appeal** in June 1991. By that time six of the family had completed their sentences, including terms of 14 years by Anne Maguire and her husband Patrick Maguire. The seventh, Giuseppe Conlon (who had received a sentence of 12 years), died in prison in 1980. The appeal had been granted on the grounds of 'innocent contamination', a ruling which led to controversy because the court declared that one of the defendants might have been so contaminated by using materials previously used by another family member. Those convicted of carrying out the 1974 bombings, the **Guildford Four**, had been released from terms of life imprisonment in October 1989.

MAJOR, JOHN

(b. 1943) **Conservative Prime Minister** since November 1990. Major entered Parliament in 1979. Under Margaret **Thatcher** he soon became a junior Social Security minister, and entered the **Cabinet** as Chief Secretary to the **Treasury** in 1987. In 1989 he served as Foreign Secretary for two months before taking over from Nigel **Lawson** as **Chancellor of the Exchequer**, when his period in office was characterized by counter-inflationary policies and the admission of Britain into the **ERM**. In November 1990 when Thatcher was forced to stand down, Major was her favoured successor and he gained enough support to beat off Michael **Heseltine** and Douglas **Hurd**. As Prime Minister he was able to enjoy immediate success on the foreign front with the successful outcome of the **Gulf War**. However, at home his government's popularity was diminished by the prolonged **recession**. While he managed to unite the party briefly in December 1991 by negotiating two **opt-outs** from the **Maastricht** Treaty, the internal differences over Europe quickly re-emerged. In the **general election** of April 1992 his chances were thought to be poor and his unexpected triumph was widely attributed to his soapbox style and emphasis on the preservation of the **UK**.

Returned to office, his respite was brief. The Conservatives were rocked by personal scandals and a **coal industry** crisis. Throughout the 1992–3 session of Parliament, it faced a **Eurosceptic** rebellion against Maastricht which culminated in a significant defeat. Major secured passage of the Treaty only by tabling a vote of confidence on the last day of the session. The growing impression of disunity now joined a pervasive sense of economic mismanagement. In September 1992 the UK had been forced out of the ERM by speculators. Although **inflation** fell the government was unpopular due to the continuing recession – the longest since the Second World War. Dismissed ministers (including his leadership campaign manager and first Chancellor Norman **Lamont**) voiced criticisms of Major's own performance. The **Downing Street Declaration** of December 1993 was a rare success on which he seemed unable to build. The coincidence of a further rash of financial and sexual scandals in his government with the ill-conceived **back to basics** campaign, successive **by-election** defeats in 1994 as well as catastrophic results in the 1994 **local government** and **European Parliament** elections, and the absence of the **feel-good factor** led to a further steep decline in the government's popularity. This was exacerbated by controversial policies such as **Post Office privatization** and the extension of **VAT** on domestic fuel which either threatened or actually prompted **backbench** revolts. Public concern about the conduct of the **executive** were heightened during the **Scott inquiry**. After a new **Euro-rebel** revolt over the financing of the **EU** in late 1994, Major withdrew the **whip** from the offenders, placing his own government in a technical minority. While the 'whipless ones' returned to the party fold in May 1995, their return appeared to be on their terms rather than his, with no commitments made on future loyalty. This fuelled the debate about his ability to lead the party and after a heated meeting with the **Fresh Start Group**, Major lost patience with the backbiters in the party and in a dramatic move on 22 June resigned the party leadership, calling on his opponents to **'put up or shut up'**. Although faced with the unexpected challenge of John Redwood, who had resigned as **Secretary of State** for Wales, rather than one of the Euro-rebels or a **stalking horse**, Major won the contest in the first round, with 218 votes to Redwood's 89 (there were eight abstentions, 12 spoiled ballot papers and two non-voters). His supporters maintained that he now enjoyed the support of the whole party, but observers remained sceptical.

Major's lack of obvious charm has led to his being characterized as 'grey' and lacking in imagination, while his leadership is criticized for its indecisiveness and lack of coherence. His family background (his father was once a trapeze artist) and his previous career in banking prompted the quip from commentator Edward Pearce that he was the only man who 'ran away from the circus to become an accountant'.

MAJORISM

The political philosophy of John **Major**, **Prime Minister** since 1990. Compared with **Thatcherism**, Major's brand of **Conservatism** has few defining characteristics, reflecting in part his own non-combative and relatively non-ideological style. Unlike Margaret **Thatcher**, Major (like Edward **Heath**) has stressed the virtues of pragmatism and consensus.

MALAYAN EMERGENCY

The state of emergency imposed in British-administered Malaya in 1948–60 in response to an insurrection led by the Communist Party of Malaya. The British counterinsurgency measures included harrying and dispersing any large concentrations of guerrilla forces, and perhaps more significantly a campaign, in the words of British general Sir Gerald Templer, to win 'the hearts and minds of the Malayan people', which included a pledge to grant independence once order had been restored. The British were assisted in their campaign by the general distrust among the country's majority ethnic Malay population of the mainly Chinese guerrillas. The insurrection was effectively broken by 1954. Malaya was granted independence in 1957.

MALVINAS *see* FALKLANDS CONFLICT

MANAGEMENT BUYOUT

The practice of selling a company with shareholdings held by or on behalf of the government, to the management (and in some instances to the employees as well) of the undertaking in question. Management buyouts have been one of the principal means by which the **Conservative** government throughout the 1980s privatized a number of former state-owned assets and public utilities, where a public **flotation** proved impossible or inappropriate. Such **privatization** measures have included the National Freight Corporation in 1982, Swan Hunter shipbuilders in 1986 and, during 1994, a number of the subsidiary companies of London Buses.

MANCHESTER AIR DISASTER

An accident which occurred on 22 August 1985, in which 55 people died when a British Airtours Boeing 737 caught fire while taking off from Manchester airport. The Department of Transport's Air Accident Investigation Branch (AAIB) issued a report on the disaster on 13 March 1989, in which it found that 48 of the deaths resulted from the inhalation of smoke and toxic gases. The report contained 31 recommendations for future safety, including the provision of passenger smoke hoods and cabin water-sprinkling systems.

MANCHESTER OLYMPIC BID

Two unsuccessful attempts by the city of Manchester to host the Olympic Games in 1996 and 2000. The first bid failed when the International Olympic Committee voted in 1991 for the 1996 games to be held in Atlanta, USA. The venue for the 2000 Games was decided in September 1993 in favour of Sydney, Australia. Manchester's second bid was acknowledged to be the more professional, with the personal backing of the **Prime Minister**, John **Major**. The Government had pledged to underwrite a capital works programme of £1,300 million to improve the area's sports facilities.

MANDARINS

The informal description used to denote the most senior civil servants (by analogy to the members of the mandarin class in imperial China and the influence which they exercised). The term, which reflects the belief that they are able to manipulate the working of government, refers specifically to the Heads of the Home **Civil Service** and of the Diplomatic Service, together with the permanent secretaries (or permanent under-secretaries) heading the main government departments and their immediate deputies.

MANIFESTO GROUP

A group formed at the end of 1974 by centre-left **Labour MPs** to counterbalance the strong influence within the Parliamentary Labour Party **(PLP)** of **left-wing** factions such as the **Tribune Group**. Manifesto backed continuing membership of the **EC**, the retention of nuclear weapons and a mixed economy – and therefore opposed further **nationalization**. It was weakened by its association with the defecting founders of the **SDP**. The Solidarity group, which shared Manifesto's values but emphasized the unity of the left, was set up in 1981.

MANPOWER SERVICES COMMISSION

The multipartite Manpower Services Commission controlled employment services from its establishment in 1973 until abolition in 1988. It took control of many financial aspects of the Industrial Training Boards during their progressive abolition in the 1980s. Eventually, however, union reluctance to co-operate in the launch of new training schemes favoured by the government precipitated its demise. Training subsequently became the province of the Training Services Agency and after that of the **TECs**.

MANSION HOUSE SPEECH

The speech delivered each year by the **Chancellor of the Exchequer** at a formal dinner at the Mansion House, the official residence of the Lord Mayor of London, attended by **City** dignitaries. The speech, usually made in June, is the most important declaration of the government's economic policy after the **budget** speech.

MANUFACTURING SECTOR

That part of the economy which produces goods. For statistical purposes the manufacturing sector consists of those industries processing raw materials but not those involved in their extraction. In political exchanges during the 1980s it came to represent wealth-creation and the ability to export, in contradistinction to the **service sector** (and especially the **financial services**) which in the eyes of the **Labour Party**, trade unions and other critics failed to do either in a genuine sense. The decline of manufacturing became synonymous with **de-industrialization**. Some **Conservatives** such as Nigel **Lawson** argued that services would take up the slack of jobs and capacity left by the decline of manufacturing, and welcomed the passing of what they regarded as obsolete 'smokestack' industries. Others, such as Michael **Heseltine**, argued the need for a strong manufacturing sector. In the 1990s, the government has come under pressure to keep down **interest rates** by interest groups like the **CBI** which maintain that borrowing charges imposed by higher rates are inimical to the fortunes of the manufacturing sector.

MAO FLU

Colloquial term for an outbreak of the Hong Kong A2 influenza virus which hit the UK in late 1969. More severe than the 1957 **Asian flu** outbreak, in the week ending 9 January it killed 2,850 people, the highest weekly figure for influenza deaths since 1933.

MARCHING SEASON

In **Northern Ireland**, the period in the summer when marches by the majority **loyalist** organizations such as the Protestant **Orange Order** culminate in the commemoration of the 1690 Battle of the Boyne on 12 July and the 1689 relief of Londonderry on 12 August. They have frequently been marked by clashes between the loyalist and **republican** communities.

MARCHIONESS DISASTER

A collision between the pleasure cruiser *Marchioness* and the sand dredger *Bowbelle* on the river Thames in the early hours of 20 August 1989. The collision took place near Southwark bridge when the 90-ton *Marchioness*, which had been chartered for a private party, was struck from behind by the 1,475-ton *Bowbelle* and quickly sank. A total of 51 of the vessel's passengers and crew died, while more than 80 survived. The seven crew members of the dredger escaped unhurt. The incident led to the adoption of a number of measures to improve river navigation and safety, and to a protracted legal struggle to apportion responsibility for the disaster. Two juries failed to agree a verdict when the master of the *Bowbelle* was tried for failing to keep a sufficient look out. However, on 7 April 1995 an inquest jury returned a verdict of unlawful killing on those who died in the tragedy.

MAREVA INJUNCTION

An injunction restraining a defendant from transferring assets abroad. Such an injunction is granted when a court believes a defendant may try to thwart a claim against him or her by moving assets abroad or hiding them so as to avoid their being seized to pay damages. The injunction takes its name from the 1980 case of *Mareva Comania Naviera SA* v. *International Bulkcarriers SA* when such an order was first issued. Mareva injunctions are sometimes used in conjunction with an **Anton Pillar Order**.

MARGARET, PRINCESS

(b. 1930) The Countess of Snowdon and younger sister of Queen **Elizabeth II**. As a child Princess Margaret Rose figured in the re-establishment of the **Royal Family** after the 1936 abdication crisis. After her sister ascended the throne, however, Princess Margaret gained a reputation for high society living. **Establishment** disapproval prevented her marriage to the divorced Group-Captain Peter Townsend. She later married the photographer Anthony Armstrong-Jones (created Earl of Snowdon) by whom she had two children, but the marriage ended in divorce in 1978, the first of a close member of the Royal Family.

MARKOV AFFAIR

The controversy associated with the assassination in London on 7 September 1978 of Georgi Markov, a Bulgarian journalist employed by the **BBC World Service**. In an apparent accident on a London street, a Bulgarian secret service agent posing as a passer-by allegedly injected with Markov with a poison pellet, using a specially adapted umbrella. For the public, the Markov Affair seemed to typify the subterfuge and skullduggery of **Cold War** undercover operations.

MARSHALL PLAN

A plan to assist the economic recovery of post-war Europe, proposed by US Secretary of State George Marshall in 1947. The scheme offered US funding to the **UK** and other European countries if they co-operated with each other in drafting recovery programmes. It was intended to preempt communist influence in Western Europe, and interim aid to France and Italy in late 1947 helped these countries overcome communist-led strikes. Because of opposition to its conditions from the Soviet Union, the Marshall Plan was confined to the 16 countries of Western Europe which met in Paris from July to September 1947 to draft a recovery programme, and which then formed the Organization for European Economic Co-operation (OEEC). Between 1948 and 1952 the Marshall Plan was responsible for the provision of aid worth US$17 billion.

MASTER OF THE ROLLS

The president of the civil division of the **Court of Appeal** in **England** and **Wales**. The holder of the post is third in the judicial hierarchy, beneath the **Lord Chancellor** and the **Lord Chief Justice**. The Master of the Rolls, appointed by the Crown on the advice of the **Prime Minister**, is the nominal official guardian of the national records at the **PRO** and is a member of the **Privy Council**.

MATERNITY BENEFIT

The payments that employers are required to make to pregnant workers. There are two types, statutory maternity pay and lower-rate maternity allowance, paid according to the worker's length of service and **national insurance** contribution record. New more generous regulations approved in April 1994 and effective from October 1994 were introduced to implement the **EC** pregnant workers' directive, which specified that a woman on maternity leave should receive no less pay than if she were on sick leave, whatever her length of service in the job. At the same time, the government announced that from September 1994 it would refund only 92 per cent rather than 100 per cent of statutory maternity payments made by larger employers (those paying more than £20,000 in gross NI contributions).

MATRIX CHURCHILL

The UK machine tool company at the centre of the events leading to the **Scott inquiry** into defence-related exports to Iraq. Paul Henderson, Trevor Abrahams and Peter Allen, executives of Matrix Churchill (then Iraqi-owned), were arrested in October 1990 shortly after the Iraqi invasion of Kuwait and charged with illegally exporting machine tools and computer equipment to Iraq. Their trial was halted after a month and all three were acquitted on 9 November 1992, after Alan Clark, Minister of Trade in 1986–9 and Minister of State for Defence Procurement in 1989–92, retracted evidence given to customs investigators, and the judge found that documents suppressed by ministerial **gagging orders** established that the defendants that been acting with the support of the government. It also emerged that Henderson had acted as an **MI6** agent.

MAU MAU

The secret political society in Kenya which developed into a violent anti-colonial rebellion in the early 1950s. The term first appeared in the late 1940s; its exact meaning, and the origins of the movement, remain controversial. Mau Mau was confined almost entirely to the Kikuyu, the dominant ethnic group in Kenya, and its aims were to drive out the European settlers. The clandestine nature and violent methods of the militant movement attracted much attention. A full-scale rebellion broke out in October 1952 with a series of terrible killings, and the colonial authorities in the same month declared a state of emergency. More than 100 leading nationalist figures were arrested, including Jomo Kenyatta, who was sentenced to seven years' imprisonment as a Mau Mau leader in 1954. The colonial government also launched military operations against Mau Mau; reinforcements from neighbouring colonies were brought in and at the height of the rebellion some 10,000 British troops were deployed. Increasingly tough security measures halted most Mau Mau activity and by 1956 the emergency was ended, although isolated incidents were reported until 1959. By the end of the conflict Mau Mau had killed 100 Europeans and 2,000 Africans and had suffered over loses of over 11,500. When Kenya obtained independence in December 1963, Kenyatta was its first President.

MAUDLING, REGINALD

(1917–79) The genial **Conservative Chancellor of the Exchequer** 1962–4. After being Commons spokesman on power, Maudling moved in 1959 to the **Board of Trade** and in 1961 became Colonial Secretary. He was appointed Chancellor in 1962 in the wake of **Prime Minister** Harold **Macmillan's Night of the Long Knives** and his **Emergency Budget** signalled the determination of the government to jump-start the economy. In 1963, many Conservative **MPs** unavailingly wished him to succeed Macmillan but he continued as Chancellor under Sir Alec **Douglas-Home**. His **Treasury** expansionism brought the Conservatives close to victory in 1964, though the trade balance deteriorated. In 1965 Edward **Heath** defeated him in the party's first formal election of the leader, probably because the party wanted someone in the Harold **Wilson** mould. As Deputy thereafter, he gave more time to business interests, but in 1970 went to the **Home Office** where he was preoccupied with **Northern Ireland** and introduced the **Immigration** Act 1971. Tainted by the **Poulson affair**, indeed under police investigation, he resigned in July 1972. Apart from a brief period in the **Shadow Cabinet** under Margaret **Thatcher**, he remained on the **backbenches** until his death in 1979.

MAXWELL, ROBERT

(1923–91) A Czech-born businessman, publisher and larger-than-life media figure, who died in mysterious circumstances off the Canary Islands in November 1991 after having gone missing from his luxury yacht. Coming from a poor Jewish family, Maxwell was evacuated to the **UK** in 1939 and joined the British army. For Maxwell the post-war period was a frenzied activity of business expansion in the publishing industry, centred around his own Pergamon Press. He enjoyed a short career in politics, being **Labour** MP for Buckingham during 1964–70. Maxwell lost control of Pergamon in 1971 after a controversial merger, culminating in a much-quoted Department of Trade and Industry report which concluded that he could not be relied on 'to exercise proper stewardship of a publicly quoted company'. Nonetheless, he regained control of Pergamon in 1974 and 10 years later became the proprietor of **Mirror Group Newspapers**. During 1991 speculation had mounted that Maxwell was in financial difficulties, and only a few days after his death it became clear that he had indulged in huge transfers of money – the **Maxwell millions** – between company pension funds and his own private interests, the latter being clouded by a labyrinth of private companies and trusts, many of which were based in Liechtenstein.

MAXWELL FYFE, SIR DAVID

(1890–1967) Home Secretary and Welsh Affairs Minister in Sir Winston **Churchill**'s **Conservative** government in 1951–54. In 1954 he was appointed **Lord Chancellor**, when he was created a viscount, continuing in that post until 1962, when he was made Earl of Kilmuir.

MAXWELL MILLIONS

A popular term for the scandal surrounding the conduct and death of media magnate Robert **Maxwell** in 1991, and the collapse of companies controlled by him. Maxwell, who had suffered business setbacks in the late 1960s, had recovered to create a vast network of media and financial interests. However, in the course of 1991 rumours began circulating which cast doubt upon the viability of his empire, and in November of that year he fell overboard to his death from his yacht near the Canary Islands. Immediately after his death, facts emerged of massive fraud, involving in particular the use of pension funds under his control to bolster up his private and public companies; two of his sons were subsequently charged with complicity in their father's frauds. One repercussion of the affair was a close review of the whole framework of the law and regulations within which occupational pensions schemes operate in the UK.

MAZE BREAKOUT

A breakout of republican inmates from the **Maze prison** near Belfast in **Northern Ireland**. On 25 September 1983 a total of 38 prisoners, serving lengthy terms, escaped from the prison; one prison officer was stabbed and killed. Half of the prisoners were recaptured within a matter of days, some others were arrested either in Northern Ireland, in Ireland or elsewhere over the succeeding years, and at least three were killed by the security forces, but a number remained at liberty.

MAZE PRISON

The high-security prison built in the early 1970s near Lisburn, in **Northern Ireland**. Originally Long Kesh prison camp, it was used to hold those detained after the introduction of **internment** in August 1971 by the provincial government. From 1976 prisoners were housed along sectarian lines in single-storey **H blocks**, notorious during the late 1970s for the staging of the **dirty protest**, a campaign which culminated in 1981 in the hunger strikes in which 10 prisoners died. This was followed in 1983 by the **Maze breakout**.

MEBYON KERNOW

'Sons of Cornwall' – the Cornish nationalist movement. Originally an organization designed to promote Cornish language and culture, *Mebyon Kernow* became a political party in 1951. It first began campaigning in parliamentary elections in 1974 but has not stood at national level since the 1983 **general election**.

MEN IN GREY SUITS

A term for senior figures in the major political parties, and particularly the **Conservative Party**, who may not hold high office but who wield considerable influence behind the scenes in both party policy and tactics. The men in grey suits are satirized as faceless manipulators, striking deals in **smoke-filled rooms**. They reputedly played a key role in persuading Margaret **Thatcher** to step down as Conservative Party leader and **Prime Minister** in 1990. Although the **Labour Party** organization is theoretically more accountable, senior trade union figures have wielded considerable influence.

MEP

A Member of the European Parliament. There are 87 UK MEPs, of whom 84 are elected (every five years since 1979) in single-member constituencies in **Great Britain** using the **first past the post** system, and three are elected in **Northern Ireland** in a single multi-member constituency using the **single transferable vote** system of proportional representation. Following the June 1994 elections there were 62 **Labour** MEPs, 18 **Conservatives**, two **Liberal Democrats**, two **Scottish Nationalists**, and one each from the (Northern Ireland) **SDLP**, the **DUP** and the **UUP**. MEPs sit with their European colleagues by political grouping in the Parliament (Labour with the Party of European Socialists, Conservatives with the European People's Party, etc.). MEPs, whose salaries and expense accounts are very enviable by UK standards, may also be **MPs** at **Westminster**, although some parties (including Labour) have their own rules against this.

METHODISTS

The members of the Methodist Church, the movement founded in the eighteenth century by John Wesley, a priest of the **Church of England**, and his brother Charles who resolved to conduct their lives 'by zeal and method'. The first Methodist chapel was founded in 1739. Doctrinal emphases included repentance, faith, the assurance of salvation, social concern and the priesthood of all believers. Methodists are also distinguished by the zeal with which they have tended to profess their faith and spread the Gospel. Their evangelical style became the subject of considerable public comment in the 1980s when the fervour with which Margaret **Thatcher** pursued her policies was attributed in part to her Methodist upbringing.

METROPOLITAN DISTRICT COUNCILS

In metropolitan areas of **England** outside Greater London, the locally elected bodies that manage the provision of specified local services. They are also known as metropolitan boroughs. Under the Local Government Act 1972 there are 36 metropolitan district councils in city areas of England outside London (and 32 borough councils and the Corporation of the **City** of London in Greater London).

From 1974–86, there were also six metropolitan county councils – Greater Manchester, Merseyside, South Yorkshire, Tyne and Wear, West Midlands and West Yorkshire – but these were abolished under the Local Government Act 1985 and most of their functions were devolved onto the metropolitan district councils. Metropolitan district councils largely combine the functions performed by **county councils** and **district councils** in non-metropolitan areas.

MI5

The Security Service, responsible for protecting national security. The counterintelligence service was originally established in 1909. In the post-1945 era and until the end of the Cold War, its attention was directed particularly towards the Soviet Union and its allies. In 1992 it was given responsibility for leading the offensive against **IRA** activity on the British mainland (i.e. excluding **Northern Ireland** itself). Counterterrorism activities account for 70 per cent of its work, 25 per cent involves counter-espionage and counter-proliferation activities, and the remaining 5 per cent involves the monitoring of subversive organizations. It is split into two sections, Operations and Administration. MI5 was placed on a statutory basis by the Security Service Act 1989, and the name of its director general was first officially acknowledged in December 1991. Details purporting to describe some of MI5's operations were published in the controversial book **Spycatcher** in 1987.

MI6

The Secret Intelligence Service (SIS). MI6 was originally formed in 1909 (together with the counter-intelligence service which evolved into **MI5**). Its present role is to produce secret intelligence in support of the government's security, defence, foreign and economic policies. The existence of MI6 in peacetime was traditionally not acknowledged by the government, and the name of its chief was officially disclosed only in May 1992. MI6 was put on a statutory footing by the Intelligence Services Act 1994.

MIDDLE ENGLAND

Literally the suburban and rural areas of central England, although more commonly a reference to the silent majority of English middle-class and upper-working-class voters which forms the greater part of the electorate, but whose supposed preoccupations are sometimes neglected by the main political parties. Since the 1970s, Middle England has formed the backbone of **Tory** support in **general elections**. Under the leadership of Tony **Blair**, the **Labour Party** has begun a battle for the hearts and minds of Middle England over the issues of the economy, education and **family values**.

MILITANT

The far-left Trotskyist group, associated with the *Militant Tendency* newspaper, which formed a faction within the **Labour Party** until the late 1980s. Militant activists stirred controversy by allegedly using ruthless tactics to ensure that allies were nominated as prospective parliamentary candidates, sometimes at the expense of incumbent Labour **MPs**. Under the leadership of Neil **Kinnock**, Labour began to expel Militant members in 1983, and by the early 1990s Militant influence had declined.

MILK MARKETING BOARD

An independent body established under the Agricultural Marketing Act 1931 to supervise and control the marketing of milk in **England** and **Wales**. Until it was superseded by the farmers' co-operative **Milk Marque** on 1 November 1994, the MMB controlled the buying and selling of all milk except for the small amount that was sold by farmers directly to consumers. It also provided consultancy and artificial insemination services for breeders and owned Dairy Crest, a subsidiary making dairy products. There was a separate MMB for **Northern Ireland**, set up under the Milk Marketing Scheme (Northern Ireland) Approval Act 1955.

MILK MARQUE

A farmers' co-operative that on 1 November 1994 largely took over the functions of the **Milk Marketing Board** (MMB). The change was part of the deregulation of the milk industry, under which farmers were allowed to sell their milk to the highest bidder rather being required to deal with a central distributor, the MMB. Milk Marque is the largest of a number of non-profit-making farmers' co-operatives established following deregulation. Dairy farmers are free not to join these co-operatives and instead to make independent deals with dairy companies, but most have joined.

MILK SNATCHER

An abusive rhyming epithet for Margaret **Thatcher** dating from the controversial withdrawal of free school milk for eight- to 11-year-olds under the October 1970 **budget**. Although she was essentially implementing the policy of the **Conservative** government, Thatcher, then Education Secretary, was popularly perceived as wholly responsible. The tabloid-inflicted label 'milk snatcher' quickly entered the national vocabulary and first brought her to wide public attention.

MILLTOWN MURDERS

A grenade and gun attack by two **loyalist** terrorists in March 1988 on mourners attending the funeral in Milltown cemetery in Belfast, **Northern Ireland**, of three **IRA** members shot dead in **Gibraltar** earlier that month by British security forces. Three people were killed and some 68 others were injured during the attack. Michael Stone, whose accomplice had escaped, was sentenced to six concurrent terms of life imprisonment in March 1989 after being found guilty of the three Milltown murders and more than 30 other terrorist offences.

MIND

A leading mental health campaigning organization. Mind (the National Association for Mental Health) is long-established and is the principal provider of **care in the community** services to the mentally ill after the **NHS**. In most cases it would rather see people supported in the community than see them in psychiatric hospitals. Mind also combines direct provision with an aggressive programme of awareness-raising over issues raised by mental health.

MINERS' STRIKE

The year-long strike by members of the UK National Union of Mineworkers (**NUM**) in 1984–5. While there had been a history of industrial conflict in the coal mining industry (for instance leading to the imposition of the **three-day week** in 1973–4), the situation was intensified in the early years of the 1979 **Conservative** government when it was characterized by the contrasting personalities of the NUM president Arthur **Scargill** and the National Coal Board chair Sir Ian MacGregor who had the full support of the **Prime Minister** Margaret **Thatcher**. At issue were not only pay claims but plans for a drastic reduction in the size of the industry, while accusations were made against Scargill and his supporters as representing the **enemy within**. The strike, which started in March 1984, was not based on a national ballot of NUM members, and this feature continued to be a point of controversy and led to a number of complicated legal cases. The strikers, who enjoyed considerable popular support, came frequently into sharp confrontation with the police, notably through the action of pickets at **Orgreave** coking plant and other sites. Limited mining continued, especially by members of the breakaway **UDM**, and the existence of large stocks of coal at pitheads and power stations reduced the effect of the restriction of coal production. The strike was eventually called off in March 1985. Over the succeeding years the role of coal in the economy was further reduced, with the number of miners falling from around 200,000 to about 10,000 and the number of deep-mined pits from around 170 to under 20. Legislation was passed in 1993–4 for the **privatization** of the coal industry.

Minimum wage

A statutorily set floor for the hourly wage rate. The uncommon absence of a minimum wage in Britain reflects past reliance on **collective bargaining** to set wage rates, and the progressive dismantling of the **Wages Councils** system. From the 1980s, however, concern for the low-paid has stimulated calls for regulation to assist those unable to help themselves due to lack of access to unions or unequal work relations. The call is resisted by the **Conservatives**, the **CBI** and most employers who claim that it will introduce rigidities into the labour market and price the low-paid out of jobs. This view is rejected by the **Labour Party** which has promised to institute a statutory minimum wage level when in government. However, it has been reluctant to specify exactly how a minimum wage would be formulated. One formulation, favoured by several unions, is half median manual earnings which in mid-1995 would result in a minimum wage of around £4.10.

Organizations like the Low Pay Unit estimated in March 1995 that one million people were paid under £2.50 an hour with one-third of these earning less than £1.50 an hour.

Minister of state

A government minister, who may occasionally be of **Cabinet** rank, but who is normally second in charge in a department. The Minister of State holds specific responsibilities within the department and deputises for the chief minister and Cabinet member – the Secretary of State. Some larger departments, including the Foreign and Commonwealth Office (**FCO**) and the **Home Office**, have more than one minister of state.

Miras

Mortgage interest relief at source, a UK government scheme that allows home-buyers to claim tax relief on the mortgage interest payments they make. It is restricted to the first £30,000 of the loan. It is often the subject of controversy when tax rates are discussed: opponents suggest that this concession unfairly benefits relatively prosperous homeowners and that the money conceded to the tax relief could be better spent on more needy groups.

Mirror Group Newspapers

The group of newspapers owned by the late Robert **Maxwell**, including the *Daily Mirror*, *Sunday Mirror*, *Sunday People* and *Sporting Life*, and (in **Scotland**) the *Daily Record* and *Sunday Mail*. Mirror Group Newspapers (MGN) had in July 1984 been bought from Reed International by Maxwell's Pergamon Press. After his death in November 1991, the sale of 54.8 per cent of MGN shares was completed in September 1993. The shares had been held by four banks as surety for loans advanced to Maxwell interests. In October 1992 David Montgomery, former editor of the *News of the World* and *Today* newspapers, was appointed chief executive of MGN.

Mixed economy

The term used to describe the presence of a large public sector in a predominantly market economy. Britain had a mixed economy after the **nationalization** measures of the **Attlee** government had established public ownership in the utilities, transport and some sectors of **manufacturing**. For a quarter of a century the existence of this large state-owned zone was not politically controversial. From the 1970s, however, the boundaries of the mixed economy were challenged by the left of the **Labour Party** (which wished to extend the public sector) and on the right by Margaret **Thatcher** and her allies in the **Conservative Party** (who wished to reduce the state's involvement). The mixed economy finally came to an end after 1979 when successive Conservative governments achieved an ambitious programme of **privatization**.

MOBILE THEATRE RESERVE

A **UN**-commanded rapid reaction force for deployment in Bosnia-Hercegovina, whose creation was agreed in June 1995 by defence ministers from 15 – principally **NATO** – countries and rapidly approved by the UN **Security Council**. The force was created largely in response to a crisis which erupted in May and June when Bosnian Serb forces seized hundreds of UN personnel, and its object was to provide enhanced protection to troops of the UN Protection Force (**UNPROFOR**). The new force, which became operational in July, comprised around 12,500 personnel organized in two brigades, one of which was the 5,000-strong British 24 Air Mobile Brigade and the other was a French-led multinational brigade which included further British and also Dutch personnel.

MOD

The Ministry of Defence. The ministry was formally established in 1947, although the post of Minister of Defence had been held by the **Prime Minister** since 1940.

MODERNIZERS

Those centre-left **Labour** politicians, closely associated with Tony **Blair** and Gordon Brown and taking inspiration from former leader Neil **Kinnock**. Kinnock backed 'modernization' of the party, or – as Blair put it – taking Labour's traditional values and reapplying them to the modern world. The modernizers, influenced by US communitarian political theorists such as Amitai Etzioni, seek to abandon class-based politics and aim to redefine the party's sense of identity and purpose and convert Labour from its previous position as the party of minorities to **new Labour** – the party of **Middle England**. Their constant themes are community, social justice and equality of opportunity coupled with 'responsible' economic policies. The modernizers' cause attracted considerable opposition from traditionalists in the party who suspect an attempt to transform the party into a new **SDP**.

MOLE

A term used to describe an individual who penetrates an organization in order to acquire sensitive information. It is most often applied to infiltrators into the security services who feed back classified information to their home country. By extension, it is also used to describe employees of government and similar bodies who 'whistle blow' by leaking information, generally to the media, in order to expose what they see as illegal or unethical conduct in those organizations.

MOLYNEAUX, JAMES

(b. 1920) The leader of the (Official) Ulster Unionist Party (**UUP**) since 1979. He was elected **MP** for Antrim South in 1970 and for Lagan Valley in 1983. Molyneaux is widely portrayed by the media as dour and uninspiring, although his **unionist** beliefs and convictions on the future of **Northern Ireland** have long been shared, on the surface at least, by successive **UK Conservative** governments. He firmly believes that the political status of the province cannot and should not be changed without the consent of a majority of the population in the North. Molyneaux welcomed the **IRA ceasefire** declaration of August 1994, but has continued to remain suspicious of **republican** long-term intentions and of the detail of any joint British-Irish document on future political arrangements for Northern Ireland. A consistent supporter of the Conservative government in the UK parliament, the UUP has been particularly courted by the Conservative Party since it won only a narrow majority in the 1992 **general election**. Molyneaux survived a leadership challenge from a UUP 'young turk' in early 1995.

MONDAY CLUB

A right-wing grouping of the **Conservative Party**, formed in 1960. Established in reaction to Harold **Macmillan's wind of change** speech in Cape Town, the Club was characterized by support for the South African regime, and subsequently the Rhodesian **UDI** regime, by advocacy of voluntary repatriation of black **Commonwealth** immigrants, and by opposition to anti-apartheid activities such as sporting boycotts. It had a revival in 1968 at the time of tension over increased Commonwealth immigration and Enoch Powell's **rivers of blood** speech. It has numbered several Conservative **MPs** among its membership.

MONETARISM

The branch of economics which argues that control of the money supply is the key to ensuring a stable economy. The theory of monetarism was formulated by **Friedmanite** economists as a challenge to standard **Keynesian** theories, which had failed to explain the emergence of sustained high **inflation** and **unemployment** in the stagflation of the 1970s. Monetarism was arguably first adopted by the **Labour** government of James **Callaghan**, which in 1976 introduced a package of cuts in public expenditure in order to win an **IMF** loan to support the pound following the **sterling crisis**. Monetarism was a key component of the economic policies associated with the **New Right** in the 1980s.

MONOPOLIES AND MERGERS COMMISSION

An independent body whose function is to investigate intended or actual monopolies and mergers deemed to be operating against the public interest. Established in 1948, it consists of industrialists, academics and trade unionists, supported by a staff of **civil service** economists and accountants. With its powers defined within the terms of the Monopolies and Mergers Act of 1965, and subsequently within the Fair Trading Act of 1973, the Commission has legal powers of enforcement and investigates whether a monopoly or merger (defined in respect of market share) is against the public interest. Cases are referred to the Commission by the **Secretary of State** for Trade and Industry. Within the atmosphere of **deregulation** since the 1980s, the criteria by which such references are made have become less strictly defined while the number of cases qualifying for investigation has dropped.

MONSTER RAVING LOONY PARTY

The political party founded by Screaming Lord Sutch in the early 1960s, which has put up candidates (most often Sutch himself) at **by-elections**, in prominent seats in **general elections** and selected local council elections since 1963 when Sutch stood at the Stratford-on-Avon by-election. An anti-**establishment** party which prides itself on its idiosyncratic manifesto, curiously many of its original pledges (such as lowering the voting age to 18, liberation of the pub licensing laws, granting licences for **commercial radio**, the abolition of the **11-plus** exam) have been taken up by the mainstream parties and implemented. The party has thus moved into increasingly eccentric territory: calling for joggers to generate electricity and for the **butter mountain** to be used to lubricate artificial ski slopes. Despite its outlandish approach, the party has had some electoral success. Its deputy leader Alan Hope has been a local councillor since 1986, its chief **whip** Stuart Hughes polled more than the **Labour** candidate in Devon county elections in 1989, while in 1995 Sutch came within 410 votes of beating the **Conservative** candidate in the Islwyn by-election.

In May 1995 it emerged that a failed property deal had left Sutch facing bankruptcy. However, it was hoped that a financial rescue package put together by the bookmaker William Hill would ensure that the party would continue to fight elections.

MONSTROUS CARBUNCLE

The phrase coined by Prince **Charles** in 1984 to describe plans for a new modernist edifice in central London. The phrase gained wider currency among the many opponents of modern architecture to describe actual or planned buildings. Charles derided the plans, which referred to modernist architect Richard Rogers's design for an extension to the National Gallery in Trafalgar Square as like 'a monstrous carbuncle on the face of a well-loved friend'. Charles berated property developers for their lack of respect for Britain's architectural heritage and their degradation of the built environment. He called for a return to traditional architectural types and low-rise, small-scale and mixed-use developments.

MOORGATE TUBE DISASTER

The worst ever accident on the London Underground. On 28 February 1975 a crowded early morning tube train failed to stop in Moorgate station and accelerated into a dead-end tunnel. The train crashed into a wall, killing the driver and 34 passengers. The first three of the train's six carriages were badly telescoped, and rescuers had to spend all day struggling to free survivors from the wreckage.

MOORS MURDERS

A brutal series of murders of young people that caused a public outcry in 1965–6. Some of the victims, whose total number is not known, were buried in the Pennine moors near Manchester. Ian Brady and his girlfriend Myra Hindley were charged in October 1965 with the murder of a 10-year-old girl, Lesley-Ann Downey. It subsequently emerged that they had abused and tortured the girl, taken nude pictures of her and made a sound recording of her cries for help. Brady was sentenced in April 1966 to three concurrent life prison sentences for the murder of Downey, a boy of 12 and a young man of 17. Hindley received two concurrent life sentences. Both subsequently admitted more killings, and another body was found on the moors in July 1987. Since the 1980s Hindley has said that she has reformed and is no longer a danger to the public, but despite a high-profile campaign for her release – supported by Lord Longford, the prison reformer – she has remained in custody.

MORNING STAR

The daily newspaper of the **Democratic Left**, formerly the Communist Party of Great Britain **(CPGB)**. The Party had founded the *Daily Worker* in 1930; it was relaunched in 1966 as the *Morning Star*, in the hope of broadening the appeal of communism. The paper became more hard-line than the party, however, and with the collapse of the Soviet bloc in 1991 lost a large part of its guaranteed overseas market. It continues to exist, but with a declining circulation.

MORRISON, HERBERT

(1888–1965) The **Labour** Deputy **Prime Minister** in 1945–51 and Foreign Secretary in 1951. The son of a policeman, Morrison had a firm grounding in **local government** having served as a member (1922–45) and leader (1934–40) of the London County Council (**LCC**). He served in Ramsey Macdonald's second Labour **Cabinet** (1929–31), Winston **Churchill**'s War Cabinet and Clement **Attlee's** first and second Labour Cabinets. In 1936 Attlee had defeated Morrison in elections for the Labour party leadership. The defeat lost him for ever the chance of becoming Prime Minister, although he went on to play a vital behind-the-scenes role acting as the liaison between government, the **PLP** and the National Executive. He was made a **life peer** in 1959.

MOSS SIDE

An **inner city** area of Manchester. It was the scene of rioting in 1981, one of a wave of similar riots that broke out in **Brixton** (south London), Handsworth (Birmingham) and **Toxteth** (Liverpool). In 1986 Moss Side was one of eight inner city areas (including **Notting Hill** in London, **St Paul's** in Bristol and Handsworth) targeted for a government programme designed to improve local employment opportunities, attract private sector investment and focus on the difficulties of young people from **ethnic minorities**. The visible street trade in illegal drugs and related violence in the area provoked public concern in the mid-1990s.

MOTOR INDUSTRY

The UK motor vehicle manufacturing concerns. At one time a source of great national pride, it has more recently become the subject of controversy following the well-publicized difficulties of the UK's leading truck manufacturer **Leyland Daf** in 1993 and the sale by **British Aerospace** (BAe) of its 80 per cent shareholding in Rover Group to the German BMW company, finalized in March 1994.

UK government shareholding in Rover Group (formerly **British Leyland**) was sold to BAe in a deal finalized on 14 July 1988. BAe suffered increasingly severe financial difficulties and under the terms of the sale to BMW, the German firm assumed almost £1 billion of Rover's debts as well as paying £800 million for the 80 per cent stake. It subsequently also acquired the other 20 per cent of Rover Group from the Japanese motor manufacturer Honda.

MOUNTBATTEN, EARL

(1900–79) The last Viceroy of India. Lord Louis Mountbatten, of royal blood, served in the Royal Navy in the First World War as a destroyer commander; in the Second World War he become Chief of Combined Operations in 1942–3 and Supreme Allied Commander, South-East Asia, in 1943–5. In 1947 he was appointed the last Viceroy of India and then its first Governor-General (when he was also created Earl Mountbatten of Burma), delicately easing the sub-continent through the last stages of British rule to independence in 1947. Mountbatten resumed his military career in 1952, becoming First Sea Lord in 1955 and Chief of Defence Staff in 1959. In retirement he was known to be the confidant and mentor of his nephew Prince **Charles**. Mountbatten was murdered in August 1979 when his boat was blown up by the **IRA** off Mullaghmore, County Sligo, in the Irish Republic.

MP

Member of Parliament. An MP is elected for the duration of a Parliament to act as a representative of all those who live in his or her **constituency**. Paid a salary and secretarial expenses from the public purse, they are expected to serve local interests, their political party and the nation. There are currently 651 MPs, although following approval of the 1995 **Boundary Commissions** review this number will rise to 659. British subjects and citizens of the Irish Republic are entitled to stand as an MP provided they are 21 or over and are not disqualified through belonging to any of the following groups: undischarged bankrupts; clergy; peers; members of the judiciary, the armed forces, the police force, the Civil Service and some local government offices. Technically, MPs may not resign mid-term, and must formally apply for an office of profit under the Crown, such as that of steward or bailiff of the three **Chiltern Hundreds** or the Manor of Northstead.

MPS' PAY

Increases in **MPs'** pay were dealt with in the immediate postwar years by **select committee** inquiries or government announcements. The Government accepted a select committee recommendation in 1981 that a review body should consider MPs' pay in the fourth year of each Parliament. From the beginning of 1988, MPs' pay was linked to that of the senior principal grade of the **civil service**, so that it is now reviewed by the Senior Salaries Review Body. The **House of Commons** voted to freeze MPs' pay for a year in 1992 in line with the Government's public-sector pay policy. MPs started being paid in 1911, when they received £400 a year. They were paid £1,000 a year in 1946; in 1995 MPs' pay was £33,176.

MSF

The white-collar Manufacturing, Science and Finance Union (MSF) is the 1980s product of a merger of the draughtsmen's union TASS and the scientific and technical union ASTMS. Around 50 per cent of members are in a wide range of manufacturing occupations, and the remainder are professional staff in universities, sales, financial services and the **NHS**. The union negotiates with 8,000 companies annually. It now eschews the militancy which characterized TASS under its communist leader Ken Gill and ASTMS under the flamboyant Clive Jenkins, and in 1994–5 consulted the membership on moving to a sector-based or federal structure.

MULTI-SPEED EUROPE

A defensive **Conservative** formula devised to answer charges that Britain is in the 'slow lane' to **EU convergence**. A multi-speed Europe would allow some EU member states, such as France, Germany and the Benelux countries, to move rapidly to a single European currency and closer co-operation over defence and foreign policy without waiting for unanimity. Each individual country would follow its own convergence programme.

MUNICH AIR CRASH *see* BUSBY BABES

MURDOCH, RUPERT

(b. 1931) The Australian-born media figure and chief executive of **News International**, who began in the family newspaper business in 1952 and who has since built up a worldwide newspaper and communications empire. Murdoch applied a simple but enormously successful formula to the selling of papers. By ensuring that they emphasized scandal, gossip and sport he was able to expand throughout Australia. He then moved on to the UK, first buying two **tabloid** newspapers – the *News of the World* in 1969 and the **Sun** in 1970, raising the sales of the latter to the 4,000,000 mark. In 1981 he acquired the Times Newspaper Group, thereby entering the **broadsheet** market. Production of the titles was in 1986 moved to east London, precipitating the **Wapping dispute** and transforming the British printing industry. Murdoch, now a US citizen, has interests in Australia, Hong Kong, Europe and the USA, and until the death of Robert **Maxwell** in November 1990, vied with the latter for the title of the world's biggest newspaper magnate.

MUSLIM INSTITUTE

A Muslim research organization. It was founded in 1973 by Kalim **Siddiqui**, its current director, and gained widespread publicity in 1989 for its role in mobilizing British Muslim support in favour of the death sentence imposed by the late Ayatollah Khomeini on the Indian born British author Salman Rushdie for his book *The* **Satanic Verses**. It is a registered charity, with annual donations from across the Muslim world estimated at between £200,000 and £300,000. Its main publication is *Crescent International*.

MUSLIM PARLIAMENT

A nominally representative Muslim assembly. It was launched in London on 14 July 1990 by Kalim **Siddiqui**, and formally inaugurated at Kensington Town Hall, London, on 4 January 1992. Its bicameral structure provides for up to 700 members, the majority of whom remain to be elected by local Muslim associations. Although it formally acknowledges the supremacy of British law as enacted by Parliament, it is committed to a more energetic defense and promotion of Muslim interests along the lines of the **Board of Deputies of British Jews**. Unlike the Board, however, it has failed so far to win official recognition as a representative body.

MYXOMATOSIS

An infectious and usually fatal disease of rabbits and hares, naturally occurring in some South American rabbits and deliberately spread among wild rabbits in the UK, Western Europe and Australia in the 1950s to reduce their fast-increasing populations. The number of wild rabbits was drastically reduced at the time, but has grown back over subsequent decades.

NADIR, ASIL

The controversial chairman and chief executive of Polly Peck International. In 1993 Nadir, a Turkish Cypriot, dramatically absconded from Britain to the self-declared Turkish Republic of Northern Cyprus to avoid trial for theft and false accounting. He was fleeing the attentions of the Serious Fraud Office whom he subsequently claimed had improperly handled his case. The **Conservative Party** was later embarrassed by disclosures that Nadir had donated £440,000 to its funds.

NAFF *see* FREEDOM ASSOCIATION

NALGO

The National Association of Local Government Officers. NALGO was not certified as a trade union until 1920, and only gradually assumed conventional character, growing by absorption and the extension of friendly society activities. After the Second World War it organized staff in the **nationalized** industries, established a position in the Whitley Council, the negotiating body for **NHS** workers other than doctors and nurses, and conducted national negotiations. Only in 1961 did it take the right to strike under rule, mounting its first official strike in 1970. Thereafter it was increasingly militant, growing in influence and size through campaigns against public expenditure. NALGO had joined the **TUC** in 1964, but in 1982 the membership rejected **Labour Party** affiliation. Six years later a political fund was established to facilitate general non-partisan agitation only. From 1988 NALGO sought a merger with **NUPE**, and in 1993 co-founded **Unison**, a move backed by three-quarters of the membership.

NAME

An investor in **Lloyd's of London** insurance market. Names invest according to the principle of unlimited liability. There are some 20,000 Names grouped into around 400 syndicates of varying sizes. Members of industry, commerce and the professions are strongly represented, while some investors work at Lloyd's for brokerage firms or underwriting agencies. Lloyd's was traditionally a source of high profits but these turned into heavy losses during the late 1980s, leading to financial ruin for many Names. Extensive legal action was taken against Lloyd's by groups of Names, who alleged that they had been placed in loss-making syndicates by those investors who worked in the market.

NANNY STATE

The pejorative term employed to denote what is perceived as over-involvement of government (especially central government) in the day-to-day decisions of individuals and industry. Those using the phrase are normally on the right of the political spectrum, and regard the excessive powers of government as undermining self-reliance and as stifling enterprise and initiative.

NASSAU CONFERENCE

The December 1962 meeting in the capital of the Bahamas between **Prime Minister** Harold **Macmillan** and US President John F. Kennedy, where Kennedy offered the **Polaris** missile as the means of modernizing the UK's nuclear weapons capability. The meeting had been made necessary when the US side decided to scrap development of the **Skybolt** air-to-ground missile unless the UK was willing to meet significant development costs.

NATIONAL ASSISTANCE ACT 1948

Social welfare legislation. This Act swept away the last vestiges of the Poor Law, under which a safety net for those ineligible for other state benefits was provided by local bodies. Under the terms of the Act, a new National Assistance Board, with regional and local offices, was created, providing means-tested relief.

NATIONAL ASSOCIATION FOR FREEDOM

see FREEDOM ASSOCIATION

NATIONAL AUDIT OFFICE

The agency established in 1983 which examines the efficiency of government. The Comptroller and Auditor General considers the accounts of government departments, certain public bodies and international organizations. He or she then reports to Parliament detailing how value for money is being achieved in public spending.

NATIONAL BLOOD AUTHORITY

The government body which runs the blood transfusion service in **England**, with the Scottish National Blood Transfusion Service and the Common Health Services Agency in **Wales** providing similar services in their respective areas. Around 2,500,000 donations are given each year by voluntary unpaid donors. Since October 1985 each donation has been tested for the **HIV** virus, although by this time a number of people (mainly haemophiliacs) had contracted the virus. There are now strict limitations on potential donors, and people who fall into at-risk categories (including homosexuals, bisexuals, intravenous drug-users, prostitutes and people recently arrived from certain countries) and their sexual partners are asked not to give blood.

In 1994 proposals to rationalize the service were published, envisaging a dramatic reduction in the number of donor centres and staff. The changes were condemned by many who regarded cost-cutting rather than efficiency as the driving force behind them. These fears heightened in mid-1995, when a number of people became seriously ill after receiving contaminated blood, and up to 7,000 pints of blood (about 20 per cent of total blood stocks) stored in potentially faulty bags had to be destroyed. The NBA was criticized for introducing the Australian-made Tuta bags which did not carry a certificate guaranteeing that they complied with NBA standards; the purchase of the bags had reportedly resulted in savings of £700,000.

NATIONAL CHURCH

A legally established creed. It is commonly applied to the **Church of England** whose establishment under the Second Act of Supremacy of 1559 and subsequently the Settlement Act of 1701 confirmed the inter-relationship between Church and State. Its most symbolic manifestation is the acknowledgement of the headship of the monarch, who in turn is crowned by the **Archbishop of Canterbury**. The **Church of Scotland**, which was established by an Act of Parliament in 1921, is also a national church though free from state interference.

NATIONAL COUNCIL FOR CIVIL LIBERTIES *see* LIBERTY

NATIONAL COUNCIL FOR VOCATIONAL QUALIFICATIONS *see* NCVQ

NATIONAL CURRICULUM

A curriculum to be followed by all state school pupils between the ages of five and 16, as prescribed by the **Education Reform Act 1988**, and to be phased in in primary and secondary schools from autumn 1989. There were three core subjects – mathematics, English and science – and seven other foundation subjects – history, geography, technology, music, art, physical education and (for pupils at secondary school) a modern foreign language. Attainment targets and testing procedures were to be phased in for pupils at the ages of seven, 11 and 14. The Welsh language would continue as a core subject in Welsh-speaking schools and as a foundation subject in other schools in **Wales**.

Teachers objected strongly to the amount of teaching time taken up by the curriculum, the level of compulsory content and the amount of time taking up by testing procedures – tests for 14-year-olds which were to have taken place in May 1994 were severely disrupted. In response, and following the publication of the **Dearing report** in January 1994, Education Minister Gillian Shephard introduced a revised national curriculum in November 1994. The amount of compulsory work was cut by 20 per cent for pupils aged between five and 14, and by 40 per cent in the following two years. The scale of measuring progress was reduced from 10 levels to eight, and history and geography would no longer be compulsory after the age of 14.

NATIONAL DEMOCRATS *see* NATIONAL FRONT

NATIONAL ECONOMIC DEVELOPMENT COUNCIL *see* NEDDY

NATIONAL ENTERPRISE BOARD *see* NEB

NATIONAL FRONT

A fringe nationalist and **racist** party founded in 1967 from small neo-fascist groups, including the League of Empire Loyalists, the British National Party, and the Racial Preservation Society. The NF opposed non-white immigration into **Britain**, and also had strong **anti-Semitic** leanings. It fought national elections during the 1970s and received some 3 per cent of the vote, but was hampered by organized opposition, such as the **Anti-Nazi League**. It fragmented in the 1980s after its leading figure, John Tyndall, left to found a new **BNP**. The party does not provide figures, but it is now believed to have fewer than 1,000 members. In July 1995 the National Front, now led by Ian Anderson, changed its name to the National Democrats in order to appeal to people who 'have been previously put off because of our name'. The name change was agreed after the May 1995 local elections when it put up candidates in just 15 seats who polled an average of less than 4 per cent of the vote. As an experiment an NF candidate stood as a National Democrat in South Staffordshire and won 8 per cent of the vote.

NATIONAL INCOMES COMMISSION

The **Conservative** precursor of the **Prices and Incomes Board**. The National Incomes Commission ('Nicky' – to distinguish it from **'Neddy'**, the National Economic Development Council) was established in 1962 after the collapse of the 'pay-pause' of the previous year and was an early attempt at a voluntary **Incomes Policy**. **Labour** replaced it with the more powerful Prices and Incomes Board in 1965.

NATIONAL INSURANCE

The social security system in which **pensions** and **unemployment**, sickness and

maternity benefits are paid in return for graduated salary-related contributions paid by individuals and their employers. The existing graduated contributions were introduced under the **Social Security** Act 1975. Previously, under the National Insurance Act 1946 effective July 1948, flat-rate contributions were paid and marked by stamps stuck to a card (hence often known as paying a national insurance stamp). Under the 1975 Act the self-employed pay flat-rate contributions and also make a second earnings-related payment. Reforms to the system which took effect in April 1995 reduced the level of contribution for employers while increasing that made by employees.

NATIONAL LOTTERY

The state-backed weekly betting scheme promoted as a means of funding good causes. Established under the National Lottery etc. Act 1993, the lottery was the first government-sponsored gambling scheme to be introduced since **Premium Bonds** in the 1950s. It was launched in spite of fears expressed by the football pools companies concerned about competition, charities fearing a decline in direct public donations, and those opposed on moral grounds. The first televised weekly draw was held in October 1994 following extensive advertising. High participation rates allowed exceptionally large prizes to accumulate. A single prize of over £17,000,000 was won within the first few weeks. Camelot, the private firm controversially selected to run the lottery, takes a proportion of the proceeds and was thought to have recouped £100 million of its initial £125 million outlay in the first 18 weeks. Future profits for the company were estimated at over £2,000,000 per week. Camelot sends 28 per cent of income in equal parts to the five designated 'good causes': the Sports Council, the **Arts Council**, the Charities Board, the National Heritage Memorial Fund and the Millennium Commission which in turn distribute funds. There were complaints in mid-1995 that funds had still to be disbursed. The lottery regulator is **Oflot**.

THE NATIONAL PLAN

A five-year economic development blueprint issued in 1965 by the **Labour** government. The Plan was the key responsibility of the newly established Department of Economic Affairs (DEA) and was meant to express Labour's preference for socialist organization as opposed to **Treasury** laissez-faire. Powerfully advocated by George **Brown**, the Secretary of State for Economic Affairs, it aimed at 3.8 per cent growth annually to 1970. By late 1966, however, it had, in the words of **Prime Minister** Harold **Wilson**, 'been blown off course' by Treasury scepticism, **balance of payments** difficulties and a lack of detailed preparation on the means of achieving its objectives.

NATIONAL RIVERS AUTHORITY

The organization responsible for the monitoring of water quality and the control of pollution, and the management of rivers, water resources, land drainage, flood protection, conservation and recreation, fisheries, and navigation. The NRA was established under the Water Act 1989, which had enabled the **privatization** in November 1989 of the 10 water authorities in **England** and **Wales**.

NATIONAL SERVICE

A system of compulsory conscription of men for the armed forces. National service was introduced in the UK in 1939, and reorganized in 1948 under the National Service Act, which covered all young men of 18 and over (subject to certain exemptions and to provision for conscientious objection). The period of full-time service was increased from 12 to 18 months at the end of 1948, and to 24 months in 1950 (following the outbreak of the Korean War), but by the late 1950s service requirements were being met largely through voluntary engagement, and the last recruits were called up for their two-year period of service in 1960.

NATIONAL TRUST

A registered charity, founded in 1895, to preserve places of historic interest or natural beauty for the benefit of the nation. It is one of the largest landowners in Britain, with more than 200 historic houses, 160 gardens and over 590,000 acres of countryside, most of which are open to the public. Its property is uniquely protected by statute (originally under the National Trust Act 1907), and cannot be sold or compulsorily purchased without special parliamentary procedure. It is not government funded although like many other owners of historic properties it receives substantial maintenance grants from **English Heritage**. By May 1995 it had over two million members.

NATIONAL VOCATIONAL QUALIFICATIONS *see* NCVQ

NATIONALITY

An individual's status in relation to a state as conferred either by birth or naturalization. Traditionally the UK has followed a policy whereby nationality was based on place of birth rather than parenthood (*jus soli* rather than *jus sanguinis*). Indeed, the British **Nationality Act of 1948** granted British nationality not only to those who were British by virtue of their connection to the UK itself but also to those deemed British by virtue of their connection to a British colony. Since then, however, restrictions on the granting of British nationality have progressively been introduced as the country's **immigration** policies have become more restrictive. By the time of the British Nationality Act 1981 adherence to the *jus soli* principle was abandoned. As a result, a child born in the UK after 1 January 1983 is only a British citizen if he or she has a parent who is either a British citizen or who is permanently settled in the UK. The Act defines five categories of British nationality: British citizen, British dependent territories citizen, British overseas citizen, British subject and British protected person. Only someone possessing British **citizenship** has the right of abode in the UK.

NATIONALIZATION

Taking privately owned industries or other activities into public ownership, normally by acquiring their assets (with or without compensation), and usually to create state-owned monopolies. Nationalization is generally undertaken by **left-wing** governments; however, it may sometimes also be carried out by right-wing and essentially nationalistic regimes, especially in respect of foreign-owned undertakings. In the UK the 1945–51 **Labour** governments nationalized large sections of productive industry and of services. Thereafter, nationalization was pursued on a piecemeal basis, usually in an effort to preserve economically ailing enterprises. This policy was reversed after the election in 1979 of the **Conservative** government of Margaret **Thatcher**, which undertook wholesale **privatization**. During the 1980s and early 1990s industries and utilities were transferred to the private sector, often at only a fraction of their true value. The initial popularity of this policy, however, has been undermined by rising consumer prices, inflated salary increases for senior managers and the absence of any real competition in many of the privatized industries.

NATO

The Brussels-based North Atlantic Treaty Organization, formed in April 1949. NATO was the basic Western alliance in the subsequent four decades of the **Cold War**, and the context within which British defence policy was framed. The idea of an Anglo-US **special relationship** in the postwar world was based partly on common views about the importance of NATO.

Reflecting fears of Communist aggression, NATO took as its basic tenet that an armed attack on any member country would be seen as an attack on them all. The Soviet bloc in turn saw NATO as its principal threat. The US nuclear capability was the centrepiece of NATO strategy, although the UK, with its **independent nuclear deterrent**, also contributed a nuclear element to the alliance's integrated planning.

NATO grew from the original 12 members to include Greece and Turkey (1952), Germany (1955) and Spain (1982), but France withdrew in 1966 from NATO military structures. Rooted in the geopolitics of the Cold War, NATO faced an identity crisis in the 1990s following the collapse of communism. Several formerly communist countries began pressing to be allowed to join, and the partnerships for peace programme was introduced in early 1994 in response to this pressure. Almost simultaneously, NATO forces became involved in the first-ever direct military action in NATO's own name, to enforce a UN-backed no-fly zone over Bosnia.

NATURALIZATION

The act of giving a foreigner the status of a natural-born **citizen**, as defined most recently in the 1981 British **Nationality** Act.

NATURE CONSERVANCY COUNCIL (NCC)

The UK government's leading adviser on nature conservation and wildlife protection, which was controversially replaced under the Environmental Protection Act 1990 and the Natural Heritage (**Scotland**) Act 1991 by three country agencies: the NCC for **England** (also known as English Nature), Scottish Natural Heritage and the Countryside Council for **Wales**. As well as advising the government on nature conservation in their areas, the three new bodies designate sites of special scientific interest (**SSSIs**). A joint committee of the three agencies – the Joint Nature Conservation Committee – sets scientific standards and advises on nature conservation issues affecting the whole of the UK.

NCCL *see* LIBERTY

NCVQ

The National Council for Vocations Qualifications, the body established in 1986 charged with reforming and rationalizing vocational qualifications. Since then National Vocational Qualifications (NVQs) have been established in **England, Wales** and **Northern Ireland**. These are job-specific and are based on national standards of competence set by industry and assessed in the workplace. There are five levels of NVQs, each made up of units. Possession of an NVQ is a guarantee that the holder is competent to carry out particular tasks. Although designed mainly for people in employment, they can also be studied for full-time. In **Scotland** the Scottish Vocational Education Council (SCOTVEC) has established parallel Scottish Vocational Qualifications (SVQs).

NEAVE, AIREY

(1916–79) The senior **Conservative** politician and Thatcherite murdered by **INLA** in 1979. Neave was a war hero who successfully escaped from the notorious Colditz castle, served in British intelligence, and was several times decorated for his bravery. He entered Parliament in 1953 as the **MP** for Abingdon and became a prominent **backbencher**. He played a key role in ousting Edward **Heath** as Conservative Party leader in 1975 and backed Margaret **Thatcher** as Heath's successor. Neave became head of Thatcher's private office and **Shadow** Secretary of State for **Northern Ireland**, in which capacity he firmly rejected power-sharing proposals. In March 1979 he was assassinated when a bomb in his car exploded in a car park in the **Palace of Westminster**.

NEB

The National Enterprise Board, created by the **Labour Government** under the Industry Act of 1975, which acted as a holding company with subsidiaries in **manufacturing**, for the purpose of assisting in economic expansion. Its forerunner was the Industrial Reorganization Corporation, established by Labour in 1966 but then dissolved by the **Conservative** Government of Edward **Heath** in 1971. The NEB was created to establish, develop and maintain any industrial enterprise or carry out the reorganization of an industry. It would extend public ownership into new areas, promote industrial democracy, and hold and manage securities in public ownership. However, with the **election** of the Conservatives in 1979, it soon became clear that the role of the NEB was to be reduced to one of providing temporary assistance in a limited number of cases. The NEB was merged in 1981 with the British Technology Group, which was to concentrate on the translation into commercial products of new research ideas. The Group was sold to the private sector in March 1992.

NEC

The Labour Party's national executive committee. The NEC is the key policy-making and administrative organ of the Labour Party between annual conferences. Its composition, reflecting the nature and history of the party, includes the leader and deputy leader of the party (both directly elected by the entire party under special **OMOV** arrangements), the treasurer (elected by the whole annual conference), one youth member elected at the national youth conference, one member elected by the Black and Asian Socialist Society, and representatives of various divisions (12 elected by trade union delegates, one elected by socialist, co-operative and other organizations, seven nominated by constituency parties and elected by individual members under a system of OMOV, and five women members elected by annual conference as a whole). By 1995 a given proportion of NEC trade union and constituency members must be women.

NEDDY

The National Economic Development Council. NEDDY was formed by the **Conservative** government in 1962 as a tripartite body bringing together representatives of government, employers and employees to examine economic performance, while some 20 'little Neddies' examined specific industrial sectors. In 1987 the frequency of meetings of the full council was greatly reduced, and it was announced in June 1992 that NEDDY was itself to be wound up at the end of that year, since the 'era of **corporatism** has long passed'.

NEGATIVE EQUITY

The term used to describe the position of those whose house or property is worth less than the value of the mortgage on the property. The term gained frequency following the slump in the housing market in the early 1990s. Those who bought property in the south of England during the housing boom of late 1988 were the worst affected. In the first quarter of 1995 there were some 1,200,000 householders in the UK with negative equity, of whom 73 per cent had been first-time buyers, with an average equity shortfall of £4,700. At this time, the total value of negative equity was £5.5 billion, well down on the peak of £12 billion at the beginning of 1993. The inability of these people snared in the equity trap to move has had a profound effect on the housing market, with almost an entire generation of house buyers unable to move.

NEIGHBOURHOOD WATCH

A network of crime-prevention schemes introduced in the 1980s whereby householders in a street or area agree to keep a watch on their own neighbourhood. The schemes are designed especially to guard against burglary or other offences to property, but also to ensure that no harm comes to the elderly and vulnerable. Although the schemes have the support of the local **police** forces, they are essentially citizens' organizations. The Police Federation is opposed to the use of volunteer neighbourhood watch patrols to cover housing estates and streets, on the grounds that such an extension might result in incidents of vigilantism. By mid-1995 there were more than 130,000 neighbourhood watch schemes nationwide, covering some five million households.

THE NET *see* INTERNET

NEUBERGER, RABBI JULIA

(b. 1950) Arguably the most prominent female rabbi in Britain. Best known for her spirited campaign in favour of Liberal Judaism, she has also been actively involved in promoting women's issues and has played a distinguished role in the improvement of the **NHS**. She trained as a liberal rabbi at the Leo Baeck College in London. From 1983–5 she was chair of the Rabbinic Conference Union of Liberal and Progressive Synagogues where her radical stance on matters of Jewish personal law incurred the wrath of her more orthodox and conservative co-religionists. In the 1990s, especially in her capacity as a Trustee of the Runnymede Trust, she has won respect for her commitment to greater understanding between different religious faiths in the UK.

NEW AGE TRAVELLERS

The term used to describe (generally young) people choosing not to settle in permanent housing but to travel the country from one makeshift campsite to another. Their lifestyle attracted wide publicity in the early 1990s. In newspaper and television interviews some members of the group stressed the philosophical basis of their behaviour and their links with more widely respected alternative movements – such as environmentalists – while others said that they travelled because they were **homeless** and trespassed on private land because there were too few council campsites. But the media coverage also focused on irate landowners, communities who claimed that the travellers had left a mess behind when they moved on, and clashes between the travellers and the **police** at new age festivals and **raves**.

Political pressure grew for the law to be changed, particularly from **backbench Conservative MPs**. In discussion the new age travellers were often improperly lumped together with traditional gypsies, a distinct group with a well-established travelling lifestyle. The **Criminal Justice** and Public Order Act 1994 gave the police new powers to impound vehicles and order trespassers to leave private land, and removed the duty on councils under the Caravan Sites Act 1968 to provide campsites for **gypsies**.

NEW COMMONWEALTH

A term applied to former British colonies in Asia, Africa and the Caribbean which became members of the **Commonwealth** on independence in the years following the Second World War. It was used to distinguish these countries from the 'old Commonwealth' or **White Commonwealth** representing the 'white' dominions (Australia, Canada, New Zealand and South Africa), whose sovereignty was confirmed under the 1931 Statute of Westminster.

NEW IRELAND FORUM

An organization created by the Irish government in May 1983 to facilitate discussions between the **Social Democratic and Labour Party** of **Northern Ireland** and the three main Irish parties – *Fianna Fáil*, *Fine Gael* and the Labour Party – on future political developments. After a year of deliberation, the Forum published in May 1984 a report which outlined three potential frameworks for the island of Ireland: a unitary Irish state, a federal relationship between the North and South, and joint sovereignty over the province between Ireland and the **UK**. The report was severely criticized by **unionist** politicians in Northern Ireland. Although the British government argued that there was little prospect for agreement on any of the three proposals, it welcomed the recognition of the need for Irish unity to be freely agreed and negotiated by the people of the North and the South.

NEW LABOUR

The designation for the **Labour Party** often repeated in **sound bites** by the **modernizers** in its leadership, and by party **spin doctors**, after the election of Tony **Blair** as party leader in July 1994. Blair argued that the party's basic objectives should remain unchanged, but added that new Labour would 'reapply' them to modern circumstances. Thus **Clause IV** of the party's constitution (which had tied the party to **nationalization**) was replaced and party members were awarded increased voting power at the expense of the trade unions. Other policy changes, particularly on education and the economy, followed. The phrase 'new Labour' was intended to underline the change in the party, to trumpet Labour's return to the political mainstream as a party of the majority, and to overcome the electorate's suspicion that the party's left wing remained pre-eminent.

NEW REALISM

A term used to describe the reappraised aims of trade unions after the **Labour Party's** 1983 **general election** defeat. The phrase 'new realism' was used by industrial correspondents to label the dominant approach at the 1983 **TUC** gathering. It implied refurbishing the unions' appeal to a changing workforce, the eschewing of the strike weapon, and pluralistic political links, and was most strongly urged by unions on the right of the labour movement. The new realism was shaken by the prohibition of unions at **GCHQ** and by the **miners' strike**, but survived in the changing role of the TUC and the unwillingness of the Labour Party to commit itself to repealing **trade union legislation**.

NEW RIGHT

The group of Western European and US theorists who, in the 1970s and 1980s, propounded a political agenda founded on laissez faire and **monetarist** economic policies and a reduced role for the state in both economic and social life. The New Right's emphasis on individualism sets it apart from traditional conservative paternalism (the 'old right'), but part of its political dynamism stems from its advocacy of moral conservatism and its criticism of the permissive society of the 1960s as the root of contemporary social ills. Unlike the New Left two decades earlier, the New Right attained political power, with the election of Margaret **Thatcher's** government in 1979 and of Ronald Reagan, who became US President in 1980.

NEW TOWNS

A group of five existing and 28 new towns throughout the **UK**, designated as such by the New Town Act of 1946 and subsequent legislation. They were created to relieve housing problems (for example in the greater London area), to serve the specific needs of the area (Corby), to help check the problem of rural depopulation, to meet overspill needs (Runcorn near Liverpool, Telford near Birmingham and Cumbernauld near Glasgow), or to serve as centres of special economic development (Antrim and **Derry**). The housing and community facilities of the new town development corporations were eventually transferred to the relevant local authorities, with their industrial and commercial property taken over by the Commission for the New Towns (for England and Wales only), under the New Towns Act of 1959. Under the New Towns and Urban Development Corporations Act of 1985, the Commission embarked on a disposals programme, which also involved the dissolution of the corporations (completed by 1992), in line with the **Conservative** government's policy of transferring assets from the public to the private sector. The Commission itself is scheduled for winding-up in March 1998.

NEWS INTERNATIONAL

An international media group, whose chief executive is Rupert **Murdoch** and which owns *The Times*, the *Sunday Times*, the **Sun**, the *News of the World* and *Today* newspapers, together with a multitude of worldwide interests. The group acquired notoriety in the UK during 1986–7, when it transferred production of its titles from **Fleet Street** to its new plant in east London, sparking off the violent **Wapping dispute** and at the same time initiating a revolution in British newspaper printing. News International has throughout the 1980s and 1990s established a firm grip on the communications industry worldwide, securing interests in radio and television as well as in publishing, and expanding the **BSkyB satellite television** company, following the merger of **Sky TV** and British Satellite Broadcasting in November 1990.

NF *see* NATIONAL FRONT

NGO

A non-governmental organization – a body (national or international) which is outside the framework of any national government. NGOs may frequently be involved in international relations not only through their own activities but also especially through full or observer status with specific international organizations (especially those concerned with developmental, social, humanitarian and cultural matters, such as **Amnesty International** and **Oxfam**).

NHS

The National Health Service, the **UK's** state health care system. The architect of the service was Aneurin **Bevan**, health minister in the **Labour government** of Clement **Attlee**, drawing from the **Beveridge Report** of 1942 on the **welfare state**. The 1946 National Health Service Act aimed to institute universally available, free or inexpensive health care, funded by **national insurance** payments and other taxation. The NHS was officially inaugurated on 5 July 1948.

The health service is a key political issue in the 1990s, with both Labour and **Conservative** claiming to be guardians of the NHS. In the 1980s the **Thatcher** government imposed strict curbs on the escalating cost of health care. A series of Conservative reforms in the 1980s and 1990s, including the establishment of **NHS trusts** and an internal market, was designed to improve the efficiency of the NHS but provoked criticism that the quality of aspects of NHS treatment had declined and that the government was **privatizing** the health service by stealth. Figures disclosed in May 1995 revealed that since 1990 (when the market reforms were initiated) 304 hospitals had been closed – one in eight of hospitals open before 1990. The figures, compiled by the **House of Commons** library, showed that just 21 hospitals had been opened in the same period.

NHS TRUSTS

The controversial 1991 reform of state hospital services designed to create an internal market by freeing **NHS** hospitals from the regional health bureaucracy and converting them into self-governing trusts. NHS trusts would then be expected to compete to offer services at the lowest possible price to district health authorities and some general practitioners ('fundholders' responsible for their own budgets under a linked reform). NHS trusts were designed to give hospitals a stake in improved efficiency, and to this end the trusts employed a new generation of managers, many from the private sector. The reform was criticized as adding unnecessary layers of bureaucracy, with wide public belief that hospital managers were being recruited at the expense of medical staff. In January 1995 it was revealed that it had cost £120,300,000 simply to set up trusts as self-governing units. Moreover, the trusts have not, by some measures, lived up to government expectations. In 1992–3, 72 of the 156 trusts missed at least one in three of the financial targets which they are obliged to meet, while an independent study revealed in January 1995 that 22 English trusts had made losses in 1994 with more than 50 running a cumulative deficit.

NI *see* NATIONAL INSURANCE

NIGHT OF THE LONG KNIVES

A term (echoing the Nazi purge of 1934) used to describe the sacking of seven **Cabinet** ministers, including **Chancellor of the Exchequer** Selwyn **Lloyd** by **Prime Minister** Harold **Macmillan** on 12 July 1962.

NIMBY

Acronym for 'Not In My Back Yard'. The expression was coined in 1986 to describe individuals and groups who are notionally in favour of progress and new construction, but vociferously oppose projects they think will have a directly adverse effect on their quality of life. Initially it referred to supporters of nuclear power or of the storage of nuclear waste, whose attitude suddenly changed in the face of a proposal to site such facilities locally.

NIMROD

A British-built defence early warning system cancelled controversially in 1986 and precipitating a row about defence procurement. The system, comprising Nimrod aircraft and a newly developed radar system, had been adopted by the government in 1977, when it was scheduled to be ready for operational use in 1984. The row erupted when the government announced its decision to cancel the contract with the General Electric Company (GEC) for Nimrod aircraft, because of escalating costs, and to purchase instead the Airborne Warning and Control Systems (**AWACS**) produced by the Boeing company in the USA. Nimrod had cost almost £1 billion since its inception and by 1986 had still failed to meet the minimum initial operating capability requirements of the RAF. The government estimated that the remaining costs of the project could be used to buy a minimum of six of the Boeing aircraft. The **Cabinet** immediately announced that an inquiry team was being appointed to investigate the future management of all large-scale defence procurement projects.

THE NINE

A synonym for the European Community (**EC**) from the time when the UK became a member (along with Denmark and Ireland) in the 1973 enlargement. The nine became the **twelve** in the 1980s, with the accession of Greece in 1981 and Spain and Portugal in 1986.

1922 COMMITTEE

A body consisting of all **Conservative backbench MPs** in the **House of Commons**. The name commemorates the decision in 1922, forced on the party leadership by Conservative backbenchers, to bring down Lloyd George's coalition government. Elections to the 1922 Committee's 12-member executive, held at the beginning of a parliamentary session, serve as a barometer for the mood of the party. Chaired in recent years by deceptively bluff Yorkshireman Sir Marcus Fox, the 1922 Committee prides itself on being able to keep its finger on the pulse of the party and as such plays a pivotal political role. The chairman of the 1922 Committee organizes the party leadership election.

1968

A year of political turmoil and unrest throughout Western Europe and the USA, when young **left-wing** radicals were inspired to challenge the old order but, ultimately, failed to overturn it. In the UK protests were limited to street demonstrations and 'sit-ins' on university and college campuses against routine targets, including capitalist exploitation of the Third World and US military adventure in Indo-China. In retrospect, Britain's rather parochial 1968 does not stand comparison with the May *évènements* in Paris or the Prague Spring in Czechoslovakia.

1984

A date with a unique resonance, evoking the nightmare **totalitarian** future. It was George Orwell, writing in 1948 at the onset of the **Cold War**, who gave the year 1984 this special significance by using it as the title of his most famous political novel. *1984*, first published in 1949, depicted a world dominated by three superpowers in a state of permanent conflict. Each superpower strongly resembled its rivals, being run strictly according to a state ideology which borrowed from the extreme right and left, and which aimed at the total subordination of the individual to the state. Social conformity was ensured by a comprehensive system of surveillance. The state was dominated by a party elite, supported by a propaganda machine that promoted a cult of personality surrounding the state's leader, **Big Brother**. A counterpart to this bleak vision was Aldous Huxley's ironically titled view of a future *Brave New World*, where social control was effected through the distribution of synthetic pleasure.

1992

The year in which the **EU** completed the preparation of the **single market,** as defined in the **Single European Act**. Publicity was generated in member states to alert businesses in particular to the challenges and opportunities that this created. The key date was 31 December 1992, and the publicity campaign in the UK fastened on 1992, whereas in France the slogans all referred to 1993, the year when the single market would come into being.

92 GROUP

A group of **Conservative MPs** on the party's right. One of the aims of the 92 Group is to maximize members' representation on committees. The group achieved a notable success in securing a majority on the executive of the **1922 Committee** elected after the 1992 **general election**. Although the members of the group have a wide range of views, they have been noted in the 1990s for their tendency to **Euroscepticism** and for championing **Thatcherite** economic policies such as continued **privatization.** The group grew out of a **Tory** dining club founded in the 1960s and takes it name from 92 Cheyne Walk, Chelsea, one of the places where the group dined.

NO-FLY ZONE

A prohibited area for fixed-wing aircraft or helicopter flight. In August 1992 France, Russia, the UK and the USA proclaimed a 'no-fly zone' over southern Iraq (south of the 32nd parallel), aimed at protecting the Shia Marsh Arab population from Iraqi forces. In the first incident of its kind, a US aircraft in December 1992 shot down an Iraqi fighter plane within this zone. In October 1992 the **UN** imposed a no-fly zone in Bosnian airspace as part of efforts to contain the conflict there.

NO TURNING BACK GROUP

A right-wing grouping of **Conservatives** in the late 1980s which supported the philosophy of the then **Prime Minister**, Margaret **Thatcher**. Shortly before her removal from office in November 1990, the group issued a document setting out its ideas for a radical **general election** manifesto to include further **privatization** and **deregulation**, tax incentives and reliefs, a reshaping of health insurance and pension benefits, and the introduction of education vouchers. Thereafter it has continued to stress the achievements of **Thatcherism** and to present itself as the keeper of the Conservative Party's true conscience. It brings together powerful **Eurosceptics** in the party, including Michael **Portillo**, Peter Lilley and Michael Forsyth. It also includes John Redwood, who stood against **Prime Minister** John **Major** for the party leadership in June–July 1995.

NOLAN COMMITTEE

The **standing committee** established by **Prime Minister** John **Major** in October 1994 to examine standards of conduct in public life in the wake of a string of scandals and allegations of government '**sleaze**', including the **cash for questions** controversy. The committee is chaired by Lord Nolan and includes academic Anthony King and former **Labour** and **Conservative Cabinet** Ministers. Its first report, published in May 1995, recommended independent scrutiny of **MPs'** conduct and of appointments to **quangos**; a complete ban on MPs working for lobbying companies; full disclosure of MPs' earnings and contracts for parliamentary services; codes of conduct for MPs and ministers; protection for whistle-blowers in the **civil service**, quangos or **NHS**; and that former ministers be required to seek permission before taking posts in the private sector within two years of leaving office. These recommendations were welcomed by Labour, which demanded their implementation in full. However, the Conservative government was reluctant to comply and controversially established a second committee comprising serving MPs to consider the recommendations. This **select committee** later split along party lines over the implementation of key proposals of the Nolan Committee, with the majority Conservatives and the **Liberal Democrats** arguing that more time was needed to consider banning MPs from working for lobbying firms and forcing them to disclose earnings from parliamentary consultancy work. Labour accused the two parties of stalling. The select committee did, however, agree on another main Nolan proposal – the establishment of a Parliamentary Commissioner for Standards to monitor the Register of Members' Interests and investigate complaints.

NON

The one-word summary of the comments made at a press conference by French President Charles de Gaulle on 14 January 1963, which effectively vetoed the UK's first application for membership of the **EC** at the end of one and a half years of negotiation. 'England', he argued, had a psychological attitude to the EC which was at odds with that of the **inner six** original members; moreover, the UK would have great difficulty in abandoning its existing and very different approach to agriculture and international trade. Most fundamentally, the entry of the UK, which simultaneously claimed a **special relationship** with the USA, would 'completely change' the EC into 'a colossal Atlantic Community under American domination'. De Gaulle's stance once again proved an obstacle when a second UK approach was launched in 1967, holding up substantive negotiations which were not completed until 1971 (i.e. after de Gaulle's retirement), leading to UK **accession** in January 1973.

NORAID

Irish Northern Aid – a controversial fund-raising organization based in the USA, which was created in 1969 for the express purpose of providing financial relief for those families deprived of a main wage-earner as a result of the British presence in Northern Ireland; it has channelled millions of dollars to **Sinn Feín** and the **IRA** since the early 1970s. While the organization insists that the funds are for non-military use, this is not the view taken by the British government, which has criticized NORAID for what it describes as its 'naive' support for 'terrorists'.

NORTH SEA OIL

The petroleum reserves found in the North Sea in the late 1960s and exploited from the early 1970s. The term is generally used to cover also natural gas deposits, whose discovery predate those of oil by some years. Oil and gas have been brought ashore by tanker or piped to land in the UK, Norway, the Netherlands and Germany. Development was given a sharp impetus by the temporary Arab oil sanctions of 1973 and the subsequent longer-term oil price increases instigated by **OPEC**, although North Sea oil prices are in line with those charged on the international markets both by OPEC and by other producers. In the main, countries with North Sea oil and gas have failed to use the revenue for major investment purposes. The reserves are still far from exhausted. However, the prospect that they will eventually dry up leaves a question-mark against the maintenance of current levels of prosperity, in the absence of the development of new indigenous energy sources.

NORTHERN IRELAND

The north-eastern part of the island of Ireland forming a component of the **United Kingdom** of **Great Britain** and Northern Ireland. In the seventeenth century the first major settlement of Ireland by British Protestants, particularly Presbyterians from **Scotland**, occurred, mainly in the nine counties of the province of Ulster, and Protestant supremacy was gradually established. Under the Government of Ireland Act 1920 a legislature was set up for **six counties** forming part of Ulster, while in 1922 the Irish Free State was established covering the other **26 counties** which now comprise the Republic of Ireland. About 58 per cent of the current population of Northern Ireland is Protestant and largely **unionist**, The remaining 42 per cent is **Roman Catholic** and includes a republican element spearheaded on the political front by **Sinn Féin** and in the military field by the **IRA**. The advent of the **Troubles** in 1969 has been the latest manifestation of the sectarian tension which has characterized Ireland's history since the seventeenth century, and since 1969 there has been a state of civil unrest in Northern Ireland which has caused the loss of more than 3,000 lives. Not only has there been violence between members of the two communities, but also attacks particularly by the IRA and other republican organizations against the Royal Ulster Constabulary (**RUC**) and the British Army presence. Ireland's constitutional claim to the whole island has proved a stumbling block in discussions over the future of the province. However, in December 1993 as part of the **Downing Street Declaration** the Irish government expressed its willingness to amend the constitution to end its territorial claims to the north. The ceasefires declared by the IRA and the **loyalist** paramilitary organizations in 1994 and the **joint framework document** put forward by the Irish and UK governments in February 1995 have advanced the prospects for peace in Northern Ireland.

NORTHERN IRELAND ASSEMBLY

An organization twice created in the recent past in **Northern Ireland** as part of a failed power-sharing equation. The first attempt arose out of the Northern Ireland Constitution Act of 1973. An Assembly was elected in June of that year but a strike in May 1974 forced a return to **direct rule** from the **UK** Parliament. The Northern Ireland Act of 1982 created a second Assembly as part of a wider scheme of **rolling devolution**. Although all of the main constitutional parties won seats in the Assembly **elections** in October 1982, the **SDLP** and **Sinn Féin** withdrew, while most of the 26 **OUP** representatives withdrew in November 1983 after **republican** gunmen killed three men in a gospel hall in Armagh.

NORTHERN IRELAND (EMERGENCY PROVISIONS) ACT 1991

The Act which provides for the bringing together in one piece of legislation all those anti-terrorism provisions which apply uniquely to **Northern Ireland**. It was introduced in the **House of Commons** in November 1990, receiving the **royal assent** in June 1991. The Act includes relevant parts of the **Prevention of Terrorism (Temporary Provisions) Acts**. It further includes powers enabling the police, in situations where terrorist offenses or their preparation were suspected, to examine documents and other recorded data, to take fingerprints without consent and to confiscate assets of those benefitting from terrorist-related activities. A new offence was created of bypassing closed border crossing points. The unlawful collection of information likely to be useful to terrorists, as well as training in the use of firearms and explosives, and the wearing of masks, hoods or other articles to conceal identity were also made illegal.

NORTHERN IRELAND OFFICE

The office, or department, of the Secretary of State for **Northern Ireland**. It was created in 1972 under the Northern Ireland (Temporary Provisions) Act (**TPA**), which effected the transfer to the **UK** Parliament of the executive and legislative authority of the Northern Ireland Parliament (**Stormont**), following the collapse of the latter that year. The province then came under the **direct rule** of the British government. The Northern Ireland Office has primary responsibility for issues of security, the administration of justice and prisons, and for any matters relating to political developments within the province. It also administers UK government policies on economic, social and industrial affairs, for example, in the field of economic development, education, agriculture and the environment. The current Secretary of State for Northern Ireland is Sir Patrick Mayhew.

NORTH-SOUTH DIVIDE

The phenomenon whereby, with deindustrialization and the decline of traditional manufacturing, the southern part of England has prospered through the establishment of new and more high-technology industry while living standards in the north and in other parts of the UK have been relatively static or have declined. This divide was accentuated by the growth in overall unemployment during the 1980s, although in the early 1990s the continued 'shake-out' in employment has begun to affect also the more favoured south-east. The use of the term is a domestic extension of the North-South split in world terms between the developed 'north' and the developing 'south'.

NO-STRIKE AGREEMENTS

Union undertakings not to take industrial action. No-strike agreements were pioneered by the **EETPU** during the **new realism** of the 1980s. They were usually only one component in a package embracing flexibility at the workplace, single status, participation and so-called 'pendulum' arbitration (resolving a dispute by an award to the company or the union but not through a compromise). Opponents of the EETPU accused it of using the no-strike undertaking as a means of obtaining members through **single-union agreements**, and suggested that the right to strike was an essential freedom. The EETPU replied that such agreements were not legally binding but were adhered to because of the advantages they brought.

A no-strike policy was also operated by the Royal College of Nursing (RCN). However, the controversial 1995 nurses' pay award, which moved towards locally negotiated pay, prompted a reassessment of this policy; in June 1995 the RCN voted to abandon the policy.

NOTTING HILL CARNIVAL

A two-day celebration of Caribbean culture held on the last weekend in August in the Notting Hill area of west London. The carnival is Europe's largest street festival, attracting 1,500,000 people from around the world. The first carnival was held in 1965 when large numbers of **immigrants** from the Caribbean had arrived in, and were still coming to, Britain. Despite the large crowds, in recent years the carnival has been a notably peaceful event in stark contrast to the **Notting Hill riots** that took place in 1976 when predominantly black youths clashed with **police**.

NOTTING HILL RIOTS

A series of violent racial clashes between white people and black immigrants in Notting Hill Gate, west London, in September 1958. Police suggested they might have been started by right-wing political groups such as the White Defence League (a forerunner of the **British Movement**) The fighting began after a gang of white youths gathered to taunt the black occupants of a house in the area and were repulsed with a petrol bomb and milk bottles. It continued through the night. The police came under violent attack and a black couple were chased down the street by a mob of whites. **Race relations** were strained in the area, in which a large number of black, largely Caribbean immigrants had settled.

NUCLEAR-FREE ZONE

A zone where there are either no nuclear weapons (more precisely termed a nuclear weapons-free zone), or no nuclear installations of any kind. Originally used of nuclear-free regions of the world, the term was adopted in the UK in the 1970s and 1980s by local communities and local authorities such as the **GLC** as a way of showing support for campaigns against **nuclear power**. Their declarations, frequently accompanied by road signs at the council boundary proclaiming 'you are now entering a nuclear-free zone', lacked the legal force to prevent, for example, the transit of nuclear waste material.

NUCLEAR POWER *see* ENERGY SOURCES

NUCLEAR REPROCESSING

The extraction of unused uranium and newly formed plutonium from spent uranium fuel rods in nuclear reactors. One third of the fuel rods in a reactor must be replaced annually. The spent fuel rods are transported to nuclear reprocessing sites where they are dissolved in nitric acid to produce uranium nitrate, plutonium nitrate, and other salts. The uranium and plutonium are then recovered, but in the process highly radioactive wastes are generated. Nuclear reprocessing is highly controversial because of the potential dangers, and the difficulty of disposing of the nuclear wastes safely. Plants such as **Thorp** at **Sellafield** are therefore opposed by environmentalists.

NUCLEAR TEST BAN TREATY

The first specific treaty on nuclear arms control, signed by the Soviet Union, the USA and the UK in Moscow on 5 August 1963 after five years of talks (and a year after the end of the UK's testing programme). It was only ever a partial ban on **nuclear tests**, prohibiting them in the atmosphere, under water and in space, but allowing underground tests provided that they caused no radiation damage outside the testing state's territory. Most countries joined the treaty, but not the other two nuclear weapons states, France and China, although both stopped atmospheric testing eventually (in 1974 and 1980 respectively). Talks on a comprehensive test ban treaty stopped and started over the period from 1974 onwards, with some prospect as of 1995 that a treaty might be concluded by the end of the following year. Meanwhile Russia declared a moratorium in October 1991 and France and the USA followed suit the following year; China continued testing underground; but the UK government opposed a formal moratorium in the absence of a general treaty.

NUCLEAR TESTS

Test explosions of nuclear weapons, of which there have been some 1,300 since 1945. The UK carried out 21 above ground in 1952–58, the first at the Monte Bello Islands 85 miles off the north-west Australian coast on 3 October 1952, thereafter at Emu Plains near **Woomera** in South Australia (1953), at Monte Bello again (1956), at Maralinga in South Australia (1956–7) and at Malden Island and Christmas Island in the central Pacific (the hydrogen bomb tests of 1957–8). The tests were suspended after September 1958 to promote British–US–Soviet negotiations on a test ban. Much later, in 1993, the UK government agreed to pay the costs of the clean-up of Maralinga, and to compensate Aboriginal inhabitants for displacement, while it also faced compensation claims for damage to the health of participating servicemen and, prospectively, Aborigines.

Atmospheric testing was banned under the Partial Test Ban Treaty in 1963 (although France and China were not signatories). A limited programme of some 20 British underground tests was conducted jointly with the USA in Nevada between 1962 and the early 1990s.

NUCLEAR UMBRELLA

Originally a Soviet proposal made at the **UN** in 1963, that both superpowers should retain a limited number of missiles armed with nuclear weapons, until the completion of a three-stage 'programme of general and complete disarmament'. At the UN Disarmament Conference in 1964, the Soviet Union insisted that this nuclear umbrella idea should be the sole basis for discussion. The USA wanted more open terms of reference, and the ensuing deadlock effectively blocked the discussion of any proposals on complete disarmament. The term nuclear umbrella was later used loosely to refer to an overt or implicit defence commitment by a nuclear power to a non-nuclear ally; for example, the USA was represented as providing a nuclear umbrella in Western Europe.

NUM

The National Union of Mineworkers, a militant **left-wing** miners' union. The NUM emerged from the Miners' Federation of **Great Britain** on the eve of the **nationalization** of the **coal industry**. Once the largest **TUC** affiliate, the NUM had shrunk by 1994 to less than 10,000 members following the industry's accelerated contraction and preparations for **privatization**. Its history is punctuated by four large national disputes: that of 1926, which precipitated the General Strike; those of 1972 and 1974 which restored mining as one of best paid manual occupations and expedited the demise of the **Heath** government; and the miners' strike of 1984–5 called by the charismatic but demonized Arthur **Scargill** . Scargill was the first miners' leader for 50 years to combine advocacy of industrial militancy with support for left-wing causes. His handling of the 1984–5 strike, which resulted in the establishment of the breakaway **UDM**, however, was widely criticized within the **Labour Party**. Though unable to prevent the industry's decline in the 1980s, Scargill and the NUM enjoyed a revival in popular support before the **Coal White Paper** of 1993 but this proved ephemeral.

NUPE

The National Union of Public Employees. The steady growth of the NUPE became exponential in the 1960s as the union grew to dominate manual **local government** and **NHS** employment. Forceful general secretaries like Bryn Roberts, Alan Fisher and Rodney Bickerstaffe agitated effectively against low pay, and NUPE attracted the women who became the majority of its membership. It was the principal union mounting action during the 1978–9 **winter of discontent**, and for a time coupled this militancy with support for the **Labour** left. After 1983,however, its Deputy General Secretary Tom Sawyer facilitated the efforts of Neil **Kinnock** to reposition the Labour Party (later becoming its general secretary). NUPE was prominent in the 1980s disputes over the pay and conditions of NHS staff and the consequences of **NHS trusts**, and in resisting the **privatization** of local government services. In 1993 its membership voted by more than 10:1 to merge with **NALGO** to form **Unison**.

NUR

The National Union of Railwaymen, the mainstream union of railway operatives. The NUR was an industrial union of all **British Rail** employees, except some drivers and white-collar staff, which mounted frequent effective industrial action. It merged with the National Union of Seamen in 1990 to form the National Union of Rail, Maritime and Transport Workers (RMT) and its members were involved in the 1994 **Railtrack/RMT strike**.

NURSERY VOUCHERS

A controversial government initiative to offer nursery vouchers for four-year-olds. The plan was launched in July 1995 by the newly established Department of Education and Employment. The vouchers, to be launched in pilot areas in 1996, will give parents £1,100 towards the cost of pre-school education, and, if they so choose, parents will be able to 'top-up' their value to buy the education they want. The apparent blurring between state and private funding for education aroused protests from sections of the **Labour Party**, while other critics argued that the scheme would be a bureaucratic irrelevance which would do nothing to create more nursery places and would simply subsidise those who have already opted for private provision.

NURSES' STRIKE

A rare example of nurses' strike action. Widespread local stoppages by **COHSE** and **NUPE** nurses against low pay occurred early in 1988, but were halted by a pay award of 15.3 per cent and the promise of a grading review. Margaret **Thatcher** specifically tied a promise to fully fund the award to the **no-strike** policy of the Royal College of Nursing

(RCN), reaffirmed that March. However, the review outcome contained extensive anomalies and caused disappointment over regradings. The **TUC**-affiliated unions began new strikes later that year, a tactic denounced by the RCN which in December claimed to have recruited 5,000 new members on this policy. The dispute lasted until February 1989 when the government announced a new increase of 6.8 per cent and the restructuring of nurses' pay on regional lines.

The 1995 controversial nurses' pay award, which moved away from nationally negotiated increases, prompted the RCN to reassess its no-strike policy. It voted overwhelmingly in June 1995 to abandon the policy.

NUS

The National Union of Students, formed in 1922 to represent students in higher education. Its leaders negotiate with **universities**, **polytechnics** and the government over issues such as **student grants**, and it acts as a pressure group on a variety of educational and political matters. The government attempted to limit the political activities of student unions, which it claimed had little to do with student life, but was forced to drop the measures from the Education Act 1994, substituting a code of practice governing the operation of student unions.

Former national officers of the NUS, such as Jack Straw and Sue Slipman, have gone on to pursue a political career.

NUT

The National Union of Teachers. The NUT joined the **TUC** in 1970 and is the biggest teachers' union. Facing several sectoral rivals for different grades of teacher, the NUT's distinctiveness lies in the breadth of its membership and its willingness to mount industrial action to resist unwelcome or what it considers harmful change. It was the last teachers' union to be reconciled to **testing** within the **national curriculum**, abandoning an effective boycott of several years' duration only in January 1995. The union is not affiliated to the **Labour Party** but has a political fund which it uses to mount non-partisan campaigns.

NVLA

The National Viewers' and Listeners' Association, an organization whose aim is to reduce the incidence of violent and sexually explicit material on UK television and radio. The NVLA was established in 1965 with Mary Whitehouse as its secretary-general (president from 1980 to 1994). It meticulously monitors programmes and regularly produces statistics in support of its claim that the broadcasting authorities and companies allow unacceptable material to be transmitted, especially before the 9 p.m. 'watershed', when young children are likely to be watching and listening. In part in response to the activities of the NVLA, the government in 1988 set up the Broadcasting Standards Council, which was placed on a statutory basis under the Broadcasting Act 1990.

NVQs

National Vocational Qualifications, established by the National Council for Vocations Qualifications (**NCVQ**).

O MY DARLING CLEMENTINE

The song which the **Secretary of State** for **Northern Ireland**, Peter Brooke, was persuaded to sing in January 1992 on an Irish television late-night chat show, a few hours after seven construction workers had been killed by an **IRA** roadside bomb in **Northern Ireland**. Brooke was castigated as insensitive by furious Northern Ireland politicians who demanded his resignation. Brooke himself apologized and announced his willingness to step down. Although **Prime Minister** John **Major** insisted that he remain in office, Brooke was not reappointed to the Cabinet following the April 1992 **general election**.

OBSCENE PUBLICATIONS ACT 1959

The primary obscenity law in the **UK**. Under it, for the first time, obscenity became a statutory offence if published matter was deemed to have a tendency to 'deprave or corrupt'. Previously it had been an infringement of common law. However, the Act was perceived as a relatively liberal measure since it gave publishers and authors a defence – the common good – which they could present in court to defend works of merit, with the support of expert witnesses. Enacted at a time of concern over works such as Nabokov's *Lolita*, the Act was soon put to the test in the **Lady Chatterley trial** and the **Oz trial**.

ODA

The Overseas Development Administration – the government department responsible for the administration of British development assistance to overseas countries and international agencies in the form of both capital and technical assistance. The ODA draws up and carries out policies to promote growth and alleviate poverty in developing countries. It also negotiates with other countries and international bodies on the terms under which aid and loans are granted and finances research by bodies connected with overseas development. Since 1989 Baroness Chalker of Wallasey has served as Minister for Overseas Development.

OFFER

The Office of Electricity Regulation, responsible for regulating and monitoring the electricity supply industry in **England** and **Wales**. The Office is operated by the Director General of Electricity Supply. It encourages competition in both the generation and supply of electricity, ensures that electricity companies observe the provisions of the licences under which they operate and protects interests of consumers. Created under the Electricity Act 1989, the Office is independent of ministerial control. The post of director-general of the Office is currently held by Stephen Littlechild.

OFFICE OF FAIR TRADING

The principal organization responsible for general consumer protection in the **UK**. The OFT was established under the Fair Trading Act of 1973 and is headed by the Director General of Fair Trading (a post currently held by Sir Bryan Carsberg). The director general collects information on any business activities which are or could be harmful to consumers, which limit or prevent competition and which are against the general public interest. The OFT also publishes information to consumers which outlines their rights, and is responsible for the regulation of the credit industry. It has the power to bring civil action for an injunction to prevent restrictive practices, and can prosecute organizations which repeatedly commit offences in breach of consumer protection law.

OFFICE OF PUBLIC SERVICE AND SCIENCE *see* CABINET OFFICE

OFFICIAL SECRETS ACT 1989

The better-targeted replacement of Official Secrets Act 1911. The infamous 'catch-all' Section 2 of the 1911 Act gave wide powers to government to infringe the personal liberties of state employees. It enjoyed a revival under the **Conservatives** in the 1980s in the cases of Sarah Tisdall (who was imprisoned after a conviction under it), **Zircon** and the **Ponting affair**. Decisions to prosecute (or not) under the Act were increasingly controversial and it was finally reduced to an object of ridicule by the **Spycatcher affair**. The 1989 Act narrowed the definition of official secrets but removed inconsistencies of the kind which had permitted Ponting's acquittal.

(OFFICIAL) ULSTER UNIONIST PARTY *see* UUP

OFGAS

The Office of Gas Supply, responsible for regulating the supply and pricing of gas for domestic tariff consumers. Created under the Gas Act of 1986, it is run by the Director General of Gas Supply. The privatization of British Gas in April 1986 was one of the more prominent transfers to the private sector of public utilities during Margaret **Thatcher's** second term of office, with net proceeds amounting to some £5.5 billion.

OFLOT

The regulator of the **National Lottery**.

OFSTED

The Office for Standards in Education, an independent agency established under the Education (Schools) Act 1992 to inspect schools and colleges in **England**. Its duty is to establish and regulate a system of independent inspections of maintained schools, voluntary schools, special schools, independent schools designated as suitable for children with special needs and **city technology colleges**. OFSTED also publishes an annual report on education. The Office is headed by Her Majesty's Chief Inspector of Schools, a post currently held by Prof. Stewart Sutherland.

OFTEL

The Office of Telecommunications, responsible for the supervision of telecommunications activities in the **UK**. Established under the Telecommunications Act 1984, which enabled the sale of **BT** in one of the **Conservative** Government's largest **privatization** measures, OFTEL operates under a Director General (a post currently held by Don Cruickshank) whose duties include monitoring of anti-competitive practices and having regard for all complaints made in respect of telecommunications equipment.

OFWAT

The Office of Water Services, responsible for supporting the Director General of Water Services in respect of the regulation of the water industry in **England** and **Wales**. The Director General (a post held in 1995 by Ian Byatt) ensures that the 10 privatized water supply companies observe the terms of their appointments or licences and protects consumer interests. Established in September 1989 under the terms of the Water Act of that year, both the Office and the Director General are directly accountable to Parliament.

OLD BAILEY

The building housing, and the popular name for, the Central Criminal Court, London, taking its name from the street in which it stands in the **City**. The first court on the site was built in 1539. The present building was completed in 1905 and opened in 1907. The Central Criminal Court is the **Crown Court** with jurisdiction over Greater London.

OMAN

A post-**Suez** military intervention. British troops suppressed a rebellion against the pro-British Sultan of Oman in 1957, apparently signalling that the capacity for intervention, though limited, had survived the Suez crisis.

OMBUDSMAN

A term of Swedish origin, indicating a commissioner appointed by a parliament, whose role it is to investigate and report on complaints against government and its officials. The post of ombudsman has been created in a number of countries. In the UK the first Parliamentary Commissioner for Administration took up office in 1967; responsibility for investigating and reporting on similar complaints in the National Health Service (**NHS**) was added in 1973, while subsequently separate local government ombudsmen (Commissioners for Local Administration) were set up for **England**, **Wales** and **Scotland**.

OMOV

One-member-one-vote, the controversial package of reforms of the **Labour Party**, passed at its conference in September 1993, which reduced the voting power of the trade unions in three key aspects of party affairs: the nomination of parliamentary candidates was to be made by a poll of constituency party members alone; the **block vote** at the party conference was reformed to give trade unions a reduced, fixed 70 per cent share of the vote; and elections to the party leadership were to be organized on the basis of an electoral college awarding only one-third of the votes to levy-paying union members. The adoption of OMOV was regarded as a victory for the party's then leader, John Smith, and for the party's '**modernizers**'.

'ON YER BIKE'

An abusive exhortation to the unemployed associated with Norman **Tebbit**. While Employment Secretary in the **Thatcher** government in 1981–3, Tebbit condemned unemployed people who were involved in **inner city** riots. Recalling his father's experience of **unemployment** in the Depression of the 1930s he commented 'he didn't riot – he got on his bike and looked for work', an observation rendered as 'On Yer Bike' by the **tabloids** and turned against him thereafter by hostile demonstrators.

ONE NATION GROUP

An informal but influential faction within the **Conservative Party** from the

1950s to the 1970s, basing itself on the 'one nation' concept of Victorian politician Benjamin Disraeli and seeking to pursue policies designed to heal social divisions within the country. Its members included both a number of grandees of the party who perpetuated a tradition of patrician obligation towards less favoured sections of society, and reformers who identified the development of cohesion within society as being essential for the achievement of balanced economic progress. One of the foremost exponents of the philosophy was Iain **Macleod**, who died in 1970. Under the leadership of Margaret **Thatcher** the Conservative Party was generally seen as moving away from the one nation concept, whose adherents were perceived as being not **one of us.**

ONE OF US

The tacit description of **Conservatives** who belonged to the circle in favour with Margaret **Thatcher** while **Prime Minister** in 1979–90. While her first **Cabinet** formed in May 1979 was representative of a relatively wide spectrum of Conservative thought and ideology, most of those ministers who did not share her particular political outlook were gradually excluded from positions of influence as being 'not one of us' and therefore of suspect loyalty.

110-DAY RULE

A rule of **Scottish** law requiring that a prisoner committed for **jury trial** must receive his or her indictment setting out the charges brought within 80 days and that the trial must begin within 110 days. If the 80-day limit is breached the prisoner has to be released but may still be prosecuted. If the 110-day limit is exceeded he or she must be released unconditionally and proceedings are closed.

OPEN GOVERNMENT

The ideal of 'transparency' in the making and implementation of government policy. This concept was brought to the fore with a **White Paper** on open government in 1993, followed by the issuing of a code of practice on access to information held by central government, effective from April 1994. The code is administered by the **Cabinet Office** (and therefore falls under the responsibility of the Chancellor of the **Duchy of Lancaster**) and independently policed by the **ombudsman**. The code fell short of proposals for any US-type **freedom of information** legislation, but covered a new statutory right of access for subjects to see personal information held about them by government, access to health and safety information held by public authorities and new provisions relating to the **30-year rule**. The policy also included a new openness about the existence of security organizations such as the internal intelligence agency **MI5**, the existence of which was acknowledged for the first time.

OPEN UNIVERSITY

A distance-learning university for mature students. The Open University (OU) was established in 1969 by the **Labour** government (and regarded by Prime Minister Harold **Wilson** as his greatest achievement) to provide degree courses by correspondence for students of 21 years or over, regardless of whether they have the entrance qualifications normally required in higher education. Most course work is carried out by self-instructional textbooks, supplemented by television and radio broadcasts and some face-to-face tuition. By 1995 around 200,000 first degrees had been awarded since the OU started its courses.

OPERATION IRMA

The media term for the airlift in August 1993 of some 40 people seriously injured in the war in Bosnia–Hercegovina to hospitals in the UK as well as Sweden and Italy. The operation was named after Irma Hadzimuratovic, a seriously injured five-year-old girl whose plight was given extensive coverage by the Western media, and who was flown out of Sarajevo on the personal initiative of **Prime Minister** John **Major**. Bosnian doctors pointed out that the high cost of the airlift would have been more effectively spent on improving medical facilities within Bosnia. Irma herself died in a London hospital in early 1995.

OPERATION SHEEPSKIN

The invasion of Anguilla in March 1969 by 300 British troops and 50 police to restore British rule. The **Caribbean** island had long resented rule by St Kitts-Nevis and in May 1967 seized control by forcibly expelling the Kittitian police. A declaration of independence in February 1969 provoked the British intervention, and British police remained until 1972. The UK administered the island directly from 1971 until it formally assumed the status of a British **dependent territory**, separate from St Kitts-Nevis, in 1980.

OPPORTUNITY 2000

A public campaign launched in October 1991 to improve women's employment prospects and in particular to increase the number of women in senior public jobs, at the time just 23 per cent of the total.

OPPOSITION DAYS

The 20 days allocated in each session of Parliament when the Opposition may choose subjects for debate. Of these days, 17 are at the disposal of the **Leader of the Opposition**, while three are at the disposal of the second-largest opposition party.

OPPS *see* CABINET OFFICE

OPTING OUT

The term used loosely from the late 1980s in relation variously to schools, **NHS** units, the **Social Chapter** of the **Maastricht** Treaty and the treaty's provisions on **EMU**. For schools, opting out implies the achievement of **grant-maintained** status outside the control of local education authorities, under the terms of the Education Reform Act 1988 (**GERBIL**). For hospitals, other health care units and general medical practices, the expression is less accurately used to indicate the acquisition of the status of **NHS trusts** and fundholding practices, with their own financial accountability but still as integral components of the NHS itself. As regards the 1991 Maastricht agreement, the UK 'opted out' of the application of the provisions of the Social Chapter and of EMU.

ORANGE ORDER

A Protestant organization in **Northern Ireland**. Its members (**loyalists** and **unionists**) support the retention of Northern Ireland within the **UK**. Its name derives from King William III, Prince of Orange, who defeated the Catholic James II in 1689–90. Many of the order's annual demonstrations, during the **marching season**, commemorate battles and other events of that period.

ORDINATION OF WOMEN PRIESTS

The fiercely controversial Priests (Ordination of Women) Measure received royal assent on 5 November 1993, and the **General Synod** of the **Church of England** gave formal approval to the parallel ecclesiastical measure in February 1994. Together these acts cleared the way for women to become priests in the Church of England for the first time. During their passage through the General Synod and Parliament the ordination of women was vigorously opposed by traditionalists and sections of the **Conservative Party**, especially those with reported **High Church** affiliations, some disaffected Church of England members left for the **Roman Catholic Church**. The first 32 women priests were ordained in March 1994 in Bristol Cathedral.

ORGREAVE

The British Steel Corporation's coking plant near Rotherham, Yorkshire, which was the site in May–June 1984 of some of the most bitter and violent clashes between pickets and police during the 1984–5 **miners' strike**. The **NUM** sought to block deliveries of coal to the plant by road in an attempt to broaden the effect of the strike to involve production in other industrial sectors.

ORKNEY CHILD ABUSE AFFAIR

A controversy involving suspected child sexual abuse in the Orkney Islands, in **Scotland**. Nine children were removed from their families on the island of South Ronaldsay by social workers in February 1991 after allegations of ritualistic abuse. The social work department was severely criticized in early April in a court judgement which said that its procedures had been 'so fatally flawed as to be incompetent'; the children were immediately returned to their homes. A judicial inquiry headed by Lord Clyde concluded in October 1992 that the social workers had acted irrationally and too quickly and had not considered alternatives to taking the children into care. Changes to the law and training of social workers were recommended.

OUP *see* UUP

THE OUTER SEVEN

An expression to distinguish the seven original member countries of the European Free Trade Area (**EFTA**) in 1959 – namely Denmark, Norway, Sweden, Austria, Portugal, Switzerland and the UK – from the **inner six** original countries of the more integrationist European Community – namely Belgium, the Netherlands, Luxembourg, France, (West) Germany and Italy.

OUTING

The public declaration by militant homosexual campaigners that a prominent person is homosexual. The term derives from the expression 'to come out of the closet', describing the voluntary acknowledgement by an individual that he or she is homosexual. The Outing movement began in the late 1980s when militant homosexual campaigners, especially in the USA, felt that homosexuals who concealed their sexuality were adding to the prevailing climate of shame and prejudice which had escalated as a result of the **AIDS** epidemic. In the UK outing has most often been used by **Outrage!**. In 1995 fear of exposure as part of an Outrage! campaign to focus attention on the **Church of England's** attitude to homosexuality prompted a number of prominent clerics to make statements about their sexual orientation.

OUTRAGE!

A militant gay pressure group founded in 1990 and associated with Peter Tatchell. Outrage! seeks to combat what it perceives as the hypocrisy of homosexuals in public life who outwardly conform to a heterosexual lifestyle. It uses **outing** to achieve its ends. In 1994 it initiated a controversial campaign to force the **Church of England** to reassess its attitude to such issues as the homosexual **age of consent** and the recognition of homosexual clergy. In early March 1995, Derek Rawcliffe, the retired bishop of Glasgow and Galloway, apparently fearing exposure by Outrage!, declared that he was homosexual. A week later, under more overt pressure from the organization, the then Bishop of London, David Hope, who was subsequently appointed Archbishop of York, described his own sexuality as 'ambiguous'.

OVERSEAS AID

The resources transferred to foster development in other countries. British overseas aid takes the form of projects, finance for essential materials and equipment, **know-how**, support for British and international research in diverse fields, and emergency aid. The lead agency is the Overseas Development Administration, a division of the **FCO**, but it does not handle other forms of aid such as debt write-offs. Around 55 per cent of British aid is bilateral (£1.3 billion in 1993–4) with the balance multilateral (i.e. passing through international and local agencies and organizations). Half of all multilateral aid (worth £1 billion in 1993–4) currently passes through the **EU**, but the UK is seeking to raise the bilateral proportion.

OVERSEAS TRADING AREA

The collection of countries accepting sterling as reserve currency. From the collapse of the gold standard until the late 1970s sterling vied with the US dollar as a global reserve currency. Sterling dominated a steadily shrinking trading area which finally disappeared when Ireland joined the **EMS** in 1978 and British **foreign exchange controls** were abolished the following year.

OWEN, DAVID

(b. 1938) The centre-left politician and founder member of the **SDP**, who was awarded a **life peerage** in 1992. Owen was born in Devon and trained as a doctor in London in the 1960s. He contested Torrington for the **Labour Party** in 1964, and served as **MP** for Plymouth Sutton from 1966–74 and for Plymouth Devonport from 1974–92. Owen was opposition defence spokesman in 1970–2, became a junior minister in 1974 and in May 1977 was appointed Foreign Secretary, thus becoming the youngest person to hold that office since Anthony **Eden** in 1935.

The Labour Party's swing to the left in the late 1970s and early 1980s persuaded Owen to join the **Gang of Four** in founding the SDP in 1981. Owen became leader of the SDP in 1983 and campaigned in **alliance** with the **Liberal Party**, when his collaboration with Liberal leader David Steel led to their being dubbed the **Two Davids**. Owen opposed the merger of the two parties in 1988, but dissolved the rump SDP in 1990.

Owen was appointed in 1992 as the senior peace negotiator for the **EU** in the former Yugoslavia, but announced his resignation from the position in his maiden speech in the **House of Lords** on 31 May 1995.

OWN RESOURCES

The money in the **EU** budget. Under an agreement concluded in 1988, this comes from a combination of import tariffs and agricultural levies (the two original 'own resources'), a proportion of the **VAT** collected by member states, and a 'fourth resource' involving payments by member states proportionate to their **GNP**. The **European Council** summit in Edinburgh in 1992 approved the so-called 'Delors package' on future Community financing, under which the ceiling for the EU budget would rise by 1999 from 1.2 to 1.27 per cent of the joint GNP of the member states.

OXBRIDGE

A portmanteau word blending Oxford and Cambridge, the country's oldest and most prestigious universities. An Oxbridge education is an essential characteristic of a member of the **Establishment**.

OXFAM

A UK-based charity which funds both disaster relief and long-term aid in the fields of health (particularly clean water), agriculture and training in some 70 underdeveloped countries. Oxfam, based in Oxford, was founded in 1942 to help women and children in Nazi-occupied Greece; it now has some 40 overseas field offices. It is funded by donations and by trade with overseas producers and disadvantaged groups in the UK.

OZ TRIAL

The highly publicised proceedings at the **Old Bailey** in 1971 in which the editors of the Australian-founded satirical magazine *Oz* were acquitted of conspiracy to corrupt morals but were convicted of **obscenity** and of despatching indecent materials through the post. The editors – magazine founder Richard Neville and Jim Anderson, both Australians, and Briton Felix Dennis – had published in April 1970 an edition largely written and illustrated by young readers, which contained sexually graphic articles and cartoons. The three received short prison sentences and Neville and Anderson were ordered to be deported, but in the **Court of Appeal** the single and minor charge of sending indecent materials through the post was upheld and they were released.

Like the **Lady Chatterley trial** of 1960, the proceedings were celebrated as a clash between old and new moralities. In this case the new values were those of the **hippies**.

In June 1995 Dennis enjoyed a partial, if belated, victory against the trial judge. He won a substantial sum (believed to be £10,000) and an apology from the *Spectator* magazine, following the publication in May 1995 of an article by Judge Michael Argyle in which he alleged that the defendants had sold drugs to schoolchildren. Although the magazine apologized profusely, Argyle declined to put his name to the apology, and Dennis indicated that he would pursue a libel action against Argyle alone.

OZONE LAYER

A stratum of the atmosphere, 10–20 miles (15–30 km) above the earth, which is rich in ozone, a form of oxygen which protects the earth from the most harmful effects of ultraviolet radiation from the sun. The reduction in the concentration of ozone in the ozone layer resulting from environmental pollution, particularly **CFCs**, has become one of the principal concerns of the environmental movement since a 'hole in the ozone layer' over Antarctica was first discovered in the early 1980s. The consequences of the thinning of the ozone layer include increasing occurrence of skin cancers, and damage to plants and crops. The depletion of ozone is most serious over Antarctica, but the concentration of ozone in the northern hemisphere has been estimated to have declined by 14 per cent since 1969. The 1987 Montreal Protocol (subsequently strengthened in 1992) represented an attempted to limit damage to the ozone layer; under the protocol countries undertook to halve CFC production, initially by 1999 and then by 1996.

PAIRING

The convention in Parliament whereby pairs of **MPs**, one each from the government and opposition sides, agree that if one is unable to be present to vote the other will abstain. This convention is generally arranged by the relevant whips, and in particular it enables ministers to be absent on government business without risking the reduction of the government's majority. The arrangement may on occasion be suspended by the opposition as a means of bringing pressure to bear upon the government.

PAISLEY, IAN

(b. 1926) The outspoken and controversial leader of the **Democratic Unionist Party** (DUP) in **Northern Ireland** since 1974, and member of the **European Parliament** since 1979. Paisley is the most emphatic and visible representative the Protestant **unionist** cause in the province. Elected to the British Parliament for Antrim North in 1970, he resigned in 1985 in protest over that year's **Anglo-Irish Treaty** and was re-elected at a **by-election** in January 1986. Throughout the period of the **Brooke initiative** during 1990–2 and further peace efforts leading up to and beyond the **IRA ceasefire** of August 1994, Paisley continued to insist that the Irish government renounce its claim – under Articles 2 and 3 of its constitution – to the North. He characteristically described the **Downing Street Declaration** of December 1993 as an act of treachery, and continues to express his deep concern over the involvement of nationalist paramilitaries in political negotiations.

PALACE OF WESTMINSTER

The location of Parliament, accommodating the **House of Commons** and **House of Lords,** as well as the various parliamentary committees. The neo-gothic parliament building by the river Thames was designed by Sir Charles Barry after the medieval palace originally occupying the site was razed to the ground in 1834. Westminster Hall, constructed in 1099, is the only part of the original palace which survived the fire. The building accommodates some 3,000 **MPs**, secretaries, maintenance and catering staff.

PALESTINE

The former British mandate in the Middle East. Palestine (today's Israel) was administered by Britain from the end of the First World War on behalf of the League of Nations. Britain had commitments to the Jews (to whom Lord Balfour had in his Declaration of 1917 promised a homeland), and to the majority Arab population. The inter-war years witnessed a rapidly expanding Jewish population but also growing frequency of communal riot. After the Second World War mass **immigration** of Jewish people (legal and illegal) grew exponentially, racial clashes proliferated and there were many casualties among British **police** and soldiers. Foreign Minister Ernest **Bevin** reluctantly came to accept that order could not be maintained. Following a vote at the **UN** of November 1947 for Partition of Palestine the British withdrew. In the aftermath Israel gained its independence and fought its first war with its Arab neighbours. Palestine is generally considered the greatest blot on Bevin's remarkable record as **Foreign Secretary**.

PARENT'S CHARTER

An initiative to provide more information for parents of children at maintained schools. The Parent's Charter was launched in September 1991 as part of the government's wider **Citizen's Charter** programme. Under it schools were required to give a written annual report to parents on their child's progress; governors' annual reports would have to include more information; parents would be given reports on schools' performances based on a four-yearly inspection;

and **league tables** of schools would be published. The government distributed 3,000,000 copies of the Charter to schools libraries and post offices at a cost of £2,000,000 – a sum criticized by many who said that it would have been better spent directly on education. Opposition from the educational establishment was underlined by advice from the National Association of Head Teachers (NAHT), telling its members not to comply with the government's request to distribute the Charter to parents, on the grounds that it was a political document.

PARIS CLUB

The informal grouping of industrialized countries which deals with debts owed to its member countries by developing countries and by severely indebted middle-income countries. In the 1990s much of its attention has been focused on the deferment of repayment of the huge debts of the former Soviet Union. The Paris Club was first created by the main west European countries in the context of dealing with Argentina's debt problems in 1957, building on arrangements initiated earlier in the decade. It grew to become the principal international forum for considering arrangements for renegotiation, consolidation and debt rescheduling. It deals with debts arising from loans made or guaranteed by official bilateral creditors, as distinct from purely commercial bilateral debts which are covered by the **London Club**.

PARLIAMENT ACT 1949

Legislation providing for circumstances under which legislation passed by the **House of Commons** could be enacted without the agreement of the **House of Lords**. The Parliament Act 1949 and its predecessor of the same name passed in 1911 allow that a money bill (dealing with government revenue) can be passed without the concurrence of the Lords, who can delay it by only one month. If any other public bill is passed by the Commons in two successive sessions and is rejected by the Lords in these sessions, it can be presented to the sovereign for the **royal assent** and so become law. This provision cannot take effect unless one year has elapsed between the date of the **second reading** in the first of the sessions in the Commons and the date the bill is passed in the second session.

PARLIAMENTARY PRIVILEGE

The rights, most notably freedom of speech, enjoyed by members of the **Houses of Parliament** to allow them to carrying out their duties without obstruction. Parliament also has first call on the attendance of its members, who thus may not be subject to arrest in civil actions and are exempt from serving on **juries** and from being compelled to attend court as witnesses. As a result **MPs** are able to make statements within the confines of the **Palace of Westminster** which could be considered libellous if uttered outside, and MPs are able to circumvent certain legal injunctions. During the **Zircon** affair, MPs, by means of citing parliamentary privilege, were able to view a copy of the banned programme, and the subsequent decision of the **Speaker** to prohibit a repeat showing provoked a row over parliamentary privilege.

PARLIAMENTARY SECRETARY

A third-ranking departmental minister. Some government departments have one or more parliamentary secretaries with specific ministerial responsibilities. The post ranks below the secretary of state and **minister of state** but above a parliamentary under-secretary.

PARTITION

The division of a country. Although its current usage is sometimes applied to **Northern Ireland** and Ireland, its most famous example was the partition of the Indian subcontinent in 1947 resulting in the independent states of India and Pakistan. Regarded by many historians as a desperate expedient adopted by the departing British imperial power after its failure to reconcile Muslim leaders to a 'one-India' solution, it failed to prevent large-scale communal violence or avert the still further partition of Pakistan following the secession of its eastern wing (Bangladesh) in 1971.

PARTNERSHIPS FOR PEACE *see* NATO

PATRIALITY
A concept introduced by the UK government under the **Immigration** Act 1971 and built upon by the British **Nationality** Act 1981. Broadly, for the purposes of immigration and right of abode under the 1971 Act, 'patriality' was enjoyed by a person who was a citizen of the UK and colonies by birth or naturalization, by a British or Commonwealth citizen who had one or more parents or grandparents born in the UK, and by a citizen of the UK and colonies with continuous residence in the UK. Stricter interpretation was provided for in the 1981 Act, which redefined British citizenship and which limited the transmission of such citizenship. At the time of the 1971 Act, accusations were made that the definition relating to the place of birth of a parent or grandparent was racial, in that the majority of people enjoying patriality under those conditions were likely to be white.

PAVING BILL
Draft legislation preparing the way for more substantial measures. Such bills prepare the ground for an issue to be dealt with in more detail later on, either by more primary legislation or by administrative action. A government minister can be given powers under a paving bill to issue regulations on a particular subject.

PAYE
Acronym for 'Pay As You Earn'– the system of collecting income tax through regular deductions by the employer from weekly or monthly earnings. The amount of tax deductible is calculated by the use of code numbers in conjunction with tax tables. The system, recommended by John Maynard **Keynes**, was introduced in 1944. It was regarded as a stabilizing factor in the economy, since tax yield automatically varied directly and rapidly with income and employment, whereby the government tended to spend proportionately more tax yield in recession.

PAYMASTER GENERAL
A ministerial post at the **Treasury** with miscellaneous duties. The minister acts as a paying agent for government departments and deals with taxes raised by **Customs and Excise**. The office is also responsible for the payment of many types of public service pensions.

PEACE PEOPLE *see* COMMUNITY OF THE PEACE PEOPLE

PEACE WALL
A barrier erected by British soldiers in **Northern Ireland** between the **Roman Catholic Falls Road** and the Protestant **Shankill** areas of Belfast, following riots and house-burning there in 1969.

PEACH, BLAIR
A New Zealand-born teacher who died as a result of injuries sustained in clashes with **police** while protesting against a rally by the **National Front**, an extreme right-wing political group, in Southall, west London, in April 1979. Peach was a member of the **Anti-Nazi League** pressure group, and its members claimed that he was a victim of an unprovoked attack by officers of the Metropolitan Police **SPG**. An inquest jury found in May 1980 that Peach had died through 'misadventure', effectively clearing the police of blame, but Peach was by this time established as a martyr by **left-wing** protest groups.

PEARCE COMMISSION
The government body established in November 1971 to investigate whether proposals to settle the dispute with **Rhodesia** over **UDI** were acceptable to the whole Rhodesian population. After the failed **Fearless Talks** of October 1968 there had been an interval in negotiations until early 1971. Eventually in mid-November Sir Alec **Douglas-Home**, the UK Foreign and Commonwealth Secretary, signed the Anglo-Rhodesian Settlement with Rhodesian leader Ian Smith. The settlement provided for the gradual but slow increase in black political power, leading to majority rule by the beginning of the next century. The Pearce Commission, headed by Lord Pearce, a retired Lord of Appeal, arrived in Salisbury (now Harare) on 11 January 1972. It canvassed opinion for two months and published a report on 23 May 1972, which revealed that of the 120,730 people questioned, 106,309 had opposed the Settlement; 97 per cent of Africans questioned were strongly opposed to the Settlement.

Thus rejected, the proposals were officially abandoned by the UK government.

PERGAU DAM AFFAIR

A political scandal concerning the links between an aid package given by the **UK** to Malaysia for the construction there of the Pergau dam and the purchase by Malaysia of UK defence equipment. The arms deal, signed in 1988, covered large-scale weapons purchases over a number of years, worth more than £1 billion. The decision to provide £234 million of aid to the construction of the Pergau hydroelectric scheme was made in 1991, but was in line with an offer made by **Prime Minister** Margaret **Thatcher** in 1989. The affair subsequently led to a rift in relations between the two countries as, following the publication of a *Sunday Times* article which alleged that the affair had involved 'special payments' to high-ranking Malaysian politicians, Malaysia imposed a ban between February and September 1994 on UK companies bidding for public contracts. On 20 July 1994 the **House of Commons' select committee** on foreign affairs published a report on the matter. It was particularly critical of George Younger, the Secretary of Defence in 1988, for having negotiated the defence and aid agreements. His 'reprehensible' conduct was cited as having created a 'moral obligation' which had committed other ministers to a linkage between aid and the sale of arms which was 'contrary to stated government policy'. The report also criticized Thatcher and Chris Patten, who at the time had been Minister of Overseas Development, for having failed to keep parliament properly informed.

PERMANENT SECRETARY

The most senior civil servant in a government department. A unified grading system was introduced in the **civil service** in 1984, technically replacing titles such as permanent secretary, second permanent secretary, deputy secretary, under-secretary and so on with grades, grade 1 being the highest. In practice the old titles are still widely used.

PERMISSIVE SOCIETY

A largely derogatory term used to describe a society that has undergone a **sexual revolution**. The term suggests a loss of morality and free sex, and to a lesser extent an abundance of drugs and alcohol. The existence of the permissive society since the mid-1960s has been seen by some as the prime reason for the increase in the number of single parents, a breakdown of **family values** and increasing levels of crime.

PENKOVSKY AFFAIR

A Soviet double agent, Oleg Penkovsky, who was a senior figure in Soviet intelligence, supplied **MI6** with information about Soviet military capabilities in the early 1960s. He was discovered by the Soviets in 1962 and it is believed that he was shot. Peter Wright, author of **Spycatcher**, cast doubt on this **MI6** success, suggesting that Penkovsky was a plant associated with double agents during the **Hollis** regime.

PHILBY, HAROLD (Kim)

(1911–88) A double agent and the notorious **Third Man** involved in the defection of Guy **Burgess** and Donald **Maclean**. Like Burgess and Maclean, Philby was recruited by Soviet intelligence while at Cambridge University in the 1930s. Thereafter he professed **right-wing** views, gained entry to the pro-Hitler Anglo-German Fellowship, and reported for *The Times* in Spain, all the time maintaining his Soviet contacts. In 1940, on the recommendation of Burgess, he was recruited by Section D of the (British) Secret Intelligence Service, and by stages to **MI6** itself. From the later years of the Second World War onward Philby was instrumental in the leaking of the secrets of the atomic weapons programme (code-named Tube Alloys) to the Soviet Union, a task made easier when he rose to be head of Section Nine, the department responsible for penetrating Soviet intelligence. Despite American suspicions that the British had double agents and **MI5's** 1945 discovery that Philby's first wife was a Soviet spy, no suspicion attached to him. In 1949 he was sent to Washington as liaison officer with the CIA and two years later warned Burgess that Maclean was about to be unmasked. Suspicion of him now hardened. He was forced into premature retirement and interrogated but without success. In 1955 a

Labour MP Marcus Lipton named him in the **House of Commons** as the 'Third Man'. However, Harold **Macmillan** (then Foreign Secretary), while conceding Philby's past communist associations, denied that he had played a role in the escape of Burgess and Maclean or that he was a traitor. This clearance allowed him to begin a last career in 1956 in Beirut as Middle East correspondent of both the *Observer* and the *Economist*, obtaining the posts with the assistance of the Foreign Office (later the **FCO**). Compelling evidence as to his identity was finally gained from Soviet defectors. He was confronted and admitted the truth but escaped to the Soviet Union in January 1963 where he was granted citizenship.

PII *see* GAGGING ORDER

THE PILL

The contraceptive or birth control pill of which the active ingredients are oestrogen and/or progesterone. The pill was developed by chemists in the USA in the 1950s and was soon available in the UK. After contraceptives were made available under the **NHS** in 1961 its use grew wider, although at a cost of just under £1 a month it was used primarily by middle class women, most of whom were married. The position altered after October 1966 when the Family Planning Association began giving advice on birth control to single people. However, the most dramatic change came in April 1974 when contraceptives, including the pill, were made available free under the NHS.

Its general availability has effectively revolutionized women's sexual behaviour, giving women control over their fertility and allowing them to choose if and when they have children. The sexual independence brought by the pill has had far-reaching effects, particularly when combined with the increasing economic independence of women from the 1960s onwards and is regarded as a contributory factor in the **sexual revolution** and in the **women's liberation** movement. In recent years there has been some disquiet about the use of the pill because of a number of worrying side effects, including greater susceptibility to thrombosis.

PIN DOWN

The discredited technique, used in certain residential children's homes in the mid-1980s, of controlling the behaviour of disturbed adolescents by placing them in solitary confinement for considerable periods of time, often dressed only in their nightclothes. The practice was banned in 1991 following publication of a report on children's homes in Staffordshire, which described it as 'harsh, restrictive and punitive' and as being 'unethical, unprofessional and unacceptable'.

PINK POUND

A term used to describe the significant economic power of homosexual men and women. The notion is based on the fact that gays are often successful professionals with few or no family financial commitments. Gay organizations have at various times called on homosexuals to use their purchasing power as a campaigning weapon.

PIPER ALPHA

An offshore oil platform located some 125 miles (200 km) north-east of Aberdeen, Scotland, on which in 1988 an explosion and fire caused 167 deaths. The disaster, on the night of 6 July 1988, was the worst in the history of **North Sea oil** exploration and exploitation. The Cullen report on the disaster, published in November 1990, was critical both of the operators of the platform (Occidental Petroleum) and of the UK Department of Energy. Following the disaster the Department of Energy in 1991 relinquished responsibility for health and safety matters on offshore installations within the British continental shelf to the Health and Safety Executive (**HSE**).

PIRATE RADIO

A term used to describe illegal offshore radio stations which in the 1960s and 1970s defied the broadcasting duopoly of the **BBC** and **commercial radio**, transmitting programmes from ships anchored in the North Sea. The stations, operating without a licence, played popular music all day and collected substantial amounts of advertising revenue. The most famous 'pirate' was undoubtedly Radio Caroline, which began to transmit in 1964 and provided generations of teenagers with a means of expressing their rebellious instincts. The BBC responded to them with the creation in 1967 of the pop and rock station Radio 1.

Plaid Cymru

(Welsh, the Party of Wales) The main Welsh nationalist political party. Set up in 1925 to secure self-government for **Wales**, it gained its first parliamentary seat in 1966. Despite the overwhelming 'no' from the Welsh electorate in the 1979 **devolution** referendum, the party continued to campaign. It made its strongest showing in the 1992 local elections when it took four seats in the Welsh-speaking north-west of the principality, making a total of 113 seats in all. In the 1995 local elections it held on to the same number of seats.

Plant report

The report of the **Labour Party's** commission on electoral reform, chaired by Lord Plant of Highfield, professor of politics at the University of Southampton, which was released on 31 March 1993. This recommended a move away from the present **first-past-the-post** system of elections to the **House of Commons** towards the 'supplementary' form of preferential voting, and a regional list system for elections to the **European Parliament**. However, no formal decision was taken on the proposals, and further work by the commission, including looking at electoral systems for local government and for any future regional assemblies, was effectively suspended by the party's **NEC** in October 1993.

Plastic bullet

One of the principal offensive weapons used by the security forces in **Northern Ireland**, generally under conditions of rioting. Also known as the 'rubber bullet' or the 'baton round', its use has often been highly controversial. One notable recent example was the killing in August 1989 of a civilian, Seamus Duffy, fired on by an apparently unidentified member of the **RUC** during clashes between the **police** and **republicans** in Belfast on the anniversary of the introduction of internment in 1971. Duffy's parents joined the United Campaign Against Plastic Bullets, while in March 1990 the Director of Public Prosecutions decided not to bring charges against anyone in the matter. Duffy had been the fourteenth person to be killed by a plastic bullet since their introduction in 1973.

Plea bargaining

Also known as sentence discounting, the practice more common in the USA and not formally used in the UK whereby lower sentences are offered to defendants willing to plead guilty early in the judicial process. The **Runciman Report** on Criminal Justice published in July 1993 recommended that a formal sentence discounting system should be established.

Plowden report

An official inquiry into overseas diplomatic representation. Sir Edwin (Lord) Plowden's committee reported in 1962, one of several committees to inquire into the Foreign Office (later the **FCO**)'s extensive network abroad. Plowden found that diplomats were often still in the amateur tradition and needed specialized training, but the report failed to recommend drastic action. The most fundamental attack on overseas representation awaited a 1977 **think-tank** report.

PLP

The Parliamentary **Labour Party**, or Labour **MPs**. The PLP has traditionally been more right-wing than the Labour movement as a whole. **Left-wing**-inspired constitutional reforms in 1981 diminished the PLP's influence by ending its sole responsibility for electing the party leader, introducing instead an electoral college system, and initiating the mandatory **reselection** of MPs, thus leaving their voting records to be scrutinized by increasingly radical constituency parties. Under Neil **Kinnock** the PLP was increasingly dominated by the party leadership.

Polaris

A submarine-launched inter-continental ballistic missile carrying nuclear warheads, which the US Navy began using from 1960 and which was also offered to the UK, becoming the basis of the UK independent nuclear capability. This aspect of the UK–US **special relationship**, agreed at the December 1962 **Nassau Conference** between **Prime Minister** Harold **Macmillan** and US President John F. Kennedy, precipitated French President Charles de Gaulle to pronounce his famous '**non**' to UK membership of the **EC**. The first of the Royal Navy's Polaris submarines, HMS *Renown*, was completed in 1968. Upgraded in the **Chevaline** programme in the 1970s and early 1980s, three Polaris submarines remain in service as of 1995 alongside the first submarine of the controversial successor programme, **Trident**.

POLICE

The UK service responsible for maintaining public order and preventing and investigating crime. In **England** and **Wales** prosecutions are carried out on behalf of the police by the **CPS**. The UK police service is organized into 52 local forces each commanded by a Chief Constable. The 43 forces in England and are maintained by a local police authority. The Metropolitan Police ('the Met') is the force for Greater London (save in the **City**, where the independent City of London Police Force has power). The police authority for the Met is the Home Secretary who has ultimate responsibility for all policing in England and Wales. The authorities for the eight forces in **Scotland** are the regional and islands councils with final responsibility resting with the Scottish Secretary, while the **RUC** in **Northern Ireland** is responsible to a government-appointed body, in turn accountable to the Northern Ireland Secretary.

The police in England, Scotland and Wales are not routinely armed with guns, although a limited number of officers are given firearms training. A survey of members of the Police Federation of England and Wales published in May 1995 found that 80 per cent of officers did not believe that they should routinely carry arms, with 11 per cent declaring that they would not be prepared to carry guns. Predictably a higher number of officers from **inner city** areas, where most of the 19 police deaths in the preceding 10 years had occurred, favoured routine arming. Since April 1994 all RUC officers have been armed. Prior to that arms were carried by male officers only.

In 1993–4 there was considerable controversy over government plans to reform the structure of the force following the publication of the **Sheehy report** and of a **White Paper** on police reform in June 1993. The Police and Magistrates Courts Act 1994 introduced new smaller police authorities independent of local authority control and gave the Home Secretary powers to set key objectives for policing.

See also Appendix VI.

POLICE COMPLAINTS AUTHORITY

The body established under the Police and Criminal Evidence Act 1984 through which members of the public can make complaints about police officers in **England** and **Wales**. The members of the Authority are appointed by the Home Secretary, and its claim to be an independent body has been called into question by critics. It not only investigates complaints from members of the public, but reviews the decisions of deputy chief constables with regard to disciplinary action taken against particular officers. It can also call for disciplinary hearings and has the power to inflict penalties on an officer found guilty of misconduct. In **Scotland** chief constables are obliged to investigate a complaint against one of their officers, and in **Northern Ireland** complaints are investigated by the Independent Commission for Police Complaints.

POLICY STUDIES INSTITUTE

An independent research organization which undertakes studies of economic, industrial and social policy and of the workings of political institutions. It is a registered charity and is not associated with any political party or pressure group. The Institute's declared mission is to inform policy by establishing facts.

POLITICAL CORRECTNESS

The doctrine of political correctness (PC) originated among US academics in the 1980s, involving the proscription of language – particularly that relating to gender and race – to ensure that it is acceptable to the self-appointed representatives of minority groups. It rapidly developed beyond the elimination of terms likely to cause offence, and became susceptible to caricature with the coining of expressions – such as 'terminally challenged' to describe the dead – which are widely considered absurd. The authoritarian fashion with which it has been pursued on campuses, together with the tendency of many of its adherents to denigrate the works of 'dead white males' in favour of studying the cultural products of minorities, regardless of their merit, have led many to criticize PC as a form of intellectual fascism. While PC poses a threat to academic freedom and independence, its impact outside academic, media and liberal-left circles remains extremely limited. It has also gained much less of a foothold in the UK than in the USA.

POLL TAX *see* COMMUNITY CHARGE

POLLUTER PAYS

The principle which states that those who cause industrial pollution should offset its effects by compensating for the damage incurred or by implementing measures to avoid the pollution being caused in the first place. The policy is difficult to enforce, mainly because atmospheric transboundary pollution can be hard to trace to its source. More localized pollution, such as oil spillage from a tanker, is more easily identifiable. The principle of polluter pays was endorsed in the Rio Declaration signed at the 1992 Earth Summit.

POLLY PECK *see* NADIR, ASIL

POLYTECHNICS

Institutes of higher education. Thirty polytechnics were created in **England** and **Wales** in 1966, largely by merging existing colleges. They offered courses at degree level and below, generally placing more emphasis than most **universities** on science and technology courses. The Further and Higher Education Act 1992 and parallel legislation in **Scotland** removed the distinction between the two types of institution, engendering changes which brought the non-university sector in line with the universities and allowing polytechnics which satisfied the necessary criteria to adopt the title of university; all the polytechnics have now done so.

PONTING AFFAIR

The trial under the 1911 **Official Secrets Act** and acquittal of Clive Ponting in 1985. Ponting, a high-flying civil servant in the Ministry of Defence (**MOD**), was accused of leaking classified information to Labour MP Tam **Dalyell**, relating to the sinking of the Argentinian cruiser **Belgrano** during the 1982 **Falklands conflict**. His motive had been to make public what he considered to be attempts by the government to avoid acknowledgment of changes in the rules of engagement prior to the sinking of the cruiser. Ponting's acquittal, although generally unexpected, was widely acclaimed in 'right-to-know' circles.

POPPLEWELL REPORT

The report by a committee of inquiry, chaired by Mr Justice Popplewell, into the 1985 **Bradford football fire**. It also covered violence which had occurred at a Birmingham City match on the same day as the fire, and the **Heysel Stadium disaster** in Brussels on May 29. The inquiry produced an interim report in July 1985 and its final report on 16 January 1986. The report made a number of recommendations for the improvement of crowd safety at sports venues, including the proposal – later deemed impractical – that supporters of visiting football teams should be required to show club membership cards.

POPULATION

The number of inhabitants of a specified area. In the UK an official census has been taken every 10 years since 1801 (save in 1941 during the Second World War); population has risen from 41,459,000 in 1901 to 50,225,000 in 1951 and 57,649,000 in 1991. The report of the Royal Commission on Population published in June 1949 forecast a slow growth in the proportion of the elderly in the population and called for an extension of state assistance to families, including a system of rent and rate rebates, and better services for mothers and young children.

See also Appendix IV.

PORRITT, JONATHON

(b. 1950) Environmentalist and author. He was director of the environmental campaigning group **Friends of the Earth** from 1984–90 and proved himself a very successful popularizer of **green** issues. Prior to that he had been Chair of the Ecology Party from 1979–80 and 1982–84, and stood unsuccessfully as a parliamentary candidate for the party in the **general elections** of 1979 and 1983. His books include *Seeing Green: The Politics of Ecology Explained* (1984), *Where on Earth Are We Going?* (1991) and, for children, *Captain Eco* (1991).

PORTILLO, MICHAEL

(b. 1953) The **Conservative Secretary of State** for Defence since July 1995, and the leading Cabinet **right-winger** and **Eurosceptic**. Widely tipped as a prospective successor to the **Prime Minister** John **Major**, Portillo nevertheless supported Major during his successful June–July 1995 leadership contest against John Redwood. However, despite his pledge of support, it was reported that Portillo had established a 'campaign headquarters' in case the contest went to a second ballot. Before his appointment as Defence Minister, Portillo had served as Employment Minister and before that as Chief Secretary to the **Treasury**.

PORTON DOWN

The familiar name for the Ministry of Defence research establishment near Salisbury. The secretive Chemical and Biological Defence Establishment was known until its formation as a defence agency in 1991 as the Porton Down Chemical Defence Establishment; in April 1995 it became part of the Defence Evaluation and Research Agency. Its function is to carry out research into defences against chemical and biological weapons.

POSITIVE DISCRIMINATION

Those policies which aim to promote members of minority or disadvantaged groups (e.g. **ethnic minorities** or women) within economic, social or political institutions. Thus, for example, where there are two candidates, one black and one white, of equal ability, the black candidate would be favoured if black people are under-represented in the organization. Positive discrimination aims to correct historical imbalances by advancing artificially individuals from groups who may have suffered from past discrimination. Proponents of positive discrimination advocate reflecting the balance of all groups in society within its institutions, while its opponents criticize it for potentially giving membership of a particular social group greater importance than individual merit.

POSITIVE EUROPE GROUP

A **Conservative** group which, as the name suggests, is on the Europhile side of the party, drawing together **Heathites** such as Ray Whitney, who actively support most things European, including, eventually, a single European currency.

POSITIVE VETTING

The often controversial process by which potential government employees and armed forces personnel are scrutinised before appointment to sensitive or high-security work. During the process, the background and personal contacts of the potential recruits are thoroughly investigated before they can be cleared for their duties.

POST OFFICE

A generic term commonly used to cover the counter service of the Post Office. In fact, three separate bodies exist. Post Office Counters Limited consists solely of the counters service. The Royal Mail covers the letters and parcels service. Parcelforce is the Post Office's parcel delivery business. The government announced in July 1992 that it was considering privatizing all or parts of the Post Office. Firm proposals finally emerged in June 1994. The government preferred the option of selling 51 per cent of its shareholding in Royal Mail and Parcelforce to the private sector by means of a public **flotation**. The Post Office itself would remain in the public sector, but introduce new commercial services and invest in new technology. The plan came unstuck in November 1994. With a number of **backbench Conservative MPs** declaring their firm opposition, and the government operating on a slim **House of Commons** majority, the proposal –

which was supposed to have formed the mainstay of the government's privatization programme before the next general election – was abandoned. At the same time plans to sell off Parcelforce were similarly abandoned because the government could not find a suitable buyer.

POST-INDUSTRIAL SOCIETY

A view of contemporary society posited on the notion of a science-based and technocentric future. This view assumes, controversially, that the constraints of industrial toil have been replaced by leisure, and that the concerns of the traditional working class with the production and distribution of material goods have been superseded by the production and distribution of in- formation technology. Other definitions include the importance of service employment; the pre-eminence accorded to the professional, scientific and technical strata; and the aspiration towards quality of life, rather than quantity of goods.

POSTMASTER GENERAL

Until 1969 the government minister responsible for the **Post Office**. The Post Office ceased to be a government department in October 1969, when it became a public corporation, and its control passed over to the Ministry of Posts and Telecommunications (which was itself wound up in March 1974). John **Stonehouse** was the last Postmaster General.

POULSON AFFAIR

The affair leading to the resignation in 1972 of Reginald **Maudling** as Home Secretary from the **Conservative Cabinet**. John Poulson was an architect who built up a major international practice in the 1960s. He became also involved in construction work, and increased his standing through contacts with influential politicians. By the early 1970s Poulson's business concerns encountered grave financial difficulties, and as a result of disclosures made during his bankruptcy examination he was charged with corruption relating to bribes given to national and local politicians aimed at winning contracts. In February–March 1974 he was sentenced to seven years' imprisonment. Others embroiled in the scandal were T. Dan Smith, a Newcastle **Labour** councillor, who was given a six-year sentence; George Pottinger, Secretary of the Scottish Department of Agriculture, who was convicted of corruption; and senior local council and health authority officials. Although Maudling resigned from the Cabinet over gifts Poulson had made to a theatre supported by his wife, he was not charged with any criminal offence. The affair also led to the imposition on **MPs** of more rigorous requirements to disclose their business and other interests.

POVERTY TRAP

A term used to describe the situation when taking up low-paid employment leaves people in a worse financial position than **unemployment** because of the loss of **welfare benefit** and the incurring of costs for travelling, meals and, often, childcare. Unemployed people who are poorly skilled and ill-educated and unable to find well-paid work may thus be trapped in the benefits system.

POWELL, ENOCH

(b. 1912) The abrasive politician famous for his views on **race relations** and his long-term opposition to **UK** membership of the **EC**. Powell left a brilliant academic career as a classicist to become a **Conservative MP** in 1950. He held ministerial positions in the governments of Anthony **Eden** and Harold **Macmillan** in the 1950s and early 1960s, and was a member of Edward **Heath**'s **shadow cabinet** but was sacked in April 1968 in the wake of his controversial **'rivers of blood'** speech. His subsequent campaign for repatriation won him astonishing public support (a **Gallup poll** in June 1968 suggested that 74 per cent of Britons supported him on the issue of immigration). In the February 1974 **general election** he withdrew as a Conservative candidate in protest at the UK's membership of the EC and actually urged his supporters to vote **Labour** as the only way to keep Britain out of Europe. That October he became an Ulster Unionist Party (**UUP**) MP and until his defeat at the 1987 general election spoke out against any settlement with the Irish Republic.

POWER SHARING

The sharing of political power, particularly between majority and minority communities, in order to allow the minority community a part in the political process which it has otherwise been denied. The term has been applied to **Northern Ireland**, where in 1974 a short-lived power sharing executive was established. It collapsed in the face of a **loyalist** strike, and **direct rule** was reimposed.

PPS

Parliamentary private secretary. This is a position held by a **backbencher** from the government party who is chosen to assist an individual minister with his or her parliamentary duties. A PPS is not paid a salary and is not a minister, but traditionally does not vote against the Government.

PREMIUM BONDS

Government savings bonds. Introduced in 1956, premium bonds can be bought at the **post office** in units of £1, redeemable at face value on demand. The return on the bond is a chance to win a cash prize in a monthly lottery.

PRESCRIPTION CHARGES

Charges levied on the purchase of medicine prescribed by a doctor. The **NHS** originally excluded all payments by patients, but means-tested charges for spectacles were introduced by the **Labour** government in 1951, prompting the resignation of the Health Minister Aneurin **Bevan**. The **Conservative** government followed this in 1952 by similar charges for dental treatment and prescriptions, which have been uprated at frequent intervals, often causing political controversy.

PRESS COMPLAINTS COMMISSION

The organization which replaced the **Press Council** in January 1991 to deal with complaints against the press. The Commission had been suggested in June 1990 by the **Calcutt reports** on privacy and press self-regulation. It is a voluntary, non-statutory body, limiting itself to dealing with complaints while not attempting to combine this role with the defence of press freedom. Early in its life the Commission was severely criticized by the January 1993 Calcutt report for not being an effective regulator of the press. This followed controversy over its role in the coverage of difficulties in the marriage of the Prince and Princess of Wales. Under continued threat of becoming a wholly statutory body, the Commission in February and May 1993 issued additions to its code of practice to provide that journalists should not obtain or publish material obtained by the use of clandestine listening devices or by intercepting private telephone conversations. Among the features of the new code was a more precise definition of the public interest.

PRESS COUNCIL

The body charged with overseeing the conduct of the press until its replacement by the **Press Complaints Commission** in January 1991, under the Broadcasting Act of 1990. The Council was set up in 1953 on the recommendation of the 1949 **Ross Royal Commission** on the press. It was funded by the newspaper industry and consisted of 36 members under an independent chairperson. In February 1989 it announced that it was to hold a review of its operation, while in June 1990 the **Calcutt reports** on privacy and press self-regulation recommended that the Council be replaced by a non-statutory commission.

PREVENTION OF TERRORISM (TEMPORARY PROVISIONS) ACTS

The legislation which allows arrest without warrant and detention for up to seven days of those suspected of being involved in terrorist offences. The original 1984 Act of the same name required parliamentary approval each year up to its maximum life of five years. The legislation was therefore re-enacted in parliament in March 1989, with its central provisions becoming fully permanent legislation and the powers contained within the Act being subject to annual renewal thereafter. The Act further enables the government, in relation to suspected involvement in terrorism, to proscribe in the UK specified organizations, to make exclusion orders against named persons, and to investigate and seize funds destined for terrorist organizations.

PRIME MINISTER

The leader of the government, currently John **Major**. The Prime Minister is appointed by the sovereign and is usually the leader of the party which can command a majority in the **House of Commons**. Other ministers are appointed by the sovereign on the advice of the Prime Minister, who assigns responsibilities among them and has the power to dismiss them individually and accept resignations. The Prime Minister informs the sovereign of state and political matters, advises on the dissolution of Parliament and makes recommendations on important Crown appointments. As chair of the **Cabinet** and leader of a political party, the Prime Minister has the task of translating party policy into government action. As leader of the government, the Prime Minister is responsible to Parliament and to the electorate for the implementation of policy. The Prime Minister also represents the country in international affairs.

See also Appendix III.

PRIMODOS CASE

The legal case surrounding the effective banning in 1981 of a television documentary on the effects of a pregnancy drug and an important example of a limitation imposed on **freedom of speech**. Broadcast of the programme was prohibited as a result of an injunction brought by the manufacturers of the drug, Schering Chemicals. The court issuing a 'prior restraint' injunction ruled that the programme relied on material the producer had gained access to while acting as a consultant for the company, and that he was therefore bound to an obligation of confidence. However, in a dissenting judgment, Lord **Denning** argued that the programme should be shown on the grounds that 'the public interest in receiving information about the drug Primodos and its effect far outweighs the private interest of the makers in preventing discussion of it'.

PRINCESS VICTORIA FERRY DISASTER

A British Rail car ferry which sank in a storm in the Irish Sea on 31 January 1953, with the loss of 128 lives; 10 crew members and 34 passengers survived. An inquest into the accident was told that the guillotine doors above the stern gates of the ferry had not been closed, and that the gates had been burst open by a wave which had then flooded the car deck and caused the vessel to sink rapidly. The death toll was increased by the difficulties experienced by rescue vessels in locating the stricken ferry which had been equipped only with a ship-to-shore link rather than a radio capable of sending out a generalized SOS to all ships in the area.

PRIVACY *see* RIGHT TO PRIVACY

PRIVATE BILL

Draft legislation for the particular benefit of a person or group. Most are local in character and allow local authorities or nationalised industries or groups of individuals to undertake works of public utility. Private bills may also deal with the affairs of an individual, such as naturalisation, marriage or the settling of estates. All private bills originate by petition and are allocated either to the **House of Commons** or the **House of Lords**, although they must eventually be passed by both houses. Individuals or groups affected by a bill may petition against the whole measure or seek to amend it.

PRIVATE EYE

A satirical magazine and self-proclaimed scourge of the **Establishment**. Published fortnightly since 1961, the *Eye* is a mixture of scurrilous gossip and investigative journalism. In its time it has exposed such government scandals as the **Profumo** and **Poulson** affairs and the Iraqi **super-gun**. It has been edited since 1988 by Ian Hislop.

PRIVATE MEMBER'S BILL

Public bills introduced by private members – or **backbenchers** – in either the **House of Commons** or the **House of Lords**. While government business is normally given precedence in the Commons, some time is set aside for private members' bills. There are also special procedures for the introduction of private members' bills, such as the **ten minute rule**. However, time constraints are so severe that it is rare for private members' bills to reach the statute book.

PRIVATE SCHOOLS *see* INDEPENDENT SCHOOLS

PRIVATIZATION

The dismantling of government ownership of industries and services, and the sale or disposal either of these enterprises or of their assets. In some cases the enterprises may have been established by the state or lower tiers of government directly; alternatively they may originally have been brought into public ownership through **nationalization**, confiscation or other methods. The wholesale privatization of public corporations and services in the UK was undertaken after 1979 by the government of Margaret **Thatcher** on both ideological and economic grounds. Industries and utilities were transferred to the private sector, often at a fraction of their true value, and the proceeds used to finance cuts in direct taxation. The policy was emulated in many other countries, in both the developed and the developing world. However, although UK privatization continued in the 1990s, its initial popularity was increasingly undermined by rising consumer prices, inflated salary increases for senior managers, and the absence of any real competition in many of the privatized entities, such as gas.

PRIVY COUNCIL

An advisory body of eminent people. The Privy Council was the chief source of executive power until the system of government by **Cabinet** developed in the eighteenth century. Now its main function is to advise the sovereign, to approve orders in council and to advise on the issue of royal proclamations. The Council's own independent statutory responsibilities include powers of supervision over the registering of bodies for the medical and allied professions. Among several Privy Council committees are those dealing with legislative matters submitted by the **Channel Islands** and the **Isle of Man** and the Judicial Committee, which is the final court of appeal from the courts of UK **dependent territories**, some **Commonwealth** countries and some disciplinary and professional bodies. Membership of the Privy Council is for life and is automatic for Cabinet ministers and certain other positions. The sovereign may accord membership to other eminent people.

PRO *see* PUBLIC RECORDS OFFICE

PROBATION ORDER

A court sentence, usually imposed on juveniles or for minor offences, under which an offender is allowed liberty subject to reporting restrictions. A probation order can last for between six months and three years. If the offender fails to comply with the order or commits another offence while on probation, he or she can be brought before court again. Orders are frequently combined with a **community service order** or a fine.

PROCURATOR FISCAL

In **Scotland**, a legally qualified civil servant who in the lower courts takes decisions to prosecute and acts as prosecutor. The **Lord Advocate** takes responsibility for these decisions and prosecutions in the **High Court**, sheriff courts and district courts. In the Scottish legal system the **police** take no part in the decision to prosecute, whereas in **England** and **Wales** prosecutions are made by the **CPS** on behalf of the police. Procurators fiscal are also responsible for privately investigating suspicious deaths in their locality and for reporting any discoveries to the Crown Agent, the head of the procurator fiscal service.

PRODUCER CHOICE

A widely publicised internal market system within the **BBC**, arising from the Broadcasting Act of 1990, which provided for some 25 per cent of programmes being made by independent producers. Producers of radio and television programmes within the Corporation became businesses from April 1993, with responsibility for their own budgets. Rather than resort to the exclusive use of services previously provided only by the BBC, such producers could buy the required services from the private sector, if they proved to be cheaper.

PROFUMO AFFAIR

The scandal leading to the resignation in 1963 of John Profumo as Secretary of State for War from the **Conservative Cabinet**. The affair was seen by many as being indicative of a perceived lack of direction and leadership in Harold **Macmillan's** government. Profumo had become involved in a relationship with a young woman called Christine Keeler, and alarm was caused by the fact that she also had a simultaneous relationship with Eugene Ivanov, a Soviet naval attaché in London. In the **House of Commons** Profumo denied any impropriety, but as increasingly lurid details emerged he was forced to resign. The security aspects of the affair were the subject of an exhaustive inquiry by senior judge Lord **Denning**.

PROGRESSIVE UNIONIST PARTY *see* PUP

PROPERTY SERVICES AGENCY

A separate agency within the Department of the Environment, established in its current form in 1972, responsible for the acquisition, leasing, management and disposal of government property, managing the design and construction of new works and the maintenance of such property. The government decided in 1988 to **privatize** the Property Services Agency (PSA), and gave effect to this intention through the Property Services Agency and Crown Suppliers Act of 1990. In April 1990 the PSA was split into two bodies – Property Holdings (performing the government's landlord functions) and PSA Services (dealing with maintenance and property management, design and project management, provision of specialist advice and overseas work). In October 1992 the PSA projects division was sold to the Tarmac construction group, while in 1993 the building management businesses of the PSA were sold.

PROPERTY-OWNING DEMOCRACY *see* HOME-OWNING DEMOCRACY

PROPORTIONAL REPRESENTATION

An alternative method of electing parliamentary representatives, advocated by **Liberal Democrats** and by some in the **Labour Party** (but rejected by the Labour-commissioned **Plant Report** in 1993) as a fairer alternative to the existing system of **first past the post** in **single-member constituencies**. Proportional representation (PR) is used in elections for the **European Parliament** in **Northern Ireland**, where three representatives are chosen in a province-wide multi-member constituency by the single transferable vote system. The term PR covers a variety of electoral systems having in common one main feature – the intention that the political parties in parliament should be represented in proportion to their overall percentage support among the electorate. Opponents of PR point to Western Europe for examples of weak and volatile coalition governments, with parliamentary support fragmented among numerous parties.

PROTECTED SPECIES

A list of animals and plants which, under the Wildlife and Countryside Act 1981, it is an offence to kill, injure, take, posses or sell. The **Nature Conservancy Council** makes recommendations to Parliament from time to time to add species to the list.

PROTEST AND SURVIVE

A slogan adopted by **CND** in the early 1980s. The slogan played on the government's civil defence pamphlet, *Protect and Survive,* which suggested that elementary precautions such as painting windows white and sheltering under tables could help people survive a nuclear attack.

PROTESTANT MAJORITY

Acknowledgment of the religious / political balance in **Northern Ireland,** in the context of numerous attempts to establish an acceptable form of political devolution there. The recognition of the Protestant majority has been given substance by both the **UK** government and the government of the Republic of Ireland. The **Anglo-Irish Agreement** of 1985 explicitly accepted that unity in Ireland could only be possible with the consent of that majority. In December 1933 the joint British-Irish **Downing Street Declaration** reaffirmed the commitment to a statutory constitutional guarantee that as long as a majority of the people of Northern Ireland wished to remain a part of the UK, the government would uphold their right to do so.

PROVISIONALS *see* IRA

PSBR

The Public Sector Borrowing Requirement, the measure of difference between the expenditure and income of the public sector. The PSBR expresses the borrowing of central government, public corporations and local authorities to fund those activities not covered by revenue. Not only conventional current and capital expenditure is included, but also loans to the private sector and the net acquisition of company securities. For more than 20 years it has been favoured by governments as the best single indicator of their fiscal stance. With the shrinkage of the public sector due to **privatization**, attention has switched to the PSBR impact on central and **local government** outlay.

In his 1994–5 **Budget**, **Chancellor** Kenneth **Clarke** foresaw a reduction in the estimated PSBR to £21.5 billion in 1995–6, compared to his revised estimate for 1994–5 of £34.4 billion. He said that further spending cuts would eliminate the PSBR by 1999–2000.

PUBLIC BILLS

Draft legislation concerning a public matter. Public bills (other than those dealing with government revenue) may be introduced into the **House of Commons** or the **House of Lords**. The government usually introduces bills of major political content into the Commons. Bills must go through both houses, except in circumstances laid down by the **Parliament Act 1949** and preceding legislation which enable a bill to be enacted without the concurrence of the Lords. Passage normally involves the stages of **first reading**, **second reading**, **committee stage**, report stage, **third reading** and **royal assent**. Most public bills are introduced by the government as part of its legislative programme, although individual **MPs** may do so by way of a **private member's bill**.

PUBLIC INTEREST IMMUNITY CERTIFICATE *see* GAGGING ORDER

PUBLIC ORDER ACT 1986

The legislation revising the law covering public assemblies and disorder, and in particular creating a new offence of 'disorderly conduct' consisting of non-violent but threatening or abusive behaviour. Statutory offences of riot, violent disorder and affray replaced existing common law offences, the **police** were given new powers to impose conditions on public meetings and marches, and the law on incitement to racial hatred was toughened.

The act followed serious violence on the **Broadwater Farm** estate in north London the previous year, as well as several riots in Britain's **inner cities** earlier in the 1980s, and violent clashes between police and workers during the **miners' strike** in 1984–5.

PUBLIC RECORDS OFFICE

The national depository of official state records and historic documents, including court records and the records of government departments. Any sensitive documentation kept at the PRO has passed the **30-year rule**. The main PRO site is at Kew in west London.

PUBLIC SCHOOLS

The term usually applied to those senior **independent schools** which belong to the Headmasters' Conference, the Governing Bodies Association or the Governing Bodies of Girls' Schools Association. Most public schools are single-sex, although an increasing number have mixed sixth-forms. Preparatory schools are so-called because they prepare children for the common entrance examination to senior independent schools, which is taken at 13 by boys and at 11–13 by girls.

PUBLIC SERVICE BROADCASTING

The principle established by the **BBC** that television in the **UK** ought to be in the business of supplying a truly public service, by providing information, education and entertainment as important features of the concept of broadcasting. Operating within a changing broadcasting environment brought about through radical **broadcasting legislation**, the BBC has come under increasing pressure to enhance its potential in the modern marketplace by ridding itself of what its critics describe as a needlessly bureaucratic structure, to harness more readily the opportunities created by new technology and to look for a realistic alternative to the **licence fee** as a source of revenue.

PUNK ROCK

A highly influential form of rock music spawned in the mid-1970s by the Sex Pistols. The Pistols, made up of Johnny Rotten, Paul Cook, Steve Jones and Sid Vicious, initiated an angry explosion of music, graphics and fashion which had a major impact on British society. While punk's trademark style ('bondage' trousers, torn clothing, safety pins and 'situationist' slogans) came out of the King's Road 'Sex' boutique, run by designer Vivien Westwood and Pistols' manager Malcom Maclaren, it was a largely urban, working class phenomenon fuelled by adolescent boredom, widespread contempt for the prevailing '**hippy**' music scene, political, social and economic discontent and, not least, copious amounts of amphetamines and alcohol. Groups such as the Clash, the Buzzcocks, Eater and X-Ray Spex were the first to emerge in the Pistols' wake. The development of the UK scene ran concurrently with the more art-based New York scene, exemplified by Richard Hell and the Voidoids, Suicide, the Ramones, and Johnny Thunders and the Heartbreakers. The first Sex Pistols' single, 'Anarchy in the UK', was released in November 1976, inciting British youth to 'destroy a passer-by'. The following year, they released an album ('Never Mind the Bollocks') and their single 'God Save the Queen' reached number two in the UK charts during the **Silver Jubilee** celebrations. The Pistols split up while spreading their nihilistic creed to a largely bewildered USA in 1978. In 1979 Sid Vicious, the bass player, died of a drug overdose and launched a posthumous career as a cult icon. With his death, the punk movement effectively ended. Even before the collapse of the Pistols, the punk diaspora had started. In the UK, this was manifested in a split between 'arties' and 'social realists' and in the establishment of the independent ('indie') sector, which generated the so-called 'second wave' (Crass, Sham 69, Siouxsie and the Banshees, Subway Sect, Alternative TV, Magazine, The Fall and Wire) and, ultimately, the emasculated 'new wave' (the Stranglers, the Jam, Elvis Costello and the Police).

PUP

The Progressive Unionist Party, an **Ulster loyalist** party formed in the late 1970s and generally regarded at that time as the political wing of the paramilitary **UVF**. Based in Protestant working-class areas of Belfast, the PUP gained a foothold on the city council but did not put up candidates in elections to the parliament in **Westminster**. In October 1994, when the **Combined Loyalist Military Command** declared a **ceasefire**, the PUP raised its profile as the political group most in touch with opinion among the paramilitaries. Preliminary meetings with British government officials in December signalled the involvement of the PUP (and the Ulster Democratic Party – **UDP**) in the **Northern Ireland** peace process, and substantial discussions took place for the first time in March 1995 between the two groups and Minister of State Michael Ancram.

PUT UP OR SHUT UP!

The gauntlet thrown down to dissenters in the **Conservative Party** by **Prime Minister** John **Major** in June 1995. In a dramatic move on 22 June, Major resigned the party leadership and invited his detractors either to put up an alternative leader or to support him. The move was apparently precipitated by a tense meeting with the **Fresh Start Group** of **Eurosceptic MPs**, but followed months of backbiting and questions about his ability to lead a party deeply divided on the issue of Europe and of speculation fuelled by critical comments by his predecessor Baroness **Thatcher**. Although the challenge was somewhat surprisingly taken up by John Redwood, who resigned as **Secretary of State** for Wales, rather than a **stalking horse**, the gamble paid off and Major won the leadership election on July 4. However, while his supporters declared that he now had the support of the entire party, objective observers remained doubtful.

PYM, FRANCIS

The Secretary of State for Foreign and Commonwealth Affairs in 1982–3 in the **Conservative** government of Margaret **Thatcher**. Pym, who was hitherto Leader of the House of Commons, replaced Lord **Carrington**, who resigned shortly after the April 1982 invasion of the **Falkland** Islands by Argentina. Pym was replaced as Foreign Secretary by Sir Geoffrey **Howe** following the Conservatives' landslide victory in the June 1983 **general election**. Pym, a **one nation Tory**, was reported to have annoyed Thatcher by observing during the campaign that 'Landslides on the whole don't produce successful government'. Following his dismissal, he announced the formation of a new inner party grouping, the Conservative Centre Forward, which aimed to curb the excesses of **Thatcherism** and press the claims of traditional Conservatism.

QUALIFIED MAJORITY VOTING

The way that **EU** decisions are made in the **Council of Ministers** and the **European Council**, except on issues where a member country claims the right to a veto because essential national interests are involved. The scope for decision making by qualified majority vote was extended under the **Single European Act** in 1987 and is to be further discussed in 1996 under the **Maastricht** Treaty framework. There is a complicated formula under which the number of votes for each member state ranges from 10 (for the four largest countries including the UK) down to two (for Luxembourg), and a specified number (the 'blocking minority') is needed to prevent a decision being taken. In March 1994 the UK reluctantly accepted the so-called **Ioannina compromise**, allowing the 'blocking minority' to be kept at the same proportion of the total when the EU was enlarged. With three new members joining in January 1995, the formula for qualified majority voting was accordingly modified, so that a decision needed 62 votes out of 87 (rather than 54 out of 76 in the 12-member EU).

QUANGO

A quasi-autonomous non-governmental organization. The description is used to indicate bodies set up by the government (through statute or otherwise), which have duties and responsibilities almost akin to government organs but which are nevertheless at arm's length from government. The term more recently favoured by the government for such organizations is 'non-departmental public bodies'. The number of quangos is a matter of some dispute and is dependent upon definition. The government maintains that between 1979 and early 1994 the number has declined from over 2,100 to under 1,400. However, these figures are disputed by government opponents, who perceive a growth of quangos as a result of increasing **privatization** and contracting out of services, and criticize the lack of accountability involved especially given the large budgets under their control. In May 1994 an independent report estimated that there were 5,521 quangos with over 70,000 non-elected 'quangocrats' controlling £46,600 million – nearly one-third of all public expenditure.

QUEEN-IN-PARLIAMENT

The legislative and constitutional functions of the sovereign, currently Queen **Elizabeth**. The Queen is formally one of the three estates of Parliament (the others being the **House of Commons** and the **House of Lords**). Legislation can reach the statute book only when the Queen has given the **royal assent**. The Queen's recommendation is required to sanction any proposal for a charge on public funds; peerages are created in her name; she is responsible for dissolving and proroguing Parliament; the functions of government are exercised in her name by ministers; and the choice of the **Prime Minister** is hers. The Queen normally attends Parliament only at the State Opening, when she delivers the **Queen's Speech** from the throne in the Lords. No sovereign has entered the Commons since Charles I.

QUEEN'S BENCH

One of three divisions of the **High Court** in **England** and **Wales**, with the **Chancery** and the Family divisions. Its president is the **Lord Chief Justice**. Its jurisdiction is primarily in commercial and maritime law, but it also hears civil cases not assigned to the High Court's other benches, and certain appeals. The Chancery division deals largely with property and financial matters. The Family division, established under the Administration of Justice Act 1970, hears cases involving family law, including divorce, maintenance and adoption.

QUEEN'S EVIDENCE

An accused person who gives evidence against accomplices in a crime. Someone who has 'turned Queen's evidence' in this way can generally expect to receive a more lenient sentence, assuming his or her evidence is in some way corroborated by unimpeachable evidence. Although the giving of Queen's evidence does not of itself secure more favourable treatment from the courts (in the same way that a guilty plea does not mitigate any sentence), the alleged leniency shown in the so-called **supergrass trials** in **Northern Ireland** has come under considerable criticism.

QUEEN'S SPEECH

The outline of the government's legislative programme, delivered annually by the sovereign. The Queen's Speech is the centrepiece of the ceremony attending the state opening of a new session of Parliament. The Speech, which is written by the government and delivered by the Queen from the throne in the **House of Lords**, outlines the main bills planned by the government for the next session. **MPs** listen to the speech having been summoned from the **House of Commons** by **Black Rod**.

QUESTION TIME

A set period of parliamentary time allotted for government ministers to answer oral questions. In the **House of Commons**, questions are answered on Mondays, Tuesdays, Wednesdays and Thursdays from 2.35 p.m. to 3.30 p.m. Ministers from different departments answer according to rota. Questions to the **Prime Minister** are put for 15 minutes on Tuesdays and Thursdays; televised live since 1990, they have developed into a ritualized exchange. Notice of questions must be given at least three days in advance and those chosen at random by computer are then printed on the order paper. Questions for written answer may be asked with a similar period of notice; the answers are printed in **Hansard**. In the **House of Lords**, up to four questions addressed to the government may be answered by an appropriate minister at the beginning of business on each sitting day.

RACE RELATIONS

The interaction of people of differing racial groups, an increasingly significant political issue in the UK in the years since the Second World War as the level of **immigration** from the **New Commonwealth** and other areas increased. The Race Relations Act 1965 established the Race Relations Board, empowered to investigate complaints of racial discrimination. The Race Relations Act 1968 widened the Board's powers and created the Community Relations Commission to promote good inter-racial relations. The Race Relations Act 1976 outlawed discrimination in education, training, employment and the delivery of services and goods. It also made incitement to racial hatred a statutory offence. The Commission for Racial Equality (**CRE**) was created under the Act to replace the Race Relations Board and the Community Relations Commission.

Despite the establishment of these bodies, **racism** remains a feature of British society, with Afro-Caribbean and Asian people in particular frequently subject to racial attack. Poor race relations have often led to unrest, particularly in the **inner cities**. Racial tension was certainly behind the **Notting Hill riots** of 1958 and a dominant factor in the rioting at **Broadwater Farm, Toxteth, Brixton** and other urban areas in the 1980s.

RACHMAN, PETER

A Polish-born private landlord, notorious for aggressive treatment of his tenants in Paddington, north London, in the early 1960s. He made his fortune by buying cheap housing and frightening tenants into leaving their homes so that he could sell them. His behaviour, which came to light during the **Profumo affair**, gave rise to the term 'Rachmanism' to denote greedy and terrorizing behaviour by landlords. It led to the establishment of an enquiry into housing in London in July 1963 and subsequently to legislation safeguarding the rights of tenants.

RACISM

The belief in the innate superiority of a particular race and the consequent practice of discrimination on the grounds of race. Although it is most often used in the UK to describe the experiences of black people subject to attack from racist groups like the **BNP**, it is appropriate to use the term to describe **anti-Semitism** and the experiences of other minorities, and to apply it to Nazi and neo-Nazi thought.

Racism remains a significant feature of British life. An opinion poll published in the *Weekly Journal*, a newspaper aimed at the black community, in March 1995 showed that 92 per cent of black people felt that they received worse treatment by the **police** than white people. A poll in the *Guardian*, also in March 1995, revealed that 79 per cent of white Britons polled believed that there was racial prejudice towards black people. A study by the **Policy Studies Institute** in early 1995 suggested that while both culturally and socially black Britons had much in common with their white peers, they nevertheless found it difficult to lay claim to being British because they felt that 'the majority of white Britons really believed that only white people could be British'. These sentiments appeared to be supported by government statistics which show that **unemployment** within the black community is twice as high as among white people.

See also Appendix IV.

RADCLIFFE REPORT

An official security inquiry. In the aftermath of the **Lonsdale** and **Blake** spy scandals, Lord Radcliffe was commissioned by **Prime Minister** Harold **Macmillan** to investigate all aspects of security in the UK. In his 1962 report Radcliffe disclosed extensive communist penetration of the **Civil Service** and the unions, and proposed tighter **positive vetting** and continuation of the **D-Notice** system. His findings were published with all-party backing, and well received at the time, but their claim that there was 'no radical defect in the system' looked hollow when the **Vassall**, **Profumo** and other affairs broke soon after.

RADIO AUTHORITY

An organization established under the Broadcasting Act of 1990. Its functions are to issue licences, supervise the performance of all independent radio stations, and allocate up to three new national **commercial radio** stations by competitive tender. New franchises were subsequently awarded to the 'non-pop' Classic FM in August 1991, to the 'rock and pop' Virgin 1215 in April 1992 and to Talk Radio UK in June 1994. In September 1993, the Authority awarded eight new franchises for radio broadcasting in London, involving the loss by the London Broadcasting Company to London Radio News of its two current licences.

RAILTRACK/RMT STRIKE 1994

A rail dispute which focused attention on the impact of the **privatization** of **British Rail**. Signal workers belonging to the National Union of Rail, Maritime and Transport Workers (RMT) staged 19 days of 24- and 48-hour stoppages over a period of four months in 1994 in pursuit of retrospective compensation for productivity gains and despite the disruption enjoyed significant public support. The cost of the strike on Railtrack, the employer, was considerable (far more than the original RMT demand) and highlighted the vulnerability of the railways to industrial action, renewing doubts about the suitability of British Rail for privatization. A settlement reached at the end of September 1994 was hailed by both sides as a victory. Negotiations before and during the strike were marked by confusion and allegations that Railtrack had been unduly influenced by the government.

RAILWAYS ACT 1993

The legislation which enabled the government to proceed with the highly controversial **privatization** of **British Rail**. It was introduced in Parliament in January 1993 and enacted in November of that year. Based on a July 1992 **White Paper**, it provided for the creation of **Railtrack**, which in April 1994 officially assumed responsibility for the provision of railway track and associated infrastructure. The government's intention was to separate the railway network into 25 companies and transfer them to private-sector operators under franchising proposals.

RAMRAIDING

A criminal activity in which a vehicle is driven into a shop-front and goods are stolen. Ramraiding became prevalent in the UK during the later 1980s and early 1990s and it is often associated with

joyriders and others involved in car theft.

RAPID REACTION FORCE *see* MOBILE THEATRE RESERVE

RATE CAPPING *see* CAPPING

RATES

The form of local taxation levied by local authorities which the **Conservative** government replaced by the **community charge** (poll tax) in **Scotland** in 1989 and in **England** and **Wales** in 1990. Rates were paid by property owners on the basis of the notional rental value of their property, at a rate in each pound specified by the local authority. The money raised funded the provision of local services. Because rates were based on property value and not on personal income, the system was perceived as having become unfairly weighted against owners living alone in large properties and paying high rates. Rates were also criticized by some homeowners and businesses in areas in which local authorities set very high rates in part to fund projects characterized by opponents as those of the **loony left**. **Capping** of local authorities was introduced under the Rates Act 1984, which gave central government the power to limit the spending of local authorities. The poll tax was itself replaced by the **council tax** (which like the rates is a property tax) in April 1993. Businesses continued to pay a modified but standardized version of the rates, the uniform business rate.

RATIONING

A means of apportioning scarce supplies to members of a group or of an entire population. Official nationwide rationing of supplies occurred during the Second World War when basic foods (though not bread), clothes and petrol were rationed under a coupon scheme. A thriving black market in unofficially sold goods developed. Popular expectations that restrictions would be lifted as soon as the war ended were dashed and rationing continued, with restrictions on certain items persisting well into the 1950s. Meat rationing was only lifted in July 1954 while restrictions on coal remained until 1958. As a consequence of the **Suez Crisis**, petrol rationing was reintroduced in December 1956 and continued until May 1957.

Preparations for petrol rationing were made during the 1973 oil crisis, but ultimately rationing was not deemed necessary.

RAVENSCRAIG

The Scottish steelworks closed in 1992 after sustained protests. Against a background of extensive restructuring of the **steel industry**, which involved widespread closures across the **EC**, and after years of vociferous opposition, British Steel closed the Ravenscraig hot strip mill at Motherwell, south of Glasgow, in June 1992. Fears for Ravenscraig's continuing existence first emerged on the closure in June 1986 of the cold strip mill at Gartcosh, near Glasgow, which was Ravenscraig's largest single customer, but its closure was not announced until May 1990. The ensuing battle to save Ravenscraig became a symbol for those advocating a self-contained economy for **Scotland** – **Scottish National Party** leader Alex Salmond described the closure as an 'outrage' – and for opponents of the decline in traditional industries in the **UK**.

RAVES

A popular term for large dance parties usually held outdoors on common or private farmland and sometimes also in large disused buildings in the early 1990s. A focus for **new age travellers**, they resulted in a series of well-publicized clashes between party-goers and the **police** and also in political pressure, particularly from **backbench Conservative MPs**, for the law to be toughened to prevent such activities. Stringent measures in the **Criminal Justice** and Public Order Act 1994 gave the police new powers to impound vehicles, order trespassers to leave private land and turn away people they believed to be travelling to a rave.

REAL LIVES

A **BBC** television documentary series which included the controversial programme, *At the edge of the union*, whose scheduled transmission in August 1985 was cancelled at the instigation of the

BBC Board of Governors. The programme included interviews with Martin McGuiness, reported to be a senior **IRA** figure. In July 1985, **Prime Minister** Margaret **Thatcher** had publicly opposed any interviews with senior **IRA** members being broadcast, while Home Secretary Leon **Brittan** wrote to the Corporation asking for the programme not to be transmitted. With **MPs** and the National Union of Journalists voicing their protests, the BBC said that there had been a failure by its management to observe detailed guidelines on the approval of programmes dealing with **Northern Ireland**, and that accordingly the programme was to be withdrawn. Transmission of an amended programme eventually took place in October 1985.

RECESSION

A cyclical downturn in the economy which formally comes into being when there have been two or more consecutive quarters of falling output. It is widely accepted that since 1945 there have been three recessions in the UK: 1974–5, 1980–1 and 1990–92. However, whereas the first two of these may partly be explained by external shocks in the form of rapid rises in the world price of oil, the third sprang directly from unsustainably rapid economic growth in the late 1980s. The closing quarters of this boom were marked by an **inflation** rate in excess of 10 per cent which the government acted on by sharp rises in **interest rates**. The recession of 1990–92 was the longest of the three, lasting for seven quarters, but it was not as deep as that of 1979–81 when output fell by 5.25 per cent. Recovery technically began in 1992 but was mitigated by a deteriorating position in European countries. Moreover, fear of **unemployment** and the absence of the **feel-good factor** combined to ensure that in the public perception the recession continued well beyond 1992.

RED HAND COMMANDOS

A loyalist paramilitary organization in **Northern Ireland**. The group was involved in a number of sectarian murders in the early 1970s and was banned in 1973. It appeared to be inactive during the 1980s, but was a party to the October 1994 **ceasefire** declaration by the **Combined Loyalist Military Command**.

RED WEDGE

A group of **left-wing** musicians who toured together in 1983–4 in a high-profile bid to raise money for the **Labour Party** and for left-wing causes, notably in support of striking **miners**. The campaign was partly an attempt to reverse the increasing apathy and drift to the right among the young demonstrated by the 1983 **general election**. Those involved included Paul Weller and Billy Bragg. Their attempts were dwarfed by comparison to the spectacular **Band Aid** and **Live Aid** campaigns of 1984–5, which raised funds to relieve African famines.

REDCLIFFE-MAUD REPORT

The report of the **Royal Commission** on Local Government Reform published in June 1969 that recommended sweeping changes to the structure of **local government**. The report suggested that **England** and **Wales** should be divided into eight provinces, each with a provincial council to take charge of economic and social planning in co-operation with the national government. Within the provinces should be 61 areas with their own controlling authorities, plus Greater London which would retain the Greater London Council (**GLC**).

Its recommendations were not effected in the Local Government Act 1972, which outside Greater London created 39 county councils, 296 district councils, six metropolitan county councils and six metropolitan district councils.

REES, MERLYN

(b. 1920) **Labour** Home Secretary in 1976–79, succeeding Roy **Jenkins**. Before his appointment as Home Secretary, Rees had served as **Secretary of State** for **Northern Ireland** in 1974–76. He was given a **life peerage** in 1992.

REFERENDUM

A ballot in which voters are asked to give a binding decision on a particular aspect of policy. While referendums are a regular feature of national life in many countries, in the UK there has been just one nationwide referendum on 5 June 1975, when the electorate was asked to vote on the question 'Do you think that the UK should stay in the European Community (Common Market)?'. The referendum was announced by the **Labour** government on 23 January. There was no precedent for it in UK history, but the Labour Party had promised at the second of the two 1974 **general elections** to submit the results of its renegotiation of **EC** membership terms to the British electorate, either by referendum or by holding yet another **general election**. Party members were free to campaign on either side. The Labour Party conference and the **TUC** in April 1975 both recommended a 'no' vote, but the government's recommendation of a 'yes' vote was eventually followed by a large majority – over 67.2 per cent of valid votes in a 64 per cent turnout. In the early 1990s, the **Major** government rejected calls for a referendum on **Maastricht**, although they were held in several other member states. The argument has, however, been sustained (with increasing support within the **Conservative Party** in particular) that the implications of joining the third stage of European monetary union (**EMU**) are sufficiently far-reaching as to require approval by referendum.

In **Scotland** and **Wales**, a referendum was held in February 1979 on the Labour government's **devolution** proposals. The proposals fell in Scotland because the narrow 'yes' majority was less than the 40 per cent of the electorate which had been specified as necessary. In Wales they were simply rejected outright.

REFUGEE

A person fleeing persecution or war. In international law a refugee is defined under the 1951 Geneva Convention on the Status of Refugees, together with its 1967 Protocol, which also defines states' obligations and responsibilities towards those granted refugee status. Although a refugee has the right to seek **asylum** in another country, it is the state which has the prerogative to grant refugee status.

In recent years the UK government has tended increasingly to grant asylum seekers **exceptional leave to remain** rather than formal refugee status (which would entail concomitant rights to housing etc.), if it is reluctant to subject them to **deportation**. There has also been a tendency in more xenophobic political circles to see the whole asylum procedure as a form of closet **immigration**. In 1993, 16 per cent of asylum seekers' applications were refused, 77 per cent were given exceptional leave to remain and 7 per cent were granted refugee status. In 1994, 74 per cent were refused, 21 per cent given exceptional leave to remain and 5 per cent granted refugee status.

REFUGEE COUNCIL

A voluntary organization formed in 1981 as a merger between the British Council for Aid to Refugees and the Standing Conference on Refugees. It is the main provider of direct services to people seeking **asylum** in the UK and also seeks to promote the rights of **refugees**. In recent years its work has included the settlement of people displaced as a result of the war in Bosnia. It has also helped in the evacuation from Bosnia of those needing medical attention and played a part in **Operation Irma**.

REGIONAL COUNCILS *see* COUNTY COUNCILS

REMAND

The practice of placing people awaiting trial in custody. Bail is most often denied to those facing serious charges and those whom the court believes to be likely to commit other offences, to abscond or to interfere with witnesses. In recent years the number of prisoners on remand has soared. Figures from the **Lord Chancellor's Department** for 1994, released in May 1995, indicated that 23,749 people were awaiting trial in prison or in police cells. Of these 6,100 had been held for more than 16 weeks, the statutory limit (compared with 4,200 in 1991), while 2,874 people had been on remand for more that six months.

RENEGOTIATION

Any process of establishing revised conditions after the conclusion of an initial agreement – but in postwar Britain more particularly the process initiated with the **EC** in 1974 by the incoming **Labour** government to reform the **CAP**, to get a better deal on UK contributions to the EC budget and on **Commonwealth** trade and aid, and to get assurances on the pace and flexibility of planned moves towards **EMU**. A UK government **White Paper** in March 1975 summarized the results of the renegotiation. It recommended, successfully, that the forthcoming **referendum** should approve continued UK membership of the EC on the revised terms.

RENT CONTROL

The imposition of limits on rents charged by landlords as a means of protecting tenants. The controversial Rent Act 1957 passed by the **Conservative** government removed controls on the letting of many houses and allowed for large increases in controlled rents. The Rent Act 1965 passed by the **Labour** government elected the previous year sought to undo these changes, guaranteeing tenants secure tenure and registered fair rents for all privately owned rented properties over a specified rateable value. Certain controls over rents charged by private landlords were relaxed by the Housing Act 1988.

REPOSSESSION

The forced return of property following payment arrears. Although often associated with hire purchase, since the collapse of the housing market in the late 1980s the term has been particularly applied to the seizure of homes by mortgage lenders as an increasing number of borrowers have fallen into arrears. A blighting of the dream of the **home-owning democracy**, more than 275,000 homes were repossessed between 1990 and July 1995, affecting 600,000 people, according to figures given by the Council of Mortgage Lenders. Although repossessions fell by an average of 13 per cent a year between 1991 and the end of 1994, the first six months of 1995 saw an upturn in the number of dwellings taken back by building societies, with some lenders increasing their repossessions by up to 15 per cent. Many of those affected were people who had bought their homes under the **Conservative** government's **right-to-buy** scheme. While high interest rates in the late 1980s and early 1990s contributed to the high levels of repossessions, **negative equity** has also now become an important factor, people in payment difficulties being unable to cut their losses by selling. Mortgage lenders expected the number of repossessions to continue to increase if the government persisted in its plans to restrict the **housing benefits** paid to unemployed mortgage borrowers.

RESELECTION

The requirement, especially in **Labour Party**, for members of parliament to undergo a formal process of readoption by their party in order to stand at a succeeding **general election**. The campaign for 'mandatory reselection' began in the 1970s, particularly among constituency Labour Parties dominated by the left wing, with a view to securing greater accountability of elected representatives. The full reselection requirement – which in fact resulted in **deselection** in only a very small number of cases – was adopted by the party's annual conferences in 1979 and 1980.

RESTRICTIVE PRACTICES

A pejorative term generally used to describe trade union influence of the work process. In his 1964 **White Heat of Technology** speech Harold **Wilson** declared he would leave 'no place for restrictive practices or outdated methods on either side of industry'. In reality restrictive practices entered the popular consciousness as analogous to rigid, union-enforced demarcation lines at the workplace. More generally they imply obstacles to efficiency in any commercial enterprise.

RETIREMENT AGE

The age at which people choose to stop working and take up their **pensions**, generally used to describe the age at which people become eligible to claim the state retirement pension – in the UK, 65 for men and 60 for women. The state pension is paid to individuals who have made sufficient **national insurance** contributions, to women on the basis of their spouse's contributions and on a non-contributory basis to those over 80. A ruling given in the European Court of Justice (**ECJ**) on 17 May 1990 stated that there should be no discrimination between men and women in occupational pension schemes. This did not directly affect state pensions, but the UK government has stated its commitment to equalizing the retirement age, although it has not announced whether the age would be 60, 65 or somewhere in between.

RHODESIA

The name used for Zimbabwe by the white minority government from the declaration of **UDI** in November 1965 to independence following the **Lancaster House Agreement** in April 1980. While under British rule the territory was known as Southern Rhodesia.

RIFKIND, MALCOLM

(b. 1946) **Conservative Foreign and Commonwealth Secretary** since July 1995, succeeding Douglas **Hurd**. The Edinburgh-born Rifkind entered Parliament in 1974. He served as Minister of State for Overseas Development in 1982–3 and as Minister of State at the Foreign Office in 1983–6. In 1986 he was appointed as Secretary of State for **Scotland**, with the task of imposing the **community charge** (poll tax) on a **Labour**-dominated country. In 1990 John **Major** moved him to Transport and in 1992 he was appointed as Secretary of State for Defence.

RIGHT TO BUY

The right of local authority and similar tenants to purchase their own homes. The right was enshrined in the Housing Act 1990 and other legislation as part of the **Conservative** government's policy of encouraging a **'home-owning democracy'**. While at first opposed vehemently by the **Labour Party**, which deplored the reduction of the stock of publicly owned housing, its general popularity meant that it gradually became part of the accepted framework of housing policy. Generous incentives are given to potential owners in the form of discounts related to the length of time during which they have been an authority's tenant. By the end of 1993 around 1,500,000 dwellings had been purchased throughout the country under right-to-buy legislation.

RIGHT TO PRIVACY

Generally construed as the entitlement of public figures such as politicians to conduct their family and social life away from the glare of the news media. This 'right' is increasingly ignored by more aggressive members of the press. More generally, an individual's freedom from interference is partially safeguarded by constraints on police powers to detain, arrest and search individuals and to gain entry to search private premises. The **Interception of Communications Act** controls official powers to eavesdrop on telephone conversations and to intercept and open private mail.

RIGHT TO SILENCE

An individual's right to refuse to answer police questions or give evidence in court, which was controversially limited under the **Criminal Justice** and Public Order Act 1994. Under the Act, courts are permitted to comment adversely on a defendant's decision to remain silent as long as he or she has been cautioned as to the possible consequences of silence. The right to silence had been defended by the **Runciman report**, the findings of the **Royal Commission** on Criminal Justice published in July 1993, which concluded that increasing the pressure on suspects to talk in police stations might result in the conviction of innocent people.

RIGHT-WING

A general term for ideologies or political standpoints including **conservatism**, the **New Right** and, in some interpretations, fascism. The term originates from the National Assembly of Revolutionary France in which more conservative elements (the nobility and clergy) sat on the right, and more radical elements on the left. Some of the key characteristics associated with the right are a defence of capitalism and private property, respect for authority, whether of the state or of tradition, and opposition to socialism and communism.

RIMINGTON, STELLA

(b. 1935) The director of **MI5** since February 1992. A one-time archivist, Rimington went on to train as an intelligence officer specializing in counter-terrorism and surveillance of militant trade unionists and other political activists. Her appointment as director of MI5 was the first to be made public, breaking a convention as old as the security services. This step was taken as part of **Prime Minister** John

Major's policy of **open government**. Rimington has overseen MI5's increasing supremacy over the **police** in important intelligence operations against the **IRA** and in advising the government on political prospects in **Northern Ireland**. In June 1995 the **Home Office** announced that Rimington would be stepping down in 1996.

RIVERS OF BLOOD

The highly controversial speech made by maverick **Conservative MP** Enoch **Powell** on 20 April 1968 in which he warned of what he saw as the social and economic consequences of continued **immigration** into the UK of black people from the **Commonwealth**. The speech was made shortly after the rapid enactment of the **Commonwealth Immigrants Act 1968** and also as the **Race Relations** Bill 1968 was about to be considered in Parliament. Urging drastic limitation of black Commonwealth immigration and the encouragement of voluntary repatriation, Powell said that as he looked ahead he was filled with foreboding, and that like the Roman, he seemed to see 'the River Tiber foaming with much blood'. As a result of this cataclysmic speech Powell was dismissed from the Conservative Party's **Shadow Cabinet**.

RMT *see* NUR

ROCK AGAINST RACISM

An informal grouping of musicians opposed to **racism** and anti-Semitism. Allied to the **Anti-Nazi League**, they aim to raise the consciousness of the public through music and pop concerts. Like the Anti-Nazi League, Rock Against Racism emerged in the late 1970s as a response to the growth in extreme right-wing and racist organizations. It lost prominence in the 1980s but was reactivated in the early 1990s as support grew for neo-Nazis across Europe.

ROLLING DEVOLUTION

The concept of representation through an elected body initially with only a consultative role, which would later extended to encompass the devolution of one or more local departments. Rolling devolution was the basis upon which the 1982 **Northern Ireland Assembly** emerged. The Assembly consisted of 78 members elected by proportional representation, and was scheduled to achieve executive powers devolved from Westminster. However, it failed to secure adequate support across the political communities in the province. The main political parties in **Northern Ireland** were extremely critical of what was generally seen as an unworkable body, and eventually withdrew.

ROLLING NEWS

The concept of a 24-hour non-stop dedicated news service. The idea had been mooted in the **UK** for the **BBC**'s new Radio 5 Live which replaced the sport, youth and education programmes of Radio 5 in March 1994. However, a new mixture emerged of news and features throughout most of the day, with emphasis on sport in the evenings and at weekends. Sports items would include journalism as well as coverage. The change in policy was based on market research showing that there was simply not enough existing demand for a rolling news service.

ROMAN CATHOLIC CHURCH

The worldwide Christian Church acknowledging as its head the Pope, who is the Bishop of Rome. Since 1534 its authority in the UK has been overridden by the **Church of England**, the **established church**, which acknowledges the monarch as its head. The uneasy relationship between the Catholic Church and the Protestant British state introduced by Henry VIII was partially resolved by the highly successful visit of Pope John Paul II in 1982. Shortly before, the Pope's representative was granted full ambassadorial status as Apostolic Nuncio. The leading prelate of the estimated 4,500,000 Roman Catholics living in **England** and **Wales** is Cardinal Basil **Hume**, who is the Archbishop of Westminster. In **Scotland** there are an estimated 750,000 adherents. The organization of the churches on the island of Ireland takes no account of its partition; both the Roman Catholic and the Church of Ireland Primates of All Ireland have their seats at Armagh, in **Northern Ireland**, where there are just over 600,000 Roman Catholic adherents, and where there has been sectarian tension since the first major settlement by British Protestants in the seventeenth century.

In an exceptional move the Pope in mid-1995 approved new rules, formulated as statutes and sent to Rome after the England and Wales Bishops' Conference in April, which would permit married former Church of England clergy to become Roman Catholic priests and work full-time in parishes. The statutes, which came into effect on 1 July and would remain in force for four years, were formulated to accommodate those of a significant number of Church of England clerics who resigned their positions in protest at the **ordination of women priests** and who might wish to become Catholic priests, some of whom had already expressed a desire to do so.

ROME, TREATY OF *see* TREATY OF ROME

RONAN POINT DISASTER

A disaster caused by a gas explosion in the 22-storey Ronan Point tower block in Newham, east London, on 16 May 1968. Three people were killed when all of the flats on one corner of the block collapsed after an explosion on the 18th floor. The explosion raised concerns over the safety of the design of the building, which had been constructed from prefabricated slabs.

ROSLA *see* SCHOOL LEAVING AGE

ROSS ROYAL COMMISSION REPORT ON THE PRESS 1949

A Commission which arose from a **House of Commons** debate on the press.It concluded that there was no evidence of a monopoly situation within the British media, although it severely criticized most newspapers for falling short of the best attainable standards. It proposed the formation of a body to encourage more public responsibility and duty among newspapers. The press eventually responded by creating a General Council of the Press in 1953, renamed the **Press Council** in 1964, which itself was replaced by the **Press Complaints Commission** in January 1991.

ROUGH JUSTICE

A **BBC** television series based on investigative journalism. It is often controversial, focusing as it does on cases where the accused or convicted in criminal cases appear to have been the victim of a miscarriage of justice.

ROWLAND, ROLAND 'TINY'

A British and international businessman and the former chief executive of **Lonrho**, the multinational trading group. Rowland has been something of an unpredictable figure in British business. He became involved in a very public row with the **Fayed** brothers after the latter had taken over the House of Fraser group in 1985, which Rowland himself had wished to acquire. In an announcement in October 1993, however, both sides declared that they had settled their differences, after an eight-year feud conducted partly through the *Observer* newspaper, at the time owned by Rowland. In May 1994 he sold the *Observer* to the Guardian and Manchester Evening News Group for £27,000,000.

ROYAL ASSENT

The action by the Crown making a bill law. The royal assent is signified by letters patent and may be given by the sovereign in person, robed, crowned and seated on the throne in the **House of Lords** (although this has not occurred since 1854) or by Royal Commissioners appointed for the purpose. However, the usual process is for the **Lord Chancellor** and the **Speaker** to interrupt proceedings in their respective chambers at a convenient time and read out the titles of bills to which the sovereign has given assent. A bill becomes an act the moment the royal assent has been granted and has the force of law from the beginning of that day, unless another date for the start of its operation has been included in the act itself.

ROYAL COMMISSION

An ad hoc advisory commission formally appointed by the Crown by virtue of its prerogative powers to investigate an issue of public concern. A commission examines written and oral evidence from government departments and other interested organizations and then submits a report with recommendations. The government will then decide whether to act on the commission's advice. A total of 34 royal commissions have been commissioned since the end of the Second World War, covering the following topics (with chair and date of appointment in parenthesis): population (Sir H. Henderson, 1946); justices of the peace (Lord du Parcq, 1946); the press (Sir D. **Ross**, 1947); betting, lotteries and gaming (H. Willink, 1949); capital punishment (Sir E. Gowers, 1949); taxation of profits and income (Lord Cohen and Lord Radcliffe, 1951); university education in Dundee (Lord Tedder, 1951); marriage and divorce (Lord Morton of Henryton, 1951); Scottish affairs (Earl of Balfour, 1952); east Africa (Sir H. Dow, 1953); the civil service (Sir R. Priestley, 1953); the law relating to mental illness and mental deficiency (Lord Percy of Newcastle, 1954); common land (Sir I. Jennings, 1955); doctors' and dentists' remuneration (Sir H. Pilkington, 1957); local government in Greater London (Sir E. Herbert, 1957); the police (Sir H. Willink, 1960); the press (Lord **Shawcross**, 1961); the penal system in England and Wales (Viscount Amory, 1964); reform of the trade unions and employers' associations (Lord Donovan, 1965); medical education (Lord Todd, 1965); tribunals of inquiry (Sir C. Salmon, 1966); the examination of assizes and quarter sessions (Lord **Beeching**, 1966); local government, England (Sir J. Maud, 1966); local government, Scotland (Lord Wheatley, 1966); the constitution (Lord Crowther and Lord Kilbrandon, 1969); civil liability and compensation (Lord Pearson, 1973); the press (Sir M. Finer and O. McGregor, 1974); standards of conduct in government (Lord Salmon, 1974); gambling (Viscount Rothschild, 1976); the National Health Service (Sir A. Merrison, 1976); legal services (Sir H. Benson, 1976); criminal procedures (Sir C. Philips, 1977); **criminal justice** (Lord **Runciman**, 1991).

ROYAL COMMISSION ON ASSIZES AND QUARTER SESSIONS *see* BEECHING ROYAL COMMISSION

ROYAL COMMISSION ON LEGAL SERVICES *see* BENSON ROYAL COMMISSION

ROYAL FACULTY OF ADVOCATES *see* BAR COUNCIL

ROYAL FAMILY

The family of the hereditary monarch. According to the practice by which the sovereign chooses the name under which they reign, Queen **Elizabeth II** declared in Council in 1952 that she and her successors should be known as the House and Family of Windsor. The name had been adopted in 1917 by King George V. In a separate Order in Council in 1960, the Queen declared that her descendants, other than those bearing royal attributes, should have the name Mountbatten-Windsor, thus preserving the family name of her husband, the Duke of **Edinburgh**.

ROYAL INSTITUTE OF INTERNATIONAL AFFAIRS *see* CHATHAM HOUSE

RPI

The retail price index, the most common measure of **inflation**. The RPI, which is published monthly by the **CSO**, measures price movements of a representative basket of commodities, each of which is weighted for its significance in the average family budget. (These weights are derived from the Family Expenditure Survey.) The outcome is intended to be a measure of the impact of price changes on the average consumer. In its early years the **Thatcher** government promoted as an alternative measure the Tax and Prices Index (TPI) which, it argued, tracked real (post-tax) purchasing power more accurately, but this grew less attractive to ministers as taxes rose and since March 1995 it has not been included in the CSO monthly release. In the 1990s controversy centred on whether or not owner-occupier housing costs should be included. Inclusion of mortgage costs can, perversely, raise the RPI when governments are pushing up **interest rates** precisely in order to cut inflation. Critics argue that the monthly comparison of the RPI with the same month one year earlier (the 'headline rate', which includes mortgage costs) should be allowed only equal status with the 'underlying rate' (which gives the trend). In March 1995 the CSO introduced a new economic yardstick, the RPI(Y), effectively RPI with mortgage interest payments and indirect taxes deducted.

ROYAL ULSTER CONSTABULARY *see* RUC

RSPCA

The Royal Society for the Prevention of Cruelty to Animals, an animal welfare charity. Founded in 1924, the RSPCA is the world's largest organization seeking to protect the welfare of animals, an aim it pursues with the assistance of a large team of inspectors. Its pronouncements tend to be authoritative. It has maintained its following despite the emergence of newer militant animal rights organizations such as the **Animal Liberation Front**. However, it has in recent years adopted a more radical approach to specific issues. Its supporters, for example, were in the forefront of the campaign to stop **live exports** which began in 1994.

RUBBER BULLETS *see* PLASTIC BULLETS

RUC

The Royal Ulster Constabulary – the **Northern Ireland** police force. The RUC was created under the Constabulary (Northern Ireland) Act of 1922 to succeed the Royal Irish Constabulary. The RUC uniquely fulfils a military as well as a civilian function, thus influencing its equipment and training. Since the advent of **the Troubles** in 1969, violence and controversy have dogged the RUC and many of its members have been killed or injured. In the aftermath of the severe rioting in the summer of 1969, the **Scarman report** recognized the fundamental animosity between the **Roman Catholic** community and the overwhelmingly Protestant RUC, perceived at its most oppressively sectarian in the form of the **B Specials**, which were disbanded in 1970. The RUC has been censured by **Amnesty International** for the use of torture, while the **super-grass trials** of the early 1980s led to accusations of RUC-led corruption within the province's legal system. In 1986 the force became involved in allegations that it was operating a **'shoot to kill'** policy, leading to the **Stalker inquiry**. With the declaration of an **IRA ceasefire** in August 1994, it would appear that the RUC's role is bound to change significantly, after some 25 years of operating as a police force within a military environment.

RUNCIMAN REPORT ON CRIMINAL JUSTICE

The report of the Royal Commission on Criminal Justice under Lord Runciman of Doxford published on 6 July 1993, which controversially recommended the abolition in certain cases of defendants' right to **jury** trial and also the creation of a tribunal to examine alleged miscarriages of justice. The commission had been announced in March 1991 by the Home Secretary Kenneth **Baker** on the grounds that the acquittal of the **Birmingham Six** raised serious issues relating to the **criminal justice system**.

Among its other recommendations were that defence lawyers should disclose the basis of their case to the prosecution before a **crown court** trial, that the use of uncorroborated confessions – which had lain behind convictions in a number of celebrated miscarriages of justice – should continue to be allowed, and that a formal system of sentence discounts (often known as **plea bargaining**) should be introduced. In September 1993 the Home Secretary Michael **Howard** underlined the government's commitment to the creation of the independent review tribunal in a speech to the **Conservative Party** conference and a government discussion paper on its composition was published on 25 March 1994.

RUSHDIE, SALMAN *see* SATANIC VERSES

RUSI

The Royal United Services Institute, the oldest of the **Establishment**'s research institutes in the foreign policy area. Participation in RUSI studies and conferences, originally confined mainly to military personnel, began increasingly to draw in other officials, academics and commentators from the 1960s onwards.

SAATCHI BROTHERS

Maurice Saatchi and his brother Charles, the country's most celebrated advertising moguls who established themselves in the 1970s but came to prominence in the 1980s as the **Conservative Party**'s agency. Typical of their style and approach was the famous 'Labour isn't working' poster depicting a dole queue; it was widely used in the 1979 election campaign which brought Margaret **Thatcher** to power. The brothers overstretched themselves in the 1980s when they made an audacious bid for Midland Bank, and in 1994 they were ousted acrimoniously from the company they established. They subsequently formed a new company, in which Maurice took the lead in order to allow his brother to devote his time and energy to his role as the nation's chief patron of modern art.

SACKS, RABBI JONATHAN

(b. 1948) The Chief Rabbi of the United Hebrew Congregations of the Commonwealth. Born in London, he was appointed as the sixth incumbent of the post by the Council of the **United Synagogue** in September 1991 in succession to the former Chief Rabbi, Immanuel Jacobovitz. Prior to assuming his current post, he had pursued a distinguished academic career and was Rabbi of Marble Arch Synagogue (1983–90). In March 1995 Sacks was at the centre of a controversy after some liberal and reformist groups called for his resignation in protest against an article in the **Jewish Chronicle** in which he questioned the faith of Jews who did not regard the Torah as the revealed word of God.

ST PAULS RIOTS

The serious disturbances in an **inner city** area of Bristol, south-west England, on 2 April 1980, consisting of fighting between black residents and **police**, and looting. The riots started after a police raid on a café and spread quickly, forcing the police to withdraw, seal the area and await reinforcements. Eight hours later they re-entered the district, but it was by then largely quiet. The unrest was widely seen as the result of years of tension between the city's black population and the police. A report by the Commission for Racial Equality (**CRE**) published in May 1980 recommended more police foot patrols, and training for officers to help them understand **ethnic minority** groups. A wave of riots hit other UK inner cities in 1981.

SALMONELLA AFFAIR

Political controversy over the incidence of salmonella food poisoning caused by eggs. Concern over the issue was heightened in December 1988 when the flamboyant junior health minister, Edwina Currie, made the following remark in a television interview: 'Most of the egg production in this country, sadly, is infected with salmonella.' The comments led to a slump in egg sales and strong protests from egg producers, several of whom issued writs against the minister. Two weeks later the controversy had grown to such proportions that Currie resigned and the government announced a scheme to compensate farmers for their lost sales.

SALVATION ARMY

A Christian evangelical sect founded in 1965 by William Booth, it took its present name in 1878. A world-wide movement, the Salvation Army is best known in the UK for its work with the homeless and in tracing missing people. Commissioner Dinsdale Pender is the current Territorial Commander in the UK, where there are 55,000 soldiers and 1,800 active officers.

SAMARITANS

A charity providing counselling for people in distress. Founded in 1953 by the Rev. Chad Varah, the Samaritans exists primarily to offer a 24-hour support service to those in despair or considering ending their lives, but also to dispel the myths surrounding depression. All work is confidential and undertaken by volunteers trained by the charity.

SAN FRANCISCO CONFERENCE

The international conference held in San Francisco, USA, in April–June 1945, at the end of which participants signed the **UN** Charter. The conference was attended by delegates from 51 countries, comprising 47 fully independent states, Byelorussia and Ukraine (which were constituent republics of the Soviet Union), and India and the Philippines (which had not at that stage achieved full independence from Britain and the USA respectively).

SANCTIONS

Measures taken by one country, or by groups of countries, to put pressure on an illegal regime or on another country deemed guilty of unacceptable behaviour. The term was first introduced in 1919 in the constitution of the League of Nations (the precursor of the **UN**). The League instituted, but could not enforce, sanctions against Italy in 1936 following its invasion of Abyssinia. More recent examples of sanctions include those levied by the USA against Cuba (from 1960), Nicaragua (in 1985–90), and the military regime in Haiti (since 1991). UN mandatory sanctions include trade restrictions placed on Rhodesia in 1966 in the wake of **UDI**, oil and arms embargoes on **apartheid** South Africa, comprehensive sanctions placed on Iraq after its 1990 invasion of Kuwait and maintained after the **Gulf War**, and sanctions against Yugoslavia. The effectiveness of sanctions may be undermined by lack of commitment in carrying them out, by weaknesses in their enforcement, and by **sanctions-busting** such as that exposed by the **Bingham report** in the case of Rhodesia.

SANCTIONS-BUSTING

Covert evasion of trade restrictions, both by a country subject to **sanctions**, and by its suppliers. Evidence of sanctions-busting operations to supply the **UDI** government of Rhodesia was revealed by the 1978 **Bingham report**. It is widely assumed that similar operations supplied the apartheid regime in South Africa. Sanctions-busting has latterly detracted from the effectiveness of sanctions against Yugoslavia.

SAOR EIRE

A little-known **left-wing republican** organization formed in Dublin in 1931. Although it appears on the UK list of proscribed organizations, it has been noted more for its involvement in armed robberies in the Irish Republic than in any documented violence. It is generally not believed to represent a real threat to security.

SAS

The Special Air Service Regiment, whose motto is 'Who dares wins' – an elite squad of soldiers largely recruited from volunteers within the Parachute Regiment of the British army. Established by Col. David Stirling during the Second World War, and subsequently maintaining a low profile, the SAS came to public notice and received much acclaim for its role in the **Iranian embassy siege** in London in 1980.

THE SATANIC VERSES

The novel by the Muslim-born British author, Salman Rushdie, published in September 1988. Variously regarded as a tale of migration and religious mythology, it became the subject of a worldwide controversy after Muslims claimed that it had blasphemed the Prophet Muhammad. The allegation triggered violent protests across the Muslim world where governments ordered the book to be banned. Muslims in North America and Europe, notably the UK, also agitated, unsuccessfully, for the book to be banned.

The novel's symbolic status as the embodiment of free speech against the tyranny of religious doctrine was finally enshrined in February 1989 when the Ayatollah Ruhollah Khomeini of Iran pronounced a **fatwa** which judged the book blasphemous and sentenced Rushdie to death for apostasy. The Iranian government was reported shortly afterwards to have despatched assassination squads abroad to implement the verdict. Rushdie obtained the official protection of the British government and has lived in hiding since February 1989. His efforts and those of his supporters to persuade world governments to impose sanctions on Iran to force it to rescind the *fatwa* have so far met with little success.

SATELLITE TELEVISION

The transmission of television signals by broadcasting satellites whose messages can be received by small domestic satellite dishes. Known as direct broadcasting by satellite (DBS), the system precludes the need for the expensive preparatory work involved in **cable television**. Satellite TV has grown in popularity by providing a multitude of specialized channels and a striking diversification in terms of programme content. The aim is to appeal to groups such as the young, women and **ethnic minorities**, thus making programmes more attractive to advertisers. Satellite TV is able to provide all-day films, sport, comedy, drama and music, with access also to US and European news services. Its main UK operator, **BSkyB**, relies heavily for funding on subscriptions from users of satellite dishes.

SAVE THE CHILDREN

The largest international voluntary agency in the UK, which works with deprived children both in the UK and in some 50 underdeveloped countries. It engages both in disaster relief and in long-term development projects, focusing on children's rights.

SBS

The Special Boat Service, a unit composed of Royal Marine Commandos. Known as an elite within an elite, the SBS was formed during the Second World War to carry out beach reconnaissance and raiding duties along European coastlines. Based at Poole in Dorset, the unit operates worldwide in great secrecy. It was known to be involved in the **Falklands conflict**.

SCARGILL, ARTHUR

(b. 1938) The **left-wing NUM** president since 1981. Scargill was a Yorkshire Area NUM militant who gained considerable publicity as a leader of the mass picket which in 1972 closed the Saltley (Birmingham) coking plant. He was soon elected youngest-ever president of the Yorkshire Area NUM, supporting a militant industrial policy, favouring the left wing of the **Labour Party** and becoming the country's best-known miner. He was comfortably elected NUM president in 1981 on a platform of resisting closures. In 1984 he led the union during the **miners' strike** during which he controversially refused to authorize a national ballot to legitimize industrial action. Then and later he urged a militant policy at the **TUC**, scornfully dismissing the **new realism**. Eventually a drastic loss of NUM membership led Scargill to lose his place on the TUC general council and his calls to action at Congress had decreasing effect. In the Labour Party Scargill continued to advocate fundamental left-wing socialism, but there his fortunes waned with those of the left. The events leading to the 1993 **coal industry White Paper** briefly revived his fortunes as the NUM benefited from widespread popular sympathy, but the final run-down of the coal industry and **privatization** (both predicted by Scargill prior to 1984) followed, leaving his influence considerably diminished.

SCARMAN REPORT

The report of a public inquiry into the April 1981 **Brixton riots**. Lord Scarman, a law lord, was appointed to carry out the public inquiry into the disorders. His report was published in November 1981. Scarman identified the causes of the riots as a breakdown in relations between the police and the community, **unemployment** and social deprivation, racial disadvantage, and a rising level of street crime. His recommendations covered not only direct matters (such as police accountability and the law on racist marches) but also more general aspects of the problems facing inner-city areas, including housing and education, with special reference to the needs of **ethnic minorities**.

SCARMAN TRIBUNAL *see* DIVIS

SCHENGEN CONVENTION

A convention providing for the abolition of passport controls on common borders, the strengthening of such controls on external borders, and co-operation on **immigration** and **police** matters. On 14 June 1985 an outline agreement to this effect was signed by Belgium, France, Germany, Luxembourg and the Netherlands and a formal accord was signed on 19 June 1990. The convention has subsequently been signed by Italy (27 November 1990), Spain and Portugal (25 June 1991), Greece (6 November 1992) and Austria (28 April 1995), which saw it as a key adjunct to the **single market** programme of the **EU**.

The convention entered into force on 26 March 1995, although Italy and Greece were granted a temporary **derogation** until their control procedures could be strengthened. The convention has not been signed by Denmark, Ireland or the UK. In 1991–2, in a move to improve EU co-operation on **asylum** policy, EU member states also signed the **Dublin Convention**.

SCHOOL LEAVING AGE

The earliest age at which a pupil can legally leave school. The **Butler Education Act 1944** raised the school leaving age from 14 to 15, a target to be achieved by 1947. It was increased to the age of 16 in 1972–3 under an initiative known as ROSLA (Raising Of the School Leaving Age). Pupils kept on at school in this interim period were known as ROSLA pupils.

SCHOOL MILK

The supply of free school milk as provided for under the **Butler Education Act 1944**. It was withdrawn from children over the age of eight, except those in special schools, in 1971 by the then Education Secretary, Margaret **Thatcher**, earning her the nickname **'milk snatcher'**. The Education Act 1980 removed any obligation on schools to provide free milk, although they retained the discretion to do so.

SCOTLAND

The country occupying the northern part of the mainland of **Great Britain**. In 1603 James VI of Scotland succeeded Elizabeth I on the throne of **England** as James I. His successors reigned as sovereigns of **Great Britain**, but political union of England and Scotland did not take place until the Act of Union of 1707, which set the framework for the modern government of Scotland. Scotland was represented at the Westminster parliament, there was a common flag and uniform coinage. However, Scotland retained its own legal and education systems and the **established church** is the **Church of Scotland**. An attempt to achieve **devolution** was defeated by referendum in 1979. Ministerial responsibility for Scotland rests with a **Secretary of State** of **Cabinet** rank. The Scottish Office has a wide range of statutory functions administered by five main departments: the Agriculture and Fisheries Department; the Education Department; the Environment Department; the Home and Health Department; and the Industry Department for Scotland.

SCOTLAND YARD

The original site of headquarters off **Whitehall** of the London Metropolitan **Police** Force. Although the 'Met' has been headquartered at a different site (New Scotland Yard, near Victoria) for over 20 years, the term Scotland Yard persists and is often used as a synonym for the criminal investigation department of the Metropolitan Police.

SCOTT AFFAIR *see* THORPE CASE

SCOTT INQUIRY

The 1993–4 inquiry into UK defence-related exports to Iraq. The inquiry under Lord Justice Scott was set up following the collapse of the **Matrix Churchill** trial, although the inquiry's terms of reference included the **super-gun** and other defence and **dual-use** sales. Much of the inquiry focused on whether the government had relaxed the arms embargo on Iraq without informing Parliament, and on the controversial use of **gagging orders** designed to prevent confidential information being revealed in court. **Prime Minister** John **Major** was called to give evidence, as were his predecessor Margaret **Thatcher** and various senior **Cabinet** ministers and **civil servants**. The main public hearings of the inquiry formally ended on 30 March 1994. Official publication of the report is not expected for some months; a series of leaks in June 1995 has suggested that Scott had questioned the behaviour of senior members of the government.

SCOTTISH GRAND COMMITTEE

A **standing committee** of the **House of Commons**. The Grand Committee comprises all 72 Scottish **MPs** and may be convened anywhere in **Scotland**. It considers the principle of Scottish **bills** referred to it at **second reading** stage. It also debates Scottish estimates and any other wholly Scottish matters referred to it. In March 1993 the government announced proposals to provide for more debates by the Grand Committee as well as to allow Scottish Office ministers to make statements to the Committee. In addition the new proposals would enable the Committee to invite the Scottish Office Minister in the **House of Lords** and the **Lord Advocate** to give evidence before it. It was believed that the initiative was a response to **Labour**'s plans for increasing Scottish autonomy.

SCOTTISH NATIONAL BLOOD TRANSFUSION SERVICE *see* NATIONAL BLOOD AUTHORITY

SCOTTISH NATIONAL PARTY

A left-of-centre political party committed to the creation of an independent parliament in **Scotland**. It began life as the National Party of Scotland in 1928, becoming the Scottish National Party (SNP) in 1934, after a merger of **home rule** and independence pressure groups. Its most notable **general election** success came in October 1974, when it won 11 seats. However, after the 1992 general election it had only three **MPs**, while Jim Sillars – one of the party's most prominent activists – had lost the Glasgow Govan seat he spectacularly won from **Labour** in a 1988 **by-election**. Under leader Alex Salmond – elected in 1990 – the aim of the SNP has been self-government for Scotland as an independent member state of the European Union. The party has struggled to maintain its challenge to Labour throughout the west of Scotland, being unable to overcome the failure to concentrate its vote. However, it increased its parliamentary representation to four in May 1995, when in a by-election it won Perth and Kinross from the **Conservatives**.

SCOTTISH VOCATIONAL EDUCATION COUNCIL *see* NCVQ

SCOTTISH VOCATIONAL QUALIFICATIONS *see* GNVQ

SCOTVEC *see* NCVQ

SCREAMING LORD SUTCH *see* MONSTER RAVING LOONY PARTY

SDLP

The Social Democratic and Labour Party – the mainly **Roman Catholic** political party based in **Northern Ireland**, closely connected to the UK **Labour Party**. Led by John **Hume** since 1979 and currently represented by four **MPs** in the UK Parliament, the SDLP has long held the view that it is within the structure of the Anglo-Irish relationship that the solution to the problems of the province can be found. The party therefore initiated the **New Ireland Forum** in 1983–4, took part in secret talks with **Sinn Féin** in 1993 and was widely credited with having done much of the political groundwork which contributed towards the **IRA ceasefire** declaration of August 1994.

SDP

The Social Democratic Party, formed in 1981 by defecting former senior **Labour Party** members, who had become alarmed at the party's drift to the left wing in the late 1970s and early 1980s. The defectors, who were known as the **Gang of Four**, launched the SDP in the **Limehouse Declaration**, backing a mixed economy, continued **EEC** membership, the maintenance of a nuclear deterrent and a renewal of **Keynesianism**. The SDP contested the 1983 **general election** in **alliance** with the **Liberal Party** and in a startling result won over one-quarter of the vote, almost beating Labour into third place in terms of share of the vote. Although some welcomed the party as a bid to break the mould of British politics, many on the centre-left accused the SDP of dividing the left and thus effectively keeping the **Conservative Party** in power in the 1980s.

The uneasy alliance between Liberals and the SDP continued until 1987 but a disappointing general election result in that year led to overwhelming pressure for a merger between the two centre parties, which became the **Social and Liberal Democrats** in 1988. SDP leader David **Owen** refused to join the new party and dissolved the rump SDP in 1990.

SECOND READING

A parliamentary debate on draft legislation. Bills which have been given a **first reading** in either the **House of Commons** or the **House of Lords** are published and the question posed 'that the bill be now read a second time'. A lengthy debate then takes place on the bill's general principles, concluding with a vote. Any member may table a 'reasoned amendment' setting out why he or she believes a bill should not get a second reading. Traditionally, a second reading in the Lords is unopposed.

SECONDARY MODERN SCHOOLS

A type of school introduced as part of the postwar reorganization of education.

The **Butler Education Act 1944** created secondary modern schools in **England** and **Wales** to be attended by those children (about 80 per cent of the total) who, by failing the **eleven-plus**, were disqualified from attending **grammar schools** or technical schools. Secondary moderns, perceived as branding those who attended them as failures, rarely enjoyed public esteem and during the 1960s and 1970s were generally subsumed into **comprehensive schools**.

SECONDARY PICKETING

The attempts by strikers to achieve stoppages of work at other sites. Secondary picketing was a feature of major national industrial disputes up to 1980, favoured by militants to maximize the impact of a stoppage during the **Winter of Discontent**. It was used for the last time in the 1980 **steel industry** strike. The Employment Act 1980 made secondary picketing unlawful by restricting picketing to union members at their own place of work.

SECRET INTELLIGENCE SERVICE *see* MI6

SECRETARY OF STATE

The formal title for a **Cabinet** minister in charge of a government department; thus the Minister of Defence is officially known as the Secretary of State for Defence. The principal exceptions to this protocol are the **Chancellor of the Exchequer** and the President of the **Board of Trade** (the title which may be used by the Secretary of State for Trade and Industry), and the Home Secretary, who is very rarely referred to by his correct title – the Secretary of State for the Home Department.

SECURITIES AND INVESTMENTS BOARD

The regulatory body for investment markets. The SIB became the designated agency under the **Financial Services Act 1986** to regulate the activities of investment businesses. Its main aims are to provide a high level of investor protection and to promote overall efficiency in the financial markets.

SECURITY COUNCIL

The **UN** Security Council, which has 'primary responsibility for the maintenance of international peace and security' under the UN Charter. There are five permanent members, and 10 non-permanent members (six until 1965) elected for two-year terms. The **UK** participates as one of the former (along with China, France, Russia and the USA), thus enjoying a '**top table**' status with veto powers. The exclusivity of this arrangement is increasingly under challenge from countries which consider it no longer realistic to treat the UK as a **first-rank power**.

SECURITY SERVICES *see* MI5, MI6

SELECT COMMITTEE

A parliamentary body of inquiry. Members are selected from the **House of Commons** or the **House of Lords** to inquire into and report on specified matters. In the Commons, select committees exist to look into the work of most government departments. There are also committees dealing with aspects of the parliamentary process such as the committee of privileges, the committee on conduct of members and a committee on procedure. Select committees are given powers to send for persons, papers and records and to question witnesses under oath. In the Lords, there are select committees on Europe and on science and technology. Further select committees may be appointed ad hoc in both houses.

SELLAFIELD

A **nuclear reprocessing** plant in Cumbria, on a site known until 1971 as **Windscale** (where the world's first known nuclear power accident occurred in 1957). Opponents of the Sellafield plant claim that radiation from it has caused cancers among the workforce, health problems in the surrounding area, and leukaemia in the children of men who work at Sellafield. Plans for a new type of reprocessing plant at Sellafield, known as **Thorp**, were finally approved in early 1994, having been delayed for many years by protests from environmental groups.

SELSDON MAN

A term coined in 1970 to denote that element of the electorate which was particularly targeted by the Conservative Party in its successful **general election** campaign of that year. Named after the location of a semi-secret meeting of the **Shadow Cabinet**, Selsdon man was seen as representing an increasingly classless section of the population which could be attracted by a party representing individualism and offering the policy of the free market, together with a programme of tax cuts, selectivity of access to social security benefits, and a more intense law and order campaign.

SEMI-HOUSETRAINED POLECAT

The epithet conferred on right-wing **Conservative MP** Norman **Tebbit** in 1977 by the then Employment Secretary Michael **Foot**, after Tebbit had provokingly asked, 'Does Mr Foot know he is a fascist?'

SEMTEX

A Czech-made plastic explosive, widely used by terrorist organizations. Semtex has been relatively easy to smuggle because it has no smell, and to handle since it cannot be exploded without a detonator. The **IRA** made extensive use of semtex throughout its long-standing campaign of violence, most spectacularly during the **Brighton bomb attack** on the **Conservative** Cabinet in October 1984.

SENTENCE DISCOUNTS *see* PLEA BARGAINING

SERETSE KHAMA AFFAIR

The connivance of the British **colonial** authorities and the white minority regimes in South Africa and **Rhodesia** to deny Seretse Khama the chieftainship of the Bamangwato tribe in Botswana (then the British protectorate of Bechualand). In 1948 Seretse Khama had married a white woman (Ruth Williams) while pursuing his legal career in London. The marriage was opposed by his uncle and regent, Tshekedi Khama, as well as by the South African and Rhodesian governments, which feared the political consequences of a mixed marriage. Under considerable pressure, in 1950 the British decided to exile Seretse Khama. He was allowed to return to Bechuanaland in 1956 after he renounced the chieftainship. However, he had widespread popular support among the Bamangwato and no other chief was appointed. Seretse Khama thus enjoyed all the traditional power of a chief while being free to act within the modern political system. In 1965 his Botswana Democratic Party won the pre-independence elections and at independence in 1966 he became President, a position he held until his death in 1980.

SERIOUS FRAUD OFFICE

The department for the investigation and prosecution of serious and complex fraud. It was created by the Criminal Justice Act 1987 with powers to operate in **England**, **Wales** and **Northern Ireland**. The SFO is staffed by lawyers, accountants and others with relevant experience, and works closely with the police, but nevertheless has had a surprisingly low 'clear-up' rate.

SERPS

The state earnings related pension scheme, under which an additional **pension** payment above the basic state retirement pension is made to retired employees who have paid **national insurance** (NI) contributions above a stipulated level. People are permitted to 'contract out' of SERPS, with the result that they and their employers pay NI at a lower rate than they would if 'contracted in'. In the 1980s and early 1990s the **Conservative** government – keen to encourage the growth of personal pensions – introduced additional incentive NI rebates and personal pension payments for young people to encourage them to contract out of SERPS and into personal pension schemes.

SERVICES SECTOR

That part of the economy concerned with intangible, non-transferable goods, such as banking, finance, telecommunications, transport, dental and medical services, education and recreation. Output and employment in the services sector has grown with the relative and absolute decline in the **manufacturing sector** since the mid-1950s. Some economists have expressed fears that a process of de-industrialization will have serious implications for Britain's economic future, while others point out that the growth of services is characteristic of all advanced economies.

SET THE PEOPLE FREE

The slogan of R. A. **Butler**'s 1952 **budget**. In his first Budget, Butler raised the Bank Rate after 20 years of **interest rate** stability, restricted imports and raised indirect taxes. He also wiped out food subsidies using the savings to make payments to the disadvantaged and to remove the burden of income tax from around 2,000,000 people. Although his principal aim was to achieve an improvement in the **balance of payments**, he was able to present the proposals as a step towards individual liberty, offering the country 'both more realism and more hope'.

SET-ASIDE

A process under the **CAP** whereby arable land is taken out of cultivation. In 1992 as part of a major CAP reform cereal prices were cut in order to pave the way for lower livestock prices. Farmers losing income as a result were compensated, but only if they 'set aside' 15 per cent of their productive land – effectively paying farmers not to produce. This reversal of the former output-maximizing thrust of the CAP owed much to **UK** pressure on Ray McSharry, the then member of the European **Commission** with responsibility for Agriculture. Set-aside payments for 1995 ranged from **ECU** 320.05 (£298.43 using the **green pound** rate as of 1 July 1994) for each hectare of land taken out of cereal production to ECU 618.76 (£576.96) per hectare of land taken out of linseed production.

SEX DISCRIMINATION ACT

The 1975 UK legislation which outlawed discrimination and victimization on the grounds of sex or marital status. The act, which applies equally to women and men, covers broadly non-contractual employment matters (contractual employment matters being already covered by the Equal Pay Act 1970), the letting of accommodation and the provision of financial and other services. Criteria are laid down for defining 'genuine occupational qualifications' which remain outside the act, and there are certain exemptions from the provisions. The enforcement of the act is entrusted to the Equal Opportunities Commission (**EOC**), which may take legal action itself or support individuals in their own actions (including before the European Court of Justice (**ECJ**)). The Sexual Discrimination Act 1986 brought the legislation broadly into line with **EC** directives on equal treatment.

SEX EDUCATION

The teaching of both the physical and ethical aspects of sexual reproduction. Always a controversial educational issue, sex education was originally envisaged as part of the **national curriculum** in 1988 but was removed as part of the Education Act 1993. It remains compulsory in secondary schools, although parents have the right to withdraw their children from some or all lessons. In primary schools, governing bodies have discretion as to how sex education is taught. Schools have often come into conflict with parents and governing bodies for providing what was regarded as 'excessive' information on sexual relations, for example discussing homosexuality, and advising on contraception and oral sex.

SEXISM

The practice of discrimination on the grounds of gender, with women almost invariably losing out to men. Sexism is based on the assumption, sometimes unconscious, that one sex is superior to another. It is vehemently challenged by **feminism**. Sexists also insist on conformity with the traditional stereotyping of social roles on the basis of gender. Attempts to counter sexism have included **positive discrimination**.

SEXUAL REVOLUTION

The general liberalization of established social and moral attitudes to sex in the UK and the **West** during the mid- to late 1960s. During this period the impact of **women's lib**, the increasing number of economically independent women and the widespread introduction of the contraceptive **pill** combined to allow women in particular to reassess their attitudes to sex and marriage.

SHADOW CABINET

The leading political figures of the principal Opposition party in Parliament, who meet on a regular basis to manage the business of opposition and scrutinize the activities of the governing party. The

Shadow Cabinet, headed by the **Leader of the Opposition** (a post held in 1995 by Tony **Blair**), has a comparatively recent history. The pre-1955 period was dominated by unofficial and unannounced arrangements, with such groups as were formed in opposition known as the 'ex-Cabinet' or the 'late Cabinet'. In July 1955, **Labour** Opposition leader Clement **Attlee** announced that members of the parliamentary committee (formed when Labour were in opposition to manage its affairs in Parliament), together with other leading Opposition figures, were to be allocated to specific policy issues. This group came to be recognized as the Labour '**front-bench** team', amounting virtually to the creation of a shadow government, or Shadow Cabinet; the bulk of them are elected annually by the **PLP** soon after the Labour Party conference. With their move into Opposition in 1964, the **Conservative Party** adopted similar arrangements, although Conservative Shadow Cabinet members are appointed by the leader of the party, rather than elected. Today, Shadow Cabinet appointments and reshuffles are given a certain prominence in the media, with political journalists commenting on such changes in the same way (although with not quite the same depth of coverage) with which ministerial changes in the government are dealt.

SHANKILL

A Protestant area of Belfast in **Northern Ireland**, from which **loyalists** are considered to glean much of their support. The area runs parallel to the mainly Catholic **Falls Road** and has been separated from it since 1969 by a **peace wall**, built following severe rioting and house-burning. The first constable of the Royal Ulster Constabulary (**RUC**) to be killed in the province, Victor Arbuckle, was shot dead in the Falls road area during a riot in 1969.

SHARE-OWNING DEMOCRACY

The **Conservative** policy, particularly during the **Thatcherite** era, to extend share ownership to ordinary families, sponsoring middle-class aspirations. A complement to the notion of a **home-owning democracy**, the policy's cornerstone was the **privatization** of state-owned utilities, beginning with **BT** in November 1984.

SHAWCROSS COMMISSION

The Royal Commission on the Press which reported in 1962. The establishment of the Commission had been prompted by the demise of the *News Chronicle* in 1960. Chaired by Lord Shawcross, Attorney General in the **Labour** government of 1945–51, its principal finding was that it could find 'no acceptable legislative or fiscal way' to remove the danger posed by monopoly control of communications. However, one eventual result of the Commission's work was the extension of the role of the **Monopolies and Mergers Commission** under the provisions of the Monopolies and Mergers Act of 1965, whereby special provision was made for its investigation of newspaper mergers.

SHEEHY REPORT

The report of an inquiry into the structure and management of the **police** force, published on 30 June 1993. Chaired by Sir Patrick Sheehy, the inquiry recommended in particular a reduction in the number of senior ranks in the police, the introduction of fixed-term contracts, payment on the basis of responsibility, performance and the difficulties of the job, the abolition of annual index-linked pay awards and also of certain allowances, and restriction of full sick pay. The proposals aroused fierce opposition throughout the police service, but most were generally accepted by the government and many were incorporated in the Police and **Magistrates'** Courts Act which came into force in July 1994.

See also Appendix VI.

SHEFFIELD STUDENT GAMES

A mishandled city rejuvenation project. Sheffield hosted the World Student Games in 1991, intending to signal a new image for a city long associated with heavy industry. The **Labour**-run city council erected impressive new sports facilities in the Lower Don Valley, a former industrial area, but public and more importantly media interest was overestimated, and costs were allowed to overrun. In the absence of central government assistance with excess costs, debt will rest with the city until the next century.

SHELTER

A pressure group highlighting the plight of homeless people and campaigning for increased provision of low-cost housing. Shelter was founded in 1966, in the wake of the screening of **Cathy Come Home**, and established itself by high-profile dramatization of **homelessness**. Its two outstanding leaders, Des Wilson and Sheila McKechnie, ably projected Shelter's aims during the 1970s and 1990s, often securing public action and always maintaining an informed critique of government policy.

SHERIFF COURT

The court hearing most criminal and civil cases under **Scotland's** separate judicial system. The Sheriff Court hears all but the most serious criminal offences and has almost unlimited jurisdiction in civil cases as well. The supreme civil court in Scotland is the **Court of Session** and the supreme criminal court is the **High Court of the Justiciary**.

SHIPBUILDING

A declining industrial sector. The security of shipbuilding, one of the bastions of British economic prosperity during the nineteenth and earlier twentieth century, was threatened from 1960, when orders began to decline. Governments pursued a subsidy policy, and in 1967, under the Shipbuilding Industry Act of that year, four yards were grouped into Upper Clyde Shipbuilders (UCS) and loans were extended to this and other undertakings. Faced with possible closure in 1971, UCS employees staged a work-in, but the general decline continued. The **Labour** government **nationalized** all the country's major shipbuilding assets in 1975, grouping them within British Shipbuilders and continuing a policy of subsidy. In the 1980s this was policy was abandoned by the **Conservatives**, and the number of yards dwindled. By the mid-1990s shipbuilding was limited to a handful of yards, most of which were building ships only for the Royal Navy and all of which faced an insecure future.

SHOOT TO KILL

The term used to describe a policy that undercover and other security forces in **Northern Ireland** were accused of pursuing, especially in the early 1980s. The allegation was that they would deliberately seek to shoot **IRA** members and other **republican** sympathizers dead rather than aiming to maim. In 1988 the UK government decided not to take any further action on the allegations of a shoot to kill policy, which were being investigated by the **Stalker inquiry**. In the same year, similar accusations were made over the 'Death on the Rock' incident, when three IRA members were killed by the security forces in **Gibraltar**, although a subsequent inquest returned a verdict of lawful killing.

SHORT SHARP SHOCK

A system designed to discourage criminal behaviour, especially among persistent juvenile offenders, through a harsh regime at special detention centres. In the UK the scheme was tried for a while in the early 1980s, and following examination of 'shock incarceration' 'boot camps' in the USA, the reintroduction of a parallel scheme as part of the government's plans to deter **young offenders** is scheduled under the **Criminal Justice** and Public Order Act 1994.

SICKLE CELL ANAEMIA

An incurable condition which affects people of African, Asian and Middle Eastern origin, causing tiredness, jaundice, and stomach and joint pains. Campaigners have claimed that research into the disease has been underfunded because the disease does not affect whites.

SIDDIQUI, KALIM

The current Director of the **Muslim Institute**. Resident in the UK since the 1960s when he began a career in journalism, he gained widespread publicity in 1989 after he called on Muslims in the UK to implement the death sentence imposed by the late Ayatollah Khomeini on Salman Rushdie (author of **The Satanic Verses**). Threatened with prosecution on charges of inciting murder, he later explained that Muslims were duty-bound to apply the fatwa only on territory under Muslim rule. In 1990 he was responsible for launching the Muslim Manifesto which highlighted the demands of UK Muslims and laid the framework for a **Muslim Parliament**, inaugurated in 1992.

SIGINT

Signals intelligence, the intelligence-gathering service whose nerve centre is at **GCHQ**. Before the Second World War most intelligence was gathered by the Admiralty by signals interception. During the war the UK and the USA agreed to share signals intelligence and divided the work. The British (based at Bletchley Park) concentrated on intercepting German communications while the USA concentrated on the Japanese. SIGINT has undergone various transformations during and after the **Cold War**, but much of the information gathered is still shared with the USA.

SILVER JUBILEE

A week-long nationwide celebration in the UK in June 1977 of the 25th anniversary of Queen **Elizabeth II**'s accession to the throne. A string of 100 bonfires were lit across the country and a Service of Thanksgiving was given in St Paul's Cathedral, London, while in many towns and cities local residents held street parties. While the celebrations were embraced by the **Establishment**, coinciding as they did with the **punk** era, they were rejected by a large proportion of disaffected youth.

SIMONSTOWN AGREEMENT

The agreement made in 1955 between South Africa and the **UK** under which the Royal Navy relinquished control of the Simonstown naval base, near Cape Town, to the South African Navy but was allowed to continue using its facilities and maintain a headquarters there. The agreement preserved and enhanced the Royal Navy's position in the South Atlantic and Indian Ocean, but was a target of anti-apartheid campaigns against military contact with the South African regime. The agreement was terminated by the UK **Labour** government in 1975.

SINGLE EUROPEAN ACT

A package of revisions to the **EC** treaties, worked out in the mid-1980s, signed on 17 February 1986, ratified by the UK on 19 November 1986, and implemented, once all the member states had ratified it, from July 1987. Setting out the objective of making 'concrete progress towards European unity', it introduced institutional changes, with more qualified majority voting in place of a requirement for unanimity in the **Council of Ministers** and more involvement for the **European Parliament**. It also set out specific policies, with commitments on creating the **single market**, on 'economic and social cohesion', on research and technology, on environmental protection and, most controversially, on **EMU** or economic and monetary union. A separate section (Title III) contained an intergovernmental agreement on European political co-operation, to encourage cohesive foreign policies among member states, and to promote consultation and joint policy-making and implementation. The integration represented by the Single European Act was taken further by the **Maastricht** agreement in the 1990s, but it has been argued that the adoption of the Single European Act, rather than Maastricht, was the key moment in compromising the sovereignty of **Westminster** over political decision-making in the UK.

SINGLE MARKET

A term widely used in the **EU** in the run-up to **1992**, after which there were to be no physical, technical or fiscal barriers to the free movement of goods, services, capital and labour among the member states, creating a single internal market of over 320 million people. The single market programme, implemented under the **Single European Act**, also included a **Social Charter** with guarantees on workers' rights.

SINGLE PARENTS

Those individuals, generally women, raising children on their own, the subject of concerted public criticism by certain **Conservative MPs** in the early 1990s. The group includes widows, divorcees and women or men otherwise abandoned by their partners, but the term as used by the MPs tended to refer to young single women who, they claimed, had deliberately or irresponsibly become pregnant with no intention of settling with their child's father, with no apparent means of supporting their offspring and – some suggested – with the intention of jumping the 'housing queue' by forcing local authorities to house them because they were now in priority need. According to the National Council of One Parent Families, in 1992, 21 per cent of all families in Britain were headed by a lone parent, compared to eight per cent in 1971. Around 90 per cent of one-parent families were headed by lone mothers and, despite the impression often given in the media, 73 per cent of one-parent families result from divorce, separation or death and only one-fifth of lone parents were under 25. Moreover the number of births to teenage mothers actually declined in 1992.

Concern was also expressed about the large amount of **welfare benefits** paid to single parents; the Child Support Act 1991 created the controversial Child Support Agency (**CSA**), empowered to trace absent parents and collect and enforce maintenance payments, thus reducing the benefit bill.

SINGLE TRANSFERABLE VOTE

A voting mechanism (sometimes abbreviated to stv) in which voters not only mark their first preference, but also give their order of preference for the other options. There is a laborious count, concentrating initially on totalling the first preference votes. Thereafter, in the procedure used to elect three members for **Northern Ireland** to the **European Parliament**, the 'surplus votes' for successful candidates (above the number required for election) are reattributed in proportion to second preferences. Other variants of the system work by reattributing the votes for the least popular choice, and repeating this process until a clear conclusion is achieved.

SINGLE-MEMBER CONSTITUENCY

The basic unit of the electoral system in the UK (except that **Northern Ireland** is a multi-member constituency in **Euroelections**). The single-member constituency system is linked with the doctrine that parliamentarians are accountable to the particular interests of the local electorate. This view has been eroded, however, by the development of the party system and the importance of national rather than individual constituency campaigns in the age of the mass media. Proponents of **proportional representation** stigmatize the single-member constituency system as unfair in that the composition of parliament does not reflect the proportion of the vote cast nationwide, to the disadvantage of smaller parties.

SINGLE-UNION AGREEMENTS

The policy adopted by an employer and a trade union whereby one union alone is recognized by the employer for negotiating and representational purposes either for a company as a whole or at a particular location. In the UK the issue came to the fore in the late 1980s, when such agreements were concluded in particular at 'greenfield sites' and when the matter became entangled with the question of no-strike deals. As a result of the Electrical, Electronic, Telecommunication and Plumbing Union (**EETPU**) entering into a number of such agreements in apparent breach of the **TUC's Bridlington Rules** on inter-union relations, the EETPU was expelled from the TUC in 1988, being readmitted only in 1992.

SINN FÉIN

(**Gaelic**, 'Ourselves alone') One of the most prominent revolutionary parties fighting initially for the republican independence of Ireland, and since partition in 1922 for the reunification of the country. First formed in 1907, after a long absence from the polls *Sinn Féin* was represented in the Irish *Dáil* (legislature) in 1957–61. In 1969 *Sinn Féin* split, as did its military wing, the **IRA**. One part became *Sinn Féin*-The Workers' Party (later just Workers' Party), which was represented in the *Dáil* between 1981 and 1992, while the other retained the name *Sinn Féin*. The latter was represented in the **UK House of Commons** from 1981 to 1992 (Owen Carron being elected in 1981 as anti-**H Block** and Gerry **Adams**, *Sinn Féin* president, being elected in 1983 and 1987 but not taking up his seat). The organization is also represented on a number of local councils in **Northern Ireland**. Although not proscribed either in the UK or in Ireland, *Sinn Féin* has, because of its association with the IRA, experienced a number of sanctions against its participation in public life, including being subject to a **broadcasting ban**. In 1993 its leadership entered into partly clandestine discussions with the UK government. Following the Anglo-Irish **Downing Street Declaration** of December 1993 and the **ceasefire** declaration by the IRA in August 1994, *Sinn Féin* entered into direct and open talks with the UK government. These began in December 1994, when *Sinn Féin* leaders met with senior civil servants. Direct talks with ministers were stalled over the timing of the disarming of the IRA, but eventually took place in May 1995.

THE SIX *see* INNER SIX, THE

SIX COUNTIES

The six counties comprising **Northern Ireland** and forming part of the **UK**. At the time of partition of Ireland the Irish Free State, created in 1922, consisted of 26 counties and Northern Ireland (under the Government of Ireland Act 1920) the remaining six (Antrim, Armagh, Down, Fermanagh, Londonderry and Tyrone). Although the term **Ulster** is commonly used to denote Northern Ireland, three of the counties of the province of Ulster (Cavan, Donegal and Monaghan) remained within the Free State (and now in the Republic of Ireland). Ireland's constitutional claim to the whole island of Ireland has proved a stumbling block in discussions over Northern Ireland, particularly among **unionist** politicians.

SIXTH FORM COLLEGES

Educational institutions in **England** and **Wales** catering only for sixth-form students. Such colleges take pupils in the 16-plus age group from schools in the catchment area of a particular local education authority, aiming to offer them a wider range of staff, facilities and courses than individual schools. Courses offered include **A-levels** and A-S levels. The Further and Higher Education Act 1992 removed all further education and sixth form colleges from local authority control as of April 1993, and provided for them to be funded directly by central government through the Further Education Funding Council for England and the Further Education Funding Council for Wales.

SIZEWELL

The site in Suffolk on the east coast of England where the UK's first **PWR**-type nuclear power station has been built, known as Sizewell B. It was due to reach full operating capacity in February 1995, but in April 1994 its opening was delayed to allow studies balancing the need for the plant with the danger of pollution from its routine radioactive discharges. The controversial Sizewell B project, originally intended as the first in a new generation of nuclear power stations in the UK, had been approved after a protracted public enquiry which ended in 1988. Plans for Sizewell C, which would double the capacity of Sizewell B and replace six existing ageing nuclear power stations, were submitted to the government by Nuclear Electric in October 1993.

SKINHEADS

A subcultural group originating in the UK in the 1960s and with a reputation for street violence and association with extreme right-wing political groups such as the **National Front**. Often grouped in gangs, skinheads typically have shaved heads or very short clipped hair and wear heavy work boots and jeans.

SKINNER, DENNIS

(b. 1932) The **left-wing Labour MP** for the Derbyshire seat of Bolsover. He entered the **House of Commons** in 1970 after working as a miner for 21 years. He vocally supported the rebel **Clay Cross** councillors and quickly earned a reputation for his passionate support for the working class and outspokenness. He has clashed with the **Speaker** on numerous occasions and is a famous heckler in the Chamber. A skilled parliamentarian, his honourable, independent and consistent approach on all matters has won the respect even of **Tories**, although his refusal to conform at all times to the party line has brought him into conflict with the Labour leadership.

SKY TV

A **satellite television** company launched in February 1989 by Rupert **Murdoch**, chief executive of **News International**.

Sky TV consisted of four channels of satellite television linked to homes either through existing cable networks or by means of new satellite dishes. The four new channels covered entertainment, news, sport and films, with a Disney and an arts channel to be launched later. Following financial problems and disappointing sales of satellite dishes, Sky TV merged with British Satellite Broadcasting (BSB) in November 1990, creating **BSkyB**.

SKYBOLT

A long-range airborne ballistic missile which the UK ordered from the USA following the collapse of its own **Blue Streak** project in 1960. In early 1963 the USA itself cancelled the Skybolt project after disappointing performances in initial test flights. At their **Nassau conference** in the Bahamas in December 1962 **Prime Minister** Harold **Macmillan** and President John Kennedy agreed that in place of Skybolt the UK should purchase the submarine-launched **Polaris** missile to which it would attach its own nuclear warheads.

SKYTRAIN

An innovative low-cost transatlantic air service operated by Laker Airways in the late 1970s and early 1980s. Freddie Laker applied in the early 1970s for a licence to operate a scheduled service for which advance reservation would not be necessary, and in the face of considerable UK government opposition the airline was eventually in 1977 allowed 'dual designation' under the **Bermuda Convention**. Flights started in September of that year, but Laker Airways subsequently ran into financial difficulties and collapsed in 1982.

SLEAZE FACTOR

A term originally used to characterize the low ethical standards of the Reagan administration in the USA (1981–89), it has more recently been widely used to describe the **Conservative** government of **Prime Minister** John **Major**. The term referred to the numerous scandals of the early 1990s, which led to the departure for non-political reasons of at least 17 government members between 1992 and April 1995. In many cases the scandals concerned the private lives of **MPs** and frequently involved allegations of sexual impropriety. These included the resignations of David Mellor as National Heritage Secretary in September 1992; Tim Yeo as Minister for the Environment and Countryside in January 1994; the Earl of Caithness as Minister for Aviation and Shipping, also in January 1994; and the loss of several parliamentary private secretaries (**PPS**). The most bizarre departure in this latter group was that of Stephen Milligan, who in February 1994 died as a result of auto-erotic asphyxiation. Others were felled by allegations of unethical financial practices either in their private lives – such as Alan Duncan who resigned as a PPS in January 1994 – or while performing political duties such as in the case of the **cash for questions** scandal. The rising tide of sleaze led Major to establish the **Nolan Committee** in October 1994, to examine the conduct of public life.

SMALL IS BEAUTIFUL

The title of a book published in 1973 by Ernst Schumacher, which became a slogan of environmentalists in their campaign against the mass industrial society and its wasteful use of resources. The book, subtitled *'A Study of Economics as if People Mattered'*, criticized industrialism for losing sight of the spiritual aspect in human lives.

SMART WEAPONS

Weapons which use 'intelligent' guidance systems, including laser technology, to avoid interception and home in on targets. This expression caught the imagination of weapons enthusiasts in early 1991, when the **Gulf War** gave the US led allies an opportunity to demonstrate the sophistication of their equipment. However, initial reports seem to have over-estimated their hit-rate rather badly on this occasion.

SMITH, JOHN

(1938–94)The **Labour** politician who died prematurely of a heart attack in May 1994 after leading the party for only 21 months. Smith, a Scottish lawyer educated at Dunoon Grammar School and Glasgow University, served as **MP** for Lanarkshire East from 1970–83 and for

Monklands East from 1983. He was appointed as **Secretary of State** for Trade in 1978 and when Labour moved into Opposition Smith served as Labour's spokesperson successively on trade, energy and employment, eventually becoming **Shadow Chancellor**. His detailed tax plans revealed in advance of the 1992 **general election** were criticized as having handed the **Conservatives** a propaganda coup. Although Smith was firmly on the pragmatic right of the party, he remained extremely popular with both left and right, and was elected Labour leader with over 91 per cent of the vote in 1992, replacing Neil **Kinnock**. Smith had suffered a major heart attack in 1988 and appeared to make a full recovery. His sudden death revealed the extent of public regard for his decency and honesty at a time when other politicians were widely vilified.

SMITHSONIAN AGREEMENT

An agreement reached in New York on 17–18 December 1971 by the finance ministers and central bank governors of the **G-10** countries, which signalled the beginning of the break-up of the international monetary conventions in operation since the end of the Second World War. In the months before the Smithsonian meeting, foreign exchange markets had suffered serious disruption, and in August 1971 the USA had suspended the convertibility of the US dollar for gold, a serious blow to the **gold standard**. The meeting reached agreement on three main points. The US dollar was to be devalued against gold (from $35 to $38 per ounce). Wider exchange rate fluctuations were to be allowed for G-10 country currencies, up to 2.25 per cent above or below par rather than just 1.0 per cent. Finally, discussions should begin promptly, especially within the **IMF** framework, to consider reform of the international monetary system over the longer term.

SMOG

A form of air pollution caused by stagnant atmospheric conditions combined with emissions from fossil fuel. Often exacerbated by fog, smog was common in UK cities until the 1960s and caused numerous deaths, especially among those with heart and lung conditions. In November 1953 smog masks were made available on the **NHS** for those most at risk, while in December 1962 some 60 deaths were attributed to smog in London over a three-day period. The problem was gradually overcome by **clean air legislation** passed in 1956 and 1968 which established smokeless zones. However, the increasing prevalence of **VOCs** has led in recent years to summer smogs.

SMOKE-FILLED ROOMS

A pejorative phrase denoting deals between groups made in private and for the sake of expediency, implying compromise and horse-trading. The **corporatist** politics of the 1970s, the internal politics of the **Labour Party** and the supposed politics of the electoral system of **proportional representation**, for example, have all been denounced for reducing politics to deals in smoke-filled rooms between **men in grey suits**.

SNAKE IN THE TUNNEL

The **EC** currency arrangement adopted in 1972, following the **Smithsonian agreement** of December 1971. The Smithsonian agreement had established 2.25 per cent margins of fluctuation above and below fixed exchange rates. The EC countries (i.e. the **Six**) agreed in March 1972 that within this 'tunnel' or framework, the maximum permitted gap between the currencies of any two EC member states should not exceed 2.25 per cent, thus creating a form of joint community float, or 'snake'. Moreover, the three Benelux countries operated a 'worm within the snake' of a maximum mutual divergence of 1.5 per cent. The four countries which were at that time applicants to join the EC (Denmark, Ireland, Norway and the UK) associated themselves with the 'snake'. A few months later, however, the UK was forced to withdraw from the arrangement, and sterling floated independently, together with the Irish punt. The French franc was withdrawn from the snake arrangements in March 1976. The snake was more formally superseded by the **EMS** effective March 1979.

SNP *see* SCOTTISH NATIONAL PARTY

SOAMES AFFAIR

A dispute between the UK and France in February 1969, when the British application for **EC** membership was pending. The affair erupted over the future of the Western European Union (**WEU**), comprising the UK and the then six EC members. The French opposed moves for the WEU to become a framework for a seven-member European 'foreign policy community', and began boycotting the WEU ministerial council. Alternative proposals outlined by President Charles de Gaulle at a private lunch with Christopher (later Lord) Soames, the British ambassador in Paris, were then leaked in an unfavourable light to other WEU members and to the press. This elicited an official French protest, a denial of the leaked reports and a restatement of de Gaulle's view that the admission of the UK 'would lead to a complete change of the Community and, in practice, to its disappearance'.

SOCIAL AFFAIRS UNIT

A **right-wing think tank** formed in 1980 as an offshoot of the **Institute of Economic Affairs** (IEA). Led by Digby Anderson, the Unit concentrates on social issues, but has been partly overshadowed by the IEA's own influential health and welfare unit.

SOCIAL AND LIBERAL DEMOCRATS

The centre party created in March 1988 from a merger of the **Liberal Party** and the **SDP**. The party abbreviated its working title to the **Liberal Democrats** in October 1989 following a postal ballot of its members and soon after formally changed its name to the Liberal Democrats.

SOCIAL CHAPTER

The section in the original draft of the **Maastricht** treaty which covered social rights (and particularly workers' rights), intended to be applied across the **EU**. The **Conservative** government strongly resisted the inclusion of the social chapter, having already made its position clear by **opting out** over the 1989 **social charter** which embodied essentially the same ideas. In the eventual denouement, at the Maastricht summit on the night of 10–11 December 1991, the other 11 member countries agreed to omit the social chapter from the treaty itself. Instead they confirmed their 'desire to continue down the path indicated by the Social Charter', and added a social policy annexe to the treaty which would enable them to do this through Community institutions for application in their respective countries.

SOCIAL CHARTER

The 'Community charter of fundamental social rights', approved by the **EU** at a **European Council** meeting in December 1989, but with the UK opting out. The charter, drafted by the **Commission** under the presidency of Jacques Delors, was regarded by **Prime Minister** Margaret **Thatcher** as a 'socialist charter'. Its proposals included guarantees on workers' rights to union membership, to information and consultation, and to decent wages and health and safety standards at work – much of which was carried forward into the **social chapter** of the **Maastricht** Treaty.

SOCIAL CONTRACT

An agreement between the **Labour** government and the **TUC** in the mid-1970s concerning social and economic policy. The concept had its origins in a document agreed between the TUC and the Labour Party (then in opposition) in January 1973, which set out the economic policy to be followed by a future Labour government. It was then embodied in a set of TUC guidelines in June 1974 describing the factors which were expected to be taken into account in wage negotiations. This 'contract', involving voluntary **wage restraint** within a form of **incomes policy**, was extended with certain adjustments in successive years, but collapsed in 1978 in the context of the approaching **winter of discontent** with its serious industrial conflict.

SOCIAL DEMOCRATIC AND LABOUR PARTY *see* SDLP

SOCIAL FUND

The **social security** scheme in which loans and grants are made to **welfare benefit** claimants. Under the discretionary social fund (DSF), applicants – however deserving – have no right to payments and funds are strictly budget-limited on a local basis. Many payments are loans which must be repaid week by week by deduction from benefit. Despite an annual budget of £366 million in 1993–4, more than one million applicants for loans from the DSF were turned down in 1993–4 because of budgetary constraints. The DSF had been controversially introduced under the Social Security Act 1988 to replace a system of special grants to cover single items such as clothing and furniture.

Under the regulated social fund, qualifying applicants are entitled to payments to cover maternity and funeral expenses and those incurred during cold weather.

SOCIAL JUSTICE COMMISSION

An independent research body set up by **Labour Party** leader John **Smith** in December 1992 and chaired by Sir Gordon Borrie. Not itself a Labour Party body and including non-Labour members, its purpose was to provide a fundamental and wide-ranging assessment of taxation, **welfare benefits** and employment issues. Its existence was seen as one of the vehicles through which Smith's successor, Tony **Blair**, would attempt to win the next **general election** on the basis on new 'modernist' policy initiatives. Publishing its principal report in October 1994, it proposed the introduction of a national **minimum wage** of £3.50 per hour; that the basic state pension be superseded by an income-related universal 'Minimum Pension Guarantee'; the establishment of a 'learning bank' with compulsory employer contributions; national voluntary community service for young people; part-time unemployment benefit to encourage people into the labour market; a national housing bank to support social housing; the retention of the **Child Support Agency**; the abolition of the tax allowance for married couples; and the gradual phasing out of **MIRAS**. Several of these themes were echoed in the **Liberal Democrat**-inspired report of the **Dahrendorf Commission, published in July 1995.**

SOCIAL MARKET FOUNDATION

A non-libertarian free market **think tank** relaunched in 1992. Its director Daniel Finkelstein espouses gradualism and, in stark contrast to **Thatcherism**, accepts the existence of 'society'. In early 1995 Finkelstein he was rumoured to be seeking a **Conservative** seat. The foundation claims considerable interest from members of John **Major's Cabinet**.

SOCIAL SECURITY

The system of state benefits designed to protect individuals from the worst consequences of ill-health and poverty arising from **unemployment**, old age or the death of one's spouse. The basis of the existing system was laid in the National Insurance Act 1946, largely based on the **Beveridge Report** on National Insurance of 1942.

Benefits are either contributory and paid according to an individual's **national insurance** contributions, such as unemployment benefit and retirement pension, or non-contributory (sometimes known as **welfare benefits**, and generally means-tested), such as **income support**, family credit and **housing benefit**.

SOCIALIST WORKERS' PARTY *see* SWP

SOFT LEFT

The pragmatic socialists located on the political spectrum between the **Labour Party's** hard left, represented by the **Campaign** group, and its **modernizers** on the right wing. The soft left (sometimes even known as the 'cuddly left' in contrast to the class politics of the hard left) is associated with the **Tribune** group. Prominent soft-left politicians include David **Blunkett**, Harriet Harman and Robin Cook.

SOLAR POWER *see* ENERGY SOURCES

SOLICITOR GENERAL

The deputy to the **Attorney General**, permitted under the Law Officers Act of 1944 to fulfil the Attorney General's duties in his or her absence. The holder of the post must be qualified as a barrister, is appointed by the **Prime Minister** and is an **MP**. Sir Derek Spencer QC has served as Solicitor General since 1992.

SONS OF GLYNDWR

A group of ardent Welsh nationalists. In 1982–3 it claimed responsibility for a number of fire-bomb attacks on English-owned second homes in **Wales**.

SOSKICE, SIR FRANK

(1902–79) **Labour** Home Secretary in the first **Wilson** government from October 1964 until December 1965, when he was replaced by Roy **Jenkins**. Soskice, who had served in the 1945–50 **Attlee** government as Solicitor-General, was given a **life peerage** in 1966.

SOUND BITE

A short phrase or sentence, designed for maximum impact, which is extracted for use in broadcast news reports from a recorded speech by a political leader. The practice of writing speeches to include sound bites developed in the 1970s and 1980s, bringing with it the criticism that complex issues are being reduced to catchphrases.

SPEAKER

The presiding officer of the **House of Commons**, a post currently held by Betty Boothroyd. The Speaker is an **MP** elected to the post by fellow members at the beginning of each new Parliament or when an incumbent has resigned. The Speaker holds office until the dissolution of the Parliament. He or she ceases to be a member of a political party and is expected to act impartially for the duration of the office. The Speaker controls proceedings of the Commons by using his or her authority to maintain order. The Speaker's powers are also supplemented by Standing Orders. Rulings on matters of order may be challenged by the tabling of a motion and the outcome of such a challenge establishes a precedent for future conduct. In the event of a tied vote in the Commons the Speaker is required to use his or her casting vote to maintain the status quo. In July 1993 a **Labour** motion that the government should not ratify the **Maastricht** treaty until it had committed itself to the **social chapter** appeared to result in a tied vote, and Boothroyd was called upon to cast her vote against the motion, the decision that the UK would **opt out** of the social chapter having already been taken. However, a final count gave the government a majority of one, so that Boothroyd, elected as a Labour MP, was relieved of the embarrassment of voting against the party.

SPECIAL BRANCH

The **police** department dedicated to investigating and countering terrorism, spying and subversion as well as providing protection for national figures. Its monitoring and investigative methods have sometimes been called into question and represented as a threat to civil liberties. The **Interception of Communications Act 1985** introduced statutory limits on such activities.

SPECIAL RELATIONSHIP

The bond of cultural heritage and shared national interest between the UK and the USA during and after the Second World War. The reality, equality and durability of the special relationship was soon called into question, notably in the **Suez crisis** of 1956, but it continued to be invoked through the **Cold War** period as the UK provided support for US foreign policy and nuclear strategy. The idea appeared to have most substance when it was reinforced by personal relationships between heads of government, as between Winston **Churchill** and President Roosevelt, between Harold **Macmillan** and President Kennedy and, in a later flowering, between Margaret **Thatcher** and President Reagan. However, the UK's membership of the **EU** since 1973, the ending of the Cold War and changing US perceptions of the nature of its strategic interests all served to diminish the relationship's significance. President Clinton signalled in Berlin in July 1994 his perception that Germany could be more of a partner than Britain, and in March 1995 there seemed little reason to give credence to any enduring special relationship as a rift opened up between Clinton and John **Major** over **Northern Ireland**.

SPG

A special patrol group, a mobile unit in the Metropolitan **Police**, which is trained and equipped to deal with incidents threatening the public order. They were abolished in 1987 but essentially recreated in the Territorial Support Groups that succeeded them. SPGs were established by the Metropolitan Police in

London in 1965, and Police Support Units – created by provincial and other UK city forces from the mid-1970s – were largely based on them. Their actions were sometimes controversial, as in the Blair **Peach** case and in 1987 after an internal Metropolitan Police investigation SPGs were officially disbanded.

SPIN DOCTOR

A member of an election candidate's campaign team who interprets for the media, as favourably as possible, the candidate's performance in a particular event. The term became part of the political vocabulary during the 1988 US presidential campaign. At that time it was used specifically with reference to the set-piece debates which are a traditional aspect of US presidential contests, and after which the spin doctors attempted to influence the media in assessing the performance of candidates. Thereafter it acquired a wider political usage, and although it remains primarily a US term, it has been increasingly applied to UK politics.

SPORTING ACADEMY *see* BRITISH ACADEMY OF SPORT

SPYCATCHER AFFAIR

The controversy over the memoirs of retired **MI5** agent Peter Wright. In the early 1980s Wright wrote his memoirs, *Spycatcher*, which were to be published in Australia where he was then living. The book itself was critical of many aspects of the nature and conduct of MI5, and contained a number of lurid allegations concerning the service's activities. The UK authorities were granted an interim injunction in the Australian courts in September 1985 preventing publication, having argued that the memoirs represented a breach of official secrets legislation and of Wright's duty to the British Crown. However, they were subsequently refused a permanent injunction. There then followed a series of court actions, not only in Australia and the UK but also in other countries, to prevent publication of the book's contents in newspapers. As details came increasingly into circulation, the **House of Lords** ruled in October 1988 against a ban on publication, although it upheld the duty of members of the security services not to disclose information about their work.

SQUATTERS

Those people illegally occupying private property, properly known as trespassers. Landlords may obtain court orders for eviction but squatters are protected to a certain extent by clauses in the Criminal Law Act 1977 outlawing the use of violence against trespassers. The **Criminal Justice** and Public Order Act 1994 made it a criminal offence for squatters to fail to leave a building within 24 hours of a court issuing an interim possession order.

SSP *see* STATUTORY SICK PAY

SSSI

A site of special scientific interest, an official designation for land in **England**, **Wales** and **Scotland** that is of particular conservation value. English Nature, Scottish Natural Heritage and the Countryside Council for Wales – the bodies created in 1991 to replace the **Nature Conservancy Council** – designate SSSIs. They are required to notify the landowner and the local planning authority and to specify activities which may not be undertaken on the site without written consent. In some cases compensation is paid to landowners and as a final resort a site may be compulsorily purchased.

SSSIs were created under the National Parks and Access to the Countryside Act 1949. The measures protecting them strengthened under the Wildlife and Countryside Act 1981.

STAINES AIR CRASH

The worst disaster in UK aviation history, which occurred on 18 June 1972. A BEA Trident airliner crashed in a field near Staines, Middlesex, at 5.15 p.m., shortly after taking off on a flight to Brussels. All 118 people on board the aircraft died in the accident.

STALKER INQUIRY

The inquiry into alleged **shoot to kill** operations by the security forces in **Northern Ireland** in late 1982. The inquiry, under the deputy chief constable of Greater Manchester John Stalker, was set up in 1984 to examine such allegations.

Stalker's report was submitted to the chief constable of the Royal Ulster Constabulary (**RUC**)in September 1985 and to the Northern Ireland Director of Public Prosecutions in February 1986. However, in May 1986 Stalker was removed from the inquiry team in controversial circumstances involving alleged unrelated misconduct, and was replaced by the chief constable of West Yorkshire Colin Sampson. No criminal proceedings were taken as a result of the Stalker-Sampson inquiry, although some members of the RUC were disciplined.

STALKING HORSE

A candidate with little prospect of victory who enters an election in order to establish the level of support for a challenge by a more serious contender. The term was particularly applied to Sir Anthony Meyer, the **Tory wet** who challenged Margaret **Thatcher** for the party leadership in 1989. Meyer received just 31 votes, and it was widely believed that his challenge had been purely an exercise to test the water for Michael **Heseltine**. Indeed, in the following year Heseltine himself stood against Thatcher, a challenge which brought about her downfall, though it failed to win Heseltine the ultimate prize of the premiership.

STAMP DUTY

A government tax on documents. There are several separate duties on different types of paperwork, such as property sales, lease agreements and share transactions. From December 1991 to August 1992 the government allowed an eight-month 'holiday' in which stamp duty was not charged on the majority of house purchases as an attempt to revive a sluggish housing market.

STANDING COMMITTEE

A parliamentary body which gives detailed consideration to draft legislation. Bills are normally assigned to standing committees in the **House of Commons** for their **committee stage**. The composition of a standing committee is chosen to reflect the make-up of the House itself. The chairman has the power to control proceedings and to select amendments. As many standing committees are appointed as necessary. There are special standing committees to deal with **private members' bills**, statutory instruments, and matters relating to **Scotland**, **Wales**, **Northern Ireland** and Europe.

STAR CHAMBER

The **Cabinet** committee established in the 1980s by **Prime Minister** Margaret **Thatcher** to determine public spending programmes for the forthcoming year. Nicknamed after the powerful Star Chamber of the fourteenth-seventeenth centuries, the discussions were frequently heated as departmental ministers, during the early summer months, defended their budgets in the light of the financial and economic constraints of the time. In 1993 the process was largely replaced by a procedure whereby the Chief Secretary to the **Treasury**, responsible for expenditure, carries out in-depth discussions with individual ministers; in addition new and more sophisticated measures of spending projections have been also developed.

STATUTORY REGULATORY BODY

A public authority with a regulatory function established by legislation. One example is the **ITC** (Independent Television Commission), set up to regulate the commercial television industry.

STATUTORY SICK PAY

A government scheme under which employers are required to pay employees who are sick for four or more consecutive days up to a maximum of 28 weeks. Prior to the Statutory Sick Pay Act 1994, these payments were refunded by the government up to 80 per cent for larger employers (with a **national insurance** bill of more than £16,000 a year) and for smaller employers in full for absences of over six weeks. However, the 1994 Act controversially abolished refunds for all larger employers and raised the threshold for qualification as a small firm to £20,000. Payments continued to be refunded in full to small firms.

STEEL INDUSTRY

A major metal **manufacturing sector** whose ownership for many years symbolized partisan differences over the mixed economy. Much of the British steel industry was **nationalized** by the **Labour** government in 1951 in a move bitterly resisted by the employers. From 1953 the **Conservative** administration restored it piecemeal to the private sector. In 1967 Labour re-nationalized all major steel firms grouping them into the British Steel Corporation (BSC). An ambitious expansion programme ('the Ten Year Strategy') followed in the 1970s. However, in the 1980s losses, **recession** and a major strike compounded steel's difficulties and the industry was drastically slimmed down. In 1988 the BSC was **privatized** in a public share issue and the entire industry is now privately owned. Few in politics now advocate its return to the public sector.

STERLING AREA

Traditionally those countries, principally British territories or independent members of the **Commonwealth**, which held their reserves in the form of sterling balances rather than in gold or other foreign currencies. There were over 60 countries in the sterling area. From the mid-1960s, as the UK began experiencing severe balance of payments problems, a series of arrangements were concluded to protect those countries against potential losses arising from fluctuations in the external value of sterling. These arrangements were successively extended until, following the 1973–4 oil price rises and the emergence of massive flows of petrodollars, they were terminated at the end of 1974. Meanwhile increasing numbers of countries had broken their link with sterling in the aftermath of the Smithsonian agreement of 1971 and subsequent upheavals in the exchange markets.

STERLING CRISIS

The rapid depreciation of sterling against other currencies, usually the US dollar. Sterling crises are generally the result of a sudden outflow of capital following a loss of confidence in sterling. In periods when the government is committed to a fixed exchange rate or to keeping sterling within a set band (as within the **ERM**), policy generally dictates intervention in the market using public money to defend the currency. One alternative is to abandon the target level through **devaluation**. *See also* Appendix V.

STERLING M3

A measure of money supply. M3 is defined as all notes and coins in circulation plus sterling deposits in the private sector. Setting targets for the money supply was a central feature of government economic policy of the early to mid-1980s, in accordance with the doctrine of **monetarism**.

STEWART, MICHAEL

(1906–90) A **Labour** Foreign and Commonwealth Secretary. Stewart replaced Patrick **Gordon-Walker** as Foreign Secretary in Harold **Wilson's** first government in early 1965. He was replaced in August 1966 by George **Brown**, but took over the portfolio again following Brown's resignation in October 1968. He held the post until Labour's defeat in the 1970 **general election**. His secretaryship coincided with the Soviet invasion of Czechoslovakia and the dispatch of British troops to **Northern Ireland**. Stewart entered the **House of Lords** as a **life peer** in 1979.

STONEHENGE *see* THE CONVOY

STONEHOUSE AFFAIR

The circumstances surrounding the disappearance of **Labour MP** John Stonehouse in 1974. Stonehouse was a middle-ranking minister in 1967–70. After Labour went into opposition in 1970 he sought to develop wide-ranging business interests. However, for a variety of reasons these combined to put him in a desperate financial situation, and in November 1974 he faked his suicide off the Miami coast. Shortly afterwards he was arrested in Australia and was extradited to the UK. In August 1976 he was convicted in the UK of fraud, theft and forgery; he was sentenced to seven years' imprisonment and only then resigned as an MP.

STONEWALL

An organization formed in the USA in the wake of the 1969 Stonewall riot in New York, which lobbies and campaigns for the legal and social equality of homosexual men and women. A branch of the organization was founded in 1988 in the UK in response to anti-homosexual measures contained in **Clause 28** of the 1988 Local Government Act. In the UK the group lobbies vigorously for equality in the **age of consent** for homosexuals and heterosexuals, and rejected the 'compromise' reduction of the age of consent for homosexuals from 21 to 18, which was adopted in February 1994 as a clause in the Criminal Justice and Public Order Bill.

STORMONT

The government and parliament buildings of **Northern Ireland** in Belfast. Stormont was the seat of the Northern Ireland parliament from 1932 until the introduction of **direct rule** in 1972, and this term denoted both the legislative and the executive identities of Northern Ireland, and Northern Ireland's limited form of self-government.

STRANGEWAYS RIOTS

The prolonged disturbances in April 1990 at Strangeways Prison, Manchester, that led to a rash of protests in other prisons and drew attention to overcrowding of inmates. More than 1,000 prisoners joined the riot at Strangeways, which after a violent beginning when the chapel and gymnasium were set on fire and convicted sex offenders in a segregated wing were attacked and injured, settled into a stalemate lasting more than three weeks as prisoners occupying the roof were besieged by the **police**. 'Copycat' riots took place in Durham, Cardiff, Bristol and Dartmoor prisons. An official inquiry into the riots was ordered and the findings published in the **Woolf Report**.

STREAMING

A form of organizing school classes, whereby children in a particular year group are divided into ranked classes according to an estimate of their overall academic ability. Many teachers believe a class is easier to teach if its members are of similar ability; others believe that streaming encourages social divisions and confirms low aspirations among children in lower streams. Streaming should be distinguished from setting, whereby children are divided into ranked classes for individual subjects.

STUDENT GRANTS

A system of financial support for students in higher and further education. Grants are paid by local education authorities in **England**, **Wales** and **Northern Ireland**, which are reimbursed by central government, and by the Scottish Office in **Scotland**. A parental contribution towards the grant of students is deductible on a sliding scale dependent on income. Tuition fees are paid in full for all students receiving a grant. Local education authorities have discretion in deciding policy over the payment of some grants. The main rates of mandatory grants were frozen in 1991–2 because it was envisaged that **student loans** would take a larger share of student support.

STUDENT LOANS

The controversial partial replacement of the **student grant** with 'top-up' loans to be repaid by the student after graduation. The Education (Student Loans) Act 1990 stated the objective of sharing the burden of supporting students in higher education more equitably between their parents and the taxpayer. A Student Loans Company, comprising 10 banks, was set up by the government to administer the scheme. The loans would be repaid over a five-year period, or seven years for those taking longer courses. The **Labour Party's** principal spokesperson on education, Jack Straw, described the scheme as 'a mortgage on knowledge and a debt-charge on skills'.

STV *see* SINGLE TRANSFERABLE VOTE

SUBSIDIARITY

The resolution of problems at the lowest appropriate level. The term has come to be associated particularly with the **EU** since the late 1980s. It is given particular emphasis in the **Maastricht** documents on **European Political Union**, and goes together with the idea of promoting 'a union closer to its citizens'. Subsidiarity is supposed to be the governing principle in determining whether decisions should be handled at the local, regional, national or Community level. In the UK, where central government has stronger powers than in most other EU member states, the **Major** government nevertheless invokes the principle of subsidiarity in the sense of national rather than Community decision-making. **Eurosceptics** see **federalism** as the real antithesis of subsidiarity.

SUEZ CRISIS

The Middle East crisis precipitated by the nationalization of the Suez Canal by Egyptian President Gamal Abd el-Nasser in July 1956. Nasser had acted after the USA had reneged on their commitment to help finance the construction of the Aswan High Dam. His action angered the UK and France, who feared for the stability of Middle Eastern oil supplies to Europe. With diplomatic efforts to solve the crisis under way, the UK and France, with the assistance of Israel, formulated plans for the military seizure of the canal. Israeli forces invaded Egypt on 29 October 1956. British and French troops followed (on the pretext of supporting a **UN** ceasefire call) and occupied the canal zone. However, the combined opposition expressed by the USA and the Soviet Union to the invasion brought a swift end to the Anglo-French action, principally because of political and economic pressure which the US administration was able to exert on the British government. The Europeans withdrew in December 1956 and the Israelis withdrew from the Sinai and Gaza Strip in March 1957. Domestically, the episode served to underline Britain's decline as an imperial power, severely strained the UK's **special relationship** with the USA, split public opinion and led to tension in the **Conservative Party**, effectively ending the career of the then **Prime Minister** Anthony **Eden**.

SUN

A **right-wing tabloid** daily newspaper with a circulation of 3½ million. Its forerunner was the **Labour**-supporting *Daily Herald*, established as a strike newspaper during a printing dispute in 1911 and taken over by the Odhams Press in 1929. In 1964 its name was changed to the *Sun* as part of an attempt to revive its flagging sales, and in 1969 it was bought by Rupert **Murdoch**. Murdoch was responsible for turning the paper into an extremely successful tabloid, using his well-established formula of scandal, gossip and sport. The paper has been battling ever since, largely successfully, with the left-of-centre *Daily Mirror* to capture the tabloid market. Its headlines are notorious, from the ludicrous – 'Freddie Starr ate my hamster' – to the brutishly concise – 'Gotcha!' (following the 1982 sinking of the **Belgrano**). The revelations appearing in the *Sun* in recent years – focusing on the private lives of celebrities and latterly of the **Royal Family** – led to the paper being cited as an example of the inability of the tabloid press to engage in the kind of self-regulation which would prevent statutory controls.

SUNDAY TRADING

Legislation regulating the opening of shops and stores on Sunday. The Shops Act 1950 laid down which goods could be sold from which types of shops on Sundays. However, by the 1980s the Act was widely regarded as outdated and open to ridicule because of numerous anomalies: fish and chips could be bought, but not from a fish and chip shop; shops could sell pornographic magazines, but not bibles. The law came to be widely flouted, particularly by do-it-yourself and gardening centres, but when the government tried to reform it in 1986 it failed to win the approval of the 'keep Sunday special' lobby. The government made another, successful, attempt to reform the law in 1994. **MPs** were given a choice of three options: deregulation – allowing all shops to open on Sunday; regulation – allowing only limited categories of shops to open; and partial deregulation – allowing all smaller shops to open, but placing restrictions on the hours of larger stores. The latter proposal was accepted and included in the Sunday Trading Act 1994.

SUNNINGDALE AGREEMENT

The abortive December 1973 agreement on the future of **Northern Ireland**. The agreement was the result of a tripartite conference between representatives of the Irish and UK governments and of the short-lived **power-sharing** Northern Ireland executive-designate. It envisaged the establishment of a joint Council of Ireland, and changes in the relationship between Northern Ireland and the Republic of Ireland. Although all three sides approved implementation of the agreement, there was strong opposition from **loyalist** workers, who staged a widely observed strike. In the face of this resistance, the power-sharing executive collapsed in May 1974 and **direct rule** was reimposed.

SUNNY JIM

One of the nicknames for James **Callaghan**, **Prime Minister** from 1976 to 1979. The name derives from a character used to advertise Force breakfast cereal at the beginning of the century, and was a reference to his unflappable demeanour.

SUPER-GRASS TRIALS

A method used by the **RUC** in **Northern Ireland** in the early 1980s to secure convictions against those suspected of terrorist activities by persuading other suspects to betray the accused in return for a promised reward. An individual – or 'super-grass' – would be encouraged to supply evidence to convict terrorist colleagues. In return, reduced sentences, freedom from the threat of prosecution or money to start a new life abroad would be promised. With many people being charged on the word of one 'super-grass', the system became open to widespread abuse and corruption and added to the problems of the already contentious legal system in the province. It was generally abandoned for those reasons in the late 1980s.

SUPER-GUN

An enormous cannon which was reportedly in the process of development by Iraq. Details of the weapon first emerged in April 1990 when it became the focus of international attention after British customs officials seized a consignment of steel cylinders manufactured by two UK-based companies and bound for Iraq. It was alleged at the time that the cylinders were to be fitted together to form the barrel of a giant 40-metre 'super-gun', possibly with the intention of launching missiles or satellites. Iraq maintained that the cylinders were for use in its petrochemical industry.

SUPERMAC

A popular nickname for **Conservative Prime Minister** Harold **Macmillan**. It was prompted by a cartoon in the London *Evening Standard* newspaper in November 1958, which depicted him in the guise of the US comic-strip hero Superman.

SUPPER CLUB

A secret dining club of **Labour MPs**, exposed in early 1991 when a copy of the agenda for a meeting of the club was left in a **House of Commons** photocopy room. The Supper Club, which was mainly although not exclusively **left-wing** and included several **front-bench** party spokespersons, was critical of the leadership of Neil **Kinnock**. Its existence came to light during the **Gulf War**, which its members opposed.

SUPPLY SIDE ECONOMICS

A body of economic theory which first gained wide currency in the 1970s, based on the proposition that an economy is driven primarily through the efficiency of markets, at the micro level, rather than through management of demand at the macro level. An essential element of the application of supply side economic policy is a reduction in marginal income tax rates in order to improve incentives – a course followed by the **Conservative** government since 1979.

SUPRANATIONAL

A term associated with international organizations, and especially the **EC** or **EU**, which have organs such as the **Commission** with a remit to pursue policy at the Community level. There is a tension between this supranational perspective and the individual national interest propounded by member governments. In the EU context, **federalists** seek to further the scope of supranational decision-making. In this they encounter resistance from the defenders of national sovereignty.

SUPREME COURT OF JUDICATURE *see* HIGH COURT

SURFING

A term appropriated from outdoor sport to glamorize the activity of computer communications enthusiasts. Surfing the **Internet**, an expression which began to be popularized in Britain in 1994, involves neither physical exertion nor water. It simply means following a chain of connections among linked computers, to discover what information or entertainment they may have on offer. With the rapid proliferation of computer sites linked to the Internet, this surfing often appears to be a random wander through a labyrinth, rather than a purposeful journey down an 'information superhighway'.

SUS

A popular term for the former offence of being a person suspected of loitering with intent to commit an offence as provided for under the 1824 Vagrancy Act. Increasingly the use by the **police** of 'sus' to arrest male (predominantly black) youths in the late 1970s prompted widespread public opposition, and the offence was abolished by the Criminal Attempts Act in 1981.

SVQs *see* NCVQ

SWEETENERS

The payments and concessions made by the UK government to **British Aerospace** (BAe) in 1988 when BAe bought the government's shareholding in the Rover Group (formerly **British Leyland**). The government paid £11 million towards buying out minority Rover Group shareholders and other costs, and allowed BAe to defer payment of the £150 million purchase price until March 1990.

The inducements first came to light when a confidential memorandum from the **National Audit Office** was leaked and published in the *Guardian* newspaper on 30 November 1989. The Commission of the **EC** on 9 March 1994 ordered BAe to repay the money with interest, since the government concessions infringed EC regulations outlawing state aid to companies.

SWP

The Socialist Workers' Party, a fringe revolutionary socialist party. It was founded in 1977, although the *Socialist Worker* newspaper, an organ of the International Socialist movement, had been published since 1968. The SWP emphasized industrial disputes as a barometer of labour unrest and, by extension, of revolutionary fervour; the party was active during the **winter of discontent** of 1979–80 and the **miners' strike** of 1984–5. Its fanatical followers number only a few thousand, but the numerous volunteer vendors of the *Socialist Worker* have helped raise the party's profile. SWP activists also habitually attend protest demonstrations and membership has increasingly overlapped with other groups such as the **Anti-Nazi League**.

TA *see* TERRITORIAL ARMY

TABLOIDS

Popular national daily or weekly newspapers normally produced in small-size or 'tabloid' format. They specialise in human interest stories presented in a snappy, compact way, preferably sensationalist with a sexual flavour, and with abundant photographs. Known also as the 'popular' press, the group comprises the (daily) **Sun**, the *Star*, the *Sport*, the *Daily Mirror*, the *Daily Express* and *Today*, and the (weekly) *News of the World* and the *Sunday People*. They contrast with the **broadsheets**, which are commonly described as the 'quality press', and are aimed at readers wanting extensive information on politics, economics and current affairs.

TALK OUT

A filibustering parliamentary strategy adopted by **MPs** opposed to legislation being debated in the **House of Commons**, whereby they continue to debate a bill until such a time that there is no time to put it to a vote.

TARZAN

A nickname given to **Conservative** politician Michael **Heseltine**, reflecting his political daring and his physical appearance, as well as personal charisma.

TASK FORCE

A common military term which was given a special resonance in the **UK** at the time of the 1982 **Falklands**/Malvinas conflict, when a hurriedly assembled task force sailed 8,000 miles south-west to the South Atlantic and joined battle with Argentina. The high-profile send-off for the task force helped to create a mood of patriotic enthusiasm which encouraged the **Thatcher** government's subsequent pursuit of military victory. The force itself consisted of 30 warships, supporting aircraft and auxiliary vessels, with its operational nerve centre aboard the aircraft carrier *Hermes*. The passenger liner *Canberra* and the container ship *Atlantic Conveyor* were among the vessels requisitioned as troop and arms ships.

TASS *see* AEEU

TAURUS

A plan to convert the **London Stock Exchange** to paperless dealing. The intention behind TAURUS was to move to a 'book entry transfer' system for shareholdings under which the share certificate would lose its legal status and ownership of equity would be transferred by electronic means. In May 1994 implementation difficulties and mounting costs at the Stock Exchange forced reconsideration of TAURUS in favour of less ambitious proposals.

TAYLOR REPORT

The report of the inquiry set up under the chairmanship of Lord Chief Justice Taylor into the **Hillsborough disaster**. The inquiry opened on 15 May 1989, and produced an interim report on 4 August which was sharply critical of the South Yorkshire police and made 43 recommendations for the improvement of safety at football grounds. The final report, published on 29 January 1990, found that the main cause of the disaster had been the failure of the police to control the movement of supporters into the Hillsborough stadium in Sheffield. The report also made a total of 76 recommendations for the improvement of safety at sports grounds, including the phasing in of all-seater football stadia.

TEBBIT, NORMAN

(b. 1931) The former chairman of the **Conservative Party** and a leading advocate of **privatization** and of radical **trade union legislation**. He was elected to the **House of Commons** in 1970, and became notable in the late 1970s for the ferocity of his attacks from the **backbenches** on the economic and industrial policies of James **Callaghan's** dying **Labour** administration. Joining Margaret **Thatcher's** first government in 1979 as a trade minister, he held the **Cabinet** posts of employment and trade and industry between 1981 and 1985. A victim, with his wife, of the **IRA's Brighton bomb attack** on a hotel during the Conservative Party conference in 1984, Tebbit recovered to serve as Chancellor of the **Duchy of Lancaster** from 1985–7, combining the post with that of party chairman. During his time in the Cabinet he was responsible for the early employment laws curbing the power of the trade unions and privatized **BT**. He withdrew from the political front line to care for his wife, who was left seriously disabled by the Brighton bomb attack. He left the Commons in 1992 and became a **life peer** and a pundit on **satellite television**. Since then he has publicly criticized John **Major's** stance over **Maastricht**, claiming that the government should have renegotiated the Treaty to exclude the objectives of economic and monetary union. His disapproval of Major's stance on Europe led him publicly to support **Eurosceptic** John Redwood in the mid-1995 **Tory** leadership battle, urging Conservative MPs to vote against the Prime Minister.

TEC

The training and enterprise councils. A TEC in **England** and **Wales** (or a local enterprise company (LEC) in **Scotland**) is one of a network of local employer-led training bodies established throughout **Great Britain** since 1990 with the role of planning and delivering training, and of promoting and supporting the development of small businesses and self-employment within their areas. Two-thirds of the membership of each TEC/LEC is drawn from senior management of local industry and commerce and the remainder from education, the voluntary sector, trade unions and other interests. TECs and LECs – of which there are 82 and 22 respectively – are funded largely through the Department of Employment. They do not operate training programmes themselves, but sub-contract to local providers.

TECHNOLOGY COLLEGES

In autumn 1993, building on the technology schools initiative which ran from 1991 to 1993, the government published a detailed prospectus for **grant-maintained** and voluntary aided secondary schools wishing to become technology colleges. Between September 1994 and May 1995, 67 schools had begun operating as technology colleges, specializing in technology, mathematics and science, with up to four 'sponsor governors', and capital and annual grants from central government to assist in the operation of an enhanced curriculum.

TELECOMMUTING

New technology-assisted **home working**. Telecommuting became feasible from the 1980s when new modes of information transfer allowed certain grades of employees to operate from home rather than from the office. The journey between the two sites was undertaken not by the individual but by his or her output in electronic form. The rapid development of the **Internet** from the early 1990s made telecommuting an option for increasing numbers of workers.

TELEPHONE TAPPING

A practice conflicting with the **right to privacy** but permissible with a warrant from a Secretary of State. In 1979 the practice, which at that stage was not regulated by any statutory authority, came under public scrutiny in a case against James Malone, when a **police** officer gave evidence indicating that the Home Secretary had authorized the tapping of Malone's telephone. When Malone, who was alleged to have stolen antiques, brought a case before the **European Court of Human Rights**, it found that the warrant procedure violated the right to privacy which was enshrined in the **European Convention on Human Rights**. The ruling obliged the **UK** government to introduce legislation to regulate the practice. The resulting **Interception of Communications Act** 1985 permits interceptions in the interests of national security, to prevent or detect serious crime and to safeguard the economic well-being of the UK. This Act regulates interceptions authorized by a Secretary of State but communications can also be intercepted by **GCHQ**.

TEN MINUTE RULE

A colloquial term for Standing Order No. 19, under which a **private member's bill** may be introduced in the **House of Commons**. An **MP** may seek leave to introduce a bill by making a speech of no more than 10 minutes in duration at the beginning of public business on Tuesdays or Wednesdays. If the bill is opposed, a 10-minute speech against it is allowed before the House votes on the issue. Even if the bill is introduced it is unlikely to become law because of the lack of parliamentary time allocated for private members' bills.

TERRITORIAL ARMY

Army reserve forces. The TA, with a current establishment of approximately 59,000, provides a trained and equipped force ready to fill mainly home defence roles, alongside the Home Service Front, such as guarding installations, reconnaissance, and maintenance of communications in times of national emergency.

TERRITORIAL WATERS

The offshore area in which a coastal state claims sovereign jurisdiction, save for the customary rights of freedom of navigation for merchant shipping. Various limits were applied by different countries until 1930 when a conference in The Hague (Netherlands) agreed by a narrow majority on a three-mile limit. Since then coastal states have claimed jurisdiction up to 200 nautical miles, but by the time of the **UN** Conference on the Law of the Sea (UNCLOS) in 1982 an intermediate position, under which territorial waters extended 12 miles offshore (along with a **continental shelf** of up to 350 nautical miles and a 200-mile **EEZ**), had gained widespread acceptance. In **UK** law the 1987 Territorial Sea Act established the breadth of the UK's territorial waters as 12 nautical miles. In November 1994 the Law of the Sea Convention came into force.

TESSA

A tax-exempt special savings account introduced by John **Major**, then **Chancellor of the Exchequer**, in the 1990 **budget**. Under the TESSA scheme, which took effect from 1 January 1991, individuals may make deposits up to given annual ceilings in special savings accounts over a five-year period. At the end of that period the amount saved, and all interest accrued, is repayable free of income tax, thus affording an incentive to regular saving; some interest may be withdrawn during the five-year term, but prior withdrawal of capital means surrendering the tax-exempt status of the funds.

TESTING

The name given to the procedure for assessing the educational progress of children in schools. The **Education Reform Act 1988** laid down the **national curriculum** and the system of testing to monitor pupils' attainment. The first statutory tests in **England** and **Wales** were held in 1990–1 but were disrupted by a sporadic boycott by teachers and by opposition from some parents. Pilot tests for 14-year-olds were held in 1991–2. All three main teaching unions, the **NUT**, the National Association of Schoolmasters Union of Women Teachers (NASUWT) and the Association of Teachers and Lecturers (ATL), voted in March and April 1993 to boycott testing on the grounds that the procedure was flawed and imposed too great a workload on teachers. The unions relented after widespread changes to the testing regime and the national curriculum.

TGWU

The Transport and General Workers' Union, often also known as the T&G, a large **left-wing** general union with around 900,000 members. For many years Britain's biggest union, the TGWU was in 1993 overtaken by **Unison**. It remains, however, the principal organization of the unskilled and semi-skilled and has a large female membership. Its founder in 1922 and guiding spirit for many years was Ernest **Bevin**; for 30 years the TGWU was central to the **TUC** and the **Labour Party**, its headquarters (Transport House) famously also hosting the Party. After 1955 the TGWU was headed by leaders who advocated vigorous industrial action and supported left-wing causes, among them Frank Cousins and Jack Jones. It strengthened itself by replacing centralized control with a shop steward infrastructure which became especially powerful in the car and engineering industries. For a time the TGWU backed the 1974 Labour government and **incomes policy**, but disenchantment led to industrial action at **Ford** in 1978. In 1990 the TGWU elected as its general secretary Bill Morris, Britain's first black union leader. He controversially voted against the amendment to **Clause IV** of the Labour Party's constitution in April 1995, without having balloted the membership. His action a provoked a leadership challenge by Jack Dromey. During the bitter campaign Dromey, husband of Harriet Harman, Labour's **shadow** employment minister, and representing Tony **Blair's new Labour** with considerable support from **Walworth Road**, cast Morris in the role of dinosaur, unwilling to progress. Nevertheless, the results of the election released in late June showed that Morris had the backing of the membership, winning a clear majority over his rival.

THALIDOMIDE

An infamous drug which as a side effect caused grievous physical disabilities to unborn children. It became widely available in 1960 as a remedy for pregnant women suffering morning sickness. In November 1961 the drug's manufacturers, Distillers (then owned by Chemie Grunenathal), withdrew thalidomide after doctors traced a link with the birth in 46 countries of thousands of children with a variety of abnormalities. Many were born with stunted limbs and misshapen hands and feet. The scandal drew attention to the procedures for testing drugs. The *Sunday Times* led a campaign in 1972–3 for adequate compensation payments to people affected by thalidomide. In May 1995 Guinness, which acquired Distillers in 1986, agreed to contribute an extra £37.5 million over 15 years to a trust fund for the 458 UK survivors of the drug.

It emerged in 1994 that the drug was being used successfully for the treatment of leprosy.

THAMES FLOOD BARRIER

A barrier across the River Thames built to protect London from tidal flooding from the North Sea. The barrier consists of 10 concrete gates which, when closed, form a 475 metre dam across the Thames at Woolwich Reach, 14 km down-river from central London. It took 11 years to construct, cost £450 million, and was opened by Queen **Elizabeth II** on 8 May 1984. Experts had calculated that the UK's capital was vulnerable to major flooding on average once every 50 years.

After some 300 people died in London in 1953, legislation was approved authorizing the **LCC** to build the flood barrier. The final design was for a movable barrier which allowed easy navigation during normal weather conditions, but which could be raised to provide protection against an imminent flood.

THAT WAS THE WEEK THAT WAS

The pioneering television programme of the early 1960s which introduced British audiences to an innovative blend of entertainment, satire and investigative journalism, and critically undermined the **Macmillan** government. Among its most controversial innovations was perhaps the first case of 'trial by TV', the live exposure of the alleged frauds of a businessman in front of an audience composed of his alleged victims. However, it was also celebrated for its spontaneous and moving tribute to President John F. Kennedy on his assassination. The show shot to prominence David Frost, its presenter, and also Ned Sherrin, its producer; among others who made their name on the programme were Bernard Levin, Millicent Martin and Willie Rushton. *That Was The Week That Was* ran intermittently from November 1962 until, a **general election** looming, the **BBC** took it off the air just over a year later.

THATCHER, MARGARET

(b. 1925) The **right-wing Conservative Prime Minister** 1979–90. Thatcher entered Parliament as **MP** for Finchley in North London in 1959 after a career in the law and industrial chemistry. After junior office in the 1960s, she became Education Secretary in the **Heath** government where she earned the epithet the **milk snatcher**. When in 1975 her mentor Keith **Joseph** declined to stand for the Conservative leadership she was nominated, unexpectedly led Edward Heath on the first ballot and beat four others to win outright. After four years as **Leader of the Opposition** she moved the no confidence motion lost by the **Labour** government in March 1979. That May she became Britain's first woman Prime Minister, The Conservatives having comfortably won the **general election**.

She stayed for more than 11 years, winning general elections in 1983 and 1987 and becoming Britain's longest-serving peacetime leader. Unusually, her radical instincts were not blunted by office. A **monetarist**, she sought throughout her terms of office to apply market-led criteria to social and economic issues, coming up with solutions such as the **right to buy**, **privatization**, the abolition of **exchange controls** and floating **sterling**. She faced down many **public sector** strikes, including the 1984–5 **miners' strike**.

Thatcherism, which she maintains was developed by Joseph, became synonymous with rigorous control of public spending and determination to overcome **inflation** despite short-term unpopularity. It also signified strong centralized control and full exploitation of the powers of the Prime Minister's office. In international affairs she was aggressively nationalistic, even jingoistic, turning an initial reverse to her advantage in the **Falklands conflict**, hailing military strength as the right response to communism (for which the Soviets dubbed her the **Iron Lady**) and asserting British sovereignty in the **EU**. The period of her government saw a blossoming of the **special relationship** with the USA, thanks in part to her good personal relations with Ronald Reagan and later with George Bush.

In 1990 the mid-term trough of Conservative unpopularity was aggravated by the **Poll Tax** and disarray over her estrangement from other EU states. A powerful resignation speech by her **Chancellor** Sir Geoffrey **Howe** triggered a leadership challenge from Michael **Heseltine** who narrowly denied her a first ballot victory. She decided, reluctantly, not to fight on, and resigned on 28 November to be succeeded by John **Major**, her favoured candidate. She left **Downing Street** in tears, a rare display of vulnerability. She remained on the **backbenches** until the April 1992 general election after which she took a life peerage as Baroness Thatcher of Grantham, but continued to encourage the Conservative right by advocating a **referendum** on **EMU**.

THATCHERISM

The political philosophy of Margaret **Thatcher**, **Prime Minister** from 1979 to 1990. This was typified by the pursuit of **conviction politics**, and its economic basis was largely founded on **Friedmanite** theories. It stressed the role of the individual and the importance of personal incentives, and spearheaded the process of **privatization**. The period of Thatcherism was, however, accompanied by generally rising unemployment and the effective deindustrialization of the economy. Thatcher's lengthy term of office was characterized by the dominance of the Prime Minister within the **Cabinet**, in contrast with the less confrontational attitude of her successor, John **Major**.

THATCHER'S CHILDREN

The generation having political knowledge only of right-wing **Conservatism** as espoused by Margaret **Thatcher**. Thatcher's children is a pejorative phrase, employed by diverse groups to lament the supposed disrespect for collective or social values of the young.

THINK TANK

A colloquial term used to describe a group of experts who gather to consider particular issues (generally social, political and economic) with a view to providing possible solutions and/or new directions. Notable examples include **Demos** and the **Social Market Foundation**.

THIRD FORCE

A vigilante group set up in **Northern Ireland** in the early 1980s. It was supported by the **Democratic Unionist Party**, which claimed that the organization had helped to reduce the number of Protestant murders in the area near the border with the Irish Republic. The party claimed at one point that the group had some 15,000–20,000 members, but its significance faded by the mid-1980s.

THIRD MAN

Kim **Philby**, the former diplomat and spy who defected to the Soviet Union in January 1963. After the defection of diplomats Guy **Burgess** and Donald **Maclean** in 1951, a prolonged investigation was held to identify the person, the 'third man', who had warned them of their imminent discovery. Philby, like Burgess a member of the pre-war Cambridge **apostles**, was interrogated but no proof could be found. He was required, however, to leave the diplomatic service and he subsequently worked as a journalist in Lebanon, from where he flew to Moscow after being confronted by the **UK** intelligence services.

In 1979 Anthony **Blunt** was revealed to have been the 'fourth man' who had acted as a talent-spotter for the Soviet Union and had passed secret information to that country while working for the counterintelligence security service **MI5**.

THIRD READING

The final parliamentary debate on draft legislation. Once a bill has passed its **committee stage** and report stage in either the **House of Commons** or the **House of Lords** a final debate takes place on its general principles. Amendments may, subject to certain restrictions, be tabled at third reading. A bill which has passed all its stages in both Houses remains with the Lords prior to its enactment by **royal assent**.

30-YEAR RULE

The practice whereby most public records are only released for general access 30 years after their date of origin. Certain exceptions are made even to this rule in respect of issues thought to be particularly sensitive, especially those relating to the **Royal Family** and to intelligence matters, to which a longer period may apply. Some relaxation was promised in July 1993 within the context of the government's policy of **open government**.

THORNEYCROFT, PETER

(1909–94) A **Conservative Chancellor of the Exchequer** under Harold **Macmillan**. Thorneycroft delivered his one and only **budget** in 1957. In what Macmillan memorably termed 'a little local difficulty', Thorneycroft, Enoch **Powell** and Nigel Birch all resigned from the **Treasury** in early 1958 in protest against a lack of monetary stringency. Thorneycroft, who was replaced as Chancellor by Derick **Heathcoat-Amory**, was made a **life peer** in 1967 and went on to chair the Conservative Party in 1975–81.

THORP

Thermal oxide reprocessing plant – the highly controversial **nuclear reprocessing** plant for which British Nuclear Fuels (**BNFL**) eventually obtained the go-ahead in early 1994. Spent nuclear fuel rods from nuclear power stations in the UK and abroad, particularly Germany and Japan, will be brought to Thorp, which is situated near **Sellafield** in Cumbria, in order to have the plutonium extracted from them. British, German, Irish, Japanese and US politicians and environmentalists have raised objections on the grounds that it is not economically viable and will produce quantities of plutonium which could encourage nuclear proliferation. There are also complaints of inadequate public consultation. The original plan to build Thorp prompted a campaign of protest by environmental pressure groups led by **Friends of the Earth**, and culminating in the 1977 **Windscale** enquiry – the UK's first public enquiry into a nuclear power development. The project was approved, but when construction was completed in 1992 commissioning was delayed because the British Nuclear Installation Inspectorate insisted on a reduction in its proposed levels of radioactive emissions.

THORPE CASE

The 1979 court case which spelt the end of the political career of Jeremy Thorpe, the former leader of the **Liberal Party**. Thorpe had resigned as party leader in May 1976, five months after Norman Scott, a former male model, had stated in court (in an unrelated case) that he and Thorpe had some years previously had a homosexual relationship. Thorpe, who denied the allegation, was subsequently charged with conspiracy and incitement to kill Scott, but was acquitted in June 1979.

THREE-DAY WEEK

The period of restricted economic activity resulting from the 1973–4 miners' strike and other industrial action in the UK. In November 1973 the National Union of Mineworkers began an overtime ban in support of a wage claim in breach of the current **incomes policy**, and this developed into a full stoppage of work in February-March 1974. The economic position was also gravely affected by the embargo imposed by member countries of the Organization of Petroleum Exporting Countries (OPEC) in October–November 1973 and the simultaneous oil price explosion, and by industrial action on the part of power engineers, railway employees and other workers. Meanwhile, a state of emergency was proclaimed in mid-November, under which in mid-December a package of measures was introduced limiting electricity supplies by a third and effectively imposing three-day working. In the context of this situation, the **Conservative Prime Minister** Edward **Heath** called a premature **general election** for 28 February 1974 on the issue of 'Who governs Britain?'. The election was lost by the Conservatives and resulted in the formation of a (minority) **Labour** government.

THREE-LINE WHIP *see* WHIP

300 GROUP

British all-party campaign launched in the 1970s to get more women into parliament, local government and other areas of public life. Of the 651 MPs elected in the **general election** held in April 1992, 60 were women compared with 44 in the outgoing parliament.

THRESHERGATE

An incident in November 1992 involving the beleaguered **Chancellor of the Exchequer** Norman **Lamont**. Lamont was reported to have bought by credit card a bottle of Bricout champagne and a packet of cigarettes at a Thresher's off-licence in Paddington in London. The story was denied by the **Treasury**, which insisted that Lamont had bought three bottles of wine at another branch of Thresher's the previous day. The claims were later withdrawn by the Thresher staff and a till receipt for the wine was produced. The story was pounced on by the media which had pursued Lamont since his refusal to resign after **Black Wednesday**. It coincided with revelations that Lamont had breached his credit card limit on over 20 occasions in eight years, and followed the disclosure that the Treasury and an anonymous contributor to the **Conservative Party** had covered the legal expenses for evicting a 'sex therapist' from a flat owned by Lamont and for answering press questions about the eviction. With the press baying for his blood, when Lamont made his **Je ne regrette rien** gaffe the following April, it was clear that he could not remain in office much longer.

TIED AID

Aid which is conditional on the recipient using the money to buy goods from the donor country or, more recently, using it in some other way specified by the donor. The most notorious recent UK example of this was the **Pergau Dam** affair where foreign aid to Malaysia was tied to the purchase of British arms.

TIGER TALKS

The negotiations held aboard HMS *Tiger* off Gibraltar on 2–4 December 1966 between **Prime Minister** Harold **Wilson** and Rhodesian leader Ian Smith, which failed to end Rhodesian **UDI**. Although Wilson virtually conceded independence to Smith's government in return for a commitment to make progress towards black majority rule, the deal was rejected by Smith's obdurate Rhodesian Front. Wilson responded by calling on the **UN** to impose mandatory economic **sanctions**. The next official round of talks, the **Fearless Talks**, took place in 1968.

TIMEX DISPUTE

A bitter industrial dispute in 1993. The workforce of the Dundee-based (but ultimately Norwegian-controlled) Timex plant went on strike on 29 January 1993 after negotiations over short-time working had broken down. They were effectively locked out by their employers, who brought in replacement non-union employees, and were dismissed in mid-February. Violent scenes occurred on the picket lines in mid-May, and the plant closed abruptly at the end of August, some months ahead of the scheduled ending of production there.

TIT-FOR-TAT KILLINGS

A pattern of killing of Catholic and Protestant civilians in **Northern Ireland**, when one and then another person or persons of alternative religion is murdered in a spiralling process of sectarian violence. In recent years, there have been two notable examples of this phenomenon. Following the killing of 10 people (including one of the bombers) by an **IRA** bomb in a fishmonger's shop in west Belfast in October 1993, a total of 13 people were shot dead during the next seven days in what appeared to be sectarian killings by loyalists. During the period May–June 1994, six Catholics were killed in one incident and a total of 13 others – including Protestants – died at the hands of **loyalist** or republican gunmen.

TOMLINSON REPORT

The report on health care in London written by Professor Bernard Tomlinson and published in October 1992. The report recommended a shift in the allocation of **NHS** resources from hospital care to primary and community care, and proposed a range of reforms including the closure or merger of 15 hospitals.

The government eventually announced in April 1995 the closure of the UK's oldest teaching hospital, St Bartholemew's, as part of its response to the report. The opposition **Labour Party** alleged that the aim of the reforms was primarily to cut health spending, and that the quality of both health care and medical training in London would decline as a result. Conservative **backbench** critics expressed scepticism over the government claim that the reforms were purely designed to improve clinical provision and were not a financial measure.

TOP TABLE

The highest level at which negotiations are conducted. In international diplomacy in the post-1945 period Britain aspired to participation at this level, as a permanent member of the **UN Security Council**, as (arguably) a **first-rank power**, and (above all, in **Cold War** terms) as the possessor of an **independent nuclear deterrent**. The desire to retain 'a place at the top table' was cited, indeed, as a reason for retaining this independent deterrent.

TORREY CANYON DISASTER

An oil spill from the 61,000-ton tanker *Torrey Canyon* when it ran aground off Lands End on 19 March 1967. The vessel's 100,000-ton cargo of crude oil began to be washed ashore from 24 March onwards, polluting more than 100 miles of the UK's coastline and causing grave damage to seabirds and marine life. On 30 March RAF aircraft bombed the remains of the stricken vessel in an attempt to reduce the pollution by burning the escaping oil.

TORY PARTY

A colloquial term for the **Conservative Party** which has acquired such wide usage that the two names are now interchangeable. It derives from a sixteenth century Irish word used abusively of Catholic outlaws. The modern Tory Party emerged in the nineteenth century with the 1834 Tamworth Manifesto, in which Sir Robert Peel urged his supporters to accept a widening of the franchise.

TORY REFORM GROUP

The **Conservative** grouping formed and funded by Peter Walker in the 1980s. The group occupies the middle ground of the party, its members tending to be interventionist and liberal leaning. Its current patrons include Michael **Heseltine**, Douglas **Hurd**, Malcolm **Rifkind** and Virginia Bottomley.

TOTE

The common name for the Horserace Totalisator Board, the state body which organizes an official race betting system at racecourses. The Tote, which runs side by side with profit-making betting operations, was established by the state in the period before commercial betting was legal. A review of the future of the Tote was announced in 1995 following a recommendation of the **House of Commons** home affairs committee that it be incorporated into an appropriate racing organization. It has been chaired since 1976 by Lord (Woodrow) Wyatt.

TOTTENHAM RIOTS *see* BROADWATER FARM

TOWN AND COUNTRY PLANNING ACT

The 1947 legislation which declared all future increment in land value caused by development was the property of the state. The Act was repealed in 1954 as part of the **Conservative** government's plan to build more houses. The repeal, together with the relaxing of building regulations, prompted a property boom, with more offices and homes being built and the price of land markedly increasing.

TOXTETH RIOTS

Serious **inner-city** disturbances in Toxteth, a deprived area of Liverpool in 1981, three months after the **Brixton riots**. The Toxteth disturbances, which started on 3 July after police stopped a black motorcyclist for a routine check, continued for three days and involved the calling in of large police reinforcements. As an immediate response, the personal protection of police officers was generally improved. While the **Scarman Report** on the Brixton disorders concentrated on the situation in Brixton itself, Lord Scarman invited and received evidence from organizations and individuals in other areas, including Liverpool.

TRADE UNION LEGISLATION

Industrial relations laws, most often used to describe **Conservative** trade union reform in the 1980s and 1990s. The traditional system whereby unions were immune from action in tort was ended when a long series of primary statutes redefined employment rights and regulated the unions themselves. The principal legislative enactments of the series were the Employment Act 1980, the Employment Act 1982, the Trade Union Act 1984, the Employment Act 1988, the Employment Act 1990, and the Trade Union Reform and Employment Rights Acts of 1992 and 1993. **Labour** was initially committed to repealing this legislation but gradually acquiesced in most of it, opting instead for a European-model framework of 'positive rights' at work.

TRAFFIC IN TOWNS *see* BUCHANAN REPORT

TRANSPORT 2000

A high-profile campaigning group of supported by trade associations, trade unions and environmental groups, founded in 1972. The group argues strongly for the public transport system, and campaigns for the railway network to be retained in the public sector. It also campaigns on behalf of pedestrians and cyclists.

TRANSPORT ACTS

A number of pieces of legislation enacted by the **Conservative** government since 1979 to implement its policy of the transfer where appropriate of public transport utilities to the private sector. Thus the Transport Act of 1980 enabled inter-city express bus routes to be de-licensed and allowed more competition between local bus services. **British Rail** (BR) was empowered to dispose of its shares in BR subsidiaries under the Transport Act of 1981. In 1982 a further Transport Act provided for the injection of private capital into the National Bus Company, which had by March 1988 sold all its 72 subsidiaries, a sale provided for under the Transport Act of 1985. The Transport (**Scotland**) Act of 1989 provided for the **privatization** of the Scottish Bus Group. Associated legislation includes the controversial **Railways Act 1993**.

TREASURY

The government department responsible for public finances. It deals with the raising of revenue through **Inland Revenue** taxes and **Customs and Excise** duties, with public expenditure planning and control, with public-sector and **civil service** pay, with competition and deregulation policy, with supervision of the banking and financial services sectors, with relations with the European Union in financial matters, and with the Royal Mint. Overall ministerial responsibility for the Treasury rests with the **Chancellor of the Exchequer**, a post currently held by Kenneth **Clarke**.

TREASURY BENCH *see* FRONT BENCH

TREATY OF ROME

The treaty signed in March 1957 creating the European Economic Community (**EEC**), and strictly speaking the separate treaty signed at the same time creating **Euratom**. The original signatories were the **Inner Six**. The UK became a party to the Treaty of Rome (and the Treaty of Paris establishing the **ECSC**) with effect from 1973, having signed the Treaty of **Accession** in January 1972.

TREVI GROUP

An informal network of **EC** justice and interior ministers set up in 1976 to combat *Terrorisme, Radicalisme, Extrémisme, Violence Internationale*. The Trevi group co-ordinates policy on matters such as **policing**, the law, **immigration, asylum**, measures to combat drug trafficking and terrorism, and preparatory work to establish **Europol**. It held 227 meetings in 1991–2. Since the entry into force of the **Maastricht** Treaty on European Union in November 1993 it has been replaced by the **K4 Committee** which operates as one of the 'intergovernmental pillars' of the Treaty. Like the K4 Committee, the Trevi Group operated outside the scrutiny of the **European Parliament** and **European Commission**.

TRIBUNE GROUP

The **Labour Party's** leading 'soft left' faction, particularly influential in the 1960s, which took its name from the *Tribune* newspaper first published in 1937. The Group has historically supported further nationalization and a withdrawal from the **EC**. Its most prominent supporters have (at one time or another) included Aneurin **Bevan**, former party leaders Michael **Foot** and Neil **Kinnock**, and latterly Gordon **Brown** and John Prescott.

TRIDENT

A US-made multiple-warhead submarine-launched nuclear missile, which **Thatcher's Conservative** government decided in 1980 to adopt as the replacement for the UK's **Polaris** missile (and the **Chevaline** upgrade). In March 1982 the Royal Navy decided to buy the D5 or Trident II missile, 16 of which could give a launch capacity of up to 128 warheads per submarine. Successive Conservative governments stood by the plan for four Trident submarines, despite escalating costs (estimated in 1995 at some £10 billion). The first Vanguard-class Trident submarine entered service in September 1993, with a second completed and due to join it in late 1995 and the others by 1998. Hostility to Trident within the opposition **Labour Party** was reflected in conference majorities in 1993 and 1994 for its immediate abandonment, although the Labour leadership resisted making a commitment to do this in its next **election** manifesto.

In a climate of international arms reduction, the UK government agreed in November 1993 to a ceiling of 96 warheads (four per missile) under the Trident programme. A decision announced in April 1995, to end the nuclear role of the RAF's Tornado bombers entirely by withdrawing its remaining free-fall nuclear bombs by 1998, would leave Trident as the sole element of the UK's strategic and sub-strategic nuclear deterrent.

TRINIDAD TERMS

An official debt reduction scheme launched by John **Major**, then **UK Chancellor of the Exchequer**, in 1990. Under this scheme, it was proposed, some 20 extremely poor countries (especially in sub-Saharan Africa) would see two-thirds of their aggregate government-to-government debt written off, provided they had an active economic programme agreed with the **IMF**. They would also be granted a five-year 'interest holiday' on their remaining debt, whose repayment would be rescheduled over up to 25 years. By early 1994 a total of 22 countries had benefited under these arrangements.

TROOPS OUT!

The slogan used from the 1970s to encapsulate the call for the unilateral and unconditional withdrawal of the British army from **Northern Ireland**. A Troops Out movement campaigns on this issue.

THE TROUBLES

A term used collectively to describe the situation which has existed since mid-1969 in **Northern Ireland**, of sectarian unrest, terrorist activities, the presence there of British Army soldiers and the murder of some 3,000 people up to the time of the **IRA ceasefire** declaration of August 1994. Division has existed for many years between Protestants, who in the main wish to see the province remain part of the **UK**, and Catholics, who want the **six counties** to be reunited with the **26 counties** of the south. The continuous political impasse in the province has led to the attempted implementation of various proposed solutions, in the form of the **Northern Ireland Assembly**, a **Council of Ireland**, a Parliament (**Stormont**), and the **Anglo-Irish Treaty**. The period of the Troubles has seen the emergence of a number of **loyalist** and **republican** paramilitary groups. There have also been incidents of bombing and murder on the British mainland as well as in continental Europe, largely instigated by the **IRA**, aimed at the British armed forces and their premises as well as at British politicians. These included the 1984 **Brighton bombing** and the **Harrods bomb** later in the same year.

TSR-2

The proposed British-built main RAF strike and reconnaissance aircraft whose cancellation was announced in the 1965 **budget** speech (in favour of buying US F-111s, although this was also later cancelled). Development of the TSR-2 had already cost some £750 million, but it had failed to win international orders, without which it would not have a long enough production run to make it economic.

TUC

The Trades Union Congress, the key umbrella employees' organization, originally founded in 1868. In mid-1994 a total of 68 individual trade unions were affiliated to the TUC, with an affiliated membership of just over 7,500,000; comparative figures for 1979 were 109 and about 12,000,000. Over this period the decline in individual unions largely reflected mergers, while the drop in membership was affected by the increase in unemployment – particularly in the traditionally highly-unionized heavy industries – and by the growth in self-employment. In the late 1970s the TUC still had a major role in consultation with government on a wide range of economic and social matters. However, its influence in these areas was restricted under the succeeding Conservative governments which introduced a series of legislative measures on industrial relations and on trade union regulation. In 1994 the TUC sought to 'relaunch' itself around a tightly defined set of priorities.

TUMIM REPORT

The report, published on 5 August 1991, into the escape of two **IRA** terrorist suspects (Pearse Gerard McAuley and Nessan Quinlivan) from Brixton Prison in south-east London on 7 July of that year. The inquiry was carried out by Judge Stephen Tumim, the Chief Inspector of Prisons for England and Wales, who had made a number of critical reports on prison conditions since his appointment in 1987. In his August 1991 report Tumim noted a series of operational failures at Brixton and recommended a wide range of security and procedural improvements. (McAuley and Quinlivan were both arrested in Ireland in April 1993 and were later sentenced in Dublin on firearms charges.)

TUNA WAR

A term referring to the clashes between Spanish fishing fleets and French, **UK** and Irish fleets over fishing rights in the Bay of Biscay in mid-1994. Differences centred on the fishing methods employed by Spanish fishermen, who used traditional rods and lines with live bait, while their **EU** counterparts used **drift nets** in the exploitation of albacore tuna stocks. The tuna war, which takes its name from the earlier so-called **cod wars** in the North Atlantic, preceded clashes off the Newfoundland coast over the exploitation of diminishing stocks of Greenland halibut in March 1995.

TURNER PRIZE

A self-consciously controversial art prize. It was established in 1984 when an anonymous member of the Tate Gallery's Patrons of New Art contributed £10,000 as prize money. The first winner was a US-based painter, Malcolm Morley. The New York dealers Drexel Burnham Lambert stepped in as sponsors in 1986. That year the prize was won by Gilbert and George, and a mild note of controversy entered the proceedings for the first time as the **tabloids** mocked the duo's winning montage – a picture of themselves gazing admiringly up at a shower of soiled Y-fronts. However, other winners in the 1980s were more 'established' artists. Channel 4 Television became the new sponsor in 1990 and they raised the prize money to £20,000. At the same time, the judges, under the chairmanship of Nicholas Serota, director of the Tate Gallery, announced their commitment to the newest of conceptual contemporary art. By 1992 the prize was firmly established in the television age thanks to Channel 4's coverage. Damien Hirst's dead fish in tanks of formaldehyde caused a mild sensation, as did the winner Grenville Davey's over-sized tin cans. In 1993 Rachel Whiteread won the prize with a cast of an East London house. Media coverage of the 1993 award was massive, boosted by a series of mysterious advertisements in the press, formulated by the so-called K Foundation, asking people to vote for the artists who had produced the 'worst' work during the last year. The 1994 award was won by sculptor Antony Gormley with a series of casts of himself in segments of lead.

THE TWELVE

A synonym sometimes used for the **EC**, and latterly the **EU**, between 1986 (when Spain and Portugal became the eleventh and twelfth members) and 1995 (when membership rose to 15).

26 COUNTIES

A term for the Republic of Ireland, used with the connotation that the division of the island of Ireland (Eire) into the 26 counties of the South and the **six counties** of the North is temporary and undesirable. The division dates from 1922, when the Irish Free State was created in the 26 counties. This included three of Ireland's four historic provinces – Leinster, Munster and Connacht – and three of the nine counties of **Ulster**. The 1937 Constitution establishing an independent Ireland nominally applies to the whole of Ireland. However, pending the 'reintegration of the national territory' the laws enacted by the Irish Parliament apply only in the 26 counties. Although Ireland's constitutional claim to the whole island has proved a stumbling block in discussions over **Northern Ireland**, the Irish government's recent expression of its willingness to amend the Constitution, dropping its territorial claim, have gone some way to assuaging the **UK** government and **unionist** politicians.

TW3 *see* THAT WAS THE WEEK THAT WAS

TWO DAVIDS

The popular term for David **Owen** and David Steel, the respective leaders of the

SDP and the **Liberal Party**, who jointly campaigned as the **Alliance** in 1983–7. Owen, a flamboyant conviction politician, and Steel, a modest pragmatist, formed an uneasy partnership and were mercilessly satirized, notably by **ITV's** *Spitting Image* programme. Following the disappointing **general election** result of 1987 the two Davids broke with each other in 1988 when Steel backed a merger of the two parties to form the **Liberal Democrats**, while Owen remained leader of the rump SDP.

TWO-SPEED EUROPE

An idea floated by the then French President François Mitterrand in a speech to the **European Parliament** in 1984, that the relaunched process of European integration in the **EC** (later the **EU**) could proceed faster for certain countries, with the remaining members possibly taking the same steps at a later date. The suggestion was highly controversial, implying that the EU would be shaped by 'core' countries (particularly France and Germany) which provided the 'motor' for integration. The two-speed idea resurfaced in the 1990s with regard to both **EMU** and the enlargement of the EU. It has also become a reality in areas such as the lifting of border controls, where the **UK** and some other member countries stand apart from the **Schengen** process. The 'two-speed' formulation has never been popular in the UK, since it generally implies a peripheral role for the UK, but in reality it is the other side of the same coin as retaining the **opt-out** as a benchmark of national sovereignty.

TWYFORD DOWN

An area in Wiltshire containing two **SSSIs** and a SAM (Scheduled Ancient Monument) which in the early 1990s became the focus of a fierce contest over the extension of the M3 motorway, with **new age travellers**, environmentalists and local residents uniting to halt the project. In a test case for **EC** environmental law, the EC **Commission** threatened the **UK** government with legal action for allegedly pressing ahead with construction without conducting an Environmental Impact Assessment as required by EC law. However, the EC dropped the case in July 1992, claiming that it was satisfied that the UK government's environmental studies satisfied the spirit of EC directives.

TYNWALD

The parliament of the **crown dependency** of the **Isle of Man**. The principal chamber of Tynwald is the 24-member directly elected House of Keys. The Legislative Council has four ex officio members, and eight elected by and from the House of Keys. Tynwald celebrated its millennium in 1979. Only the *Althing* of Iceland claims to be older (dating back to at least 930).

U-TURN

Usually a reference to a political reversal of policy. The term came to prominence after **Prime Minister** Margaret **Thatcher**'s speech on government economic policy at the **Conservative Party** conference of 1980 when, faced by frantic media calls that she should moderate her policies, her reply contained no sign of vacillation: 'To those waiting with baited breath for that favourite media catchphrase, the U-turn, I have only one thing to say: you turn if you want to. The lady's not for turning.'

UB40

The document issued by the government Employment Service to people claiming unemployment benefit or income support.

UDA

The Ulster Defence Association, the dominant paramilitary Protestant organization in **Northern Ireland**. The UDA came to the fore in the early 1970s and has been assigned responsibility – either directly or indirectly – for about a third of civilian killings in Northern Ireland since the outbreak of major disturbances in 1969. Most, but not all, of its victims have been Catholics. However, it was only in August 1992 that it was officially proscribed. The UDA, which is closely linked with the **UFF**, was one of the **loyalist** organizations which declared a cessation of 'military operations' in October 1994.

UDI

Unilateral Declaration of Independence, the proclamation by Prime Minister Ian Smith on 11 November 1965 that Southern **Rhodesia** was rejecting its status as a self-governing colony and would henceforth be an independent monarchy within the **Commonwealth**. The declaration was signed by Smith, leader of the Rhodesian Front Party, and by all 15 members of his Cabinet, who rejected British government insistence that they should accept black majority rule. UDI met international condemnation. No country formally recognized the Smith regime, although the apartheid regime in South Africa was sympathetic to it. Britain declared the regime 'illegal' and imposed unilateral sanctions which were soon given international application through the **UN**. Despite negotiations beginning with the **Tiger Talks**, UDI continued until 12 December 1979. It ended with the (temporary) resumption of British sovereignty under the **Lancaster House Agreement**, with Lord Soames as Governor.

UDM

The Union of Democratic Miners (UDM). A breakaway Nottinghamshire-based miners' union which originated in defiance of the 1984 **miners' strike** call by the **NUM**. The majority of the Nottingham area NUM membership stayed at work during the 1984–5 **miners' strike** which their output helped to defeat. Most of these members adhered to the new organization after it ended, although the NUM retained the loyalty of most miners nationally. After 1992 UDM leaders strongly voiced a sense of betrayal at the run-down of the **coal industry** which caused a drastic diminution of membership.

UDP

The **Ulster** Democratic Party, formed in the early 1980s (when it was known as the Ulster **Loyalist** Democratic Party) as the political wing of the loyalist paramilitary Ulster Defence Association (**UDA**). Since the loyalist **ceasefire** of October 1994 the UDP has become involved in discussions with British government representatives as part of the **Northern Ireland** peace process, although it is generally seen as being overshadowed by the emergence of the **PUP** as the political group most in touch with opinion among the paramilitaries.

UFF

The Ulster Freedom Fighters, a paramilitary Protestant organization in **Northern Ireland**. Since the early 1970s the UFF has carried out large numbers of killings, especially of Catholics. It is widely considered to be the main military wing of the **UDA**. The organization was proscribed in November 1973. The UDA was one of the **loyalist** organizations to declare a **ceasefire** in October 1994.

UGANDAN ASIANS

A term used to describe the 80,000 Ugandans of Asian (predominantly Indian) descent who were expelled from Uganda in 1972; they were given 90 days to leave by Idi Amin. The Asian community was identified in the mind of many Ugandans with British colonialism, and the move was widely supported. By December 1972, 90 per cent of the Asians had left, the majority, as British passport holders, going to the UK and others to India. They left behind assets worth an estimated £500,000,000.

In October 1992 Ugandan President Yoweri Museveni asked for the forgiveness of the Ugandan Asians and invited all of them to return, promising that they would be able to recover their property or seek compensation for their losses. The first property was returned in February 1993.

UK

United Kingdom, the official title of the country often loosely referred to as Britain. **Great Britain** and Ireland were unified as the United Kingdom of Great Britain and Ireland under the 1800 Act of Union. The creation of the Irish Free State in 1922 made it necessary to amend the full title of the UK to the United Kingdom of Great Britain and **Northern Ireland**.

UK ACTION COMMITTEE ON ISLAMIC AFFAIRS

A Muslim pressure group. It was founded in 1989 as the campaigning arm of the **Union of Muslim Organizations** to mobilize British Muslim opinion in favour of endorsing the death sentence pronounced by the Ayatollah Khomeini on the author, Salman Rushdie for his novel *The* **Satanic Verses**. Its convener was Mughram al-Ghamdi of Saudi Arabia, the then Director-General of the **London Central Mosque**. Its chief support was alleged to lie among Muslim groups with close links to the Pakistan-based religious party, the *Jamaat-i-Islami* Pakistan.

UK COUNCIL OF IMAMS AND MOSQUES

An Islamic pressure group founded in 1985 to provide practical support for religious leaders and promote inter-faith relations. In 1989 it played a prominent part in the campaign to ban **The Satanic Verses** by Salman Rushdie although it was opposed to the death sentence imposed on Rushdie by the Ayatollah Khomeini. It recently launched the Islamic Renewal Campaign which seeks to counter moves by the **Church of England** to revive popular interest in Christianity.

UKIAS

The UK Immigrants' Advisory Service, a government-funded body providing advice to prospective immigrants to the UK. Founded in 1970 by the second **Wilson** government, the UKIAS currently provides advice and legal representation on **immigration** questions for some 2,000 families a month on an annual government grant of £1,500,000. In July 1991 the Home Secretary, Kenneth **Baker**, who had been embarrassed in judicial review proceedings by several independent solicitors, announced plans to withdraw the green form **legal aid** system of public funding from all independent solicitors and impose a UKIAS monopoly over immigration cases. However, public opposition to such a move forced the government to withdraw the plans in February 1992. The UKIAS's work contrasts with that of the independent **Joint Council for the Welfare of Immigrants**.

ULSTER

One of the four historic provinces of Ireland, comprising the island's nine north-eastern counties. Ulster has the largest concentration of Protestants in the island, and showed the strongest determination to remain within the **UK**. At the time of partition in 1922 most of Ulster – the **six counties** (Antrim, Armagh, Down, Fermanagh, Londonderry and Tyrone) – became **Northern Ireland** as part of the UK, whereas the counties of Cavan, Donegal and Monaghan were among the **26 counties** included within the Irish Free State. 'Ulster' is commonly if inaccurately used by **unionists** as synonymous with Northern Ireland.

ULSTER DEMOCRATIC PARTY *see* UDP

UN

The United Nations, the most significant international organization in the period since the Second World War. The UN emerged originally from wartime co-ordination among the **UK** and the Allies and their declarations – in particular the Atlantic Charter of August 1941, the Washington Declaration by 26 allied countries on 1 January 1942, the Dumbarton Oaks conference of the **Big Four** in 1944, the Yalta conference of the **Big Three** in February 1945, and the **San Francisco Conference** from 25 April to 25 June 1945 – formally entitled the United Nations Conference on International Organization. The UN Charter was signed by 50 countries at the end of this meeting on 26 June, and entered into force on 24 October 1945, when the UN was formally established with its headquarters in New York. Since its inception, the UK has (along with the USA, the Soviet Union – latterly Russia – China and France) held a permanent seat on the **Security Council**, the UN's principal organ to preserve peace and security.

UN ASSOCIATION

An all-party parliamentary **lobby** group which also has a broad educational objective of promoting public support for the **UN**, especially for the UN's role in disarmament. It has its headquarters in London and counterpart organizations in many other countries.

UNEMPLOYMENT

The economic term for the predicament of people capable of, and seeking, work who are unable to find it. Wide-scale unemployment is now a familiar UK problem. The number of registered unemployed exceeded two million in 1981 and three million in 1984. The **Conservative** governments of Margaret **Thatcher** and John **Major** have claimed success in reducing the unemployment rate, and the official figures fell sharply to about 1.6 million in July 1990 (although they rose again to more than two million). However, opponents have suggested that this fall is the result of changes to the rules governing the unemployment register which have excluded certain groups and thus significantly reduced the total.

UNILATERALISM

The belief that individual states should independently renounce the use of nuclear weapons. Unilateral nuclear disarmament has been advocated in Britain from the mid-1950s by the anti-nuclear campaign group **CND** and by radical elements of the **Labour Party**, briefly becoming official party policy in 1960 and again in the early 1980s.

UNION OF MUSLIM ORGANIZATIONS

A Muslim umbrella organization. Founded in 1970, it claimed to be a representative forum of diverse Muslim opinion in the **UK**. After some initial success, however, it lost the support of most major Muslim organizations resulting in a rapidly dwindling membership consisting mainly of some 200 or so local mosques and associations. In 1988 it re-emerged, through its affiliated body, the **UK Action Committee on Islamic Affairs**, to play a key role in the campaign against the publication of **The Satanic Verses**, and lobbied energetically for the prosecution of its author, Salman Rushdie, and his publisher, Penguin, under the Public Order and **Race Relations** Act.

UNIONISTS

The members of political parties and other organizations in **Northern Ireland** committed to the maintenance of the union between Northern Ireland and the rest of the **UK**. Traditionally, the unionist movement was closely identified with the **Conservative Party**. The majority of Northern Ireland members of the **House of Commons** from 1921 were unionist supporters of the Conservatives, while unionists also dominated the Northern Ireland parliament at **Stormont**. However, by 1969 the Democratic Unionists (**DUP**) had been formed as a dissident **loyalist** Protestant grouping, and in 1972, with the imposition of **direct rule** in Northern Ireland, **MPs** of the Ulster Unionist Council (now commonly referred to as the official Ulster Unionists – **OUP**) ceased to take the Conservative **whip**. However, the **Major** government's small and shrinking majority following the 1992 **general election** have made the unionists a key group in parliament. They have supported the government in a number of crucial votes. In December 1993 the government promised to establish a **select committee** on Northern Ireland. The concession of this principal unionist demand was regarded as a reward for the support the unionists had given the government in vital votes on Europe. Currently in the House of Commons both the OUP and the DUP are represented.

UNISON

The giant public service union formed in 1993 by a merger of **COHSE**, **NALGO** and **NUPE**. With 1.4 million members, it is the largest British union and the third largest in Europe. Unison organizes one in six of all trade unionists and one-third of all women members. Some 800,000 members work in **local government**, 400,000 in the **NHS**, and others work for higher education, gas, electricity, water and the **police** authorities. Two-thirds of its members are women, and an estimated 800,000 members earn less than £10,000 annually. The contentious issue of reconciling the non-partisan NALGO with the **Labour**-affiliated COHSE and NUPE was resolved by the novel device of creating two Unison political funds. The General Fund pays for non-partisan campaigns and the Affiliated Fund, which bankrolls links with the Labour Party including Unison's 20 sponsored **MPs**.

UNIT FINES

The controversial system introduced in October 1992 under the **Criminal Justice** Act 1991, in which courts imposed fines on the basis of a sliding scale according to the weekly disposable income of the offender. The scheme was widely criticized by **magistrates** as unfair to those on middle incomes and on 13 May 1993 Home Secretary Kenneth **Clarke** announced that it was to be withdrawn.

UNITED KINGDOM *see* UK

UNITED KINGDOM IMMIGRANTS' ADVISORY SERVICE *see* UKIAS

UNITED SYNAGOGUE

The largest orthodox Jewish religious grouping. It was established by an Act of Parliament in 1870 and is recognized as the main body representing the Anglo-Jewish religious **Establishment**. It maintains the Chief Rabbinate, the Council of which appoints the Chief Rabbi or the religious head of Jewry in the **UK**, a post currently occupied by Rabbi Jonathan **Sacks**. Through the London Board of Religious Education, the United Synagogue controls most part-time religious education and provides chaplaincies to hospitals, prisons, the military and universities.

UNIVERSITIES

Institutions of higher education. Most universities are self-governing institutions established by Royal Charter, some dating back centuries. They have academic freedom, employ their own staff and award their own degrees. Overall responsibility for universities in the **UK** rests with the Secretary of State for Education, although the role is filled by the Secretary of State for **Northern Ireland** in that province. The Further and Higher Education Act 1992 abolished the so-called 'binary' system based on a distinction between universities and **polytechnics**. In June of that year, 28 polytechnics adopted the title 'university' in addition to the 46 universities already existing. The funding of higher education institutions was brought under a single structure, the Higher Education Funding Councils for **England**, **Wales** and **Scotland**.

UNPROFOR

The **UN** Protection Force, whose establishment was authorized by the **UN Security Council** in January 1992. A 14,000-strong force, drawn from 30 countries, including France, Russia and the **UK**, was dispatched to **Croatia** in March 1992 to monitor a ceasefire between Croatia and the **Krajina** Serbs. UNPROFOR's mandate was enlarged in June 1992, when troops were also deployed in **Bosnia-Hercegovina** (with the principal object of protecting the means of aid distribution) and, in smaller numbers, in **Macedonia**. UNPROFOR troops have been subject to persistent harassment by all parties in the war.

UNSINKABLE AIRCRAFT CARRIER

A cynical term for the facilities which Britain provided for the US Air Force in the Second World War, giving it access to airfields conveniently located for the European theatre of war. The role was revived within the **NATO** alliance structure in the subsequent **Cold War**, not only for aircraft but also, in the 1980s, for nuclear-armed **cruise** missiles.

UPUP

The Ulster Popular Unionist Party, founded in 1980 by the rebel **unionist** Sir James Kilfedder, who was the party's sole representative in the **House of Commons** until his death in March 1995. The **by-election** in Sir James's Down North constituency which took place in mid-June 1995, won by Robert McCartney, an independent describing himself as a United Kingdom Unionist, was the first election in **Northern Ireland** since the 1994 paramilitary **ceasefire**.

URUGUAY ROUND

The final stage of **GATT** talks on liberalizing world trade. An agreement marking the end of the 7½ years of the Uruguay Round was signed by the **UK** and 123 other countries and the **European Union** at a conference in Marrakesh in April 1994. It provided for a 40 per cent cut in global tariffs, wider access to imported goods, a clearer framework for conducting trade and the extension of GATT rules to agricultural goods, services and intellectual property rights. However, negotiators failed to agree in the areas of financial services, telecommunication and shipping, and important bilateral issues were unresolved, notably a protracted dispute between the USA and Japan.

UUP

The Ulster Unionist Party, the principal **unionist** party in **Northern Ireland**. Under the cautious leadership of James **Molyneaux**, the UUP has usually supported the **Conservative Party** in the **House of Commons**. However, the UUP has always made known its concern over a number of aspects of future political arrangements in the province. It has in particular been anxious about the extent of involvement by the Irish government in the affairs of the north. In a document published in February 1994, entitled *Blueprint for Stability*, the party called for the abandonment of the 1985 **Anglo-Irish Treaty** and the setting up of a new **Northern Ireland Assembly**. The UUP is often referred to as the 'official' Unionists (and abbreviated to 'OUP'), to differentiate it from the **Democratic Unionist Party**.

UVF

The **Ulster** Volunteer Force, a paramilitary Protestant organization in **Northern Ireland**. The UVF is one of the oldest such organizations, having been formed in 1912. It was banned in 1966 (before the outbreak of major disturbances in Northern Ireland in 1969) but its proscription was lifted in May 1974. However, it was once again proscribed in November 1975 after it had been involved in various acts of violence. The UVF was one the **loyalist** organizations to declare a cessation of 'operational hostilities' in October 1994.

VASSALL AFFAIR

The circumstances surrounding the conviction of William John Vassall, an Admiralty clerk, for spying for the Soviet Union. Vassall was blackmailed into cooperating with the Soviet authorities after compromising photographs of him in a homosexual relationship were taken in Moscow in the mid-1950s. His activities were revealed by a Soviet defector, and he was sentenced in 1962 to 18 years' imprisonment. A tribunal of inquiry was established in 1962 under a senior judge, Lord Radcliffe, which absolved the government of blame for failing to identify Vassall's homosexuality but which was critical of Admiralty personnel procedures.

VAT

Value added tax, a form of indirect taxation, which was introduced in the **UK** on 1 April 1973. It involves taxing each stage of production or provision through which goods or services pass and is levied on the basis of 'value added' during that stage. It is collected by requiring traders to charge the assigned percentage VAT on their output sales (sales of goods which leave them after being processed), and then to pay the money over to the government after subtracting their input tax, i.e. the VAT which they paid to the traders from whom they received goods prior to processing. Specific goods and services may be either exempt or zero-rated.

The **Conservative** government severely dented its popular support when it announced in March 1993 that domestic fuel and power would cease to be zero-rated. Although VAT was charged on domestic fuel and power at 8 per cent from April 1994, the government was defeated in the **House of Commons** in December 1994 when it attempted to increase the rate to 17.5 per cent.

The **EC** (now **EU**) decided in 1992 that there should be a minimum standard rate of VAT of 15 per cent throughout the Community, within the framework of the **single market**. A portion of the VAT receipts of the individual member states is allocated to the EU, and this provides around half of the EU's 'own resources' for its general budget.

VICEROY

The governor of a country – such as India under British rule (the Raj) – or province who rules on behalf of the sovereign. Earl **Mountbatten** was the last Viceroy of India, in 1947–8, his immediate predecessor being Lord Wavell in 1943–7.

VICTORIAN VALUES

The resonant expression taken up by **Prime Minister** Margaret **Thatcher** in 1982 to sum up a series of qualities – such as hard work, frugality and self-reliance – which she considered to have been key strengths of the British people in the nineteenth century, when the country occupied a more prominent position in the world, and to which she felt the country should return.

VIDEO NASTIES

A commonplace description of video films which largely feature particularly distasteful violent or sexually explicit scenes. They became more widespread as well as more notorious in the early 1980s. Video nasties have been the subject of legal action which has resulted in their withdrawal from the market, although their circulation has not been prevented in any effective way, despite the existence of the **Obscene Publications Act** of 1959, and attempts by the **Conservative** government to introduce stricter controls through legislation introduced with all-party support, the Video Recordings Act of 1984. The belief that video nasties lead to violence and degradation has been expressed in some quarters. Such views intensified during the trial of the two children involved in the **Bulger affair**, when it emerged that they had watched an extremely unsavoury video (*Child's Play*).

VIENNA CONVENTION 1961

The international agreement under which all signatories guarantee the immunity, rights and privileges of diplomatic staff and the integrity of embassies within their countries. The convention formalized a longstanding recognition of the need for immunity in the conduct of diplomatic relations.

VOC

A volatile organic compound. VOCs are contained in fumes from traffic, paint and solvents and are a principal constituent of low-level ozone 'summer **smog**'. They are carcinogenic and cause breathing difficulties by attacking the lining of the lungs. The government is committed to reducing VOC emissions by 1999 by 30 per cent compared to 1988. However, this target has been attacked as too low by environmental groups demanding **clean air** who say that ozone smogs are unacceptable when one in seven British children suffers from asthma, a condition severely aggravated by the smogs.

VOX POP

(from Latin *vox populi*, 'the voice of the people') Interviews conducted with members of the public, usually in the street, in order to elicit their views on a variety of topics. Since the 1960s broadcasters and journalists have increasingly resorted to this technique as a means of gauging the 'mood of the people'.

VSO

Voluntary Service Overseas, a charitable organization founded in 1958 which sends volunteers from the **UK** to work in developing countries with government and community organizations. Volunteers, who spend two years abroad, are skilled individuals, qualified and experienced in their field and include midwives, accountants, carpenters and teachers. They range between 20 and 70 years old, though the average age is 33. The fundamental philosophy of the organization is that volunteers should contribute towards the long-term, sustainable development of the groups with which they work. Consequently volunteers devote a large part of their time to training and sharing skills with local colleagues. At the end of 1994 VSO had 1,720 volunteers in 57 countries.

VTOL

Vertical take-off and landing, a term used to describe fixed-wing aircraft which do not require a runway and which can thus be used in confined areas including on seaborne aircraft carriers. Extensive research into the design of such craft began in the 1950s; the first successful VTOL was the SC1 built in 1960 by Shorts Brothers of Belfast, Northern Ireland. However, the first VTOL to go into operational use as a combat jet was the Harrier Jump Jet. The RAF took delivery of the first Jump Jet on 18 April 1969.

VULCAN

An RAF jet-powered bomber, capable of delivering conventional or nuclear bombs. It was ordered by the RAF in 1947 and the first one entered service in February 1957. Improved Mark 2 Vulcans were equipped in 1962 with 'Blue Steel' stand-off nuclear missiles, which they carried beneath the fuselage. In 1969 Royal Navy **Polaris** boats took over the UK nuclear strike role from the Vulcans. The RAF withdrew the last Vulcans from front-line service in 1983 after using them the previous year to fly long-range conventional bombing missions during the **Falklands conflict**.

WADDINGTON, DAVID

(b. 1929) For a brief period **Conservative** Home Secretary at the tail end of Margaret **Thatcher**'s premiership, from October 1989 to November 1990. Prior to his appointment he had served for two years as Government Chief **Whip**. Waddington was replaced as Home Secretary in John **Major**'s first government (formed in November 1990) by Kenneth **Baker** while he, given a **life peerage**, served in the government for two further years as **Lord Privy Seal** and **Leader of the House of Lords**.

WAGE RESTRAINT

A climate in which trade unions agree to lower pay increases than could be secured by collective bargaining, as a means of controlling inflation. The **Conservative** government in 1972–4 imposed a statutory **incomes policy** in three stages, the third stage of which indexed wages to the cost of living. The policy was resisted by the trade unions and was a major factor in the Conservative election defeat of 1974. The subsequent **Labour** Government opted for voluntary wage restraint under the **Social Contract**, but this too foundered in 1978 as a result of union opposition.

WAGES COUNCILS

The boards with statutory powers to set rates and conditions in certain industries. Wages Councils were established early in the twentieth century for the 'sweated' trades and came to cover more than 4,000,000 workers. In 1985 their number and scope were considerable and in 1993 all remaining Councils were abolished with the single exception of the Agricultural Wages Board. In the absence of a **minimum wage** this step left Britain one of the most deregulated economies of the developed world.

WAITE, TERRY

(b. 1939) The **Church of England** envoy held captive in Lebanon from 1987–91 by pro-Iranian militants. Waite, the **Archbishop of Canterbury's** special representative in Lebanon, was negotiating for the release of existing hostages when he was himself seized by members of Islamic *Jihad*, a faction of the radical pro-Iranian group *Hezbollah* ('the Party of God'). He was released with fellow-hostage Thomas Sutherland, a US academic, on 19 November 1991, just over three months after another British hostage John **McCarthy**. The release was part of a complex three-way international hostage deal brokered by the **UN** and involving also the release of Shia Muslims held in Israel and Israeli military personnel held in the Lebanon.

WALES

The principality occupying the extreme west of the mainland of **Great Britain**. The integration of Wales was achieved through the Acts of Union in 1536 and 1542 which made the **Westminster** parliament sovereign over Wales. Despite subsequent fluctuating Welsh nationalist sentiment, these constitutional arrangements have remained basically unchanged. An attempt to establish **devolution** was defeated in a referendum in 1979. Cardiff was proclaimed the national capital in 1954 and ministerial responsibility for Wales was taken over by a Secretary of State with Cabinet rank in 1964. The Welsh Office administers policies on health, social services, education, local government, housing, the environment, agriculture, sport, and regional and economic planning.

WALWORTH ROAD

The South London location, since 1980, of the **Labour Party** head office, which was named John **Smith** House in September 1994 in commemoration of the party's late leader. The Walworth Road offices serve as the administrative hub of the party, hosting meetings of the **NEC** and co-ordinating party fund-raising and campaigns. Party researchers based at Walworth Road play an advisory role in policy-making. Between 1928 and 1980 the party central office had been Transport House, the headquarters of the **TGWU**.

WAPPING DISPUTE

A pivotal and bitter industrial dispute in the newspaper industry lasting just over a year in 1986–7. The dispute was centred around the relocation of the editorial offices and printing works of **News International**, the publishers of *The Times*, the **Sun** and other newspapers, from **Fleet Street** to a new site at Wapping further east – the move being associated with radical changes in technology and working practices. Despite firm employee opposition to management attitudes, and support from many other trades unions, work finally resumed in February 1987. The course of the dispute was widely seen as clear evidence of the determination of management, not only in newspapers but also in other industries, to break free from hardened and entrenched industrial practices on the part of labour.

WAR CRIMES ACT 1991

Legislation providing for the prosecution of British residents alleged to have committed atrocities in Nazi-occupied Europe during the Second World War, which was passed without the approval of the **House of Lords**. It was opposed in some quarters on the grounds that the prosecutions would be based on events that occurred more than 40 years ago and that defendants would not receive a fair trial. It was defeated in the House of Lords in June 1990, reintroduced the following year and rejected for a second time in April 1991. It was passed on 9 May 1991, under the **Parliament Act 1949** and that of 1991, which permitted bills that had been approved twice by the **House of Commons** to be passed without the agreement of the House of Lords. The first British war crimes prosecution was launched in July 1995, when Szymon Serafinowicz, formerly a Byelorussian but now a British citizen, was charged with the murder of four unknown Jews.

WAR WIDOWS PENSION

A weekly payment made to dependants of men killed in UK army service at a rate depending on her age and her late husband's service rank and set each tax year. Widows whose husbands served in the UK armed forces on or after 1 January 1973 are entitled to a supplementary earnings-related payment under the service pensions scheme.

A late amendment to the Pensions Bill in late April 1995 provided for the payment of a pension to war widows who had remarried and whose marriages had ended through bereavement, divorce or legal separation. The amendment followed a long campaign supported by the **British Legion**, and the concession was made in the run-up to the celebrations for the 50th anniversary of the end of the War in Europe (VE Day).

WARNOCK REPORT

A report published in July 1984, on **bioethics** as well as the social and legal implications of recent and potential developments in the field of human-assisted reproduction. Chaired by Baroness Warnock, the committee recommended in particular that certain forms of infertility treatment, such as artificial insemination by donor and **IVF**, were ethically acceptable, that 'surrogate' motherhood was open to strong moral objections and that the provision of surrogacy services should be banned, and that research on human embryos should be permitted only up to the fourteenth day after fertilization. Most of the report's conclusions were incorporated in the Human Fertilization and Embryology Act 1990.

WARRINGTON DISPUTE

The bitter 1983 conflict between National Graphical Association (NGA) and Messenger Group. The Warrington dispute was a first serious defeat for the powerful NGA which had hitherto operated a formidable pre-entry **closed shop**. It was achieved by the use of non-union labour to maintain output and with extensive **police** assistance to resist mass picketing, often resulting in violence. The role of the police presaged their use in the **miners' strike** while the dispute itself was a major early development under the **new realism**.

WATER POWER *see* ENERGY SOURCES

WAVE POWER *see* ENERGY SOURCES

THE WEB *see* WORLD WIDE WEB

WELFARE BENEFITS

The payments made under the government **social security** system to those suffering from ill-health or poverty. They are non-contributory benefits, unlinked to an individual's **national insurance** contribution record, and are generally means-tested. **Income support**, which replaced supplementary benefit under the Social Security Act 1986, is paid to the unemployed who do not qualify for the contributory unemployment benefit and is the best known. Others include **housing benefit** and family credit for low-paid workers with children.

WELFARE STATE

A state **social security** system designed to provide basic means to all, and incorporating benefit payments to the unemployed, the sick, the elderly and the disabled, and free or inexpensive health care.

The welfare state in the **UK** was rooted in the radical **Beveridge Report** of 1942, which recommended the establishment of a comprehensive system of social insurance and a national health service. Although accepted in principle by the wartime coalition government of Winston **Churchill**, the institution of the welfare state was the accomplishment of the post-war **Labour** government of Clement **Attlee**. The continued protection of the welfare state became, with full employment and a mixed economy, one of the shibboleths of postwar politics, until the **Thatcherite** era shattered the consensus with a new emphasis on individual responsibility and a repudiation of the **nanny state**.

WELSH DEVELOPMENT AGENCY

The government body charged with promoting industrial development in **Wales**. Created in 1976, the WDA under successive **Conservative** governments has sought to encourage inward investment from overseas and to raise private loan capital for industrial projects. Like its sister organization, the **Scottish Development Agency**, the WDA has also undertaken land reclamation and urban renewal.

WELSH GRAND COMMITTEE

A **standing committee** of the **House of Commons** which comprises all 38 Welsh **MPs** and up to five others. The Committee considers **bills** referred to it at **second reading** stage and matters concerning **Wales** only.

WELSH LANGUAGE SOCIETY

A pressure group for the preservation of the Welsh language. The Society was founded in 1962 and describes itself as a 'socialist organization to ensure the future of the Welsh Language'. It has branches throughout **Wales** and is affiliated to other linguistic and political groups in Europe.

WELSH OFFICE *see* WALES

WEST

A misleading term in a variety of usages in international affairs. Never strictly geographical even when applied to Europe and North America, it was extended in its **Cold War** usage to include Australia and New Zealand, in contradistinction to 'East', a similarly inaccurate synonym for the communist bloc. In the categorization of the world according to types of economic system, West also loosely corresponds to countries with developed market economies, leading to its use sometimes to include Japan. In the language of world development the North-South distinction, which has gained general acceptance, places the West and much of the East in the same category, the North.

WEST MIDLANDS SERIOUS CRIME SQUAD

A controversial unit within the West Midlands **Police** Force (WMP) that was disbanded in August 1989 amid allegations that its detectives had fabricated confessions to secure convictions and following the failure of six cases based on WMSCS evidence in two years. 0n 13 October 1993 and 28 July 1984 WMP agreed substantial compensation payments to individuals alleging mistreatment by WMSCS officers. A WMSCS officer involved in a number of controversial cases took the confession of Patrick Molloy, crucial to the conviction of the **Bridgewater Three**.

WESTERN ALLIES

The USA, the UK and France in the period after 1945 when, with the onset of the **Cold War**, the Soviet Union became estranged from its wartime allies and there was no longer a common purpose uniting the **Big Three** or the **Big Four**.

Westland affair

The **Cabinet** crisis in 1985–6 over the future of the sole remaining British helicopter manufacturer. Westland, which had been experiencing financial difficulties, was the subject of rival bids, principally from the US Sikorsky's parent company UTC together with the Italian Fiat, and from a European consortium. The Defence Secretary Michael **Heseltine**, who favoured the European solution, perceived a bias on the part of his Cabinet colleagues in favour of the Sikorsky/UTC bid, and resigned over the Cabinet's handling of the matter. The Trade and Industry Secretary Leon **Brittan** also resigned after it emerged that he had sanctioned the leaking to the press of a confidential letter written to Heseltine by the **Attorney General**, Sir Patrick Mayhew. In the event, UTC/Fiat took a substantial minority holding in Westland, while after further problems Westland was acquired in early 1994 by the UK engineering and defence group GKN, which already held a considerable minority stake.

Westminster

The overall term for the world of Parliament. It derives from the location of the Houses of Parliament – the **Palace of Westminster** – and the immediate area (and borough) in which it is situated. The term is used in contradistinction to **Whitehall**, the adjacent area housing the offices of many of the most important government departments, which indicates the bureaucratic and administrative structure of government. 'Westminster' also signifies central as distinct from local, regional (or **Northern Ireland**) government, and increasingly indicates political powers exercised on a national as opposed to European level.

Westminster City Council

One of London's 32 borough councils, which was at the centre of a political storm in early 1994 when it was accused of **gerrymandering**. An independent district auditor's report suggested that the council, under the leadership of Dame Shirley Porter, had illegally attempted to use housing policy to raise the proportion of **Conservative** voters in the borough. In 1987–9, under an illegal programme, inducements were offered to council tenants to vacate their homes. These were sold to private purchasers considered more likely than the previous residents to vote Conservative and thus ensure a Conservative majority on the council in the four-yearly elections. Many homes remained empty, although the number of registered homeless in Westminster was high. In the 1990 elections the Conservatives greatly extended their representation on the council.

The council and Porter had first come to notoriety in the mid-1980s, when it was revealed that three council-owned cemeteries had been sold to a property developer for 5 pence each. The sales were subsequently declared illegal by the courts.

Westminster Foundation for Democracy

An organization to assist in building and strengthening pluralistic democratic institutions overseas, established in 1992 by the government after consultations with the main political parties. With representatives on the Board of Governors from each of the three main political parties as well as a representative of the smaller parties and non-party figures from business, trade unions and the academic world, the Foundation is independent and the government cannot veto projects the Foundation chooses to support. Projects include the development of electoral systems, of legislatures, of political parties and of free trade unions, and the Foundation currently concentrates its efforts on central and south-eastern Europe, the former Soviet Union and on anglophone Africa.

Wet

A member of the **Conservative Party**, particularly during the period of Margaret **Thatcher's** premiership in 1979–90, who disputed **Thatcherite** policies and called for the restoration of a more pragmatic and traditional brand of **Conservatism**. The term was used pejoratively by Thatcherite loyalists (who themselves became known as **dries**) to imply a lack of moral courage.

The wets generally backed close co-operation with the **EC** and, alarmed over the damage to the industrial base wrought by the **recession** of the early 1980s, backed a relaxation of anti-**inflation** austerity measures. There was also disquiet among the wets over Thatcher's inflexible leadership style. Prominent **backbench** wets included former **Prime Minister** Edward **Heath**. Thatcher's first **Cabinet**, formed in May 1979, included a number of wets, for instance Francis **Pym**, Sir Ian Gilmour and Peter Walker, but their number and influence diminished over succeeding years.

WEU

The Western European Union, a forum for European military co-operation set up in 1954. Its seven original members were the **UK** plus the **Inner Six** founder members of the European Community (**EC**). It foundered in the 1960s essentially over the divergent **British** and French attitudes to the Atlantic Alliance which were epitomized in the **Soames affair**. It was 'reactivated' in 1984 and subsequently enlarged, so that by February 1995 it had 10 of the **EU** member states as full members and the other five as observers.

WHAT'S LEFT?

A discreet **Labour Party** group formed in mid-1995 by **MPs** concerned by the party's drift to the right. The group counts around 30 MPs as adherents, and several **Shadow Cabinet** members, including Robin Cook, David **Blunkett** and Clare Short, were reported to have attended meetings. The group is regarded by insiders as the true heir to the **Tribune** Group, purged of 'old left' elements and in favour of a stronger commitment to full employment and to a high national **minimum wage**. While some What's Left? adherents, anxious not to be perceived as treacherous, are reluctant to discuss their activities, the group has nevertheless caused concern among **new Labour** MPs who foresee the beginnings of internal opposition to a future **Blair** government.

WHEEL CLAMPS

A device used to immobilize illegally parked cars, both by the police and by an increasing number of private clamping firms. The use of wheel clamps on vehicles parked illegally in central London was introduced in 1984 and was based on a strategy first adopted in the US city of Denver. During the first full year, the Metropolitan Police clamped 44,101 vehicles, but the figure fell to 34,810 vehicles in 1985 and to 26,028 in 1986. At the end of 1986 the police brought in private contractors to carry out clamping, and the number of vehicles clamped increased dramatically. Between 1 December 1986 (when the private contractors took over) and 8 November 1987, a total of 107,709 vehicles were clamped in central London. In 1992 the government began examining what could be done to curb the activities of 'cowboy clampers' in **England** and **Wales** after a finding of the Scottish **High Court of the Justiciary** that private wheel-clamping amounted to 'extortion and theft'.

WHIPS

MPs and peers who maintain party discipline in Parliament. Whips of the government and opposition parties are officially recognized by both the **House of Commons** and the **House of Lords** and are provided with offices and salaries from public funds. The whips' function is to ensure the attendance of MPs and peers on important occasions, particularly when votes are called. The circular letter sent by whips to MPs is also known as a 'whip', its urgency being determined by the number of times it is underlined. A three-line whip is the most important, and failure to comply is likely to result in withdrawal of the whip, which is equivalent to expulsion, at least temporarily, from the parliamentary party. As a result of their failure to support John **Major's** government on its European policy, the whip was withdrawn from eight '**Euro-rebel**' **Conservative** MPs from November 1994 to April 1995.

WHITE COMMONWEALTH

A popular term used to describe the former British dominions of Australia, Canada, New Zealand and South Africa, colonized by European settlers, which gained independence as members of the **Commonwealth** under the 1931 Statute of Westminster. It was synonymous with 'old Commonwealth', while British colonies in Asia, Africa and the Caribbean which became independent after the Second World War acquired the label '**New Commonwealth**'.

WHITE HEAT OF TECHNOLOGY

The theme of a famous speech by Harold **Wilson**. Soon after becoming **Labour** leader, Wilson used his speech at the party conference in October 1963 to identify himself with white-collar workers, scientists and technicians and to plead for modernization of training. He told the conference that the party was redefining its socialism in terms of the scientific revolution and that 'the Britain that is going to be forged in the white heat of this revolution will be no place for restrictive practices or for outdated methods on either side of industry'.

WHITE PAPER

A document issued by the government containing policy and/or legislative decisions. A White Paper may or may not be preceded by a consultative **Green Paper** setting out proposals (and frequently alternative courses of action) on which representations and expressions of view are invited. The contents of important White Papers are themselves often debated in Parliament, prior to the introduction of legislation implementing the detail of the broad policy conclusions.

WHITEHALL

The collective machinery of government. The term derives from the street of that name in London, just east of the **Houses of Parliament**, in which the offices of some of the most important government departments have traditionally been sited. It is used to denote the bureaucratic and administrative structure of government, as opposed to the political decision-making elements which are encapsulated in the term **Westminster**. It also signifies central as distinct from local or regional administration.

WHITEHOUSE, MARY *see* NVLA

WHITELAW, WILLIAM

(b. 1918) A Conservative elder statesman and long-time party mediator and fixer. Born into a wealthy Scottish family, Whitelaw progressed through Winchester, Cambridge and the Scots Guards before arriving in the **House of Commons** in 1955. Among the posts he held during 30 years at the forefront of **Conservative** politics were **Northern Ireland** Secretary (1972–3), Home Secretary (1979–83) and **Leader of the House** of Lords (1983–88). The highest office eluded him, even though in 1975 he was widely regarded as a natural successor to Edward **Heath**. His trademark loyalty prevented him from standing in the first round of the leadership voting, by which time Margaret **Thatcher** had built an unassailable lead. Subsequently, Whitelaw became one of Thatcher's most trusted lieutenants. A true Conservative grandee and a representative of the **'one nation'** brand of Conservatism of a bygone age, Whitelaw was given an hereditary peerage in 1983, becoming the first Viscount Whitelaw.

WIDGERY TRIBUNAL *see* BLOODY SUNDAY

WILLIAMS COMMITTEE REPORT ON OBSCENITY AND FILM CENSORSHIP

The report of a committee established in 1977 by the then **Labour** Home Secretary, Merlyn **Rees**, to review the laws relating to obscenity, indecency and violence in publications, displays and entertainments (with the exception of broadcasting). The committee, which reported in 1979, emphasized the urgent need to translate proposals into legislation, even though it was of the opinion that pornography played only a minor part in influencing society. It concluded that pornography through the printed word ought not to be prohibited since it is not immediately offensive, while pornographic films and photographs should be prohibited where their production appears to have involved exploitation for sexual purposes. The report further recommended that the powers of the **BBFC** ought to be encapsulated within a film examining board to establish a policy and criteria for film censorship. Any legislative intentions which may have arisen from the report were lost with the change of government in May 1979.

WILSON, HAROLD

(1916–95) Leader of the **Labour Party** from 1963 until 1976 and **Prime Minister** in 1964–70 and 1974–6, The Yorkshire-born Wilson's trademarks were his pipe, his Gannex raincoat and his homespun speaking style. After a brilliant academic career (he was an Oxford don at 21 and a **Whitehall** economist under the wartime coalition) Wilson was elected to Parliament in 1945 and at 31 became President of the **Board of Trade**. In 1951 he resigned with Aneurin **Bevan** over the imposition of **prescription charges**, thus gaining credibility as a **left-winger**. He stood unsuccessfully for the party leadership in 1960, but achieved the post in 1963 when Hugh **Gaitskell** died. Under Wilson, Labour won a narrow electoral victory in 1964, but his ambitious plans for economic expansion were hamstrung by the government's small majority and poor trade figures. He called a snap **general election** in 1966 and increased his majority to almost 100, but Labour's hopes were again frustrated by further economic problems leading to **devaluation** in November 1967. Wilson's style of government was controversial, particularly his reliance on a small **kitchen cabinet**, and his deteriorating relations with the press, stemming – some said – from paranoia on his part. In spring 1970, with the economy recovering, Wilson went to the country, but lost unexpectedly. He returned at the head of a minority government early in 1974 which he converted into a small majority in the second general election of the year held in October. The main achievement of his final term was renegotiation of Britain's membership of the **EEC**, confirmed by a referendum. In April 1976 Wilson suddenly resigned, prompting conspiracy theories and speculation that some dark secret was about to emerge, but none did. He was created Baron Wilson of Rievaulx in 1983.

WILTON PARK

An executive agency under the Foreign and Commonwealth Office (**FCO**), whose purpose is to hold international conferences at Wilton House in Steyning, Sussex, to stimulate 'off-the-record' discussion between UK foreign policy practitioners and a range of other participants from the UK and abroad.

WIND OF CHANGE

The resounding phrase used by **Prime Minister** Harold **Macmillan** in a speech to the South African parliament on 3 February 1960. Macmillan told the white minority legislature: 'The wind of change is blowing through this continent, and whether we like it or not, this growth of national consciousness is a political fact. We must all accept it as a fact, and our national policies must take account of it.' He made it clear that the South African government's policy of apartheid would not be supported by his government, and called for a greater share in political power for the black population. The speech highlighted the growing rift between the UK and South African governments, marked by the departure of South Africa from the **Commonwealth** the following year.

WIND POWER *see* ENERGY SOURCES

WINDSCALE

A nuclear reactor in Cumbria, which produced plutonium and was the site of one of the world's first nuclear accidents, a serious fire on 8 October 1957. The overheating of graphite bricks which encased the uranium fuel rods in the reactor, caused 11 tons of uranium to oxidise, releasing radioactive materials into the atmosphere and igniting a fire in the reactor core. The fire burned for 16 hours before it was extinguished. The UK government sought to minimise publicity, and did little to acknowledge the scale of the accident, beyond ordering the destruction of milk from an area of land seven miles long by two wide close to the site. No records were kept on people living near Windscale at the time, and therefore it is impossible to quantify the incidence of cancers attributable to exposure to radiation released in the accident. Windscale was renamed **Sellafield** in 1971 under a reorganization of the UK's nuclear agencies.

WINDSOR CASTLE

One of the principal royal residences, it is situated on a site in Berkshire first fortified by William the Conqueror. It was converted by Edward III into a luxurious palace, the headquarters of the Order of the Garter, whose Chapel of St George was rebuilt under Edward IV and his successors. The castle was substantially damaged by fire in November 1992, and it was agreed that Queen **Elizabeth** would personally foot the bill for the repairs. The cost of the repairs was given as a reason for opening parts of **Buckingham Palace** to the public for a few months of each year from 1993.

WINE LAKE

The huge surplus **EC** stocks of poor-quality wine built up under the **CAP**. In British eyes this, even more than the corresponding **butter mountain** and the other 'mountains' (of beef, cereals, even sultanas), symbolized how the system was loaded to the detriment of consumers and the advantage of farmers elsewhere in the Community. By the mid-1980s the wine lake had reached 3 billion litres. Subsequent reforms of the CAP emphasized tackling overproduction problems by measures to eliminate surplus capacity, in this case the payment of premiums to grub up poor quality vines.

WINNING THE WELFARE DEBATE

A series of proposals on the reform of the **welfare state** put forward by the **Social Market Foundation** since late 1993. Although the Foundation is an independent **think tank**, its proposals reflect the views of the **Conservative** government; indeed, all four of the main policy proposals were delivered in speeches made by Peter Lilley, **Secretary of State** for Social Security. The proposals call for people to be encouraged to provide through the tax system for retirement, as the value of state **pensions** diminishes; greater incentives for **single parents** to work through tax breaks for childcare; more local variation in the provision of welfare in for example housing and community care; and improvements in education and training in the state system, through the **national curriculum** and technology colleges. The proposals rejected the principle of a national **minimum wage**, instead calling for minimal employer obligations to increase demands for labour.

WINTER OF DISCONTENT

The time of industrial unrest over the winter of 1978–9. Within the framework of the lengthy period of **incomes policy** which had continued almost unabated since 1972, in August 1978 the **Labour** government introduced a strict 5 per cent guideline for pay increases in the coming pay round. This policy was rejected by the **TUC** and by the Labour Party itself, and sparked off a series of stoppages of work, especially in transport and the public services, gravely damaging the image of the Labour Party as the 1979 **general election** approached.

WINTER OF '47

A period of crisis for the post-war **Labour Government**. The early months of 1947 were climatically the most severe since 1880–1. The problems brought by snow and ice were compounded by a fuel crisis. In February Emmanuel Shinwell, the Minister of Fuel and Power, announced rationing of electricity and a progressive slow-down of industry followed. The March thaw brought the new hazard of flood with its attendant handicap of drowned livestock and ruined crops. Much contemporary opinion blamed Shinwell for the winter's economic impact, arguing that he had failed to provide for the higher coal output needed to sustain electricity supply.

WINTERTON RULE

A rule devised by **whips** of the **Conservative Party** in the **House of Commons** to exclude long-serving members from **select committees**. The rule, accepted by the committee of selection, states that no Conservative **MP** should be allowed to serve on a committee for the duration of more than three parliaments. The rule was formulated to prevent Nicholas Winterton, the MP for Macclesfield, to be re-elected as chair of the health select committee in July 1992, after he had spoken out against government health policies.

WOLFENDEN REPORT

The report of a committee chaired by Sir John Wolfenden, which recommended in particular the decriminalization of homosexual acts between males and an increase in penalties for soliciting by prostitutes. The landmark report, published on 4 September 1957, led to the Street Offences Act 1959 (introduced by the government) and to the Sexual Offences Act 1967. The latter, introduced by Labour backbencher Leo Abse, permitted homosexual acts in private between consenting male adults (in **England** and **Wales**). The **age of consent** under the Sexual Offences Act was reduced from 21 to 18 under the **Criminal Justice** and Public Order Act 1994.

WOMEN'S LIB

The informal women's liberation movement based on **feminism**, which emerged in the West in the late 1960s. It coincided with the entry of greater numbers of women into the workforce and the consequent increase in the number of economically independent women. Although the movement covered a broad spectrum of views, its basic aim was to challenge **sexism**. All so-called 'women's libbers' argued that women should have equal rights with men, enjoy equal access to education and employment, and receive equal pay for equal work. Other issues on which they campaigned included **abortion** rights. By questioning traditional social mores, Women's Lib also played a major role in the **sexual revolution**.

See also Appendix VI.

WOMEN'S ORDINATION *see* ORDINATION OF WOMEN PRIESTS

WOOLF REPORT

The report, published on 25 February 1991, of the inquiry by Lord Justice Woolf into the massive disturbances in April 1990 at **Strangeways** Prison, Manchester. The report not only covered the circumstances of the riot at Strangeways and steps taken to restore order there, but also contained a series of recommendations relating to the structure and to the administration of the prison system and to conditions within prisons themselves. In particular, Woolf recommended closer co-operation between different parts of the **criminal justice system**; greater devolution of responsibilities to individual prison governors; better training of prison officers; greatly improved standards and conditions within prisons (including an accelerated programme for installing integral sanitation); and improved standards of justice within prisons. The Woolf report led to a series of legislative and administrative actions by the government over the succeeding years.

WOOMERA

The site of British **nuclear weapon tests** in southern Australia in October 1953, part of a series of tests that became the subject of controversy in the 1980s as the UK government came under pressure to pay the costs of decontaminating the area. In July 1984, following a period of mounting concern over the tests and their lingering aftermath, the Australian government established the **Royal Commission** into British Nuclear Tests in Australia. It reported in December 1985 that the tests had been carried out in unsafe conditions and recommended that the UK should pay the costs (estimated at between £50 million and £100 million) of decontaminating the sites. In November 1990 the UK government stated that it had made agreements with the Australian authorities in 1968 and 1979 clearing it of further responsibility for the sites. Aborigines, who in 1984 had been handed back much of the contaminated territory, visited the UK in 1991 to press for compensation.

WORKERS' REVOLUTIONARY PARTY

A Trotskyite political party founded in 1973. The WRP (described as 'containing more revolutionaries than workers'), which has its roots in the communist Militant Group formed in the 1930s, advocates a revolutionary general strike, the creation of a workers' militia in place of the **police**, the formation of soviets, and the **nationalization** without compensation of major industries and financial institutions. The party first contested a general election in 1974 and in 1987 fielded 110 candidates, although the number of candidates has been drastically reduced since then. The party was seriously split in 1985 when party leader Gerry Healy was expelled for alleged debauchery and formed another party by the same name. Among his supporters, who were also expelled, were the actors Vanessa and Corin Redgrave. Further in-fighting resulted in a faction led by Mike Banda forming the Communist Forum in 1986. The WRP is currently led by Cliff Slaughter and the dissident WRP by Sheila Torrance.

WORKFARE

A concept developed in the USA in the 1980s, but as yet largely untried, whereby recipients of welfare are required to work in return for assistance which they receive from the state. The aim of the policy – which is particularly popular with, but by no means confined to, the right wing of the Republican Party – is to break a perceived pattern of welfare-dependency by re-establishing a degree of individual responsibility in welfare matters. In the 1990s the idea has found increasing popularity in the UK within the **right wing** of the **Conservative Party**. In a speech at the **Carlton Club** on 3 February 1993, **Prime Minister** John **Major** indicated that it might be right to require unemployed people to undertake some form of activity in return for the receipt of unemployment benefit. Since then an experimental voluntary scheme has begun in Norfolk.

WORKING FOR PATIENTS

A controversial White Paper published in 1989 and containing proposals for the reorganization and 'reform' of the **NHS**. The Paper proposed a decentralization of control of hospitals, the largest of which should have self-governing status; an increase in the number of senior consultants; the delegation of more financial and professional responsibility to larger general practices of doctors; more professional and business representatives on health authorities; changes to the management structure within the **DOH**; and tax incentives to encourage the taking out of private medical insurance by the elderly. While the Paper was strongly criticized by influential sections of the medical profession, including the **BMA**, many of the proposals were subsequently implemented by the government.

WORLD POWER

A major player in global politics. After the Second World War Britain sought to maintain equal status with the USA and Soviet Union as co-arbiter of world affairs, a strategy which implied continuing high defence expenditure and global diplomatic activity despite relative economic weakness and **decolonization**. The **independent nuclear deterrent** was maintained to give Britain a 'place at the **top table**' and to cement the **special relationship**. However, the **Suez Crisis** brutally clarified Britain's inability to mount a military adventure independently of the USA. After this the attempt to maintain world power status grew increasingly unconvincing though Britain joined the disarmament talks of the early 1960s as one of the **Big Three**. Global pretentions were effectively ended after 1967 when British detachments were brought home from **East of Suez**, against US objections.

WORLD TRADE ORGANIZATION *see* GATT

WORLD WIDE WEB

An aspect of the computer communications revolution, and the development which prompted much of the explosion of interest in the **Internet** in **Britain** in late 1994 and 1995. Abbreviated variously as WWW or The Web, and based on software developed by Tim Berners-Lee at CERN in Switzerland, it allows the creation of a 'user-friendly' graphical environment to which users can gain access by computerized dial-up. A 'point and click' convention gives them wide-ranging opportunities to pursue topics which interest them. The software then makes the link, showing a new screen (of words, pictures or video) which may actually be held on any one of millions of interconnected computers around the world. The World Wide Web could revolutionize the provision of public information, commercial publishing, entertainment, and the advertising and sales media. Its potential is constrained by the data handling capacity of communications networks, with much of the traffic currently still using lines designed just for telephone calls. Its commercial exploitation requires the development of secure methods of online payment, and also raises fundamental issues about copyright and intellectual property.

WRP *see* WORKERS' REVOLUTIONARY PARTY

WWW *see* WORLD WIDE WEB

YALTA
The summit meeting between the **Big Three** wartime Allies – the Soviet Union, the **UK** and the USA – held on 4–12 February 1945 in the Crimean resort of Yalta. The summit achieved Soviet agreement to join the war against Japan three months after victory in Europe, in return for concessions in the Far East, the admission of France as a joint occupier of Germany – whose defeat was imminent, Soviet participation in the UN and the extension of the Soviet border into eastern Poland, which would itself be compensated by territory from Germany. The participants also signed the 'Declaration on Liberated Europe', which promised the restoration of sovereignty in all European countries, free elections and economic reconstruction. Thus, although it became a cliché to identify the Yalta summit with the West's 'betrayal' of Eastern Europe, it did not, in fact, enshrine the division of the region into spheres of influence.

YARDIES
A slang expression, originally Jamaican, for underground gangs of armed Jamaican criminals which became notorious in the UK in the early 1990s. Speculation that the gangs were entering the UK to take over the illegal drugs trade in cities lent colour to continuing debates over **immigration** controls and deportation procedures in 1993–4. Deportation was particularly under scrutiny at this time following the death in August 1993 of Jamaican woman Joy **Gardner** from injuries sustained while being arrested prior to deportation.

YOB
The slang term current for a badly behaved young person, almost exclusively male, disrespectful to authority figures such as **police** officers. The term, in use since the 1960s, has been applied to widely diverse groups such as **young offenders**, **new age travellers**, **skinheads**, football fans and people on protest marches.

YOMPING
A slang phrase used in the British army for moving at speed across a muddy or mountainous landscape while carrying a heavy pack. It became current in the 1982 **Falklands conflict**.

YOPS
The youth opportunities programme, a scheme introduced in the UK in February 1978 designed to provide work openings for unemployed school leavers.

YORKSHIRE RIPPER
The British criminal who murdered 13 women, mostly prostitutes, in 1977–81. Peter Sutcliffe, a lorry driver from Bradford, northern England, was dubbed the 'Yorkshire Ripper' because of the resemblance of his crimes to those of the notorious Jack the Ripper, the unidentified vicious murderer of a series of prostitutes in London in the 1880s. Sutcliffe pleaded that murder charges should be reduced to manslaughter on the grounds of diminished responsibility, but he was found guilty of murder and sentenced to life imprisonment on 22 May 1981.

YOUNG OFFENDERS
Juvenile criminals, the subject of increasing government concern in the face of an apparent rise in persistent youth crime, the highly publicised activities of **joyriders** in 1991 and the **Bulger affair** in early 1993. The **Criminal Justice** Act 1990 gave courts powers to force parents of 16- and 17-year-old offenders to pay their children's fines. The **Criminal Justice** and Public Order Act 1994 controversially introduced a range of tough new penalties for young offenders: a new 'secure training order' of a maximum of two years, including one year's imprisonment, was created for those aged between 12 and 14 who had committed three or more imprisonable offences; the range of offences for which young people aged between 10 and 13 might be imprisoned was extended from murder or manslaughter to include rape, robbery, arson and domestic burglary.

In May 1995 government plans for a 'boot camp' were revealed. Although based on the US model, the camp would not have the military overtones associated with US schemes, although the inmates would engage in strenuous physical activity. It was envisaged that 60 young male offenders would volunteer to attend the camp where they would also receive educational training and be forced to confront their crimes by qualified psychologists. **Home Office** officials insisted that the camp was fundamentally different from the failed **short sharp shock** initiative.

YOU'VE NEVER HAD IT SO GOOD

The slogan coined by US President Harry S. Truman in 1952 but taken up later in the decade by UK **Prime Minister** Harold **Macmillan**. Macmillan successfully captured the mood of the nation and was re-elected in 1959 with a 100-plus Commons majority.

YTS

The Youth Training Scheme designed to provide young unemployed people with skills. It was eventually transformed in 1991 into Youth Training, under the auspices of **TECs**.

YUPPIE

A young urban professional person. The term first surfaced in the USA in 1983 to identify a new generation of young, ambitious, hard-working high-fliers, generally in the finance, advertising and hi-tech industries. In the **UK** yuppies were often also described as '**Thatcher's Children**' as they appeared to embody the ideals of **Thatcherism**. The term (which spawned numerous more or less humorous variants) is still in common usage, but yuppies were really a phenomenon of the boom years of the mid- to late 1980s.

ZIRCON

The code-name for a satellite surveillance system developed by the **MOD**. The system came to public attention in 1987 when a television programme about the system, designed to 'eavesdrop' on civilian and military communications, caused a political storm. Transmission of the programme was halted by the Director-General of the **BBC** Alasdair Milne, a decision widely believed to have been made under pressure from the government. An article about the programme was subsequently printed in the *New Statesman* and **MPs** were given a private showing. When a repeat showing was prohibited by the **Speaker**, a row over **parliamentary privilege** broke out. On 31 January the **police** raided the BBC Glasgow studios and seized tapes not only of the programme but of the entire series of which it was a part. In August 1987 the press reported that the project had been abandoned, after it was determined that it would be obsolete by the time it was operational.

APPENDIX I

Members of the British Empire or under British control which have been granted independence since 1945

Country	Year	Changes of status	Former name
*Bahamas	1973	Independence	
*Bangladesh	1971	Broke away from Pakistan	East Pakistan (from 1947)
*Barbados	1966	Independence	
*Belize	1981	Independence	British Honduras
*Botswana	1966	Independence	Bechuanaland
*Brunei	1984	Independence	
Burma	1948	Independence	
†Cameroon	1961	Independence as Federal Republic of Cameroon with French-administered territory	British Cameroons
*Cyprus	1960	Independence	
*Dominica	1978	Independence	
Fiji	1970	Independence	
*Gambia	1965	Independence	
*Ghana	1957	Independence	Gold Coast
*Grenada	1974	Independence	
*Guyana	1966	Independence	British Guiana
*India	1947	Independence	
*Jamaica	1962	Independence	
*Kenya	1963	Independence	
*Kiribati	1979	Independence	Gilbert Islands
*Lesotho	1966	Independence	Basutoland
*Malawi	1964	Independence	Nyasaland
Malaysia	1957	Independence	Malaya (until 1963)
	1963	Formation with Singapore, Sarawak and Sabah of Malaysia Federation	
*Maldives	1965	Independence	
*Malta	1964	Independence	
*Mauritius	1968	Independence	
*†Nauru	1968	Independence	
*Nigeria	1960	Independence	
*Pakistan	1947	Independence	
†Israel	1948	Independence	Palestine
*St Christopher (St Kitts) and Nevis	1983	Independence	
*St Lucia	1979	Independence	
*St Vincent & the Grenadines	1979	Independence	
*Seychelles	1976	Independence	
Sierra Leone	1961	Independence	

*Currently a member of the Commonwealth.
†Administered by the UK on behalf of the UN/League of Nations.

Country	Year	Changes of status	Former name
*Singapore	1963	Independence as part of Malaysian Federation	
	1965	Seceded to form independent republic	
*Solomon Islands	1978	Independence	
*Sri Lanka	1948	Independence	Ceylon (until 1972)
Sudan	1956	Independence (formerly jointly ruled with Egypt)	
*Swaziland	1968	Independence	
*Tanzania	1964	Merger of †Tanganika (independent in 1961) with Zanzibar	
*Tonga	1970	Independence	
*Trinidad & Tobago	1962	Independence	
*Tuvalu	1978	Independence	Ellice Islands
*Uganda	1962	Independence	
*Vanuatu	1980	Independence (formerly jointly ruled with France)	New Hebrides
*Zambia	1964	Independence	Northern Rhodesia
*Zimbabwe	1980	Independence	Rhodesia (until 1964 Southern Rhodesia)

Aden: In1963 Aden acceded to the South Arabian Federation, becoming the People's Republic of South Yemen (1967) and subsequently merging with North Yemen (1990).

*Currently a member of the Commonwealth.
†Administered by the UK on behalf of the UN/League of Nations.

APPENDIX II

General election results 1945–1992

A general election is customarily held on a Thursday.

1945 5 July

	No. of votes	% of votes	MPs†
Labour	11,995,152	47.8	393 (2)
Conservative	9,988,306	39.8	213 (1)
Liberal	2,248,226	9.0	12
Communist	102,780	0.4	2
Common Wealth	110,634	0.4	1
Others	640,880	2.0	19
Total	25,085,978	100.0	640 (3)

Turnout: 72.7 per cent.

1950 23 February

	No. of votes	% of votes	MPs†
Labour	13,266,592	46.1	315
Conservative	12,502,567	43.5	298 (2)
Liberal	2,621,548	9.1	9
Others	381,964	1.3	3
Total	28,772,671	100.0	625 (2)

Turnout: 84.0 per cent.

1951 25 October

	No. of votes	% of votes	MPs†
Conservative	13,717,538	48.0	321 (4)
Labour	13,948,605	48.8	295
Liberal	730,556	2.5	6
Others	198,969	0.7	3
Total	28,595,668	100.0	625 (4)

Turnout: 82.5 per cent.

1955 26 May

	No. of votes	% of votes	MPs
Conservative	13,286,569	49.7	344
Labour	12,404,970	46.4	277
Liberal	722,405	2.7	6
Others	346,554	1.2	3
Total	26,760,498	100.0	630

Turnout: 76.7 per cent.

†Figures in parentheses indicate MPs returned unopposed.

1959 8 October

	Total votes	% of votes	MPs
Conservative	13,749,830	49.4	365
Labour	12,215,538	43.8	258
Liberal	1,638,571	5.9	6
Others	142,670	0.9	1
Total	27,859,241	100.0	630

Turnout: 78.8 per cent.

1964 15 October

	Total votes	% of votes	MPs
Labour	12,205,814	44.1	317
Conservative	12,001,396	43.4	304
Liberal	3,092,878	11.2	9
Others	347,905	1.3	0
Total	27,655,374	100.0	630

Turnout: 77.1 per cent.

1966 31 March

	Total votes	% of votes	MPs
Labour	13,064,951	47.9	363
Conservative	11,418,433	41.9	253
Liberal	2,327,533	8.5	12
Others	452,959	1.2	2
Total	27,263,606	100.0	630

Turnout: 75.8 per cent.

1970 18 June

	Total votes	% of votes	MPs
Conservative	13,145,123	46.4	330
Labour	12,179,341	43.0	287
Liberal	2,117,035	7.5	6
Scot. Nat. Party	306,802	1.1	1
Others	596,497	2.0	6
Total	28,344,798	100.0	630

Turnout: 72.0 per cent.

1974 28 February

	Total votes	**% of votes**	**MPs**
Labour	11,639,243	37.1	301
Conservative	11,868,906	37.9	297
Liberal	6,063,470	19.3	14
Scot. Nat. Party	632,032	2.0	7
Plaid Cymru	171,364	0.6	2
Others (NI)*	717,986	2.3	12
Others (GB)	240,665	0.8	2
Total	31,333,226	100.0	635

Turnout: 78.7 per cent.

1974 10 October

	Total votes	**% of votes**	**MPs**
Labour	11,457,079	39.2	319
Conservative	10,464,817	35.8	276
Liberal	5,346,754	18.3	13
Scot. Nat. Party	839,617	2.9	11
Plaid Cymru	166,321	0.6	3
Others (NI)*	702,094	2.4	12
Others (GB)	212,496	0.8	1
Total	29,189,178	100.0	635

Turnout: 72.8 per cent.

1979 3 May

	Total votes	**% of votes**	**MPs**
Conservative	13,697,690	43.9	339
Labour	11,532,148	36.9	268
Liberal	4,313,811	13.8	11
Scot. Nat. Party	504,259	1.6	2
Plaid Cymru	132,544	0.4	2
Others (NI)*	695,889	2.2	12
Others (GB)	343,674	1.2	1
Total	31,220,010	100.0	635

Turnout: 76.0 per cent.

*From 1974 onwards, no candidates in Northern Ireland are included in the major party totals.

1983 9 June

	Total votes	% of votes	MPs
Conservative	13,012,315	42.4	397
Labour	8,456,934	27.6	209
Alliance	7,780,949	25.4	23
Liberal	(4,210,115)	(13.7)	(17)
Social Democrat	(3,570,834)	(11.6)	(6)
Scot. Nat. Party	331,975	1.1	2
Plaid Cymru	125,309	0.4	2
Others (NI)*	764,925	2.5	17
Others (GB)	232,054	0.6	0
Total	30,704.461	100.0	650

Turnout: 72.7 per cent.

1987 11 June

	Total votes	% of votes	MPs
Conservative	13,763,066	42.3	376
Labour	10,029,778	30.8	229
Alliance	7,341,290	22.5	22
Liberal	(4,173,450)	(12.8)	(17)
Social Democrat	(3,168,183)	(9.7)	(5)
Scot. Nat. Party	416,473	1.3	3
Plaid Cymru	123,599	0.4	3
Others (NI)*	730,152	2.2	17
Others (GB)	151,519	0.5	0
Total	32,556,220	100.0	650

Turnout: 75.3 per cent.

1992 9 April

	Total votes	% of votes	MPs
Conservative	14,092,891	41.9	336
Labour	11,559,735	34.4	271
Lib. Dem.	5,999,384	17.8	20
Scot. Nat. Party	629,552	1.9	3
Plaid Cymru	154,439	0.5	4
Others (NI)*	740,485	2.2	17
Others (GB)	436,207	1.3	0
Total	33,612,693	100.0	651

Turnout: 77.7 per cent.

*From 1974 onwards, no candidates in Northern Ireland are included in the major party totals.

APPENDIX III

Senior government members since 1945

Prime Minister	Deputy Prime Minister	Chancellor of the Exchequer	Home Secretary	Foreign Secretary
26 July 1945 **Clement Attlee** **(Labour)**	26 July 1945– 24 February 1951 Herbert Morrison	27 July 1945 Hugh Dalton 13 November 1947 Sir Stafford Cripps 19 October 1950 Hugh Gaitskell	3 August 1945 James Chuter Ede	27 July 1945 Ernest Bevin 9 March 1951 Herbert Morrison
26 October 1951 **Winston Churchill** **(Conservative)**	26 October 51– 6 April 1955 Sir Anthony Eden	28 October 1951 R. A. Butler	28 October 1951 Sir David Maxwell Fyfe 18 October 1954 Maj. Gwilym Lloyd-George	28 October 1951 Sir Anthony Eden
6 April 1955 **Sir Anthony Eden** **(Conservative)**		20 December 1955 Harold Macmillan		7 April 1955 Harold Macmillan 20 December 1955 Selwyn Lloyd
10 January 1957 **Harold Macmillan** **(Conservative)**	13 July 1962– 18 October 1963 R. A. Butler	13 January 1957 Peter Thorneycroft 6 January1958 Derick Heathcoat -Amory 27 July 1960 Selwyn Lloyd 13 July 1962 Reginald Maudling	13 January 1957 R. A. Butler 13 July 1962 Henry Brooke	27 July 1960 Earl of Home (Sir Alec Douglas-Home)

Prime Minister	Deputy Prime Minister	Chancellor of the Exchequer	Home Secretary	Foreign Secretary
18 October 1963 **Sir Alec Douglas-Home** **(Conservative)**				20 October 1963 R. A. Butler
16 October 1964 **Harold Wilson** **(Labour)**		16 October 1964 James Callaghan	18 October 1964 Sir Frank Soskice	16 October 1964 Patrick Gordon Walker 22 January 1965 Michael Stewart
			23 December 1965 Roy Jenkins	
				11 August 1966 George Brown
		30 November 1967 Roy Jenkins	30 November 1967 James Callaghan	
				16 March 1968 Michael Stewart
19 June 1970 **Edward Heath** **(Conservative)**		20 June 1970 Iain Macleod 25 July 1970 Anthony Barber	20 June 1970 Reginald Maudling	20 June 1970 Sir Alec Douglas-Home
			19 July 1972 Robert Carr	

Prime Minister	Deputy Prime Minister	Chancellor of the Exchequer	Home Secretary	Foreign Secretary
4 March 1974 **Harold Wilson** **(Labour)**		25 March 1974 Denis Healey	5 March 1974 Roy Jenkins	5 March 1974 James Callaghan
5 April 1976 **James Callaghan** **(Labour)**			10 September 1976 Merlin Rees	8 April 1976 Anthony Crosland 21 February 1977 David Owen
4 May 1979 **Magaret Thatcher** **(Conservative)**	4 May 1979– 10 January 1988 William Whitelaw	5 May 1979 Sir Geoffrey Howe	5 May 1979 William Whitelaw	5 May 1979 Lord Carrington 5 April 1982 Francis Pym
		11 June 1983 Nigel Lawson	11 June 1983 Leon Brittan 2 September 1985 Douglas Hurd	11 June 1983 Sir Geoffrey Howe
				14 June 1989 John Major
	24 July 1889– 1 November 1990 Sir Geoffrey Howe	26 October 1989 John Major	26 October 1989 David Waddington	26 October 1989 Douglas Hurd
28 November 1990 **John Major** **(Conservative)**		28 November 1990 Norman Lamont	28 November 1990 Kenneth Baker 11 April 1992 Kenneth Clarke	
		27 May 1993 Kenneth Clarke	27 May 1993 Michael Howard	
	5 July 1995 Michael Heseltine			5 July 1995 Malcolm Rifkind

APPENDIX IV

UK population 1941–1991

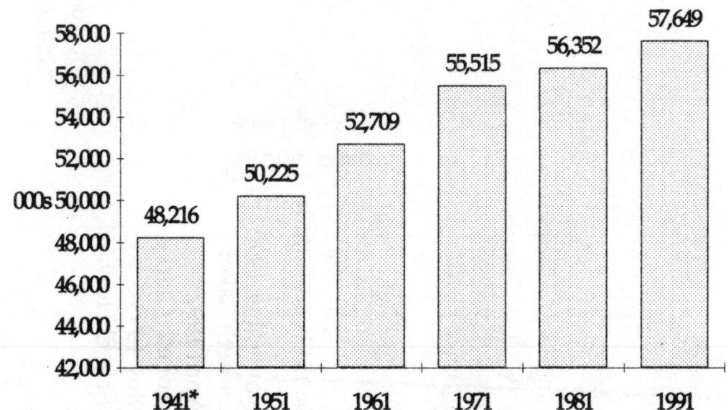

*Mid-year estimate, civilian population only; census figures are given for other years.

Sources: *Censuses of Population* and *Annual Abstract of Statistics.*

UK ethnic minorities 1991

In 1991 ethnic minorities constituted 5 per cent of the population as a whole.

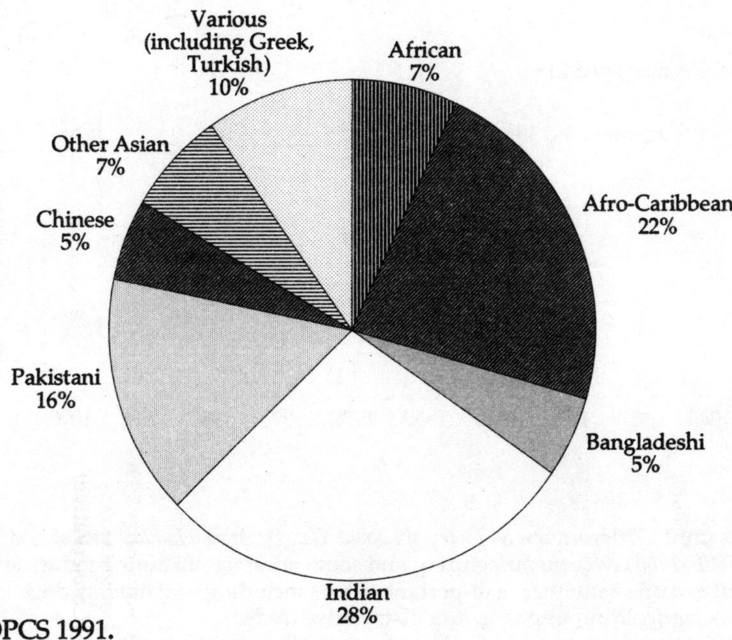

Source: OPCS 1991.

APPENDIX V

National income and prices 1948–1992

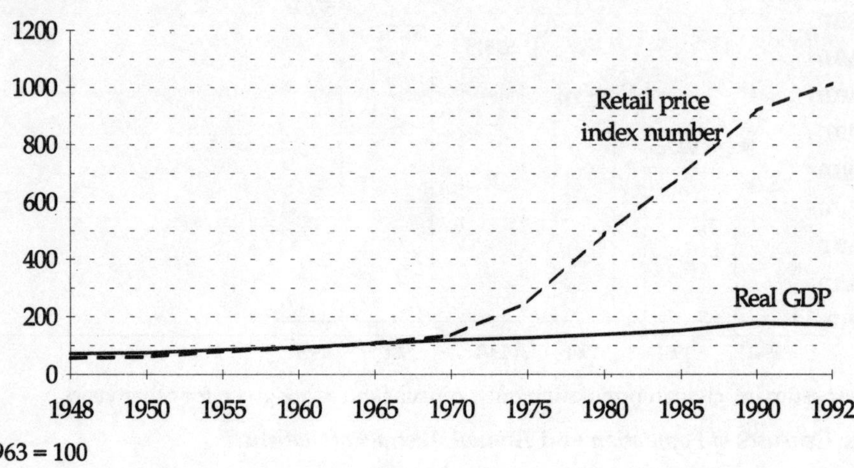

1963 = 100

Average weekly earnings of manual workers 1945–1992

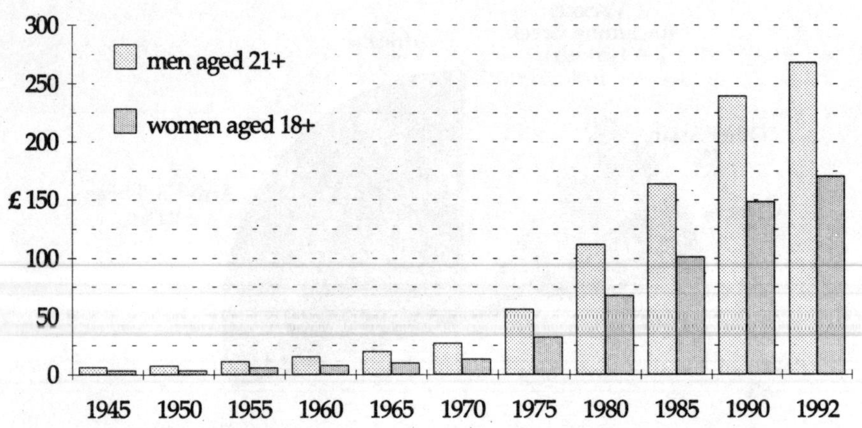

Figures until 1970 from the *Ministry of Labour Gazette British Labour Statistics: Historical Abstract 1886–1968* cover manufacturing and some non-manufacturing industries and services, but exclude a number of important sectors including coal mining, dock labour, railways, agriculture, shipping, and distributive trades.
From 1970 figures come from the New Earnings Survey of a sample of all employees and are thus not strictly comparable with earlier period.

Dollar and Deutschmark annnualized exchange rates 1945–1994

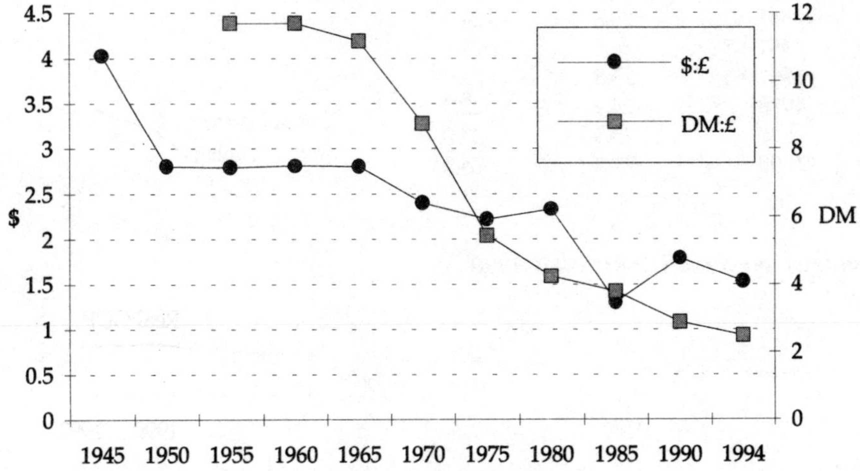

APPENDIX VI

Average age at first marriage in England and Wales 1941–1990

Year	Bachelors	Spinsters
1941–45	26.8	24.6
1951–55	26.5	24.2
1961–65	25.5	22.9
1970	24.4	22.7
1980	25.3	23.0
1990	27.2	25.2

Divorces in Great Britain 1940–1990

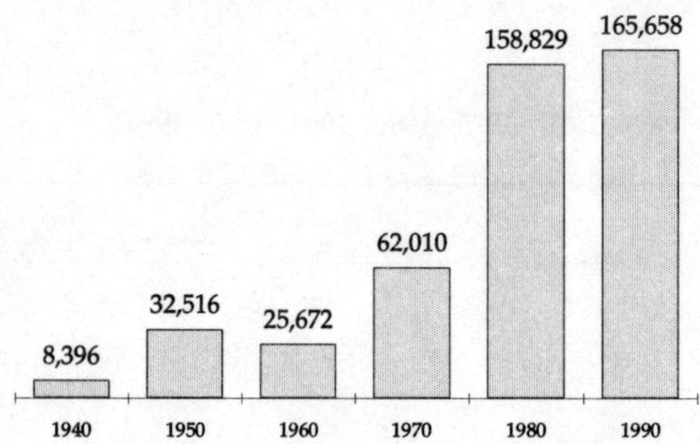

Legal abortion in England and Wales 1968–1990

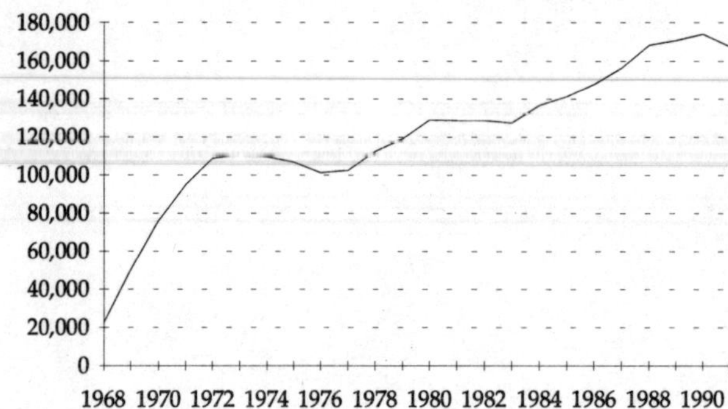

Recorded crime in Great Britain 1950–1990

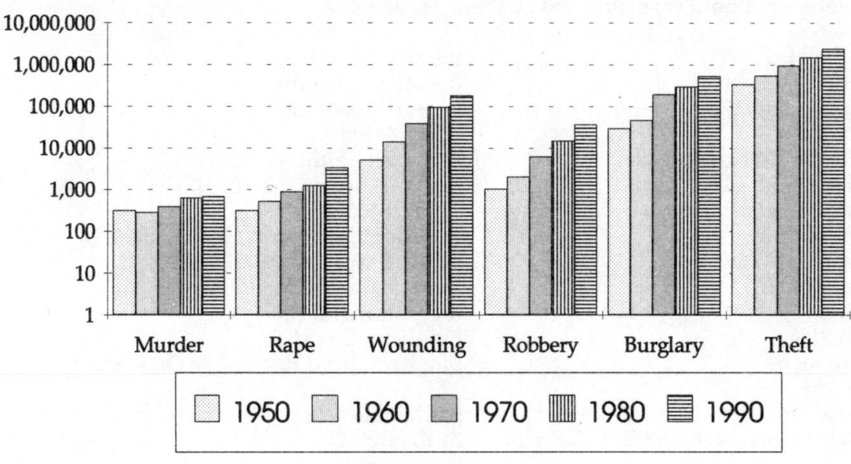

Prison sentences and prison population in England and Wales 1950–1990

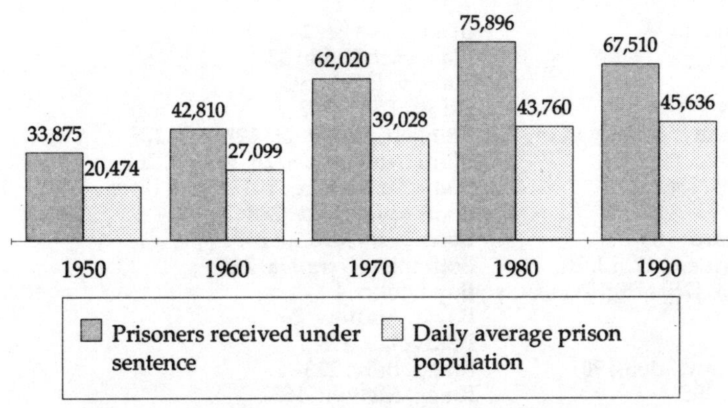

Police force strength in Great Britain 1950–1990

Year	Number of forces	Number of police
1950	163	72,600
1960	159	83,900
1970	68	107,700
1980	52	136,000
1990	52	147,870

Source: *British Political Facts 1900–1994*, David Butler and Gareth Butler, Macmillan, 1994

INDEX OF PERSONAL NAMES

A page reference in **bold** type indicates a biographical entry